Mastering Securities Lending Documentation

A guide to the main European and US master securities lending agreements

PAUL C. HARDING AND CHRISTIAN A. JOHNSON

**Financial Times
Prentice Hall
is an imprint of**

PEARSON

Harlow, England • London • New York • Boston • San Francisco • Toronto • Sydney • Singapore • Hong Kong
Tokyo • Seoul • Taipei • New Delhi • Cape Town • Madrid • Mexico City • Amsterdam • Munich • Paris • Milan

PEARSON EDUCATION LIMITED

Edinburgh Gate
Harlow CM20 2JE
Tel: +44 (0)1279 623623
Fax: +44 (0)1279 431059
Website: www.pearsoned.co.uk

First published in Great Britain in 2011

© Pearson Education Limited 2011

The rights of Paul C. Harding and Christian A. Johnson to be identified as authors of this work has been asserted by them in accordance with the Copyright, Designs and Patents Act 1988.

Pearson Education is not responsible for the content of third party internet sites.

ISBN: 978-0-273-73497-0

British Library Cataloguing-in-Publication Data
A catalogue record for this book is available from the British Library

Library of Congress Cataloging-in-Publication Data
A catalog record for this book is available from the Library of Congress

All rights reserved. No part of this publication may be reproduced, stored in a retrieval system, or transmitted in any form or by any means, electronic, mechanical, photocopying, recording or otherwise, without either the prior written permission of the publisher or a licence permitting restricted copying in the United Kingdom issued by the Copyright Licensing Agency Ltd, Saffron House, 6–10 Kirby Street, London EC1N 8TS. This book may not be lent, resold, hired out or otherwise disposed of by way of trade in any form of binding or cover other than that in which it is published, without the prior consent of the Publishers.

10 9 8 7 6 5 4 3 2 1
15 14 13 12 11

Typeset in 11.5pt Garamond by 30
Printed by Ashford Colour Press Ltd., Gosport

About the authors

Paul C. Harding is a graduate of London University and has worked in several UK and foreign banks in London in credit, marketing and documentation roles. Since 1990 he has been involved with derivatives documentation and was a well-known negotiator in the City of London with Barclays Capital Securities Limited and Hill Samuel Bank Limited where he was head of Treasury Documentation.

In February 1997 he founded Derivatives Documentation Limited, a derivatives consultancy and project management company based in the City of London and providing negotiation, recruitment and in-house training services in derivatives documentation (see www.derivsdocu.com). Its clients include many of the world's leading banks.

In November 2001 Paul's book, *Mastering the ISDA Master Agreement,* was published by Financial Times-Prentice Hall. This was followed by his *Mastering Collateral Management and Documentation,* in conjunction with Christian Johnson, which was published by Financial Times-Prentice Hall in November 2002. In 2004 he co-wrote *A Practical Guide to Using Repo Master Agreements* published by Euromoney Books.

His book on the 2002 ISDA Master Agreement was published in December 2003 also by Financial Times-Prentice Hall and in June 2004 his *A Practical Guide to the 2003 ISDA Credit Derivatives Definitions* was published by Euromoney Books.

A third edition of *Mastering the ISDA Master Agreements (1992 and 2002)* was published by Financial Times-Prentice Hall in April 2010.

Christian A. Johnson is a professor at the University of Utah and was previously a professor at Loyola University Chicago School of Law for 13 years. Professor Johnson teaches courses on corporate finance, banking and taxation. He graduated from Columbia Law School and was the Executive Editor of the *Columbia Law Review*. He practised law with Milbank Tweed Hadley & McCloy in New York and Mayer Brown Rowe & Maw in Chicago before teaching.

Christian has published extensively on corporate finance, lending and banking. He is also a frequent speaker and panelist on corporate finance and banking issues and has served as an expert witness in these areas. Christian is also a regular instructor for Euromoney Training on these subjects. Finally he brings over 18 years in negotiating and documenting corporate finance transactions such as securities lending, repurchase transactions and over-the-counter derivatives, having represented several large money centre banks, Federal Home Loan Banks and hedge funds in negotiations.

His previous collaboration with Paul Harding was in 2002 when he co-wrote *Mastering Collateral Management and Documentation* which was published by Financial Times-Prentice Hall and in 2004 when he co-wrote *A Practical Guide to Using Repo Master Agreements* published by Euromoney Books.

Disclaimer

This book is intended to provide an informational and illustrative overview of its subject mainly to non-lawyers. It should in no way be relied upon, for any reason, including but not limited to the provision of legal or tax advice in respect of any particular situation, contractual relationship or contemplated transaction. Users of this book must consult such legal and other advisers as they deem appropriate in the preparation and negotiation of securities lending documentation.

Any examples given herein are illustrative only and neither the authors of this book nor the publisher assumes any responsibility for any use to which ISLA, SIFMA or FBE securities lending documentation, or any definition or provision set forth in this book, may be put.

Contents

Acknowledgements	viii
Publisher's acknowledgements	ix
Preface	xi

1 Introduction — 1

History and development of the securities lending market	2
The short selling controversy	2
The Lehman Brothers collapse	4
How a securities lending transaction works	8
The importance of intermediaries	10
Reasons and strategies for borrowing securities	14
How a deal is done from start to finish	17
Basic tax issues for the UK	21
Basic tax issues for the US	23
Risks with securities lending	24
Differences between repos and securities loans	27

2 Legal issues: UK and US perspectives — 29

UK perspective by Paul C. Harding	31
Legal capacity	31
Title transfer and recharacterisation risk	32
The enforceability of close-out netting	35
Agency arrangements	36
The English Law securities lending master agreements	43
The ICMA and SIFMA legal opinions	43
US perspective by Christian A. Johnson	44
Enforcement of New York Choice of Law	44
Enforceability of the US Master Securities Loan Agreement	45
US Bankruptcy and banking insolvency law	46
FDICIA	53

	Legal capacity	54
	Severability	55
	Use of employee plan assets	55
3	**The Global Master Securities Lending Agreement (2000)**	**59**
	Paragraph by paragraph analysis of the Global Master Securities Lending Agreement (2000) and its Schedule	61
	Amendments sometimes proposed to the GMSLA 2000	162
	UK Tax Addendum	185
	The Clifford Chance Legal Opinion on the GMSLA 2000	185
4	**The Global Master Securities Lending Agreement (2010)**	**187**
	ISLA's Securities Lending Set Off Protocol (March 2009)	188
	Introduction to the Global Master Securities Lending Agreement (2010) and main differences from the GMSLA 2000	188
	Paragraph by paragraph analysis of the Global Master Securities Lending Agreement 2010 and its Schedule	189
	Agency Annex	313
	Addendum for Pooled Principal Agency Loans	321
	UK Tax Addendum	336
5	**The European Master Agreement**	**337**
	Background to the European Master Agreement (the "EMA")	338
	Goals and benefits of the EMA	338
	Structure of the EMA	340
	Clause by clause analysis of the EMA	343
	Comparison of the EMA with the GMSLA 2010	425
6	**The US Master Securities Loan Agreement (2000)**	**429**
	Christian A. Johnson	
	Commentary on the Master Securities Loan Agreement (2000 Version) (the "MSLA")	430
	Section by section analysis of the MSLA 2000	433
	Annexes to the MSLA 2000	571
	Schedules A and B of the MSLA 2000	593

7 The credit crunch and possible future developments in the securities lending market — **615**

Origins — 616
What happened? — 616
The current position — 617
Possible future developments — 619

Appendices — 621
Bibliography — 763
Index — 765

Acknowledgements

Paul Harding

I should like to thank my wife, Sheila, for all her encouragement and patience in the writing of this book. Our dining room table is once again empty of drafts and research materials, which appeals to her minimalist tendencies. I thank her for all her sacrifices over the past year.

I also thank my daughter, Abigail, for much typing at the later stages of producing this book.

I should like to thank Kevin McNulty, Chief Executive of the International Securities Lending Association for assistance on three questions during the writing of this book.

Christian Johnson and I should like to thank the International Securities Lending Association and the Securities Industry and Financial Markets Association for kindly permitting the reproduction of their documentation in Appendices 1, 2 and 4 of this book. We are also grateful to the European Banking Federation for permission to reproduce their European Master Agreement in Appendix 3. All these institutions gave their permissions most readily and we are pleased to express our grateful thanks to them here. Any errors remain my own.

We should like to thank the editorial staff at Euromoney Books for all their excellent editing and support. Special thanks are due to Christopher Cudmore and Linda Dhondy.

Finally, it has been a real pleasure to work with Christian Johnson on another book. To my mind, Christian is a teacher with a real love of imparting knowledge, a characteristic which has enhanced this book enormously.

Christian Johnson

I begin by thanking my lovely wife Cori and my three wonderful children, Bethany, Katherine and Henry for their patience with me and the late nights as the book progressed and took shape.

I would also like to thank Fred Engler and Yolanda Guzman at the Royal Bank of Scotland and Jelena Novakova for their patience in answering endless questions about the finer points of documenting securities lending transactions. Any errors in the book, however, are all my own.

I extend special thanks to Dean Hiram Chodosh and the faculty of the University of Utah College of Law for providing me with financial and moral support. I would also like to thank my assistant Cynthia Lane at the Law School and Chayce Clark, my student research assistant, for able research assistance and help in editing and proofing the manuscript.

Finally, I want to thank Paul Harding for inviting me to work with him on this book. This book is Paul's brainchild and he brought tremendous energy, enthusiasm, knowledge and work to completing it. He was also tremendously helpful in editing my contributions regarding the Master Securities Lending Agreement (2000) and the effect of US federal and New York law on the agreements. It has been an honour to collaborate with one of the most prolific and able commentators on securities lending, repurchase agreements and derivatives.

Publisher's acknowledgements

We are grateful to the following for permission to reproduce copyright material:

The European Master Agreement is printed with the permission of the European Banking Federation; the US Master Securities Loan Agreement is printed with the permission of the Securities Industry and Financial Markets Association (SIFMA); reproduction of the GMSLA 2009 and 2010 by permission of the International Securities Lending Association (ISLA). The commentary on the agreement does not reflect the ISLA's views and has not been approved by the ISLA.

Preface

When Christian and I were writing this course we wondered whether to start with the master agreements or the market. It reminded us of the traveller arriving in the square of an Irish village and seeing two hotels opposite each other. So he asks a local which one he should stay at. 'Ah well', he replied, 'whichever one you choose you'll wish you had stayed at the other.' We are starting with the market.

Securities lending is a significant global business with a current estimated volume of US$ 2.5 trillion (US$ 2,500 billion). It is also a fully collateralised business with most loans on an open or on demand basis. In the USA cash collateral is most often taken for securities loans; in Europe non-cash collateral predominates.

In this book we have concentrated on securities lending master agreements in English. There is a significant master agreement for securities loans in France but regrettably the authors' shortcomings in that language prevent its inclusion here.

The book does not deal with tax, regulatory or accountancy issues to any extent except where they touch on documentation. Readers should refer to more specialised publications for commentary on these matters or, of course, to experts in these fields.

This book comprises seven chapters and four appendices.

Chapter 1 sets the scene and describes the development of the UK and US securities lending markets; the short selling controversy; the nature of a securities loan and how it works; the importance of intermediaries in this market; risk issues and the differences between securities loans and repos (sales and repurchase agreements).

Chapter 2 describes the legal issues surrounding securities lending in Europe and the United States.

Chapter 3 provides detailed and clear commentary on the Global Master Securities Lending Agreement (2000) which is still very much used in Europe.

Chapter 4 does the same with the Global Master Securities Lending Agreement (2010) which was published on 20 January 2010 and is being actively promoted by the International Securities Lending Association.

In Chapter 5 we review the European Master Agreement which contains Annexes for repos, securities loans and derivatives. Our focus is, of course, mostly upon securities loans.

Chapter 6 provides detailed commentary upon the US Master Securities Loan Agreement (2000) which is the master agreement used for securities lending in the United States.

Chapter 7 is a short final chapter on the effects of the credit crunch and possible future trends both generally and for the securities lending market.

The four appendices aim to provide practical information in one place for easy reference. They are:

- **Appendix 1**: A facsimile of the Global Master Securities Lending Agreement (2000) reproduced with the kind permission of the International Securities Lending Association.
- **Appendix 2**: A facsimile of the Global Master Securities Lending Agreement (2010) reproduced with the kind permission of the International Securities Lending Association.
- **Appendix 3**: A facsimile of the European Master Agreement reproduced with the kind permission of the European Banking Federation.
- **Appendix 4**: A facsimile of the Master Securities Lending Agreement reproduced by kind permission of the Securities Industry and Financial Markets Association.

We believe this book has something to offer to seasoned practitioners and beginners. We hope you enjoy it and find it useful.

Paul C. Harding and Christian A. Johnson

1

Introduction

History and development of the securities lending market

The short selling controversy

The Lehman Brothers collapse

How a securities lending transaction works

The importance of intermediaries

Reasons and strategies for borrowing securities

How a deal is done from start to finish

Basic tax issues for the UK

Basic tax issues for the US

Risks with securities lending

Differences between repos and securities loans

HISTORY AND DEVELOPMENT OF THE SECURITIES LENDING MARKET

First of all, the terms "securities lending" and "stock lending" mean the same thing.

Securities lending developed from the 19th century UK securities trading markets. This involved gilt-edged securities (i.e. government stocks) sourced by specialist intermediaries being borrowed by market makers. They, in turn, typically provided non-cash collateral at the end of the trading day so that lenders had some protection against default.

Securities lending is older than repo trading which was first conducted by the US Federal Reserve System in 1918. It allows lenders to generate extra savings from otherwise idle securities.

Broadly speaking, in the securities lending market, transactions are either "cash driven" or "securities driven". In cash driven transactions, securities are lent or borrowed for cash which is reinvested. Any agreed eligible securities are acceptable in these deals. Typical securities might be G7 government bonds, corporate bonds (with agreed credit ratings levels), agreed equities and certificates of deposit drawn on highly rated financial institutions.

With securities driven transactions, institutions will seek to lend or borrow particular securities against collateral, perhaps to cover a short sale where they have previously sold the securities to a third party without owning them in the hope that the price would fall before they needed to deliver them. Securities driven transactions are equivalent to special repos.

THE SHORT SELLING CONTROVERSY

In normal times short selling improves market liquidity and helps efficient pricing but in distressed markets it can lead to disorderly markets and systemic risks and this is what concerns regulators.

In late 2008 short selling was a controversial subject resulting in a short selling ban on financial stocks by the Financial Services Authority in the UK until 16th January 2009 and then a regulatory requirement that short positions of 0.25% in financial services companies or those carrying out a rights issue have to be publicly disclosed. The Securities & Exchange Commission in the US held a two-day meeting on the subject at the end of September 2009. This resulted in SEC Rule 201 where short selling will be restricted on the day that a company's stock falls by more than 10% and for the day after. Then short selling will only be allowed at a price above the national best available bid price for the stock concerned. The rule applies to all equities listed on exchanges and in the OTC market.

On 2nd March 2010 the Paris based Committee of European Securities Regulators recommended disclosure of net short positions by traders to their regulators where these crossed a threshold of 0.2% of the outstanding equity in issue. Positions greater than 0.5% would have to be publicly disclosed to the whole market as would any additional increases in steps of 0.1% in each case. There was an exemption for market makers. BAFIN in Germany introduced these limits on 4th March. On 18th May BAFIN followed this up by publishing decrees prohibiting naked short sales of shares in 10 German financial stocks and Eurozone government bonds until 31st March 2011.

So far in the UK (November 2010) this has not had much effect as there has been little activity in the German markets although it has led some lenders to question if they should be doing securities lending business at all. Hong Kong has also introduced a reporting threshold in net short positions of 0.02% of a listed company's issued share capital or a market value of HK 30 million (US$ 3.8 million) whichever is lower. Naked short selling of stocks is banned in Spain.

On 15th September 2010 the European Commission adopted the 0.2% and 0.5% levels (with further disclosure each time they rise by 0.1%). They now go to the European Council and Parliament for negotiation and adoption, scheduled for 1st July 2012. This will be in the form of a Short Selling Directive which will also include a prohibition on the naked short selling of any European quoted share whose main trading venue is in the EU. ISLA thinks the public disclosure threshold of 0.5% for short sales is too low.

Regulators will also be able to introduce a circuit breaker where they can forbid the short sale of a share for 24 hours where that share has suffered a 10% decline in value on a single trading day. They can also temporarily prohibit or apply conditions on short selling of bonds or shares of European issuers or the sovereign debt of EU member states.

In addition, the proposed European Directive on Alternative Investment Fund Managers also contains short selling provisions which may impose additional disclosure requirements or limitations.

The Dodd-Frank Wall Street Reform and Consumer Protection Act which provides for a comprehensive reform of the US financial industry was signed into law by President Barack Obama on 21st July 2010.

As regards securities lending an important provision of this Act proposes to amend the Securities Exchange Act (1934) to prohibit "manipulative" short sales of securities and directs the SEC to design rules to implement this prohibition. The term "manipulative" is not yet defined. To avoid potential liability for violating this prohibition, a securities lender might well consider obtaining sufficient contractual or other assurances from the borrower that it is not borrowing securities for the purpose of engaging in a manipulative short sale.

The Act requires registered brokers and dealers to notify their customers that they may choose not to allow their fully paid securities to be used in short sales. If, however, they do use a customer's securities in short sales, they must notify the customer that they may receive fees for lending the customer's securities in this way. The SEC can prescribe the form, content, timing and delivery method for such notices.

Moreover, the SEC is required to issue rules for the disclosure of short sales by certain large institutional investment managers at least once a month.

The Act requires the SEC to produce these rules by no later than 21st July 2012. These rules will be designed to increase the transparency of information available to brokers, dealers and investors for securities lending transactions. Moreover, the Act amends Section 10 of the Securities Exchange Act to prohibit any securities lending being entered into in contravention of any applicable SEC rules and regulations. However, this provision does not stop any federal banking agency also prescribing rules relating to securities lending.

The Act also requires the SEC to introduce rules for providing monthly public disclosure of short sales by institutional investment managers subject to Section 13(f) of the Securities Exchange Act. In addition, it also requires the SEC to complete a study by 21st July 2011 on whether short sale positions in real time should only be reported to the SEC and the Financial Industry Regulatory Authority (to be established) or to the public as a whole. This additional disclosure of short selling activity may, of course, lower securities lending volume in the market.

A separate development from the new Act is a concept release issued by the SEC on 14th July 2010. This seeks public comment on the US proxy system for shareholder voting.

In a typical securities loan the right to vote the loaned securities is transferred along with legal title to those securities to the borrower. If a lender wishes to vote those loaned securities he must recall them from the borrower before the vote takes place. The concept release points out that proxy statements are typically posted after the dividend or coupon record date for the securities and therefore an institutional lender must be very alert to the timing of the record date in order to be able to recall the securities in time to vote them. The release raises the question whether decisions to recall loaned securities for voting purposes might be more timely and better informed. The release considers the possibility of addressing this issue by requiring issuers to report to those regulators the dates of meetings and their agendas before the record date so that lenders can decide if they wish to recall loan securities for voting purposes at those meetings.

THE LEHMAN BROTHERS COLLAPSE

Usually there is not much point in reinventing the wheel. The analysis in the next seven paragraphs owes much to the account which appeared in ISLA's publication *Securities Lending: Your Questions Answered* (April 2009).

Lehman Brothers, which was a major prime broker and borrower of equities and bonds, collapsed in mid-September 2008. In the weeks before its failure, many lenders had eliminated or reduced their securities lending risk exposures to them, taking advantage of the fact that most loans are callable so that lent securities must be returned within the normal settlement cycle following demand. Others had tightened collateral eligibility guidelines or margin levels.

On the morning of 15th September 2008, administrators were appointed to Lehman Brothers International Europe (Lehman) and most securities lenders immediately declared an event of default based either on the appointment of the administrators or the admission by Lehman that it was unable to perform its obligations under the relevant securities lending agreement.

Most lending agents took the approach of selling collateral in order to buy back lent securities in the market. In this way, lenders were restored to their original position of owning the lent securities. Any net exposure to Lehman was then calculated as the cost of repurchasing the lent securities less the funds raised from sales of collateral. Given the usual over-collateralisation with securities lending, most lenders were left with a surplus, even after deducting their costs, which was owed to Lehman's administrators. Some, however, may have been left with a deficit, and therefore had a claim on Lehman in administration. This was more likely to have been the case if they had been holding collateral that fell in market value relative to the securities that had been lent. However, ISLA believes few lenders in fact suffered material losses. Many lenders had indemnities from their agents which would have protected them from losses.

In some cases it was not sensible to sell collateral securities and/or repurchase lent securities in the market. This was typically because the markets in those particular securities were illiquid. Legal agreements, however, gave the non-defaulting parties the alternative approach of valuing their securities using dealer quotations in order to calculate their net risk exposure to a defaulting party.

Those lenders were subsequently left holding the collateral securities until such time as it was sensible to replace them with the lent securities. Again, lenders that had indemnities from agents would have been protected from losses.

Lehman was the biggest counterparty default in the history of the securities lending market. In general, the mechanisms designed to protect lenders against counterparty risk (collateral quality, margining, the close-out netting process under the legal agreement, etc.) worked well.

The lessons of the Lehman insolvency highlighted the importance of:

- active management of counterparty risk exposures;
- quality of collateral in relation to the lent securities;

- liquidity of lent securities and of collateral; and
- indemnities from agent lenders and their scope.

Following the Lehman Brothers' insolvency and downsizing in the hedge fund industry, some institutions reconsidered the risks of securities lending and withdrew from the market although this was expected to be temporary and some have already returned. As in the repo market there was a major decline in outstanding volumes as institutions reduced their exposure. Those that stayed tended to increase their haircuts (i.e. discounts on security value), and limited the range of collateral they were willing to accept and the stocks they were prepared to lend – usually just "specials" or "hot stocks" because they command higher fees as they are most in demand. There was also increased focus on counterparty risk and daylight exposure (i.e. same day settlement risk) and a shortening of the period for term loans. Estimates of the fall in volume of securities lent varied from 13–30%.

The main players in the securities lending market are securities houses, investment banks, fund managers, pension funds, central banks, insurance companies, broker dealers, hedge funds and even some corporate treasurers with large securities portfolios.

Securities lending is considered a money market instrument in most countries because transactions are for less than one year. Many are on an open or on demand basis but term loans also occur.

The International Securities Lenders Association ("ISLA") is the trade association for securities lenders. It was established in 1989 and has about 100 members, most of whom are based in the UK. In the UK securities lending is regulated by the Financial Services Authority ("FSA") under the terms of the Financial Services and Markets Act 2000 ("FSMA 2000"). Borrowers and lenders need to be authorised persons under the FSMA 2000 and be subject to the FSA Handbook and Code of Market Conduct. In the US, the Securities & Exchange Commission regulates securities lending (especially with respect to mutual fund activity).

In addition the UK's Securities Lending and Repo Committee has drawn up a Securities Borrowing and Lending Code (latest edition July 2009) which all UK based market participants are expected to observe. It applies to market players even when they have outsourced functions to a custodian.

In the 1950s an informal practice began among brokers where they did not hold enough physical share certificates to settle sale transactions. This was because their clients had either mislaid them or failed to provide them by the transaction's settlement date.

To cover this the selling broker would borrow the stock from another broker (the "lending broker") and when the certificate was received from the client he would pass it on to the lending broker and the transaction would be completed. This was a very informal business arrangement and no formal written agreement was put in place and no collateral was provided. "My word is my bond" (the London Stock Exchange motto) was the watchword.

The first formal equity lending transactions took place in London in the 1960s at the same time as an active interdealer market (back office to back office) developed in the US. The settlement systems in both markets were paper based which led to backlogs of settlement failures and back offices borrowing securities to cover open positions. Up to this time the US market focused upon equity lending but towards the end of the 1960s bond financing became more prominent there.

In the 1970s the US market developed along the lines of its present form but the UK market had to wait until deregulation with Big Bang on 27th October 1986 before it could evolve further because of previous tighter market regulation.

In the US custodian banks began to lend securities on behalf of their insurance company clients. Arbitrage trading became more prominent and the first international offshore securities lending transactions were undertaken. This trend grew rapidly in the 1980s partly due to the international expansion of US broker dealers and custodian banks and the willingness of US and UK lenders to expand their programmes beyond domestic securities. At the same time, increases in G10 government debt fuelled the growth of the gilt-edged securities lending and the repo markets.

In the 1980s US pension funds joined the market for the first time (following amendments to the Employee Retirement Income Security Act (1974) ("ERISA")) in 1981. In addition securities settlement systems usefully introduced book entry settlement rather than the delivery of certificates which led to greater volumes of transactions being processed.

There were, however, two "scandals" in the 1980s. In May 1982 Drysdale Securities, a US bond dealer, collapsed with over US$ 2 billion in US Treasury securities loans outstanding. Counterparties ultimately lost US$ 300 million due to being undercollateralised. This led to caution in the market which only revived later in the decade through the passing of the US Government Securities Act of 1986 and the publication of the PSA Master Securities Lending Agreement in 1987 which brought some standardisation in documentation to the market.

From November 1988 the late Robert Maxwell authorised securities lending transactions from the Mirror Group pension fund. The Mirror Group was a publicly quoted national newspaper publisher in the UK. (It is now owned by Trinity Mirror PLC.) Maxwell used blue chip shares in the pension funds as collateral for bank loans to private companies in his business empire. The problem was that no collateral was provided to the pension funds for these shares so that after his death in 1991, the pension funds were insolvent to the tune of £480 million and the debacle was investigated by the UK's Department of Trade and Industry. However, Maxwell's activities gave an impetus to the formation of corporate governance rules. Disclosures, funding arrangements, and protection of members' rights are now an important consideration in the operation of every pension fund.

During the 1990s securities lending grew through a combination of the lifting of regulatory and tax barriers particularly in the UK and through the growth of hedge funds, although the market paused following the near collapse of Long Term Capital Management in the US in September 1998.

Since 2000 there has been an increase in automated trading though platforms like Equilend and SecFinex; greater use of third party securities lending agents i.e. major custodians like Euroclear, Clearstream, The Bank of New York Mellon and JPMorgan Chase Bank, N.A.; and deregulation and development of new markets in Brazil, India, South Korea and Taiwan.

The European securities lending market itself is very large. In its half yearly survey of 54 financial institutions on 9th December 2009, ICMA's European Repo Council estimated total outstandings of €837 billion for securities loans transacted from repo desks in the European securities lending market. ISLA itself does not make volume figures publicly available. DataExplorers, a global provider of securities lending data, estimates current total global outstandings of securities lending of approximately US$2.5 trillion.

Like repos, securities lending represents a significant proportion of daily settlement value in many settlement systems and plays an important role in maintaining liquidity in the securities markets.

HOW A SECURITIES LENDING TRANSACTION WORKS

In a securities lending transaction a lender lends securities to a borrower on an open basis or for an agreed period of time against a transfer of collateral from the borrower to the lender. This collateral may be cash or securities (bonds or shares), certificates of deposits or a bank letter of credit.

Despite the terms "borrower" and "lender" and "collateral", the contract structure adopted in the UK and US market agreements is to have an outright transfer of legal title in the borrowed securities to the borrower and an outright transfer of legal title in the collateral to the lender. This enables the borrowed securities and collateral to be sold or on-lent if desired.

Upon maturity of the transaction, each party has a contractual obligation to return equivalent securities or equivalent cash or securities collateral to its counterparty. In this context "equivalent" means of an identical type, class, nominal value, issue, issuer, description and amount as the securities or securities collateral originally transferred. You do not have to return the identically numbered securities or the selfsame collateral you received. The word most commonly used in the market itself to describe such equivalent securities is *fungible*.

Therefore a securities lending transaction like a repo involves a temporary transfer of assets.

The borrower pays an agreed fee quoted as an annualised percentage of the value of the loaned securities to the lender normally on a monthly basis (normally within seven calendar days of the end of the previous month). Calls and returns of collateral may take place during the life of the loan but have no effect on the fee. However, lenders can review their portfolios during the life of a loan (many of which are on demand) and if a security is in great demand, they can negotiate a higher fee with the borrower for the remainder of the loan or recall the security.

The borrower would receive interest from the lender on any cash deposit he placed with the lender as collateral. However, the rate is likely to be below market rate so that the lender can reinvest the cash at a higher rate elsewhere in the market and make a profit. If the agreed form of collateral is cash, then the fee may be quoted as a "rebate", meaning that the lender will earn all of the interest which accrues on the cash collateral, and will "rebate" an agreed rate of interest to the borrower.

This is an important factor in US securities lending where cash collateral is the norm. In Europe non-cash collateral is usually taken.

Figure 1.1 illustrates a seven-day term securities lending transaction.

Pricing is negotiated between the parties and would reflect:

- the supply and demand of the particular securities (the scarcer the security the higher the lender's fee can be);
- the scope and flexibility of the collateral concerned (the borrower may be willing to pay a higher fee if the lender is more flexible on the collateral it will agree to take);
- the size of any manufactured dividend (please see page 21 for an explanation of this term) – the lower the manufactured dividend required by the lender due to its tax status, the higher the fee it can negotiate; and

A seven-day term securities lending transaction   **Figure 1.1**

Day 1

Lender → Securities → Borrower

Lender ← Cash or other agreed collateral

Day 7

Lender → Equivalent securities → Borrower

Lender ← Cash or other agreed collateral (plus interest if cash)

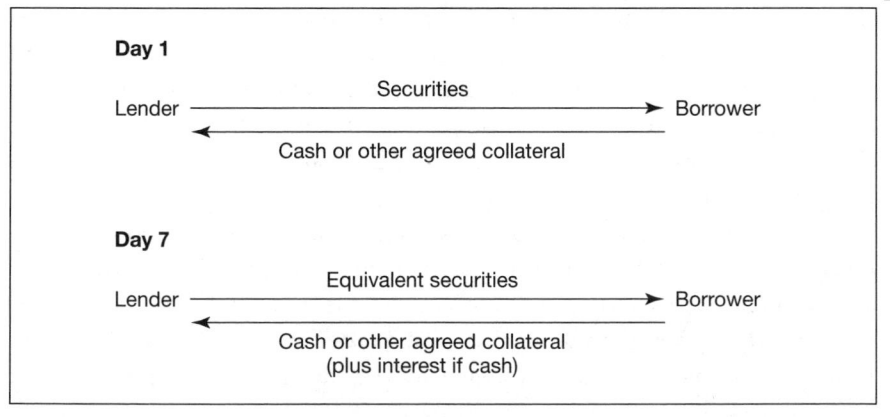

- the likelihood that the lender will recall the securities early. (The lender could charge a premium if it guaranteed there would be no early recall.)

This last point is important because most securities loans are normally "on demand" and could be recalled by giving short notice. This enables a lender who is a fund manager to be able to sell at any time to a third party and recall the securities out on loan to meet its delivery obligations. However, there are also some term loans in the market.

Repos and buy/sellbacks also flourish alongside securities lending in the UK and US markets. However, many fund managers and institutions such as insurance companies prefer to lend securities in return for a fixed fee rather than engage in repo which requires setting up a dealing desk and exposes the seller to market risk although this is alleviated through margining.

THE IMPORTANCE OF INTERMEDIARIES

Many lenders and borrowers regard securities lending as a secondary activity and prefer to use intermediaries such as the following:

- custodian banks which lend securities from the portfolios they hold on behalf of institutional investors;
- prime brokers which give their clients (e.g. hedge funds) access to lendable securities;
- clearing houses and central securities depositories which clear and settle securities and provide a number of automated services such as stock identification and tracking. Most settlement of securities lending transactions goes through a few big central securities depositories (e.g. Euroclear, Clearstream and Bank of New York Mellon).

Intermediaries typically provide valuable services such as supplying liquidity, i.e. borrowing securities on demand and lending them on a term basis. They also offer credit enhancement and comprehensive administrative services covering mark to market calculations (advised to both the borrower and lender), checking collateral eligibility and managing it, custody of securities, inter account transfers, dealing with dividends and other corporate actions, daily reporting and protecting borrowers from recalls. Finally, they offer economies of scale due to the heavy sunk costs of their previous investment in technology.

Arrangements are usually formalised under a triparty custodial undertaking among the borrower, the lender and the custodian. Under this arrangement the custodian will receive eligible collateral from a borrower and hold it in a segregated account to the order of the lender. The process is highly automated as the custodian can identify the loan requirement of a borrower and loan availability from a lender. Normally the borrower pays the custodian's fees.

Custodians also act as agents in managing securities lending programmes for their lending clients. Such clients gain from the custodian's economies of scale and established relationships with borrowers.

Custodians performing this function will typically benchmark potential borrowers against pre-agreed credit criteria; monitor loans; mark to market exposure daily to ensure the required level of collateral coverage; collect borrowers' fees when due and provide reports on outstanding loans and revenue on portfolios. Typically a lender will place limitations on which counterparties can borrow its securities; on what is acceptable collateral and risk concentration levels for securities; and the level of haircut it requires.

Most custodians acting as agents can provide indemnities against borrower default either for the full return of lent securities to a lender or the payment of cash compensation equal to the value of the securities at the time the default occurred.

Agent intermediaries such as custodians separate the underlying owners of securities (e.g. pension funds or insurance companies) from the borrowers of these securities. Economies of scale offered by these custodians ease market entry to smaller securities portfolio owners who would otherwise find the costs of running an efficient securities lending book too high. Lenders and custodians often split revenues received from securities lending between them.

As well as agent intermediaries such as custodian banks there are also principal intermediaries in the securities lending market.

While there is nothing to stop securities lending taking place directly between a beneficial owner of securities, i.e. lender and a borrower, normally an intermediary is involved. The three main species of principal intermediaries are:

- broker-dealers,
- specialist intermediaries, and
- prime brokers.

They perform a number of useful roles such as:

- *Credit risk assumption.* An owner of securities could be an insurance company or a pension scheme while a borrower might be a hedge fund. Institutions are often reluctant to take on credit exposures to borrowers that are not well known or who are lightly regulated or who do not have a good credit rating. In these circumstances, a principal intermediary (often acting as prime broker) performs a credit intermediation service in taking a principal position between the lending institution and the hedge fund.

- *Providing liquidity.* A principal intermediary will often borrow from institutions on an open basis. This gives the institutions scope to recall the securities if they want to sell them.
- *Matching of owners and borrowers.* Principal intermediaries also match beneficial owners who have large stable securities portfolios with counterparties with a high borrowing requirement. They can distribute securities to a wider range of borrowers than underlying lenders who may not be geared up to deal with a large number of market counterparties.

These activities leave principal intermediaries exposed to liquidity risk if lenders recall securities that have been lent to borrowers on a term basis. This risk is mitigated by using in-house inventory wherever possible. This is because proprietary trading positions can be a stable source of lending supply. Efficient inventory management is therefore critical and many securities lending desks act as central clearers of inventory within their organisations, only borrowing externally when netting of in-house positions is complete. This can require significant technology investment. Other ways of mitigating 'recall risk' include arrangements to borrow securities from affiliated investment management firms, where regulations permit, and bidding for exclusive access to securities from other lenders.

Let us look at the roles of these principal intermediaries in a little more detail.

Broker-dealers

Broker-dealers borrow securities for the following purposes:

- market making,
- to support proprietary trading,
- on behalf of clients.

Many broker-dealers combine their securities lending activities with their prime brokerage business (i.e. the servicing the requirements of hedge funds). This can bring significant efficiency and cost benefits.

Specialist intermediaries

Historically, regulatory controls on who could participate in securities lending markets meant that globally there were many intermediaries. Some specialised in acting as middlemen between stock lenders and market makers, e.g. the former UK Stock Exchange Money Brokers. With deregulation, these niches have almost all disappeared and some of the specialists are now part of larger financial organisations. Others have become part of a group and expanded into proprietary trading.

Prime brokers

Prime brokers usually provide the following range of services to their hedge fund customers:

- securities lending,
- repo trading,
- finance,
- trade execution,
- securities clearance,
- custody,
- reporting,
- risk management,
- fund accounting.

The cost associated with the establishment of a full service prime broker is high and recognised providers such as UBS and Goldman Sachs have a big advantage. Some of the newer entrants have been using total return swaps, contracts for differences and other derivative transaction types to offer what has become known as "synthetic prime brokerage".

Securities lending is a key component of the service as the prime broker will still need to borrow securities in order to hedge the derivatives positions it has entered into with hedge funds, for example, to cover short positions. However, this is done internally within the prime broker organisation and is less obvious to the client.

As mentioned before, main lenders in the securities lending market are pension funds, insurance companies and mutual funds or unit trusts. Their "customers" are borrowers who often have the following preferences when dealing with a lender direct:

- Large portfolios with significant borrowing opportunities.
- Minimum deal size of about US$ 250,000.
- Passive investment strategies to minimise the risk of recalls.
- Global portfolios with good liquidity and a better chance to find a match although specialist lenders in particular markets can also be valuable.

- Favourable tax profile. Borrowers are responsible for "making good" any benefits of share ownership (excluding voting rights) as if the securities had not been lent. They must "manufacture" (i.e. pay) the economic value of dividends received to the lender. A lender's tax position compared to that of other possible lenders is therefore an important consideration. If the cost of manufacturing dividends or coupons to a lender is low then its securities portfolio will be in greater demand.
- Supply of "hot stocks". "Hot" portfolios are much sought after by borrowers and offer higher fee earning potential to lenders.
- Exclusive access. Borrowers value portfolios where they have exclusive access and are willing to pay for this privilege.

Securities lending thrives when new issues are frequent and merger and acquisition activity is high. When this fell off between 2000 and 2003 and in 2007–2008 it depressed equity securities lending.

Borrowers do not need to disclose to lenders and their agents why they are borrowing securities. Indeed they may not know the full story themselves where they are on-lending to proprietary traders and secretive hedge funds or prime brokers.

REASONS AND STRATEGIES FOR BORROWING SECURITIES

Generally speaking securities borrowing is done for three reasons viz:

- to cover a short position;
- to make two-way prices, i.e. market-making;
- to take advantage of arbitrage opportunities.

Covering a short position

Short selling can be defined as borrowing securities in order to sell them in the expectation that they can be bought back at a lower price by the time they need to be returned to the lender. Short selling is a directional strategy, speculating that prices will fall rather than a part of a wider trading strategy, usually involving a corresponding long position in a related security.

Market making

Market makers play a central role in many securities markets around the world by providing two-way price liquidity. They need to be able to borrow securities in order to settle "buy orders" from customers and to make tight, two-way prices.

The ability to make markets in illiquid securities is sometimes impeded by poor access to borrowing and some of the specialist borrowers in these less liquid securities have put in place special arrangements to access such securities including guaranteed exclusive bids with securities lenders.

Securities borrowing is typically short term and on an open basis. This means that the level of communication between market makers and the securities lending business has to be highly automated in order to ensure that the necessary securities are available on loan. A market maker that goes short and then finds that there is no loan available would have to buy that security in the market to flatten its book.

Arbitrage

Securities are often borrowed to cover a short position in one security which has been taken to hedge a long position in another as part of an 'arbitrage' strategy. Some common arbitrage transactions involving securities lending are as follows.

Convertible bond arbitrage

Convertible bond arbitrage involves buying a convertible bond and simultaneously selling the underlying equity short and borrowing the shares to cover the short position. Leverage can be used to increase the return on this type of transaction. Prime brokers like hedge funds that engage in convertible bond arbitrage as they offer scope for several revenue sources, e.g.:

- securities lending revenues;
- provision of finance (i.e. leverage);
- execution of the convertible bond;
- execution of the equity.

Relative value arbitrage

This in an investment strategy that seeks to identify two companies with similar characteristics whose equity securities are currently trading at prices outside their normal historical trading range. The strategy involves buying the apparently undervalued security while selling the ostensibly overvalued security short and then borrowing that overvalued security to cover the short position.

Focusing on securities in the same sector or industry should normally reduce the risks in this strategy.

Index arbitrage

Index arbitrage involves the simultaneous purchase and sale of the same commodity or stock in two different markets in order to profit from price differentials between those markets.

An arbitrage opportunity arises when the same security trades at different prices in different markets. Then investors buy the security in one market at a lower price and sell it in another for more. However, these opportunities vanish quickly as investors rush to take advantage of the price differential.

As these transactions normally have thin margins, they are often executed in large sizes.

Tax arbitrage

Markets that have historically provided the best opportunities for tax arbitrage include those with significant tax credits that are not available to all investors (e.g. Italy, Germany and France).

The different tax positions of investors around the world have opened up opportunities for borrowers to use securities lending transactions for the mutual benefit of borrower and lender. The lender's reward comes in one of two ways: either a higher lending fee if they require a lower manufactured dividend or a higher manufactured dividend than the post tax dividend they would normally receive (quoted as an "all-in rate").

For example, an offshore lender that would normally receive 75% of a German dividend and incur 25% withholding tax (with no possibility to reclaim) could lend the security to a borrower that, in turn, could sell it to a German investor who was able to obtain a tax credit rather than incurring withholding tax. If the offshore lender claimed 95% of the dividend that it would otherwise have received, it would be making a significant pick up (20% of the dividend yield), while the borrower might make a spread of between 95% and whatever the German investor was bidding.

This example, for which I am grateful, comes from Max C. Faulkner's *An Introduction to Securities Lending* (ISLA, 2004).

Dividend reinvestment plan arbitrage

Many securities issuers create an arbitrage opportunity when they offer shareholders the choice of taking a dividend or reinvesting in additional securities at a discount. One way that they can share in the potential profitability here is to lend securities to borrowers who then do the following:

- borrow as many existing shares as possible, as cheaply as possible;
- tender the borrowed securities to receive the new discounted shares;
- sell the new shares to realise the 'profit' between the discounted share price and the market price;
- return the shares and manufacture the cash dividend to the lender.

So what was once a back office low profile activity is now actually a thriving business for many asset managers and securities lending is now an integral part of modern financial markets impacting as it does on investors, issuers, market intermediaries and regulators globally.

HOW A DEAL IS DONE FROM START TO FINISH

First of all credit departments will approve dealing lines for individual counterparties based upon their creditworthiness. They will also approve the type of collateral acceptable from borrower counterparties generally and also in specific cases (e.g. from emerging markets counterparties).

Traditionally securities loans have been negotiated between the counterparties on the telephone and followed up with written or electronic confirmations. Normally the borrower makes the call to the lender with a borrowing request. However, proactive lenders may also offer securities in demand to their approved counterparties. This would happen particularly where a borrower returns a security and the lender is still lending it to others in the market. The lender would contact those other borrowers to see if they want to borrow more of those securities.

Today, there is an increasing amount of bilateral and multilateral automated lending where securities are broadcast as available at particular rates by email or other electronic means. Where lending terms are agreed automatic matching can take place. This is called contract and compare.

As mentioned before, loans may either be for a fixed term or open. Open loans have no fixed maturity date and they are the most common securities loans especially for equities because lenders often wish to preserve the flexibility to be able to sell at any time. Lenders are able to sell securities because they can recall them from the borrower within the settlement period for the market concerned. However, if not recalled, open loans can continue for a long time.

If the term of the loan is fixed the lender does not have to accept the early return of the securities from the borrower nor does the borrower have to accede to an early return request from the lender. Accordingly securities in these fixed term loans are not on-sold.

Indicative term trades are also possible where the borrower has a long-term need for the securities but the lender finds it too risky to fix for a specific term and retains the right to recall the securities if necessary. It is also possible for securities to be put on hold – a practice also called "icing" the securities. Here the lender will reserve securities at the borrower's request against the borrower's expected need to borrow those securities at a future date. This is because the borrower must be sure that the securities will be available before committing to a trade with a third party which will require their delivery.

While some details can be agreed between the parties, it is normal for any price quoted to be purely indicative and for securities to be held until the following business day. The borrower can "roll over" the arrangement (i.e. continue to ice the securities) by contacting the lender before 9 a.m. on the next business day. Otherwise the arrangement terminates.

With icing the lender does not receive a fee for reserving the securities and they are generally open to challenge by another borrower making a firm bid. In this case the first borrower would have 30 minutes to decide whether to take the securities at that time or to release them.

A variation on icing is 'pay-to-hold'. Here the lender receives a fee for putting the securities on hold. This constitutes a contractual agreement and securities are not open to challenge by other borrowers.

Confirmations

Written or electronic confirmations are issued, whenever possible, on the day the trade is done so that any queries by the other party can be addressed as quickly as possible. Significant changes (e.g. collateral substitutions or adjustments) during the life of the transaction are agreed between the parties as they occur and may also be confirmed if either party wishes. The parties agree who will be responsible for issuing loan confirmations.

Confirmations normally contain the following information:

- contract and settlement dates;
- details of loaned securities;
- identities of lender and borrower (and any underlying principal where the lender is acting as agent);
- acceptable collateral and margin percentages;
- terms and rates;
- bank and settlement account details of the lender and borrower.

Most confirmations are electronic and very brief. Paper confirmations are rarely sent. With much automated trading often confirmations are not sent at all and deals are just matched electronically.

Settlements

Securities lenders may sometimes need to settle transactions on a shorter timescale than the customary settlement period in the underlying securities market. Settlement will normally be through the lender's custodian bank whether the lender is acting as principal or agent. The lender will usually have agreed a schedule of guaranteed settlement times for its securities lending activity with its custodians. Prompt settlement information is crucial for the efficient monitoring and control of a securities lending programme where reports are needed for both loans and collateral every business day.

In most settlement systems securities loans are delivered on a 'free-of-payment' basis and the collateral is taken separately, perhaps through a different payment or settlement system and maybe a different country and time zone. For example, UK equities might be lent against collateral provided in a European international central securities depository such as Euroclear or on US dollar cash collateral paid in New York. This can give rise to 'daylight exposure' (i.e. the risk that the second party will not return cash or securities after receiving securities from the first party). To avoid this risk some lenders will insist that their borrowers transfer their collateral in advance and this transfers the lender's daylight risk on the lender (see Chapter 3, page 87 for appropriate wording to cover this).

The CREST system for settling UK and Irish securities is an exception to this as collateral is available within that system and intra-day settlement is possible. CREST also has specific settlement arrangements for securities loans, requiring the independent input of instructions by both parties who each complete a number of matching fields including the amount and currency of any cash collateral together with the percentage value of the applicable loan margin. Loans may be made against sterling, euro or dollar consideration or be made free-of-payment.

Immediately after the settlement of the loan, CREST automatically creates a pre-matched securities loan return transaction with an intended settlement date of the next business day. The return is prevented from settling until the borrower intervenes to raise the settlement priority of the transaction. The securities lender may freeze the transaction in order to prevent the stock from returning.

CREST provides a full revaluation service for all securities out on loan. On the original creation of the return and every night that the loan is open thereafter, it is marked to market against the prevailing CREST offer price. Any deficit or surplus of cash collateral of a securities loan return arising from price movements is corrected by CREST which automatically generates payment instructions between the parties and simultaneously alters the value of the return consideration. Users may opt out of the revaluation process by completing the relevant field of the loan transaction or by settling loans on a free-of-payment basis.

Terminations

On demand loans may be terminated by the borrower returning securities or by the lender recalling them. A borrower will sometimes refinance its loan positions by borrowing more cheaply elsewhere and returning securities to the original lender. The borrower may, however, give the original lender the opportunity to reduce the fee being charged on the loan before borrowing elsewhere.

Delivery failures

When deciding which markets and what size to lend in, securities lenders will consider how certain they can be of having their securities returned punctually when recalled and what legal remedies are available where a return of securities fails.

Procedures to be followed with a failed redelivery are usually covered in legal agreements or otherwise agreed between the parties at the start of their relationship. Financial redress is usually available to the lender if the borrower fails to redeliver loaned securities or collateral on the intended settlement date and would typically include:

- direct interest and/or overdraft interest incurred;
- costs reasonably and properly incurred as a result of the borrower's failure to meet its sale or delivery obligations;
- total costs and expenses reasonably incurred by the lender as a result of a "buy-in" (i.e. where the lender has to purchase securities in the open market following the borrower's failure to return them).

Costs that would usually be excluded are any indirect or consequential losses. An example of that would be when the non-return of loaned securities causes an onward trade for a larger amount to fail. The norm is for only the proportion of the total costs which relates to the unreturned securities or collateral to be claimed. It is good practice, where possible, to consider 'shaping' or 'partialling' larger transactions (i.e. breaking them down into a number of smaller amounts for settlement purposes) so as to avoid the whole transaction failing if the transferor cannot redeliver the loaned securities or collateral on the intended settlement date.

Unfortunately, failures to deliver and return securities are a daily occurrence in the repo and securities lending markets.

The commentaries on the individual master agreements in Chapters 3–6 describe the scope of compensation available for failed redeliveries in each individual agreement.

Corporate actions and votes

A basic principle with securities lending is that it represents a temporary transfer of securities from the lender to the borrower and that the lender should continue to enjoy the benefit of any dividends or rights or bonus issues. This is achieved by the borrower making equivalent payments to the lender. These payments are called "manufactured dividends".

However, where equities are involved, a shareholder's right to vote as part owner of a company cannot be manufactured.

When securities are lent, legal ownership and the right to vote in shareholder meetings passes to the borrower who will often on sell the securities. Where lenders have the right to recall securities, they can use this option to restore the holdings and voting rights. The onus is then on the borrower to find the securities by borrowing or buying them in the market if necessary.

It is important that beneficial owners are aware that when shares are lent the right to vote is also transferred. This is emphasised in Section 7.3 of the Bank of England's Stock Lending and Repo Committee's Code of Guidance. A balance needs to be struck between the importance of voting and the benefits of lending the securities. Beneficial owners need to ensure that any agents they have made responsible for their voting and stock lending act in a co-ordinated way.

Borrowing securities in order to build a holding in a company with the deliberate purpose of influencing a shareholder vote is not necessarily illegal in the UK. However, institutional leaders and regulators do not see this as a legitimate use of securities borrowing. This is emphasised in Section 7.4 of the above Code of Guidance and is now a standard borrower warranty in Paragraph 14(e) of the Global Master Securities Lending Agreement (2010) that it will not do this.

Hedge funds are increasingly active as borrowers in securities lending transactions and voting rights are important to them in respect of target companies.

Further attention to this issue is possible from international regulators and corporate governance bodies.

BASIC TAX ISSUES FOR THE UK

We shall look at some of these again during commentary on the various agreements but as far as the UK is concerned, briefly the tax regime is basically benign towards securities lending. The main issues are as follows.

Transfer and re-transfer of borrowed securities

This would normally constitute an acquisition and disposal for UK capital gains tax purposes. However, this is not a problem in the UK but would need to be checked in other jurisdictions if the transaction is to make economic sense.

Following lobbying by the industry, tax authorities in the UK and USA have agreed that the disposal of lent securities following a default should not be treated as a sale for capital gains tax purposes provided equivalent securities are repurchased in the market.

Payment of stamp duty

London Stock Exchange rules require securities lending arrangements on which UK Stamp Duty/Stamp Duty Reserve Tax is chargeable to be reported to the Exchange. This enables firms to bring their borrowing and lending activity "on Exchange"; and to allow them to be exempt from Stamp Duty/Stamp Duty Reserve Tax. Firms which are not members of the Exchange but which conduct borrowing and lending through a member firm are also eligible for relief from stock lending Stamp Duty/Stamp Duty Reserve Tax. On Exchange lending arrangements are evidenced by regulatory reports that are transmitted to the Exchange by close of business on the day the lending arrangement is agreed. Therefore payment of Stamp Duty on the transfer and re-transfer of borrowed securities is not a problem in the UK but again this would need checking elsewhere.

Before entering into a lending arrangement, member firms are required to sign a formal master agreement with the other party, e.g. a Global Master Securities Lending Agreement (2000) or (2010).

It is also important to note that UK Stamp Duty does not apply to the sale of collateral and the purchase of lent securities following a default.

Treatment of manufactured coupons

In some jurisdictions there is the issue of withholding tax on manufactured coupons. Where the issuer of borrowed securities pays income on the securities and the borrower is receives such income it is required to compensate the lender by paying the lender an amount equal to it (the "manufactured dividend"). In some jurisdictions payment of the manufactured dividend is subject to withholding tax. It is necessary to check the laws of the borrower's tax jurisdiction to see if there is any withholding tax on the payment of a manufactured dividend in respect of the borrowed securities and the laws of the lender's tax jurisdiction in connection with payments of manufactured dividends arising from securities held as collateral. If there is withholding tax there may be exemptions available. If no exemptions are available then the parties much decide who bears the tax burden. Again this is not a problem in the UK but the matter needs to be explored in other jurisdictions.

BASIC TAX ISSUES FOR THE US

The following is a brief and summary discussion of the US tax rules governing the treatment of a securities lending transaction.

The US Internal Revenue Code essentially treats a securities lending transaction as a secured loan. Because it is treated as a secured loan, the loan is not treated as a disposition or transfer since the borrower will be returning the loaned securities at the end of the term of the loan. As discussed below, in the event that the loaned securities are not returned to the lender, it is still not treated as a disposition provided that the lender purchases equivalent replacement securities.

With respect to the fees paid under a transaction, the lender will have gross income when it receives a fee payment from the borrower. In the event that the borrower pledges cash collateral, the lender would have gross income for the income earned when it reinvests the cash collateral. The lender would have a deduction when it pays the rebate to the borrower. The borrower would have a deduction when it pays the fee to the lender. The borrower would also have gross income when it receives the rebate from the lender.

Although the general tax rules with respect to securities lending are relatively straightforward, many of the tax rules regarding payments in securities lending transactions can be complex and counter-intuitive, especially when cross-border payments are made.

Unfortunately, a thorough discussion of the various US tax issues is beyond the scope of this chapter. *Parties should always consult tax counsel when analysing the US tax consequences of securities lending transactions, especially with respect to cross-border payments.*

The main issues of concern are as follows:

Transfer and re-transfer of borrowed securities

Section 1058 of the US Internal Revenue Code provides, similar to the UK rules, that the disposal of lent securities following a default should not be treated as a sale for capital gains tax purposes provided equivalent securities are repurchased in the market. In other words, if a borrower were to fail to return the loaned securities, the transaction would not be treated as a disposition for the lender. The lender would thus avoid recognising a gain or loss when the loaned securities are not returned, provided that the lender purchases equivalent replacement securities as required under the terms of Section 1058.

Treatment of manufactured coupons

Significant care should be taken under US law with respect to the treatment of manufactured coupons, such as dividend payments. Although dividend payments on lent securities are in substance passed through to the lender, the process of paying the manufactured payment by the borrower to the lender can result in the dividend losing its character as a dividend. For example, a dividend in the hands of the recipient may be characterised as qualified dividend income for capital gains purposes under US tax law but the subsequent passing through of that dividend as a manufactured payment may result in such payment losing its character as a qualified dividend. This would result in the payment being taxed at ordinary income tax rates as opposed to the preferential lower tax rate currently available for qualified dividend income.

Cross-border payment issues

There has been significant concern about how US tax withholding rules should be applied to cross-border transfers of manufactured income or coupons, which are referred to in the rules as "dividend equivalents". Congress enacted Internal Revenue Code Section 871(l) and enacted regulations that affect how these types of payments are characterised for purposes of US tax rules. Recently, the US Internal Revenue Service issued Notice 2010-46 that attempts to deal with some of these concerns. The end result, however, is that it is becoming more likely that dividend equivalent payments (i.e. manufactured payments) made by a US payor to a non US taxpayer may be subject to withholding tax risks.

RISKS WITH SECURITIES LENDING

While the credit risk with securities lending is less than with unsecured transactions, it still exists in the forms detailed below.

Counterparty risk

This is where a securities lending counterparty defaults by not returning cash or securities on the maturity date. With the borrower acquiring full title to the bonds under a securities lending transaction there is the additional risk that the value of the bonds will have fallen below the original purchase price when the default occurs. Counterparty risk can be reduced through margining and agreeing upon appropriate initial margin or haircuts.

During the credit crunch another form of counterparty risk arose where lenders either directly or through an intermediary invested their cash collateral in toxic mortgage backed securities and other bonds through money market funds. Here the reinvestment risk was, and still is, the lender's as the intermediary would not indemnify against such losses.

In turbulent market conditions the on demand nature of most stock loans means they can be recalled so that a lender can reduce or even eliminate his risk exposure on a troubled borrower. This is what happened to Lehman Brothers (see page 5)

Market risk

This is the risk that the value of a financial instrument will fall due to market price movements. With a bond this would arise where market interest rates rise.

Margining reduces the lender's risk in this respect. However, the lender is still exposed to this risk and it will mark the loss on its balance sheet during the securities loan's life. The lent securities normally remain on the lender's balance sheet. Margin takes the form of initial margin and top-up margin.

The amount of margin required will be influenced by the following factors:

- the credit quality of the margin giver;
- the term of the securities loan (shorter is better);
- the margin's price volatility; and
- the presence of a legal agreement such as the Global Master Securities Lending Agreement (2000) or (2010).

Collateral is not the be all and end all. It is still vitally important to do a full credit analysis of your counterparty; adopt regular marking to market or revaluation (ideally daily) and have a suitable collateral cushion to mitigate sudden market price falls and avoid frequent margin calls.

The basic question, of course, is if my counterparty fails, will the collateral I hold protect me against financial loss?

Operational risk

This risk arises from system failure, human error, fraud, accident or natural disaster. ISDA defines it as: "the risk of direct or indirect loss resulting from inadequate or failed internal processes, people and systems and from external events". Operational risk also includes settlement risk which is eliminated where a delivery-versus-payment system or delivery-versus-delivery system is the norm.

Where overseas securities are being borrowed or lent and settlement is proposed in a local clearing system other than Euroclear or Clearstream, it is important to consider whether there are particular requirements relating to payments or deliveries under that settlement system which need to be reflected in the master agreement schedule. If so, the relevant master agreement should be amended accordingly. This might well happen with emerging markets trades.

It is also important to consider the settlement period for the delivery of the relevant borrowed securities or collateral. The period stated in the master agreement for the delivery of the securities must not be shorter than the standard settlement period for such securities in the relevant market.

Another issue referred to before is 'daylight exposure'. This is the exposure which may be suffered by one party to a securities lending transaction where the securities and collateral are located in different time zones or are delivered through different settlement systems. For instance, it will be difficult to achieve simultaneous delivery of securities and collateral if, for instance, the borrower is located in London and the lender is located in Hong Kong. As a result of the time difference between the two cities, the lender would have delivered the borrowed securities several hours before it receives the collateral. The risk is often accepted in the market where the party has trust and confidence in the credit of its counterparty. Alternatively the borrower may be required to agree to a delivery versus delivery system or to deliver pre-deal collateral, such as a letter of credit or to deliver collateral before the delivery of the borrowed securities.

In the rare circumstances where local regulations require that cash collateral be delivered in the local currency, it is important to consider whether such currency is readily available. If not, it may be expensive and inconvenient to obtain the local currency at the start of the transaction and to reconvert it to the preferred currency at the end. This is only likely where the borrower is paying cash collateral to a lender in an emerging market.

Legal risk

This risk arises from a failure to agree on the interpretation of a legal document or such a document being unfit for purpose or difficulty in enforcing a legal agreement when a default occurs. Fortunately, the Global Master Securities Lending Agreement (2000) and its close-out netting mechanism have not been challenged in this way.

If a securities lending master agreement is entered into by the parties and the enforceability of its close-out netting provisions is supported by a robust legal opinion from a reputable law firm in the country where the counterparty type is incorporated, regulators will allow exposure to be reported on a net basis for regulatory capital savings purposes which will lead to a reduction in the capital to be allocated to securities lending in a bank's trading book.

One area where risk has reduced over the years is in documentation as we shall see in the following chapters.

DIFFERENCES BETWEEN REPOS AND SECURITIES LOANS

It is now useful to end this chapter by distinguishing repos from securities loans, which share many of their mechanics, e.g. outright transfer of title, margining and the right to retransfer equivalent securities as follows:

Type of transaction

A repo is a sale and repurchase contract while securities lending is more of a lending and borrowing relationship and contract, despite the fact that full legal title and ownership passes with the securities and collateral.

Scope of collateral

In a classic repo cash is paid by the buyer in return for bond collateral while in securities lending stock is given in return for collateral which may be in the form of cash, bonds, equities, certificates of deposit or letters of credit. There is therefore a greater range of collateral available with securities lending.

Payment

In a repo, the seller pays a repo rate to the buyer for his cash which is accounted for on the repurchase date.

In a securities loan, the borrower pays a fee to the lender for the use of the securities based on their value. It is usually paid monthly in arrears. Interest is paid on any cash collateral.

Type of securities

With a repo (unless it is special repo) the precise nature of the securities transferred is of secondary importance being mainly there to provide some assurance to the buyer that the seller will perform its obligation to pay the repurchase price on the repurchase date. With a securities loan the borrower will be very specific about the securities he wants to borrow probably because usually he needs them to settle a transaction with a third party.

Specials

Demand for particular securities is reflected in a repo by the lower repo rate paid by the seller for the buyer's cash, but in a securities loan it is reflected in the higher fee paid by the borrower.

Income

In a classic repo, income is paid over to the seller in the form of a manufactured dividend by the buyer. In a stock loan the stock is either recalled over the coupon date or the coupon is passed through to the lender if there are no tax implications for the other party.

Term

Most repos are for a fixed term even if that is only overnight. Most securities loans are open or on demand.

Underlying transactions

Most repos have bonds as the underlying security. Most securities loans have equities. Indeed 70% of securities lending income comes from equities securities lending in Europe.

In Chapter 2 we will examine legal issues relating to securities lending in Europe and the US.

2

Legal issues: UK and US perspectives

UK PERSPECTIVE BY PAUL C. HARDING

Legal capacity

Title transfer and recharacterisation risk

The enforceability of close-out netting

Agency arrangements

The English Law securities lending master agreements

The ICMA and SIFMA legal opinions

US PERSPECTIVE BY CHRISTIAN A. JOHNSON

Enforcement of New York Choice of Law

Enforceability of the US Master Securities Loan Agreement

US bankruptcy and banking insolvency law

FDICIA

Legal capacity

Severability

Use of employee plan assets

UK PERSPECTIVE BY PAUL C. HARDING

The UK legal framework for securities lending is very similar to that for repos.
The three key issues in the UK and in many other jurisdictions are:

- legal capacity;
- title transfer and recharacterisation risk;
- the enforceability of close-out netting.

We shall also be dealing with other matters but these are the main ones.

LEGAL CAPACITY

Capacity is the legal ability of an individual or an entity such as a company to enter into a legally binding contract.

It is vital to establish that the party with whom you wish to sign a Global Master Securities Lending Agreement ("GMSLA") (either a 2000 or 2010 version) has the necessary legal capacity to enter into it and any transactions under it. If not, then your counterparty would be acting *ultra vires* by entering into such transactions under a GMSLA and those transactions would be invalid.

Banks will have specific authorisation from their regulators to enter into securities loans. In the UK this would be from the Financial Services Authority ("FSA") under the terms of the Financial Services and Markets Act (2000). Borrowers and lenders need to be authorised persons under this Act and be subject to the FSA Handbook and Code of Market Conduct. They are also expected to adhere to the Securities Borrowing and Lending Code of Guidance (latest version July 2009) which is issued by the Bank of England's Securities Lending and Repo Committee.

As regards funds, evidence of their capacity to enter into securities loans should be looked for in their constituting documents and prospectuses.

Corporate contracting parties incorporated in England and Wales provide some statutory comfort to their counterparties. This is because Section 39 of the UK's 2006 Companies Act will generally protect third parties against *ultra vires* (beyond their powers) acts of their English corporate counterparties but this is not the case in many other countries.

TITLE TRANSFER AND RECHARACTERISATION RISK

The various UK master agreements for securities loans (please see page 43 for details) have always been based upon full legal title transfer of lent securities and collateral between the parties to a securities loan.

During the period of the securities loan the borrower obtains full legal title and ownership of the securities and can use them as he thinks fit and the lender obtains full legal title and ownership of the collateral and can use it as he thinks fit. Unfortunately use of terms like "borrow", "lend", "loan" and "collateral" obscures this legal reality.

A number of factors differentiate a securities loan conducted on a title transfer basis from a pledge. These are:

- insolvency risk;
- recharacterisation risk;
- the right to deal with the securities;
- the right to the coupon;
- proceeds on enforcement.

Insolvency risk

Under a pledge the party pledging the asset is called the pledgor and the party receiving the asset is called the pledgee. It is important to remember that the pledgor retains an ownership interest in the asset pledged to the pledgee. The pledgee also has fiduciary obligations to the pledgor for the safe custody of the asset.

Under title transfer collateral arrangements like the GMSLA, the borrower as collateral giver would be the transferor and lender as the collateral taker would be the transferee. Because the transferee of collateral in the form of securities becomes their legal owner, it is entitled to do what it likes with them, subject only to a contractual obligation to return equivalent fungible securities to the transferor (the borrower) when the loan matures. Because it is the owner, it is also free of fiduciary obligations to the transferor for the safe custody of the collateral.

However, it is important to note that the transferor (borrower) has a risk on the transferee (lender) if he became insolvent. As the lender owns the collateral, the transferor will only rank as an unsecured creditor in his liquidation for the amount by which the lent securities do not cover the value of the collateral transferred. Under a pledge, as noted above, a pledgee only has a partial interest in the pledged asset and the pledgor remains the owner of that asset. Therefore in the insolvency of the pledgee, the pledgor should generally be able to redeem the asset out of the pledgee's bankruptcy estate on the basis of its continuing ownership interest in it and so that asset is therefore not available to the pledgee's general creditors. This issue has come out sharply in the recent rehypothecation (re-use) debate in the US where there is a right to redeem provided that you have not given the insolvent party the right to use the collateral. In addition, it is also important that the secured party has not commingled any cash collateral with its other assets. As a practical matter, the parties would set off what was owed and then the pledgor would sue for damages for any amount that could not be offset.

Recharacterisation risk

Recharacterisation arises from a court decision that the nature of a transaction is different from the way it is presented or characterised in its documentation. Recharacterisation undermines legal certainty.

Under English law, the nature of transactions is decided or characterised by looking at the intentions of the parties concerned. This is normally gauged from the wording of the documentation. This approach is one of "substance over form". In the past the English courts might have recharacterised a title transfer stock loan as secured loan or pledge if the form of the transaction did not match its substance or the conduct of the parties indicated this. Areas they might have looked at to gauge this were:

- the right to deal with the securities;
- the right to the coupon;
- proceeds on enforcement.

The right to deal with the securities

This right arises where legal title to the lent securities passes from lender to borrower who is then entitled to sell them, relend them, repo them out to a third party or hold on to them – in other words, to deal with them as he thinks fit.

Under a secured loan the lender obtains a partial ownership interest in the security which is subject to the borrower's "equity of redemption" (i.e. the right, when the loan is repaid, to the return of the same assets previously charged to the lender).

Because under a stock loan the borrower does not return the selfsame securities at the end of the deal but equivalent fungible securities instead, this reflects the title transfer nature of the stock loan contract.

The right to the coupon

An underlying principle of stock loan transactions is that lender should not be disadvantaged by them and should be put in the same position as if he had never entered into them. An area where he potentially could be disadvantaged is in the payment of income by the bond issuer. As legal ownership of the bonds has passed to the borrower he is recorded as their holder in the books of the bond issuer. Therefore he will receive any interest coupons on the bonds.

However, since a stock loan is only a temporary transfer of securities and the deal will end at some point, it was considered fair that the lender should receive equivalent income from the borrower who will remit a "manufactured dividend" to the lender by way of a separate payment shortly after an interest coupon is paid on the securities. Similarly a lender would remit a manufactured dividend to a borrower for income paid by a securities issuer on collateral securities. This again reinforces the title transfer nature of the stock loan contract.

Proceeds on enforcement

Where following a lender's default or insolvency, the borrower sells the securities on the open market and obtains less than the value of the collateral he has previously given to the lender, he will base his residual claim on cash damages and not refer to unpaid indebtedness. The close-out netting mechanism of the GMSLA documents promotes the cash damages concept and again indicates the title transfer nature of the stock loan contract.

Disadvantages of recharacterisation as a secured loan

In the past if an English court decided that a particular stock loan transaction was in reality a secured loan or pledge the consequences could potentially have been serious and could have entailed the following:

Inability to deal with securities

If the stock loan was recharacterised as a secured loan or pledge, a borrower who had entered into a stock loan to cover a short position would have been unable to pass the securities unencumbered to its client as the lender would retain an ownership interest in them.

Enforcement formalities

If a stock loan is a title transfer arrangement, the borrower as absolute owner of the securities can dispose of them at any time. However, if the borrower only held a security interest in them while the lender retained the ownership rights then he probably could only enforce his security in a prescribed legal procedure and may find other creditors such as the receiver and the tax authorities ranking ahead of him. He may, in fact, be prevented from selling the securities by the lender's liquidator because he did not have sufficient legal title to sell them if they were recharacterised.

Breach of negative pledge

A negative pledge is an undertaking given by a borrower to a lending bank that it will not give security to any of its lenders. The title transfer of a stock loan does not cut across a negative pledge but if a stock loan were recharacterised as a secured loan or pledge it would undoubtedly breach any negative pledge given by a lender to a bank. This would then allow that bank to accelerate its loan to that lender and demand immediate repayment.

Administration freezes

Under English insolvency law administration is a rehabilitative process, similar to the US's Chapter 11 bankruptcy legislation, whereby the court allows an insolvent company breathing space to re-order its affairs under the supervision of an insolvency official called an administrator. During this period of typically three or six months, secured creditors cannot enforce their charges but securities subject to stock loan arrangements would be unaffected by administration freezes unless they were recharacterised as a secured loan or pledge.

In England and Wales the creation of security interests required certain formalities to perfect them such as registration within 21 days of creation at Companies House. Failure to do this would render a security interest void against a liquidator. However, a pledge or charge over securities is not one of the list of registrable charges set out in Section 860(7) of the Companies Act 2006 and therefore for securities this would not have been a drawback where a stock loan was recharacterised as a secured loan but would be if it had been recharacterised as a floating charge although this would have been unlikely.

However, the problem of recharacterisation has disappeared in the EU for repo and collateralised derivative transactions because the UK and all other EU states except Bulgaria have adopted the European Directive on Collateral Financial Arrangements which grants protection against recharacterisation claims. However, it is unclear whether securities loans are also covered under this Directive.

THE ENFORCEABILITY OF CLOSE-OUT NETTING

Close-out netting is very important because it is against the closed-out net exposure that the collateral is applied in a default situation. So close-out netting needs to be robust if collateral is to be enforced successfully. There must be no risk of local insolvency officials trying to ringfence collateral assets given so an insolvent bank branch in their jurisdiction for a stock loan.

Many jurisdictions have acted to clarify the enforceability of close-out netting for securities lending (e.g. France (1996), Switzerland (1997) and

Italy and Japan (1998)). However, in all cases it is necessary to refer to the country opinion concerned to see if there are any conditions applying to the enforceability of close-out netting (e.g. that the collateral has to be cash).

Under the GMSLA (2010), when an event of default occurs and a non-defaulting party exercises its termination rights, both parties' payment and delivery obligations and any other obligations they have under the Agreement between them are accelerated to the Termination Date (i.e. as at the time of the event of default) and the values of all loans and collateral are calculated and converted into a common base currency and netted off against each other so as to produce a single cash sum due to one party or the other.

The non-defaulting party therefore has no claim on the defaulting party for the return of any lent securities, reflecting the fact that securities lending involves a full legal transfer of those securities. Only cash damages will be paid in respect of the terminated transactions. So where the borrower defaults, the lender nets off the market value of its collateral against the market value of its lent securities. Assuming that markets are normal and the margining levels on the collateral have been conservatively pitched, the lender should have a net liability to the borrower.

AGENCY ARRANGEMENTS

Chapter 1 referred to the widespread use of intermediaries in the securities lending market. Typically a custodian bank lends securities as its lending customer's agent to its borrowing customers. Usually two agreements are needed to cover this type of arrangement viz:

- an agreement between the agent and the underlying lender setting out the agency's terms and any special lending criteria required by the lender, especially the range of acceptable collateral and the haircuts to be applied to it plus the lender's refusal rights; and
- a triparty agreement (sometimes called an escrow agreement or a triparty custodial undertaking) among the lender, the agent and the borrower which sets out the terms for lending and the parties' respective roles under the arrangement.

The agent usually performs the following functions:

- He receives requests from potential borrowers and notifies the lender of the proposed deal terms;
- if the lender agrees the deal, the agent then transfers the securities to the borrower's account with him against simultaneous delivery of agreed collateral which would be credited to the lender's account with the agent;

- the agent revalues the collateral every business day and, where appropriate, calls for additional collateral from the borrower or returns surplus collateral if the borrower requests this and there is no dispute;
- the agent will reverse the loan when it ends by simultaneously transferring equivalent securities to the lender's account against the transfer of equivalent collateral to borrower's account.

During the lives of deals the agent will also:

- check collateral eligibility;
- allocate collateral among underlying principals as instructed by the lender;
- make manufactured dividends to the borrower for income received from the issuers of collateral securities;
- collect monthly fees from the borrower;
- deal with the borrower's substitution requests, if any;
- have absolute discretion to take any necessary action regarding collateral held;
- use sub-custodians, where necessary; and
- provide the lender with a daily reconciliation of the total collateral deposited with the agent and the collateral allocated to each underlying principal in its individual account.

The lender and borrower would normally give wide ranging indemnities to the agent under the triparty agreement.

Normally the agent would NOT do the following:

- exercise any voting rights or deal with corporate actions for collateral securities unless instructed in writing by the borrower;
- advise the borrower or the lender on the investment merits of any collateral;
- give any warranties on the borrower's or lender's capacity to pass full legal and beneficial ownership of collateral or equivalent collateral to each other or opine on the validity, efficacy or enforceability of any rights under the collateral;
- inquire if the borrower or lender had defaulted under the securities lending master agreement concerned or breached its terms; and
- insure the collateral.

These triparty agreements also contain events of default covering the lender and borrower and the agent's termination rights in those circumstances. In addition, there is normally a standard non-reliance representation given by both the lender and borrower to the agent.

The Bank of England's Securities Lending and Repo Committee's Securities Borrowing and Lending Code of Guidance (latest version July 2009) makes the following points about agency lending in its Section B3:

- When dealing with a client for the first time, the agent should either confirm that the client is already aware of the Code and its key contents or draw them to its attention.
- Agents should state the capacity in which they are acting (i.e. as agent) and there should be a clear legal agreement setting out the agent's authority to lend securities, agreed lending criteria and the range of eligible collateral.
- Agents should inform underlying principals that securities lending involves transfer of full legal ownership of securities to borrowers and voting rights are lost unless the loaned securities are recalled.
- Agents should agree with underlying principals the arrangements for the safekeeping of collateral and how income on that collateral will be allocated or shared.
- Where acting for multiple principals, agents should establish systems clearly showing which principals' securities are on loan and for allocating collateral among them.
- Agents should provide regular detailed reports to principals on the amount of securities lending conducted on their behalf.

Section C.10 of the Code refers to Best Execution and Agency Lending which, of course, is influenced by the Markets in Financial Instruments Directive ("MiFID"), which came into force on 1st November 2007.

The Implementing Directive for MiFID (2006/73 EC) imposes an obligation that all reasonable steps be taken to obtain, when executing an order, the best possible result for the client concerned depending upon their status (as retail, professional or eligible counterparties). Greatest protection in this respect is extended to retail clients. As far as securities lending is concerned, the Financial Services Authority expects best execution to apply to the securities lending transaction as a whole and not necessarily to each leg of the transaction.

Transactions with clients classified as eligible counterparties (e.g. investment firms, banks, insurance companies, pension funds, UCITS and national governments) are not subject to the best execution requirements unless they specifically request this (MiFID Article 24(2)).

Where best execution requirements apply, agents are obliged to draw up a procedure stating how they will take all reasonable steps to obtain best execution for their clients in line with the execution factors listed in MiFID Article 21 of which the most relevant are:

- *Price.* This relates to the lending fee. Generally competitive fee quotations are not obtained by agent lenders in the market although lending fees can be compared to those in similarly executed recent deals in that market. Distinction would be made between securities trading at general collateral rates and those trading at special rates.
- *Costs.* These focus on settlement arrangements and costs – i.e. the ability of borrowers to deliver collateral efficiently and in line with the lenders' requirements, e.g. delivery to a custodian under a tri-party arrangement.
- *Likelihood of execution and settlement.* Factors to consider here are borrower demand and how reliable borrowers are (from past trading history) in returning securities if a lender recalls them.
- *Size of the transaction.*
- *Other order execution factors.* These include borrowers and lenders each approving the other as counterparties and marking appropriate credit limits; specifying a lender's collateral requirements; considering diversification of the lender's credit risk on its borrowers; deciding the duration of loans; and reviewing the tax status of borrowers and lenders.
- *Speed.* This is less relevant than in share dealing because agent lenders are responding to borrowing requests rather than executing specific client orders.

The Code of Guidance also mentions other factors relating to best execution viz:

- *Execution venues.* These include:
  - bilateral execution with approved counterparties following telephone negotiation or the use of an electronic system;
  - execution through a multilateral trading platform or central counterparty (e.g. a clearing house);
  - execution on a regulated market.

  Most securities lending is negotiated outside regulated markets according to the Code of Guidance and so agents need to obtain clients' permission beforehand to deal through execution venues and this is typically done by a written agreement between them.
- *Reinvestment of cash collateral by the agent.* This activity might be treated as portfolio management under MiFID and therefore be subject to best execution for the agent's order execution policy for that function.

- *Review of execution policy.* The agent needs to establish a written policy on how it will monitor and review its own order execution policy and who will be responsible for doing so.
- *Compliance with COBS rules.* At clients' request, agents should provide them with appropriate information so they can satisfy themselves that the agent's order execution policy follows the FSA's Conduct of Business Sourcebook ("COBS") rules. This is useful because the absence of centralised market prices makes it difficult to compare lending fees, for example, with prevailing market levels at a particular time.
- *Pooling arrangements.* Agents engaged in pooled securities lending normally have separate policies for allocating transactions fairly among clients.

This neatly leads on to the question of collateral allocation letters by agent lenders and borrowers, and in November 2007 ISLA published some core principles on this matter.

Within the master agreement used by the parties there should be an exhibit identifying each principal lender to the borrower by legal name, address, entity type and jurisdiction of incorporation. This information must be provided before any trading is done.

ISLA recommends that the text of collateral allocation letters should be based as far as possible on the relevant wording of the Global Master Repurchase Agreement 2000's Agency Annex and Addendum. However, now that the Global Master Securities Lending Agreement 2010 has been published it is better to make its Agency Annex and Addendum for Pooled Principal Transactions the basis of a collateral allocation letter.

Where the agent has entered into securities loans on behalf of two of more principals, the collateral delivered to the agent from the borrower will be deemed to be allocated among these principals in proportion to the relevant required collateral value applying to each principal lender for all securities loans outstanding from such principal lender.

Furthermore, the separate types of securities comprising the collateral will also be deemed to be allocated pro rata among the relevant principals. These arrangements will only apply to those principals with the same acceptable collateral criteria.

Where different principals have different acceptable collateral criteria, the relevant collateral will be "pooled" according to those requirements. The agent should inform the borrower which principals relate to which collateral pools.

Collateral will be rebalanced (i.e. where collateral deliveries are to be made by the borrower to multiple lenders and by multiple lenders to the borrower) and netted off to minimise collateral redeliveries. This means that collateral deliveries to lenders will be maintained on a pro rata basis with only a net surplus amount of collateral to be delivered by the borrower or redelivered by the agent on behalf of the relevant lender(s).

The agent must keep an up-to-date record or statement of net collateral deliveries so as to ensure that it always has an accurate statement of all collateral that it holds on behalf of lenders. The agent will also agree to make that statement available to the borrower when requested.

Maintaining an accurate, up-to-date statement and having an agreed method of collateral allocation and an agreed method of rebalancing collateral movements so that the amount of collateral allocated to each underlying principal lender can always be determined will be useful where an event of default occurs and close-out follows. This is because the amount of such collateral can then be determined for the purposes of the close-out calculation.

If the borrower requires, the agent should provide regular (e.g. month end) statements of the actual collateral allocation among underlying principal lenders for reconciliation purposes.

ISLA Model for Agent Lender Disclosure ("ALD") in Europe

Since 2006 in the US agent lenders have provided data that allows SEC registered borrowers' credit and regulatory capital sections to monitor counterparty credit exposure and calculate regulatory capital requirements based upon securities loans with underlying principal lenders covered by securities lending agreements.

In the US, borrowers have to perform regulatory capital calculations at the principal rather than the agent lender level (cf. SEC rule 15c3-1, Net Capital Requirements for Brokers and Dealers).

There are three main elements to the US ALD model viz:

- exchange of files between firms;
- credit pre-qualification before trading; and
- regulatory capital calculation.

Data is transmitted daily from agent lenders to borrowers using standard text formatted files. The Depository Trust and Clearing Corporation ("DTCC") serves as a transmission hub for this purpose. Many agent lenders use vendors such as Equilend and SunGard to manage this process although it is possible to submit files directly to DTCC and receive them directly from DTCC.

Underlying principal lenders are identified using unique codes which agent lenders obtain from DTCC using a web based application. For US entities these codes are their US tax reference numbers.

The borrower uses the information contained in the files provided by the agent lender to calculate their regulatory capital requirements in order to comply with ALD regulations daily. Files are also sent from agent lenders and borrowers to each other to add or remove a principal lender to or from their borrowing programme. Where a principal is proposed to be added, borrowers must send back an approval to the agent lender for the principal before any borrowing can take place.

In its paper on the *ISLA Model for Agent Lender Disclosure in Europe* (March 2009) the ISLA proposed that key elements of the US ALD model be replicated in Europe, especially:

- *Identical file types and formats.* This would allow firms to use them for both US and European data. Of course, agent lenders would send separate files containing European and US data to the European and US offices of borrowers respectively.
- *Use of DTCC's data exchange hub for both European and US reporting.* Agent lenders need to decide whether to connect to the DTCC hub directly or via a vendor.

  ISLA has recommended a 9.00 a.m. CET Settlement + one day deadline for borrowers to receive daily loan and non-cash collateral files in Europe. As this coincides with the US deadline, it allows agent lenders to send all data files at the same time. Daily capital and credit reconciliation files are also sent.
- *Use of DTCC's unique identifiers for underlying principal lenders and counterparties.* Clearly agent lenders need to subscribe to DTCC for the issue of these identifiers.
- *Adoption of the US credit process.* Agent lenders would need to obtain credit approval for their current European principal lenders from borrowers using an incremental add/delete standardised file before starting to exchange daily European data files. Most borrowers will have already approved those lenders for credit purposes outside the ALD model. Nonetheless the ALD credit approval process still needs to be completed and the same process is used for securities lending, repo and reverse repo principals (if relevant). Where a borrower cannot approve one of these products, it has to reject the credit approval application and contact the agent lender directly.

This model has applied to all agent lenders operating on a pooled basis for clients in the European securities lending market from 1st January 2010. It does not need to apply to agent lenders who segregate principals and collateral.

THE ENGLISH LAW SECURITIES LENDING MASTER AGREEMENTS

Master agreements in the securities markets provide the following benefits:

- credit and legal protection;
- detailed collateral arrangements;
- a close-out netting mechanism for counterparty default or bankruptcy.

In the past the market standard agreement for documenting securities lending transactions in the UK and European market varied depending on the type of securities being borrowed. With UK gilts, the appropriate agreement was the Master Gilt Edged Stock Lending Agreement ("GESLA"). For overseas securities (i.e. securities not issued in the UK) the appropriate agreement was the Overseas Securities Lenders' Agreement ("OSLA") and where the securities were issued in the UK (but were not gilt edged securities) the appropriate agreement was the Master Equity and Fixed Interest Stock Lending Agreement ("MEFISLA").

However, in May 2000 the International Securities Lenders' Association ("ISLA") published its Global Master Securities Lending Agreement (the "GMSLA 2000") which combined these three agreements into one. Clifford Chance provided an English law legal opinion at the end of August 2000 and large numbers of market players moved over to the GMSLA 2000 which also had a tax addendum in relation to overseas securities. However, the OSLA is still also used in the market particularly for agency trades.

On 24th July 2009 ISLA published the Global Master Securities Lending Agreement 2009 ("GMSLA 2009") and a new UK Tax Addendum. Unfortunately there were market objections to the terms of the GMSLA 2009's paragraphs 5.4 and 5.5 concerning the pre-collateralisation of manufactured dividends on the Income Record Date (i.e. before Income was actually paid) and paragraph 6.2 concerning an aspect of manufactured dividends.

This meant that on 20th January 2010 ISLA published the Global Securities Lending Agreement 2010 ("GMSLA 2010") to replace the GMSLA 2009.

THE ICMA AND SIFMA LEGAL OPINIONS

Securities lending legal opinions are provided under the auspices of the Securities Lending and Repo Committee ("SLRC") chaired by the Bank of England. The opinions are obtained by the law firm, Freshfields Bruckhaus Deringer LLP, who also obtain them for ICMA at the same time.

ICMA opinions (of which there are currently 62) are available to ICMA members only. Securities lending opinions are available on the SLRC Extranet on a subscription basis which is run by Freshfields Bruckhaus Deringer LLP.

There are currently securities lending opinions for 58 jurisdictions.

US PERSPECTIVE
BY CHRISTIAN A. JOHNSON

As a practical matter, the enforcement of one's rights under a securities lending transaction will be substantively similar whether the US Master Securities Loan Agreement (2000 version) (the "MSLA") or the Global Master Securities Lending Agreement is selected by the parties with respect to US Federal and New York state law. However, there are important regulatory and insolvency considerations under New York and US Federal law that either do not exist under English law or take a different form. When negotiating the MSLA and securities lending transactions it is important to understand and appreciate those differences.

The following discussion is limited to the MSLA entered into by a party with any of the following types of entities:

- banks and savings associations organised or chartered under federal or state law and that take FDIC insured deposits;
- corporations, limited liability companies and partnerships organised under state law;
- broker-dealers that carry customer accounts insured by the Securities Investor Protection Corporation.

Although the legal treatment of the MSLA and securities lending transactions is favourable under US Federal law and New York law, the application of these legal principles to specific transactions can be complex.

The discussion below is by its nature general and provided in a summary form. Peculiarities with respect to a particular transaction may influence its treatment under US Federal law or New York state law. Experienced legal counsel should always be sought to review the specific terms of individual securities lending transactions and their relationship to the MSLA.

ENFORCEMENT OF NEW YORK CHOICE OF LAW

The MSLA is governed by New York law (see its Section 19). Indeed, the agreement was written on the basis of the common law and statutory provisions of the State of New York. Non-US parties often question whether such a choice of law would be enforced by the courts of the State of New York or the United States District Courts located in the State of New York ("New York Courts").

This is an especially important question if the party has no contacts with New York or is not incorporated or organised under New York law. There appears to be little doubt, however, that a New York Court would enforce the selection of New York law and would grant jurisdiction to the parties in the event of any litigation. In fact, New York Courts are required by the laws of the State of New York to enforce the choice of New York law. The aggregate amount of obligations arising out of the contract, however, cannot be less than $250,000 (N.Y. General Obligation Law §5-1401(1)). Because the amount at issue in the litigation should be more than the "Market Value" of the securities transferred, the $250,000 threshold should be easily satisfied.

New York Courts are also required by the laws of the State of New York to enforce New York as the forum for litigation "for which a choice of New York has been made" (N.Y. General Obligation Law § 5-1402(1)). The aggregate amount of obligations arising out of the contract, however, cannot be less than $1,000,000. Because the amount at issue in the litigation should be more than the "Market Value" of the securities transferred, the $1,000,000 threshold should be easily satisfied. The MSLA in Section 23.1 also expressly provides that the parties have agreed to the non-exclusive jurisidiction of the State of New York.

ENFORCEABILITY OF THE US MASTER SECURITIES LOAN AGREEMENT

Parties should be able to enforce their rights under the MSLA, assuming that both are solvent. Both US Federal law and New York State law should characterise a securities lending transaction governed by the MSLA as a title transfer arrangement between the seller and buyer. Similarly, the transfer of cash or securities under the collateral provisions (Section 4) would also be characterised by both US federal and New York State law as a transfer of title. Finally, there is no reason to believe that any provision of the MSLA would violate any public policies of the US government or the State of New York.

However, it might be asserted that a securities lending transaction could be recharacterised under New York State law as a secured loan. Although such an argument has been made with respect to the characterisation of repurchase transactions,[1] there are no reported decisions of such an argument for securities lending. Even for repurchase transactions, however, more recent decisions and commentators follow the widespread thinking that a repurchase transaction should not be recharacterised in such a way.[2]

---

[1] See *In Lombard-Wall Inc. v. Columbus Bank & Trust co.*, No. 82-B-11556 (Bankr. S.D.N.Y. 1982); Gary Walters, *Securities lending agreements and the Bankruptcy Code: The Need for Legislative Action*, 52 Fordham L.Rev. 828 (April, 1984).

[2] See, e.g., *In Re Bevill, Bresler & Schulman Asset Management Corp.*, 67B.R. 557 (D.N.J. 1986); *SEC v. Drysdale Sec. Corp.*, 785 F.2d 38 (2d Cir. 1986); Jeanne L. Schroeder, *Repo Madness: The Characterization of Securities lending agreements under the Bankruptcy Code and the U.C.C.*, 46 Syracuse L.Rev. 999 (1996).

Although a recent bankruptcy court decision has introduced some ambiguity,[3] its result has been criticised and dealt with a limited factual scenario.[4]

Similar to the practice in the derivative area where the International Swaps and Derivatives Association has solicited legal opinions on behalf of its members, SIFMA (through its predecessors) has solicited a legal opinion which opined that the MSLA was enforceable under New York law. However, a party wishing to rely upon such an opinion would be required to become a member of SIFMA given that the opinions were addressed expressly to their membership only.

US BANKRUPTCY AND BANKING INSOLVENCY LAW

A key concern for a solvent party is whether, upon the bankruptcy or insolvency of its counterparty under the MSLA, it will still be able to enforce its rights under the agreement without being subject to various limitations imposed under different insolvency regimes. Such party's rights will depend upon the bankruptcy or insolvency regime that expressly applies to it.

Most corporates organised under state law in the United States are subject to the US Bankruptcy Code. Financial institutions that take federally insured deposits, such as banks and savings institutions, however, are not subject to the US Bankruptcy Code. Instead, they are subject to insolvency rules found in the Federal Deposit Insurance Act ("FDIA"). Broker dealers that carry customer accounts insured by the Securities Investor Protection Corporation ("SIPC") are subject to special insolvency rules in addition to those under the US Bankruptcy Code.

Apart from these three classes of parties, there are other parties that are not subject to these insolvency rules. For example, insurance companies are subject to the insolvency rules of the insurance laws of the state under which they are organised. Quasi-government entities such as Federal Home Loan Banks have their own insolvency rules. Municipalities and other government subdivisions also have their own insolvency regimes. A discussion of these rules is beyond the scope of this chapter.

US Bankruptcy Code

The US Bankruptcy Code has special rules dealing with a bankrupt party that has entered into a securities lending agreement (referred to as a "securities contract" in the US Bankruptcy Code) with a financial institution, stockbroker, financial participant or securities clearing agency, all as

---

[3] *In re: Criimi Mae,Inc.*, 251 B.R. 796 (Bankr. D. Md. 2000).
[4] Jeanne L. Schroeder, *A Repo Opera: How Criimi Mae Got Repos Backwards*, 76 Am. Bankr. L.J. 565 (Fall, 2002). The Schroeder article is important in that she criticises the Criimi Mae Court for misinterpreting her prior commentary.

defined in the US Bankruptcy Code. These rules are very creditor friendly and provide important protections for an eligible creditor.

Securities contract

The definition of a securities contract in the US Bankruptcy Code expressly includes a "contract for the purchase, sale or *loan* of a security".[5] The definition also includes "a master agreement that provides for an agreement or transaction" with respect to a contract for the purchase, sale or loan of a security. A security is defined in Section 11 USC 101(49) of the Code to include a stock, note, bond, and debenture, in addition to other instruments.

---

[5] The US Bankruptcy Code defines "securities contract" in 11 USC 741(7):

(7) "securities contract" – (A) means – (i) a contract for the purchase, sale, or loan of a security, a certificate of deposit, a mortgage loan, any interest in a mortgage loan, a group or index of securities, certificates of deposit, or mortgage loans or interests therein (including an interest therein or based on the value thereof), or option on any of the foregoing, including an option to purchase or sell any such security, certificate of deposit, mortgage loan, interest, group or index, or option, and including any repurchase or reverse repurchase transaction on any such security, certificate of deposit, mortgage loan, interest, group or index, or option (whether or not such repurchase or reverse repurchase transaction is a "repurchase agreement", as defined in section 101); (ii) any option entered into on a national securities exchange relating to foreign currencies; (iii) the guarantee (including by novation) by or to any securities clearing agency of a settlement of cash, securities, certificates of deposit, mortgage loans or interests therein, group or index of securities, or mortgage loans or interests therein (including any interest therein or based on the value thereof), or option on any of the foregoing, including an option to purchase or sell any such security, certificate of deposit, mortgage loan, interest, group or index, or option (whether or not such settlement is in connection with any agreement or transaction referred to in clauses (i) through (xi)); (iv) any margin loan; (v) any extension of credit for the clearance or settlement of securities transactions; (vi) any loan transaction coupled with a securities collar transaction, any prepaid forward securities transaction, or any total return swap transaction coupled with a securities sale transaction; (vii) any other agreement or transaction that is similar to an agreement or transaction referred to in this subparagraph; (viii) any combination of the agreements or transactions referred to in this subparagraph; (ix) any option to enter into any agreement or transaction referred to in this subparagraph; (x) a master agreement that provides for an agreement or transaction referred to in clause (i), (ii), (iii), (iv), (v), (vi), (vii), (viii), or (ix), together with all supplements to any such master agreement, without regard to whether the master agreement provides for an agreement or transaction that is not a securities contract under this subparagraph, except that such master agreement shall be considered to be a securities contract under this subparagraph only with respect to each agreement or transaction under such master agreement that is referred to in clause (i), (ii), (iii), (iv), (v), (vi), (vii), (viii), or (ix); or (xi) any security agreement or arrangement or other credit enhancement related to any agreement or transaction referred to in this subparagraph, including any guarantee or reimbursement obligation by or to a stockbroker, securities clearing agency, financial institution, or financial participant in connection with any agreement or transaction referred to in this subparagraph, but not to exceed the damages in connection with any such agreement or transaction, measured in accordance with section 562; and (B) does not include any purchase, sale, or repurchase obligation under a participation in a commercial mortgage loan.

Solvent parties eligible for special treatment under the Code

Parties facing bankrupt counterparties in securities lending transactions are eligible for special treatment under the Code. To qualify for the special treatments available for securities contracts, however, a solvent counterparty needs to be characterised as a stockbroker (which includes both brokers and dealers),[6] a financial institution,[7] a financial participant[8] or a securities clearing agency (11 USC §741(7)). To qualify as a financial participant, the participant must either be a clearing organisation or meet one of two quantitative tests with respect to its aggregate trading activity in securities contracts, swap agreements, repurchase agreements or forward contracts. It must have outstanding at least $1,000,000,000 "in notional or actual principal amount on any day during the previous 15-month period". It may also qualify if it has "gross mark-to-market positions of not less than $100,000,000" in such contracts.

---

[6] The term "stockbroker" means person—
(A) with respect to which there is a customer, as defined in section 741 of this title; and
(B) that is engaged in the business of effecting transactions in securities—
(i) for the account of others; or
(ii) with members of the general public, from or for such person's own account. 11 USC 101(53A)

[7] The term "financial institution" means—
(A) a Federal reserve bank, or an entity that is a commercial or savings bank, industrial savings bank, savings and loan association, trust company, federally-insured credit union, or receiver, liquidating agent, or conservator for such entity and, when any such Federal reserve bank, receiver, liquidating agent, conservator or entity is acting as agent or custodian for a customer (whether or not a "customer", as defined in section 741) in connection with a securities contract (as defined in section 741) such customer; or
(B) in connection with a securities contract (as defined in section 741) an investment company registered under the Investment Company Act of 1940. 11 USC 101(22)

[8] The term "financial participant" means—
(A) an entity that, at the time it enters into a securities contract, commodity contract, swap agreement, repurchase agreement, or forward contract, or at the time of the date of the filing of the petition, has one or more agreements or transactions described in paragraph (1), (2), (3), (4), (5), or (6) of section 561(a) with the debtor or any other entity (other than an affiliate) of a total gross dollar value of not less than $1,000,000,000 in notional or actual principal amount outstanding (aggregated across counterparties) at such time or on any day during the 15-month period preceding the date of the filing of the petition, or has gross mark-to-market positions of not less than $100,000,000 (aggregated across counterparties) in one or more such agreements or transactions with the debtor or any other entity (other than an affiliate) at such time or on any day during the 15-month period preceding the date of the filing of the petition; or
(B) a clearing organization (as defined in section 402 of the Federal Deposit Insurance Corporation Improvement Act of 1991). 11 USC 101(22A)

It is important to appreciate that the class of parties that can benefit from the special treatment is more limited, for example, than the protections extended for swap agreements, given that the vast majority of commercial entities would not qualify under these categories. Securities lending, however, tends to be limited by its nature to the group of participants listed above. Few non-financial entities (that do not otherwise qualify as a financial participant) have either large inventories of lendable securities or a need to borrow securities on a large scale.

Right to terminate and liquidate

When a debtor files for bankruptcy under the US Bankruptcy Code, the law imposes an automatic stay under its Section 11 USC §362. The stay ordinarily prevents the creditor of a bankrupt debtor from exercising the majority of its legal rights and remedies (i.e. to terminate and liquidate) under the relevant contract. Generally, the automatic stay remains in effect until the case is dismissed or completed, or the judge grants relief, unless a specific exemption from the automatic stay applies.

For example, assuming there was no relevant exemption, upon the filing of a bankruptcy petition, a party to the MSLA would normally be automatically stayed from exercising any of the self-help remedies found in the MSLA against its bankrupt counterparty. Without a specific exemption, the solvent party would be prevented from terminating and liquidating transactions under the MSLA.

Congress, however, has eliminated many of these concerns through the passage of Section 555 of the Code.[9] If the counterparty of the debtor is a

---

[9] Section 555 reads as follows:
The exercise of a contractual right of a stockbroker, financial institution, financial participant, or securities clearing agency to cause the liquidation, termination, or acceleration of a securities contract, as defined in section 741 of this title, because of a condition of the kind specified in section 365 (e)(1) of this title shall not be stayed, avoided, or otherwise limited by operation of any provision of this title or by order of a court or administrative agency in any proceeding under this title unless such order is authorized under the provisions of the Securities Investor Protection Act of 1970 or any statute administered by the Securities and Exchange Commission. As used in this section, the term "contractual right" includes a right set forth in a rule or bylaw of a derivatives clearing organization (as defined in the Commodity Exchange Act), a multilateral clearing organization (as defined in the Federal Deposit Insurance Corporation Improvement Act of 1991), a national securities exchange, a national securities association, a securities clearing agency, a contract market designated under the Commodity Exchange Act, a derivatives transaction execution facility registered under the Commodity Exchange Act, or a board of trade (as defined in the Commodity Exchange Act), or in a resolution of the governing board thereof, and a right, whether or not in writing, arising under common law, under law merchant, or by reason of normal business practice. 11 USC 555.

stockbroker, financial institution, financial participant or securities clearing agency, Section 555 provides that the "liquidation, termination, or acceleration of a securities contract" cannot be "stayed, avoided or otherwise limited". This means that a solvent party typically would not be subject to the automatic stay and could immediately exercise its rights under the MSLA.

The only exception in Section 555 is where the defaulting party is a stockbroker and a stay of such termination or liquidation is authorised under the Securities Investor Protection Act ("SIPA") or any statutory provision administered by the SEC. In discussions, the Securities Investor Protection Corporation (the "SIPC") has indicated that it will bar immediate termination and liquidation in such securities lending situations. The SIPC, however, has indicated that in the case of a securities lending agreement it would consent to termination and liquidation of transactions under it if the SIPC receives an affidavit from the solvent counterparty that it (i) "has no knowledge of any fraud involved in the transactions and that by the terms of the transaction such counterparty has either acquired the rights of an owner of assets received in the transaction . . . ".[10]

Preference payments and avoiding power

A bankruptcy trustee has the power, commonly referred to as a trustee's avoiding power, to reclaim or unwind property transfers made to a creditor prior to the bankruptcy in certain situations. The avoiding power permits a trustee to reclaim preference payments made to a creditor up to 90 days prior to the filing of a bankruptcy petition (and up to one year in the case of transfers to insiders) (11 U.S.C. § 547(b)).

Congress, however, has resolved this concern by enacting Section 546(e) of the US Bankruptcy Code, which generally exempts transfers made to a "stockbroker, financial institution, financial participant, or securities clearing agency, in connection with a securities contract" from a trustee's avoiding powers, particularly with respect to preference payments or constructive fraudulent transfers.

Master netting contracts

Parties often enter into master netting agreements when they have entered into multiple master agreements. A common form of master netting agree-

---

[10] Letter to Omer Oztan, Vice President and Assistant General Counsel of The Bond Market Association, from Michael Don, President of the SIPC, dated as of 25 June 2002. See also Order Commencing Liquidation, SIPC v. Lehman Brothers, INC>, Civil Action No. 08-CIV-8119, dated as of 19 September 2008.

ment is the Cross Product Master Agreement, developed by several trade groups. For example, the same parties may have entered into a Master Repurchase Agreement as well as a Master Securities Loan Agreement. The master netting contract provides that upon the termination of one of the underlying master agreements, it would give the non-defaulting party the right simultaneously to terminate all transactions under the other agreements subject to the master netting agreement. Section 561 of the Code provides that such provisions in a master netting agreement are enforceable with respect to a securities contract and may not be stayed by any provision of the Code, but only if a counterparty would have had such a right to terminate transactions under the securities contract under Section 555.

US banking insolvency law

As mentioned before, financial institutions are generally not subject to the US Bankruptcy Code. Instead they are subject to various banking law insolvency statutes, such as the Federal Deposit Insurance Act ("FDIA"), the National Bank Act or the New York Banking Law. Typically, if the party accepts insured deposits, it will be subject to the FDIA.

Historically, parties had many of the same concerns about US banking law as they had about the US Bankruptcy Code with respect to securities lending agreements. Congress, however, has basically resolved these concerns by amending the various banking law statutes in a manner similar (but not exactly) to the US Bankruptcy Code.

Generally, US banking law provides similar exemptions and provisions that favour the solvent counterparty with respect to "qualified financial contracts" (12 U.S.C. §1821(e)(8)). The definition of qualified financial contract includes a "securities contract". A securities contract is defined in the same manner in the FDIA as it is under the Code. A qualified financial contract also includes a repurchase agreement, forward contract and commodity contract, all defined for purposes of the FDIA in a manner consistent with how they were defined under the Code.

Termination

Under US banking law, the solvent party is generally precluded from terminating the MSLA and underlying transactions solely because of the financial institution's insolvency. The FDIA, however, provides that a qualified financial contract (e.g. a securities lending agreement) can be terminated and liquidated under certain circumstances depending upon whether the Federal Deposit Insurance Corporation ("FDIC") is appointed as a receiver or a conservator of the insolvent financial institution.

The solvent counterparty of an insolvent financial institution can terminate and liquidate a securities lending agreement upon the appointment of the FDIC as a receiver as of 5 p.m. eastern one day after such appointment (12 U.S.C. §1821(e)(8)(A)). As a receiver, the FDIC only has the power to liquidate the financial institution and wind up its affairs.

In contrast, if the FDIC is appointed as conservator of the insolvent financial institution, the solvent party will not have the right to terminate the MSLA because of the insolvency of the financial institution (12 USC §1821(e)(10)(B)(ii)). The FDIC, as conservator, has the right to operate the financial institution as a going concern. The FDIC essentially steps into the shoes of the insolvent institution. To terminate the MSLA upon appointment of the FDIC as a conservator, an Event of Default (other than an insolvency) or a Termination Event would have to occur (12 U.S.C. §1821(e)(8)(E)).

Under general insolvency rules, the FDIC has the right to repudiate the contracts of an insolvent financial institution. This could result in the FDIC cherry picking, i.e. selectively terminating or transferring the disadvantageous contracts and maintaining the advantageous ones. The FDIA, however, provides that if the FDIC is going to transfer any qualified financial contract, it must transfer all the qualified financial contracts that it has with a particular creditor to the same transferee (12 U.S.C. §1821(e)(9)). In other words, it cannot transfer the contracts that a creditor has with the insolvent financial institution to multiple transferees. The FDIC also may not selectively repudiate or terminate any individual transaction or contract under a MSLA that the insolvent financial institution had with its counterparty; rather, it must terminate the MSLA and any underlying transactions all at once if it intends to terminate any individual transaction (12 U.S.C. §1821(e)(9)).

Solvent parties have also worried in the past that the FDIC may try to avoid certain payments made before the insolvency of the financial institution as a preferential payment. Such payments, however, may not be avoided by the FDIC unless "the transferee had actual intent to hinder, delay, or defraud such institution" (12 U.S.C. §1821(e)(8)(C)). This should protect the vast majority of payments made in the normal course of business under the MSLA.

It is possible that the New York Banking Law may apply to the insolvency of a financial institution. Its rules largely parallel those described above under the FDIA. Generally speaking, an insolvency that would involve the New York Banking Law would also involve the FDIC and the FDIA rules. Although it is possible that the New York Banking Law may apply alone, such a situation is more likely to occur with a New York branch of a non-US bank that does not have deposits insured by the FDIC, a situation beyond the scope of this discussion.

FDICIA

In addition to the statutory provisions favouring creditors in both the FDIA and the US Bankruptcy Code, the US Congress enacted additional statutory provisions as part of the Federal Deposit Insurance Corporation Improvement Act of 1991 ("FDICIA") to enforce "netting contracts". FDICIA has been codified in the United States Code in Title 12, sections 4401–4406. FDICIA is important because if a court were to find that the parties were ineligible for the "securities lending" friendly provisions found in the US Bankruptcy Code or the FDIA, the parties could still enforce the netting provisions of the MSLA provided that they were "financial institutions".

Under FDICIA, netting rights are enforceable regardless of any other provisions, statutes, regulations or judicial action. The FDICIA clarifies, however, that it does not override the FDIC's power to transfer a securities lending agreement or permit a party to terminate the securities lending agreement during the time periods allowed for the FDIC to repudiate or transfer a securities lending agreement when it is appointed as a receiver or conservator.

To be enforceable, however, parties must qualify as a certain type of financial institution or be "financial institutions" as defined in FDICIA. It is not necessary, however, that the MSLA be governed by federal law or by state law (such as the laws of the State of New York) although almost invariably it will be governed by New York law if the MSLA is entered into with a US dealer.

A netting contract is defined under FDICIA as a contract that "provides for netting present or future payment obligations or payment entitlements (including liquidation or close-out values relating to the obligations or entitlements) among the parties to the agreement" (12 USC §4402(14)(a)). The MSLA should be characterised as a netting contract under FDICIA. The remedies found in its Section 13 provide that settlement amounts can be aggregated upon an Event of Default and may be set off in determining a single net amount payable. Section 26.5 (Intent) provides that both parties agree that the MSLA constitutes a "netting contract" for purposes of FDICIA.

The definition of "financial institution" includes not only financial institutions that accept federally insured deposits, but also "a broker or dealer, a depository financial institution, a futures commission merchant, or any other financial institution as determined by the Board of Governors of the Federal Reserve System" (12 U.S.C. §4402(9)). Under Federal Reserve Board regulations, a financial institution also includes parties that meet quantitative and qualitative tests that generally describe the characteristics of a dealer in the financial markets (12 CFR Part 231).

Similar to the practice in the derivatives space where the International Swaps & Derivatives Association, Inc has solicited legal opinions on behalf of its members, SIFMA (through its predecessors) has solicited a legal opinion which discusses the bankruptcy and insolvency aspects of the MSLA and its enforceability under US Federal bankruptcy law, banking law and New York state law. However, a party wishing to rely upon such an opinion would be required to become a member of SIFMA given that the opinions were addressed expressly to their membership only.

LEGAL CAPACITY

As with European documentation, it is important that a US party has the legal capacity to enter into securities lending transactions and the MSLA. Where a US entity is concerned, however, there is no precedent under New York law where a party has been found to lack this. Unfortunately, there are no statutory protections against *ultra vires* actions in this area as are found in English law. In contrast to England, US parties by and large have not suggested or pushed for such legislation in the US.

Normally, US dealers (whether they are a bank or non-bank entity) take the position that such capacity is understood and such powers are part of its business as a dealer. A party can generally eliminate such concerns, however, by requesting that its counterparty deliver a secretary's certificate that verifies that its board of directors has approved such actions.

A party may want to be especially vigilant, however, when dealing with non-dealers, such as government entities, pension plans and similar entities that are governed by special statutory rules and regulations. By entering into securities lending transactions with a counterparty that may not have the corporate capacity to do so, a party risks a court finding that the transactions are unenforceable or ordering the party to make restitution for any gains and profits from such transactions. Additional due diligence may be needed such as requesting legal opinions from the counterparty or reviewing the various statutes, regulations, orders or organisational documents that govern such an entity.

Although there is no case law with respect to securities lending on this particular issue, Orange County raised this argument in the context of repo transactions in 1995 when it sued Merrill Lynch for losses that it suffered in the repo market.[11] Orange County sued Merrill Lynch for $2 billion in restitution and other equitable relief for entering into repo agreements with Orange County that were in violation of the California state constitution and California statutes. These provisions and statutes restricted the type of transactions and the amount of investments that Orange County could make. Ultimately Merrill Lynch settled the lawsuit with Orange County. Although the Orange County litigation is unusual both in its size and nature, it illustrates the possible consequences of entering into securities lending transactions with a party that lacks corporate capacity to do so.

---

[11] *In re County of Orange, Plaintiffs Complaint*, Case No. SA-22272-JR (Bankr. C.C. Cal. Jan. 12, 1995) (complaint filed by Orange County against Merrill Lynch).

SEVERABILITY

Parties are sometimes concerned that if one provision of the MSLA is considered to be unenforceable or illegal, the entire agreement would be unenforceable. The MSLA, however, expressly provides in Section 14 that it will be enforceable even if there are provisions that are illegal or unenforceable. New York law will enforce such a clause provided that the unenforceable or illegal provisions are only incidental to the main objective of the agreement.[12]

USE OF EMPLOYEE PLAN ASSETS

The US has stringent rules that protect employee benefit plans, pension plans and similar types of arrangements (a "Plan"), as well as certain entities in which Plans invest, from being taken advantage of by parties that have an interest or certain relationships with the Plan (a "Related Party"). The principle behind this protection is that a Related Party may have an opportunity to engage in proprietary trading or similar types of business because of the special relationship it has with the Plan (e.g. serving as an investment adviser). These laws define a Related Party very broadly. For example, an entity may be considered to be a Related Party merely because of its affiliation with another entity. Section 17 of the MSLA deals explicitly with these concerns.

In certain circumstances, the law permits a Plan to avoid certain transactions with a Related Party. Parties are concerned that if its counterparty is considered to be a Plan, the Plan may be able to avoid its obligations under the MSLA if the other party is considered to be a Related Party. Because it may be difficult to determine if it is a Related Party, a party will request that its counterparty represent that it is not a Plan.

In general, a counterparty will know whether it is organised as a Plan for the purposes of US law. It is more difficult to determine if the counterparty is holding what are referred to as "plan assets", which may result in the counterparty being treated in the same manner as a Plan for purposes of the law. An entity is sometimes considered to hold plan assets if Plans have made an equity investment in the entity. If the percentage equity ownership of an entity by different Plans exceeds a certain percentage (most commonly 25 per cent), the entity itself may be treated as holding plan assets (unless the entity is an operating company or satisfies certain conditions). In particular, the assets of investment funds may inadvertently become plan assets if too many Plans have invested in them.

---

[12] See, e.g., *Donnel v. Stogel*, 161 A.D.2d 93, 97-98 (N.Y. App., Div. 2d Dept. 1990).

Fortunately, the Department of Labor has issued Prohibited Transaction Class Exemption 81-6 which provides an important exemption and important protections with respect to these concerns. Section 17 of the MSLA provides for representations and warranties to ensure that the parties are eligible for Exemption 81-6. A complete discussion of these provisions can be found in the annotations to Section 17 in Chapter 6. Exemption 81–6 is shown as Figure 2.1.

Figure 2.1

Prohibited Transaction Class Exemption 81–6

http://www.fdic.gov/regulations/examinations/trustmanual/appendix_e/e_prohibited.html

Securities Lending

January 23, 1981 (46 FR 7527)

[Amended on May 19, 1987 (52 FR 18754)]

Recap
Securities Lending: Loans by plans to banks and broker-dealers. – The lending of securities by employee benefit plans to broker-dealers and banks who are parties in interest is permitted under this class exemption. In order for such loans to be exempt from ERISA's prohibited transaction provisions, neither the borrower nor an affiliate may have discretionary authority with respect to the investment of the plan assets involved in the transaction. A 1987 amendment, which expanded the exemption to government securities dealers, is included in the Amended Exemption.
Also see:
PTE 82–63 permits payment of compensation to a fiduciary for securities lending services.

Class Exemption To Permit Certain Loans of Security by Employee Benefit Plans

Agency: Department of Labour.

Action: Grant of class exemption.

Summary: This exemption will allow the lending of securities by employee benefit plans to banks and broker-dealers who are parties in interest with respect to such plans, if the conditions specified in the exemption are met. The exemption affects participants and beneficiaries of employee benefit plans, person who manage the assets of such plans, and parties in interest who might engage in securities lending transactions with such plans. In the absence of this exemption, securities lending transactions between a plan and a party in interest would be prohibited by the Employee Retirement Income Security Act of 1974 (the Act) and the Internal Revenue Code of 1954 (the Code).

Effective Date: January 23, 1981. For purpose solely of Prohibited Transaction Exemption 79–23 (the Grumman Corp. Pension Trust, 44 FR 31750, June 1, 1979). The final disposition of this class exemption will be deemed to occur on February 23, 1981.

Amended Exemption

Effective January 23, 1981, the restrictions of section 406(a)(1)(A) through (D) of the Act and the taxes imposed by section 4975(a) and (b) of the code by reason of section 4975(c)(1)(A) through (D) of the code shall not apply to the lending of securities that are assets of an employee benefit plan to a broker-dealer registered under the Securities Exchange Act of 1934 (the 1934 Act) or exempted from registration under section 15(a)(l) of the 1934 Act as a dealer in exempted Government securities (as defined in section 3(a)(12) of the 1934 Act) or to a bank, if:

1. Neither the borrower nor an affiliate of the borrower has discretionary authority or control with respect to the investment of the plan assets involved in the transaction, or renders investment advice (within the meaning of 29 C.F.R. 2510.3–21(c) with respect to those assets;

2. The plan receives from the borrower (either by physical delivery or by, book entry in a securities depositary) by the close of lending fiduciary's business on the day in which the securities lent are delivered to the borrower, collateral consisting of cash, securities issued or guaranteed by the United States Government or its agencies, or irrevocable bank letters of credit issued by a person other than the borrower or an affiliate thereof, or any combination thereof, having, as of the close of business on the preceding business day, a market value equal to not less than 100 percent of the market value of the securities lent;

3. Prior to the making of any such loan, the borrower shall have furnished the lending fiduciary with (1) the most recent available audited statement of the borrower's financial condition, (2) the most recent available unaudited statement of its financial condition (if more recent than such audited statement), and (3) a representation that, at the time the loan is negotiated, there has been no material adverse change in its financial condition since the date of the most recent financial statement furnished to the plan that has not been disclosed to the lending fiduciary. Such representation may be made by the borrower's agreeing that each such loan shall constitute a representation by the borrower that there has been no such material adverse change;

4. The loan is made pursuant to a written agreement, the terms of which are at least as favorable to the plan as an arm's length transaction with an unrelated party, would be. Such agreement may be in the form of a master agreement covering a series of securities lending transactions;

5. (a) The plan (1) receives a reasonable fee that is related to the value of the borrowed securities and the duration of the loan, or (2) has the opportunity to derive compensation through the investment of cash collateral. Where the plan has that opportunity. The plan may pay a loan rebate or similar fee to the borrower, if such fee is not greater than the plan would pay in a comparable transaction with an unrelated party;
(b) The plan receives the equivalent of all distributions made to holders of the borrowed securities during the term of the loan, including, but not limited to, cash dividends, interest payments, shares of stock as a result of stock splits and rights to purchase additional securities;

6. If the market value of the collateral at the close of trading on a business day is less than 200 percent of the market value of the borrowed securities at the close of trading on that day, the borrower shall deliver, by the close of business on the following business day, an additional amount of collateral (as described in paragraph 2) the market value of which, together with the market value of all previously delivered collateral, equals at least 100 percent of the market value of all the borrowed securities preceding day.

Notwithstanding the foregoing, part of the collateral may be returned to the borrower if the market value of the collateral exceeds 100 percent of the market value of the borrowed securities, as long as the market value of the remaining collateral equals at least 100 percent of the market value of the borrowed securities;

7. The loan may be terminated by the plan at any time, whereupon the borrower shall deliver certificates for securities identical to the borrowed securities (or the equivalent thereof in the event of reorganization, recapitalization or merger of the issuer of the borrowed securities) to the plan with (1) the customary delivery period for such securities, (2) five business days, or (3) the time negotiated for such delivery by the plan and the borrower, whichever is lesser; and

8. In the event the loan is terminated, and the borrower fails to return the borrowed securities of the equivalent thereof within the time described in paragraph 7 above, (i) the plan may, under the terms of the loan agreement, purchase securities (or their equivalent as described above) and may apply, the collateral to the payment of the purchase price, any other obligations of the borrower under the agreement, and any expenses associated with the sale and/or purchase, and (ii) the borrower is obligated, under the terms of the loan agreement, to pay, and does pay to the plan the amount of any remaining obligations and expenses not covered by the collateral plus interest at a reasonable rate.

Notwithstanding the foregoing, the borrower may, in the event the borrower fails to return borrowed securities as described above, replace non-cash collateral with an amount of cash not less than the then current market value of the collateral, provided such replacement is approved by the lending fiduciary.

If the borrower fails to comply with any condition of this exemption in the course of engaging in a securities lending transaction, the plan fiduciary who caused the plan to engage is such transaction shall not be deemed to have caused the plan to engage in a transaction prohibited by section 406(a)(1)(A) through (D) of the Act soley by reason of the borrower's failure to comply with the conditions of the exemption.

For purposes of this class exemption the term 'affiliate' of another person shall include:

i. Any person directly of indirectly, through one or more intermediaries, controlling, controlled by, or under common control with such other person;

ii. Any officer, director, or partner, employee or relative (as defined in section 3(15) of the Act) of such other person; and

iii. Any corporation or partnership of which such other person is an officer, director or partner.

For purposes of this definition the term 'control' means the power to exercise a controlling influence over the management or policies of a person other than an individual.

The Global Master Securities Lending Agreement (2000)

Paragraph by paragraph analysis of the Global Master Securities Lending Agreement (2000) and its Schedule

Amendments sometimes proposed to the GMSLA 2000

UK Tax Addendum

The Clifford Chance Legal Opinion on the GMSLA 2000

3 · The Global Master Securities Lending Agreement (2000)

As mentioned in Chapter 2 (page 43) the GMSLA 2000 replaces the OSLA, GESLA and MEFISLA if parties want to adhere to it.

When published its aims were:

- To create an international "one stop" securities lending agreement for all types of bonds and equities.
- To reflect market rule and practice changes including clearing and settlement arrangements.
- To produce a Tax Addendum where overseas securities and collateral were involved and one of the parties was UK tax resident.

The GMSLA 2000 came with guidance notes which are worth reading carefully.

As with the GMRA 2000 for repos it is normal in the UK to sign a GMSLA 2000 before entering into any securities lending transactions.

PARAGRAPH BY PARAGRAPH ANALYSIS OF THE GLOBAL MASTER SECURITIES LENDING AGREEMENT (2000) AND ITS SCHEDULE

Let us review the 28 paragraphs of the GMSLA 2000.

AGREEMENT

BETWEEN:

                                                ("**Party A**") a company incorporated under the laws of of acting through a Designated Office; and

                                                ("**Party B**") a company incorporated under the laws of of acting through a Designated Office.

Preamble

First of all the parties state their full legal names; in which jurisdiction they are incorporated; and that they are acting through a Designated Office. Its location is stated in Part 4 of the GMSLA Schedule. Normally only one Designated Office is stated with the GMSLA 2000 but multiple Designated Offices are possible with the GMSLA 2010 (see page 191).

1. **APPLICABILITY**

1.1 From time to time the parties may enter into transactions in which one party ("**Lender**") will transfer to the other ("**Borrower**") securities and financial instruments ("**Securities**") against the transfer of Collateral (as defined in paragraph 2) with a simultaneous agreement by Borrower to transfer to Lender Securities equivalent to such Securities on a fixed date or on demand against the transfer to Borrower by Lender of assets equivalent to such Collateral.

1.2 Each such transaction shall be referred to in this Agreement as a "**Loan**" and shall be governed by the terms of this Agreement, including the supplemental terms and conditions contained in the Schedule and any Addenda or Annexures attached hereto, unless otherwise agreed in writing.

1.3 Either party may perform its obligations under this Agreement either directly or through a Nominee.

1. APPLICABILITY

1.1

The GMSLA 2000 is a master agreement governing the parties' securities lending transactions for UK and overseas bonds and equities. Contracting parties are Lenders or Borrowers under the GMSLA 2000 depending upon the terms of each transaction. A Lender lends Securities to a Borrower against the transfer of agreed Collateral. Securities loans may be on demand or for a fixed term. When a transaction ends Borrower must return Equivalent Securities to Lender and Lender must return Equivalent Collateral to Borrower simultaneously.

1.2

Transactions are technically called "Loans" and shall be governed by the terms of the GMSLA 2000 and its Schedule and any annexes or appendices which may be attached to the GMSLA 2000, unless otherwise agreed in writing which is unlikely.

1.3

Either party may perform its obligations under the GMSLA 2000 either directly or via a nominee.

2. **INTERPRETATION**

2.1 In this Agreement:-

"**Act of Insolvency**" means in relation to either Party

(i) its making a general assignment for the benefit of, or entering into a reorganisation, arrangement, or composition with creditors; or

(ii) its stating in writing that it is unable to pay its debts as they become due; or

(iii) its seeking, consenting to or acquiescing in the appointment of any trustee, administrator, receiver or liquidator or analogous officer of it or any material part of its property; or

(iv) the presentation or filing of a petition in respect of it (other than by the other Party to this Agreement in respect of any obligation under this Agreement) in any court or before any agency alleging or for the bankruptcy, winding-up or insolvency of such Party (or any analogous proceeding) or seeking any reorganisation, arrangement, composition, re-adjustment, administration, liquidation, dissolution or similar relief under any present or future statute, law or regulation, such petition not having been stayed or dismissed within 30 days of its filing (except in the case of a petition for winding-up or any analogous proceeding in respect of which no such 30 day period shall apply); or

(v) the appointment of a receiver, administrator, liquidator or trustee or analogous officer of such Party over all or any material part of such Party's property; or

(vi) the convening of any meeting of its creditors for the purpose of considering a voluntary arrangement as referred to in Section 3 of the Insolvency Act 1986 (or any analogous proceeding);

"**Alternative Collateral**" means Collateral having a Market Value equal to the Collateral delivered pursuant to paragraph 5 and provided by way of substitution in accordance with the provisions of paragraph 5.3;

2. INTERPRETATION

Paragraph 2 is an extensive definitions paragraph.

Act of Insolvency

Act of Insolvency is an important definition.
The events described in it are as follows:

- a composition with creditors;
- a written admission of inability to pay debts when due;
- steps to appoint an insolvency official;
- presentation of a bankruptcy petition by a third party which is not dismissed within 30 days. (Please note that in (iv) there is no 30-day grace period for dismissal of a third party winding up petition as there is in the 1992 ISDA Master Agreement.);
- actual appointment of an insolvency official;
- convening a creditors' meeting to propose a voluntary arrangement (a process allowed under the UK's 1986 Insolvency Act where a solvent party can make a composition of its debts or an arrangement of its financial affairs if its creditors agree).

As we shall see in paragraph 14.1 there is no grace period for Acts of Insolvency and most other Events of Default.

Alternative Collateral

Collateral being substituted for previously delivered collateral with a market value equal to that previously delivered collateral.

"**Base Currency**" means the currency indicated in paragraph 2 of the Schedule;

"**Business Day**" means a day other than a Saturday or a Sunday on which banks and securities markets are open for business generally in each place stated in paragraph 3 of the Schedule and, in relation to the delivery or redelivery of any of the following in relation to any Loan, in the place(s) where the relevant Securities, Equivalent Securities, Collateral or Equivalent Collateral are to be delivered;

"**Cash Collateral**" means Collateral that takes the form of a transfer of currency;

"**Close of Business**" means the time at which the relevant banks, securities exchanges or depositaries close in the business centre in which payment is to be made or Securities or Collateral is to be delivered;

Base Currency

This is the currency into which risk exposure under securities loans and collateral values are converted and is stated in paragraph 2 of the Schedule. As in the GMRA 2000, Base Currency is used for both margining and close-out purposes in the GMSLA 2000.

Business Day

A day (apart from Saturday and Sunday) on which banks and securities markets in the places of business of the contracting parties are open and the place to which Securities, Equivalent Securities, Collateral or Equivalent Collateral are to be delivered at the appropriate time.

Cash Collateral

Collateral in the form of agreed currencies.

Close of Business

The time or times when banks, securities exchanges and depositories close for business in the place where a payment is to be made or Securities or Collateral delivered.

"**Collateral**" means such securities or financial instruments or transfers of currency as are referred to in the table set out under paragraph 1 of the Schedule as being acceptable or any combination thereof as agreed between the Parties in relation to any particular Loan and which are delivered by Borrower to Lender in accordance with this Agreement and shall include Alternative Collateral;

"**Defaulting Party**" shall have the meaning given in paragraph 14;

"**Designated Office**" means the branch or office of a Party which is specified as such in paragraph 4 of the Schedule or such other branch or office as may be agreed to in writing by the Parties;

"**Equivalent** " or "**equivalent to**" in relation to any Securities or Collateral provided under this Agreement means securities, together with cash or other property(in the case of Collateral) as the case may be, of an identical type, nominal value, description and amount to particular Securities or Collateral, as the case may be, so provided. If and to the extent that such Securities or Collateral, as the case may be, consists of securities that are partly paid or have been converted, subdivided, consolidated, made the subject of a takeover, rights of pre-emption, rights to receive securities or a certificate which may at a future date be exchanged for securities, the expression shall include such securities or other assets to which Lender or Borrower as the case may be, is entitled following the occurrence of the relevant event, and, if appropriate, the giving of the relevant notice in accordance with paragraph 6.4 and provided that Lender or Borrower, as the case may be, has paid to the other Party all and any sums due in respect thereof. In the event that such Securities or Collateral, as the case may be, have been redeemed, are partly paid, are the subject of a capitalisation issue or are subject to an event similar to any of the foregoing events described in this paragraph, the expression shall have the following meanings:-

(a) in the case of redemption, a sum of money equivalent to the proceeds of the redemption;

(b) in the case of a call on partly paid securities, securities equivalent to the relevant Loaned Securities or Collateral, as the case may be, provided that Lender shall have paid Borrower, in respect of Loaned Securities, and Borrower shall have paid to Lender, in respect of Collateral, an amount of money equal to the sum due in respect of the call;

(c) in the case of a capitalisation issue, securities equivalent to the relevant Loaned Securities or Collateral, as the case may be, together with the securities allotted by way of bonus thereon;

(d) in the case of any event similar to any of the foregoing events described in this paragraph, securities equivalent to the Loaned Securities or the relevant Collateral, as the case may be, together with or replaced by a sum of money or securities or other property equivalent to that received in respect of such Loaned Securities or Collateral, as the case may be, resulting from such event;

Collateral

Collateral acceptable to both parties as stated in paragraph 1 of the Schedule. It will include Alternative Collateral following a substitution.

Defaulting Party

One of the two parties to the GMSLA 2000 who has committed one or more of the Events of Default described in paragraph 14.1.

Designated Office

The branch or office through which a contracting party transacts which is stated in paragraph 4 but could also be agreed in a side letter.

Equivalent

The terms "Equivalent" or "equivalent to" have a number of meanings in this definition. Firstly they relate to Equivalent Securities and Equivalent Collateral to be returned at the end of a Loan. Here "Equivalent" means of the identical type, nominal value, description and amount as the Securities and Collateral originally transferred between the parties. It does not mean the identically numbered securities originally transferred between them.

Where a corporate action has occurred and the necessary formalities have been completed (e.g. giving of notices or payment of sums due for the corporate action), "Equivalent" or "equivalent to" have the following additional meanings:

(a) where the securities are redeemed, the amount of money received;
(b) where a call takes place on partly paid securities and is paid, the Securities or Collateral due to be returned thereafter;
(c) where bonus securities are issued, those bonus securities; and
(d) in all other cases, replacement securities or redemption moneys for Securities and Collateral due to be returned.

"**Income**" means any interest, dividends or other distributions of any kind whatsoever with respect to any Securities or Collateral;

"**Income Payment Date**", with respect to any Securities or Collateral means the date on which Income is paid in respect of such Securities or Collateral, or, in the case of registered Securities or Collateral, the date by reference to which particular registered holders are identified as being entitled to payment of Income;

"**Letter of Credit**" means an irrevocable, non-negotiable letter of credit in a form, and from a bank, acceptable to Lender;

"**Loaned Securities**" means Securities which are the subject of an outstanding Loan;

"**Margin**" shall have the meaning specified in paragraph 1 of the Schedule with reference to the table set out therein;

Income

Essentially interest or dividends paid by an issuer of Securities or securities collateral to their holders.

Income Payment Date

The date on which an issuer pays interest or dividends on Securities or securities collateral it has issued to their holders. With registered Securities or securities collateral it is the day up until which interest has accrued (the record date) and when the issuer announces that the amount will be paid over to holders at an agreed future date which will be the Income Payment Date. This is a common practice with UK gilts.

Letter of Credit

A letter of credit is a non-transferable, irrevocable letter from a bank guaranteeing the obligations of Borrower to Lender up to an agreed limit and expiry date. Its terms must be acceptable to Lender.

Loaned Securities

The outstanding securities loans themselves.

Margin

The overcollateralisation required on Collateral for securities loans which is shown in the table in paragraph 1 of the Schedule.

"Market Value" means:

(a) in relation to the valuation of Securities, Equivalent Securities, Collateral or Equivalent Collateral (other than Cash Collateral or a Letter of Credit):

(i) such price as is equal to the market quotation for the bid price of such Securities, Equivalent Securities, Collateral and/or Equivalent Collateral as derived from a reputable pricing information service reasonably chosen in good faith by Lender; or

(ii) if unavailable the market value thereof as derived from the prices or rates bid by a reputable dealer for the relevant instrument reasonably chosen in good faith by Lender,

in each case at Close of Business on the previous Business Day or, at the option of either Party where in its reasonable opinion there has been an exceptional movement in the price of the asset in question since such time, the latest available price; plus (in each case)

(iii) the aggregate amount of Income which has accrued but not yet been paid in respect of the Securities, Equivalent Securities, Collateral or Equivalent Collateral concerned to the extent not included in such price,

(provided that the price of Securities, Equivalent Securities, Collateral or Equivalent Collateral that are suspended shall (for the purposes of paragraph 5) be nil unless the Parties otherwise agree and (for all other purposes) shall be the price of such Securities, Equivalent Securities, Collateral or Equivalent Collateral, as the case may be, as of Close of Business on the dealing day in the relevant market last preceding the date of suspension or a commercially reasonable price agreed between the Parties;

(b) in relation to a Letter of Credit the face or stated amount of such Letter of Credit; and

(c) in relation to Cash Collateral the amount of the currency concerned;

Market Value

One of the key definitions in the GMSLA 2000 is that of "Market Value" which is important for calculating the value of securities and collateral to be provided and the marking to market requirements for them during the loan term. Cash Collateral and Letters of Credit are always valued at their face value.

"Market Value" is generally calculated by Lender on a bid price basis by referring to a reputable pricing service chosen reasonably by him in good faith. Any accrued income is added to the valuation to the extent it is not already included in the price. Normally, the previous day's closing prices will be used but either party may choose the latest available price where in its opinion an exceptional price movement has occurred since the closing price on the previous Business Day.

Suspended securities or collateral are valued at zero for margining purposes and as at close of business on the day of suspension for other purposes. However, it would clearly be unfair for the purposes of close-out netting or substitution for the value of such securities to be zero so for these purposes the value is treated as the Market Value of the relevant securities on the Business Day immediately before the date of suspension plus accrued income if not already in the price. Alternatively they can agree a commercially reasonable price between themselves.

A Letter of Credit is valued at the amount stated in it and Cash Collateral is valued at its face value.

Different valuation provisions apply for the purposes of applying close-out netting (called set off in the GMSLA 2000) after an Event of Default.

"**Nominee**" means an agent or a nominee appointed by either Party to accept delivery of, hold or deliver Securities, Equivalent Securities, Collateral and/or Equivalent Collateral or to receive or make payments on its behalf;

"**Non-Defaulting Party**" shall have the meaning given in paragraph 14;

"**Parties**" means Lender and Borrower and "Party" shall be construed accordingly;

"**Posted Collateral**" has the meaning given in paragraph 5.4;

"**Required Collateral Value**" shall have the meaning given in paragraph 5.4;

"**Settlement Date**" means the date upon which Securities are transferred to Borrower in accordance with this Agreement.

Nominee

An agent or named party appointed by a contracting party to accept or deliver securities or collateral or to receive or make payments on their behalf.

Non-Defaulting Party

The party not at fault in an Event of Default in paragraph 14.1.

Parties

Lender and Borrower. The word "Party" refers to either of them.

Posted Collateral

Collateral delivered to cover risk exposure on outstanding securities loans.

Required Collateral Value

The basic value of the collateral plus the overcollateralisation represented by the Margin. The margin is stated in paragraph 1 of the Schedule.

Settlement Date

The date Securities are transferred to Borrower at the start of a Loan.

2.2 **Headings**

All headings appear for convenience only and shall not affect the interpretation of this Agreement.

2.3 **Market terminology**

Notwithstanding the use of expressions such as "borrow", "lend", "Collateral", "Margin", "redeliver" etc. which are used to reflect terminology used in the market for transactions of the kind provided for in this Agreement, title to Securities "borrowed" or "lent" and "Collateral" provided in accordance with this Agreement shall pass from one Party to another as provided for in this Agreement, the Party obtaining such title being obliged to redeliver Equivalent Securities or Equivalent Collateral as the case may be.

2.4 **Currency conversions**

For the purposes of determining any prices, sums or values (including Market Value, Required Collateral Value, Relevant Value, Bid Value and Offer Value for the purposes of paragraphs 5 and 10 of this Agreement) prices, sums or values stated in currencies other than the Base Currency shall be converted into the Base Currency at the latest available spot rate of exchange quoted by a bank selected by Lender (or if an Event of Default has occurred in relation to Lender, by Borrower) in the London interbank market for the purchase of the Base Currency with the currency concerned on the day on which the calculation is to be made or, if that day is not a Business Day the spot rate of exchange quoted at Close of Business on the immediately preceding Business Day.

2.5 The parties confirm that introduction of and/or substitution (in place of an existing currency) of a new currency as the lawful currency of a country shall not have the effect of altering, or discharging, or excusing performance under, any term of the Agreement or any Loan thereunder, nor give a party the right unilaterally to alter or terminate the Agreement or any Loan thereunder. Securities will for the purposes of this Agreement be regarded as equivalent to other securities notwithstanding that as a result of such introduction and/or substitution those securities have been redenominated into the new currency or the nominal value of the securities has changed in connection with such redenomination.

2.6 **Modifications etc to legislation**

Any reference in this Agreement to an act, regulation or other legislation shall include a reference to any statutory modification or re-enactment thereof for the time being in force.

2.2 Headings

Headings are for convenience only and will not affect the interpretation of the GMSLA 2000's terms.

2.3 Market terminology

Full legal title to Securities borrowed and Collateral received passes to Borrower and Lender respectively despite use of the terms "borrow", "lend", "Collateral", " Margin" and the like which could give the impression that the transaction is a secured loan. The obligations of Borrower and Lender are to return Equivalent Securities or Equivalent Collateral when called upon to do so or at the end of the Loan.

2.4 Currency conversions

For margining and close-out purposes the values of Securities and Collateral of all types shall be converted into the Base Currency agreed in the Schedule. Where such values are stated in another currency, that currency will be converted into the Base Currency by Lender obtaining a spot FX rate from a reputable bank in the London interbank market on the day the calculation is to be made. If that is not a Business Day, the spot rate of exchange between the two currencies at the close of business on the immediately preceding Business Day is used. Where Lender has committed an Event of Default, Borrower as the Non-Defaulting Party obtains the FX rate concerned.

2.5

This sub-paragraph deals with the introduction of a new currency as the lawful currency of a country in respect of parties' payment and delivery obligations under the Agreement. The result is that no obligations under the GMSLA 2000 or a Loan are avoided because of this and that Securities in an old currency transferred under a Loan shall be considered to be redenominated in an equivalent amount of the new currency. This sub-paragraph would provide for continuity of contract in the event that any further member states of the European Union participate in European monetary union. Therefore, Transactions in former currencies continue when redenominated in the euro.

2.6 Modification, etc. to legislation

Any reference to an act, regulation or other legislation shall also refer to any revisions of these in force at present.

3. **LOANS OF SECURITIES**

Lender will lend Securities to Borrower, and Borrower will borrow Securities from Lender in accordance with the terms and conditions of this Agreement. The terms of each Loan shall be agreed prior to the commencement of the relevant Loan either orally or in writing (including any agreed form of electronic communication) and confirmed in such form and on such basis as shall be agreed between the Parties. Any confirmation produced by a Party shall not supersede or prevail over the prior oral, written or electronic communication (as the case may be).

3. LOANS OF SECURITIES

This paragraph sets out how Lender will lend securities to Borrower and vice versa in accordance with the terms of the GMSLA 2000.

The terms of each Loan are agreed in advance by telephone, in writing or electronically and confirmed as agreed between the parties.

Interestingly the paragraph states any confirmation produced by a party will not supersede any previous communication between the parties agreeing the terms of the securities loan. This is because deal terms are usually electronically matched in the market and such confirmations as exist are usually sparse in detail.

In other master agreements like the ISDA Master Agreement and the GMRA 2000 the confirmation normally prevails over all other documentation where there is a clash of terms on the same subject matter.

4. **DELIVERY**

4.1 **Delivery of Securities on commencement of Loan**

Lender shall procure the delivery of Securities to Borrower or deliver such Securities in accordance with this Agreement and the terms of the relevant Loan. Such Securities shall be deemed to have been delivered by Lender to Borrower on delivery to Borrower or as it shall direct of the relevant instruments of transfer, or in the case of Securities held by an agent or within a clearing or settlement system on the effective instructions to such agent or the operator of such system which result in such Securities being held by the operator of the clearing system for the account of the Borrower or as it shall direct, or by such other means as may be agreed.

4.2 **Requirements to effect delivery**

The Parties shall execute and deliver all necessary documents and give all necessary instructions to procure that all right, title and interest in:

(a) any Securities borrowed pursuant to paragraph 3;

(b) any Equivalent Securities redelivered pursuant to paragraph 8;

(c) any Collateral delivered pursuant to paragraph 5;

(d) any Equivalent Collateral redelivered pursuant to paragraphs 5 or 8;

shall pass from one Party to the other subject to the terms and conditions set out in this Agreement, on delivery or redelivery of the same in accordance with this Agreement with full title guarantee, free from all liens, charges and encumbrances. In the case of Securities, Collateral, Equivalent Securities or Equivalent Collateral title to which is registered in a computer based system which provides for the recording and transfer of title to the same by way of book entries, delivery and transfer of title shall take place in accordance with the rules and procedures of such system as in force from time to time. The Party acquiring such right, title and interest shall have no obligation to return or redeliver any of the assets so acquired but, in so far as any Securities are borrowed or any Collateral is delivered to such Party, such Party shall be obliged, subject to the terms of this Agreement, to redeliver Equivalent Securities or Equivalent Collateral as appropriate.

4. DELIVERY

4.1 Delivery of Securities on commencement of Loan

Lender shall deliver Securities or arrange for their delivery to Borrower in accordance with the relevant Loan and GMSLA 2000 terms. Delivery takes place when the Securities and any necessary transfer documentation are received by Borrower or its agent. If Borrower wants Lender to deliver to a clearing or settlement system like Euroclear or Clearstream, delivery takes place when the Securities arrive in Borrower's account or that of its agent in such systems.

4.2 Requirements to effect delivery

The various species of Securities or Collateral which can be borrowed or delivered under the GMSLA 2000 will be delivered with full legal title free of all liens, charges or encumbrances together with all necessary transfer documentation or instructions. Under any transaction, legal title to the loaned securities is transferred outright to Borrower and legal title to the collateral is transferred outright to Lender.

Where legal title to any Securities or Collateral is registered in a book entry electronic transfer system, delivery and title transfer will take place in accordance with the current rules of that system.

At the end of the transaction, the original loaned securities and collateral are not returned, but Equivalent Securities and Equivalent Collateral are transferred between the parties.

4.3 **Deliveries to be simultaneous unless otherwise agreed**

Where under the terms of this Agreement a Party is not obliged to make a delivery unless simultaneously a delivery is made to it, subject to and without prejudice to its rights under paragraph 8.6 such Party may from time to time in accordance with market practice and in recognition of the practical difficulties in arranging simultaneous delivery of Securities, Collateral and cash transfers waive its right under this Agreement in respect of simultaneous delivery and/or payment provided that no such waiver (whether by course of conduct or otherwise) in respect of one transaction shall bind it in respect of any other transaction.

4.4 **Deliveries of Income**

In respect of Income being paid in relation to any Loaned Securities or Collateral, Borrower in the case of Income being paid in respect of Loaned Securities and Lender in the case of Income being paid in respect of Collateral shall provide to the other Party, as the case may be, any endorsements or assignments as shall be customary and appropriate to effect the delivery of money or property equivalent to the type and amount of such Income to Lender, irrespective of whether Borrower received the same in respect of any Loaned Securities or to Borrower, irrespective of whether Lender received the same in respect of any Collateral.

4.3 Deliveries to be simultaneous unless otherwise agreed

A party is not obliged to make a delivery of securities or collateral unless a simultaneous delivery is made to it by its counterparty and it is confident that this will take place. Otherwise it may exercise the rights available to it under paragraph 8.6 (i.e. withholding its own delivery). However, market practice or practical difficulties with simultaneous delivery of Securities, Collateral or cash transfers may persuade him to waive this on a case by case basis without setting any general precedent for the future.

4.4 Deliveries of Income

With securities and securities collateral, Borrower and Lender will respectively be shown as owner of these assets in the books of the issuer of the securities concerned. As a Loan is only a temporary transfer of securities, the market considers it fair that Lender (in the case of Securities) and Borrower (in the case of securities collateral) should receive any Income on these securities distributed by their issuers. This will be in the form of equivalent payments (manufactured dividends) under paragraph 6.1 made by each party to the other after receiving the relevant Income from the securities issuer. Each of them is still obliged to pay this over during the life of the Loan even if they have disposed of the Securities or the securities collateral concerned to a third party.

5. **COLLATERAL**

5.1 **Delivery of Collateral on commencement of Loan**

Subject to the other provisions of this paragraph 5, Borrower undertakes to deliver to or deposit with Lender (or in accordance with Lender's instructions) Collateral simultaneously with delivery of the Securities to which the Loan relates and in any event no later than Close of Business on the Settlement Date. In respect of Collateral comprising securities, such Collateral shall be deemed to have been delivered by Borrower to Lender on delivery to Lender or as it shall direct of the relevant instruments of transfer, or in the case of such securities being held by an agent or within a clearing or settlement system, on the effective instructions to such agent or the operator of such system, which result in such securities being held by the operator of the clearing system for the account of the Lender or as it shall direct, or by such other means as may be agreed.

5. COLLATERAL

5.1 Delivery of Collateral on commencement of Loan

This sub-paragraph contains the obligation of Borrower to provide Collateral to Lender at the same time as Lender delivers the loaned securities to it or by the end of the same Business Day if simultaneous delivery is impracticable.

In the case of securities collateral, delivery is considered to take place at the time Lender or its agent receives it together with any necessary transfer documentation or if the securities collateral is to be held within a clearing or settlement system, at the time the securities collateral is credited to Lender's account in that system.

Where the parties agree that Lender is to be pre-collateralised, the following provision could be inserted in the Schedule:

"Unless otherwise agreed in respect of any particular Loan, notwithstanding anything to the contrary in this Agreement (i) any obligation of Lender to deliver Securities in respect of any Loan to Borrower is conditional upon Lender having received the Collateral agreed to be provided in respect of such Loan and (ii) any obligation of Lender to repay or redeliver (as the case may be) Equivalent Collateral upon the termination of a Loan is conditional upon Lender verifying receipt of Equivalent Securities or upon the substitution of Alternative Collateral is conditional upon Lender verifying receipt of Equivalent Securities or Alternative Collateral, as the case may be."

5.2 **Deliveries through payment systems generating automatic payments**

Unless otherwise agreed between the Parties, where any Securities, Equivalent Securities, Collateral or Equivalent Collateral (in the form of securities) are transferred through a book entry transfer or settlement system which automatically generates a payment or delivery, or obligation to pay or deliver, against the transfer of such securities, then:-

(i) such automatically generated payment, delivery or obligation shall be treated as a payment or delivery by the transferee to the transferor, and except to the extent that it is applied to discharge an obligation of the transferee to effect payment or delivery, such payment or delivery, or obligation to pay or deliver, shall be deemed to be a transfer of Collateral or redelivery of Equivalent Collateral, as the case may be, made by the transferee until such time as the Collateral or Equivalent Collateral is substituted with other Collateral or Equivalent Collateral if an obligation to deliver other Collateral or redeliver Equivalent Collateral existed immediately prior to the transfer of Securities, Equivalent Securities, Collateral or Equivalent Collateral; and

(ii) the party receiving such substituted Collateral or Equivalent Collateral, or if no obligation to deliver other Collateral or redeliver Equivalent Collateral existed immediately prior to the transfer of Securities, Equivalent Securities, Collateral or Equivalent Collateral, the party receiving the deemed transfer of Collateral or redelivery of Equivalent Collateral, as the case may be, shall cause to be made to the other party for value the same day either, where such transfer is a payment, an irrevocable payment in the amount of such transfer or, where such transfer is a delivery, an irrevocable delivery of securities (or other property, as the case may be) equivalent to such property.

5.3 **Substitutions of Collateral**

Borrower may from time to time call for the repayment of Cash Collateral or the redelivery of Collateral equivalent to any Collateral delivered to Lender prior to the date on which the same would otherwise have been repayable or redeliverable provided that at the time of such repayment or redelivery Borrower shall have delivered or delivers Alternative Collateral acceptable to Lender and Borrower is in compliance with paragraph 5.4 or paragraph 5.5, as applicable.

5.2 Deliveries through payment systems generating automatic payments

This sub-paragraph covers the situation where a clearing or settlement system (such as the old Central Gilts Office) cannot cope with accepting securities or securities collateral on a free of payment or free of delivery basis. This means that as soon as such securities are delivered a payment equal to their value is sent to their transferor.

(i) If this happens such a payment may be used to meet an existing obligation which its recipient (the transferee) may have to the delivering transferor. Otherwise such payment will be considered to be Collateral or Equivalent Collateral, as the case may be, until it is substituted by Alternative Collateral, if a prior obligation to deliver Collateral or Equivalent Collateral exists.

(ii) Where no such obligation exists at the time, the recipient of the payment or delivery must return an equivalent payment or delivery to its counterparty on the same Business Day outside the settlement system concerned or the same thing will happen again.

5.3 Substitutions of Collateral

Borrower may at any time call for repayment of Cash Collateral or the substitution of securities collateral **and does not need Lender's consent to do so**. However, it must provide substitute Collateral which is acceptable to Lender and fully covers Lender's risk exposure on Borrower.

5.4 **Marking to Market of Collateral during the currency of a Loan on aggregated basis**

Unless paragraph 1.3 of the Schedule indicates that paragraph 5.5 shall apply in lieu of this paragraph 5.4, or unless otherwise agreed between the Parties:-

(i) the aggregate Market Value of the Collateral delivered to or deposited with Lender (excluding any Equivalent Collateral repaid or redelivered under Paragraphs 5.4(ii) or 5.5(ii) (as the case may be)) ("**Posted Collateral**") in respect of all Loans outstanding under this Agreement shall equal the aggregate of the Market Value of the Loaned Securities and the applicable Margin (the "**Required Collateral Value**") in respect of such Loans;

(ii) if at any time on any Business Day the aggregate Market Value of the Posted Collateral in respect of all Loans outstanding under this Agreement exceeds the aggregate of the Required Collateral Values in respect of such Loans, Lender shall (on demand) repay and/or redeliver, as the case may be, to Borrower such Equivalent Collateral as will eliminate the excess;

(iii) if at any time on any Business Day the aggregate Market Value of the Posted Collateral in respect of all Loans outstanding under this Agreement falls below the aggregate of Required Collateral Values in respect of all such Loans, Borrower shall (on demand) provide such further Collateral to Lender as will eliminate the deficiency.

5.4 Marking to Market of Collateral during the currency of a Loan on an aggregated basis

The GMSLA 2000 offers a choice of margining being across all Loans (as here in paragraph 5.4) or on an individual Loan basis (as in paragraph 5.5). The choice is made in paragraph 1.3 of the Schedule:

(i) In paragraph 5.4 the Market Value of the collateral to cover all Loans must be equal to the Market Value of all loaned securities plus the Margin agreed in paragraph 1.2 of the Schedule for each type of collateral acceptable to both parties. Collateral provided is called Posted Collateral. The aggregate of the Market Value of the loaned securities and the Margin is called the Required Collateral Value.

(ii) If the Market Value of the Posted Collateral is higher than the Required Collateral Value for all loaned securities, Borrower may call on Lender at any time on a Business Day to return the surplus.

(iii) If the Market Value of the Posted Collateral falls below the Required Collateral Value for all loaned securities, Lender may call on Borrower at any time on a Business Day to top up the collateral value.

5.5 **Marking to Market of Collateral during the currency of a Loan on a Loan by Loan basis**

If paragraph 1.3 of the Schedule indicates this paragraph 5.5 shall apply in lieu of paragraph 5.4, the Posted Collateral in respect of any Loan shall bear from day to day and at any time the same proportion to the Market Value of the Loaned Securities as the Posted Collateral bore at the commencement of such Loan. Accordingly:

(i) the Market Value of the Posted Collateral to be delivered or deposited while the Loan continues shall be equal to the Required Collateral Value;

(ii) if at any time on any Business Day the Market Value of the Posted Collateral in respect of any Loan exceeds the Required Collateral Value in respect of such Loan, Lender shall (on demand) repay and/or redeliver, as the case may be, to Borrower such Equivalent Collateral as will eliminate the excess; and

(iii) if at any time on any Business Day the Market Value of the Posted Collateral falls below the Required Collateral Value, Borrower shall (on demand) provide such further Collateral to Lender as will eliminate the deficiency.

5.5 Marking to Market of Collateral during the currency of a Loan on a Loan by Loan basis

This sub-paragraph covers margining on a Loan by Loan basis and once again the choice is made in paragraph 1.3 of the Schedule. In my experience most professional market players choose to have global margining across all Loans, i.e. paragraph 5.4.

However, if Loan by Loan margining is chosen:

(i) The Market Value of the Posted Collateral must be at least equal to the Required Collateral Value for each outstanding Loan;

(ii) Where the Posted Collateral is greater than the Required Collateral Value for an individual Loan, on any Business Day Borrower can call on Lender to repay the surplus; and

(iii) Where the Market Value of the Posted Collateral falls below the Required Collateral Value for an individual Loan on any Business Day, Lender can call on Borrower to transfer more collateral to eliminate the shortfall.

5.6 **Requirements to redeliver excess Collateral**

Where paragraph 5.4 applies, unless paragraph 1.4 of the Schedule indicates that this paragraph 5.6 does not apply, if a Party (the "**first Party**") would, but for this paragraph 5.6, be required under paragraph 5.4 to provide further Collateral or redeliver Equivalent Collateral in circumstances where the other Party (the "**second Party**") would, but for this paragraph 5.6, also be required to or provide Collateral or redeliver Equivalent Collateral under paragraph 5.4, then the Market Value of the Collateral or Equivalent Collateral deliverable by the first Party ("**X**") shall be set-off against the Market Value of the Collateral or Equivalent Collateral deliverable by the second Party ("**Y**") and the only obligation of the Parties under paragraph 5.4 shall be, where X exceeds Y, an obligation of the first Party, or where Y exceeds X, an obligation of the second Party to repay and/or (as the case may be) redeliver Equivalent Collateral or to deliver further Collateral having a Market Value equal to the difference between X and Y.

5.7 Where Equivalent Collateral is repaid or redelivered (as the case may be) or further Collateral is provided by a Party under paragraph 5.6, the Parties shall agree to which Loan or Loans such repayment, redelivery or further provision is to be attributed and failing agreement it shall be attributed, as determined by the Party making such repayment, redelivery or further provision to the earliest outstanding Loan and, in the case of a repayment or redelivery up to the point at which the Market Value of Collateral in respect of such Loan equals the Required Collateral Value in respect of such Loan, and then to the next earliest outstanding Loan up to the similar point and so on.

5.8 **Timing of repayments of excess Collateral or deliveries of further Collateral**

Where any Equivalent Collateral falls to be repaid or redelivered (as the case may be) or further Collateral is to be provided under this paragraph 5, unless otherwise agreed between the Parties, it shall be delivered on the same Business Day as the relevant demand. Equivalent Collateral comprising securities shall be deemed to have been delivered by Lender to Borrower on delivery to Borrower or as it shall direct of the relevant instruments of transfer, or in the case of such securities being held by an agent or within a clearing or settlement system on the effective instructions to such agent or the operator of such system which result in such securities being held by the operator of the clearing system for the account of the Borrower or as it shall direct or by such other means as may be agreed.

5.6 Requirements to redeliver excess Collateral

Whether sub-paragraph 5.6 applies depends upon the parties choosing to apply it in paragraph 1.4 of the Schedule.

Where global margining (paragraph 5.4) applies and sub-paragraph 5.6 is selected to apply, then parties can set off the values of any amounts of Collateral each is obliged to deliver to the other for different Loans on any Business Day and the values of any amounts of Equivalent Collateral each is obliged to redeliver in respect of different Loans on any Business Day. All such transfers will be converted into the Base Currency chosen in paragraph 2 of the Schedule. Under this arrangement only the difference in the two values is transferred between the parties. **This is basically a collateral netting clause**.

5.7

Where the parties agree to global margining across all Loans and a party needs to deliver top-up collateral or return Equivalent Collateral to the other party, this paragraph allows the allocation of such collateral to individual Loans on their maturity. Where they do not agree the fallback position is that the recipient will apply it to the earliest outstanding Loan and if there is still surplus collateral after this has been done, to the next earliest outstanding Loan and so on.

5.8 Timing of repayments of excess Collateral or deliveries of further Collateral

Collateral transfers of whatever sort are to be made on the same Business Day as the demand is made unless otherwise agreed.

Once again delivery of Equivalent Collateral is confirmed to take place when received by Borrower or its agent together with any necessary transfer documentation or if a settlement or clearing system is involved upon receipt of such securities into Borrower's account or that of its agent in such system.

5.9 **Substitutions and extensions of Letters of Credit**

Where Collateral is a Letter of Credit, Lender may by notice to Borrower require that Borrower, on the Business Day following the date of delivery of such notice, substitute Collateral consisting of cash or other Collateral acceptable to Lender for the Letter of Credit. Prior to the expiration of any Letter of Credit supporting Borrower's obligations hereunder, Borrower shall, no later than 10.30a.m. UK time on the second Business Day prior to the date such Letter of Credit expires, obtain an extension of the expiration of such Letter of Credit or replace such Letter of Credit by providing Lender with a substitute Letter of Credit in an amount at least equal to the amount of the Letter of Credit for which it is substituted.

5.9 Substitutions and extensions of Letters of Credit

Lender can ask Borrower by one Business Day's notice for a Letter of Credit to be substituted by cash or other collateral acceptable to Lender.

Where a Letter of Credit is due to expire, Borrower shall obtain an extension of it no later than 10.30 a.m. UK time on the second Business Day before it is due to expire or replace it with another Letter of Credit of equivalent value.

6. DISTRIBUTIONS AND CORPORATE ACTIONS

6.1 Manufactured Payments

Where Income is paid in relation to any Loaned Securities or Collateral (other than Cash Collateral) on or by reference to an Income Payment Date Borrower, in the case of Loaned Securities, and Lender, in the case of Collateral, shall, on the date of the payment of such Income, or on such other date as the Parties may from time to time agree, (the "**Relevant Payment Date**") pay and deliver a sum of money or property equivalent to the type and amount of such Income that, in the case of Loaned Securities, Lender would have been entitled to receive had such Securities not been loaned to Borrower and had been retained by Lender on the Income Payment Date, and, in the case of Collateral, Borrower would have been entitled to receive had such Collateral not been provided to Lender and had been retained by Borrower on the Income Payment Date unless a different sum is agreed between the Parties.

6.2 Income in the form of Securities

Where Income, in the form of securities, is paid in relation to any Loaned Securities or Collateral, such securities shall be added to such Loaned Securities or Collateral (and shall constitute Loaned Securities or Collateral, as the case may be, and be part of the relevant Loan) and will not be delivered to Lender, in the case of Loaned Securities, or to Borrower, in the case of Collateral, until the end of the relevant Loan, provided that the Lender or Borrower (as the case may be) fulfils their obligations under paragraph 5.4 or 5.5 (as applicable) with respect to the additional Loaned Securities or Collateral, as the case may be.

DISTRIBUTIONS AND CORPORATE ACTIONS

6.1 Manufactured Payments

This sub-paragraph provides that any income received by Borrower on loaned securities from their issuer during the life of a Loan shall be paid over promptly to Lender by way of a separate payment (a "manufactured dividend"). Similarly any income received by Lender on securities collateral from their issuer will be paid over to Borrower as a manufactured dividend. A different sum may be agreed between the parties.

The payment to Lender of a manufactured dividend on the loaned securities or to Borrower on securities collateral held by Lender does not depend upon them holding the relevant securities or securities collateral at the time the issuer pays income on them. They may have repoed them out or lent them out elsewhere, for instance. Nonetheless they still need to pay a manufactured dividend to the other party during the life of the loan. Each party will carefully study if it could be impacted by adverse tax implications upon the payment of income by an issuer to them or any manufactured dividend they might make.

6.2 Income in the form of securities

Where a distribution of bonus securities is made in respect of any loaned securities or securities collateral, this paragraph provides for such securities to be added to the loaned securities or securities collateral, as the case may be (instead of delivering Equivalent Securities at the time of the distribution) provided that both parties comply with the collateral provisions of paragraph 5. Such bonus securities will be delivered to the relevant party at the end of the loan.

6.3 **Exercise of voting rights**

Where any voting rights fall to be exercised in relation to any Loaned Securities or Collateral, neither Borrower, in the case of Equivalent Securities, nor Lender, in the case of Equivalent Collateral, shall have any obligation to arrange for voting rights of that kind to be exercised in accordance with the instructions of the other Party in relation to the Securities borrowed by it or transferred to it by way of Collateral, as the case may be, unless otherwise agreed between the Parties.

6.4 **Corporate actions**

Where, in respect of any Loaned Securities or any Collateral, any rights relating to conversion, sub-division, consolidation, pre-emption, rights arising under a takeover offer, rights to receive securities or a certificate which may at a future date be exchanged for securities or other rights, including those requiring election by the holder for the time being of such Securities or Collateral, become exercisable prior to the redelivery of Equivalent Securities or Equivalent Collateral, then Lender or Borrower, as the case may be, may, within a reasonable time before the latest time for the exercise of the right or option give written notice to the other Party that on redelivery of Equivalent Securities or Equivalent Collateral, as the case may be, it wishes to receive Equivalent Securities or Equivalent Collateral in such form as will arise if the right is exercised or, in the case of a right which may be exercised in more than one manner, is exercised as is specified in such written notice.

6.3 Exercise of voting rights

This sub-paragraph provides that Borrower, in respect of loaned securities and Lender, in respect of securities collateral, has no obligation to arrange for any voting rights arising to be exercised in accordance with the instructions of the other party unless they agree otherwise. This is because voting rights on the securities are transferred with legal ownership to the party receiving them.

6.4 Corporate actions

If a corporate action (such as a rights issue or a takeover offer) arises before the end of a loan in respect of any loaned securities or securities collateral, this paragraph permits Lender, in the case of loaned securities and Borrower, in the case of securities collateral, to require that Equivalent Securities or Equivalent Collateral, as the case may be, which will be redelivered at the end of the Loan take the form following the corporate action being exercised in accordance with the instructions of Lender or Borrower. However, this is provided that such party gives written notice in good time to the other before rights relating to the corporate action become exercisable.

7. **RATES APPLICABLE TO LOANED SECURITIES AND CASH COLLATERAL**

7.1 **Rates in respect of Loaned Securities**

In respect of each Loan, Borrower shall pay to Lender, in the manner prescribed in sub-paragraph 7.3, sums calculated by applying such rate as shall be agreed between the Parties from time to time to the daily Market Value of the Loaned Securities.

7.2 **Rates in respect of Cash Collateral**

Where Cash Collateral is deposited with Lender in respect of any Loan, Lender shall pay to Borrower, in the manner prescribed in paragraph 7.3, sums calculated by applying such rates as shall be agreed between the Parties from time to time to the amount of such Cash Collateral. Any such payment due to Borrower may be set-off against any payment due to Lender pursuant to paragraph 7.1.

7.3 **Payment of rates**

In respect of each Loan, the payments referred to in paragraph 7.1 and 7.2 shall accrue daily in respect of the period commencing on and inclusive of the Settlement Date and terminating on and exclusive of the Business Day upon which Equivalent Securities are redelivered or Cash Collateral is repaid. Unless otherwise agreed, the sums so accruing in respect of each calendar month shall be paid in arrear by the relevant Party not later than the Business Day which is one week after the last Business Day of the calendar month to which such payments relate or such other date as the Parties shall from time to time agree.

7. RATES APPLICABLE TO LOANED SECURITIES AND CASH COLLATERAL

7.1 Rates in respect of Loaned Securities

This relates to the agreed fee Borrower must pay Lender for the securities loan. It is based on the daily Market Value of the securities borrowed and the fee is normally set out in a confirmation or another document agreed between the parties.

7.2 Rates in respect of Cash Collateral

Interest will be paid on cash collateral to Borrower at an agreed rate and can be set off against any securities lending fee payable by Borrower to Lender.

7.3 Payment of rates

This sub-paragraph sets out the periods by which securities lending fees and interest on cash collateral are to be calculated. It also sets out the time when such sums are payable. Payments accrue from the date of delivery of securities and cash collateral up to the Business Day before redelivery. Sums accrue in respect of the previous calendar month and unless otherwise agreed, payments are due not later than one week after the last Business Day of the preceding calendar month.

8. REDELIVERY OF EQUIVALENT SECURITIES

8.1 Delivery of Equivalent Securities on termination of a Loan

Borrower shall procure the redelivery of Equivalent Securities to Lender or redeliver Equivalent Securities in accordance with this Agreement and the terms of the relevant Loan on termination of the Loan. Such Equivalent Securities shall be deemed to have been delivered by Borrower to Lender on delivery to Lender or as it shall direct of the relevant instruments of transfer, or in the case of Equivalent Securities held by an agent or within a clearing or settlement system on the effective instructions to such agent or the operator of such system which result in such Equivalent Securities being held by the operator of the clearing system for the account of the Lender or as it shall direct, or by such other means as may be agreed. For the avoidance of doubt any reference in this Agreement or in any other agreement or communication between the Parties (howsoever expressed) to an obligation to redeliver or account for or act in relation to Loaned Securities shall accordingly be construed as a reference to an obligation to redeliver or account for or act in relation to Equivalent Securities.

8.2 Lender's right to terminate a Loan

Subject to paragraph 10 and the terms of the relevant Loan, Lender shall be entitled to terminate a Loan and to call for the redelivery of all or any Equivalent Securities at any time by giving notice on any Business Day of not less than the standard settlement time for such Equivalent Securities on the exchange or in the clearing organisation through which the Loaned Securities were originally delivered. Borrower shall redeliver such Equivalent Securities not later than the expiry of such notice in accordance with Lender's instructions.

8.3 Borrower's right to terminate a Loan

Subject to the terms of the relevant Loan, Borrower shall be entitled at any time to terminate a Loan and to redeliver all and any Equivalent Securities due and outstanding to Lender in accordance with Lender's instructions and Lender shall accept such redelivery.

8. REDELIVERY OF EQUIVALENT SECURITIES

8.1 Delivery of Equivalent Securities on termination of a Loan

This sub-paragraph recites Borrower's obligation to redeliver Equivalent Securities to Lender at the end of the relevant Loan. Delivery shall be deemed to take place when Lender or its agent receives the Equivalent Securities and any necessary transfer documentation and if a clearing or settlement system is involved when the Equivalent Securities are received in Lender's account or that of its agent.

8.2 Lender's right to terminate a Loan

This sub-paragraph sets out Lender's right to terminate a loan of securities. Subject to any terms of the relevant loan (e.g. where a fixed period has been agreed) Lender may terminate on giving notice equal to the standard market settlement time for the securities concerned and Borrower must redeliver by the end of such period in line with Lender's instructions.

8.3 Borrower's right to terminate a Loan

Sub-paragraph 8.3 sets out Borrower's right to terminate a loan of securities. Except where the loan has a fixed term, Borrower may terminate and redeliver securities at any time in accordance with Lender's delivery instructions and Lender will accept such redelivery.

8.4 Redelivery of Equivalent Collateral on termination of a Loan

On the date and time that Equivalent Securities are required to be redelivered by Borrower on the termination of a Loan, Lender shall simultaneously (subject to paragraph 5.4 if applicable) repay to Borrower any Cash Collateral or, as the case may be, redeliver Collateral equivalent to the Collateral provided by Borrower pursuant to paragraph 5 in respect of such Loan. For the avoidance of doubt any reference in this Agreement or in any other agreement or communication between the Parties (however expressed) to an obligation to redeliver or account for or act in relation to Collateral shall accordingly be construed as a reference to an obligation to redeliver or account for or act in relation to Equivalent Collateral.

8.5 Redelivery of Letters of Credit

Where a Letter of Credit is provided by way of Collateral, the obligation to redeliver Equivalent Collateral is satisfied by Lender redelivering for cancellation the Letter of Credit so provided, or where the Letter of Credit is provided in respect of more than one Loan, by Lender consenting to a reduction in the value of the Letter of Credit.

8.6 Redelivery obligations to be reciprocal

Neither Party shall be obliged to make delivery (or make a payment as the case may be) to the other unless it is satisfied that the other Party will make such delivery (or make an appropriate payment as the case may be) to it. If it is not so satisfied (whether because an Event of Default has occurred in respect of the other Party or otherwise) it shall notify the other party and unless that other Party has made arrangements which are sufficient to assure full delivery (or the appropriate payment as the case may be) to the notifying Party, the notifying Party shall (provided it is itself in a position, and willing, to perform its own obligations) be entitled to withhold delivery (or payment, as the case may be) to the other Party.

8.4 Redelivery of Equivalent Collateral on termination of a Loan

This provision recites Lender's obligation to repay Cash Collateral or redeliver equivalent securities collateral simultaneously with the return of the loaned securities by Borrower at the end of the Loan.

8.5 Redelivery of Letters of Credit

This sub-paragraph sets out how the obligation to deliver Equivalent Collateral where that collateral is in the form of a Letter of Credit is to be achieved. Either the Letter of Credit is delivered for cancellation or where the Letter of Credit covers more than one Loan, Lender consents to a reduction in its value.

8.6 Redelivery obligations to be reciprocal

Neither party shall be obliged to make a payment or delivery to the other unless it is satisfied that the other party will make its payment or delivery on time as well. If it is not satisfied, it will notify the other party and seek assurances that full delivery or payment will be made by it as contractually agreed. If such assurances are not received or are unconvincing, the first party is entitled to withhold its payment or delivery (provided that it would be in a position to make them) to the other party.

This type of provision is sometimes seen in ISDA Master Agreement Schedules where it is called an Adequate Assurances provision.

9. **FAILURE TO REDELIVER**

9.1 **Borrower's failure to redeliver Equivalent Securities**

(i) If Borrower does not redeliver Equivalent Securities in accordance with paragraph 8.1 or 8.2, Lender may elect to continue the Loan (which Loan, for the avoidance of doubt, shall continue to be taken into account for the purposes of paragraph 5.4 or 5.5 as applicable) provided that if Lender does not elect to continue the Loan, Lender may either by written notice to Borrower terminate the Loan forthwith and the Parties' delivery and payment obligations in respect thereof (in which case sub-paragraph (ii) below shall apply) or serve a notice of an Event of Default in accordance with paragraph 14.

(ii) Upon service of a notice to terminate the relevant Loan pursuant to paragraph 9.1(i):-

(a) there shall be set-off against the Market Value of the Equivalent Securities concerned such amount of Posted Collateral chosen by Lender (calculated at its Market Value) as is equal thereto;

(b) the Parties delivery and payment obligations in relation to such assets which are set-off shall terminate;

(c) in the event that the Market Value of the Posted Collateral set-off is less than the Market Value of the Equivalent Securities concerned Borrower shall account to Lender for the shortfall; and

(d) Borrower shall account to Lender for the total costs and expenses incurred by Lender as a result thereof as set out in paragraphs 9.3 and 9.4 from the time the notice is effective.

9. FAILURE TO REDELIVER

9.1 Borrower's failure to redeliver Equivalent Securities

This sub-paragraph sets out Lender's remedies if Borrower fails to redeliver Equivalent Securities at the end of a Loan. If this happens Lender can choose to:

- continue the Loan (which will remain margined); or
- terminate only the affected Loan; or
- serve a notice of an Event of Default and so close out all outstanding Loans.

Where only the affected Loan is terminated, the parties' normal payment and delivery obligations are curtailed and replaced by an obligation to pay the difference between the Market Values of the relevant Equivalent Securities and the relevant Equivalent Collateral.

Borrower is liable for any shortfall and for certain of Lender's costs and expenses as laid out in paragraphs 9.3 and 9.4 from the time the notice is effective.

9.2 **Lender's failure to Redeliver Equivalent Collateral**

(i) If Lender does not redeliver Equivalent Collateral in accordance with paragraph 8.4 or 8.5, Borrower may either by written notice to Lender terminate the Loan forthwith and the Parties' delivery and payment obligations in respect thereof (in which case sub-paragraph (ii) below shall apply) or serve a notice of an Event of Default in accordance with paragraph 14.

(ii) Upon service of a notice to terminate the relevant Loan pursuant to paragraph 9.2(i):-

(a) there shall be set-off against the Market Value of the Equivalent Collateral concerned the Market Value of the Loaned Securities;

(b) the Parties delivery and payment obligations in relation to such assets which are set-off shall terminate;

(c) in the event that the Market Value of the Loaned Securities held by Borrower is less than the Market Value of the Equivalent Collateral concerned Lender shall account to Borrower for the shortfall; and

(d) Lender shall account to Borrower for the total costs and expenses incurred by Borrower as a result thereof as set out in paragraphs 9.3 and 9.4 from the time the notice is effective.

9.2 Lender's failure to Redeliver Equivalent Collateral

This sub-paragraph concerns Borrower's remedies if Lender fails to deliver Equivalent Collateral at the end of a Loan. If this happens, Borrower may:

(i) terminate only the affected Loan; or
(ii) serve notice of an Event of Default thereby closing out all outstanding Loans.

Once again where the affected Loan is terminated, the parties' normal payment and delivery obligations are terminated and replaced by an obligation to pay the difference between the Market Values of the Equivalent Collateral and the Equivalent Securities.

Lender is liable for any shortfall and for certain of Borrower's costs and expenses as set out in paragraphs 9.3 and 9.4 from the time the notice is effective.

9.3 **Failure by either Party to redeliver**

This provision applies in the event that a Party (the "**Transferor**") fails to meet a redelivery obligation within the standard settlement time for the asset concerned on the exchange or in the clearing organisation through which the asset equivalent to the asset concerned was originally delivered or within such other period as may be agreed between the Parties. In such situation, in addition to the Parties' rights under the general law and this Agreement where the other Party (the "**Transferee**") incurs interest, overdraft or similar costs and expenses the Transferor agrees to pay on demand and hold harmless the Transferee with respect to all such costs and expenses which arise directly from such failure excluding (i) such costs and expenses which arise from the negligence or wilful default of the Transferee and (ii) any indirect or consequential losses. It is agreed by the Parties that any costs reasonably and properly incurred by a Party arising in respect of the failure of a Party to meet its obligations under a transaction to sell or deliver securities resulting from the failure of the Transferor to fulfil its redelivery obligations is to be treated as a direct cost or expense for the purposes of this paragraph.

9.4 **Exercise of buy-in on failure to redeliver**

In the event that as a result of the failure of the Transferor to fulfil its redelivery obligations a "buy-in" is exercised against the Transferee, then the Transferor shall account to the Transferee for the total costs and expenses reasonably incurred by the Transferee as a result of such "buy-in".

9.3 Failure by either Party to redeliver

This sub-paragraph provides an additional remedy where a failure to deliver Equivalent Securities or Equivalent Collateral within the standard market settlement time or as agreed between the parties, has occurred. The party that has failed to deliver (the "Transferor") is liable to the other party (the "Transferee") for any interest, overdraft or similar direct costs and expenses incurred by the Transferee arising from the Transferor's failure to deliver. These include costs incurred by the Transferee for any failure by it to fulfil an onward sale or delivery obligation to a third party for the securities the Transferor was to have delivered to it. However, these costs exclude indirect or consequential losses or any arising from the Transferee's negligence or wilful default. The parties specifically agree that any direct costs incurred by the Transferee (including finance costs) because it failed to sell or redeliver securities to a third party due to the Transferor's failure to deliver to it, shall be indemnified by the Transferor.

9.4 Exercise of buy-in on failure to redeliver

In addition to the remedies set out in sub-paragraphs 9.1–9.3, the Transferor is also liable for any costs of a buy-in exercised against the Transferee. A "buy-in" is where:

(i) the Transferee was due to deliver to a third party the securities that the Transferor failed to deliver to it;

(ii) as a result of this failure, the Transferee fails to meet its delivery obligation to the third party; and

(iii) the third party goes into the market and buys in the relevant securities itself.

The GMSLA 2000 Guidance Notes point out that the Transferor is liable to the Transferee for the costs of such buy-in including the excess of the value assigned to the loaned securities by the Transferee and the third party, and the price paid by the third party together with its associated purchase expenses. This amounts to a recovery of the Transferee's profit on the deal.

10. **SET-OFF ETC**

10.1 **Definitions for paragraph 10**

In this paragraph 10:

"Bid Price" in relation to Equivalent Securities or Equivalent Collateral means the best available bid price on the most appropriate market in a standard size;

10. SET OFF, etc.

Paragraph 10 is the GMSLA 2000's close-out netting provision which is triggered by a Non-Defaulting Party exercising its rights following the occurrence of one of the Events of Default in paragraph 14 (or any other Event of Default which may be agreed in the Schedule). Where close-out occurs, both parties' payment and delivery obligations are accelerated and the values of all Loans are calculated and converted into the Base Currency and netted off against each other so as to produce a single cash sum due to one party or the other.

The Non-Defaulting Party therefore has no claim on the Defaulting Party for the return of any lent securities, reflecting the fact that securities lending involves a full legal transfer of those securities. So where Borrower defaults, Lender sets off the market value of its collateral against the market value of the lent securities. Assuming that markets are normal and the margining levels on the collateral have been conservatively pitched, Lender should have a net liability to Borrower.

It is strange that this close-out netting clause precedes its Event of Default triggers which appear in paragraph 14. The order is more logical in the GMSLA 2010.

10.1 Definitions for paragraph 10

This sub-paragraph contains certain definitions used in other parts of paragraph 10:

"Bid Price"

This means the best available buy price for Equivalent Securities or equivalent securities collateral in standard size lots in the relevant market as calculated by the Non-Defaulting Party.

"Bid Value" subject to paragraph 10.5 means:-

(a) in relation to Collateral equivalent to Collateral in the form of a Letter of Credit zero and in relation to Cash Collateral the amount of the currency concerned; and

(b) in relation to Equivalent Securities or Collateral equivalent to all other types of Collateral the amount which would be received on a sale of such Equivalent Securities or Equivalent Collateral at the Bid Price at Close of Business on the relevant Business Day less all costs, fees and expenses that would be incurred in connection therewith, calculated on the assumption that the aggregate thereof is the least that could reasonably be expected to be paid in order to carry out such sale or realisation and adding thereto the amount of any interest, dividends, distributions or other amounts, in the case of Equivalent Securities, paid to Borrower and in respect of which equivalent amounts have not been paid to Lender and in the case of Equivalent Collateral, paid to Lender and in respect of which equivalent amounts have not been paid to Borrower, in accordance with paragraph 6.1 prior to such time in respect of such Equivalent Securities, Equivalent Collateral or the original Securities or Collateral held, gross of all and any tax deducted or paid in respect thereof;

"Offer Price" in relation to Equivalent Securities or Equivalent Collateral means the best available offer price on the most appropriate market in a standard size;

"Offer Value" subject to paragraph 10.5 means:-

(a) in relation to Collateral equivalent to Collateral in the form of a Letter of Credit zero and in relation to Cash Collateral the amount of the currency concerned; and

(b) in relation to Equivalent Securities or Collateral equivalent to all other types of Collateral the amount it would cost to buy such Equivalent Securities or Equivalent Collateral at the Offer Price at Close of Business on the relevant Business Day together with all costs, fees and expenses that would be incurred in connection therewith, calculated on the assumption that the aggregate thereof is the least that could reasonably be expected to be paid in order to carry out the transaction and adding thereto the amount of any interest, dividends, distributions or other amounts, in the case of Equivalent Securities, paid to Borrower and in respect of which equivalent amounts have not been paid to Lender and in the case of Equivalent Collateral, paid to Lender and in respect of which equivalent amounts have not been paid to Borrower, in accordance with paragraph 6.1 prior to such time in respect of such Equivalent Securities, Equivalent Collateral or the original Securities or Collateral held, gross of all and any tax deducted or paid in respect thereof;

"Bid Value"

This definition concerns how Collateral and Equivalent Securities are to be valued where the Non-Defaulting Party is hypothetically buying them for close-out purposes.

On this basis:

(a) A Letter of Credit is to be valued at zero and cash collateral at its face value.

(b) Equivalent Securities and securities collateral are valued at their sale price for the Non-Defaulting Party (i.e. the bid price offered by a third party buyer) at the close of business on the relevant Business Day less all associated costs and expenses. To this would be added any income paid by a securities issuer to Lender for securities collateral and to Borrower for loaned securities provided this has not already been paid over to the other party by way of a manufactured dividend. In addition, the amount paid over will be paid gross with no withholding tax being deducted in respect of such manufactured dividends.

"Offer Price"

This means the best available sale price for Equivalent Securities or equivalent securities collateral in standard size lots in the relevant market as calculated by the Non-Defaulting Party.

"Offer Value"

This concerns how Collateral and Equivalent Securities are to be valued where the Non-Defaulting Party is hypothetically selling them for close-out purposes. On this basis:

(a) A Letter of Credit is to be valued at zero and cash collateral at its face value.

(b) Equivalent Securities and securities collateral are valued at their purchase price for the Non-Defaulting Party (i.e. the sale price offered by a third party seller) at the close of business on the relevant Business Day plus all associated costs and expenses. Once again added to this would be any income paid by a securities issuer to Lender for securities collateral and to Borrower for loaned securities which has not already been paid over to the other party by way of a manufactured dividend. In addition, such manufactured dividend will be paid over gross with no withholding tax deducted.

10.2 **Termination of delivery obligations upon Event of Default**

Subject to paragraph 9, if an Event of Default occurs in relation to either Party, the Parties' delivery and payment obligations (and any other obligations they have under this Agreement) shall be accelerated so as to require performance thereof at the time such Event of Default occurs (the date of which shall be the **"Termination Date"** for the purposes of this clause) so that performance of such delivery and payment obligations shall be effected only in accordance with the following provisions:

(i) the Relevant Value of the securities which would have been required to be delivered but for such termination (or payment to be made, as the case may be) by each Party shall be established in accordance with paragraph 10.3; and

(ii) on the basis of the Relevant Values so established, an account shall be taken (as at the Termination Date) of what is due from each Party to the other and (on the basis that each Party's claim against the other in respect of delivery of Equivalent Securities or Equivalent Collateral or any cash payment equals the Relevant Value thereof) the sums due from one Party shall be set-off against the sums due from the other and only the balance of the account shall be payable (by the Party having the claim valued at the lower amount pursuant to the foregoing) and such balance shall be payable on the Termination Date.

If the Bid Value is greater than the Offer Value, and the Non-Defaulting Party had delivered to the Defaulting Party a Letter of Credit, the Defaulting Party shall draw on the Letter of Credit to the extent of the balance due and shall subsequently redeliver for cancellation the Letter of Credit so provided.

If the Offer Value is greater than the Bid Value, and the Defaulting Party had delivered to the Non-Defaulting Party a Letter of Credit, the Non-Defaulting Party shall draw on the Letter of Credit to the extent of the balance due and shall subsequently redeliver for cancellation the Letter of Credit so provided.

10.2 Termination of delivery obligations upon Event of Default

Except where one Affected Loan is being closed out under paragraph 9, where an Event of Default occurs to a party, both parties' delivery and payment obligations and any other obligations they have under the GMSLA 2000, are accelerated so that they need to be performed on the Termination Date (i.e. the date upon which the Event of Default occurs). This is done as follows:

(i) The Relevant Value of securities which would otherwise be delivered by each party or a due payment shall be calculated as provided under paragraph 10.3 by the Non-Defaulting Party.

(ii) Once the Relevant Values have been established an account shall be taken as to what is due from one party to the other and the resultant sums are aggregated and netted off against each other in the Base Currency so that only the difference between the two sums is payable by the party having the lower aggregate valuation of its trading positions. This net amount is payable on the Termination Date.

Sub-paragraph 10.2 also describes what needs to be done on close-out where a Letter of Credit is the collateral.

Where the Defaulting Party is owed the net amount and the Non-Defaulting Party has previously delivered the Letter of Credit as collateral, the Defaulting Party will draw on the Letter of Credit for the balance due and then return it to the Non-Defaulting Party or the bank concerned for cancellation. Where the Non-Defaulting Party is owed the net amount and it has previously received a Letter of Credit from the Defaulting Party, the Non-Defaulting Party will draw on that Letter of Credit for the balance due and then return it for cancellation.

In all other circumstances, upon close-out, where a Letter of Credit has previously been delivered to a party (and perhaps it was not used because it was only offered as a sign of good faith and other collateral was used instead) it must be redelivered for cancellation.

10.3 **Determination of delivery values upon Event of Default**

For the purposes of paragraph 10.2 the "**Relevant Value**":-

(i) of any securities to be delivered by the Defaulting Party shall, subject to paragraph 10.5 below, equal the Offer Value of such securities; and

(ii) of any securities to be delivered to the Defaulting Party shall, subject to paragraph 10.5 below, equal the Bid Value of such securities.

10.3 Determination of delivery values upon Event of Default

This means that any securities to be delivered by the Defaulting Party shall equal the Offer Value of such securities (i.e. the hypothetical price the Non-Defaulting Party would have to pay to buy them in). Any securities to be delivered to the Defaulting Party shall equal the Bid Value of such securities (i.e. the hypothetical price the Non-Defaulting Party would have to pay to sell them). Transaction expenses and received but undistributed income from securities issuers with no withholding tax deducted are also factored in here. However, if sub-paragraph 10.5 applies, this will supersede the arrangements in sub-paragraphs 10.2 and 10.3.

10.4 For the purposes of paragraph 10.3, but subject to paragraph 10.5, the Bid Value and Offer Value of any securities shall be calculated for securities of the relevant description (as determined by the Non-Defaulting Party) as of the first Business Day following the Termination Date, or if the relevant Event of Default occurs outside the normal business hours of such market, on the second Business Day following the Termination Date (the **"Default Valuation Time"**);

10.4

Paragraph 10.4 seems to contradict the position in paragraph 10.2 of the net amount being payable on the Termination Date itself (which curiously is also the date the Event of Default occurred). Things would have to move abnormally quickly for this to be achieved. Paragraph 10.4 states that the Bid and Offer Values of securities are calculated on the first Business Day following the Event of Default (the Termination Date) or if the Event of Default occurred outside normal working hours, on the second Business Day following the date of the Event of Default. This seems to be a blemish in the GMSLA 2000. In my opinion, it should be clearer that the Bid and Offer Values are **as at** the close of business on the Termination Date which I think is what is meant here. A cross-reference back to paragraph 10.2(11) would have helped. This issue has been resolved in the GMSLA 2010.

A similar problem occurs with the term "Performance Date" in the OSLA and prompted one writer to call their early termination provisions "an exercise in time travel"!

The guidance notes to the GMSLA 2000 lay out how the drafters envisaged that the close-out arrangement should work although this needs to be deduced from the GMSLA 2000 text itself.

The Non-Defaulting Party makes the following calculations as of the Business Day following the date of the Event of Default (or if the Event of Default occurred outside normal working hours, on the second Business Day following the date of the Event of Default) through comparing:

(a) the value of the securities which were to have been delivered to it by the Defaulting Party being the hypothetical cost of buying such securities (together with associated fees and expenses), less any payments of manufactured dividends due (in accordance with paragraph 6.1) in respect of such securities but unpaid; with

(b) the value of the securities which it was to have delivered to the Defaulting Party being the hypothetical cost of selling such securities (less all associated costs and expenses), less any payments of manufactured dividends due in respect of such securities but unpaid.

If the amount calculated under (a), together with any cash payments due from the Defaulting Party is greater than the amount calculated under (b) together with any cash payments due to the Defaulting Party, then the Defaulting Party shall pay the difference to the Non-Defaulting party. In addition, if the amount calculated under (a) together with any cash payments due from the Defaulting Party is less than the amount calculated under (b) together with any cash payments due to the Defaulting Party, then the Non-Defaulting party shall pay the difference to the Defaulting Party.

10.5 Where the Non-Defaulting Party has following the occurrence of an Event of Default but prior to the close of business on the fifth Business Day following the Termination Date purchased securities forming part of the same issue and being of an identical type and description to those to be delivered by the Defaulting Party or sold securities forming part of the same issue and being of an identical type and description to those to be delivered by him to the Defaulting Party, the cost of such purchase or the proceeds of such sale, as the case may be, (taking into account all reasonable costs, fees and expenses that would be incurred in connection therewith) shall (together with any amounts owing pursuant to paragraph 6.1) be treated as the Offer Value or Bid Value, as the case may be, of the amount of securities to be delivered which is equivalent to the amount of the securities so bought or sold, as the case may be, for the purposes of this paragraph 10, so that where the amount of securities to be delivered is more than the amount so bought or sold as the case may be, the Offer Value or Bid Value as the case may be, of the balance shall be valued in accordance with paragraph 10.4.

10.6 Any reference in this paragraph 10 to securities shall include any asset other than cash provided by way of Collateral.

10.7 **Other costs, expenses and interest payable in consequence of an Event of Default**

The Defaulting Party shall be liable to the Non-Defaulting Party for the amount of all reasonable legal and other professional expenses incurred by the Non-Defaulting Party in connection with or as a consequence of an Event of Default, together with interest thereon at the one-month London Inter Bank Offered Rate as quoted on a reputable financial information service ("**LIBOR**") as of 11.00 am, London Time, on the date on which it is to be determined or, in the case of an expense attributable to a particular transaction and where the parties have previously agreed a rate of interest for the transaction, that rate of interest if it is greater than LIBOR. The rate of LIBOR applicable to each month or part thereof that any sum payable pursuant to this paragraph 10.7 remains outstanding is the rate of LIBOR determined on the first Business Day of any such period of one month or any part thereof. Interest will accrue daily on a compound basis and will be calculated according to the actual number of days elapsed.

10.5

Normally sub-paragraphs 10.2–10.4 rule close-out situations. However, paragraph 10.5 overrules them in the calculation of Bid and Offer Values where the Non-Defaulting Party has entered into actual purchases and sales of the same securities with other counterparties in the five Business Days after the Termination Date as follows:

> If between the date of the Event of Default (the Termination Date) and the fifth Business Day thereafter, the Non-Defaulting Party actually purchases securities to have been delivered by the Defaulting Party or sells securities to have been delivered to the Defaulting Party, then the costs of any such purchase or proceeds of sale (in each case, taking into account any associated expenses and payments of manufactured dividends due but unpaid) shall be substituted for the amounts calculated for Bid and Offer Values in sub-paragraphs 10.2 and 10.3, as the case may be (adjustments to be made depending upon the number of securities bought or sold and the number of securities to have been delivered).

However, this does not easily fit in with the requirement in paragraph 10.2(11) for the close-out payment to be made to the party owed it on the Termination Date itself.

10.6

References to securities of any kind in paragraph 10 exclude cash collateral.

10.7 Other costs, expenses and interest payable in consequence of an Event of Default

The Defaulting Party is liable for the Non-Defaulting Party's reasonable legal and other professional expenses in enforcing its rights under paragraph 10 together with interest at one-month LIBOR unless a higher rate of interest has been agreed between them. The LIBOR rate will be determined on the first Business Day of such monthly period. Interest will accrue on a daily compounded basis.

11. **TRANSFER TAXES**

Borrower hereby undertakes promptly to pay and account for any transfer or similar duties or taxes chargeable in connection with any transaction effected pursuant to or contemplated by this Agreement, and shall indemnify and keep indemnified Lender against any liability arising as a result of Borrower's failure to do so.

11. TRANSFER TAXES

Borrower undertakes to pay any transfer taxes in connection with Loans under the GMSLA 2000 and indemnifies Lender where it fails to do so.

12. LENDER'S WARRANTIES

Each Party hereby warrants and undertakes to the other on a continuing basis to the intent that such warranties shall survive the completion of any transaction contemplated herein that, where acting as a Lender:

(a) it is duly authorised and empowered to perform its duties and obligations under this Agreement;

(b) it is not restricted under the terms of its constitution or in any other manner from lending Securities in accordance with this Agreement or from otherwise performing its obligations hereunder;

(c) it is absolutely entitled to pass full legal and beneficial ownership of all Securities provided by it hereunder to Borrower free from all liens, charges and encumbrances; and

(d) it is acting as principal in respect of this Agreement or, subject to paragraph 16, as agent and the conditions referred to in paragraph 16.2 will be fulfilled in respect of any Loan which it makes as agent.

13. BORROWER'S WARRANTIES

Each Party hereby warrants and undertakes to the other on a continuing basis to the intent that such warranties shall survive the completion of any transaction contemplated herein that, where acting as a Borrower:

(a) it has all necessary licenses and approvals, and is duly authorised and empowered, to perform its duties and obligations under this Agreement and will do nothing prejudicial to the continuation of such authorisation, licences or approvals;

(b) it is not restricted under the terms of its constitution or in any other manner from borrowing Securities in accordance with this Agreement or from otherwise performing its obligations hereunder;

(c) it is absolutely entitled to pass full legal and beneficial ownership of all Collateral provided by it hereunder to Lender free from all liens, charges and encumbrances; and

(d) it is acting as principal in respect of this Agreement.

12. LENDER'S WARRANTIES

In the GMSLA 2000 Lender offers Borrower 4 warranties on a continuous basis:

(a) It is authorised to perform its duties and obligations under the GMSLA 2000.

(b) There are no restrictions upon it lending Securities or performing its obligations under the GMSLA 2000.

(c) It can pass full legal title to all Securities to Borrower without any encumbrances. And

(d) It is acting as principal under the GMSLA 2000 unless it declares to Borrower that it is acting as agent for an underlying principal in accordance with the terms of paragraph 16.

13. BORROWER'S WARRANTIES

Borrower also offers Lender 4 warranties on a continuous basis. They are:

(a) It is duly authorised to perform its duties and obligations under the GMSLA 2000 and will do nothing to prejudice this.

(b) There are no restrictions upon it borrowing Securities or performing its obligations under the GMSLA 2000.

(c) It can pass absolute unencumbered legal title in the Collateral to Lender. And

(d) It is acting as principal under the GMSLA 2000. In fact it can never act as agent.

14. **EVENTS OF DEFAULT**

14.1 Each of the following events occurring in relation to either Party (the "**Defaulting Party**", the other Party being the "**Non-Defaulting Party**") shall be an Event of Default for the purpose of paragraph 10 but only (subject to sub-paragraph (v) below) where the Non-Defaulting Party serves written notice on the Defaulting Party:-

(i) Borrower or Lender failing to pay or repay Cash Collateral or deliver Collateral or redeliver Equivalent Collateral or Lender failing to deliver Securities upon the due date;

(ii) Lender or Borrower failing to comply with its obligations under paragraph 5;

(iii) Lender or Borrower failing to comply with its obligations under paragraph 6.1;

(iv) Borrower failing to comply with its obligations to deliver Equivalent Securities in accordance with paragraph 8;

(v) an Act of Insolvency occurring with respect to Lender or Borrower, an Act of Insolvency which is the presentation of a petition for winding up or any analogous proceeding or the appointment of a liquidator or analogous officer of the Defaulting Party not requiring the Non-Defaulting Party to serve written notice on the Defaulting Party;

(vi) any representation or warranty made by Lender or Borrower being incorrect or untrue in any material respect when made or repeated or deemed to have been made or repeated;

(vii) Lender or Borrower admitting to the other that it is unable to, or it intends not to, perform any of its obligations under this Agreement and/or in respect of any Loan;

(viii) Lender (if applicable) or Borrower being declared in default or being suspended or expelled from membership of or participation in, any securities exchange or association or suspended or prohibited from dealing in securities by any regulatory authority;

(ix) any of the assets of Lender or Borrower or the assets of investors held by or to the order of Lender or Borrower being transferred or ordered to be transferred to a trustee (or a person exercising similar functions) by a regulatory authority pursuant to any securities regulating legislation, or

(x) Lender or Borrower failing to perform any other of its obligations under this Agreement and not remedying such failure within 30 days after the Non-Defaulting Party serves written notice requiring it to remedy such failure.

14. EVENTS OF DEFAULT

As mentioned before in the commentary to paragraph 10, it is strange that the Agreement's Events of Default follow the close-out netting process in paragraph 10. A more logical order applies in the GMSLA 2010.

14.1

There are 10 Events of Default which are very similar to those in the GMRA (2000). These are:

(i) failure by Borrower or Lender to deliver Collateral of any sort or redeliver Equivalent Collateral on the due date or Lender failing to deliver Securities;

(ii) failure to comply with paragraph 5 obligations re Collateral;

(iii) failure to pay manufactured dividends;

(iv) Borrower failing to redeliver Equivalent Securities under paragraph 8;

(v) an act of insolvency occurring to Borrower or Lender;

(vi) representations or warranties made by Borrower or Lender being untrue or incorrect;

(vii) failure by either party to perform its obligations under the GMSLA 2000 or in respect of any Loan;

(viii) either party being in breach of securities exchange rules or being suspended from membership of a securities exchange or other self regulatory organisation;

(ix) transfer of either party's assets to a trustee by order of its regulator under existing securities laws; and

(x) failure by either party to remedy any other breach under the GMSLA 2000 within a 30-day cure period following written notice.

There are no grace periods for Events of Default except the last one.

In each case except for the appointment of a liquidator or the presentation of a petition for winding up, the Non-Defaulting Party must serve a notice on the Defaulting Party to call an Event of Default.

14.2 Each Party shall notify the other (in writing) if an Event of Default or an event which, with the passage of time and/or upon the serving of a written notice as referred to above, would be an Event of Default, occurs in relation to it.

14.3 The provisions of this Agreement constitute a complete statement of the remedies available to each Party in respect of any Event of Default.

14.4 Subject to paragraph 9.3 and 10.7, neither Party may claim any sum by way of consequential loss or damage in the event of failure by the other party to perform any of its obligations under this Agreement.

14.2

Each party is obliged to notify its counterparty in writing if it suffers an Event of Default or a potential Event of Default.

14.3

As far as Events of Default are concerned, the GMSLA 2000 constitutes a complete statement of remedies available to the parties.

14.4

Claims for consequential losses are prohibited under the GMSLA 2000 as they are under many other master agreements.

15. **INTEREST ON OUTSTANDING PAYMENTS**

In the event of either Party failing to remit sums in accordance with this Agreement such Party hereby undertakes to pay to the other Party upon demand interest (before as well as after judgment) on the net balance due and outstanding, for the period commencing on and inclusive of the original due date for payment to (but excluding) the date of actual payment, in the same currency as the principal sum and at the rate referred to in paragraph 10.7. Interest will accrue daily on a compound basis and will be calculated according to the actual number of days elapsed.

15. INTEREST ON OUTSTANDING PAYMENTS

This sub-paragraph provides for interest to be paid on late payments at one-month LIBOR or at such higher rate as the parties may agree on a daily compounded basis from and including the date the payment was due to, but excluding, the date it was actually paid.

16. **TRANSACTIONS ENTERED INTO AS AGENT**

16.1 **Power for Lender to enter into Loans as agent**

Subject to the following provisions of this paragraph, Lender may (if so indicated in paragraph 6 of the Schedule) enter into Loans as agent (in such capacity, the "**Agent**") for a third person (a "**Principal**"), whether as custodian or investment manager or otherwise (a Loan so entered into being referred to in this paragraph as an "**Agency Transaction**").

16.2 **Conditions for agency loan**

A Lender may enter into an Agency Transaction if, but only if:-

(i) it specifies that Loan as an Agency Transaction at the time when it enters into it;

(ii) it enters into that Loan on behalf of a single Principal whose identity is disclosed to Borrower (whether by name or by reference to a code or identifier which the Parties have agreed will be used to refer to a specified Principal) at the time when it enters into the Loan or as otherwise agreed between the Parties; and

(iii) it has at the time when the Loan is entered into actual authority to enter into the Loan and to perform on behalf of that Principal all of that Principal's obligations under the agreement referred to in paragraph 16.4(ii).

16.3 **Notification by Lender of certain events affecting the principal**

Lender undertakes that, if it enters as agent into an Agency Transaction, forthwith upon becoming aware:-

(i) of any event which constitutes an Act of Insolvency with respect to the relevant Principal; or

(ii) of any breach of any of the warranties given in paragraph 16.5 or of any event or circumstance which has the result that any such warranty would be untrue if repeated by reference to the then current facts;

it will inform Borrower of that fact and will, if so required by Borrower, furnish it with such additional information as it may reasonably request.

16. TRANSACTIONS ENTERED INTO AS AGENT

16.1 Power for Lender to enter into Loans as Agent

Provided this is indicated in paragraph 6 of the Schedule, a party may act as agent for a single disclosed principal in a Transaction when it is acting as Lender. It may be acting as custodian or investment manager for such underlying principal. Under the GMSLA 2000 an agency Loan is technically called an Agency Transaction. Only the Lender may act as agent in a securities lending transaction.

16.2 Conditions for agency loan

Paragraph 16.2 sets out the conditions for an Agency Transaction.

Lender must state that the Loan is an Agency Transaction when he enters into it. He must disclose the identity of his principal to Borrower (whether by name or an agreed code) at the time he enters into the Loan. Undisclosed principals are not allowed under the GMSLA 2000. Lender must enter into the loan on behalf of a single Principal only and he must have the Principal's actual authority to enter into the Loan and perform all the Principal's obligations on his behalf under the GMSLA 2000.

16.3 Notification by Lender of certain events affecting the principal

In sub-paragraph 16.3 Lender (as Agent) undertakes immediately to inform Borrower of any Act of Insolvency affecting his Principal and of any material breach of his authority to act warranty in paragraph 16.5 (so that it is untrue) and to provide any further reasonably requested information to Borrower.

Mastering Securities Lending Documentation

16.4 **Status of agency transaction**

(i) Each Agency Transaction shall be a transaction between the relevant Principal and Borrower and no person other than the relevant Principal and Borrower shall be a party to or have any rights or obligations under an Agency Transaction. Without limiting the foregoing, Lender shall not be liable as principal for the performance of an Agency Transaction, but this is without prejudice to any liability of Lender under any other provision of this clause; and

(ii) all the provisions of the Agreement shall apply separately as between Borrower and each Principal for whom the Agent has entered into an Agency transaction or Agency Transactions as if each such Principal were a party to a separate agreement with Borrower in all respects identical with this Agreement other than this paragraph and as if the Principal were Lender in respect of that agreement;

PROVIDED THAT

if there occurs in relation to the Agent an Event of Default or an event which would constitute an Event of Default if Borrower served written notice under any sub-clause of paragraph 14, Borrower shall be entitled by giving written notice to the Principal (which notice shall be validly given if given to Lender in accordance with paragraph 21) to declare that by reason of that event an Event of Default is to be treated as occurring in relation to the Principal. If Borrower gives such a notice then an Event of Default shall be treated as occurring in relation to the Principal at the time when the notice is deemed to be given; and

if the Principal is neither incorporated in nor has established a place of business in Great Britain, the Principal shall for the purposes of the agreement referred to in paragraph 16.4(ii) be deemed to have appointed as its agent to receive on its behalf service of process in the courts of England the Agent, or if the Agent is neither incorporated nor has established a place of business in Great Britain, the person appointed by the Agent for the purposes of this Agreement, or such other person as the Principal may from time to time specify in a written notice given to the other Party.

The foregoing provisions of this paragraph do not affect the operation of the Agreement as between Borrower and Lender in respect of any transactions into which Lender may enter on its own account as principal.

16.5 **Warranty of authority by Lender acting as agent**

Lender warrants to Borrower that it will, on every occasion on which it enters or purports to enter into a transaction as an Agency Transaction, have been duly authorised to enter into that Loan and perform the obligations arising under such transaction on behalf of the person whom it specifies as the Principal in respect of that transaction and to perform on behalf of that person all the obligations of that person under the agreement referred to in paragraph 16.4(ii).

16.4 Status of agency transaction

(i) Sub-paragraph 16.4 states that despite the Agent's intermediation each Agency Transaction shall be deemed to be a Loan between the relevant Principal and Borrower who will have privity of contract. This is important because there is no mutuality of contract between the Agent and Borrower. Moreover, close-out netting under the GMSLA 2000 only works on a principal to principal basis. It is made clear that Lender shall have no liability as principal where it is acting as Agent but otherwise it will be liable as principal under the GMSLA 2000.

(ii) The relevant Principal and Borrower will be deemed to have entered into a separate GMSLA 2000 between them identical to that between Borrower and Lender.

If, however, an Event of Default occurs to Lender as Agent, Borrower may notify the relevant Principal that the Event of Default shall be deemed to affect it and treat the Event of Default as happening at the time it sent its notice of such default to that Principal.

If the Principal is not English incorporated the Agent shall be deemed to be its Process Agent and if the Agent is not English incorporated its own Process Agent will fulfil this role for the Principal. Alternatively the Principal may advise Lender of a different Process Agent.

This provision does not affect any Transactions between Borrower and Lender on a principal to principal basis.

16.5 Warranty of authority by Lender acting as agent

In sub-paragraph 16.5 the Agent warrants each time it enters into an Agency Transaction it has been authorised by its principal to do so.

17. **TERMINATION OF THIS AGREEMENT**

    Each Party shall have the right to terminate this Agreement by giving not less than 15 Business Days' notice in writing to the other Party (which notice shall specify the date of termination) subject to an obligation to ensure that all Loans which have been entered into but not discharged at the time such notice is given are duly discharged in accordance with this Agreement.

18. **SINGLE AGREEMENT**

    Each Party acknowledges that, and has entered into this Agreement and will enter into each Loan in consideration of and in reliance upon the fact that, all Loans constitute a single business and contractual relationship and are made in consideration of each other. Accordingly, each Party agrees:

    (i) to perform all of its obligations in respect of each Loan, and that a default in the performance of any such obligations shall constitute a default by it in respect of all Loans; and

    (ii) that payments, deliveries and other transfers made by either of them in respect of any Loan shall be deemed to have been made in consideration of payments, deliveries and other transfers in respect of any other Loan.

19. **SEVERANCE**

    If any provision of this Agreement is declared by any judicial or other competent authority to be void or otherwise unenforceable, that provision shall be severed from the Agreement and the remaining provisions of this Agreement shall remain in full force and effect. The Agreement shall, however, thereafter be amended by the Parties in such reasonable manner so as to achieve as far as possible, without illegality, the intention of the Parties with respect to that severed provision.

17. TERMINATION OF THIS AGREEMENT

Each party has the right to terminate the GMSLA 2000 on 15 Business Days' notice in writing stating the termination date. Any such termination will not, however, affect the parties' existing obligations for any outstanding loans of securities. All outstanding Loans must be discharged in line with the GMSLA 2000's terms.

18. SINGLE AGREEMENT

The single agreement concept is designed to prevent a liquidator indulging in a practice called "cherry picking" where he is willing to honour his obligations under transactions profitable to his insolvent client but refuses to do so under other transactions which are unprofitable to that client but insists that the Non-Defaulting Party meets his obligations under such transactions.

Under the single agreement concept all Loans depend upon each other and a default in one of them counts as defaults under all Loans under the GMSLA 2000 through the set-off process in paragraph 10. This reduces the values of all Loans to a single net payment due to one party or the other.

The language in paragraph 18 stresses (i) the interdependence of each Loan with all other Loans under the GMSLA 2000 and (ii) that payments and deliveries under one Loan are deemed to be made in consideration of payments and deliveries under other Loans thus strengthening the single agreement concept.

19. SEVERANCE

This is a relatively standard severability provision which seeks to continue the GMSLA 2000 by severing an illegal or unenforceable provision in it. The parties can later try to amend the Agreement by inserting an equivalent provision, if they can, to the one previously severed.

20. **SPECIFIC PERFORMANCE**

Each Party agrees that in relation to legal proceedings it will not seek specific performance of the other Party's obligation to deliver or redeliver Securities, Equivalent Securities, Collateral or Equivalent Collateral but without prejudice to any other rights it may have.

21. **NOTICES**

21.1 Any notice or other communication in respect of this Agreement may be given in any manner set forth below to the address or number or in accordance with the electronic messaging system details set out in paragraph 4 of the Schedule and will be deemed effective as indicated:

(i) if in writing and delivered in person or by courier, on the date it is delivered;

(ii) if sent by telex, on the date the recipient's answerback is received;

(iii) if sent by facsimile transmission, on the date that transmission is received by a responsible employee of the recipient in legible form (it being agreed that the burden of proving receipt will be on the sender and will not be met by a transmission report generated by the sender's facsimile machine);

(iv) if sent by certified or registered mail (airmail, if overseas) or the equivalent (return receipt requested), on the date that mail is delivered or its delivery is attempted; or

(v) if sent by electronic messaging system, on the date that electronic message is received,

unless the date of that delivery (or attempted delivery) or the receipt, as applicable, is not a Business Day or that communication is delivered (or attempted) or received, as applicable, after the Close of Business on a Business Day, in which case that communication shall be deemed given and effective on the first following day that is a Business Day.

21.2 Either party may by notice to the other change the address, telex or facsimile number or electronic messaging system details at which notices or other communications are to be given to it.

22. **ASSIGNMENT**

Neither Party may charge assign or transfer all or any of its rights or obligations hereunder without the prior consent of the other Party.

20. SPECIFIC PERFORMANCE

Each party agrees not to seek in any legal proceedings, specific performance of the other party's obligations to deliver securities or collateral. This reinforces the close-out netting provisions, i.e. by reducing everything to cash damages.

21. NOTICES

Paragraph 21.1 describes how notices may be delivered and when they take effect. Delivery details are given in paragraph 4 of the Schedule.

As regards a fax (Paragraph 21.1 (iii)) its receipt is only effective on the date a responsible employee receives the fax in legible form. The sender has to prove receipt and a transmission report from a fax machine is not good enough for this purpose. Receipt is normally confirmed on a recorded telephone line. There is no definition of who is a responsible employee and any doubts about this (e.g. a temporary cleaner receiving a fax late at night when everyone else has left the office) could affect the timing of receipt of the notice. An electronic message is effective on receipt. If the date of delivery or receipt is not a Business Day or takes place after close of business on one then it will only become effective on the next Business Day.

In paragraph 21.2 the parties agree to notify each other about changes in their contact details.

22. ASSIGNMENT

Neither party may assign, charge or transfer any of its rights under the GMSLA 2000 without the other party's prior consent. This does not have to be in writing but normally would be.

23. **NON-WAIVER**

   No failure or delay by either Party (whether by course of conduct or otherwise) to exercise any right, power or privilege hereunder shall operate as a waiver thereof nor shall any single or partial exercise of any right, power or privilege preclude any other or further exercise thereof or the exercise of any other right, power or privilege as herein provided.

24. **GOVERNING LAW AND JURISDICTION**

   24.1 This Agreement is governed by, and shall be construed in accordance with, English law.

   24.2 The courts of England have exclusive jurisdiction to hear and decide any suit, action or proceedings, and to settle any disputes, which may arise out of or in connection with this Agreement (respectively, "**Proceedings**" and "**Disputes**") and, for these purposes, each party irrevocably submits to the jurisdiction of the courts of England.

   24.3 Each party irrevocably waives any objection which it might at any time have to the courts of England being nominated as the forum to hear and decide any Proceedings and to settle any Disputes and agrees not to claim that the courts of England are not a convenient or appropriate forum.

   24.4 Each of Party A and Party B hereby respectively appoints the person identified in paragraph 5 of the Schedule pertaining to the relevant Party as its agent to receive on its behalf service of process in the courts of England. If such an agent ceases to be an agent of Party A or party B, as the case may be, the relevant Party shall promptly appoint, and notify the other Party of the identity of its new agent in England.

25. **TIME**

   Time shall be of the essence of the Agreement.

26. **RECORDING**

   The Parties agree that each may record all telephone conversations between them.

23. NON-WAIVER

This is a relatively standard no waiver clause which is found in many types of legal agreement. No failure or delay by a party in exercising any of its rights under the GMSLA 2000 shall constitute a waiver of such rights. Limited exercise of such rights shall not preclude any later or further exercise of them.

24. GOVERNING LAW AND JURISDICTION

24.1

The GMSLA 2000 shall be governed by English law.

24.2

The parties irrevocably submit to the exclusive jurisdiction of the English courts to decide a lawsuit or settle a dispute.

24.3

This is re-emphasised in paragraph 24.3 where the parties agree not to object to the exclusive jurisdiction of the English courts to conduct proceedings and settle disputes. They also agree not to claim that the English courts are an inconvenient forum.

24.4

Process Agents, where relevant, are stated in paragraph 5 of the Schedule for the parties. They are a necessary part of the legal formalities for commencing legal proceedings and enforcing foreign judgments in the English courts. Replacement of Process Agents will be done quickly and notified to the other party.

25. TIME

Obligations must be performed promptly under the GMSLA 2000.

26. RECORDING

The parties agree that all telephone conversations between them may be recorded. This is favoured by regulators particularly in the UK where such recording is recommended in the Financial Service Authority's *Conduct of Business Sourcebook (2007)*.

27. **WAIVER OF IMMUNITY**

Each Party hereby waives all immunity (whether on the basis of sovereignty or otherwise) from jurisdiction, attachment (both before and after judgement) and execution to which it might otherwise be entitled in any action or proceeding in the courts of England or of any other country or jurisdiction relating in any way to this Agreement and agrees that it will not raise, claim or cause to be pleaded any such immunity at or in respect of any such action or proceeding.

27. WAIVER OF IMMUNITY

This is a relatively standard waiver of sovereign or other legal immunity which a party may have in respect of the GMSLA 2000 or similar agreements. Contracting parties who are supranational entities often delete this because they are set up under charters giving them numerous tax and legal immunities. They will never surrender them but most other counterparty types are expected to do so.

28. **MISCELLANEOUS**

28.1 This Agreement constitutes the entire agreement and understanding of the Parties with respect to its subject matter and supersedes all oral communication and prior writings with respect thereto.

28.2 The Party (the "**Relevant Party**") who has prepared the text of this Agreement for execution (as indicated in paragraph 7 of the Schedule) warrants and undertakes to the other Party that such text conforms exactly to the text of the standard form Global Master Securities Lending Agreement posted by the International Securities Lenders Association on its website on 7 May 2000 except as notified by the Relevant Party to the other Party in writing prior to the execution of this Agreement.

28.3 No amendment in respect of this Agreement will be effective unless in writing (including a writing evidenced by a facsimile transmission) and executed by each of the Parties or confirmed by an exchange of telexes or electronic messages on an electronic messaging system.

28.4 The obligations of the Parties under this Agreement will survive the termination of any Loan.

28. MISCELLANEOUS

28.1

The GMSLA 2000 constitutes the entire contractual agreement between the parties and supersedes all previous oral and written communications between them.

28.2

This is a warranty and undertaking from the party that has prepared the GMSLA 2000 for execution that it conforms to the standard form GMSLA 2000 text unless it states otherwise and this has been communicated to the other party in writing before it is executed.

28.3

Amendments to the GMSLA 2000 are only effective if in writing (including faxes) and executed by both parties. Alternatively they can be confirmed by telex or via an electronic messaging system. General market practice is for amendments to the GMSLA 2000 to be in hard copy form and signed by authorised signatories of both contracting parties.

28.4

The parties' obligations under the GMSLA 2000 survive the maturity of any individual Loan under it.

28.5 The warranties contained in paragraphs 12, 13, 16 and 28.2 will survive termination of this Agreement for so long as any obligations of either of the Parties pursuant to this Agreement remain outstanding.

28.6 Except as provided in this Agreement, the rights, powers, remedies and privileges provided in this Agreement are cumulative and not exclusive of any rights, powers, remedies and privileges provided by law.

28.7 This Agreement (and each amendment in respect of it) may be executed and delivered in counterparts (including by facsimile transmission), each of which will be deemed an original.

28.8 A person who is not a party to this Agreement has no right under the Contracts (Rights of Third Parties) Act 1999 to enforce any terms of this Agreement, but this does not affect any right or remedy of a third party which exists or is available apart from that Act.

28.5

In addition Lender's warranties in paragraph 12, Borrower's warranties in paragraph 13, warranties in relation to Agency Transactions in paragraph 16 and the GMSLA 2000 text conformity warranty in paragraph 28.2 will survive the termination of the GMSLA 2000 for so long as any of the parties' obligations under it remain outstanding.

28.6

In paragraph 14.3 the GMSLA 2000 is stated as constituting a complete statement of remedies available to the parties. Notwithstanding this, parties may have recourse to general contract law if they wish.

28.7

The GMSLA 2000 and any amendments may be executed in counterparts (including by fax) and each counterpart will be considered an original.

28.8

Paragraph 28.8 is a provision excluding third party rights in order to preserve privity of contract. The Contracts (Rights of Third Parties) Act 1999 reformed this area of English law. Before the Act came into force a person could only enforce a contract if they were party to it. This law permits third parties to enforce contracts that benefit them and which were entered into on or after 11 May 2000 as long as they are identified in the contract by name, as a class or by a particular description. There are certain exceptions set out in the Act and it is possible to exclude the effect of the Act altogether to ensure that privity of contract will apply as has been done here. However, this does not affect any other legal rights and remedies a third party may have outside this Act.

EXECUTED by the **PARTIES**

SIGNED BY   )
)
DULY AUTHORISED FOR AND   )
ON BEHALF OF   )

SIGNED BY   )
)
DULY AUTHORISED FOR AND   )
ON BEHALF OF   )

Signing block

The GMSLA 2000 is signed by authorised signatories of the contracting parties. It is either dated the date the first party signs it or more commonly the date that the second party signs it.

In the European market the convention is to sign the Agreement before any trading is done under it.

1. **Collateral**

1.1 The securities, financial instruments and deposits of currency set out in the table below with a cross marked next to them are acceptable forms of Collateral under this Agreement.

1.2 Unless otherwise agreed between the Parties, the Market Value of the Collateral delivered pursuant to paragraph 5 by Borrower to Lender under the terms and conditions of this Agreement shall on each Business Day represent not less than the Market Value of the Loaned Securities together with the percentage contained in the row of the table below corresponding to the particular form of Collateral, referred to in this Agreement as the "**Margin**".

Security/Financial Instrument/Deposit of Currency	Mark "X" if acceptable form of Collateral	Margin (%)

Schedule

Various matters referred to in the main text of the GMSLA 2000 are tackled in the Schedule.

1. Collateral

1.1 and 1.2

The types of margin or collateral acceptable to both parties are stated in the table in paragraph 1.2 together with the margin percentage applying to them. Sometimes they have different margin percentages. Alternatively one margin percentage usually 5% is applied across the board even when this looks strange as with cash. The Margin is essentially the haircut or discount on the value of the collateral supplied although sometimes it is expressed as a total percentage of the collateral value, e.g. 105%: practice varied. Where G10 government bonds were taken as collateral before the collapse of Lehman Brothers, the overcollateralisation could have been 102% or 105% (depending upon whether the collateral was in the same currency as the collateral or not) while with equity collateral it was usually 110%. Equity collateral is now at least 120%. Practice varied in other ways too. Where there was likely to be significant trading between parties, they might have agreed a lower margin percentage, e.g. 102%. Indeed, on many occasions, they agreed different margin percentages whatever was stated in paragraph 1.2 of the Schedule. As indicated above, since the collapse of Lehman Brothers many institutions have increased their margin levels on collateral.

Some parties may send their counterparties very long and comprehensive lists of collateral and margin percentages. It is vital that collateral managers decide which collateral they want to give and receive and not just accept what their counterparty offers them.

1.3 Basis of Margin Maintenance:

Paragraph 5.4 (aggregation) shall not apply* ☐

The assumption is that paragraph 5.4 (aggregation) applies unless the box is ticked.

1.4 Paragraph 5.6 (netting of obligations to deliver Collateral and redeliver Equivalent Collateral) shall not apply* ☐

If paragraph 5.4 applies, the assumption is that paragraph 5.6 (netting) applies unless the box is ticked.

2. **Base Currency**

The Base Currency applicable to this Agreement is

3. **Places of Business**

(See definition of Business Day.)

1.3 Basis of Margin Maintenance

This is where you choose whether global margining (paragraph 5.4.) or individual loan margining (paragraph 5.5.) is to apply. Most people choose global margining and often they will make a positive statement to this effect which I consider to be better practice than just leaving the box unticked.

1.4

This concerns the netting of collateral movements under paragraph 5.6 if global margining applies. It would normally apply in these circumstances. Once again better practice, in my view, is to make a positive statement rather than leaving the box unticked.

2. Base Currency

The agreed Base Currency for margining and close-out purposes is stated here.

3. Places of Business

The locations through which the parties plan to trade will be stated here (e.g. London and Paris or just London if they both plan to trade through their London Designated Offices). The definition of Business Day in the GMSLA 2000 will apply to these locations, i.e. whether banks and securities markets are open in them on the Business Day concerned. They must be open in both places of business stated in order for the GMSLA 2000 to work properly. Under the GMSLA 2000 it is normal to have only one Designated Office each. However, multiple Designated Offices are possible in the GMSLA 2010.

4. **Designated Office and Address for Notices**

(A) **Designated office of Party A:**

Address for notices or communications to Party A:

Address:

Attention:

Facsimile No:

Telephone No:

Electronic Messaging System Details:

(B) **Designated office of Party B:**

Address for notices or communications to Party B:

Address:

Attention:

Facsimile No:

Telephone No:

Electronic Messaging System Details:

5. (A) **Agent of Party A for Service of Process**

Name:

Address:

(B) **Agent of Party B for Service of Process**

Name:

Address:

4 Designated Office and Address for Notices

Notice details for Designated Offices are stated here.

5 Process Agents

If one or both parties are not English incorporated, details of their Process Agents are stated here.

6. **Agency**

- Paragraph 16 may apply to Party A* ☐
- Paragraph 16 may apply to Party B* ☐

7. **Party Preparing this Agreement**

Party A* ☐

Party B* ☐

6. Agency

If a party plans to act as an agent lender, it must tick the appropriate box. The provisions of paragraph 16 will apply to any Agency Transactions although they can be supplemented by further provisions in the Schedule.

7. Party Preparing this Agreement

For the purposes of paragraph 28.2 of the GMSLA 2000, the party preparing the Agreement must identify itself by ticking the appropriate box.

AMENDMENTS SOMETIMES PROPOSED TO THE GMSLA 2000

In contrast to the ISDA Master Agreement and the GMRA 2000, many Schedules to the GMSLA 2000 may only show completion of the items shown in the GMSLA Schedule template.

However, more sophisicated counterparties may add further provisions after paragraph 7 of the Schedule which may include the following matters:

- deletion of Lender failing to deliver Securities at the start of a Loan as an Event of Default;
- deletion of Borrower failing to deliver Equivalent Securities at the end of a Loan as an Event of Default;
- inclusion of a set-off clause;
- inclusion of a grace period in relation to a winding up petition in an insolvency situation;
- inclusion of extended agency provisions for an agency GMSLA 2000.

All these provisions or amendments are reviewed in the following section and need to be carefully considered by the negotiator and whether they are acceptable will be a matter of policy in many cases.

Some of the following provisions could be negotiated in a GMSLA 2010 Schedule but there are so few of these available at the time of writing (December 2010) that meaningful commentary is not yet possible.

The provisions are reviewed in the paragraph order of the GMSLA 2000.

Paragraph 2 Interpretation

Under the Act of Insolvency definition, presentation of a bankruptcy petition by a third party has a 30-day grace period for dismissal. However, there is no 30-day grace period for dismissal of a third party winding up petition as there is in the 1992 ISDA Master Agreement.

Sometimes parties may propose that there be no grace period at all as in the following example:

> In paragraph 2.1 of this Agreement, in sub-paragraph (iv) of the definition of "Act of Insolvency":
>
> (i) the last words ", such petition not having been stayed or dismissed within 30 days of its filing (except in the case of a petition for winding-up or any analogous proceeding in respect of which no such 30 day period shall apply)" shall be deleted.

3 · The Global Master Securities Lending Agreement (2000)

Alternatively a reduced grace period of 15 calendar days is sometimes proposed as in the following:

(1) Act of Insolvency Definition

Sub-paragraph 2.1(iv) shall be amended: by deleting the words "(except in the case of a petition for winding-up or any analogous proceeding in respect of which no such 30 day period shall apply)" at the end of the sub-paragraph and substituting the following wording therefor "(or in the case of a petition for winding-up or any analogous proceeding within 15 days of the filing of such a petition)".

Letters of Credit are not often used as collateral under the GMSLA 2000 and occasionally a party will propose a stark statement on this matter such as:

Letters of Credit shall not be acceptable Collateral under this Agreement. Accordingly, the definition of "Letter of Credit" in paragraph 2.1 of this Agreement shall be deleted and any provision of this Agreement relating to a Letter of Credit shall not be applicable.

Paragraph 5 Collateral

Paragraph 5.3 concerns substitutions of collateral and an amendment sometimes seen is the following addition to the clause:

The following wording shall be added to paragraph 5.3 of the Agreement:

"At the request of Lender, Borrower shall call for the redelivery of Collateral, equivalent to such Collateral. If Lender requests Borrower no later than five Business Days beforehand to recall Collateral because Income may become payable upon this Collateral, Borrower shall call for redelivery in good time to ensure that such Equivalent Collateral may be delivered prior to any Income becoming payable to Lender. At the time of such delivery, Borrower shall deliver Alternative Collateral acceptable to Lender."

This provision might be used where the Lender would be concerned about a withholding tax being charged on income received by him on the Borrower's collateral securities. Therefore a substitution is arranged in this case involving a five Business Day notice period.

Paragraph 5.8 requires that collateral transfers should be made on the same Business Day as the collateral call. The following amendment provides that the collateral transfer can take place on the following Business Day, which might be more operationally practical:

> Timing of repayments of excess Collateral or deliveries of further Collateral
>
> Paragraph 5.8 shall be amended by deleting the first sentence thereof and replacing it with the following new sentence:
>
> Where any Equivalent Collateral falls to be repaid or redelivered (as the case may be) or further Collateral is to be provided under this paragraph 5, unless otherwise agreed between the Parties, it shall be delivered on the first Business Day after the relevant demand.

Some parties are concerned about the relative informality of collateral transfers in the securities lending market and may prefer to have these confirmed as in the following provision:

> In paragraph 5, a new sub-paragraph 5.10 "Confirmations" shall be added as follows:
>
> "5.10 Confirmations
>
> The Parties shall each confirm by fax, by telephone or by electronic communication, the terms of any delivery, payment, redelivery, repayment or top-up of Collateral (including Cash Collateral, Alternative Collateral and Equivalent Collateral) occurring on any Business Day."

Paragraph 6 Distributions and Corporate Actions

A similar amendment to the one we saw in relation to paragraph 5.8 above sometimes appears as an amendment to paragraph 6.1 as follows:

> The following wording shall be added to paragraph 6.1 of the Agreement:
>
> "Where Income (of any kind whatsoever) is pending in relation to any Loaned Securities or Collateral on or by reference to an Income Payment Date, Borrower, in the case of Loaned Securities, and Lender, in the case of Collateral, shall use its best endeavours to notify the other Party thereof as timely as possible prior thereto but not earlier than five Business Days prior to the payment of such Income."

Here the obligation is to inform the relevant party of the impending income payment rather than automatically arranging a substitution.

Other amendments seen for paragraph 6 concern corporate actions. The first of these conditionally stops a Borrower terminating a Loan where a corporate action is imminent:

3 · The Global Master Securities Lending Agreement (2000)

Impending Corporate Actions

Borrower shall not be entitled to terminate a Loan of Loaned Securities which are the subject of an impending Corporate Action unless Lender has accepted that redelivery of Equivalent Securities by Borrower in accordance with paragraph 8.3 will be received in sufficient time to allow Lender to participate in the Corporate Action.

A more elaborate provision is the following:

Collateral – Corporate Actions and Income

Where Securities are delivered as Collateral for a Loan, Borrower shall provide to Lender Alternative Collateral acceptable to Lender three Business Days prior to the record date for the happening of a Corporate Action, maturity or the payment of any Income with respect to the Collateral. If, for whatever reason, Alternative Collateral is not provided prior to the record date for the happening of such Corporate Action, maturity or the payment of any Income with respect to the Collateral, causing Lender to be the holder of record at such time, the following shall apply: (i) Lender shall have no liability to Borrower in connection with any elections or exercisable rights in respect of such Corporate Actions and Lender's obligation to redeliver Equivalent Collateral shall be revised accordingly, save that Lender shall use reasonable efforts to act in accordance with the Borrower's instructions in connection therewith provided these are given to Lender within a reasonable timeframe, as determined by Lender, as would enable Lender to comply with such instructions and (ii) Lender's obligation to account to Borrower for Income or other distributions in respect of Collateral, shall be subject to any withholding taxes or duties deducted or imposed on Lender, without reference to any amount of tax credit or reclaim which may be due or claimable by Lender. Borrower acknowledges that Income paid on non-cash Collateral may be afforded different tax treatment by the local tax authority than Borrower would have been so entitled had it not delivered the Collateral to Lender, and hereby agrees not to claim against Lender for any disparate treatment as a result of Borrower receiving the Income or other distribution from Lender (as opposed to a distribution from issuer directly).

Whether the scope of this is acceptable is a matter of policy.

Voting rights

Voting rights cannot be manufactured and therefore they pass to the Borrower fully when the Lender transfers Loaned Securities to it at the start of a Loan. If the Lender wishes to vote the securities at a meeting of the issuer's shareholders or bondholders he must recall them from the Borrower. It is **not** normal for a Borrower to be under an obligation to vote the securities in line with the Lender's instructions and so a provision such as the following will normally be resisted:

Voting Rights

The parties agree further that:

(i) the Borrower will not exercise or procure the exercise of the voting, conversion, redemption and all other rights attaching to or arising in respect of Loaned Securities that are Equities held by the Borrower or its nominee other than in accordance with the directions of the Lender. In the absence of such instructions the Borrower shall not exercise any such rights; and

(ii) the Lender will not exercise or procure the exercise of the voting, conversion, redemption and all other rights attaching to or arising in respect of Collateral Securities that are Equities held by the Lender or its nominee other than in accordance with the directions of the Borrower. In the absence of such instructions the Lender shall not exercise any such rights.

Paragraph 8 Redelivery of Equivalent Securities

Paragraph 8.3 concerns Borrower's right to terminate a Loan and this can be at any time. An amendment occasionally seen in the market adds a new sentence to the end of paragraph 8.3 as follows:

Paragraph 8.3 shall be amended by adding the following new sentence at the end. "For Securities lent for a specified time the full rate over such specified time shall, unless otherwise agreed between the Parties, be payable by the Borrower even if the Equivalent Securities are redelivered prematurely."

It is possible that not everybody will like this provision.

Most securities loans are open or on demand but some contracting parties might be concerned that this is too open ended and may propose the following provision:

Paragraph 8 shall be amended by inserting a new paragraph 8.7 that reads as follows:

"In the absence of a demand notice, the date of redelivery for a Loan terminable on demand shall be the day falling 364 days after the day the Loan was made."

Paragraph 9 Failure to Redeliver

A common amendment in paragraphs 9.1 and 9.2 is to disapply the option of an Event of Default being declared because of a failure of the Borrower to redeliver equivalent securities at the end of a Loan and the Lender failing to redeliver equivalent collateral at the same time. Typical wording for this is as follows:

> Paragraph 9.1(i) shall be amended as follows:
>
> The words "either" in line 5 and "or serve a notice of an Event of Default in accordance with paragraph 14." in lines 7 and 8 shall be deleted.

This deletion no longer gives the option of calling an Event of Default for them under the GMSLA 2010.

In paragraph 9.3 a party due to receive securities (a Transferee) who failed to fulfil his contractual obligations to redeliver these securities to a third party could be faced with a compensation claim from that third party who had been forced to buy in those securities from the market. Paragraph 9.3 gives the right for the Transferee to have recourse to the party who failed to deliver the securities to him, i.e. the Transferor.

In paragraph 9.4 the Transferor essentially gives an indemnity to make the Transferee wholly responsible for the total costs and expenses reasonably incurred by the Transferee in the third party's buy-in.

The following provision is sometimes seen in this respect:

> Exercise of buy-in on failure to redeliver
>
> In paragraph 9.4 of this Agreement, the words ", provided that reasonable notice has been given to the Transferor of the likelihood of such buy-in," shall be inserted after the words "… against the Transferee, then" in line 2.

Paragraph 11 Transfer Taxes

In paragraph 11 the Borrower provides an ongoing tax indemnity to the Lender in respect of taxes chargeable on any Loan under the GMSLA 2000. A common proposed amendment here makes each party responsible for taxes charged to it:

> Paragraph 11 shall be amended by deleting such paragraph in its entirety, except for the heading, and inserting the following: "Each of the Parties shall itself pay and account for any transfer or similar duties or taxes chargeable in connection with any transaction effected pursuant to or contemplated by this Agreement incurred by the relevant Party."

OR

Paragraph 11 shall be amended by deleting the paragraph in its entirety (including the heading) and inserting the following:

"11. TAXES

11.1 Each of the Parties shall itself pay and account for transfer or similar duties or taxes chargeable in connection with any transaction effected pursuant to or contemplated by this Agreement incurred by the relevant Party. The Parties agree that each Party will be liable for any other potential tax effects of the Agreement and any transaction hereunder for its own business and that the other Party will not be liable for any such effects.

11.2 Each of the Parties warrants to the other Party that appropriate investigations regarding the potential tax effects of the Agreement and any transaction hereunder for its own business has been made prior to entering into the Agreement."

Paragraph 12 Lender's Warranties

These warranties are continuous but sometimes parties may seek to vary this as in the following:

The representations and warranties set out in Paragraph 12 shall be deemed repeated by the Lender on the date of acceptance of each Borrowing Request issued hereunder and on the Settlement Date for any loan of borrowed Securities hereunder.

In my opinion this should be resisted.

Paragraph 14 Events of Default

Two common amendments here are to disapply as Events of Default the Lender failing to deliver Securities at the start of the Loan or the Borrower failing to deliver Equivalent Securities at its end. Operational problems beyond either party's control are a common everyday problem in this market and many market players considered these Events of Default (paragraphs 14.1(i) and 14.1(iv)) were too draconian in this respect. They are no longer Events of Default under the GMSLA 2010.

Wording commonly used to disapply them in the GMSLA 2000 is as follows:

Paragraph 14 shall be amended as follows:

(i) In Paragraph 14.1(i) the words "or Lender failing to deliver Securities" in line 2 shall be deleted.

(ii) Paragraph 14.1(iv) shall be deleted.

Scandinavian counterparties sometimes want to exclude labour lock-outs from being an Event of Default. In the 1980s there were a significant number of bank strikes in Scandinavia some of which lasted for several weeks. Possible wording to exclude these could be the following:

The following shall be inserted as a new paragraph 14.5:

A Party ("X") shall not be deemed to be in breach of this Agreement or otherwise liable to the other Party ("Y") and no Event of Default shall be deemed to occur with respect to X, as a result of any delay in performance or any non-performance by X of any obligations under this Agreement (and the time for performance shall be extended accordingly) if and to the extent that the delay or non-performance is due to lock-outs, strikes or other disputes, in each case directly or indirectly affecting or instigated by X or its workforce.

In this particular example there is no time limit on the lock-out.

Paragraph 22 Assignment

In paragraph 22 neither party can make any assignment of its rights and obligations without the other party's prior consent although it is not stated that this needs to be in writing. An amendment sometimes seen is the following:

Paragraph 22 is deleted in its entirety and replaced with the following:

"Neither party may assign, charge or otherwise deal with (including without limitation any dealing with any interest in or the creation of any interest in) its rights or obligations under this Agreement or under any Transaction without the prior written consent of the other party, except that a party may assign, charge or otherwise deal with all or any part of its interest in any sum payable to it under paragraphs 9, 10, 11 and 15."

The sums payable under the paragraphs stated in the final line relate to sums payable where a Borrower fails to redeliver Equivalent Securities or a Lender fails to redeliver Equivalent Collateral or buy-in costs become chargeable (paragraph 9); a Non-Defaulting Party receives a termination payment from a Defaulting Party (paragraph 10); a party receives a transfer tax payment (paragraph 11); or a party receives interest on a late payment (paragraph 15).

Whether these exclusions are acceptable is a matter of policy.

Paragraph 26 Recording

Regulators favour the recording of contractual business telephone conversations. There are many examples of wording for this but in certain countries (e.g. Germany) consent is needed from the people whose conversations are being recorded. An example of such wording is the following:

> Telephone Recording
>
> Paragraph 26 is deleted in its entirety and replaced with the following new provision:
>
> Each of Party A and Party B (i) consents to the recording of telephone conversations of trading personnel of the Parties and (ii) agrees to obtain any necessary consent of, and give notice of such recording to, such personnel.

Schedule

1.1 and 1.2 Collateral

Paragraph 1.2 is where the parties agree the collateral acceptable to each of them and the Margin percentages applying to them. They normally want certainty on this and so the following provision is unlikely to be acceptable to most market players:

> Notwithstanding Paragraph 1.1 above the Lender shall have the right to refuse to accept certain types of security, financial instruments and deposits of currency as Collateral under this Agreement in its absolute discretion provided reasonable notice is provided to the Borrower.

1.3 Basis of Margin Maintenance

This is where a choice is made for global margining across a whole securities lending portfolio. The template states that this will apply unless the box is ticked. This is rather confusing and it is better to state clearly whether you want it to apply or not. Most market players will apply it. A belt and braces approach to this is the following:

Basis of Margin Maintenance: paragraph 5.4 (aggregation) of this Agreement <u>shall</u> apply and paragraph 5.5 of this Agreement <u>shall not</u> apply.

5 Process Agent

Normally this is not a problem but occasionally you might have a difficult counterparty who is not English incorporated and who does not wish to appoint a Process Agent in England. Usually there is considerable negotiation on this but ultimately the following provision might be agreed if all else fails:

> For the purpose of paragraph 24.4, Party B will notify Party A in writing of the person appointed to be its agent for service of process in England provided, however, that if Party B fails to appoint an agent for service of process or such agent for service of process is not or ceases to be effectively so appointed and in the event that Party A is required to serve process on Party B in connection with any proceedings, Party B agrees to (i) co-operate with Party A, its agents or employees, as the case may be, in the service of such process; and (ii) indemnify in full and hold Party A harmless from any and all losses, costs and expenses (including, without limitation, any losses, costs and expenses incurred by Party A, its agents or employees by reason of any delay in the service of process) as a result, whether directly or indirectly, of its failure to appoint an agent for service of process hereunder.

Other provisions

Other provisions might be included in an additional paragraph 8 to the Schedule. Here are a few examples:

> Scope of Agreement
>
> Party A and Party B confirm and agree that all transactions entered into between Party A and Party B in relation to the lending of Securities prior to the date of this Agreement and still outstanding will from the date of this Agreement incorporate the terms of and be governed by this Agreement.

This provision sweeps in securities loans between the parties which are outside the GMSLA 2000. There is a similar provision in paragraph 27.4 of the GMSLA 2010 which is optional.

Threshold

A Threshold or a margin Threshold is the unsecured exposure one party grants another before any collateral call can be made. This is common in the ISDA Credit Support Annexes under English and New York law and the GMRA 2000. However, it is not common in the GMSLA 2000. Therefore, I consider that the following provisions should not be agreed because they are currently contrary to general market practice.

> Threshold applicable to Collateral Margin
>
> Notwithstanding the provisions of paragraph 5.4, a threshold amount of Euro 200,000 (the "Margin Threshold") will be applicable to Collateral, and the Lender agrees not to require Collateral in respect of its exposure to the Borrower up to and including the Margin Threshold. For the avoidance of doubt, once the Borrower's exposure to the Lender exceeds the Margin Threshold, the Borrower will provide Collateral (which, for the avoidance of doubt, shall include the appropriate Margin thereon in accordance with paragraph 1 of the Schedule) for the entire exposure the Borrower has to the Lender.

OR, more elaborately:

> Notwithstanding Paragraph 5.6, neither party may require the other party to make a Margin Transfer to it under the Agreement if its Net Exposure in respect of the other party is less than the lesser of £500,000 or 2.5% of the value outstanding under the Agreement (or its Market Value equivalent in GBP if it is not denominated in GBP) (the "Margin Threshold"), provided, however, that the Margin Threshold shall not apply if there are no Transactions outstanding under this Agreement but there remains a Net Exposure between the parties in an amount less than the Margin Threshold.

Force majeure and labour dispute events

Sometimes counterparties propose adding new paragraphs to the GMSLA 2000 such as the following provision incorporated in a new paragraph 29:

> A new paragraph 29 entitled "FORCE MAJEURE AND LABOUR DISPUTE EVENTS" shall be inserted in the Agreement reading as follows:
>
> "29.1 If a Party ("X") is prevented, hindered or delayed, by reasons of Acts of God, riots, civil commotions, insurrections, wars or, acting in good faith, any other similar causes beyond

its control (a "Force Majeure Event") or by reasons of lock-outs, strikes or other disputes, in each case directly or indirectly affecting or instigated by X or its workforce (a "Labour Dispute Event"), from fulfilling any obligation under this Agreement, X shall not be deemed to be in breach of this Agreement or otherwise liable to the other Party ("Y"), and no Event of Default shall be deemed to occur with respect to X. In case of a Force Majeure Event or a Labour Dispute Event, the time for performance shall be extended accordingly.

29.2 If X cannot receive payment from Y or Y cannot make payment to X due to a Force Majeure Event or a Labour Dispute Event, then Y shall not be deemed to be in breach of this Agreement or otherwise liable to X, and no Event of Default shall be deemed to occur with respect to Y.

29.3 If, in accordance with this paragraph, any obligation of X or Y hereunder is postponed following a Force Majeure Event or a Labour Dispute Event, interest shall accrue on the relevant amount(s) from the scheduled payment/delivery date(s) to the date of actual payment or delivery at a rate per annum in accordance with paragraph 10.7 of the Agreement.

29.4 X shall promptly notify Y of the nature and extent of the circumstances giving rise to a Force Majeure Event or a Labour Dispute Event and shall use its reasonable endeavours to make or receive payments by alternative means.

29.5 If a Force Majeure Event or a Labour Dispute Event prevails for a continuous period in excess of thirty calendar days such event shall be an Event of Default."

This expanded provision which partly covers Labour Dispute Events has a 30-day time limit in its final sub-paragraph.

Another such provision I have seen is the following:

30. GOVERNING PRACTICES

A new paragraph 30 entitled "GOVERNING PRACTICES" shall be inserted in the Agreement reading as follows:

"Each of the Parties shall use its best efforts to notify the other Party (in writing) of any material changes in legislation or practices governing or affecting the other Party's rights or obligations under this Agreement or the treatment of transactions effected pursuant to or contemplated by this Agreement."

While this seems reasonable enough, giving undertakings on a best efforts basis should be avoided as this implies quite a high standard of conduct. For example, in the case of *IBM United Kingdom Ltd v Rockware Glass Ltd* [1980] FSR 335, a best endeavours clause (which is arguably similar to a best efforts clause) was described as one in which the obligor should take "all those steps in their power which are capable of producing the desired results ... being steps which a prudent, determined and reasonable [obligee], acting in his own interests and desiring to achieve that result, would take". It may not always be possible to comply with this requirement due to operational error or lack of time. Any obligation to provide such information should be subject to the caveat that failure to provide it should not constitute an Event of Default. Alternatively best efforts could be diluted to "reasonable efforts". If a party is still uncomfortable about this I would recommend deleting this provision.

Set off and cross-collateralisation

Following the publication of the GMSLA 2000, parties regularly added a set-off clause along the lines of the one included in the Schedule of a 1992 ISDA Master Agreement based upon the wording shown on page 56 of ISDA's Users' Guide to that Agreement. Given the overcollateralisation involved with securities lending, if this is done correctly a Lender should not be exposed if its counterparty defaults or goes bankrupt unless very illiquid securities are involved. A set-off clause therefore is normally unnecessary with securities lending. However, there is now a set-off clause in paragraph 11.8 of the GMSLA 2010 and as the market is moving in this direction, I have to relax my position on this.

An example of a simple set-off clause which might be used with a GMSLA 2000 is the following:

> **Paragraph 10 shall be amended by inserting the following provision as a new clause 10.8 at the end thereof:**
>
> 10.8 In addition to any rights of set-off a party may have as a matter of law or otherwise upon the occurrence of an Event of Default, the Non-Defaulting Party shall have the right (but not be obliged) to set off any obligation of the Defaulting Party owing to the Non-Defaulting Party (whether or not arising under this Agreement, whether or not matured, whether or not contingent and regardless of the currency, place of payment or booking office of the obligation) against any obligation of the Non-Defaulting Party owing to the Defaulting Party (whether or not arising under this Agreement whether or not matured, whether or not contingent and regardless

of the currency, place of payment or booking office of the obligation). For this purpose any sums not in the Base Currency shall be converted into the Base Currency in accordance with paragraphs 2.4 and 2.5. If an obligation is unascertained, the Non-Defaulting Party may in good faith estimate that obligation and set-off in respect of the estimate, subject to the relevant party accounting to the other when the obligation is ascertained. Nothing in this paragraph shall be effective to create a security interest. This paragraph shall be without prejudice and in addition to any right of set-off, combination of accounts, lien or other right to which any party is at any time entitled (whether by operation of law, contract or otherwise).

A more elaborate one is:

The following is inserted as a new Paragraph 29:

"29 CROSS-DEFAULT, CROSS-COLLATERALISATION

Each party to this agreement (such party, "Party X") agrees that, upon the insolvency of Party X or the default of Party X under any transaction with the other party hereto (such other party a "Non-Defaulting Party"), each Non Defaulting Party may, without prior notice to Party X: (a) liquidate any transaction between party X and any Non-Defaulting Party (which liquidation may include the conversion of amounts denominated in multiple currencies into a single currency if deemed necessary or desirable by the Non Defaulting Party), (b) reduce any amounts due and owing to Party X under any transaction between Party X and any Non-Defaulting Party by setting off against such amounts any amounts due and owing to a Non-Defaulting Party by Party X, and (c) treat all security for, and all amounts due and owing to Party X under, any transaction between Party X and any Non-Defaulting Party as security for all transactions between Party X and any Non-Defaulting Party; provided, however, that the exercise of the remedies described in sub-paragraphs (a), (b), and (c) above (or in any other similar provision in any agreement between the parties) shall be deemed to occur immediately subsequent to, but independent of, the exercise of any netting, liquidation, set-off or other similar provision contained in any master agreement between the parties; provided further that each provision and agreement hereof shall be treated as independent from any other provision or agreement herein and shall be enforceable notwithstanding the unenforceability of any such other provision or agreement."

This widens the scope of the set off to any transactions under other agreements and many parties may find this too wide.

Withholding tax indemnity

The GMSLA 2000 does not include a specific withholding tax indemnity and I have seen the following proposed by a party:

> Payments and deliveries net of tax
>
> All monies, securities or other property due from the Borrower to the Lender or vice versa under this Agreement shall be paid or delivered, as the case may be, free and clear of any taxes or duties of whatsoever nature imposed, levied, collected, withheld or assessed by any authority having power to tax, unless the withholding or deduction of such taxes or duties is required by law. In that event, for greater certainty and except to the extent otherwise provided in this Agreement or as agreed in writing between the parties, the Borrower or the Lender as the case may be shall pay or deliver such additional amounts thereof as will result in the net amounts receivable by the Lender or the Borrower as the case may be being equal to such amounts as would have been received by it had no such taxes or duties been required by law to be withheld or deducted.

Again whether this is acceptable is a matter of policy.

Excess amounts under this Agreement

You would have to have excellent operational systems to agree to the following which involves setting off amounts due between the parties following the termination of all Transactions under repo and securities lending master agreements:

> Excess amounts under this Agreement
>
> Any net amount arising under this Agreement from the occurrence of an Event of Default hereunder which is:
>
> (a) due to the Non-Defaulting Party, may be set off against any net amount due from the Non-Defaulting Party pursuant to the close-out procedure under any other securities lending or repurchase agreement between the Parties arising as a result of such Event of Default; or
>
> (b) due from the Non-Defaulting Party, may be set off against any net amount due to the Non-Defaulting Party pursuant to the close-out procedure under any other securities lending or repurchase agreement between the Parties arising as result of such Event of Default.

My advice is not to agree this type of provision without a thorough discussion with your Operations Department. It could be a nightmare for them.

Agency provisions

Many securities lending transactions are undertaken by an agent acting for a group of underlying disclosed principals. In paragraph 16 of the GMSLA 2000 there are a series of agency provisions to a single disclosed principal. In the market parties either amend these to cover multiple disclosed principals or substitute them with a completely different set of such provisions. An example of the first approach is as follows:

The following shall be added to the end of paragraph 16.1:

"For the avoidance of doubt, unless specified otherwise at the time a Loan is entered into, each Loan under this Agreement shall be an Agency Transaction.

The Lender may simultaneously enter into a number of such Agency Transactions, PROVIDED THAT it identifies to the Borrower details of Loans made in respect of each Principal on or after the time each Agency Transaction is entered into. The Lender and the Borrower agree that the Lender may at any time, and without prior notice, substitute a new Principal (the "New Principal" (which has been approved by the Borrower prior to trading)) in place of the existing Principal (the "Existing Principal") for an Agency Transaction (a "Substitution") whereupon simultaneously:

(i) the Borrower and the Existing Principal shall be released from all of their respective obligations and liabilities to each other in respect of the Agency Transaction and the Existing Principal shall have no further rights in respect of the Agency Transaction;

(ii) the New Principal shall assume, and undertakes to the Borrower to perform, the obligations and liabilities in favour of the Borrower identical to all of the Existing Party's obligations and liabilities under the Agency Transaction immediately prior to the Substitution; and

(iii) the Borrower shall assume, and undertake to the New Principal to perform, the obligations and liabilities in favour of the New Principal identical to all of its obligations and liabilities to the Existing Principal under the Agency Transaction immediately prior to the Substitution."

8.3 The following shall be added as new paragraph 16.6:

"When the Agent enters into an Agency Transaction, it will allocate the Loan either to a single Principal or to several Principals, each of whom shall be responsible for only that part of the Loan which has been allocated to it. Where the allocation is to two or more Principals, a separate Loan shall be deemed to have been entered into between the other party and each such Principal with respect to the appropriate proportion of the borrowed Securities."

8.4 Party B agrees that all Confidential Information (as defined below) shall be kept strictly confidential and used solely for the purposes of identification, credit analysis and complying with all applicable financial and regulatory reporting requirements and not for any other reason or purpose, including, but limited to, the solicitation and/or pursuit of Principals for the purpose of directed lending or any other transaction or arrangement, and that no Confidential Information may be revealed to any personnel of Party B engaged in a sales or trading role, or to any person managing such personnel.

"Confidential Information" means any information which:

(i) identifies the identities of any Principal, disclosed by Party A to Party B's credit department in accordance with new paragraph 16.2 (ii) of this Agreement; or

(ii) details the outstanding loan balances between Party B and any Principal (which shall include any reports or information derived therefrom.

8.5 Agency Transactions in respect of loans of Securities may only be entered into where the Principal is acting as Lender.

An example of a comprehensive substitution of agency provisions is the following:

AGENCY ANNEX TO GLOBAL MASTER SECURITIES LENDING AGREEMENT

Supplemental terms and conditions for Agency Transactions

This Annex constitutes an Annex to the Schedule to the Global Master Securities Lending Agreement dated .... between X Bank, as Agent

and ....(referred to in this Annex as "Borrower"), (the "Agreement").

1 Scope and interpretation

(a) Borrower acknowledges that it shall not enter into Loans under the Agreement as agent for a third person, but shall act solely as principal.

(b) In relation to Agency Transactions, this Agreement is amended and supplemented as set out in paragraphs 2 to 12 of this Annex.

(c) The Parties acknowledge that a Loan may be arranged by the Agent for the account of more than one Principal and accordingly the Parties acknowledge that the Agent is required to have duly allocated that Loan to the relevant Principals before the Settlement Date for that Loan, and the Parties agree that for all purposes of this Agreement, that Loan shall be treated as a series of separate Agency Transactions entered into simultaneously between each relevant Principal and Borrower for the amount allocated to the relevant Principal, and "Agency Transaction" shall be construed accordingly.

(d) In this Annex -

   (i) If at any time on any Business Day the aggregate Market Value of Posted Collateral in respect of all Loans outstanding with a Principal under this Agreement exceeds the aggregate of the Required Collateral Value in respect of such Loans, Borrower has a "Net Transaction Exposure" to that Principal equal to that excess; if at any time on any Business Day the aggregate Market Value of Posted Collateral in respect of all Loans outstanding under this Agreement with a Principal falls below the aggregate of the Required Collateral Value in respect of such Loans, that Principal shall be deemed to have a Net Transaction Exposure for such Loans equal to that deficiency;

   (ii) "Pooled Principal" has the meaning given in paragraph 6(a) below; and

   (iii) "Pooled Transaction" has the meaning given in paragraph 6(a) below.

2 Initiation; Confirmation

The Parties agree that all Loans effected under the Agreement shall be Agency Transactions unless at the time a Loan is entered into the Agent specifies that it is entering into the Loan as principal, and this is reflected in the confirmation for the Loan.

3 Agent's representations and warranties

The Agent represents and warrants that:

(a) Before arranging any Agency Transactions it shall have disclosed generally to Borrower the identity and the jurisdiction of incorporation, organisation or establishment of each Principal (whether by name or by reference to a code or identifier which the Parties have agreed will be used to refer to a specified Principal) on behalf of which it has authority to arrange Agency Transactions. Such disclosure may be made to the legal/credit/compliance department of Borrower, and shall be promptly updated when changes in respect of any of those Principals occur;

(b) it will have, on every occasion on which it arranges an Agency Transaction and at the time when the Loan is entered into, actual authority to arrange the Loan on behalf of the relevant Principal and to act on behalf of the relevant Principal in respect of all of that Principal's rights and obligations under the Agreement;

(c) it shall, if at the time of entering into an Agency Transaction it has not duly allocated the Loan to a Principal, allocate the Loan as soon as practicable thereafter but always before the Settlement Date for that Loan either to a single Principal or to several Principals and shall consequently record the Loan as a series of Agency Transactions between each relevant Principal and Borrower;

(d) at the time of allocating an Agency Transaction in accordance with paragraph 1(c) above, no Event of Default, of which Agent is aware, has occurred in relation to any Principal or Principals to whom the Agent has allocated that Loan or any part of that Loan;

(e) where Borrower is regulated in the conduct of its investment business by the United Kingdom Financial Services Authority ("FSA") the Principal on whose behalf the Agent is acting will not be an "indirect customer" of Borrower, and the Agent, and not the Principal, will be the "customer" of Borrower, in each case for the purposes of the rules of the FSA;

(f) the Agent has obtained evidence of, and recorded, the identity of the Principal under procedures maintained by the Agent in accordance with applicable anti-money laundering regulations; and

(g) at the time of entering into an Agency Transaction in accordance with paragraph 1(c) above, it has previously received a representation on behalf of each Principal to whom the Agent has allocated that Loan or any part of that Loan, that such Principal is duly authorised to enter into the Loans contemplated by this Agreement and to perform its obligations under such Loans.

4 Allocation of Collateral

(a) Unless the Agent expressly allocates (i) a delivery or deposit of Posted Collateral or (ii) a repayment of Cash Collateral or a redelivery of Equivalent Collateral (each a "Collateral Transfer") before such time, the Agent shall, at the time of making or receiving that Collateral Transfer, be deemed to have allocated any Collateral Transfer in accordance with sub-paragraph (b) below.

   (i) If the Agent has made a Collateral Transfer on behalf of more than one Pooled Principal, that Collateral Transfer shall be allocated in proportion to Borrower's Net Transaction Exposure in respect of each Pooled Principal at the Agent's close of business on the Business Day before the Collateral Transfer is made; and

   (ii) if the Agent has received a Collateral Transfer on behalf of more than one Pooled Principal, that Collateral Transfer shall be allocated in proportion to each Pooled Principal's Net Transaction Exposure in respect of Borrower at the Agent's close of business on the Business Day before the Collateral Transfer is made.

Sub-paragraphs (a) and (b) above shall not apply in respect of any Collateral Transfer which is effected or deemed to have been effected under paragraph 6(c) below.

5 Pooled Principals: rebalancing of Collateral

(a) Where the Agent acts on behalf of more than one Principal, the Parties may agree that, as regards all (but not some only) outstanding Agency Transactions with those Principals, or with such of those Principals as they may agree ("Pooled Principals", such transactions being "Pooled Transactions"), any Collateral Transfers are to be made on an aggregate net basis.

(b) Sub-paragraphs (c) to (e) below shall have effect for the purpose of ensuring that any Posted Collateral held, Posted Collateral to be delivered or deposited, Cash Collateral to be repaid or Equivalent Collateral to be redelivered is, so far as is practicable, transferred and held proportionately, as between the respective Pooled Principals, in respect of all Pooled Transactions for the time being outstanding under the Agreement.

(c) At or as soon as practicable after the Agent's close of business on each Business Day on which Pooled Transactions are outstanding (or at such other times as the Parties may from time to time agree) there shall be effected such Collateral Transfers as shall ensure that immediately thereafter -

   (i) in respect of all Pooled Principals which have a Net Transaction Exposure to Borrower, the amount of Collateral then deliverable (or payable in the case of Cash Collateral) to each such Pooled Principal is equal to such proportion of the aggregate amount of Collateral then deliverable (or payable in the case of Cash Collateral) to all such Pooled Principals as corresponds to the proportion which the Net Transaction Exposure of the relevant Pooled Principal bears to the aggregate of the Net Transaction Exposures of all Pooled Principals to Borrower; and

   (ii) in respect of all Pooled Principals to which Borrower has a Net Transaction Exposure, the aggregate amount of Equivalent Collateral then re-deliverable (or repayable in the case of Cash Collateral) by each such Pooled Principal is equal to such proportion of the aggregate amount of Equivalent Collateral then re-deliverable (or repayable in the case of Cash Collateral) by all such Pooled Principals as corresponds to the proportion which the Net Transaction Exposure of the Borrower to the relevant Pooled Principal bears to the aggregate of the Net Transaction Exposures of Borrower to all Pooled Principals.

(d) Collateral Transfers effected under sub-paragraph (c) shall be effected (and if not so effected shall be deemed to have been so effected) by appropriations made by the Agent and shall be reflected by entries in accounting and other records maintained by the Agent. Accordingly, it shall not be necessary for delivery or deposits of Posted Collateral, repayments of Cash Collateral or redelivery of Equivalent Collateral to be made through any settlement system for the purpose of such Collateral Transfers. Without limiting the generality of the foregoing, the Agent is hereby authorised and instructed by Borrower to do all such things on behalf of the Borrower as may be necessary or expedient to effect and record the receipt on behalf of Borrower of repayments of Cash Collateral or redeliveries of Equivalent Collateral from, and the delivery or deposit of Posted Collateral on behalf of Borrower to, Pooled Principals in the course or for the purposes of any Collateral Transfer effected under that sub-paragraph.

6 Records, statements and confidentiality

(a) The Agent shall keep records capable of demonstrating at all times the outstanding Agency Transactions, the Principal that is a party to each such Agency Transaction, the Net Transaction Exposure of each Principal, the amount of Cash Collateral and/or Collateral Securities allocated to each Principal, or delivered by Borrower in respect of Loans for that Principal and such other information as may be necessary to perform its obligations as Agent.

(b) The Agent shall, at such times as have been agreed between the Parties, or otherwise upon reasonable request by Borrower, deliver a statement to Borrower in respect of all outstanding Agency Transactions, identifying the relevant Principals thereto (which may be by name or by reference to a code or identifier which the parties have agreed will be used to refer to a specified Principal) and the amount of Collateral held for each for each Principal. The information so provided by the Agent shall be kept strictly confidential by the other party and used solely for the purposes of identification, credit and risk analysis, legal due diligence, compliance with applicable financial and regulatory reporting requirements and otherwise as required by applicable law and regulation.

(c) Where the identity of a Principal has been disclosed only to the legal/credit/compliance department of the Borrower and a code or identifier is used thereafter to refer to the Principal, Borrower confirms that it shall use its best endeavours to ensure that the Principal's identity shall not be disclosed to any other persons, including without limitation the Borrower's sales, trading or marketing department, without the prior written consent of the Agent.

(d) Borrower acknowledges that if it has entered or shall enter into a separate Confidentiality Agreement with the Agent, in respect of securities lending by the Agent on behalf of its clients, that Confidentiality Agreement shall also apply in respect of information provided to Borrower by the Agent pursuant to this Agreement.

7 Rights of termination/substitution

The Parties agree that, in respect of any outstanding Agency Transaction, the Agent is hereby authorised by the Borrower to terminate any Loan between one Principal ("Principal A") and the Borrower (the "1st Loan"), and simultaneously enter into a new Loan on the same terms (the "2nd Loan") with another Principal ("Principal B") provided that:

(a) no Event of Default shall have occurred in respect of either Principal A or Principal B;

(b) Principal B shall be a Principal the identity of which has previously been disclosed to Borrower in accordance with paragraph 3 (a) of this Annex; and

(c) the termination of the 1st Loan and entry into the 2nd Loan shall be reflected by entries in accounting and other records maintained by the Agent and in the next statement provided by the Agent to the Borrower in accordance with paragraph 7(b) of this Annex.

Borrower agrees that the termination of the 1st Loan and entry into the 2nd Loan shall be effective from the time that the relevant entries are made in the Agent's records, without notice to Borrower, and at that time all rights, title, interest, obligations and liabilities of Principal A and Borrower in respect of the 1st Loan will be treated as having been performed and discharged and the obligations of Principal B and the Borrower to deliver Securities and to deliver any applicable Collateral Transfer as at that time will also be treated as having been performed and discharged.

8 General

(a) If the Agent shall fail to perform its obligations in paragraph 3(c) of this Annex in respect of allocation of Agency Transactions, then for the purposes of assessing any damage suffered by Borrower (but for no other purpose) it shall be assumed that, if the Loan concerned (to the extent not allocated) had been allocated in accordance with paragraph 3(c) all the terms of the Loan would have been duly performed.

(b) Borrower acknowledges that it is not relying on the Agent as regards any credit, legal or other due diligence in respect of any Principal and will make its own judgements with respect thereto.

9 Borrower: scope of Events of Default and Acts of Insolvency

If any Event of Default should occur to Borrower as set out in the Agreement, then each Loan entered into between Borrower and each Principal under this Agreement shall be dealt with in accordance with the provisions applicable to it under this Agreement.

10 Principals: scope of Events of Default and Acts of Insolvency

(a) If any Event of Default should occur to a Principal as set out in the Agreement then each Loan entered into between the Principal and Borrower under this Agreement shall be dealt with in accordance with the provisions applicable to it under this Agreement.

(b) For the avoidance of doubt, all Loans entered into between any other Principal and Borrower under this Agreement shall be treated as continuing in accordance with their respective terms and shall not be affected by the occurrence of an Event of Default in relation to a Principal as provided for in paragraph (a) above.

UK TAX ADDENDUM

In 2000 ISLA issued a UK Tax Addendum for use with the GMSLA 2000 where one of the parties is resident for UK tax purposes and overseas securities would be traded. The main focus of the Addendum was to ensure that no withholding tax was payable on income and manufactured dividends on such securities.

Changes in tax legislation since 2000 rendered many references in the addendum out of date. Some market players have issued updates but ISLA has taken the UK Tax Addendum off its website. It has composed a new UK Tax Addendum for use with the GMSLA 2010.

THE CLIFFORD CHANCE LEGAL OPINION ON THE GMSLA 2000

The Clifford Chance legal opinion on the GMSLA 2000 was published on 30th August 2000 and covers the following principal matters:

- It is given in respect of bodies corporate other than insurance companies and building societies.
- It covers the laws of England and Wales only.
- It applies to parties acting as principals only.

- It gives no opinions on UK tax law.
- It does not opine on questions of fact such as a party's title to transfer securities or collateral.
- The governing law of the Agreement would be recognised in the English and Welsh courts even if neither party were domiciled in England or Wales.
- Recharacterisation of title transfer as a security interest is unlikely unless the genuine intention of the parties was different.
- Close-out netting provisions of paragraph 10 are considered effective.
- Automatic Early Termination is deemed unnecessary.
- Transactions do not have to form a single agreement but as they do this is effective.
- Transactions entered into post insolvency might not be included in the close-out calculations.
- Third party creditors will be unable to intervene.
- Netting does not need to be disclosed in the parties' records.
- Close-out netting under English law will not be jeopardised by parties transacting through Designated Offices in jurisdictions unsympathetic to close-out netting.
- If global netting of Transactions applies this cannot be invalidated by a Defaulting Party's Insolvency Representative irrespective of the Designated Office through which the loans were entered.
- The opinion includes two Schedules of Assumptions and Reservations that need to be studied carefully.

It should be borne in mind that many parties are currently (December 2010) continuing to use the GMSLA 2000 although ISLA is hoping that the market will adopt the GMSLA 2010 in the foreseeable future.

4

The Global Master Securities Lending Agreement (2010)

ISLA's Securities Lending Set Off Protocol (March 2009)

Introduction to the Global Master Securities Lending Agreement (2010) and main differences from the GMSLA 2000

Paragraph by paragraph analysis of the Global Master Securities Lending Agreement 2010 and its Schedule

Agency Annex

Addendum for Pooled Principal Agency Loans

UK Tax Addendum

ISLA'S SECURITIES LENDING SET OFF PROTOCOL (MARCH 2009)

Before the GMSLA 2009 was published on 24th July 2009, ISLA published the 2009 Securities Lending Set Off Protocol in March 2009 which let parties incorporate the close-out netting provisions of paragraph 10 of the GMRA 2000 into their securities lending master agreement before the GMSLA 2009 was published. To me this was an admission that the GMSLA 2000 close-out netting procedure is flawed (see my comments on pages 121 and 125).

The amendments for the GMSLA 2000, which also included an ISDA style set-off clause, were in the Protocol's Annex 5.

The Protocol is an evergreen document meaning that it has no end date for adherence. It was likely to have been of most interest to those who did not want to disturb their current master agreement documentation by entering into a new GMSLA 2009 wholesale, although that may have been the better course. ISLA was disappointed with the response to this Protocol as only eight market players have signed up to it. No others are likely to, in my view, now that the GMSLA 2010 has been published.

INTRODUCTION TO THE GLOBAL MASTER SECURITIES LENDING AGREEMENT (2010) AND MAIN DIFFERENCES FROM THE GMSLA 2000

As mentioned before, on 24th July 2009 ISLA published a new Global Master Securities Lending Agreement – the GMSLA 2009. Incidentally the GMSLA 2009 reflected lessons learned from the financial crises of 2007–2008. Unfortunately, there were market objections to the terms of the GMSLA 2009's paragraphs 5.4 and 5.5 concerning the pre-collateralisation of manufactured dividends on the Income Record Date (i.e. before Income was actually paid) and paragraph 6.2 concerning an aspect of manufactured dividends.

This meant that on 20th January 2010 ISLA published the GMSLA 2010 to replace the GMSLA 2009. Guidance notes to the GMSLA 2010 were published by ISLA on 26th April 2010 and are worth reading. An English law netting opinion prepared by Freshfields is available to subscribers through the Bank of England's Stock Lending and Repo Committee.

The main reason for producing the GMSLA 2010 was to update the default valuation provisions from the experience of the banking crisis where those in the GMSLA 2000 were less flexible than desired.

The main differences from the GMSLA 2000 are as follows:

- Failure to deliver Equivalent Securities or Equivalent Collateral is no longer an Event of Default. Nor is a Lender failing to deliver Securities in the first place.
- Close-out netting procedures following an Event of Default broadly harmonised with those under the GMRA 2000.
- Revisions to manufactured dividend provisions.
- Indemnity for failure to redeliver Equivalent Non-Cash Collateral which is activated by a Schedule choice.
- Loan fees payable up to the 10th Business Day of the following month rather than seven calendar days after it.
- Three Business Day grace period in the failure to make a manufactured dividend Event of Default.
- Set-off clause included in the main text.
- New clauses on Stamp Tax, VAT and retrospective changes in tax law.
- New warranty by the Borrower that he is not entering into a Loan just to get voting rights.
- In the Schedule, Notification Time is quoted for transfers of collateral.
- A Schedule choice needs to be made if Automatic Early Termination is to apply.
- In the Schedule, the rate of default interest needs to be quoted.
- A new Agency Annex and Addendum for Multiple Principal Transactions.
- A new UK Tax Addendum.

PARAGRAPH BY PARAGRAPH ANALYSIS OF THE GLOBAL MASTER SECURITIES LENDING AGREEMENT 2010 AND ITS SCHEDULE

Let us review the 27 paragraphs of the GMSLA 2010.

AGREEMENT

BETWEEN:

> (*Party A*) a company incorporated under the laws of acting through one or more Designated Offices; and

> (*Party B*) a company incorporated under the laws of acting through one or more Designated Offices.

Preamble

First of all the parties state their full legal names; in which jurisdiction they are incorporated; and that they are acting through one or more Designated Offices. The locations of these are stated in paragraph 3 of the GMSLA Schedule. In the GMSLA 2000 only one Designated Office was stated but the GMSLA 2010 allows more to be included as is the practice with the GMRA 2000.

1. **APPLICABILITY**

1.1　From time to time the Parties acting through one or more Designated Offices may enter into transactions in which one party (*Lender*) will transfer to the other (*Borrower*) securities and financial instruments (*Securities*) against the transfer of Collateral (as defined in paragraph 2) with a simultaneous agreement by Borrower to transfer to Lender Securities equivalent to such Securities on a fixed date or on demand against the transfer to Borrower by Lender of assets equivalent to such Collateral.

1.2　Each such transaction shall be referred to in this Agreement as a *Loan* and shall be governed by the terms of this Agreement, including the supplemental terms and conditions contained in the Schedule and any Addenda or Annexes attached hereto, unless otherwise agreed in writing. In the event of any inconsistency between the provisions of an Addendum or Annex and this Agreement, the provisions of such Addendum or Annex shall prevail unless the Parties otherwise agree.

1.3　Either Party may perform its obligations under this Agreement either directly or through a Nominee.

1. APPLICABILITY

1.1

The GMSLA 2010 is a master agreement governing the parties' securities lending transactions for UK and overseas bonds and equities. Contracting parties are Lenders or Borrowers under the GMSLA 2010 depending upon the terms of each transaction. A Lender lends Securities to a Borrower against the transfer of agreed Collateral. Securities loans may be on demand or for a fixed term. When a transaction ends, the Borrower must return Equivalent Securities to the Lender and the Lender must return Equivalent Collateral to the Borrower simultaneously.

1.2

Transactions are technically called "Loans" and shall be governed by the terms of the GMSLA 2010 and its Schedule and any annexes or addenda which may be attached to the GMSLA 2010, unless otherwise agreed in writing which is unlikely. Where there is a clash of terms between an Annex or Addendum and the GMSLA 2010, the provisions of the Annex or Addendum will prevail unless the parties agree otherwise.

1.3

Either party may perform its obligations under the GMSLA 2010 either directly or via a nominee.

2. INTERPRETATION

2.1 In this Agreement:

Act of Insolvency means in relation to either Party:

(a) its making a general assignment for the benefit of, or entering into a reorganisation, arrangement, or composition with creditors; or

(b) its stating in writing that it is unable to pay its debts as they become due; or

(c) its seeking, consenting to or acquiescing in the appointment of any trustee, administrator, receiver or liquidator or analogous officer of it or any material part of its property; or

(d) the presentation or filing of a petition in respect of it (other than by the other Party to this Agreement in respect of any obligation under this Agreement) in any court or before any agency alleging or for the bankruptcy, winding-up or insolvency of such Party (or any analogous proceeding) or seeking any reorganisation, arrangement, composition, re-adjustment, administration, liquidation, dissolution or similar relief under any present or future statute, law or regulation, such petition not having been stayed or dismissed within 30 days of its filing (except in the case of a petition for winding-up or any analogous proceeding in respect of which no such 30 day period shall apply); or

(e) the appointment of a receiver, administrator, liquidator or trustee or analogous officer of such Party over all or any material part of such Party's property; or

(f) the convening of any meeting of its creditors for the purpose of considering a voluntary arrangement as referred to in Section 3 of the Insolvency Act 1986 (or any analogous proceeding);

2. INTERPRETATION

Act of Insolvency

Act of Insolvency is an important definition.

The events described in it are as follows:

- a composition with creditors;
- a written admission of inability to pay debts when due;
- steps to appoint an insolvency official;
- presentation of a bankruptcy petition by a third party which is not dismissed within 30 days. (Please note that in (iv) there is no 30-day grace period for dismissal of a third party winding up petition as there is in the 1992 ISDA Master Agreement.);
- actual appointment of an insolvency official;
- convening a creditors' meeting to propose a voluntary arrangement (a process allowed under the UK's 1986 Insolvency Act where a solvent party can make a composition of its debts or an arrangement of its financial affairs if its creditors agree).

As we shall see in paragraph 10 there is no grace period for Acts of Insolvency and most other Events of Default.

Agency Annex means the Annex to this Agreement published by the International Securities Lending Association and providing for Lender to act as agent for a third party in respect of one or more Loans;

Alternative Collateral means Collateral having a Market Value equal to the Collateral delivered pursuant to paragraph 5 and provided by way of substitution in accordance with the provisions of paragraph 5.3;

Applicable Law means the laws, rules and regulations (including double taxation conventions) of any relevant jurisdiction, including published practice of any government or other taxing authority in connection with such laws, rules and regulations;

Automatic Early Termination has the meaning given in paragraph 10.1(d);

Base Currency means the currency indicated in paragraph 2 of the Schedule;

Agency Annex

A new Annex published by ISLA providing for the Lender to act as agent for a third party in respect of one or more Loans. Only disclosed underlying principals are allowed.

Automatic Early Termination

Introduced into the GMSLA Schedule for the first time. It is triggered where a winding up petition is presented or an insolvency official is appointed. Selected to apply in paragraph 5 of the Schedule. No Default Notice is needed.

Base Currency

This is the currency into which risk exposure and collateral values are converted and is stated in paragraph 2 of the Schedule. As in the GMRA 2000, Base Currency is used for both margining and close-out purposes in the GMSLA 2010.

Business Day means:

(a) in relation to Delivery in respect of any Loan, a day other than a Saturday or a Sunday on which banks and securities markets are open for business generally in the place(s) where the relevant Securities, Equivalent Securities, Collateral or Equivalent Collateral are to be delivered;

(b) in relation to any payments under this Agreement, a day other than a Saturday or a Sunday on which banks are open for business generally in the principal financial centre of the country of which the currency in which the payment is denominated is the official currency and, if different, in the place where any account designated by the Parties for the making or receipt of the payment is situated (or, in the case of a payment in euro, a day on which TARGET operates);

(c) in relation to a notice or other communication served under this Agreement, any day other than a Saturday or a Sunday on which banks are open for business generally in the place designated for delivery in accordance with paragraph 3 of the Schedule; and

(d) in any other case, a day other than a Saturday or a Sunday on which banks are open for business generally in each place stated in paragraph 6 of the Schedule;

Buy-In means any arrangement under which, in the event of a seller or transferor failing to deliver securities to the buyer or transferee, the buyer or transferee of such securities is entitled under the terms of such arrangement to buy or otherwise acquire securities equivalent to such securities and to recover the cost of so doing from the seller or transferor;

Cash Collateral means Collateral taking the form of a transfer of currency;

Business Day

The term "Business Day" has four meanings in the GMSLA 2010 viz:

(a) For Loan deliveries it means a day (apart from Saturday or Sunday) when banks and securities markets are open for business in the place(s) where Securities or securities collateral have to be delivered.

(b) For payments under the GMSLA 2010 it means a day (apart from Saturday or Sunday) when banks are open for business in the main financial centre for the currency concerned or where the parties hold their main accounts for payments and receipts of that currency. For the Euro this would be a day when the TARGET (now TARGET 2) system is open for business.

(c) In relation to notices under the GMSLA 2010 it means a day (apart from Saturday or Sunday) when banks are generally open for business in the places of business for deliveries named in paragraph 3 of the Schedule. And

(d) In all other cases it means a day (apart from Saturday or Sunday) when banks are open for business in the places stated in paragraph 6 of the Schedule.

Buy-In

This enables a buyer or transferee of undelivered securities to buy such securities in from the market and recover the cost from the party who originally failed to deliver them.

Cash Collateral

This is margin in an agreed currency.

Close of Business means the time at which the relevant banks, securities settlement systems or depositaries close in the business centre in which payment is to be made or Securities or Collateral is to be delivered;

Collateral means such securities or financial instruments or transfers of currency as are referred to in the table set out under paragraph 1 of the Schedule as being acceptable or any combination thereof as agreed between the Parties in relation to any particular Loan and which are delivered by Borrower to Lender in accordance with this Agreement and shall include Alternative Collateral;

Defaulting Party has the meaning given in paragraph 10;

Delivery in relation to any Securities or Collateral or Equivalent Securities or Equivalent Collateral comprising Securities means:

(a)   in the case of Securities held by a Nominee or within a clearing or settlement system, the crediting of such Securities to an account of the Borrower or Lender, as the case may be, or as it shall direct, or,

(b)   in the case of Securities otherwise held, the delivery to Borrower or Lender, as the case may be, or as the transferee shall direct of the relevant instruments of transfer, or

(c)   by such other means as may be agreed,

and *deliver* shall be construed accordingly;

Designated Office means the branch or office of a Party which is specified as such in paragraph 6 of the Schedule or such other branch or office as may be agreed to in writing by the Parties;

Close of Business

The closing time for banks, securities settlement systems or depositories in the place where payments or deliveries of Securities and Collateral are made.

Collateral

Collateral acceptable to both parties as stated in paragraph 1.2 of the Schedule.

Defaulting Party

One of the two parties to the GMSLA 2010 who has committed one or more of the Events of Default described in paragraph 10.

Delivery

The term "Delivery" means for Securities or securities collateral:

(a) if held by a Nominee or in a clearing system, the crediting of them to the party entitled to receive them or as such party shall direct; or

(b) if held otherwise, by the delivery of them to the party entitled to receive them or as such party directs in any transfer documentation; or

(c) as the parties otherwise agree.

Designated Office

The branch or office through which a contracting party transacts which is normally stated in paragraph 6 of the Schedule.

Equivalent or ***equivalent to*** in relation to any Loaned Securities or Collateral (whether Cash Collateral or Non-Cash Collateral) provided under this Agreement means Securities or other property, of an identical type, nominal value, description and amount to particular Loaned Securities or Collateral (as the case may be) so provided. If and to the extent that such Loaned Securities or Collateral (as the case may be) consists of Securities that are partly paid or have been converted, subdivided, consolidated, made the subject of a takeover, rights of pre-emption, rights to receive securities or a certificate which may at a future date be exchanged for Securities, the expression shall include such Securities or other assets to which Lender or Borrower (as the case may be) is entitled following the occurrence of the relevant event, and, if appropriate, the giving of the relevant notice in accordance with paragraph 6.7 and provided that Lender or Borrower (as the case may be) has paid to the other Party all and any sums due in respect thereof. In the event that such Loaned Securities or Collateral (as the case may be) have been redeemed, are partly paid, are the subject of a capitalisation issue or are subject to an event similar to any of the foregoing events described in this paragraph, the expression shall have the following meanings:

(a) in the case of redemption, a sum of money equivalent to the proceeds of the redemption;

(b) in the case of a call on partly-paid Securities, Securities equivalent to the relevant Loaned Securities or Collateral, as the case may be, provided that Lender shall have paid Borrower, in respect of Loaned Securities, and Borrower shall have paid to Lender, in respect of Collateral, an amount of money equal to the sum due in respect of the call;

(c) in the case of a capitalisation issue, Securities equivalent to the relevant Loaned Securities or Collateral, as the case may be, together with the securities allotted by way of bonus thereon;

(d) in the case of any event similar to any of the foregoing events described in this paragraph, Securities equivalent to the Loaned Securities or the relevant Collateral, as the case may be, together with or replaced by a sum of money or Securities or other property equivalent to that received in respect of such Loaned Securities or Collateral, as the case may be, resulting from such event;

Equivalent

The terms "Equivalent" or "equivalent to" have a number of meanings in this definition. Firstly they relate to Equivalent Securities and Equivalent Collateral to be returned at the end of a Loan. Here "equivalent" means of the identical type, nominal value, description and amount as the Securities and Collateral originally transferred between the parties. It does not mean the identically numbered securities originally transferred between them.

Where a corporate action has occurred, "Equivalent" or "equivalent to" have the following additional meanings:

(e) where the securities are redeemed, the amount of money received;

(f) where a call takes place on partly paid securities and is paid, the Securities or Collateral due to be returned thereafter;

(g) where bonus securities are issued, those bonus securities and the Securities and Collateral due to be returned; and

(h) in all other cases, replacement securities or redemption moneys for Securities and Collateral due to be returned.

Income means any interest, dividends or other distributions of any kind whatsoever with respect to any Securities or Collateral;

Income Record Date, with respect to any Securities or Collateral, means the date by reference to which holders of such Securities or Collateral are identified as being entitled to payment of Income;

Letter of Credit means an irrevocable, non-negotiable letter of credit in a form, and from a bank, acceptable to Lender;

Loaned Securities means Securities which are the subject of an outstanding Loan;

Margin has the meaning specified in paragraph 1 of the Schedule with reference to the table set out therein;

Income

Essentially interest or dividends paid by an issuer of Securities or securities collateral to their holders.

Income Record Date

This is the date as at which holders of securities or securities collateral are identified as entitled to receive payment of income on them. The income is actually paid on an announced future date.

Letter of Credit

A letter of credit is a non-transferable, irrevocable letter from a bank guaranteeing the obligations of Borrower to Lender up to an agreed limit and expiry date.

Loaned Securities

The outstanding securities loans themselves.

Margin

The overcollateralisation or surplus required on Collateral for securities loans which is shown in the table in paragraph 1.2 of the Schedule.

Market Value means:

(a) in relation to the valuation of Securities, Equivalent Securities, Collateral or Equivalent Collateral (other than Cash Collateral or a Letter of Credit):

(i) such price as is equal to the market quotation for the mid price of such Securities, Equivalent Securities, Collateral and/or Equivalent Collateral as derived from a reputable pricing information service reasonably chosen in good faith by Lender; or

(ii) if unavailable the market value thereof as derived from the mid price or rate bid by a reputable dealer for the relevant instrument reasonably chosen in good faith by Lender,

in each case at Close of Business on the previous Business Day, or as specified in the Schedule, unless agreed otherwise or, at the option of either Party where in its reasonable opinion there has been an exceptional movement in the price of the asset in question since such time, the latest available price, plus (in each case):

(iii) the aggregate amount of Income which has accrued but not yet been paid in respect of the Securities, Equivalent Securities, Collateral or Equivalent Collateral concerned to the extent not included in such price,

provided that the price of Securities, Equivalent Securities, Collateral or Equivalent Collateral that are suspended or that cannot legally be transferred or that are transferred or required to be transferred to a government, trustee or third party (whether by reason of nationalisation, expropriation or otherwise) shall for all purposes be a commercially reasonable price agreed between the Parties, or absent agreement, be a price provided by a third party dealer agreed between the Parties, or if the Parties do not agree a third party dealer then a price based on quotations provided by the Reference Dealers. If more than three quotations are provided, the Market Value will be the arithmetic mean of the prices, without regard to the quotations having the highest and lowest prices. If three quotations are provided, the Market Value will be the quotation remaining after disregarding the highest and lowest quotations. For this purpose, if more than one quotation has the same highest or lowest price, then one of such quotations shall be disregarded. If fewer than three quotations are provided, the Market Value of the relevant Securities, Equivalent Securities, Collateral or Equivalent Collateral shall be determined by the Party making the determination of Market Value acting reasonably;

(b) in relation to a Letter of Credit the face or stated amount of such Letter of Credit; and

(c) in relation to Cash Collateral the amount of the currency concerned;

Nominee means a nominee or agent appointed by either Party to accept delivery of, hold or deliver Securities, Equivalent Securities, Collateral and/or Equivalent Collateral or to receive or make payments on its behalf;

Market Value

One of the key definitions is "Market Value" which is important for calculating the value of collateral to be provided and the marking to market requirements for collateral during the loan's life. "Market Value" under the GMSLA 2010 is to be calculated by the Lender on a mid-price basis by referring to a reputable pricing service chosen reasonably by him in good faith. It was the bid price under the GMSLA 2000 and this change caused some controversy among ISLA members who might seek to amend it in the Schedule. We shall see. Any accrued income is added to the valuation if it is not already included in the price. Normally, the previous day's closing prices will be used but either party may choose the latest available price where it considers an exceptional price movement has occurred since the closing price on the previous Business Day.

With suspended securities and those which cannot legally be transferred or can only be transferred (due to nationalisation or expropriation) to a government or trustee or third party, the parties will need to try to agree a commercially reasonable price. If they fail they will need to agree on appointing a third party dealer to establish the price. If they cannot agree on a third party dealer, then price quotations will need to be obtained from Reference Dealers, i.e. four leading dealers in the relevant securities selected by the party determining Market Value in good faith. If more than three quotations are received, the Market Value will be their arithmetic mean. If exactly three quotations are provided, the Market Value will be the quotation left after the highest and lowest have been discarded. If fewer than three quotations are obtained, the party entitled to determine the Market Value shall act reasonably in deciding it. This is new to the GMSLA 2010 and was not in the GMSLA 2000.

A Letter of Credit is valued at the amount stated in it and Cash Collateral is valued at its face value.

Of course, different valuation provisions apply for the purposes of applying close-out netting in paragraph 11 after an Event of Default.

Nominee

The term "Nominee" means an agent or a nominee appointed by either Party to accept delivery of, hold or deliver Securities, Equivalent Securities, Collateral and/or Equivalent Collateral or to receive or make payments on its behalf. Such a nominee would typically be a third party custodian.

Non-Cash Collateral means Collateral other than Cash Collateral;

Non-Defaulting Party has the meaning given in paragraph 10;

Notification Time means the time specified in paragraph 1.5 of the Schedule;

Parties means Lender and Borrower and ***Party*** shall be construed accordingly;

Posted Collateral has the meaning given in paragraph 5.4;

Reference Dealers means, in relation to any Securities, Equivalent Securities, Collateral or Equivalent Collateral, four leading dealers in the relevant securities selected by the Party making the determination of Market Value in good faith;

Required Collateral Value has the meaning given in paragraph 5.4;

Sales Tax means value added tax and any other Tax of a similar nature (including, without limitation, any sales tax of any relevant jurisdiction);

Settlement Date means the date upon which Securities are due to be transferred to Borrower in accordance with this Agreement;

Non-Cash Collateral

All other types of agreed collateral except for cash.

Non-Defaulting Party

The party not at fault in an Event of Default in paragraph 10.

Notification Time

The deadline for making a collateral call stated in paragraph 1.5 of the Schedule.

Parties

Lender and Borrower. The word "Party" refers to either of them.

Posted Collateral

Collateral delivered to cover risk exposure on outstanding securities loans.

Reference Dealers

Four leading dealers in the relevant Securities or securities collateral chosen by the party calculating Market Value in good faith.

Required Collateral Value

The basic value of the collateral plus the overcollateralisation represented by the Margin. It therefore overcollateralises the risk exposure by the margin percentage.

Sales Tax

Value Added Tax or its equivalent.

Settlement Date

The date Securities are transferred to Borrower at the start of a Loan.

Stamp Tax means any stamp, transfer, registration, documentation or similar Tax; and

Tax means any present or future tax, levy, impost, duty, charge, assessment or fee of any nature (including interest, penalties and additions thereto) imposed by any government or other taxing authority in respect of any transaction effected pursuant to or contemplated by, or any payment under or in respect of, this Agreement.

Stamp Tax

A stamp duty charged by a tax authority on Securities transfers and/or transfer documentation.

Tax

Any present or future tax charge imposed by a government or tax authority on transactions or payments under the GMSLA 2010.

2.2 **Headings**

All headings appear for convenience only and shall not affect the interpretation of this Agreement.

2.3 **Market terminology**

Notwithstanding the use of expressions such as "borrow", "lend", "Collateral", "Margin" etc. which are used to reflect terminology used in the market for transactions of the kind provided for in this Agreement, title to Securities "borrowed" or "lent" and "Collateral" provided in accordance with this Agreement shall pass from one Party to another as provided for in this Agreement, the Party obtaining such title being obliged to deliver Equivalent Securities or Equivalent Collateral as the case may be.

2.4 **Currency conversions**

Subject to paragraph 11, for the purposes of determining any prices, sums or values (including Market Value and Required Collateral Value) prices, sums or values stated in currencies other than the Base Currency shall be converted into the Base Currency at the latest available spot rate of exchange quoted by a bank selected by Lender (or if an Event of Default has occurred in relation to Lender, by Borrower) in the London inter-bank market for the purchase of the Base Currency with the currency concerned on the day on which the calculation is to be made or, if that day is not a Business Day, the spot rate of exchange quoted at Close of Business on the immediately preceding Business Day on which such a quotation was available.

2.5 The Parties confirm that introduction of and/or substitution (in place of an existing currency) of a new currency as the lawful currency of a country shall not have the effect of altering, or discharging, or excusing performance under, any term of the Agreement or any Loan thereunder, nor give a Party the right unilaterally to alter or terminate the Agreement or any Loan thereunder. Securities will for the purposes of this Agreement be regarded as equivalent to other securities notwithstanding that as a result of such introduction and/or substitution those securities have been redenominated into the new currency or the nominal value of the securities has changed in connection with such redenomination.

2.6 **Modifications etc. to legislation**

Any reference in this Agreement to an act, regulation or other legislation shall include a reference to any statutory modification or re-enactment thereof for the time being in force.

2.2

Headings are for convenience only and will not affect the interpretation of the GMSLA 2010's terms.

2.3

Legal title to Securities borrowed and Collateral received passes to the Borrower and Lender respectively despite use of the terms "borrow", "lend", "Collateral", "Margin" and the like which could give the impression that the transaction is a secured loan. The obligations of the Borrower and Lender are to return Equivalent Securities or Equivalent Collateral when called upon to do so or at the end of the Loan.

2.4

For margining and close-out purposes the values of Securities and Collateral of all types shall be converted into the Base Currency agreed in the Schedule. Where such values are stated in another currency, that currency will be converted into the Base Currency by the Lender obtaining a spot FX rate from a reputable bank in the London interbank market on the day the calculation is to be made. If that is not a Business Day, the spot rate of exchange between the two currencies at the close of business on the Business Day immediately before is used. Where the Lender has committed an Event of Default, the Borrower as the Non-Defaulting Party obtains the FX rate concerned.

2.5

This paragraph deals with the introduction of a new currency as the lawful currency of a country for the parties' payment and delivery obligations under the Agreement. The result is that no obligations under the GMSLA 2010 or a Loan are avoided because of this and that Securities in an old currency transferred under a Loan shall be considered to be redenominated in an equivalent amount of the new currency.

2.6

Any reference to an act, regulation or other legislation shall also refer to any revisions of these in force at present or in the future.

3. **LOANS OF SECURITIES**

Lender will lend Securities to Borrower, and Borrower will borrow Securities from Lender in accordance with the terms and conditions of this Agreement. The terms of each Loan shall be agreed prior to the commencement of the relevant Loan either orally or in writing (including any agreed form of electronic communication) and confirmed in such form and on such basis as shall be agreed between the Parties. Unless otherwise agreed, any confirmation produced by a Party shall not supersede or prevail over the prior oral, written or electronic communication (as the case may be).

3. LOANS OF SECURITIES

This paragraph sets out how the Lender will lend securities to the Borrower in line with the terms of the GMSLA 2010. The terms of each Loan are agreed in advance by telephone, in writing or electronically and confirmed as agreed between the parties.

Interestingly, the paragraph states any confirmation produced by a party will not supersede any previous communication between the parties agreeing the terms of the securities loan, unless they agree this. In other master agreements, the confirmation's terms normally prevail.

In the securities lending market it is not normal practice for paper confirmations to be issued as terms are usually matched electronically through a contract and compare approach.

4. DELIVERY

4.1 Delivery of Securities on commencement of Loan

Lender shall procure the Delivery of Securities to Borrower or deliver such Securities in accordance with this Agreement and the terms of the relevant Loan.

4.2 Requirements to effect Delivery

The Parties shall execute and deliver all necessary documents and give all necessary instructions to procure that all right, title and interest in:

(a) any Securities borrowed pursuant to paragraph 3;

(b) any Equivalent Securities delivered pursuant to paragraph 8;

(c) any Collateral delivered pursuant to paragraph 5;

(d) any Equivalent Collateral delivered pursuant to paragraphs 5 or 8;

shall pass from one Party to the other subject to the terms and conditions set out in this Agreement, on delivery of the same in accordance with this Agreement with full title guarantee, free from all liens, charges and encumbrances. In the case of Securities, Collateral, Equivalent Securities or Equivalent Collateral title to which is registered in a computer-based system which provides for the recording and transfer of title to the same by way of book entries, delivery and transfer of title shall take place in accordance with the rules and procedures of such system as in force from time to time. The Party acquiring such right, title and interest shall have no obligation to return or deliver any of the assets so acquired but, in so far as any Securities are borrowed by or any Collateral is delivered to such Party, such Party shall be obliged, subject to the terms of this Agreement, to deliver Equivalent Securities or Equivalent Collateral as appropriate.

4.3 Deliveries to be simultaneous unless otherwise agreed

Where under the terms of this Agreement a Party is not obliged to make a Delivery unless simultaneously a Delivery is made to it, subject to and without prejudice to its rights under paragraph 8.6, such Party may from time to time in accordance with market practice and in recognition of the practical difficulties in arranging simultaneous delivery of Securities, Collateral and cash transfers, waive its right under this Agreement in respect of simultaneous delivery and/or payment provided that no such waiver (whether by course of conduct or otherwise) in respect of one transaction shall bind it in respect of any other transaction.

4. DELIVERY

4.1

The Lender shall deliver Securities or arrange for their delivery to the Borrower in accordance with the relevant Loan and GMSLA 2010 terms. Delivery is a defined term here and takes place when the Securities and any necessary transfer documentation are received by the Borrower or its agent. If the Borrower wants the Lender to deliver to a custodian or to a clearing or settlement system like Euroclear or Clearstream, delivery takes place when the Securities arrive in the Borrower's account or that of its agent with that custodian or in such a clearing system. The definition of Delivery in paragraph 2 covers these alternatives.

4.2

The various species of Securities or Collateral which can be borrowed or delivered under the GMSLA 2010 will be delivered free of all liens, charges or encumbrances together with all necessary transfer documentation or instructions. Under any transaction, legal title to the loaned securities is transferred outright to the Borrower and legal title to the collateral is transferred outright to the Lender.

Where legal title to any Securities or Collateral is registered in a book entry electronic transfer system, delivery and title transfer will take place in accordance with the current rules of that system.

At the end of the transaction, the original loaned securities and collateral are not returned, but Equivalent Securities and Equivalent Collateral are transferred between the parties with outright title transfer.

4.3

A party is not obliged to make a delivery of securities or collateral unless a simultaneous delivery is made to it by its counterparty and it is confident that this will take place. Otherwise it may exercise the rights available to it under paragraph 8.6 (i.e. withholding its own delivery). However, market practice or practical difficulties with simultaneous delivery of Securities, Collateral or cash transfers may persuade a party to waive this on a case by case basis without setting any general precedent for the future.

4.4 **Deliveries of Income**

In respect of Income being paid in relation to any Loaned Securities or Collateral, Borrower (in the case of Income being paid in respect of Loaned Securities) and Lender (in the case of Income being paid in respect of Collateral) shall provide to the other Party, as the case may be, any endorsements or assignments as shall be customary and appropriate to effect, in accordance with paragraph 6, the payment or delivery of money or property in respect of such Income to Lender, irrespective of whether Borrower received such endorsements or assignments in respect of any Loaned Securities, or to Borrower, irrespective of whether Lender received such endorsements or assignments in respect of any Collateral.

4.4

Paragraph 4.4 sets out the mechanism for the delivery of income payments. With securities and securities collateral, the Borrower and Lender will respectively be shown as their owner in the books of the issuer of the securities concerned. As a Loan is only a temporary transfer of securities, the market considers it fair that the Lender (in the case of Securities) and the Borrower (in the case of securities collateral) should receive any Income on these securities distributed by their issuers. This will be in the form of equivalent payments (manufactured dividends) made by each party to the other after receiving Income from the securities issuer. Each of them is still obliged to pay this over during the life of the Loan even if they have disposed of the Securities or the securities collateral concerned to a third party and irrespective as to whether they received any endorsements or assignments referred to in the clause.

5. COLLATERAL

5.1 Delivery of Collateral on commencement of Loan

Subject to the other provisions of this paragraph 5, Borrower undertakes to deliver to or deposit with Lender (or in accordance with Lender's instructions) Collateral simultaneously with Delivery of the Securities to which the Loan relates and in any event no later than Close of Business on the Settlement Date.

5.2 Deliveries through securities settlement systems generating automatic payments

Unless otherwise agreed between the Parties, where any Securities, Equivalent Securities, Collateral or Equivalent Collateral (in the form of securities) are transferred through a book entry transfer or settlement system which automatically generates a payment or delivery, or obligation to pay or deliver, against the transfer of such securities, then:

(a) such automatically generated payment, delivery or obligation shall be treated as a payment or delivery by the transferee to the transferor, and except to the extent that it is applied to discharge an obligation of the transferee to effect payment or delivery, such payment or delivery, or obligation to pay or deliver, shall be deemed to be a transfer of Collateral or delivery of Equivalent Collateral, as the case may be, made by the transferee until such time as the Collateral or Equivalent Collateral is substituted with other Collateral or Equivalent Collateral if an obligation to deliver other Collateral or deliver Equivalent Collateral existed immediately prior to the transfer of Securities, Equivalent Securities, Collateral or Equivalent Collateral; and

(b) the Party receiving such substituted Collateral or Equivalent Collateral, or if no obligation to deliver other Collateral or redeliver Equivalent Collateral existed immediately prior to the transfer of Securities, Equivalent Securities, Collateral or Equivalent Collateral, the Party receiving the deemed transfer of Collateral or Delivery of Equivalent Collateral, as the case may be, shall cause to be made to the other Party for value the same day either, where such transfer is a payment, an irrevocable payment in the amount of such transfer or, where such transfer is a Delivery, an irrevocable Delivery of securities (or other property, as the case may be) equivalent to such property.

5. COLLATERAL

5.1

This sub-paragraph contains the obligation of the Borrower to provide Collateral to the Lender at the same time as the Lender delivers the loaned securities to it or by the end of the same Business Day if simultaneous delivery is impracticable.

In the case of securities collateral, delivery is considered to take place at the time the Lender or its agent receives it together with any necessary transfer documentation, or if the securities collateral is to be held within a clearing or settlement system, at the time the securities collateral is credited to the Lender's account in that system. This is in line with the definition of Delivery in paragraph 2 of the Agreement.

Where the parties agree that the Lender is to be pre-collateralised, the following provision could be inserted in the Schedule:

> "Unless otherwise agreed in respect of any particular Loan, notwithstanding anything to the contrary in this Agreement (i) any obligation of Lender to deliver Securities in respect of any Loan to Borrower is conditional upon Lender having received the Collateral agreed to be provided in respect of such Loan and (ii) any obligation of Lender to repay or redeliver (as the case may be) Equivalent Collateral upon the termination of a Loan is conditional upon Lender verifying receipt of Equivalent Securities or upon the substitution of Alternative Collateral is conditional upon Lender verifying receipt of Equivalent Securities or Alternative Collateral, as the case may be."

5.2

This paragraph covers the situation where a clearing or settlement system (such as the old UK Central Gilts Office) cannot cope with accepting securities or securities collateral on a free of payment or free of delivery basis. This means that as soon as such securities are delivered a payment equal to their value is sent to the one delivering them (the transferor).

(a) If this happens such automated payment or delivery may be used to meet an obligation which its recipient (the transferee) may have to the transferor. Otherwise such payment will be considered to be Collateral or Equivalent Collateral, as the case may be, until it is substituted by other collateral if an obligation to deliver such collateral arose immediately before the transfer.

(b) Where no such obligation exists at the time, the recipient of the automated payment or delivery must return an equivalent payment or delivery to its counterparty on the same Business Day outside the settlement system concerned or the same thing will happen again.

5.3 **Substitutions of Collateral**

Borrower may from time to time call for the repayment of Cash Collateral or the Delivery of Collateral equivalent to any Collateral delivered to Lender prior to the date on which the same would otherwise have been repayable or deliverable provided that at or prior to the time of such repayment or Delivery Borrower shall have delivered Alternative Collateral acceptable to Lender and Borrower is in compliance with paragraph 5.4 or paragraph 5.5, as applicable.

5.3

The Borrower may at any time call for repayment of Cash Collateral or the substitution of securities collateral and **does not need the Lender's consent to do so**. However, it must provide substitute Collateral which is acceptable to the Lender and fully covers the Lender's risk exposure on the Borrower.

5.4 **Marking to Market of Collateral during the currency of a Loan on aggregated basis**

Unless paragraph 1.3 of the Schedule indicates that paragraph 5.5 shall apply in lieu of this paragraph 5.4, or unless otherwise agreed between the Parties:

(a) the aggregate Market Value of the Collateral delivered to or deposited with Lender (excluding any Equivalent Collateral repaid or delivered under paragraphs 5.4(b) or 5.5(b) (as the case may be)) (*Posted Collateral*) in respect of all Loans outstanding under this Agreement shall equal the aggregate of the Market Value of Securities equivalent to the Loaned Securities and the applicable Margin (the *Required Collateral Value*) in respect of such Loans;

(b) if at any time on any Business Day the aggregate Market Value of the Posted Collateral in respect of all Loans outstanding under this Agreement together with: (i) all amounts due and payable by the Lender under this Agreement but which are unpaid; and (ii) if agreed between the parties and if the Income Record Date has occurred in respect of any Non-Cash Collateral, the amount or Market Value of Income payable in respect of such Non-Cash Collateral exceeds the aggregate of the Required Collateral Values in respect of such Loans together with: (i) all amounts due and payable by the Borrower under this Agreement but which are unpaid; and (ii) if agreed between the parties and if the Income Record Date has occurred in respect of any securities equivalent to Loaned Securities, the amount or Market Value of Income payable in respect of such Equivalent Securities, Lender shall (on demand) repay and/or deliver, as the case may be, to Borrower such Equivalent Collateral as will eliminate the excess;

(c) if at any time on any Business Day the aggregate Market Value of the Posted Collateral in respect of all Loans outstanding under this Agreement together with: (i) all amounts due and payable by the Lender under this Agreement but which are unpaid; and (ii) if agreed between the parties and if the Income Record Date has occurred in respect of any Non-Cash Collateral, the amount or Market Value of Income payable in respect of such Non-Cash Collateral falls below the aggregate of Required Collateral Values in respect of all such Loans together with: (i) all amounts due and payable by the Borrower under this Agreement but which are unpaid; and (ii) if agreed between the parties and if the Income Record Date has occurred in respect of Securities equivalent to any Loaned Securities, the amount or Market Value of Income payable in respect of such Equivalent Securities, Borrower shall (on demand) provide such further Collateral to Lender as will eliminate the deficiency;

(d) where a Party acts as both Lender and Borrower under this Agreement, the provisions of paragraphs 5.4(b) and 5.4(c) shall apply separately (and without duplication) in respect of Loans entered into by that Party as Lender and Loans entered into by that Party as Borrower.

5.4

The GMSLA 2010, like the GMSLA 2000, offers a choice of global margining being across all Loans (as here in paragraph 5.4) or on an individual Loan basis (as in paragraph 5.5). The choice is made in paragraph 1.3 of the Schedule.

(a) In paragraph 5.4 the Market Value of the collateral to cover all Loans must be equal to the Market Value of all loaned securities together with the Margin agreed in paragraph 1.2 of the Schedule for each type of collateral acceptable to both parties. Collateral provided is called Posted Collateral. The total of the Market Value of the loaned securities and the Margin is called the Required Collateral Value.

(b) If the Market Value of the Posted Collateral is higher than the Required Collateral Value for the aggregate loaned securities, the Borrower may call on the Lender to return the surplus. The Market Value will take into account, following an Income Record Date, any unpaid manufactured dividends on securities or other unpaid sums payable by the Lender or Borrower under the Agreement. This extension of the Market Value definition is new to the GMSLA 2010. However, pre-collateralisation of manufactured dividends from the Income Record Date now only applies if the parties agree.

Some major banks approached ISLA on this because reference to the Income Record Date entailed manufactured dividends relating to coupons declared but not paid falling into the collateral calculation under the GMSLA 2009. This meant that manufactured dividends would be pre-collateralised and the party due to receive the coupon from the issuer would be exposed to the risk that the issuer failed to pay it on the income payment date. Previously he only needed to manufacture the payment if he received the coupon from the issuer in the first place. The agreement approach overcomes this problem.

(c) If the Market Value of the Posted Collateral falls below the Required Collateral Value for the aggregate loaned securities, the Lender may call on the Borrower to top up the collateral value. Once again Market Value takes into account, following an Income Record Date, any unpaid manufactured dividends on securities or other unpaid sums payable by the Lender or Borrower under the Agreement. However, again pre-collateralisation of manufactured dividends from the Income Record Date only applies if the parties agree to it.

(d) It is made clear that where a party acts as both Borrower and Lender under the Agreement, paragraphs 5.4(b) and (c) will apply separately in respect of Loans a party enters into as Lender and those it enters into as Borrower. It also extends by implication to Agent Lenders. This is a new provision in the GMSLA 2010.

5.5 **Marking to Market of Collateral during the currency of a Loan on a Loan by Loan basis**

If paragraph 1.3 of the Schedule indicates this paragraph 5.5 shall apply in lieu of paragraph 5.4, the Posted Collateral in respect of any Loan shall bear from day to day and at any time the same proportion to the Market Value of Securities equivalent to the Loaned Securities as the Posted Collateral bore at the commencement of such Loan. Accordingly:

(a) the Market Value of the Posted Collateral to be delivered or deposited while the Loan continues shall be equal to the Required Collateral Value;

(b) if at any time on any Business Day the Market Value of the Posted Collateral in respect of any Loan together with: (i) all amounts due and payable by the Lender in respect of that Loan but which are unpaid; and (ii) if agreed between the parties and if the Income Record Date has occurred in respect of any Non-Cash Collateral, the amount or Market Value of Income payable in respect of such Non-Cash Collateral exceeds the Required Collateral Value in respect of such Loan together with: (i) all amounts due and payable by the Borrower in respect of that Loan; and (ii) if agreed between the parties and if the Income Record Date has occurred in respect of Securities equivalent to any Loaned Securities, the amount or Market Value of Income payable in respect of such Equivalent Securities, Lender shall (on demand) repay and/or deliver, as the case may be, to Borrower such Equivalent Collateral as will eliminate the excess; and

(c) if at any time on any Business Day the Market Value of the Posted Collateral together with: (i) all amounts due any payable by the Lender in respect of that Loan; and (ii) if agreed between the parties and if the Income Record Date has occurred in respect of any Non-Cash Collateral, the amount or Market Value of Income payable in respect of such Non-Cash Collateral falls below the Required Collateral Value together with: (i) all amounts due and payable by the Borrower in respect of that Loan; and (ii) if agreed between the parties and if the Income Record Date has occurred in respect of Securities equivalent to any Loaned Securities, the amount or Market Value of Income payable in respect of such Equivalent Securities, Borrower shall (on demand) provide such further Collateral to Lender as will eliminate the deficiency.

5.5

This paragraph covers margining on a Loan by Loan basis and once again the choice is made in paragraph 1.3 of the Schedule. In my experience most professional market players choose to have global margining across all Loans (i.e. paragraph 5.4). A party might choose loan by loan margining if they lacked the systems to do global margining efficiently.

However, if Loan by Loan margining is chosen:

(a) The Market Value of the Posted Collateral must be at least equal to the Required Collateral Value for each Loan.

(b) Where the Posted Collateral is greater than the Required Collateral Value for an individual Loan, on any Business Day the Borrower can call on the Lender to repay the surplus. Once again the Market Value will take into account any unpaid manufactured dividends on securities or other unpaid sums payable by the Lender or Borrower under the Agreement. Pre-collateralisation of manufactured dividends from the Income Record Date now only applies if the parties agree.

(c) Where the Market Value of the Posted Collateral falls below the Required Collateral Value for an individual Loan on any Business Day, the Lender can call on the Borrower to transfer more collateral to eliminate the shortfall. Once again Market Value will take into account any unpaid manufactured dividends on securities or other unpaid sums payable by the Lender or Borrower under the Agreement. Again pre-collateralisation of manufactured dividends from the Income Record Date only applies if the parties agree to it.

5.6 Requirements to deliver excess Collateral

Where paragraph 5.4 applies, unless paragraph 1.4 of the Schedule indicates that this paragraph 5.6 does not apply, if a Party (the *first Party*) would, but for this paragraph 5.6, be required under paragraph 5.4 to provide further Collateral or deliver Equivalent Collateral in circumstances where the other Party (the *second Party*) would, but for this paragraph 5.6, also be required to or provide Collateral or deliver Equivalent Collateral under paragraph 5.4, then the Market Value of the Collateral or Equivalent Collateral deliverable by the first Party (*X*) shall be set off against the Market Value of the Collateral or Equivalent Collateral deliverable by the second Party (*Y*) and the only obligation of the Parties under paragraph 5.4 shall be, where X exceeds Y, an obligation of the first Party, or where Y exceeds X, an obligation of the second Party to repay and/or (as the case may be) deliver Equivalent Collateral or to deliver further Collateral having a Market Value equal to the difference between X and Y.

5.7

Where Equivalent Collateral is repaid or delivered (as the case may be) or further Collateral is provided by a Party under paragraph 5.6, the Parties shall agree to which Loan or Loans such repayment, delivery or further provision is to be attributed and failing agreement it shall be attributed, as determined by the Party making such repayment, delivery or further provision to the earliest outstanding Loan and, in the case of a repayment or delivery up to the point at which the Market Value of Collateral in respect of such Loan equals the Required Collateral Value in respect of such Loan, and then to the next earliest outstanding Loan up to the similar point and so on.

5.8 Timing of repayments of excess Collateral or deliveries of further Collateral

Where any Equivalent Collateral falls to be repaid or delivered (as the case may be) or further Collateral is to be provided under this paragraph 5, unless otherwise provided or agreed between the Parties, if the relevant demand is received by the Notification Time specified in paragraph 1.5 of the Schedule, then the delivery shall be made not later than the Close of Business on the same Business Day; if a demand is received after the Notification Time, then the relevant delivery shall be made not later than the Close of Business on the next Business Day after the date such demand is received.

5.9 Substitutions and extensions of Letters of Credit

Where Collateral is a Letter of Credit, Lender may by notice to Borrower require that Borrower, on the third Business Day following the date of delivery of such notice (or by such other time as the Parties may agree), substitute Collateral consisting of cash or other Collateral acceptable to Lender for the Letter of Credit. Prior to the expiration of any Letter of Credit supporting Borrower's obligations hereunder, Borrower shall, no later than 10.30 a.m. UK time on the second Business Day prior to the date such Letter of Credit expires (or by such other time as the Parties may agree), obtain an extension of the expiration of such Letter of Credit or replace such Letter of Credit by providing Lender with a substitute Letter of Credit in an amount at least equal to the amount of the Letter of Credit for which it is substituted.

5.6

Whether paragraph 5.6 applies depends upon the parties choosing to apply it in paragraph 1.4 of the Schedule. **This is a collateral netting clause**.

Where global margining applies (paragraph 5.4) and paragraph 5.6 is selected to apply, then parties can net the values of any amounts of Collateral each is obliged to deliver to the other for different Loans on any Business Day and the values of any amounts of Equivalent Collateral each is obliged to redeliver for different Loans on the same Business Day. All such transfers will be converted into the Base Currency chosen in paragraph 2 of the Schedule. Under this collateral netting arrangement only the difference in the two aggregate values of the collateral to be delivered and redelivered is transferred between the parties.

5.7

Where the parties agree to global margining across all Loans and a party needs to deliver top-up collateral or return Equivalent Collateral to the other party, this paragraph allows the allocation of such collateral to individual Loans. Where they do not agree, the fallback position is that at the maturity of each loan the recipient will apply the collateral to the earliest outstanding Loan and if there is still some left over after this has been done, to the next earliest outstanding Loan and so on. This is in line with the banking rule in *Clayton's Case* (Devaynes vs Noble) (1816) (1 Mer 572) where a credit transfer into a current account extinguishes the earliest debit and so on until the value of the credit is used up.

5.8

Collateral transfers of whatever sort are to be made by the close of business on the same Business Day as the demand is made provided this is before the Notification Time stated in paragraph 1.5 of the Schedule.

If the Notification Time deadline is not met, then delivery of the Collateral will take place on the following Business Day after the demand is received.

Notification Times are new to the GMSLA 2010 but are common in the ISDA Credit Support Annexes under English and New York law.

5.9

The Lender can ask the Borrower by three Business Days' notice for a Letter of Credit to be substituted by cash or other collateral acceptable to the Lender. The notice period was one Business Day in the GMSLA 2000: so this gives the Borrower more time to obtain replacement collateral.

Where a Letter of Credit is due to expire, the Borrower is obliged to obtain an extension of it no later than 10.30 a.m. UK time on the second Business Day (or other period agreed by the parties) before it is due to expire or replace it with another Letter of Credit of equivalent value.

6. DISTRIBUTIONS AND CORPORATE ACTIONS

6.1 In this paragraph 6, references to an amount of Income *received* by any Party in respect of any Loaned Securities or Non-Cash Collateral shall be to an amount received from the issuer after any applicable withholding or deduction for or on account of Tax.

6.2 **Manufactured payments in respect of Loaned Securities**

Where the term of a Loan extends over an Income Record Date in respect of any Loaned Securities, Borrower shall, on the date such Income is paid by the issuer, or on such other date as the Parties may from time to time agree, pay or deliver to Lender such sum of money or property as is agreed between the Parties or, failing such agreement, a sum of money or property equivalent to (and in the same currency as) the type and amount of such Income that would be received by Lender in respect of such Loaned Securities assuming such Securities were not loaned to Borrower and were retained by Lender on the Income Record Date.

6. DISTRIBUTIONS AND CORPORATE ACTIONS

6.1

Paragraph 6.1 defines Income paid by an issuer of securities or securities collateral and the same income received by a party entitled to receive it.

In paragraph 6.1 Income received by any party in respect of holding securities or securities collateral shall be the amount received from the issuer after withholding tax is deducted, if it applies. In the UK we normally expect it to be received gross.

6.2 Manufactured payments in respect of Loaned Securities

This paragraph provides that any income received by the Borrower on loaned securities from their issuer during the life of a Loan shall be paid over promptly to the Lender by way of a separate payment (a "manufactured dividend") in the same currency as the income received from the issuer. A different sum or payment date is often agreed between the parties and this should be done in writing. Such payments will be made gross without deduction of withholding tax. The provision emphasises that the Lender will not be prejudiced in making the securities loan and would receive the same amount of income as if the Loan had not been made and he had owned the securities himself over the Income Record Date.

In the discussions about the GMSLA 2009, a number of large banks pointed out that where manufactured dividends were not agreed, there was an obligation and market convention to put the securities provider in the same position as if he had not transferred the securities and entered into the securities loan. They were concerned that in Paragraph 6.1(b) of the GMSLA 2009 the Lender was only obliged to pass on what he received while in its paragraph 6.2 the Borrower had to manufacture the gross dividend without regard to withholding tax. The big banks involved said that normally manufactured dividend rates were agreed but they did not believe the fallback should be a manufactured dividend grossed up for withholding tax. They considered this is unfair to the Borrower and that is why it was amended in the GMSLA 2010.

6.3 Manufactured payments in respect of Non-Cash Collateral

Where Non-Cash Collateral is delivered by Borrower to Lender and an Income Record Date in respect of such Non-Cash Collateral occurs before Equivalent Collateral is delivered by Lender to Borrower, Lender shall on the date such Income is paid, or on such other date as the Parties may from time to time agree, pay or deliver to Borrower a sum of money or property as is agreed between the Parties or, failing such agreement, a sum of money or property equivalent to (and in the same currency as) the type and amount of such Income that would be received by Lender in respect of such Non-Cash Collateral assuming Lender:

(a) retained the Non-Cash Collateral on the Income Record Date; and

(b) is not entitled to any credit, benefit or other relief in respect of Tax under any Applicable Law.

6.3 Manufactured payments in respect of Non-Cash Collateral

Similarly any income received by the Lender on securities collateral or non-cash collateral from their issuer will be paid over to the Borrower as a manufactured dividend. A different sum or payment date is often agreed between the parties for their convenience or to avoid the transfer of uneven amounts.

The payment of the manufactured dividend by the Lender is subject to two qualifications viz:

(a) that the Lender holds the Non-Cash Collateral on the Income Record Date up to which Income has been accrued and is deemed payable to the holder on a future date; and

(b) that the Lender is not entitled to any tax credit or relief under any applicable law.

These qualifications are new to the GMSLA 2010. The second condition was added to limit any tax arbitrage advantage the Lender may have. Traders often arbitrage tax credits on interest coupons. However, this a complex area beyond the scope of this book.

The payment to the Borrower of a manufactured dividend on securities held by the Lender does not depend upon it holding the relevant securities collateral at the time the issuer pays income. The Lender may have repoed the securities collateral out or lent them out elsewhere, for instance. Nonetheless the Lender still needs to pay a manufactured dividend to the Borrower as if it held the securities collateral on the Income Record Date. Where a party is concerned about the tax ramifications of making or receiving a manufactured dividend it will usually propose to substitute the securities concerned before the Income Record Date.

6.4   **Indemnity for failure to redeliver Equivalent Non-Cash Collateral**

Unless paragraph 1.6 of the Schedule indicates that this paragraph does not apply, where:

(a)   prior to any Income Record Date in relation to Non-Cash Collateral, Borrower has in accordance with paragraph 5.3 called for the Delivery of Equivalent Non-Cash Collateral;

(b)   Borrower has given notice of such call to Lender so as to be effective, at the latest, five hours before the Close of Business on the last Business Day on which Lender would customarily be required to initiate settlement of the Non-Cash Collateral to enable settlement to take place on the Business Day immediately preceding the relevant Income Record Date;

(c)   Borrower has provided reasonable details to Lender of the Non-Cash Collateral, the relevant Income Record Date and the proposed Alternative Collateral;

(d)   Lender, acting reasonably, has determined that such Alternative Collateral is acceptable to it and Borrower shall have delivered or delivers such Alternative Collateral to Lender; and

(e)   Lender has failed to make reasonable efforts to transfer Equivalent Non-Cash Collateral to Borrower prior to such Income Record Date,

Lender shall indemnify Borrower in respect of any cost, loss or damage (excluding any indirect or consequential loss or damage or any amount otherwise compensated by Lender, including pursuant to paragraphs 6.3 and/or 9.3) suffered by Borrower that it would not have suffered had the relevant Equivalent Non-Cash Collateral been transferred to Borrower prior to such Income Record Date.

6.4 Indemnity for failure to redeliver Equivalent Non-Cash Collateral

This is new to the GMSLA 2010 and is an optional indemnity (selected in paragraph 1.6 of the Schedule) covering the situation where the Lender fails to return Non-Cash Collateral when agreed with the Borrower before an Income Record Date. This provision should be useful where the Borrower fears he may be hit by a withholding tax on the manufactured dividend the Lender will need to pay him. The steps involved in the process outlined here are as follows:

(a) The Borrower calls for a substitution of securities collateral with Alternative Collateral before the Income Record Date.

(b) The Borrower has given the Lender notice of this at least five hours before close of business on the last Business Day on which the Lender could return securities collateral so that settlement could occur on the Business Day immediately before the Income Record Date.

(c) The Borrower has provided the Lender with reasonable details of the securities collateral, the Income Record Date concerned and the proposed Alternative Collateral.

(d) The Lender has reasonably decided that the Alternative Collateral is acceptable to it and it is delivered to the Lender. And

(e) Then the Lender fails to make reasonable efforts to transfer the original securities collateral to the Borrower before the Income Record Date.

If (e) happens the Lender agrees to indemnify the Borrower against any cost or damage (except indirect costs or consequential loss or damage) that the Borrower has suffered because the Lender failed to transfer the equivalent securities collateral.

These provisions are modelled on those in the GMRA 2000's Equities Annex.

6.5 Income in the form of Securities

Where Income, in the form of securities, is paid in relation to any Loaned Securities or Collateral, such securities shall be added to such Loaned Securities or Collateral (and shall constitute Loaned Securities or Collateral, as the case may be, and be part of the relevant Loan) and will not be delivered to Lender, in the case of Loaned Securities, or to Borrower, in the case of Collateral, until the end of the relevant Loan, provided that the Lender or Borrower (as the case may be) fulfils its obligations under paragraph 5.4 or 5.5 (as applicable) with respect to the additional Loaned Securities or Collateral, as the case may be.

6.6 Exercise of voting rights

Where any voting rights fall to be exercised in relation to any Loaned Securities or Collateral, neither Borrower, in the case of Equivalent Securities, nor Lender, in the case of Equivalent Collateral, shall have any obligation to arrange for voting rights of that kind to be exercised in accordance with the instructions of the other Party in relation to the Securities borrowed by it or transferred to it by way of Collateral, as the case may be, unless otherwise agreed between the Parties.

6.7 Corporate actions

Where, in respect of any Loaned Securities or any Collateral, any rights relating to conversion, sub-division, consolidation, pre-emption, rights arising under a takeover offer, rights to receive securities or a certificate which may at a future date be exchanged for securities or other rights, including those requiring election by the holder for the time being of such Securities or Collateral, become exercisable prior to the delivery of Equivalent Securities or Equivalent Collateral, then Lender or Borrower, as the case may be, may, within a reasonable time before the latest time for the exercise of the right or option give written notice to the other Party that on delivery of Equivalent Securities or Equivalent Collateral, as the case may be, it wishes to receive Equivalent Securities or Equivalent Collateral in such form as will arise if the right is exercised or, in the case of a right which may be exercised in more than one manner, is exercised as is specified in such written notice.

6.5

Where a distribution of bonus securities is made for any loaned securities or securities collateral, this paragraph provides for such bonus securities to be added to the loaned securities or securities collateral, as the case may be, provided that the collateral provisions in paragraph 5 are complied with. Such bonus securities will be delivered to the relevant party at the end of the loan.

6.6

This paragraph provides that the Borrower, in respect of loaned securities, and the Lender, in respect of securities collateral, has no obligation to arrange for any voting rights arising to be exercised in accordance with the instructions of the other party unless they have agreed otherwise.

6.7

If a corporate action (such as a rights issue or a takeover offer) arises in respect of any loaned securities or securities collateral, this paragraph permits the Lender, in the case of loaned securities, and the Borrower, in the case of securities collateral, to require that Equivalent Securities or Equivalent Collateral which will be redelivered at the end of the Loan take the form following the corporate action being exercised in line with the instructions of either Lender or Borrower. However, this is provided that such party gives written notice in good time to the other before rights relating to the corporate action become exercisable.

7. RATES APPLICABLE TO LOANED SECURITIES AND CASH COLLATERAL

7.1 Rates in respect of Loaned Securities

In respect of each Loan, Borrower shall pay to Lender, in the manner prescribed in sub-paragraph 7.3, sums calculated by applying such rate as shall be agreed between the Parties from time to time to the daily Market Value of the Loaned Securities.

7.2 Rates in respect of Cash Collateral

Where Cash Collateral is deposited with Lender in respect of any Loan, Lender shall pay to Borrower, in the manner prescribed in paragraph 7.3, sums calculated by applying such rates as shall be agreed between the Parties from time to time to the amount of such Cash Collateral. Any such payment due to Borrower may be set-off against any payment due to Lender pursuant to paragraph 7.1.

7.3 Payment of rates

In respect of each Loan, the payments referred to in paragraph 7.1 and 7.2 shall accrue daily in respect of the period commencing on and inclusive of the Settlement Date and terminating on and exclusive of the Business Day upon which Equivalent Securities are delivered or Cash Collateral is repaid. Unless otherwise agreed, the sums so accruing in respect of each calendar month shall be paid in arrears by the relevant Party not later than the Business Day which is the tenth Business Day after the last Business Day of the calendar month to which such payments relate or such other date as the Parties shall from time to time agree.

7. RATES APPLICABLE TO LOANED SECURITIES AND CASH COLLATERAL

7.1

This relates to the agreed fee the Borrower must pay the Lender for the securities loan. It is based on the value of the securities borrowed and the fee is set out in the deal terms agreed between the parties.

7.2

Interest will be paid on cash collateral to the Borrower at an agreed rate and can be netted off against any securities lending fee payable by Borrower to Lender.

7.3

This paragraph sets out the periods by which securities lending fees and interest on cash collateral are to be calculated. It also sets out the time when such sums are payable. Payments accrue from the date of delivery of securities and cash collateral up to the Business Day before redelivery. Sums accrue for the previous calendar month and unless otherwise agreed, payments are due not later than 10 Business Days after the end of the last Business Day of that month. In the GMSLA 2000 the deadline was one week after the end of the last Business Day of the preceding calendar month but the 10 Business Days is apparently more in line with current market practice.

8. DELIVERY OF EQUIVALENT SECURITIES

8.1 Lender's right to terminate a Loan

Subject to paragraph 11 and the terms of the relevant Loan, Lender shall be entitled to terminate a Loan and to call for the delivery of all or any Equivalent Securities at any time by giving notice on any Business Day of not less than the standard settlement time for such Equivalent Securities on the exchange or in the clearing organisation through which the Loaned Securities were originally delivered. Borrower shall deliver such Equivalent Securities not later than the expiry of such notice in accordance with Lender's instructions.

8.2 Borrower's right to terminate a Loan

Subject to the terms of the relevant Loan, Borrower shall be entitled at any time to terminate a Loan and to deliver all and any Equivalent Securities due and outstanding to Lender in accordance with Lender's instructions and Lender shall accept such delivery.

8.3 Delivery of Equivalent Securities on termination of a Loan

Borrower shall procure the Delivery of Equivalent Securities to Lender or deliver Equivalent Securities in accordance with this Agreement and the terms of the relevant Loan on termination of the Loan. For the avoidance of doubt any reference in this Agreement or in any other agreement or communication between the Parties (howsoever expressed) to an obligation to deliver or account for or act in relation to Loaned Securities shall accordingly be construed as a reference to an obligation to deliver or account for or act in relation to Equivalent Securities.

8. DELIVERY OF EQUIVALENT SECURITIES

8.1

This paragraph sets out the Lender's right to terminate a loan of securities. Subject to any terms of the relevant loan (for example, where a fixed period has been agreed) the Lender may terminate on giving notice equal to the standard market settlement time for the securities concerned and the Borrower must redeliver by the end of such period in line with the Lender's instructions.

8.2

This paragraph sets out the Borrower's right to terminate a loan of securities. Subject to the terms of the relevant loan, the Borrower may terminate and redeliver securities at any time in line with the Lender's delivery instructions and the Lender will accept such redelivery.

8.3

The Borrower will deliver or arrange delivery of Equivalent Securities to the Lender at the end of the Loan. For the avoidance of doubt, any reference in the Agreement or other communications to the delivery of or accounting for Loaned Securities shall constitute a parallel obligation to redeliver, deal with or account for Equivalent Securities at the appropriate time.

8.4 Delivery of Equivalent Collateral on termination of a Loan

On the date and time that Equivalent Securities are required to be delivered by Borrower on the termination of a Loan, Lender shall simultaneously (subject to paragraph 5.4 if applicable) repay to Borrower any Cash Collateral or, as the case may be, deliver Collateral equivalent to the Collateral provided by Borrower pursuant to paragraph 5 in respect of such Loan. For the avoidance of doubt any reference in this Agreement or in any other agreement or communication between the Parties (however expressed) to an obligation to deliver or account for or act in relation to Collateral shall accordingly be construed as a reference to an obligation to deliver or account for or act in relation to Equivalent Collateral.

8.5 Delivery of Letters of Credit

Where a Letter of Credit is provided by way of Collateral, the obligation to deliver Equivalent Collateral is satisfied by Lender delivering for cancellation the Letter of Credit so provided, or where the Letter of Credit is provided in respect of more than one Loan, by Lender consenting to a reduction in the value of the Letter of Credit.

8.6 Delivery obligations to be reciprocal

Neither Party shall be obliged to make delivery (or make a payment as the case may be) to the other unless it is satisfied that the other Party will make such delivery (or make an appropriate payment as the case may be) to it. If it is not so satisfied (whether because an Event of Default has occurred in respect of the other Party or otherwise) it shall notify the other Party and unless that other Party has made arrangements which are sufficient to assure full delivery (or the appropriate payment as the case may be) to the notifying Party, the notifying Party shall (provided it is itself in a position, and willing, to perform its own obligations) be entitled to withhold delivery (or payment, as the case may be) to the other Party until such arrangements to assure full delivery (or the appropriate payment as the case may be) are made.

8.4

This provision recites the Lender's obligation to repay Cash Collateral or redeliver equivalent securities collateral simultaneously with the return of the loaned securities by the Borrower at the end of the Loan. Once again any reference in the Agreement or in any communication between the parties to deliver or account for collateral shall include a parallel obligation to redeliver, deal with or account for Equivalent Collateral at the appropriate time.

8.5

This sub-paragraph sets out the obligation of how to deliver Equivalent Collateral in the form of a Letter of Credit. Either the Letter of Credit is delivered for cancellation or where it covers more than one Loan, the Lender consents to a reduction in its value.

8.6

Neither party shall be obliged to make a payment or delivery to the other unless it is satisfied that its counterparty will make its payment or delivery on time as well. If it is not satisfied, it will notify its counterparty and seek assurances that full delivery or payment will be made by it as contractually agreed. If such assurances are not received or are unconvincing, the first party is entitled to withhold its payment or delivery to its counterparty until arrangements to ensure full delivery or payment are made. This is rarely implemented but if it was an innocent party would withhold its own payments and deliveries and insist upon pre-collateralisation from its counterparty. While it would be concerned about a potential default, pre-collateralisation would give it more confidence to continue the relationship.

9. FAILURE TO DELIVER

9.1 Borrower's failure to deliver Equivalent Securities

If Borrower fails to deliver Equivalent Securities in accordance with paragraph 8.3 Lender may:

(a) elect to continue the Loan (which, for the avoidance of doubt, shall continue to be taken into account for the purposes of paragraph 5.4 or 5.5 as applicable); or

(b) at any time while such failure continues, by written notice to Borrower declare that that Loan (but only that Loan) shall be terminated immediately in accordance with paragraph 11.2 as if (i) an Event of Default had occurred in relation to the Borrower, (ii) references to the Termination Date were to the date on which notice was given under this sub-paragraph, and (iii) the Loan were the only Loan outstanding. For the avoidance of doubt, any such failure shall not constitute an Event of Default (including under paragraph 10.1(i)) unless the Parties otherwise agree.

9. FAILURE TO DELIVER

Sub-paragraphs 9.1 and 9.2 are the GMSLA 2010's mini close-out provisions. Under the GMSLA 2010, failures to deliver Securities or Equivalent Securities are no longer Events of Default as they were under the GMSLA 2000. The market regarded the termination of all Transactions because there was a failure to deliver securities under one of them as too draconian a penalty. The mini close-out of individual Transactions for this reason was deemed preferable.

9.1

This sub-paragraph sets out the Lender's remedies if the Borrower fails to redeliver Equivalent Securities at the end of a Loan (perhaps because he has repoed or lent them elsewhere and there is a sudden market shortage of them). If this happens the Lender can choose to:

(a) continue the Loan (which will still be margined); or

(b) serve notice on the Borrower and terminate only the affected Loan.

Technically an Event of Default is deemed to have occurred to the Borrower; the Termination Date is deemed to be the date the notice was given to the Borrower under this paragraph 9.1(b); and the Loan concerned is deemed to be the only one outstanding. It is stressed that this failure will not be an Event of Default under paragraph 10.1(i) unless the parties otherwise agree in the Schedule.

9.2 **Lender's failure to deliver Equivalent Collateral**

If Lender fails to deliver Equivalent Collateral comprising Non-Cash Collateral in accordance with paragraph 8.4 or 8.5, Borrower may:

(a) elect to continue the Loan (which, for the avoidance of doubt, shall continue to be taken into account for the purposes of paragraph 5.4 or 5.5 as applicable); or

(b) at any time while such failure continues, by written notice to Lender declare that that Loan (but only that Loan) shall be terminated immediately in accordance with paragraph 11.2 as if (i) an Event of Default had occurred in relation to the Lender, (ii) references to the Termination Date were to the date on which notice was given under this sub-paragraph, and (iii) the Loan were the only Loan outstanding. For the avoidance of doubt, any such failure shall not constitute an Event of Default (including under paragraph 10.1(i)) unless the Parties otherwise agree.

9.2

This sub-paragraph sets out the Borrower's remedies if the Lender fails to deliver Equivalent Collateral (i.e. equivalent securities collateral) upon the termination of a Loan (again perhaps because he has repoed or lent them elsewhere and there is a sudden market shortage of them). If this happens, the Borrower may:

(a) **continue the loan (which will still be margined);**

(b) **serve notice on the lender and terminate only the affected Loan.**

Once again, technically an Event of Default is deemed to have occurred but this time to the Lender; the Termination Date is deemed to be the date the notice was given to the Lender under paragraph 9.2(b); and the Loan concerned is deemed to be the only one outstanding. It is again stressed that this failure will not be an Event of Default under paragraph 10.1(i) unless the parties otherwise agree in the Schedule. In the GMSLA 2000 paragraphs 9.1 and 9.2 were Events of Default but no longer because the market generally regarded this as too severe a penalty where the failure to deliver was unrelated to a party's default – financial deterioration.

9.3 Failure by either Party to deliver

Where a Party (the *Transferor*) fails to deliver Equivalent Securities or Equivalent Collateral by the time required under this Agreement or within such other period as may be agreed between the Transferor and the other Party (the *Transferee*) and the Transferee:

(a) incurs interest, overdraft or similar costs and expenses; or

(b) incurs costs and expenses as a direct result of a Buy-in exercised against it by a third party,

then the Transferor agrees to pay within one Business Day of a demand from the Transferee and hold harmless the Transferee with respect to all reasonable costs and expenses listed in sub-paragraphs (a) and (b) above properly incurred which arise directly from such failure other than (i) such costs and expenses which arise from the negligence or wilful default of the Transferee and (ii) any indirect or consequential losses.

9.3

Paragraph 9.3 is an abbreviated revamp of paragraphs 9.3 and 9.4 of the GMSLA 2000.

Paragraph 9.3 covers where a party (the "Transferor") fails to deliver Equivalent Securities or Equivalent Collateral within timescales agreed with its counterparty or at the end of a Loan. If the party not receiving delivery (the "Transferee") incurs interest and banking charges or buy-in costs or expenses are charged to it because a third party to whom it had contracted to deliver securities did not receive them, then the Transferor who originally failed to deliver these securities agrees to indemnify the Transferee. He will pay within one Business Day of demand the Transferee's banking expenses and the buy-in costs charged to it which arise directly from the Transferor's original failure to deliver. However, it does not indemnify against any costs or expenses arising from the Transferee's own negligence or wilful default or any indirect or consequential losses.

10. EVENTS OF DEFAULT

10.1 Each of the following events occurring and continuing in relation to either Party (the ***Defaulting Party***, the other Party being the ***Non-Defaulting Party***) shall be an Event of Default but only (subject to sub-paragraph 10.1(d)) where the Non-Defaulting Party serves written notice on the Defaulting Party:

(a) Borrower or Lender failing to pay or repay Cash Collateral or to deliver Collateral on commencement of the Loan under paragraph 5.1 or to deliver further Collateral under paragraph 5.4 or 5.5;

(b) Lender or Borrower failing to comply with its obligations under paragraph 6.2 or 6.3 upon the due date and not remedying such failure within three Business Days after the Non-Defaulting Party serves written notice requiring it to remedy such failure;

(c) Lender or Borrower failing to pay any sum due under paragraph 9.1(b), 9.2(b) or 9.3 upon the due date;

(d) an Act of Insolvency occurring with respect to Lender or Borrower, provided that, where the Parties have specified in paragraph 5 of the Schedule that Automatic Early Termination shall apply, an Act of Insolvency which is the presentation of a petition for winding up or any analogous proceeding or the appointment of a liquidator or analogous officer of the Defaulting Party shall not require the Non-Defaulting Party to serve written notice on the Defaulting Party (***Automatic Early Termination***);

(e) any warranty made by Lender or Borrower in paragraph 13 or paragraphs 14(a) to 14(d) being incorrect or untrue in any material respect when made or repeated or deemed to have been made or repeated;

(f) Lender or Borrower admitting to the other that it is unable to, or it intends not to, perform any of its obligations under this Agreement and/or in respect of any Loan where such failure to perform would with the service of notice or lapse of time constitute an Event of Default;

(g) all or any material part of the assets of Lender or Borrower being transferred or ordered to be transferred to a trustee (or a person exercising similar functions) by a regulatory authority pursuant to any legislation;

(h) Lender (if applicable) or Borrower being declared in default or being suspended or expelled from membership of or participation in, any securities exchange or suspended or prohibited from dealing in securities by any regulatory authority, in each case on the grounds that it has failed to meet any requirements relating to financial resources or credit rating; or

(i) Lender or Borrower failing to perform any other of its obligations under this Agreement and not remedying such failure within 30 days after the Non-Defaulting Party serves written notice requiring it to remedy such failure.

10. EVENTS OF DEFAULT

10.1

There are nine Events of Default which are very similar to those in the GMRA (2000). **In the GMSLA 2000 the events only had to occur. Here they have to occur and be continuing.** They are:

(a) Failure by Borrower or Lender to deliver Cash Collateral or other Collateral at the start of the loan or to deliver or redeliver Cash Collateral; or to deliver further collateral when called under the paragraph 5.4 or 5.5 margining provisions.

(b) Failure to pay manufactured dividends on their due date and not remedying this within three Business Days of a written notice from the Non-Defaulting Party. This grace period was not in the GMSLA 2000.

(c) The Borrower or Lender failing to pay any sum due in mini close-outs, buy-ins and related direct expenses.

(d) An Act of Insolvency occurring to the Borrower or Lender.

(e) Warranties made by the Borrower or Lender being materially untrue or incorrect.

(f) Either party intending not to perform its obligations under the GMSLA 2010 or under any Loan resulting in a potential Event of Default.

(g) Transfer of all or most of either party's assets to a trustee by order of its regulator following applicable law.

(h) Either party being in breach of securities exchange rules or being suspended from membership of a securities exchange or being forbidden to deal by a regulator, in each case because it has failed to meet requirements in relation to its financial substance or external credit rating.

(i) Failure by either party to remedy any other breach under the GMSLA 2010 within a 30-day cure period following notice.

There are no grace periods for Events of Default except for 10.1((b) and the last one.

In each case, except for the appointment of a liquidator or the presentation of a petition for winding up in 10.1(d) where Automatic Early Termination is chosen to apply in Section 1.5 of the Schedule, the Non-Defaulting Party must serve a notice on the Defaulting Party to call an Event of Default.

Please note that, as mentioned before, failure to deliver Equivalent Securities is no longer an Event of Default under the GMSLA 2010. The Non-Defaulting Party may choose to terminate only the affected securities loan (a mini close-out).

10.2 Each Party shall notify the other (in writing) if an Event of Default or an event which, with the passage of time and/or upon the serving of a written notice as referred to above, would be an Event of Default, occurs in relation to it.

10.3 The provisions of this Agreement constitute a complete statement of the remedies available to each Party in respect of any Event of Default.

10.4 Subject to paragraphs 9 and 11, neither Party may claim any sum by way of consequential loss or damage in the event of failure by the other Party to perform any of its obligations under this Agreement.

10.2

Each party is obliged to notify its counterparty in writing if it suffers an Event of Default or a potential Event of Default.

10.3

As far as Events of Default are concerned, the GMSLA 2010 constitutes a complete statement of remedies available to the parties.

10.4

Claims for consequential losses are prohibited under the GMSLA 2010 as they are under many other master agreements.

11. CONSEQUENCES OF AN EVENT OF DEFAULT

11.1   If an Event of Default occurs in relation to either Party then paragraphs 11.2 to 11.7 below shall apply.

11.2   The Parties' delivery and payment obligations (and any other obligations they have under this Agreement) shall be accelerated so as to require performance thereof at the time such Event of Default occurs (the date of which shall be the *Termination Date*) so that performance of such delivery and payment obligations shall be effected only in accordance with the following provisions.

   (a)   The Default Market Value of the Equivalent Securities and Equivalent Non-Cash Collateral to be delivered and the amount of any Cash Collateral (including sums accrued) to be repaid and any other cash (including interest accrued) to be paid by each Party shall be established by the Non-Defaulting Party in accordance with paragraph 11.4 and deemed as at the Termination Date.

   (b)   On the basis of the sums so established, an account shall be taken (as at the Termination Date) of what is due from each Party to the other under this Agreement (on the basis that each Party's claim against the other in respect of delivery of Equivalent Securities or Equivalent Non-Cash Collateral equal to the Default Market Value thereof) and the sums due from one Party shall be set off against the sums due from the other and only the balance of the account shall be payable (by the Party having the claim valued at the lower amount pursuant to the foregoing) and such balance shall be payable on the next following Business Day after such account has been taken and such sums have been set off in accordance with this paragraph. For the purposes of this calculation, any sum not denominated in the Base Currency shall be converted into the Base Currency at the Spot Rate prevailing at such dates and times determined by the Non-Defaulting Party acting reasonably.

11. CONSEQUENCES OF AN EVENT OF DEFAULT

Paragraph 11 is the close-out netting provision and is entitled Consequences of an Event of Default and not Set Off as it was confusingly called in the GMSLA 2000. The text has been substantially revised from the GMSLA 2000 and closely follows that in the GMRA 2000.

11.1

Paragraph 11.1 states that if an Event of Default happens to a party, close-out will follow the process outlined in paragraphs 11.2–11.7.

11.2

When an Event of Default occurs and a Non-Defaulting Party exercises its close-out rights, both parties' payment and delivery obligations and any other obligations they have under the Agreement are accelerated to the Termination Date (i.e. as at the time of the Event of Default) and the values of all Loans are calculated and converted into the Base Currency and netted off against each other so as to produce a single cash sum due to one party or the other.

The Non-Defaulting Party therefore has no claim on the Defaulting Party for the return of any lent securities, reflecting the fact that securities lending involves a full legal transfer of those securities. So where the Borrower defaults, the Lender offsets the market value of its collateral against the market value of its lent securities. Assuming that markets are normal and the margining levels on the collateral have been conservatively pitched, the Lender should have a net liability to the Borrower.

The detailed process starts in paragraph 11.2(a).

(a) The Default Market Values of Equivalent Securities and securities and cash collateral (including accrued interest) are calculated by the Non-Defaulting Party as at the Termination Date on the basis of the alternative valuation approaches in paragraph 11.4.

(b) On the basis of these calculations, the Non-Defaulting Party will then net off the amounts due to and from each party (on the basis of their Default Market Values) and arrive at a single net figure payable by the party with the lower valuation for its Transactions on the following Business Day. If Transactions are in different currencies these will be converted into the Base Currency at the prevailing Spot Rate.

Please note that the Non-Defaulting Party has the flexibility to make currency conversions but must act reasonably in calculating the Spot Rate.

(c) If the balance under sub-paragraph (b) above is payable by the Non-Defaulting Party and the Non-Defaulting Party had delivered to the Defaulting Party a Letter of Credit, the Defaulting Party shall draw on the Letter of Credit to the extent of the balance due and shall subsequently deliver for cancellation the Letter of Credit so provided.

(d) If the balance under sub-paragraph (b) above is payable by the Defaulting Party and the Defaulting Party had delivered to the Non-Defaulting Party a Letter of Credit, the Non-Defaulting Party shall draw on the Letter of Credit to the extent of the balance due and shall subsequently deliver for cancellation the Letter of Credit so provided.

(e) In all other circumstances, where a Letter of Credit has been provided to a Party, such Party shall deliver for cancellation the Letter of Credit so provided.

(c) Where the Defaulting Party is owed the net amount and the Non-Defaulting Party has previously delivered a Letter of Credit as collateral, the Defaulting Party will draw on the Letter of Credit for the balance due and then return it to the Non-Defaulting Party or the bank concerned for cancellation.

(d) Where the Non-Defaulting Party is owed the net amount and it has previously received a Letter of Credit from the Defaulting Party, the Non-Defaulting Party will draw on that Letter of Credit for the balance due and then return it for cancellation.

(e) In all other circumstances, upon close-out, where a Letter of Credit has previously been delivered to a party (and perhaps it was not used because it was only offered as a sign of good faith and other collateral was used instead) it must be redelivered for cancellation.

11.3　For the purposes of this Agreement, the *Default Market Value* of any Equivalent Collateral in the form of a Letter of Credit shall be zero and of any Equivalent Securities or any other Equivalent Non-Cash Collateral shall be determined in accordance with paragraphs 11.4 to 11.6 below, and for this purpose:

(a) the *Appropriate Market* means, in relation to securities of any description, the market which is the most appropriate market for securities of that description, as determined by the Non-Defaulting Party;

(b) the *Default Valuation Time* means, in relation to an Event of Default, the close of business in the Appropriate Market on the fifth dealing day after the day on which that Event of Default occurs or, where that Event of Default is the occurrence of an Act of Insolvency in respect of which under paragraph 10.1(d) no notice is required from the Non-Defaulting Party in order for such event to constitute an Event of Default, the close of business on the fifth dealing day after the day on which the Non-Defaulting Party first became aware of the occurrence of such Event of Default;

(c) *Deliverable Securities* means Equivalent Securities or Equivalent Non-Cash Collateral to be delivered by the Defaulting Party;

(d) *Net Value* means at any time, in relation to any Deliverable Securities or Receivable Securities, the amount which, in the reasonable opinion of the Non-Defaulting Party, represents their fair market value, having regard to such pricing sources and methods (which may include, without limitation, available prices for securities with similar maturities, terms and credit characteristics as the relevant Equivalent Securities or Equivalent Collateral) Transaction Costs incurred or reasonably anticipated in connection with the purchase or sale of such securities;

(e) *Receivable Securities* means Equivalent Securities or Equivalent Non-Cash Collateral to be delivered to the Defaulting Party; and

(f) *Transaction Costs* in relation to any transaction contemplated in paragraph 11.4 or 11.5 means the reasonable costs, commissions (including internal commissions), fees and expenses (including any mark-up or mark-down or premium paid for guaranteed delivery) incurred or reasonably anticipated in connection with the purchase of Deliverable Securities or sale of Receivable Securities, calculated on the assumption that the aggregate thereof is the least that could reasonably be expected to be paid in order to carry out the transaction.

11.3

A series of definitions are set out in paragraph 11.3. They are:

Appropriate Market

In valuing Securities for the purposes of close-out of Transactions under paragraph 11 following an Event of Default, "Appropriate Market" is the one deemed most relevant by the Non-Defaulting Party for obtaining prices from dealers.

Default Valuation Time

Where an Act of Insolvency has occurred, this is up to the close of business on the fifth dealing day after the Non-Defaulting Party first becomes aware of the Act of Insolvency. With other Events of Default the Default Valuation Time is up to the close of business on the fifth dealing day in the Appropriate Market (determined by the Non-Defaulting Party) after the Event of Default occurs.

Deliverable Securities

At close-out the securities or securities collateral the Defaulting Party is notionally obliged to deliver to the Non-Defaulting Party. The Non-Defaulting Party would value them at their Default Market Value.

Net Value

This is the Non-Defaulting Party's reasonable opinion of the fair market value of securities or securities collateral notionally to be delivered by or to the Defaulting Party upon close-out. Reasonable Transaction costs are also accounted for in the definition of Net Value.

Receivable Securities

At close-out these are the securities or securities collateral the Non-Defaulting Party is notionally obliged to deliver to the Defaulting Party. The Non-Defaulting Party would value them at their Default Market Value.

Transaction Costs

These are the costs, commissions, fees or premia due for the purchase or sale of Securities at close-out in order for the parties to settle their obligations to each other. The aggregate of these costs should be reasonable in the context of transactions to be executed.

11.4 If between the Termination Date and the Default Valuation Time:

   (a) the Non-Defaulting Party has sold, in the case of Receivable Securities, or purchased, in the case of Deliverable Securities, securities which form part of the same issue and are of an identical type and description as those Equivalent Securities or that Equivalent Collateral, (and regardless as to whether or not such sales or purchases have settled) the Non-Defaulting Party may elect to treat as the Default Market Value:

   (i) in the case of Receivable Securities, the net proceeds of such sale after deducting all Transaction Costs; provided that, where the securities sold are not identical in amount to the Equivalent Securities or Equivalent Collateral, the Non-Defaulting Party may, acting in good faith, either (A) elect to treat such net proceeds of sale divided by the amount of securities sold and multiplied by the amount of the Equivalent Securities or Equivalent Collateral as the Default Market Value or (B) elect to treat such net proceeds of sale of the Equivalent Securities or Equivalent Collateral actually sold as the Default Market Value of that proportion of the Equivalent Securities or Equivalent Collateral, and, in the case of (B), the Default Market Value of the balance of the Equivalent Securities or Equivalent Collateral shall be determined separately in accordance with the provisions of this paragraph 11.4; or

   (ii) in the case of Deliverable Securities, the aggregate cost of such purchase, including all Transaction Costs; provided that, where the securities purchased are not identical in amount to the Equivalent Securities or Equivalent Collateral, the Non-Defaulting Party may, acting in good faith, either (A) elect to treat such aggregate cost divided by the amount of securities purchased and multiplied by the amount of the Equivalent Securities or Equivalent Collateral as the Default Market Value or (B) elect to treat the aggregate cost of purchasing the Equivalent Securities or Equivalent Collateral actually purchased as the Default Market Value of that proportion of the Equivalent Securities or Equivalent Collateral, and, in the case of (B), the Default Market Value of the balance of the Equivalent Securities or Equivalent Collateral shall be determined separately in accordance with the provisions of this paragraph 11.4;

11.4

Paragraphs 11.4 and 11.5 set out the three choices the Non-Defaulting Party has in calculating the Default Market Value of securities and securities collateral during the period between the Termination Date and the Default Valuation Time.

Firstly in paragraph 11.4(a) the Non-Defaulting Party may calculate the Default Market Value by referring to the prices of actual sales and purchases of the same securities or securities collateral made to or from other counterparties during the five Business Day Default Valuation Time period. Account is taken in each case of reasonable fees, commissions or expenses incurred in these sales and purchases. So we are talking about the net proceeds of these actual sales and purchases.

Where the securities sold or purchased are not identical in amount to the securities or securities collateral subject to termination, the Non-Defaulting Party may, in good faith, either divide the net sale proceeds by the number of securities sold or bought and multiply this figure by the actual number of Equivalent Securities or securities collateral subject to termination, or it may take these net sale proceeds as a base figure and value the rest of the Equivalent Securities or securities collateral separately in line with this sub-paragraph 11.4(a).

(b) the Non-Defaulting Party has received, in the case of Deliverable Securities, offer quotations or, in the case of Receivable Securities, bid quotations in respect of securities of the relevant description from two or more market makers or regular dealers in the Appropriate Market in a commercially reasonable size (as determined by the Non-Defaulting Party) the Non-Defaulting Party may elect to treat as the Default Market Value of the relevant Equivalent Securities or Equivalent Collateral:

(i) the price quoted (or where more than one price is so quoted, the arithmetic mean of the prices so quoted) by each of them for, in the case of Deliverable Securities, the sale by the relevant market marker or dealer of such securities or, in the case of Receivable Securities, the purchase by the relevant market maker or dealer of such securities, provided that such price or prices quoted may be adjusted in a commercially reasonable manner by the Non-Defaulting Party to reflect accrued but unpaid coupons not reflected in the price or prices quoted in respect of such Securities;

(ii) after deducting, in the case of Receivable Securities or adding in the case of Deliverable Securities the Transaction Costs which would be incurred or reasonably anticipated in connection with such transaction.

Alternatively in paragraph 11.4(b) the Non-Defaulting Party may request and receive offer quotations for the securities it must notionally deliver to the Defaulting Party or bid quotations for securities the Defaulting Party is notionally obliged to deliver to it from two or more regular dealers in the Appropriate Market for a commercially reasonable sized block of such securities.

The Non-Defaulting Party may then either take the price quoted as the Default Market Value or where more than one price has been quoted, the arithmetic mean of such prices. Where Deliverable Securities are concerned (i.e. those which the Defaulting Party needs notionally to deliver to the Non-Defaulting Party on close-out), the dealer's offer or sale price is taken and where Receivable Securities are involved (i.e. those which the Non-Defaulting Party needs notionally to deliver to the Defaulting Party on close-out), the dealer's bid or buy price is taken to which the Non-Defaulting Party may add accrued interest or coupons not already included in such prices.

Finally in paragraph 11.4(b)(ii) reasonable Transaction Costs would be deducted in relation to Receivable Securities and added in respect of Deliverable Securities.

11.5 If, acting in good faith, either (A) the Non-Defaulting Party has endeavoured but been unable to sell or purchase securities in accordance with paragraph 11.4(a) above or to obtain quotations in accordance with paragraph 11.4(b) above (or both) or (B) the Non-Defaulting Party has determined that it would not be commercially reasonable to sell or purchase securities at the prices bid or offered or to obtain such quotations, or that it would not be commercially reasonable to use any quotations which it has obtained under paragraph 11.4(b) above the Non-Defaulting Party may determine the Net Value of the relevant Equivalent Securities or Equivalent Collateral (which shall be specified) and the Non-Defaulting Party may elect to treat such Net Value as the Default Market Value of the relevant Equivalent Securities or Equivalent Collateral.

11.6 To the extent that the Non-Defaulting Party has not determined the Default Market Value in accordance with paragraph 11.4, the Default Market Value of the relevant Equivalent Securities or Equivalent Collateral shall be an amount equal to their Net Value at the Default Valuation Time; provided that, if at the Default Valuation Time the Non-Defaulting Party reasonably determines that, owing to circumstances affecting the market in the Equivalent Securities or Equivalent Collateral in question, it is not reasonably practicable for the Non-Defaulting Party to determine a Net Value of such Equivalent Securities or Equivalent Collateral which is commercially reasonable (by reason of lack of tradable prices or otherwise), the Default Market Value of such Equivalent Securities or Equivalent Collateral shall be an amount equal to their Net Value as determined by the Non-Defaulting Party as soon as reasonably practicable after the Default Valuation Time.

11.5

However, paragraph 11.5 says that if, acting in good faith, the Non-Defaulting Party has been unable to buy or sell securities under paragraph 11.4(a) or failed to obtain quotations under paragraph 11.4(b), or both, or secondly believes that it would not be commercially reasonable to buy or sell at those prices or to obtain quotations or, if they were obtained, to use them, then the Non-Defaulting Party can fall back to Net Value as the Default Market Value. This is the fair market value of the securities or securities collateral reasonably determined by the Non-Defaulting Party and derived from such pricing methods or pricing sources as he thinks appropriate.

Circumstances where it might not be appropriate to obtain quotations would be where the position is so large it would materially affect the quotations obtained. Circumstances where it might be inappropriate to use them would be where the securities were not very liquid and there are big differences between the quotations obtained.

11.6

Paragraph 11.6 confirms that Net Value will be the fallback Default Market Value if the Non-Defaulting Party does not calculate this otherwise under paragraph 11.4. However, if at the Default Valuation Time the Non-Defaulting Party reasonably decides that given market conditions for the securities or securities collateral in question it is not reasonable to calculate a commercially feasible Net Value for these securities (perhaps because there is a shortage of trading prices), the Net Value shall be calculated by the Non-Defaulting Party as soon as reasonably practicable after the Default Valuation Time.

Other costs, expenses and interest payable in consequence of an Event of Default

11.7　The Defaulting Party shall be liable to the Non-Defaulting Party for the amount of all reasonable legal and other professional expenses incurred by the Non-Defaulting Party in connection with or as a consequence of an Event of Default, together with interest thereon at such rate as is agreed by the Parties and specified in paragraph 10 of the Schedule or, failing such agreement, the overnight London Inter Bank Offered Rate as quoted on a reputable financial information service (***LIBOR***) as at 11.00 a.m., London time, on the date on which it is to be determined or, in the case of an expense attributable to a particular transaction and, where the Parties have previously agreed a rate of interest for the transaction, that rate of interest if it is greater than LIBOR. Interest will accrue daily on a compound basis.

Set-off

11.8　Any amount payable to one Party (the ***Payee***) by the other Party (the ***Payer***) under paragraph 11.2(b) may, at the option of the Non-Defaulting Party, be reduced by its set-off against any amount payable (whether at such time or in the future or upon the occurrence of a contingency) by the Payee to the Payer (irrespective of the currency, place of payment or booking office of the obligation) under any other agreement between the Payee and the Payer or instrument or undertaking issued or executed by one Party to, or in favour of, the other Party. If an obligation is unascertained, the Non-Defaulting Party may in good faith estimate that obligation and set off in respect of the estimate, subject to accounting to the other Party when the obligation is ascertained. Nothing in this paragraph shall be effective to create a charge or other security interest. This paragraph shall be without prejudice and in addition to any right of set-off, combination of accounts, lien or other right to which any Party is at any time otherwise entitled (whether by operation of law, contract or otherwise).

11.7

The Defaulting Party will be liable to the Non-Defaulting Party for its reasonable legal and professional expenses in enforcing its early termination rights under the Agreement together with any default interest on late payment of the close-out amount as stated in paragraph 10 of the Schedule. If this is not agreed, the fallback will be the overnight LIBOR quoted by a reputable financial information service such as Reuters or Bloomberg as at 11.00 a.m. London time on the date the interest is calculated. A rate greater than LIBOR will apply to expenses for individual transactions where this has previously been agreed by the parties. Accrued interest will be compounded on a daily basis.

11.8

Paragraph 11.8 is a set-off clause and was not in the GMSLA 2000 main text. This was because it was considered that if the Loan was sufficiently overcollateralised, the Non-Defaulting Party would be paid out fully on an Event of Default and indeed would have a liability to repay any surplus to the Defaulting Party. A set-off clause was therefore deemed unnecessary although some parties added one in the Schedule. Of course, where the Loan involved illiquid securities or securities collateral, then a set-off clause was more justifiable. The set-off clause gives the Non-Defaulting Party more flexibility but a liquidator could challenge it.

The set-off clause here applies just to the contracting parties (Party A and Party B) and there is no extension to the Non-Defaulting Party's Affiliates (other group companies) as there is sometimes in an ISDA Master Agreement Schedule.

The set off can take place without prior notice and is wide-ranging. It can cover amounts owing under other agreements between the same parties and can involve currency conversion provided this is conducted in a commercially reasonable manner.

Difficult to value obligations can be estimated and set off but there has to be a final settlement when the value of the obligation is ultimately calculated.

The set off is stated not to constitute any kind of security interest and is a separate legal right to a list of other rights contained in the final sentence.

ISLA members decided to include a set-off clause to give the Non-Defaulting Party more flexibility on close-out.

12. TAXES

Withholding, gross-up and provision of information

12.1 All payments under this Agreement shall be made without any deduction or withholding for or on account of any Tax unless such deduction or withholding is required by any Applicable Law.

12.2 Except as otherwise agreed, if the paying Party is so required to deduct or withhold, then that Party (*Payer*) shall:

(a) promptly notify the other Party (*Recipient*) of such requirement;

(b) pay or otherwise account for the full amount required to be deducted or withheld to the relevant authority;

(c) upon written demand of Recipient, forward to Recipient documentation reasonably acceptable to Recipient, evidencing such payment to such authorities; and

(d) other than in respect of any payment made by Lender to Borrower under paragraph 6.3, pay to Recipient, in addition to the payment to which Recipient is otherwise entitled under this Agreement, such additional amount as is necessary to ensure that the amount actually received by Recipient (after taking account of such withholding or deduction) will equal the amount Recipient would have received had no such deduction or withholding been required; provided Payer will not be required to pay any additional amount to Recipient under this sub-paragraph (d) to the extent it would not be required to be paid but for the failure by Recipient to comply with or perform any obligation under paragraph 12.3.

12.3 Each Party agrees that it will upon written demand of the other Party deliver to such other Party (or to any government or other taxing authority as such other Party directs), any form or document and provide such other cooperation or assistance as may (in either case) reasonably be required in order to allow such other Party to make a payment under this Agreement without any deduction or withholding for or on account of any Tax or with such deduction or withholding at a reduced rate (so long as the completion, execution or submission of such form or document, or the provision of such cooperation or assistance, would not materially prejudice the legal or commercial position of the Party in receipt of such demand). Any such form or document shall be accurate and completed in a manner reasonably satisfactory to such other Party and shall be executed and delivered with any reasonably required certification by such date as is agreed between the Parties or, failing such agreement, as soon as reasonably practicable.

12. TAXES

12.1

All payments under the GMSLA 2010 shall be made gross of any withholding tax unless such tax is legally required to be deducted.

12.2

However, where a payer has to deduct withholding tax it must take the following steps:

(a) promptly notify the payee of this;
(b) promptly pay the withholding tax calculated or assessed to the tax authorities;
(c) upon its written request, promptly send the payee satisfactory documentation evidencing the tax payment to the authorities; and
(d) except in the case of manufactured dividends for securities collateral as per paragraph 6.3, make the gross payment to the payee so that it ends up with the amount it originally anticipated.

This is new to the GMSLA 2010.

12.3

This is also new to the GMSLA 2010.

Paragraph 12.3 records the agreement of each party to supply certain tax related and contractual information and to co-operate to enable such party to make payments under the GMSLA 2010 with no withholding tax or with such withholding tax at a reduced rate.

However, a party need not send its counterparty tax forms to reduce or eliminate withholding tax on payments under the Agreement if doing so would "materially prejudice" its "legal or commercial position". In practice, it would probably need to provide some convincing proof of this to its counterparty.

Such document will be accurate and completed to the other party's satisfaction and executed and delivered with any appropriate certification on or before any date agreed by the parties or otherwise as soon as reasonably practicable.

This clause is to help avoid withholding tax as opposed to obtaining tax refunds.

Stamp Tax

12.4 Unless otherwise agreed, Borrower hereby undertakes promptly to pay and account for any Stamp Tax chargeable in connection with any transaction effected pursuant to or contemplated by this Agreement (other than any Stamp Tax that would not be chargeable but for Lender's failure to comply with its obligations under this Agreement).

12.5 Borrower shall indemnify and keep indemnified Lender against any liability arising as a result of Borrower's failure to comply with its obligations under paragraph 12.4.

Sales Tax

12.6 All sums payable by one Party to another under this Agreement are exclusive of any Sales Tax chargeable on any supply to which such sums relate and an amount equal to such Sales Tax shall in each case be paid by the Party making such payment on receipt of an appropriate Sales Tax invoice.

Retrospective changes in law

12.7 Unless otherwise agreed, amounts payable by one Party to another under this Agreement shall be determined by reference to Applicable Law as at the date of the relevant payment and no adjustment shall be made to amounts paid under this Agreement as a result of:

(a) any retrospective change in Applicable Law which is announced or enacted after the date of the relevant payment; or

(b) any decision of a court of competent jurisdiction which is made after the date of the relevant payment (other than where such decision results from an action taken with respect to this Agreement or amounts paid or payable under this Agreement).

12.4

Paragraph 12.4 states the Borrower's liability promptly to pay any stamp duty applying to a Loan except where the Lender fails to comply with its obligations under the GMSLA 2010.

12.5

Moreover, in paragraph 12.5, the Borrower indemnifies and agrees to keep the Lender indemnified for any failure by the Borrower to pay stamp duty under paragraph 12.4.

12.6

This provision is new to the GMSLA 2010. All sums payable under the Agreement exclude Value Added Tax (VAT) or sales tax. Where VAT is due on a payment that will be subject to a separate VAT invoice being sent and received.

12.7

This provision is also new to the GMSLA 2010. Existing tax law will apply to all payments under the GMSLA on their due date and no later adjustments will be made to such payments because of:

(a) any retrospective change in such tax law which is announced or comes into force after the date of payment; or

(b) any court decision made after the payment date (unless this relates to legal action taken with respect to the Agreement itself or amounts due or paid under it).

This means that you cannot ask a counterparty for money because you have suffered a retrospective tax law change.

13. **LENDER'S WARRANTIES**

Each Party hereby warrants and undertakes to the other on a continuing basis to the intent that such warranties shall survive the completion of any transaction contemplated herein that, where acting as a Lender:

(a) it is duly authorised and empowered to perform its duties and obligations under this Agreement;

(b) it is not restricted under the terms of its constitution or in any other manner from lending Securities in accordance with this Agreement or from otherwise performing its obligations hereunder;

(c) it is absolutely entitled to pass full legal and beneficial ownership of all Securities provided by it hereunder to Borrower free from all liens, charges and encumbrances; and

(d) it is acting as principal in respect of this Agreement, other than in respect of an Agency Loan.

13. LENDER'S WARRANTIES

In the GMSLA 2010, the Lender offers the Borrower four warranties on a continuous basis:

(a) It is authorised to perform its duties and obligations under the GMSLA 2010.
(b) There are no restrictions upon it lending Securities or performing its obligations under the GMSLA 2010.
(c) It can pass full legal title to all Securities to Borrower without any encumbrances.
(d) It is acting as principal under the GMSLA 2010 unless it declares to the Borrower that it is acting as agent for an underlying principal under an Agency Loan.

14. BORROWER'S WARRANTIES

Each Party hereby warrants and undertakes to the other on a continuing basis to the intent that such warranties shall survive the completion of any transaction contemplated herein that, where acting as a Borrower:

(a) it has all necessary licences and approvals, and is duly authorised and empowered, to perform its duties and obligations under this Agreement and will do nothing prejudicial to the continuation of such authorisation, licences or approvals;

(b) it is not restricted under the terms of its constitution or in any other manner from borrowing Securities in accordance with this Agreement or from otherwise performing its obligations hereunder;

(c) it is absolutely entitled to pass full legal and beneficial ownership of all Collateral provided by it hereunder to Lender free from all liens, charges and encumbrances;

(d) it is acting as principal in respect of this Agreement; and

(e) it is not entering into a Loan for the primary purpose of obtaining or exercising voting rights in respect of the Loaned Securities.

14. BORROWER'S WARRANTIES

The Borrower also offers the Lender five warranties on a continuous basis. They are:

(a) It has obtained all necessary approvals and is duly authorised to perform its duties and obligations under the GMSLA 2010 and will do nothing to prejudice this.

(b) There are no restrictions upon it borrowing Securities or performing its obligations under the GMSLA 2010.

(c) It can pass absolute unencumbered legal title in the Collateral to Lender.

(d) It is acting as principal under the GMSLA 2010. In fact it can never act as agent; and

(e) Its main purpose in entering into a Loan is not to obtain or exercise voting rights over the Loaned Securities. This is an addition to the GMSLA 2010 reflecting regulatory concerns that hedge funds and others were stake building with a view to influencing market prices in takeover situations. It is also consistent with the best practice stated in the UK's Securities Lending and Repo Committee's Code of Guidance.

15. INTEREST ON OUTSTANDING PAYMENTS

In the event of either Party failing to remit sums in accordance with this Agreement such Party hereby undertakes to pay to the other Party upon demand interest (before as well as after judgment) on the net balance due and outstanding, for the period commencing on and inclusive of the original due date for payment to (but excluding) the date of actual payment, in the same currency as the principal sum and at the rate referred to in paragraph 11.7. Interest will accrue daily on a compound basis and will be calculated according to the actual number of days elapsed. No interest shall be payable under this paragraph in respect of any day on which one Party endeavours to make a payment to the other Party but the other Party is unable to receive it.

16. TERMINATION OF THIS AGREEMENT

Each Party shall have the right to terminate this Agreement by giving not less than 15 Business Days' notice in writing to the other Party (which notice shall specify the date of termination) subject to an obligation to ensure that all Loans which have been entered into but not discharged at the time such notice is given are duly discharged in accordance with this Agreement.

15. INTEREST ON OUTSTANDING PAYMENTS

This paragraph provides for interest to be paid on late payments at the default interest rate referred to in paragraph 10 of the Schedule or if that is not agreed at one-month LIBOR on a daily compounded basis from and including the date the payment was due to, but excluding, the date it was actually paid. However, no interest is payable for any day when one party tries to make a payment to the other who cannot receive it, probably due to operational problems.

16. TERMINATION OF THIS AGREEMENT

Each party has the right to terminate the GMSLA 2010 on 15 Business Days' notice in writing. Any such termination will not, however, affect the parties' existing obligations for any outstanding loans of securities. All outstanding Loans must be discharged in line with the GMSLA 2010's terms.

17. **SINGLE AGREEMENT**

Each Party acknowledges that, and has entered into this Agreement and will enter into each Loan in consideration of and in reliance upon the fact that, all Loans constitute a single business and contractual relationship and are made in consideration of each other. Accordingly, each Party agrees:

(a) to perform all of its obligations in respect of each Loan, and that a default in the performance of any such obligations shall constitute a default by it in respect of all Loans, subject always to the other provisions of the Agreement; and

(b) that payments, deliveries and other transfers made by either of them in respect of any Loan shall be deemed to have been made in consideration of payments, deliveries and other transfers in respect of any other Loan.

17. SINGLE AGREEMENT

The single agreement concept is the basis of close-out netting.

This paragraph provides that all loans form part of a single contractual relationship.

The single agreement concept is designed to prevent a liquidator indulging in a practice called "cherry picking" where he is willing to honour his obligations under transactions which are profitable to his insolvent client but refuses to do so on other transactions which are unprofitable to that client, but insisting that the Non-Defaulting Party meets his obligations under such transactions.

Under the single agreement concept, subject to other provisions of the Agreement, all Loans depend upon each other and a default under one of them counts as defaults under all Loans under the GMSLA 2010 through the close-out netting process in paragraph 11. This reduces the values of all Loans to a single net payment due to one party or the other.

The language in paragraph 17 stresses (a) the interdependence of each Loan with all other Loans under the GMSLA 2010 and (b) that payments and deliveries under one Loan are deemed to be made in consideration of payments and deliveries under other Loans thus strengthening the single agreement concept.

18. **SEVERANCE**

If any provision of this Agreement is declared by any judicial or other competent authority to be void or otherwise unenforceable, that provision shall be severed from the Agreement and the remaining provisions of this Agreement shall remain in full force and effect. The Agreement shall, however, thereafter be amended by the Parties in such reasonable manner so as to achieve as far as possible, without illegality, the intention of the Parties with respect to that severed provision.

19. **SPECIFIC PERFORMANCE**

Each Party agrees that in relation to legal proceedings it will not seek specific performance of the other Party's obligation to deliver Securities, Equivalent Securities, Collateral or Equivalent Collateral but without prejudice to any other rights it may have.

20. **NOTICES**

20.1 Any notice or other communication in respect of this Agreement may be given in any manner set forth below to the address or number or in accordance with the electronic messaging system details set out in paragraph 5 of the Schedule and will be deemed effective as indicated:

(a) if in writing and delivered in person or by courier, on the date it is delivered;

(b) if sent by facsimile transmission, on the date that transmission is received by a responsible employee of the recipient in legible form (it being agreed that the burden of proving receipt will be on the sender and will not be met by a transmission report generated by the sender's facsimile machine);

(c) if sent by certified or registered mail (airmail, if overseas) or the equivalent (return receipt requested), on the date that mail is delivered or its delivery is attempted; or

(d) if sent by electronic messaging system, on the date that electronic message is received,

unless the date of that delivery (or attempted delivery) or the receipt, as applicable, is not a Business Day or that communication is delivered (or attempted) or received, as applicable, after the Close of Business on a Business Day, in which case that communication shall be deemed given and effective on the first following day that is a Business Day.

20.2 Either Party may by notice to the other change the address or facsimile number or electronic messaging system details at which notices or other communications are to be given to it.

18. SEVERANCE

This is a relatively standard severability provision which seeks to continue the GMSLA 2010 by severing or amending an illegal or unenforceable provision in it.

19. SPECIFIC PERFORMANCE

Each party agrees in legal proceedings not to seek specific performance of the other party's obligations to deliver or redeliver securities or collateral. This reinforces the close-out netting provisions, i.e. by reducing everything to cash damages.

20. NOTICES

Paragraph 20.1 describes how notices may be delivered and when they take effect. Delivery details are given in paragraph 6 (**not** 5) of the Schedule.

As regards a fax (Paragraph 20.1 (b)) its receipt is only effective on the date a responsible employee receives the fax in legible form. The sender has to prove receipt and a transmission report from a fax machine is not good enough for this purpose. Receipt is normally confirmed on a recorded telephone line where this is required. There is no definition of who is a responsible employee and any doubts about this (e.g. a temporary cleaner receiving a fax late at night when everybody else is out of the office) could affect the timing of receipt of the notice. An electronic message is effective on receipt. If the date of delivery or receipt is not a Business Day, or takes place after close of business on one, then it will only become effective on the next Business Day.

In paragraph 20.2 the parties agree to notify each other about changes in their contact details.

21. ASSIGNMENT

21.1 Subject to paragraph 21.2, neither Party may charge, assign or otherwise deal with all or any of its rights or obligations hereunder without the prior consent of the other Party.

21.2 Paragraph 21.1 shall not preclude a party from charging, assigning or otherwise dealing with all or any part of its interest in any sum payable to it under paragraph 11.2(b) or 11.7.

22. NON-WAIVER

No failure or delay by either Party (whether by course of conduct or otherwise) to exercise any right, power or privilege hereunder shall operate as a waiver thereof nor shall any single or partial exercise of any right, power or privilege preclude any other or further exercise thereof or the exercise of any other right, power or privilege as herein provided.

23. GOVERNING LAW AND JURISDICTION

23.1 This Agreement and any non-contractual obligations arising out of or in connection with this Agreement shall be governed by, and shall be construed in accordance with, English law.

23.2 The courts of England have exclusive jurisdiction to hear and decide any suit, action or proceedings, and to settle any disputes or any non-contractual obligation which may arise out of or in connection with this Agreement (respectively, *Proceedings* and *Disputes*) and, for these purposes, each Party irrevocably submits to the jurisdiction of the courts of England.

23.3 Each Party irrevocably waives any objection which it might at any time have to the courts of England being nominated as the forum to hear and decide any Proceedings and to settle any Disputes and agrees not to claim that the courts of England are not a convenient or appropriate forum.

23.4 Each Party hereby respectively appoints the person identified in paragraph 7 of the Schedule pertaining to the relevant Party as its agent to receive on its behalf service of process in the courts of England. If such an agent ceases to be an agent of a Party, the relevant Party shall promptly appoint, and notify the other Party of the identity of its new agent in England.

21. ASSIGNMENT

21.1

Subject to paragraph 21.2, neither party may assign, charge or transfer any of its rights under the GMSLA 2010 without the other party's prior consent.

21.2

However, paragraph 21.2 permits this for any close-out amount due to it under paragraph 11.2(b) or any default interest, costs or expenses due to it under paragraph 11.7.

22. NON-WAIVER

This is a relatively standard no waiver clause which is found in many types of legal agreement. No failure or delay by a party in exercising any of its rights under the GMSLA 2010 shall constitute a waiver of such rights. Limited exercise of such rights shall not preclude any later or further exercise of them.

23. GOVERNING LAW AND JURISDICTION

23.1

The GMSLA 2010 and any non-contractual obligations arising from it shall be governed by English law.

23.2

The parties irrevocably submit to the exclusive jurisdiction of the English courts.

23.3

This is re-emphasised here in paragraph 23.3 where the parties agree not to object to the exclusive jurisdiction of the English courts to conduct proceedings and settle disputes. They also agree not to claim that the English courts are an inconvenient forum.

23.4

Process Agents, where relevant, are stated in paragraph 7 of the Schedule for the parties if they are not English incorporated. They are a necessary part of the legal formalities for commencing legal proceedings and enforcing foreign judgments in the English courts. Replacement of Process Agents will be done quickly and notified to the other party.

24. **TIME**

Time shall be of the essence of the Agreement.

25. **RECORDING**

The Parties agree that each may record all telephone conversations between them.

24. TIME

Obligations must be performed promptly under the GMSLA 2010.

25. RECORDING

The parties agree that all telephone conversations between them may be recorded. This is favoured by regulators particularly in the UK where such recording is recommended in the Financial Service Authority's *Conduct of Business Sourcebook (2007)*.

26. **WAIVER OF IMMUNITY**

Each Party hereby waives all immunity (whether on the basis of sovereignty or otherwise) from jurisdiction, attachment (both before and after judgement) and execution to which it might otherwise be entitled in any action or proceeding in the courts of England or of any other country or jurisdiction relating in any way to this Agreement and agrees that it will not raise, claim or cause to be pleaded any such immunity at or in respect of any such action or proceeding.

26. WAIVER OF IMMUNITY

This is a relatively standard waiver of sovereign or other legal immunity which a party may have in respect of the GMSLA 2010 or similar agreements. Supranationals (e.g. the European Bank for Reconstruction and Development) are often established by charters giving them numerous legal and tax immunities. They will not waive these but everyone else is expected to do so.

27. MISCELLANEOUS

27.1 This Agreement constitutes the entire agreement and understanding of the Parties with respect to its subject matter and supersedes all oral communication and prior writings with respect thereto.

27.2 The Party (the ***Relevant Party***) who has prepared the text of this Agreement for execution (as indicated in paragraph 9 of the Schedule) warrants and undertakes to the other Party that such text conforms exactly to the text of the standard form Global Master Securities Lending Agreement (2009 version) posted by the International Securities Lending Association on its website except as notified by the Relevant Party to the other Party in writing prior to the execution of this Agreement.

27.3 Unless otherwise provided for in this Agreement, no amendment in respect of this Agreement will be effective unless in writing (including a writing evidenced by a facsimile transmission) and executed by each of the Parties or confirmed by an exchange of telexes or electronic messages on an electronic messaging system.

27.4 The Parties agree that where paragraph 11 of the Schedule indicates that this paragraph 27.4 applies, this Agreement shall apply to all loans which are outstanding as at the date of this Agreement and which are subject to the securities lending agreement or agreements specified in paragraph 11 of the Schedule, and such Loans shall be treated as if they had been entered into under this Agreement, and the terms of such loans are amended accordingly with effect from the date of this Agreement.

27. MISCELLANEOUS

27.1

The GMSLA 2010 constitutes the entire contractual agreement between the parties and supersedes all previous oral and written communications between them.

27.2

This is a warranty and undertaking from the party that has prepared the GMSLA 2010 for execution that it conforms to the standard form GMSLA 2010 text unless it states otherwise and this has been communicated to the other party in writing before it is executed. Please note that the reference to the GMSLA 2009 is incorrect.

27.3

Amendments to the GMSLA 2010 are only effective if in writing (including faxes) and executed by both parties. Alternatively they can be confirmed by telex or via an electronic messaging system. General market practice is for amendments to the GMSLA 2000 or 2010 to be signed by authorised signatories of both contracting parties.

27.4

Paragraph 27.4 is new to the GMSLA 2010 and is optional. It is a kind of Scope of Agreement clause which sweeps Loans documented under other securities lending agreements into the GMSLA 2010 and such loans then become subject to the GMSLA 2010 and its terms. The original master agreements under which these loans were documented are stated in paragraph 11 of the Schedule if it applies.

27.5 The Parties agree that where paragraph 12 of the Schedule indicates that this paragraph 27.5 applies, each may use the services of a third party vendor to automate the processing of Loans under this Agreement and that any data relating to such Loans received from the other Party may be disclosed to such third party vendors.

27.6 The obligations of the Parties under this Agreement will survive the termination of any Loan.

27.7 The warranties contained in paragraphs 13, 14 and 27.2 and in the Agency Annex will survive termination of this Agreement for so long as any obligations of either of the Parties pursuant to this Agreement remain outstanding.

27.8 Except as provided in this Agreement, the rights, powers, remedies and privileges provided in this Agreement are cumulative and not exclusive of any rights, powers, remedies and privileges provided by law.

27.9 This Agreement (and each amendment in respect of it) may be executed and delivered in counterparts (including by facsimile transmission), each of which will be deemed an original.

27.10 A person who is not a party to this Agreement has no right under the Contracts (Rights of Third Parties) Act 1999 to enforce any terms of this Agreement, but this does not affect any right or remedy of a third party which exists or is available apart from that Act.

27.5

Paragraph 27.5 is also new to the GMSLA 2010. You select in paragraph 12 of the Schedule if it is to apply and it is optional. It relates to the automation of loan processing by third party vendors. If it applies, both parties consent to this and to the disclosure of any data or information about such loans to these third party service providers.

27.6

The parties' obligations under the GMSLA 2010 survive the maturity of any individual Loan under it.

27.7

In addition, Lender's warranties in paragraph 13, Borrower's warranties in paragraph 14, the GMSLA 2010 text conformity warranty in paragraph 27.2 and the warranties in the Agency Annex will survive the termination of the GMSLA 2010 for so long as any of the parties' obligations under it remain outstanding.

27.8

In paragraph 10.3 the GMSLA 2010 is stated as constituting a complete statement of remedies available to the parties. Notwithstanding this, parties may have recourse to general contract law if they wish.

27.9

The GMSLA 2010 and any amendments may be executed in counterparts (including by fax) and each counterpart will be considered an original.

27.10

Paragraph 27.10 is a provision excluding third party rights in order to preserve privity of contract. The Contracts (Rights of Third Parties) Act 1999 reformed this area of English law. Before the Act came into force a person could only enforce a contract if they were party to it. This law permits third parties to enforce contracts that benefit them and which were entered into on or after 11 May 2000 as long as they are identified in the contract by name, as a class or by a particular description. There are certain exceptions set out in the Act and it is possible to exclude the effect of the Act altogether to ensure that privity of contract will apply as has been done here. However, this does not affect any right or remedy such a party has outside the Act.

EXECUTED by the **PARTIES**

SIGNED by)
)
duly authorised for and)
on behalf of)

SIGNED by)
)
duly authorised for and)
on behalf of)

Signing block

The GMSLA 2010 is signed by authorised signatories of the contracting parties. It is either dated the date the first party signs it or more commonly the date that the second party signs it.

In the European market the convention is to sign the Agreement before any trading is done under it.

SCHEDULE

1. **COLLATERAL**

    1.1 The securities, financial instruments and deposits of currency set out in the table below with a cross marked next to them are acceptable forms of Collateral under this Agreement.

    1.2 Unless otherwise agreed between the Parties, the Market Value of the Collateral delivered pursuant to paragraph 5 by Borrower to Lender under the terms and conditions of this Agreement shall on each Business Day represent not less than the Market Value of the Loaned Securities together with the percentage contained in the row of the table below corresponding to the particular form of Collateral, referred to in this Agreement as the *Margin*.

Security/Financial Instrument/ Deposit of Currency	Mark "X" if acceptable form of Collateral	Margin (%)

Schedule

Various matters referred to in the main text of the GMSLA 2010 are tackled in the Schedule.

1.1 and 1.2

The types of margin or collateral acceptable to both parties are stated in the table in paragraph 1.2 together with the margin percentage applying to them. Alternatively one margin percentage, usually 5%, is applied across the board even when this looks strange as with cash. The Margin is essentially the haircut or discount on the value of the collateral supplied although sometimes it is expressed as a total percentage of the collateral value (e.g. 105%): practice varies. Where G10 government bonds were taken as collateral in normal times, the overcollateralisation could have been 102% or 105% (depending upon whether the collateral was in the same currency as the collateral or not) while with equity collateral it was usually 110%. Now it is more like 120%. Practice varied in other ways too. Where there was likely to be significant trading between parties, they might have agreed a lower margin percentage (e.g. 102%). Indeed, on many occasions, they agreed different margin percentages whatever was stated in paragraph 1.2 of the Schedule. Since the collapse of Lehman Brothers many institutions have increased their margin levels on collateral so this needs to be more carefully considered than it perhaps was in the past.

1.3 Basis of Margin Maintenance:

Paragraph 5.4 (aggregation) shall not apply* ☐

Paragraph 5.4 (aggregation) applies unless the box is ticked.

1.4 Paragraph 5.6 (netting of obligations to deliver
Collateral and redeliver Equivalent Collateral) shall not apply* ☐

Paragraph 5.6 (netting) applies unless the box is ticked

---

* Delete as appropriate.
* Delete as appropriate.

1.3

This is where you choose whether global margining (paragraph 5.4) or individual loan margining (paragraph 5.5) is to apply. Most people choose global margining and often they will make a positive statement to this effect which I consider to be better practice than just leaving the box unticked.

1.4

This concerns the netting of collateral movements under paragraph 5.6 if global margining applies. It would normally apply in these circumstances. Once again better practice, in my view, is to make a positive statement rather than leaving the box unticked.

1.5 For the purposes of Paragraph 5.8, Notification Time means by ☐ , London time.

1.6 Paragraph 6.4 (indemnity for failure to redeliver
Equivalent Non-Cash Collateral) shall not apply* ☐

Paragraph 6.4 (indemnity for failure to redeliver Equivalent Non-Cash Collateral) applies unless the box is ticked.

---

* Delete as appropriate.

1.5

Paragraph 1.5 is new to the GMSLA 2010 Schedule. The Notification Time is the deadline for calling for collateral if that collateral is to be delivered by the close of business on that same Business Day. If the deadline is missed, the collateral will not be due for delivery until the following Business Day.

1.6

Paragraph 1.6 is also new to the GMSLA 2010 Schedule and is optional. It is an indemnity given by the Lender to the Borrower where the Lender fails to return Non-Cash Collateral when agreed with the Borrower before an Income Record Date. This may be because the Borrower fears he may be hit by a withholding tax on the manufactured dividend the Lender will need to pay to him. Once again, I consider it better practice to make a positive statement about this rather than leaving the box unticked.

2. **BASE CURRENCY**

The Base Currency applicable to this Agreement is   provided that if that currency ceases to be freely convertible the Base Currency shall be [US Dollars] [Euro] [specify other currency]*

2. Base Currency

The agreed Base Currency for margining and close-out purposes is stated here. Where it ceases to be convertible, there is the opportunity to name a major fallback currency here.

3. **PLACES OF BUSINESS**

   (See definition of Business Day.)

4. **MARKET VALUE**

   (See definition of Market Value.)

3. Places of Business

The locations through which the parties plan to trade will be stated here, for example London and Paris or just London if they both plan to trade through their London Designated Offices. The definition of Business Day in the GMSLA 2010 will apply to these locations, i.e. whether banks and securities markets are open in them on the Business Day concerned. They must be open in both places of business stated in order for the GMSLA 2010 to work properly. Under the GMSLA 2000 it is normal to have only one Designated Office each. However, under the GMSLA 2010 multiple Designated Offices are possible. This is to reflect that big Lenders can operate out of several offices and custodians could deal in London but collateralise in New York.

4. Market Value

This is new to the GMSLA 2010 Schedule and allows for any agreed redefinition of the time at which a price or value is to be taken for the purpose of Market Value. If no time is stated the fallback is close of business on the previous Business Day.

5. **EVENTS OF DEFAULT**

   Automatic Early Termination shall apply in respect of Party A ☐

   Automatic Early Termination shall apply in respect of Party B ☐

5. Events of Default

This is also new to the GMSLA 2010 Schedule. In Paragraph 10.1(d) no default notice is needed where an Act of Insolvency has occurred and resulted in a winding-up petition being presented or a liquidator appointed because termination is automatic. You can choose whether you want that to apply here. In most cases parties will choose this for these circumstances.

In the world of ISDA the focus of Automatic Early Termination is on where a particular counterparty is incorporated which will determine if Automatic Early Termination will apply to them. This is because in some countries bankruptcy laws can override contractual close-out netting provisions and therefore it is better to terminate automatically rather than by notice in bankruptcy situations. However, that does not appear to be the focus under the GMSLA 2010, although parties may make a decision to apply Automatic Early Termination based on a netting opinion they have obtained.

6. **DESIGNATED OFFICE AND ADDRESS FOR NOTICES**

(a) **Designated office of Party A**:

Address for notices or communications to Party A:

Address:

Attention:

Facsimile No:

Telephone No:

Electronic Messaging System Details:

(b) **Designated office of Party B**:

Address for notices or communications to Party B:

Address:

Attention:

Facsimile No:

Telephone No:

Electronic Messaging System Details:

7. (a) **Agent of Party A for Service of Process**

Name:

Address:

(b) **Agent of Party B for Service of Process**

Name:

Address:

6 Designated Office and Addresses for Notice

Notice details for Designated Offices are stated here.

7

If one or both parties are not English incorporated, details of their Process Agents are stated here.

8. **AGENCY**

– Party A [may][will always]* act as agent ☐

– Party B [may][will always]* act as agent ☐

– The Addendum for Pooled Principal Transactions
may apply to Party A ☐

– The Addendum for Pooled Principal Transactions
may apply to Party B ☐

9. **PARTY PREPARING THIS AGREEMENT**

Party A ☐

Party B ☐

8 Agency

If a party plans to act as an agent lender, it must tick the appropriate box and the Agency Annex will apply to it. If it will always act as Agent this will mean that it will not need to identify a Loan as an Agency Loan (see paragraph 1.1 of the Agency Annex). If there are to be multiple disclosed principals for an Agency Loan, the party/parties entering into such loans will need to tick the appropriate box because the Addendum to Pooled Principal Transactions covers such loans.

9 Party Preparing this Agreement

For the purposes of paragraph 27.2 of the GMSLA 2010, the party preparing the Agreement must identify itself by ticking the appropriate box.

10. **DEFAULT INTEREST**

   Rate of default interest:

11. **EXISTING LOANS**

   Paragraph 27.4 applies* ☐

   [Overseas Securities Lenders Agreement dated   ]*

   [Global Master Securities Lending Agreements dated   ]*

12. **AUTOMATION**

   Paragraph 27.5 applies* ☐

---

* Delete as appropriate.

Paragraphs 10–12 are new to the GMSLA 2010 Schedule.

10. Default Interest

There is the opportunity to state a level of default interest here for late payments after close-out referred to in paragraph 11.7 of the Agreement. Some care is needed because an English court can throw out any default interest level which it deems to be a penalty.

11. Existing Loans

This is an optional Scope of Agreement clause sweeping securities loans under other master agreements into the GMSLA 2010.

12. Automation

This is an optional provision agreeing to third party loan processing and the provision of loan data to such service providers.

In contrast to the ISDA Master Agreement and the GMRA 2000, many Schedules to the GMSLA 2000, or eventually the GMSLA 2010, may only show completion of the items shown in its template.

AGENCY ANNEX

1. **TRANSACTIONS ENTERED INTO AS AGENT**

1.1 **Power for Lender to enter into Loans as agent**

Subject to the following provisions of this paragraph, Lender may enter into Loans as agent (in such capacity, the *Agent*) for a third person (a *Principal*), whether as custodian or investment manager or otherwise (a Loan so entered into being referred to in this paragraph as an *Agency Loan*).

If the Lender has indicated in paragraph 8 of the Schedule that it may act as Agent, it must identify each Loan in respect of which it acts as Agent as an Agency Loan at the time it is entered into. If the Lender has indicated in paragraph 8 of the Schedule that it will always act as Agent, it need not identify each Loan as an Agency Loan.

1.2 **[Pooled Principal transactions**

The Lender may enter into an Agency Loan on behalf of more than [one] Principal and accordingly the addendum hereto for pooled principal transactions shall apply.][*]

---

[*] Delete as appropriate.

AGENCY ANNEX

The Agency Annex and Addendum for Pooled Transactions are closely modelled on the same documents used for the GMRA 2000 subject to changes in terminology.

The Agency Annex's opening paragraph reflects paragraph 16.1. of the GMSLA 2000.

1.1

A party may act as agent for a single disclosed principal in a Transaction when it is acting as Lender. It may be acting as custodian or investment manager for such underlying principal. Under the GMSLA 2010 such a transaction is technically called an Agency Loan. Only the Lender may act as agent in a securities lending transaction.

Where the Lender has stated in paragraph 8 of the Schedule that it may act as Agent, it must specify each Agency Loan as such when it enters into it. If it indicates in Schedule paragraph 8 that it will always act as Agent it does not need to do this.

1.2

Where the Lender wants to enter into an Agency Loan on behalf of a number of underlying principals then the Addendum will be used.

1.3 Conditions for Agency Loan

A Lender may enter into an Agency Loan if, but only if:

(a) it provides to Borrower, prior to effecting any Agency Loan, such information in its possession necessary to complete all required fields in the format generally used in the industry, or as otherwise agreed by Agent and Borrower (***Agreed Format***), and will use its best efforts to provide to Borrower any optional information that may be requested by the Borrower for the purpose of identifying such Principal (all such information being the ***Principal Information***). Agent represents and warrants that the Principal Information is true and accurate to the best of its knowledge and has been provided to it by Principal;

(b) it enters into that Loan on behalf of a single Principal whose identity is disclosed to Borrower (whether by name or by reference to a code or identifier which the Parties have agreed will be used to refer to a specified Principal) either at the time when it enters into the Loan or before the Close of Business on the next Business Day after the date on which Loaned Securities are transferred to the Borrower in the Agreed Format or as otherwise agreed between the Parties; and

(c) it has at the time when the Loan is entered into actual authority to enter into the Loan and to perform on behalf of that Principal all of that Principal's obligations under the agreement referred to in paragraph 1.5(b) below.

Agent agrees that it will not effect any Loan with Borrower on behalf of any Principal unless Borrower has notified Agent of Borrower's approval of such Principal, and has not notified Agent that it has withdrawn such approval (such Principal, an ***Approved Principal***), with both such notifications in the Agreed Format.

Borrower acknowledges that Agent shall not have any obligation to provide it with confidential information regarding the financial status of its Principals; Agent agrees, however, that it will assist Borrower in obtaining from Agent's Principals such information regarding the financial status of such Principals as Borrower may reasonably request.

1.3 Conditions for Agency Loan

The Lender may enter into an Agency Loan only if:

(a) It provides to the Borrower beforehand information it possesses to complete files for agent lender disclosure in Europe as agreed in the securities lending industry. These files concern outstanding loans, allocation of collateral and credit approval of underlying principals. The Lender also agrees to provide any optional information needed by the Borrower to identify the Principal. The Agent represents and warrants that such information is to its knowledge true and accurate and has been supplied by the Principal.

(b) It is entering into an Agency Loan for a single principal disclosed to the Borrower by name or by an agreed code or identifier the parties have agreed for that Principal either at the time it enters the Loan or before the close of business on the next Business Day on which Loaned Securities are transferred to the Borrower. The Agreed Format refers to the European Agent Lender Disclosure process which involves information transmission via DTCC (see page 42).

(c) When entering the loan the Lender has actual authority from the Principal to do so.

The Agent agrees that it will not enter into any Agency Loan with the Borrower unless the Borrower has approved the Principal and not withdrawn that approval using the industry agreed transmission files. In practice the Lender will send the Borrower a list of principals and will request approval by the following Business Day.

The Borrower agrees that the Lender has no obligation to provide it with any confidential financial information on a principal but the Lender will try to assist the Borrower in obtaining reasonable financial information from such a principal.

1.4 **Notification by Agent of certain events affecting any Principal**

Agent undertakes that, if it enters as agent into an Agency Loan, forthwith upon becoming aware:

(a) of any event which constitutes an Act of Insolvency with respect to the relevant Principal; or

(b) of any breach of any of the warranties given in paragraph 1.6 below or of any event or circumstance which results in any such warranty being untrue if repeated by reference to the then current facts,

it will inform Borrower of that fact and will, if so required by Borrower, furnish it with such additional information as it may reasonably request to the extent that such information is readily obtainable by Agent.

1.4

The Agent undertakes to advise the Borrower immediately if:

(a) it becomes aware of an Act of Insolvency afflicting the principal; or

(b) it breaches its warranty of authority to act on behalf of the principal.

In such case it informs the Borrower of this and, if requested by the Borrower, provides it with readily available additional information.

1.5 **Status of Agency Loan**

(a) Each Agency Loan shall be a transaction between the relevant Principal and Borrower and no person other than the relevant Principal and Borrower shall be a party to or have any rights or obligations under an Agency Loan. Without limiting the foregoing, Agent shall not be liable as principal for the performance of an Agency Loan, but this is without prejudice to any liability of Agent under any other provision of this Annex; and

(b) all the provisions of the Agreement shall apply separately as between Borrower and each Principal for whom the Agent has entered into an Agency Loan or Agency Loans as if each such Principal were a party to a separate agreement with Borrower in all respects identical with this Agreement other than this Annex and as if the Principal were Lender in respect of that agreement; provided that

(i) if there occurs in relation to the Agent an Event of Default or an event which would constitute an Event of Default if Borrower served written notice under any sub-clause of paragraph 10 of the Agreement, Borrower shall be entitled by giving written notice to the Principal (which notice shall be validly given if given in accordance with paragraph 20 of the Agreement) to declare that by reason of that event an Event of Default is to be treated as occurring in relation to the Principal. If Borrower gives such a notice then an Event of Default shall be treated as occurring in relation to the Principal at the time when the notice is deemed to be given; and

(ii) if the Principal is neither incorporated in nor has established a place of business in Great Britain, the Principal shall for the purposes of the agreement referred to in paragraph 1.5(b) above be deemed to have appointed as its agent to receive on its behalf service of process in the courts of England the Agent, or if the Agent is neither incorporated nor has established a place of business in Great Britain, the person appointed by the Agent for the purposes of this Agreement, or such other person as the Principal may from time to time specify in a written notice given to the other Party.

If Lender has indicated in paragraph 6 of the Schedule that it may enter into Loans as agent, the foregoing provisions of this paragraph do not affect the operation of the Agreement as between Borrower and Lender in respect of any Loans into which Lender may enter on its own account as principal.

1.6 **Warranty of authority by Lender acting as Agent**

Agent warrants to Borrower that it will, on every occasion on which it enters or purports to enter into a Loan as an Agency Loan, have been duly authorised to enter into that Loan and perform the obligations arising under such Loan on behalf of the Principal in respect of that Loan and to perform on behalf of the Principal all the obligations of that person under the agreement referred to in paragraph 1.5(b) above.

1.5

(a) Each Agency Loan is a private transaction between the Borrower and the underlying principal and no third party shall intervene. When acting as Agent, the Lender is not liable for loan performance but this is without prejudice to any other liability the Agent may have under this Annex.

(b) All GMSLA provisions will apply separately between the Borrower and each underlying principal as if each such principal had entered into a separate identical GMSLA with the Borrower (except for this Annex) and as if such a principal was the Lender under such GMSLA, provided that:

  (i) if an Event of Default happens to the Agent, the Borrower shall be entitled to serve a written default notice on the underlying principal and such Event of Default shall be treated as applying to the principal at the time the notice was deemed to be given; and

  (ii) if the principal is not incorporated or established in business in Great Britain, the Agent will be appointed as its Process Agent, failing which the Lender's own Process Agent will fulfil this role or such other person as the principal may notify to the Borrower.

Agency Loans do not affect any Loans that Lender and Borrower have entered into on a principal to principal basis.

1.6

This is the Agent's continuing warranty of authority to act on behalf of a principal which he gives to the Borrower each time he enters an Agency Loan.

ADDENDUM FOR POOLED PRINCIPAL AGENCY LOANS

1. SCOPE

This addendum applies where the Agent wishes to enter into an Agency Loan on behalf of more than one Principal. The Agency Annex shall apply to such a Loan subject to the modifications and additional terms and conditions contained in paragraph 2 to 7 below.

2. INTERPRETATION

2.1 In this addendum:

(a) *Collateral Transfer* has the meaning given in paragraph 5.1 below;

(b) if at any time on any Business Day the aggregate Market Value of Posted Collateral in respect of all Agency Loans outstanding with a Principal under the Agreement exceeds the aggregate of the Required Collateral Value in respect of such Agency Loans, Borrower has a *Net Loan Exposure* to that Principal equal to that excess; if at any time on any Business Day the aggregate Market Value of Posted Collateral in respect of all Agency Loans outstanding under the Agreement with a Principal falls below the aggregate of the Required Collateral Value in respect of such Agency Loans, that Principal has a *Net Loan Exposure* to Borrower for such Agency Loans equal to that deficiency;

(c) *Pooled Principal* has the meaning given in paragraph 6(a) below; and

(d) *Pooled Loan* has the meaning given in paragraph 6(a) below.

ADDENDUM FOR POOLED PRINCIPAL AGENCY LOANS

1. SCOPE

As mentioned before, the Agency Annex is used where a party is acting on behalf of a single disclosed Principal. The Addendum for Pooled Principal Agency Loans is used where it is proposed to enter into an Agency Loan with multiple disclosed Principals. Paragraph 1 also states that paragraphs 2–7 modify the terms of the Agency Annex in various ways.

2. INTERPRETATION

2.1

Various defined terms are briefly referenced. In 2.1(b) the margin call rules of paragraphs 5.4(b) and (c) and 5.5(b) and (c) are recited again but this time in relation to the risk exposure a Borrower has on a principal or a principal has on a Borrower in Agency Loans. In a pooled arrangement, collateral is allocated pro rata across Pooled Principals as we shall see.

3. MODIFICATIONS TO THE AGENCY ANNEX

3.1 Paragraph 1.3(b) of the Agency Annex is deleted and replaced by the following:

"it enters into that Loan on behalf of one or more Principals and at or before the time when it enters into the Loan it discloses to Borrower the identity and the jurisdiction of incorporation, organisation or establishment of each such Principal (and such disclosure may be made either directly or by reference to a code or identifier which the Parties have agreed will be used to refer to a specified Principal);".

3.2 Paragraph 1.3(c) of the Agency Annex is deleted and replaced by the following:

"it has at the time when the Loan is entered into actual authority to enter into the Loan on behalf of each Principal and to perform on behalf of each Principal all of that Principal's obligations under the Agreement".

3. MODIFICATION TO THE AGENCY ANNEX

Paragraph 3 contains a couple of amendments to the Agency Annex text:

- In 3.1, paragraph 1.3(b) is amended to cater for the disclosure of the identities of multiple principals as opposed to just a single principal under the Agency Annex.
- In 3.2, the Agent's authority to act as warranty is extended from a single principal to each principal.

4. ALLOCATION OF AGENCY LOANS

4.1 The Agent undertakes that if, at the time of entering into an Agency Loan, the Agent has not allocated the Loan to a Principal, it will allocate the Loan before the Settlement Date for that Agency Loan either to a single Principal or to several Principals, each of whom shall be responsible for only that part of the Agency Loan which has been allocated to it. Promptly following such allocation, the Agent shall notify Borrower of the Principal or Principals (whether by name or reference to a code or identifier which the Parties have agreed will be used to refer to a specified Principal) to which that Loan or part of that Loan has been allocated.

4.2 Upon allocation of a Loan in accordance with paragraph 4.1 above or otherwise, with effect from the date on which the Loan was entered into:

(a) where the allocation is to a single Principal, the Loan shall be deemed to have been entered into between Borrower and that Principal; and

(b) where the allocation is to two or more Principals, a separate Loan shall be deemed to have been entered into between Borrower and each such Principal with respect to the appropriate proportion of the Loan.

4.3 If the Agent shall fail to perform its obligations under paragraph 4.2 above then for the purposes of assessing any damage suffered by Borrower (but for no other purpose) it shall be assumed that, if the Loan concerned (to the extent not allocated) had been allocated in accordance with that paragraph, all the terms of the Loan would have been duly performed.

4. ALLOCATION OF AGENCY LOANS

4.1

The Agent undertakes to allocate the Agency Loan to a single principal or several principals before its Settlement Date if it has not already done so when it first entered into the Agency Loan. Each principal is only responsible for that part of an Agency Loan which has been allocated to it.

Promptly after allocation, the Lender must notify the Borrower of the identity of the principals and the amount of the Agency Loan allocated to them.

The Agent must allocate the Agency Loan among the various principals *before* the Settlement Date and when allocated the Borrower shall be deemed to have a contract with each principal. This is to avoid legal uncertainty about the status of the Agency Loan if it is not allocated before the Settlement Date and the relevant principal becomes insolvent. Until the allocation is done, your risk is on the Agent.

4.2

(a) Where the allocation is to a single principal, the Loan is deemed to have been entered into by the Borrower and that principal with effect from the date the Loan was entered into; and

(b) Where multiple principals are involved, a separate Loan shall be deemed to have been entered into between the Borrower and each principal up to the amount allocated to that principal.

4.3

If the Agent fails to make an allocation, the Borrower's damages shall be limited to any direct losses caused by such non-allocation.

5. ALLOCATION OF COLLATERAL

5.1 Unless the Agent expressly allocates (a) a deposit or delivery of Posted Collateral or (b) a repayment of Cash Collateral or a redelivery of Equivalent Collateral (each a *Collateral Transfer*) before such time, the Agent shall, at the time of making or receiving that Collateral Transfer, be deemed to have allocated any Collateral Transfer in accordance with paragraph 6.3 below.

5.2 (a) If the Agent has made a Collateral Transfer on behalf of more than one Pooled Principal, that Collateral Transfer shall be allocated in proportion to Borrower's Net Loan Exposure in respect of each Pooled Principal at the Agent's close of business on the Business Day before the Collateral Transfer is made; and

(b) if the Agent has received a Collateral Transfer on behalf of more than one Pooled Principal, that Collateral Transfer shall be allocated in proportion to each Pooled Principal's Net Loan Exposure in respect of Borrower at the Agent's close of business on the Business Day before the Collateral Transfer is made.

(c) Sub-paragraphs (a) and (b) shall not apply in respect of any Collateral Transfer which is effected or deemed to have been effected under paragraph 6.3 below.

5. ALLOCATION OF COLLATERAL

5.1

Collateral transfers shall be deemed to be made at the close of business on each Business Day in accordance with paragraph 6.3 unless the Agent makes a specific allocation beforehand.

5.2

(a) If the Agent has made a collateral transfer on behalf of more than one Pooled Principal, it shall be allocated to the Borrower pro rata to the Borrower's net risk exposure on each principal at the Agent's close of business on the Business Day before the collateral transfer is made.

(b) Conversely if the Agent has received a collateral transfer for the Pooled Principals, it is deemed to allocate it pro rata to them according to their individual net risk exposure on the Borrower and this will be done at the Agent's close of business on the Business Day before the collateral transfer is made.

(c) Neither of the above sub-paragraphs will apply if collateral transfers are dealt with under paragraph 6.3.

6. POOLED PRINCIPALS: REBALANCING OF MARGIN

6.1 Where the Agent acts on behalf of more than one Principal, the Parties may agree that, as regards all (but not some only) outstanding Agency Loans with those Principals, or with such of those Principals as they may agree (*Pooled Principals*, such Agency Loans being *Pooled Loans*), any Collateral Transfers are to be made on an aggregate net basis.

6.2 Paragraphs 6.3 to 6.5 below shall have effect for the purpose of ensuring that Posted Collateral is, so far as is practicable, transferred and held uniformly, as between the respective Pooled Principals, in respect of all Pooled Loans for the time being outstanding under the Agreement.

6. POOLED PRINCIPALS: REBALANCING OF MARGIN

It is common for fund managers and agency lenders to operate the collateral provisions on a pooled basis for all underlying principals rather than on an individual principal basis.

By way of introduction to paragraph 6 let me abbreviate the collateral pooling process outlined as follows.

Collateral transfers are allocated pro rata between each Pooled Principal at the end of each Business Day according to the proportion this represents of the aggregate Net Exposure outstanding. Therefore margin calls would be on a net aggregate basis. This involves an automatic rebalancing of margin between the Principals and, as mentioned above, is common practice in the fund management industry. Therefore the positions of all Principals are taken into account in aggregate rather than on an individual Principal basis. In addition, rather than making individual margin transfers from one Principal to another or from a Principal to the other party, Agents rebalance or reallocate margin already held by book entries rather than making actual payments or deliveries.

The purpose of the pooling provisions is to ensure that margin is held uniformly for all underlying principals. Paragraph 6 provides the legal basis for margining in this way.

The detailed process is as follows:

6.1

By agreement between the parties, netting of collateral transfers among all Agency Loans to designated principals can be done.

6.2

As far as practicable, collateral is to be transferred and held in the same manner (e.g. by a custodian) for all Pooled Loans for each Pooled Principal.

6.3 At or as soon as practicable after the Agent's close of business on each Business Day on which Pooled Loans are outstanding (or at such other times as the Parties may from time to time agree) there shall be effected such Collateral Transfers as shall ensure that immediately thereafter:

(a) in respect of all Pooled Principals which have a Net Loan Exposure to Borrower, the amount of Collateral then deliverable or Cash Collateral then payable by Borrower to each such Pooled Principal is equal to such proportion of the aggregate amount of Collateral then deliverable or Cash Collateral then payable, to all such Pooled Principals as corresponds to the proportion which the Net Loan Exposure of the relevant Pooled Principal bears to the aggregate of the Net Loan Exposures of all Pooled Principals to Borrower; and

(b) in respect of all Pooled Principals to which Borrower has a Net Loan Exposure, the aggregate amount of Equivalent Collateral then deliverable or repayable by each such Pooled Principal to Borrower is equal to such proportion of the aggregate amount of Equivalent Collateral then deliverable or repayable by all such Pooled Principals as corresponds to the proportion which the Net Loan Exposure of Borrower to the relevant Pooled Principal bears to the aggregate of the Net Loan Exposures of Borrower to all Pooled Principals.

6.3

Collateral transfers shall be made at the Agent's close of business on each Business Day so that immediately afterwards:

(a) the net risk exposure each Pooled Principal has on the Borrower shall be collateralised pro rata to the total risk exposure all Pooled Principals have on the Borrower under all Pooled Loans; and

(b) the net risk exposure that the Borrower has on each Pooled Principal shall be collateralised pro rata to the total risk exposure the Borrower has on all Pooled Principals under all Pooled Loans.

6.4 Collateral Transfers effected under paragraph 6.3 shall be effected (and if not so effected shall be deemed to have been so effected) by appropriations made by the Agent and shall be reflected by entries in accounting and other records maintained by the Agent. Accordingly, it shall not be necessary for payments of cash or deliveries of Securities to be made through any settlement system for the purpose of such Collateral Transfers. Without limiting the generality of the foregoing, the Agent is hereby authorised and instructed by Borrower to do all such things on behalf of Borrower as may be necessary or expedient to effect and record the receipt on behalf of Borrower of cash and Securities from, and the delivery on behalf of Borrower of cash and Securities to, Pooled Principals in the course or for the purposes of any Collateral Transfer effected under that paragraph.

6.5 Promptly following the Collateral Transfers effected under paragraph 6.3 above, and as at the Agent's close of business on any Business Day, the Agent shall prepare a statement showing in respect of each Pooled Principal the amount of cash Collateral which has been paid, and the amount of non-cash Collateral of each description which have been transferred, by or to that Pooled Principal immediately after those Collateral Transfers. If Borrower so requests, the Agent shall deliver to Borrower a copy of the statement so prepared in a format and to a timetable generally used in the market.

6.4

Collateral transfers shall be allocated by book entries to the relevant party's Loan by the Agent rather than making actual payments and deliveries. Authority is given to the Agent to do this and record these book entry transfers.

6.5

The Agent must maintain accounting records of the various collateral transfers made by and to each Pooled Principal as at the Agent's close of business on any Business Day and promptly prepare a statement of them.

If the Borrower requests a statement of collateral transfers, the Agent will provide this in an industry standard form.

7. WARRANTIES

7.1 The Agent warrants to Borrower that:

(a) all notifications provided to Borrower under paragraph 4.1 above and all statements provided to the other party under paragraph 6.5 above shall be complete and accurate in all material respects;

(b) at the time of allocating an Agency Loan in accordance with paragraph 4.1 above, each Principal or Principals to whom the Agent has allocated that Agency Loan or any part of that Agency Loan is duly authorised to enter into the Agency Loans contemplated by this Agreement and to perform its obligations thereunder; and

(c) at the time of allocating an Agency Loan in accordance with paragraph 4.1 above, no Event of Default or event which would constitute an Event of Default with the service of a Default Notice or other written notice under paragraph 14 of the Agreement has occurred in relation to any Principal or Principals to whom the Agent has allocated that Agency Loan or any part of that Agency Loan.

7. WARRANTIES

7.1

(a) All notifications to the Borrower about loan allocations and all collateral transfer statements shall be complete and accurate in all material respects;

(b) upon allocation each underlying principal is duly authorised to enter into Agency Loans and perform their obligations under them; and

(c) at the time allocation is made, no actual or potential Event of Default has occurred to any principal.

UK TAX ADDENDUM

In 2000 ISLA issued a UK Tax Addendum for use with the GMSLA 2000 where one of the parties is resident for UK tax purposes and overseas securities would be traded. The main focus of the Addendum was to ensure that no withholding tax was payable on income and manufactured dividends on such securities.

Changes in tax legislation since 2000 made many references in the addendum out of date. Some market players issued updates but eventually ISLA took the UK Tax Addendum off its website. However, another Tax Addendum has been composed for use with the GMSLA 2010. It has the same broad purpose as the previous Tax Addendum but as well as covering manufactured dividends for Overseas Securities it also covers those for Net Paying UK Securities, REIT shares and PAIF shares any of which can be disapplied by the Borrower or Lender.

The two main functions of the Addendum are:

(a) to disapply the gross up provisions in paragraph 12 of the GMSLA 2010 where it applies to manufactured dividends on loaned securities; and

(b) to require the payer to consider carefully representations and other information provided by his counterparty when deciding if he should withhold tax on his payment.

ISLA has published a commentary on the UK Tax Addendum on pages 26–28 of its GMSLA 2010 Guidance Notes but as I am not a tax specialist, it would be inappropriate for me to comment further.

The European Master Agreement

- Background to the European Master Agreement (the "EMA")
- Goals and benefits of the EMA
- Structure of the EMA
- Clause by clause analysis of the EMA
- Comparison of the EMA with the GMSLA 2010

BACKGROUND TO THE EUROPEAN MASTER AGREEMENT (THE "EMA")

The European Master Agreement (the "EMA") was published on 29th October 1999. It was jointly sponsored by the Banking Federation of the European Union (the "FBE") and the European Savings Banks Group and the European Association of Co-operative Banks. The EMA underwent minor revision in January 2001 and major revision of some of its parts in early 2004.

The full text of the EMA is available on the FBE's website on www.fbe.be. It is available in seven languages (English, French, German, Greek, Italian, Portuguese and Spanish). Legal opinions have been commissioned from law firms in 19 countries. France and Germany were the main promoters of the EMA.

GOALS AND BENEFITS OF THE EMA

Goals

The EMA was created to provide a common standard text which could be used in different languages and under different national laws within and outside the European Union. The aim is to encourage replacement of the many domestic agreements currently in use. Initially the EMA focused on agreements covering repos and securities lending. Indeed one goal was to use the EMA in developing a single euro denominated repo and securities lending market. The European Central Bank has solely used the EMA since November 2001 for repo transactions with its EU and Swiss counterparties.

The EMA is designed to be a multiproduct agreement like the ISDA Master Agreement. The eventual aim is to document all trading transactions under one master agreement. Initially the EMA covered repo and securities lending transactions but in early 2004 this was extended to interest rate derivatives transactions, options and foreign exchange transactions with the possibility of other products being added in the future.

The EMA is also designed to be multi-jurisdictional. This means that contracting parties may choose the particular governing law under which it is to operate and its contractual language, in this way taking into account individual national legal requirements.

Benefits

The EMA:

- proposes a standard multiproduct agreement with uniform Events of Default;
- aims to avoid inconsistencies among numerous single product master agreements;
- aims to speed up the negotiation process by reducing the volume of master agreements handled and the number of legal opinions required;
- promotes the single agreement approach and includes a close-out netting mechanism which reduces credit risk and hence regulatory capital requirements for financial institutions;
- reduces the risk of "cherry picking" (which could happen where the parties may have several single product master agreements in existence in jurisdictions unfriendly to close-out netting);
- could potentially reduce documentation backlogs;
- facilitates cross-product netting and margining (for those who can do it);
- simplifies and potentially reduces the number of domestic and cross-border European master agreements into one document. (Ultimately the use of the EMA could result in further harmonisation of operational provisions among the New York or English law master agreements developed by ISDA, SIFMA, ICMA and ISLA. This issue is particularly relevant with back to back transactions where mismatches and documentation basis risk can arise through inconsistencies.)
- possibly increases trading with more European counterparties which want to use an agreement which is standard in their country: this is in line with the EMA's goal to become the common basic agreement text very close to home country standard documentation;
- could offer a standard for documentation in countries lacking their own standard forms;
- offers flexibility through choice of governing law and submission to courts in agreed jurisdictions;
- may offer cost savings;
- possibly lends itself more easily to computerisation (e.g. formation of databases of standard and non-standard terms); and
- could be used in new countries acceding to the European Union.

STRUCTURE OF THE EMA

The EMA is composed of the following elements:

- General Provisions (which are always incorporated into the Agreement);
- separate Product Annexes for Repurchase Transactions, Securities Loans and Derivatives: the Derivatives Annex also has three specialist Supplements for Foreign Exchange Transactions, Interest Rate Transactions and Options;
- a Margin Maintenance Annex for Repurchase Transactions, Securities Loans and Derivatives;
- Special Provisions (which consist of individually negotiated terms).

This structure of the EMA is shown in Figure 5.1.

Figure 5.1   **Overview of EMA structure**

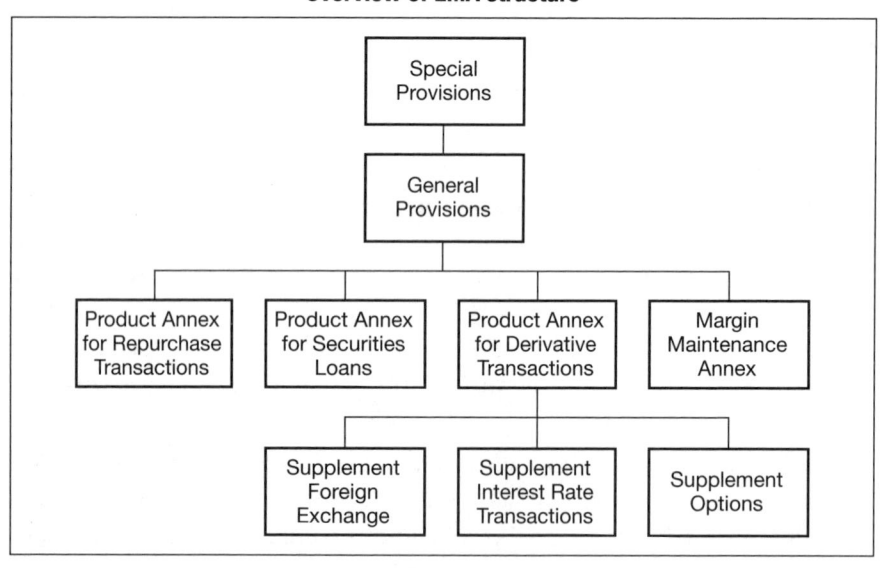

```
                    ┌─────────────┐
                    │   Special   │
                    │  Provisions │
                    └──────┬──────┘
                           │
                    ┌──────┴──────┐
                    │   General   │
                    │  Provisions │
                    └──────┬──────┘
     ┌─────────────┬───────┼───────┬─────────────┐
┌────┴────┐  ┌─────┴────┐ ┌┴──────┐ ┌───────────┐
│ Product │  │ Product  │ │Product│ │  Margin   │
│  Annex  │  │  Annex   │ │ Annex │ │Maintenance│
│   for   │  │   for    │ │  for  │ │   Annex   │
│Repurchase│ │Securities│ │Deriv. │ │           │
│  Trans. │  │  Loans   │ │ Trans.│ │           │
└─────────┘  └──────────┘ └───┬───┘ └───────────┘
                    ┌─────────┼─────────┐
              ┌─────┴────┐ ┌──┴────┐ ┌──┴─────┐
              │Supplement│ │Suppl. │ │Suppl.  │
              │ Foreign  │ │Int.Rt.│ │Options │
              │ Exchange │ │ Trans.│ │        │
              └──────────┘ └───────┘ └────────┘
```

General Provisions

The General Provisions and Annexes are essentially terms of business which are not signed as such but are incorporated into the EMA. The Special Provisions are what the parties sign. Exceptionally the General Provisions may be incorporated into the terms of a Transaction usually where the Special Provisions are not yet agreed and signed. In Section 1(2) the second sentence addresses such situations.

The General Provisions are a multiproduct document broadly similar to an ISDA Master Agreement. They contain contractual principles common to repos, securities loans and derivatives. Duplications and inconsistencies which could arise where parties enter into different master agreements with each other are therefore avoided. A further benefit is that the Annexes which deal specifically with repos, securities loans, derivatives and margin maintenance are relatively brief and focused technical documents.

The General Provisions contain the following 11 Sections:

1 Purpose, Structure, Interpretation
2 Transactions
3 Payments, Deliveries and Related Definitions
4 Taxes
5 Representations
6 Termination
7 Final Settlement Amount
8 Notices
9 Booking Offices
10 Miscellaneous
11 Governing Law, Settlement of Disputes, Jurisdiction, Arbitration.

Generally these provisions are in line with existing market documentation standards. Where this is not so (e.g. with default and no default termination events) a choice has to be made or a new approach taken.

Special Provisions

The Special Provisions are the only part of the EMA which is signed by the parties. It will normally constitute the master agreement, incorporate Product Annexes, Supplements and the Margin Maintenance Annex and include bilaterally agreed provisions, including choice of law and any amendments and additions to terms in the General Provisions. It may be quite short if the parties are satisfied with the General Provisions of the EMA and do not amend them. It sets the scope of the contractual arrangements between the parties.

Product Annexes

The three Product Annexes apply to repos, securities lending transactions and derivatives transactions respectively and address issues arising under them in a consistent manner e.g. definitions, deliveries and payments, corporate and other special events, subscription rights (for repos and securities loans) and market disruption.

The following comments apply to the Product Annexes for repos and securities loans.

Under these Annexes consequential damages arising from late delivery are excluded on principle but costs incurred in borrowing substitute securities by the party entitled to receive them may be charged.

Generally subscription rights will need to be transferred to the Seller or Lender of the securities whether or not the Buyer or Borrower then holds the securities. Often the Buyer or Borrower will need to purchase subscription rights in the market in order to transfer them. The treatment of subscription rights is therefore broadly in line with the way income distributions are normally treated under repo and securities lending transactions.

Because the EMA is silent on voting rights, the person who owns the securities at the relevant time may freely exercise such rights. Unless expressly agreed, the Seller or Lender is not entitled to give voting instructions. The fact that the Buyer or Borrower may be holding the securities of the same kind as those purchased at the relevant time will have no impact. We will revisit these matters later in the chapter where we examine the Annexes more closely.

Margin Maintenance Annex

The Margin Maintenance Annex for Repurchase Transactions, Securities Loans and Derivatives Transactions sets out common rules on margining for these types of transactions. This is a new approach in the market. The Margin Maintenance Annex states in its Section 1(1) that margining may occur globally for all Transactions or for each individual Transaction or for specified groups of Transactions (e.g. by distinguishing among repos, securities loans and derivatives transactions or between equity and debt transactions) on each Business Day. It allows margin calculations to be made on a net basis for all transactions governed by the EMA.

The commentary on the EMA in this chapter will be confined to the General Provisions, Special Provisions, the Product Annex for Securities Loans and the Margin Maintenance Annex. It will not discuss the Repurchase Transactions Annex nor the Derivatives Annex nor its Supplements because they are not the focus of this book.

CLAUSE BY CLAUSE ANALYSIS OF THE EMA

Let us now review the clauses of the EMA.

MASTER AGREEMENT
FOR FINANCIAL TRANSACTIONS

GENERAL PROVISIONS
Edition 2004

1. Purpose, Structure, Interpretation

(1) *Purpose, Applicability.* The provisions set out in this document (the "General Provisions") are intended to govern financial transactions (each a "Transaction") under any Master Agreement for Financial Transactions (each a "Master Agreement") based on the form published by the Banking Federation of the European Union ("FBE"). The provisions of a Master Agreement shall apply to the extent that they are incorporated by the parties into the terms of a Transaction or type of Transactions between them.

(2) *Structure.* A Master Agreement consists of (i) an agreement between the parties thereto providing a basis for Transactions between them (the "Special Provisions"), (ii) these General Provisions, (iii) any annexes thereto (each an "Annex"), being Annexes concerning particular types of Transactions ("Product Annexes") or concerning other matters and (iv) any supplements to the Product Annexes (each a "Supplement"). If no Special Provisions have been agreed, these General Provisions (together with, if applicable, any Annexes and any Supplements thereto) shall constitute a Master Agreement governing all Transactions into the terms of which they have been incorporated. Each Master Agreement and the terms agreed in respect of all Transactions thereunder shall collectively be referred to herein as the "Agreement".

(3) *Interpretation.* In the event of any conflict between different parts of the Agreement, (i) any Annex shall prevail over the General Provisions, (ii) the Special Provisions shall prevail over the General Provisions and any Annex and (iii) the terms agreed in respect of an individual Transaction shall, in respect of that Transaction only, prevail over all other terms of the Agreement. Unless otherwise specified, all references herein or in any Annex to Sections are to Sections of these General Provisions or such Annex, respectively. Certain expressions used in the Agreement are defined at the places indicated in the Index of Defined Terms published by the FBE in connection with these General Provisions.

1. Purpose, Structure, Interpretation

(1) Purpose, Applicability

The broad, general sweep of the EMA is apparent in this very first subsection. The General Provisions can govern financial transactions under any master agreement based on but not identical to the EMA. The provisions of such a master agreement shall apply provided the parties state this in the Transaction terms (i.e. in any oral agreement between dealers and in the Transaction Confirmation).

(2) Structure

A Master Agreement comprises the Special Provisions, the General Provisions, any Product Annexes or Supplements and any other Annexes. Where no Special Provisions have been agreed, the General Provisions and any agreed Annexes will constitute a Master Agreement which will govern all Transactions which state that it does so. The Master Agreement and the agreed Transaction terms shall be collectively referred to as the Agreement. Note that the Confirmation is not referred to directly but, as you will see when we discuss the General Provisions in more detail, it is an important part of the Agreement.

(3) Interpretation

This is primarily an Inconsistency clause. Where there is any conflict between parts of the EMA:

- any Annex shall prevail over the General Provisions;
- the Special Provisions shall prevail over the General Provisions and any Annex; and
- agreed terms for an individual Transaction shall prevail over all other terms of the EMA in respect of that Transaction only.

This hierarchy corresponds to the basic approach of the ISDA Master Agreement.

Please note that there is no Definitions Section as such in the General Provisions. Definitions appear in the body of the EMA. However, at the end of the EMA there is an Index of Defined Terms which refers to the location of definitions within it.

(4) *Single Agreement.* The Agreement constitutes a single contractual relationship. Accordingly, (i) each obligation of a party under any Transaction is incurred and performed in consideration of the obligations incurred and to be performed by the other party under all Transactions, and (ii) unless otherwise agreed, a failure by a party to perform an obligation under any Transaction shall constitute a failure to perform under the Agreement as a whole.

The parties enter into the Master Agreement between them and each Transaction thereunder in reliance on these principles, which they consider fundamental to their risk assessment.

(5) *Modifications.* Any modification of these General Provisions or any modified or new Annex which the FBE may promulgate in the future may become effective between the parties to a Master Agreement by each party notifying its acceptance in the manner designated by the FBE.

(4) Single Agreement

This single agreement wording closely resembles that in the GMSLA 2010.

The provision starts with a statement that Transaction obligations are entered into by one party in consideration of corresponding Transaction Obligations being undertaken by its counterparty. This is, therefore, a type of consideration clause.

This sub-section also acknowledges that the EMA and each Transaction under it constitutes a single contractual relationship and where a party fails to perform an obligation under one Transaction this constitutes a failure to perform under the whole EMA and consequently gives grounds to close out all Transactions under it. Therefore all Transactions depend upon each other for the single agreement concept.

The final sentence emphasises that the parties have entered into the EMA and the Transactions in reliance on the above principles which are fundamental to their risk assessment.

The purpose of the single agreement provision is to prevent liquidators cherry picking. Cherry picking is a practice where a liquidator will honour payments on those Transactions which are profitable to his insolvent client and refuse to do so on other Transactions which are not profitable to them but will insist that the non-defaulting counterparty performs its obligations in respect of those Transactions.

(5) Modifications

If the FBE modifies the terms of the General Provisions or amends or issues new Annexes in the future, parties can adhere to them by notifying each other in the manner to be prescribed by the FBE. This could be by way of an amendment agreement or even by the protocol route used by ISDA, for instance, for various important market issues.

2. Transactions

(1) *Form.* A Transaction may be entered into orally or by any other means of communication.

(2) *Confirmation.* Upon the parties having agreed on a Transaction each party shall promptly send to the other a confirmation (a "Confirmation") of such Transaction in the manner specified in Section 8(1). The absence of either or both Confirmations shall not affect the validity of the Transaction.

2. Transactions

(1) Form

This self-explanatory clause gives some flexibility for entering into Transactions.

(2) Confirmation

This clause anticipates that both parties will promptly send each other a Confirmation of the Transaction terms by letter, telex, fax or electronic messaging system (the methods mentioned in Section 8(1)) although telex is no longer used in the market for this purpose. However, the Transaction remains valid even if one or both parties fails to issue a Confirmation.

In the UK, the Financial Services Authority's *Conduct of Business Sourcebook (2007)* requires parties to exchange Confirmations no later than the following Business Day.

3. Payments, Deliveries and Related Definitions

(1) *Date. Place. Manner.* Each party shall make the payments and deliveries to be made by it at the time, date and place and to the account agreed in respect of the Transaction concerned and in the manner customary for payments or deliveries of the relevant kind. Each payment shall be made in the currency agreed in respect thereof (the "Contractual Currency"), free of all costs and in funds which are freely available on the due date. Each party may change its account for receiving a payment or delivery by giving notice to the other at least ten Business Days prior to the scheduled date for the relevant payment or delivery, unless the other party reasonably objects to such change and gives timely notice thereof.

(2) *Transfer of Title. Retransfer of Securities*.

(a) *Transfer of Title.* Unless otherwise agreed, any delivery or transfer of securities or other financial instruments ("Securities") or any other assets (including, in respect of Derivative Transactions, any other underlying assets of such Transactions) by a party to the other pursuant to the Agreement shall constitute a transfer to such other party of the unrestricted title to such Securities and/or assets or, if customary in the place where delivery is to be effected, of a legal position (such as a co-ownership interest in a collective holding of Securities, the position as beneficiary of a trust or another form of beneficial ownership) which is the functional equivalent of such title (including, in each case, an unrestricted right to dispose of such Securities and/or assets) and not the creation of a security interest; the use of the terms "margin" or "substitution" shall not be construed as indicating an agreement to the contrary. The transferor of any Securities and/or assets shall, accordingly, (i) not retain in respect of those Securities and/or assets any ownership interest, security interest or right to dispose and (ii) execute all documents reasonably required to effect such full transfer. As far as transfer of Securities is concerned, if registered Securities are to be transferred, the transferee may dispose of the Securities received before the transfer is entered into the relevant register; if the entry depends upon a circumstance beyond the transferor's reasonable control, the transferor does not warrant that such entry will be effected.

3. Payments, Deliveries and Related Definitions

(1) Date, Place, Manner

The EMA envisages cash payments and physical delivery as do the GMRA (2000), GMSLA (2010) and the ISDA Master Agreement.

Payments and deliveries must be made punctually, to the agreed account and in the customary manner for such payments and deliveries. Each payment must be in cleared funds in the agreed currency. Either party may, by giving not less than 10 Business Days' prior notice to the other, change its account for payments or deliveries unless the other party promptly and reasonably objects to it. A party might object, for instance, if such a change of account is to an overseas office of the first party and the change might cause a withholding tax to arise on payments. It might also object to an overseas transfer of account if there was a risk of exchange controls being imposed on payments from that account.

(2) Transfer of Title, Retransfer of Securities

(a) Transfer of Title The provision confirms the absolute right to transfer title from the transferor to the other party in a repo, securities lending or derivative transaction. This includes any pro-rated co-ownership rights in a collective pool of securities as in the Euroclear or Clearstream systems or being a beneficiary under a trust in each case with the unfettered right to dispose of such securities. It is stressed that no security interest is thereby created and the terms "margin" or "substitution" shall not in themselves cause such title transfer to be called into question or recharacterised into another arrangement.

The transferor cedes all its ownership, charging or sale rights to the transferee and agrees to execute all necessary transfer documentation. If the transfer involves registered securities the transferee is free to sell or transfer the securities before the original transfer is recorded by the registrar. The transferor does not have to warrant that the entry will be registered if there is a circumstance beyond its reasonable control.

(b) *Retransfer of Securities.* An obligation to return or retransfer any Securities is an obligation to transfer Securities of the same kind as such Securities. Securities are "of the same kind" as other Securities if they are of the same issuer and the same type and nominal value and represent identical rights as such other Securities; if all such other Securities have been redeemed, redenominated, exchanged, converted, subdivided, consolidated or been the subject of a capital increase, capital reduction, call on partly paid securities or event similar to any of the foregoing, Securities "of the same kind" means the amount of Securities, money and other property (together "Substitute Assets") received in respect of such other Securities as a result of such event (provided that if any sum had to be paid in order to receive such Substitute Assets, an obligation to transfer them shall be conditional upon payment by the transferee of such sum to the transferor).

(3) *Conditions Precedent.* Each payment or delivery obligation of a party is subject to the conditions precedent that (i) no Event of Default or event which by the lapse of time or the giving of notice (or both) may become an Event of Default with respect to the other party has occurred and is continuing and (ii) no notice of termination has been given in respect of the relevant Transaction because of a Change of Circumstances.

(4) *Payment Netting.* If on any date both parties would otherwise be required to make payments in the same currency in respect of the same Transaction, the mutual payment obligations shall automatically be set off against each other and the party owing the higher amount shall pay to the other the difference between the amounts owed. The parties may agree that this principle shall apply in respect of two or more Transactions or one or more types of Transactions or that it shall apply also in respect of mutual obligations to deliver assets which are fungible with each other. If and so long as a single currency can be expressed in different currency units (such as the euro unit and national currency units under the principles governing the transition to European Economic and Monetary Union), the principle set forth in the first sentence of this subsection shall apply only if both payments are to be made in the same unit.

(b) Retransfer of Securities It is stated that securities of the same type, issuer, nominal value and with equivalent rights must be retransferred in a repo or securities lending transaction, but not the identically numbered securities. In the market these are often referred to as *fungible* securities. This requirement also applies if the securities concerned have been subject to a corporate event whereupon equivalent securities reflecting the corporate event must be retransferred. However, if payment is due to be made for such substitute assets, the transferee should make such payment before retransferring them to the transferor on the basis that a repo or securities lending transaction (which is essentially a temporary transfer of securities) aims to place the transferor in the same position he would have been in if he had held the securities and not entered into the repo or securities loan at all.

(3) Conditions Precedent

This provision reflects two thirds of a similar provision in the ISDA Master Agreement (i.e. Section 2(a)(iii)). A party's payment or delivery obligations are subject to no actual or potential Event of Default having occurred and no notice of termination having been issued due to a Change of Circumstances as listed in General Provisions Section 6(2).

(4) Payment Netting

This provision permits single Transaction, multiple Transaction and cross-product payment netting where only the difference is payable by the party owing the higher amount to the other party. This procedure applies to cash payments and delivery of fungible securities (i.e. securities of the same type and class). Payments must occur on the same day and in the same currency and this even applied where euros and national currencies were involved. They cannot now be netted off against each other and indeed this has not been possible since 1st January 2002 in any case.

(5) *Late Payment.* If in respect of a Transaction a party fails to make a payment to the other when due (and, for the avoidance of doubt, without being entitled to withhold such payment), interest, payable on demand, shall accrue (before and after judgment) at the Default Rate on the amount outstanding, calculated for the period from (and including) the due date to (but excluding) the day on which such payment is received. "Default Rate" means the higher of (a) the Interbank Rate and (b) the cost to the other party, as certified by it, of funding the relevant amount, in each case plus any interest surcharge which may be agreed in the Special Provisions. "Interbank Rate" means the interbank offered interest rate charged by prime banks to each other for overnight deposits at the place of payment and in the currency of the amount outstanding for each day on which interest is to be charged (being, if an amount in euros is outstanding, the Euro Overnight Index Average ("EONIA") Rate calculated by the European Central Bank).

(6) *Business Day Convention.* If any payment or delivery date, any determination or valuation date, any commencement or termination date or any exercise date agreed between the parties which is deemed to be a Business Day is not a Business Day, payments, deliveries, determinations or valuations shall be made or, as the case may be, the commencement date, the termination date or the exercise date shall be deemed to occur, as elected in respect of the relevant Transaction, on (a) the immediately preceding Business Day ("Preceding"), (b) the immediately following Business Day ("Following"), or (c) the immediately following Business Day, unless such day falls in the next calendar month, in which case the relevant payment, delivery, determination or valuation shall be made or, as the case may be, the relevant commencement date, termination date or exercise date shall be deemed to occur on the immediately preceding Business Day ("Modified Following" or "Modified"), provided that failing such election, (b) shall apply.

(5) Late Payment

This provision states that interest will be chargeable on overdue payments at the Default Rate from and including the due date to but excluding the date payment is received as is the normal practice in the derivatives markets. The Default Rate is defined as the higher of the overnight interbank rate for the currency concerned (e.g. EONIA for the euro) or the Non-Defaulting Party's self-certified funding cost plus any interest surcharge agreed in the Special Provisions.

(6) Business Day Convention

A Business Day Convention must be chosen for payments, deliveries and valuations. The options are Preceding, Following or Modified Following. If no choice is made the fallback is the Following Business Day Convention.

(7) *Business Day Definition:* "Business Day" means (a) in relation to any payment in euros a day on which all relevant parts of TARGET are operational to effect such a payment, (b) in relation to any payment in any other currency a day (other than a Saturday or a Sunday) on which commercial banks are open for business (including payments in the currency concerned as well as dealings in foreign exchange and foreign currency deposits) in the place(s) agreed in relation to the relevant Transaction or, if not so agreed, in the place where the relevant account is located and, if different, in the principal financial centre, if any, of the currency of such payment, (c) in relation to any delivery of Securities, (i) where a Transaction is to be settled through a securities settlement system, a day on which such securities settlement system is open for business in the place where delivery of the Securities is to be effected, and (ii) where a Transaction is to be settled in a way other than (i), a day (other than a Saturday or a Sunday) on which commercial banks are open for business in the place where delivery of the Securities is to be effected, (d) in relation to any delivery of any assets other than Securities, a day (other than a Saturday or a Sunday) on which commercial banks are open for business in the place where delivery of the relevant assets is to be effected or any other day agreed between the parties in the Confirmation of the relevant Transactions or otherwise, (e) in relation to any valuation, a day on which an up-to-date valuation based on the agreed price sources can reasonably be carried out, and (f) in relation to any notice or other communication, a day (other than a Saturday or Sunday) on which commercial banks are open for business in the city specified in the address provided by the recipient pursuant to Section 8(1).

(8) *Market Value.* "Market Value" means in respect of any Securities as of any time on any date, (a) the price for such Securities then quoted through and obtainable from a generally recognised source agreed to by the parties and (b) failing such agreement or such quotation (i) if the Securities are listed on a stock exchange and not then suspended, their price last quoted on such exchange; (ii) if the Securities are not so listed, but have, on the main market on which they are traded, the price published or made public by a central bank or an entity of undisputed authority on such day, such price last published or made public; and (iii) in any other case, the average of the bid and offer prices for such Securities, as of such time on such date, as established by two leading market participants other than the parties, in each of the cases listed in (a) and (b) together with (if not included in such price) any interest accrued on such Securities as of that date.

(7) Business Day Definition

This standard provision covers cash payments, securities transfers, valuations and notices. It defines Business Day as follows:

(a) a day when the TARGET 2 payment system is open for euro settlements;

(b) for other currencies, a non-weekend day when commercial banks are open for foreign exchange dealings in the place where the Transaction is to be made, failing which the principal financial centre for the currency concerned;

(c) for securities, a day when the relevant securities settlement system in the place where the securities are to be delivered is open for business, failing which a non-weekend day when commercial banks are open for the delivery of securities;

(d) for other assets, a non-weekend day on which commercial banks can take delivery of such other assets: the timing of their delivery may also be stated in a Confirmation between the two parties;

(e) for up-to-date valuations, a day when the necessary price sources are available for the valuation to be carried out; and

(f) for notices, a non-weekend day when commercial banks are open for business.

(8) Market Value

This provision concerns the valuation of securities. In the first two instances mentioned, valuation shall be determined by current market prices. Otherwise an average of the bid and offer prices provided by two independent market makers (i.e. a mid-price) shall be used to determine the Market Value. If accrued interest is not included in the price (called a "dirty price"), it must be added to any "clean price" obtained.

4. Taxes

(1) *Withholding Tax.* If a party is or will be obliged to deduct or withhold an amount for or on account of any tax or other duty from a payment which it is to make, it shall pay to the other party such additional amounts as are necessary to ensure that such other party receives the full amount to which it would have been entitled at the time of such payment if no deduction or withholding had been required. This shall not apply if the tax or duty concerned is imposed or levied (a) by or on behalf or for the account of the jurisdiction (or a tax authority of or resident in the jurisdiction) in which the Booking Office of the payee (or its place of residence, if the payee is an individual) is located, (b) pursuant to (directly or indirectly) an obligation imposed by a treaty to which such jurisdiction is a party, or by a regulation or directive enacted under such treaty, or (c) because the payee has failed to perform its obligation under Section 10(4)(b).

(2) *Documentary Tax.* Subject to Section 10(2), each party shall pay any stamp, documentary or similar tax or duty payable with respect to the Agreement (a "Documentary Tax") and imposed upon it in the jurisdiction in which its Booking Office or place of residence is located and shall indemnify the other party for any Documentary Tax payable in such jurisdiction and imposed upon the other party, unless the Booking Office of such other party (or its place of residence, if the other party is an individual) is also located in such jurisdiction.

4. Taxes

(1) Withholding Tax

Compared to the ISDA Master Agreement or the GMSLA 2010, this is a relatively brief withholding tax gross up provision. If a payer is obliged by his tax authority to withhold tax on a payment, this clause requires him to gross up or increase his payment so that the payee receives what he expected to receive. However, the gross up will not apply where it arises in a domestic income tax situation or where there is a failure to follow treaty obligations or where the payee fails to provide the necessary documentation to enable the payer to make a payment free of withholding tax or at a reduced rate. Withholding tax only applies to cross-border transactions.

(2) Documentary Tax

This provision states that in a non-default situation each party shall pay any stamp or similar tax imposed by its local tax jurisdiction on the Agreement. However, each party shall also indemnify the other party against such taxes in such jurisdiction provided that the first party's tax jurisdiction is not the same as its counterparty's tax jurisdiction.

5. Representations

(1) *Representations.* Each party represents to the other, as of the date on which it enters into a Master Agreement and as of each date on which a Transaction is entered into, that:

(a) *Status.* It is validly existing under the laws of its organisation or incorporation;

(b) *Corporate Action.* It is duly authorised to execute and deliver, and perform its obligations under, the Agreement;

(c) *No Violation or Conflict.* The execution, delivery and performance of the Agreement do not violate or conflict with any provision of law, judgment or government or court order applicable to it, or any provision of its constitutional documents;

(d) *Consents.* All governmental and other consents which are required to be obtained by it with respect to the Agreement have been obtained and are in full force and effect;

(e) *Obligations Binding.* Its obligations under the Agreement are legal, valid and binding;

(f) *Absence of Certain Events.* No Event of Default or event which by the lapse of time or the giving of notice (or both) may become an Event of Default and, to its knowledge, no Change of Circumstances with respect to it has occurred and is continuing;

(g) *Absence of Litigation.* There is not pending or, to its knowledge, threatened against it any action, suit or proceeding before any court, tribunal, arbitrator or governmental or other authority that is likely to affect the legality, validity, binding effect or enforceability against it of the Agreement or its ability to perform its obligations under the Agreement;

(h) *No Reliance.* It has the necessary knowledge and experience to assess the benefits and risks incurred in each Transaction and has not relied for such purpose on the other party;

(i) *Margin.* It has full title to the Securities transferred, as margin or collateral, to the other party under the Agreement and that such Securities shall be free and clear of any lien, security interest or any other right which may affect the right of the other party to dispose freely of such Securities.

(2) *Applicability to Guarantor.* If a third person specified in the Special Provisions or in a Confirmation as Guarantor (a "Guarantor") has, in an instrument specified in the Special Provisions or otherwise agreed between the parties, given a guarantee or other credit support in respect of any obligations of either party under the Agreement (a "Guarantee"), then the representations of such party in respect of itself and the Agreement pursuant to subsection l (a) through (i) shall *mutatis mutandis* apply also to the Guarantor and the Guarantee.

5. Representations

(1)(a)–(i) Representations

The representations apply mutually, as is normal, both when the EMA is signed and each time a Transaction is executed. Items (a)–(g) are common in most types of agreements and concern status, authority, no conflicts, consents obtained, binding obligations, absence of adverse events and litigation. Item (f) includes Change of Circumstances as well as actual and potential Events of Default. Item (g) – absence of litigation – has no explicit materiality test for the effect of the litigation although the stated results would clearly be adverse. Item (h) is a short non-reliance provision. Item (i) represents that a collateral giver has full legal title to Securities it is to transfer to a collateral receiver and that it can make that transfer free and clear of any security interest, i.e. unencumbered.

(2) Applicability to Guarantor

This provision extends the representations in Section 5(1) to any guarantor or credit support provider, *mutatis mutandis*. Reference to the guarantor may be made in the Special Provisions or in a Confirmation.

6. Termination

(1) *Termination due to an Event of Default.*

(a) *Event of Default.* The occurrence of any of the following events in respect of a party shall constitute an event of default ("Event of Default"):

(i) *Failure to Pay or Deliver.* The party fails to make, when due, any payment or delivery under the Agreement and such failure continues for three Business Days after the day on which notice of such failure is given to the party;

(ii) *Failure to Provide or Return Margin or Collateral.* The party fails to provide or return, when due, margin or collateral required to be provided or returned by it under the Agreement;

(iii) *Other Breach of Agreement.* The party fails to perform, when due, any other obligation under the Agreement and such failure continues for thirty days after the day on which notice of such failure is given to the party;

(iv) *Misrepresentation.* Any representation by the party in the Agreement proves to have been incorrect on the date as of which it was made and the other party determines in good faith that, as a result thereof (or of the matters of fact or law which were not correctly stated), the balance of its risks and benefits under the Agreement is materially adversely affected;

(v) *Default under Specified Transactions.* If the parties have, in the Special Provisions, specified any Transactions ("Specified Transactions") to which this Section 6(1)(a)(v) will apply, the party fails to make a payment or a delivery under any such Specified Transaction and such failure (A) results in the liquidation or early termination of, or an acceleration of obligations under, such Specified Transaction or (B) continues beyond any applicable grace period (or, if there is no such period, for at least three Business Days) after the last payment or delivery date of such Specified Transaction, provided, in either case, that such failure is not caused by circumstances which, if occurring under the Agreement, would constitute a Change of Circumstances as described in subsection 2(a)(ii);

6. Termination

(1) Termination due to an Event of Default

Ten Events of Default are stated viz:

- Failure to Pay or Deliver
- Failure to Provide or Return Margin or Collateral
- Other Breach of Agreement
- Misrepresentation
- Default under Specified Transactions
- Cross Default
- Restructuring Without Assumption
- Insolvency Events
- Repudiation of Obligations
- Guarantee Ineffective.

(a) Event of Default An Event of Default is caused by one party only and gives the right to a Non-Defaulting Party to close out all Transactions under their EMA.

(i) Failure to Pay or Deliver A three Business Day grace period following notice by the Non-Defaulting Party is allowed as in the 1992 ISDA Master Agreement. Please note that the notice must be given or the grace period does not start.

(ii) Failure to Provide or Return Margin or Collateral No grace period is allowed for a party which has failed to provide or return collateral.

(iii) Other Breach of Agreement This Event of Default covers a party's failure to fulfil any other obligation under the EMA. This provision allows a remedial period of 30 calendar days after the Non-Defaulting Party gives notice to the Defaulting Party. Please note again that the notice must be given or the grace period does not start.

(iv) Misrepresentation A party makes a misrepresentation which the other party judges in good faith to affect the EMA in a materially adverse way.

(v) Default under Specified Transactions This is a concept from the ISDA Master Agreement where it means a default under an OTC derivatives type transaction between the two parties to the ISDA Master Agreement but governed by terms outside of it, i.e. possibly under a long form Confirmation, market terms or another master agreement.

Under the EMA the scope of Specified Transactions must be stated in the Special Provisions.

The default "tests" here are where the failure to pay or deliver results in early termination or acceleration of the Specified Transaction or where the failure occurs following the expiry of a grace period after the last payment under the Specified Transaction is due. A three Business Day grace period applies if none exists in the Specified Transaction documentation.

This default is deemed not to have occurred if the failure is due to Illegality or Impossibility.

(vi) *Cross Default.* Any payment obligation of the party in respect of borrowed money (whether incurred by it as primary or secondary obligor and whether arising from one or more contracts or instruments) in an aggregate amount of not less than the applicable Default Threshold (A) has become, or may be declared, due and payable prior to the stated maturity thereof as a result of any default or similar event (however described) which has occurred in respect of the party or (B) has not been performed for more than seven days after its due date and, in either case, the other party has reasonable grounds to conclude that the financial obligations of the party under the Agreement may not be performed. "Default Threshold" means the amount specified as such in the Special Provisions in respect of a party or, in the absence of such specification, 1 per cent of such party's equity (meaning the sum of its capital, disclosed reserves and retained earnings, determined in accordance with generally accepted accounting principles applicable to that party, as reported in its most recent published audited financial statements);

(vii) *Restructuring Without Assumption.* The party is subject to a Corporate Restructuring and the Successor Entity fails to assume all obligations of such party under the Agreement. "Corporate Restructuring" means, with respect to such party, any consolidation or amalgamation with, or merger into, or demerger, or transfer of all or substantially all assets to, another person, or an agreement providing for any of the foregoing, and "Successor Entity" means the person which results from, survives or is the transferee in, such Corporate Restructuring;

(viii) *Insolvency Events.* (1) The party is dissolved or has a resolution passed for its dissolution (other than, in either case, pursuant to a Corporate Restructuring resulting in a solvent Successor Entity); (2) the party commences an Insolvency Proceeding against itself or takes any corporate action to authorize such Insolvency Proceeding; (3) a governmental or judicial authority or self-regulatory organisation having jurisdiction over the party in a Specified Jurisdiction (a "Competent Authority") commences an Insolvency Proceeding with respect to the party; (4) a Competent Authority takes any action under any bankruptcy, insolvency or similar law or any banking, insurance or similar law governing the operation of the party which is likely to prevent the party from performing when due its payment or delivery obligations under the Agreement; (5) a person other than a Competent Authority commences an Insolvency Proceeding against the party in a Specified Jurisdiction and such action (A) results in a Judgment of Insolvency, or (B) is not dismissed or stayed within thirty days following the action or event commencing the Insolvency Proceeding, unless the commencement of such Proceedings by such person or under the given circumstances is obviously inadmissible or frivolous; (6) the party is bankrupt or insolvent as defined under any bankruptcy or insolvency law applicable to it in a Specified Jurisdiction; (7) the party makes a general assignment for the benefit of, or enters into a composition or amicable settlement with, its creditors generally; (8) the party is generally unable to pay its debts as they fall due; or (9) the party causes or is subject to any event which, under the laws of the Specified Jurisdiction, has an effect which is analogous to any of the events specified in Nos. (1) to (8). "Insolvency Proceeding"; means a mandatory or voluntary proceeding seeking a judgment, order or arrangement of insolvency, bankruptcy, composition, amicable settlement, rehabilitation, reorganisation, administration, dissolution or liquidation with respect to a party or its assets or seeking the appointment of a receiver, liquidator, administrator or similar official for such party or for all or any substantial part its assets under any bankruptcy, insolvency or similar law or any banking, insurance or similar law governing the operation of the party;the expression does not include a solvent corporate reorganisation. An Insolvency Proceeding is "commenced" if a petition to conduct such proceeding is presented to or filed with, or (where no such petition is required) a decision to conduct such proceeding is taken by, a competent court, authority, corporate body or person. "Judgment of Insolvency" means any judgment, order or arrangement instituting an Insolvency Proceeding. "Specified Jurisdiction" in relation to a party means the jurisdiction of that party's organisation, incorporation, principal office or residence and any additional jurisdiction that may be specified with respect to that party in the Special Provisions;

(vi) Cross Default This clause covers the non-repayment of borrowed money in debt agreements above a Default Threshold stated in the Special Provisions with a fallback to 1% of the Defaulting Party's equity as defined if no Default Threshold is stated. The Cross Default tests are (i) potential acceleration under a debt agreement or (ii) non-payment more than seven days after its due date with the other party having reasonable grounds to believe that the Defaulting Party will not perform its financial obligations.

(vii) Restructuring Without Assumption This sub-section partly reflects the ISDA Master Agreement Merger without Assumption provision (Section 5(a)(viii)). It states that an Event of Default will occur if a Successor Entity fails to take over all the restructured party's obligations under the EMA following a merger type event or a major asset transfer.

(viii) Insolvency Events The usual long list of insolvency events with which we are familiar from the ISDA Master Agreement and the GMSLA 2010 is recited in this clause. Three things are notable. First, in 5(1) a dissolution following a Corporate Restructuring which results in a solvent Successor Entity is not an Insolvency Event. Second, in 5(B) there is an exclusion for frivolous proceedings. Third, at the end of the definition of Specified Jurisdiction the insolvency events are limited to a party's home jurisdiction and any other jurisdiction agreed by the parties in the Special Provisions.

In contrast, insolvency provisions in other market documentation seem to suggest that insolvency proceedings in any country, irrespective of whether the party is present there or not, may trigger termination.

(ix) *Repudiation of Obligations.* The party declares that it will not perform any material obligation under the Agreement or under any Specified Transaction (otherwise than as part of a bona fide dispute as to the existence, nature or extent of such obligation);

(x) *Guarantee Ineffective.* A Guarantee given with respect to the party is not in full force and effect, except if it has ceased to be in effect (i) in accordance with its terms, (ii) upon satisfaction of all of the party's obligations secured by such Guarantee or (iii) with the consent of the other party.

(b) *Termination.* If an Event of Default occurs with respect to a party (the "Defaulting Party") and is continuing, the other party (the "Non-Defaulting Party") may, by giving not more than twenty days' notice specifying the relevant Event of Default, terminate all outstanding Transactions, but not part thereof only, with effect as from a date (the "Early Termination Date") to be designated by it in such notice. Notwithstanding the foregoing, unless otherwise specified in the Special Provisions, all Transactions shall terminate, and the Early Termination Date shall occur, automatically in the case of an Event of Default mentioned in paragraph (a) (viii)(l), (2), (3), (5)(A) or, to the extent analogous thereto, (9) as of the time immediately preceding the relevant event or action.

(ix) Repudiation of Obligations Apart from bona fide disputes, it will be an Event of Default if a party wilfully repudiates material obligations under the EMA or a Specified Transaction.

(x) Guarantee Ineffective It will be an Event of Default if a guarantee ceases to be effective except where this occurs in accordance with its terms; all obligations covered by it are satisfied; or the other party agrees that the guarantee need not be in full force and effect.

(b) Termination This provision states that if an Event of Default occurs the Non-Defaulting Party may give the Defaulting Party up to 20 days' notice stating an Early Termination Date on which all Transactions under the EMA will be terminated. Automatic termination will occur with certain Insolvency Events. This process closely follows that outlined in Section 6(a) of the ISDA Master Agreement.

(2) *Termination due to Change of Circumstances.*

(a) *Change of Circumstances.* The occurrence of any of the following events or circumstances in respect of a party shall constitute a change of circumstances ("Change of Circumstances"):

(i) *Tax Event.* As a result of the entry into force of any new law or regulation or of any change in law or any other provision of mandatory effect or change in the application or official interpretation thereof occurring after the date on which a Transaction is entered into, or as a result of a Corporate Restructuring of either party not falling under subsection 1 (a)(vii), the party would, on or before the next due date relating to such Transaction, (A) be required to pay additional amounts pursuant to Section 4(1) with regard to a payment which it is obliged to make, other than a payment of interest pursuant to Section 3(5), or (B) receive a payment, other than a payment of interest pursuant to Section 3(5), from which an amount is required to be deducted for or on account of a tax or duty and no additional amount is required to be paid in respect of such tax or duty under Section 4(1), other than by reason of Section 4(1)(c);

(ii) *Illegality, Impossibility.* As a result of the entry into force of any new law or regulation or of any change in law or any other provision of mandatory effect or change in the application or official interpretation thereof or, if so specified in the Special Provisions, as a result of an Impossibility Event, in each case occurring after the date on which a Transaction is entered into, it becomes, or is likely to become, unlawful or impossible for the party (A) to make, or receive, a payment or delivery in respect of such Transaction when due or to punctually comply with any other material obligation under the Agreement relating to such Transaction or (B) to perform any obligation to provide margin or collateral as and when required to be provided by it under the Agreement; "Impossibility Event" means any catastrophe, armed conflict, act of terrorism, riot or any other circumstance beyond the party's reasonable control affecting the operations of the party;

(iii) *Credit Event upon Restructuring.* If the party is subject to a Corporate Restructuring, the creditworthiness of the Successor Entity is materially weaker than that of the party immediately before the Corporate Restructuring.

(2) Termination due to Change of Circumstances

(a)(i)–(iii) The Change of Circumstances events are:

- **Tax Event**
- **Illegality, Impossibility**
- **Credit Event Upon Restructuring.**

These equate to corresponding Termination Events or Additional Termination Events in the ISDA Master Agreement.

Under the Tax Event if a withholding tax is charged (due to a change in tax law or regulation or following a Corporate Restructuring) after a Transaction has been entered into and that tax results in a payment having to be grossed up or increased or a receipt being received net (except in either case where a payment of default interest is involved) a Change of Circumstances will be deemed to have occurred.

Sub-section 6(2)(a)(ii) provides that if following a change of law or its interpretation it becomes unlawful or impossible for a party to make or receive payments or deliveries under the EMA or punctually to comply with any important obligation under the EMA including the provision of collateral then that will also constitute a Change of Circumstances. Impossibility Events (which are defined) need to be stated in the Special Provisions.

The Credit Event Upon Restructuring event is a short form simplified version of the similar Credit Event Upon Merger provision in the 1992 ISDA Master Agreement. It applies if the creditworthiness of the Successor Entity is far worse than that of the original contracting party immediately before the Corporate Restructuring took place.

(b) _Termination._ If a Change of Circumstances occurs with respect to a party (the "Affected Party"), the Affected Party in the case of paragraph (a)(i) or (ii), and the other party (the "Non-Affected Party") in the case of paragraph (a)(ii) or (iii) may, subject to the limitations set forth below, by giving not more than twenty days' notice, terminate the Transaction(s) affected by such change, with effect as from a date (the "Early Termination Date") to be designated by it in such notice, it being understood that, in the case of paragraph (a)(iii), all Transactions will be deemed so affected. If, without prejudice to any agreement between the parties on the provision of margin or collateral, either party determines that as a result of such termination its credit exposure to the other party is significantly increased, it may, not later than one week after the effective date of the notice of termination, by giving notice to the other party require such other party to provide, within one week after receipt of such last-mentioned notice, margin or collateral reasonably acceptable to it in such amount as to be at least equal to the increase in credit exposure under the Agreement, as determined by it. In the cases of paragraph (a)(i) and (ii), the right to terminate shall be subject to the following limitations: (i) the Early Termination Date may not be earlier than thirty days before the date on which the Change of Circumstances becomes effective, and (ii) the Affected Party may, unless it would otherwise be required to pay additional amounts as contemplated by paragraph (a)(i)(A), give notice of termination only after a period of thirty days has expired following a notice by it informing the other party of such event and if the situation (if capable of remedy) has not been remedied within such period (by way of an agreed transfer of the affected Transactions to another Booking Office or otherwise).

(b) Termination The Affected Party may give notice of a Change of Circumstances for a Tax Event and either party may give notice with respect to an Illegality or Impossibility. However, only the Non-Affected Party may give notice for a Credit Event Upon Restructuring. The notice may state that only affected Transactions in the case of Tax Event or Illegality or Impossibility but all Transactions with a Credit Event Upon Restructuring will be terminated on a specific Early Termination Date no later than 20 days after the notice is issued. If the Non-Affected Party decides that its risk exposure is significantly increased by the proposed termination, it may give a notice to the Affected Party not later than one week after the termination notice is issued to transfer to it within seven days sufficient reasonably acceptable collateral to offset the increase in counterparty risk exposure it has calculated.

Certain other conditions also apply. The Termination Date may not be earlier than 30 days before the date on which the Change of Circumstances takes effect and, barring any obligation to gross up for a withholding tax, an Affected Party may only give a termination notice when 30 days have passed from when it advised the other party of the Tax Event or Illegality or Impossibility and if the position remains unremedied (e.g. by trying to transfer affected Transactions to another of the Affected Party's Booking Offices).

(3) *Applicability to Guarantor.* If a Guarantee has been given with respect to a party and any of the events described in subsections l(a)(iii) through (ix) and 2(a) occurs with respect to the relevant Guarantor or such Guarantee, the occurrence of such event shall have the same effect as if it had occurred with respect to such party or the Agreement, respectively.

(4) *Effect of Termination.* In the event of a termination pursuant to this Section 6, neither party shall be obliged to make any further payment or delivery under the terminated Transaction(s) which would have become due on or after the Early Termination Date or to provide or return margin or collateral which would otherwise be required to be provided or returned under the Agreement and related to the terminated Transaction(s). These obligations shall be replaced by an obligation of either party to pay the Final Settlement Amount in accordance with Section 7.

(5) *Event of Default and Change of Circumstances.* If an event or circumstance which would otherwise constitute or give rise to an Event of Default also constitutes a Change of Circumstances as referred to in subsection 2(a)(ii), it will be treated as a Change of Circumstances and will not constitute an Event of Default, except that any event as described in subsection l(a)(viii) will always be treated as an Event of Default and not as a Change of Circumstances.

(3) Applicability to Guarantor

This provision extends the application of termination for most Events of Default or all Change of Circumstances events to a party's guarantor.

(4) Effect of Termination

In a termination situation neither party makes any normal payments or deliveries nor transfers collateral in respect of terminated Transactions. The parties proceed to the close-out netting mechanism of Section 7 of the EMA.

(5) Event of Default and Change of Circumstances

Where an event could be deemed to be either an Event of Default, an Illegality or an Impossibility it will be treated as an Illegality or Impossibility in line with the normal market practice of trying to mitigate the effects of such events and only closing out affected Transactions. However, any Insolvency Event will always be treated as an Event of Default.

7. Final Settlement Amount

(1) *Calculation.*

(a) *Procedure and Bases of Calculation.* Upon termination pursuant to Section 6, the Non-Defaulting Party or, as the case may be, the Non-Affected Party or, if there are two Affected Patties, each party (each the "Calculation Party") shall as soon as reasonably possible calculate the Final Settlement Amount.

"Final Settlement Amount" means, subject to subsection 2(b)(i), the amount determined by the Calculation Party to be equal to, as of the Early Termination Date, (A) the sum of all Transaction Values which are positive for it, the Amounts Due owed to it and its Margin Claims less (B) the sum of the absolute amounts of all Transaction Values which are negative for it, the Amounts Due owed by it and the Margin Claims of the other party;

"Amounts Due" owed by a party means the sum of (i) any amounts that were required to be paid by such party under any Transaction, but not paid, (ii) the Default Value, as of the agreed delivery date, of each asset that was required to be delivered by such party under any Transaction, but not delivered (in either case regardless of whether or not the party was entitled to withhold such payment or delivery, by virtue of Section 3(3) or for any other reason) and (iii) interest on the amounts specified in (i) and (ii) from (and including) the due date of the relevant payment or delivery to (but excluding) the Early Termination Date at the Interbank Rate or, if Section 3(5) is applicable, the Default Rate; Margin Claims shall be disregarded for the determination of Amounts Due;

"Default Value" means, in respect of any assets (including Securities or, in respect of Derivative Transactions, any other underlying assets of such Transactions) on any given date, an amount equal to (A) if the assets are or were to be delivered by the Calculation Party, the net proceeds (after deducting fees and expenses) which the Calculation Party has or could have reasonably received when selling assets of the same kind and quantity in the market on such date, (B) if the assets are or were to be delivered to the Calculation Party, the cost (including fees and expenses) which the Calculation Party has or would have reasonably incurred in purchasing assets of the same kind and quantity in the market on such date, and (C) if a market price for such assets cannot be determined, an amount which the Calculation Party determines in good faith to be its total losses and costs (or gains, in which case expressed as a negative number) in connection with such assets;

"Margin Claims" means, as of the Early Termination Date, the aggregate of the amount of cash paid and the Default Value of Securities transferred, as margin or collateral, by a party and not repaid or retransferred to it, plus any interest accrued on such cash at the rate agreed in respect thereof;

"Transaction Value" means, with respect to any Transaction or group of Transactions, an amount equal to, at the option of the Calculation Party, (i) the loss incurred (expressed as a positive number) or gain realized (expressed as a negative number) by the Calculation Party as a result of the termination of such Transaction(s), or (ii) the arithmetic mean of the quotations for replacement or hedge transactions on the Quotation Date obtained by the Calculation Party from not less than two leading market participants. In the case of (ii), each such quotation shall be expressed as the amount which the market participant would pay or receive on the Quotation Date if such market participant were to assume, as from the Quotation Date, the rights and obligations of the other party (or their economic equivalent) under the relevant Transaction(s); the resulting amount shall be expressed as a positive number if it would be payable to the market participant, and shall otherwise be expressed as a negative number. If, in such case, no or only one quotation can reasonably be obtained, the Transaction Value shall be determined pursuant to (i),

"Quotation Date" means the Early Termination Date, except that in the event of an automatic termination as provided in Section 6(1)(b), the Quotation Date shall be the date designated as such by the Non-Defaulting Party, which shall be not later than the fifth Business Day after the day on which the Non-Defaulting Party became aware of the event which caused such automatic termination.

7. Final Settlement Amount

(1) Calculation

(a) Procedure and Bases of Calculation The party or parties not at fault have the right to calculate the Final Settlement Amount.

The Final Settlement Amount is calculated as of the Termination Date by offsetting the values of each party's Transactions, Margin Claims and Amounts Due (i.e. cash payments or securities deliveries due but not made because of the termination) and calculating one net figure payable one way or the other.

Each term is defined according to its various constituents.

Default Value relates to the value of Securities or assets underlying Derivative Transactions. If the assets are deliverable by the Calculation Party the net proceeds are reduced by selling fees and expenses. If the assets are to be delivered to the Calculation Party the purchase fees and expenses are added to the amount receivable. If the market price of assets cannot be ascertained the Calculation Party's good faith determination of its losses and costs (minus its gains) in respect of such assets will be used to determine the Default Market Value.

Margin Claims include accrued interest on cash deposits.

Apart from Transaction losses and costs, Transaction Values take into account the cost of replacement hedging transactions (calculated by averaging at least two market quotations). If only one quotation is available, the calculation of Transaction Value will be made in good faith by the Calculation Party himself.

The Quotation Date is the Early Termination Date but with automatic termination for an Insolvency Event, the Quotation Date may be set by the Non-Defaulting Party but not later than the fifth Business Day after it became aware of the Insolvency Event which caused the automatic termination.

(b) *Conversion.* Any Amounts Due, Default Value, Margin Claims and Transaction Value not denominated in the Base Currency shall be converted into the Base Currency at the Applicable Exchange Rate. "Base Currency" means the euro, unless otherwise agreed. "Applicable Exchange Rate" means the arithmetic mean of the respective rates at which the person calculating or converting an amount pursuant to the Agreement is reasonably able to (i) purchase the relevant other currency with, and (ii) sell such currency for, the Base Currency on the date as of which such amount is calculated or converted.

(2) *Payment Obligations.*

(a) *One Calculation Party.* If one party only acts as Calculation Party, the Final Settlement Amount, as calculated by it, shall be paid (i) to that party by the other party if it is a positive number and (ii) by that party to the other party if it is a negative number; in the latter case the amount payable shall be the absolute value of the Final Settlement Amount.

(b) *Two Calculation Parties.* If both parties act as Calculation Party and their calculations of the Final Settlement Amount differ from each other, the Final Settlement Amount shall (i) be equal to one-half of the difference between the amounts so calculated by both parties (such difference being, for the avoidance of doubt, the sum of the absolute values of such amounts if one is positive and the other negative) and (ii) be paid by the party which has calculated a negative or the lower positive amount.

(b) Conversion All calculations of the constituent elements of the Final Settlement Amount are to be converted at prevailing market exchange rates into the Base Currency which shall be the euro unless otherwise agreed in the Special Provisions.

(2) Payment Obligations

(a) One Calculation Party This provision is equivalent to the Second Method in the 1992 ISDA Master Agreement. If the Final Settlement Amount is positive, the Defaulting Party pays it to the Non-Defaulting Party. If it is negative, then the Non-Defaulting Party pays it to the Defaulting Party. In either case the full amount due must be paid over.

An easy way to remember who gets what is to view the positive and negative amounts from the Non-Defaulting Party's viewpoint. If the close-out amount is positive the Non-Defaulting Party receives it and could be said to view the situation positively. If the close-out amount is negative, the Non-Defaulting Party has to pay it over and so views the situation negatively.

(b) Two Calculation Parties In a "no fault" termination both parties will act as Calculation Parties. It is likely their calculations of the Final Settlement Amount will differ. In that case the amount payable is calculated as one half of the difference between the amounts calculated by them both and is paid by the party who has calculated a negative amount or a lower positive amount.

(3) *Notification and Due Date.*

(a) *Notification.* The Calculation Party shall notify as soon as reasonably possible the other party of the Final Settlement Amount calculated by it and provide to such other party a statement setting forth in reasonable detail the basis upon which the Final Settlement Amount was determined.

(b) *Due Date.* The Final Settlement Amount shall be payable immediately upon receipt of the notification mentioned in paragraph (a) if termination occurs as a result of an Event of Default, and otherwise within two Business Days following such receipt, but in either case not before the Early Termination Date, It shall bear interest as from the Early Termination Date to the date on which the payment is due at the Interbank Rate and thereafter at the Default Rate.

(4) *Set-Off.* The Non-Defaulting Party may set off its obligation (if any) to pay the Final Settlement Amount against any actual or contingent claims ("Counterclaims") which it has against the Defaulting Party on any legal grounds whatsoever (including by virtue of any financing or other contract). For the purpose of calculating the value of the Counterclaims, the Non-Defaulting Party shall, (i) to the extent that they are not payable in the Base Currency, convert them into the Base Currency at the Applicable Exchange Rate, (ii) to the extent that they are contingent or unascertained, take into account for such calculation their potential amount, if ascertainable, or otherwise a reasonable estimate thereof, (iii) to the extent that they are claims other than for the payment of money, determine their value in money and convert them into a money claim expressed in the Base Currency and (iv) to the extent that they are not yet due and payable, determine their present value (also having regard to interest claims), The provisions of this subsection 4 relating to Counterclaims against a Defaulting Party shall apply *mutatis mutandis* to Counterclaims against an Affected Party if termination occurred pursuant to Section 6(2)(a)(ii) or (iii).

(3) Notification and Due Date

(a) Notification The Calculation Party has a duty promptly to provide the other party with a statement showing, in reasonable detail, how he has calculated the Final Settlement Amount.

(b) Due Date The Final Settlement Amount shall be payable immediately upon receipt of the Calculation Party's notification of it if the termination is due to an Event of Default or within two Business Days of its receipt if termination is due to some other reason but in any case it will not be payable before the Termination Date. Interest is payable on the Final Settlement Amount from the Termination Date up to the time it is due at the rate designated. The Default Rate applies if the payment is made late.

(4) Set-Off

Once the Final Settlement Amount has been calculated, if it is negative and the Non-Defaulting Party is obliged to pay it over to the Defaulting Party, the Non-Defaulting Party has the right to calculate and offset any Counterclaims it has against the Defaulting Party (including under other contracts). Counterclaims in other currencies can be converted into the Base Currency (e.g. into euros); a reasonable estimate can be made for contingent claims; non-money claims can be converted into monetary terms in the Base Currency; and future claims can be discounted back to their net present value, having regard to interest claims.

The set-off clause also applies to Counterclaims against an Affected Party if termination is due to Illegality, Impossibility or Credit Event Upon Restructuring Change of Circumstances events.

8. Notices

(1) *Manner of Giving Notices.* Unless otherwise specified in the Agreement, any notice or other communication under the Agreement shall be made by letter, telex, telefax or any electronic messaging system agreed to by the parties in the Special Provisions to the address (if any) previously specified by the addressee.

(2) *Effectiveness.* Every notice or other communication made in accordance with subsection 1 shall be effective (a) if made by letter or telefax, upon receipt by the addressee, (b) if made by telex, upon receipt by the sender of the addressee's answerback at the end of transmission, and (c) if made by an electronic messaging system, upon receipt of that electronic message, provided that if, in any such case, such notice or other communication is not received on a Business Day or is received after the close of business on a Business Day, it shall take effect on the first following day that is a Business Day.

(3) *Change of Address.* Either party may by notice to the other change the address, telex or telefax number or electronic messaging system details at which notices or other communications are to be given to it.

8. Notices

(1) Manner of Giving Notices

Notices between the parties may be made by letter, telex or fax. Any electronic messaging system agreed to between the parties must be stated in the Special Provisions.

(2) Effectiveness

This provision determines the timing of receipt of notices by the addressee depending upon the medium used to communicate them. Any notices not received on a Business Day or after close of business on it, shall be effective only from the following Business Day.

(3) Change of Address

Changes in contact details should be notified to the other party.

9. Booking Offices

(1) *Extent of Obligations.* If a party enters into a Transaction through a Booking Office other than its principal office, its obligations in respect of that Transaction shall constitute obligations of such party as a whole, to the same extent as if they had been entered through such party's principal office. Such party shall not be obliged, however, to perform such obligations through any of its other offices if performance through that Booking Office is unlawful or impossible by virtue of any of the events described in Section 6(2)(a)(ii).

(2) *Change of Booking Office.* Neither party may change a Booking Office without the prior written consent of the other.

(3) *Definition.* "Booking Office" of a party means the office agreed by the parties through which such party is acting for the relevant Transaction, provided that if no such office is agreed in respect of a party, such party's principal office (or, in the absence of a principal office, such party's registered office or place of residence) shall be deemed to be the Booking Office.

9. Booking Offices

(1) Extent of Obligations

The first sentence states that a counterparty may regard entry into of a Transaction by a party through one of its branches as an obligation of the organisation as a whole, as though the Transaction had been entered into by the party's Head Office. However, that party is not obliged to perform such obligations through any of its other offices (including its Head Office) if performance is illegal or impossible through the Transaction's original Booking Office.

(2) Change of Booking Office

Prior written consent of the other party is needed for a party to change its Booking Office. Consent is necessary because such a change could have adverse tax consequences for the other party.

(3) Definition

The Booking Office is the office agreed by the parties for the relevant Transaction and payments under it. If no Booking Office is stated, the fallback is a party's Head Office or registered office in its place of residence.

10. Miscellaneous

(1) *Transfer of Rights and Obligations.* No rights or obligations under the Agreement may be transferred, charged or otherwise disposed of to or in favour of any third person without the prior consent of the other party given in the manner specified in Section 8(1), except that no such consent shall be required in the case of a transfer of all or substantially all assets of a party in connection with a Corporate Restructuring which does not involve a change of the tax status relevant to the Agreement and does not otherwise adversely affect the interests of the other party to any significant extent. The limitation provided in the preceding sentence shall not apply to a party's right to receive the Final Settlement Amount or to be indemnified pursuant to subsection 2.

(2) *Expenses.* A Defaulting Party and a party failing to make a payment or delivery when due shall on demand indemnify the other party for all reasonable expenses, including legal fees, incurred by the other party for the enforcement or protection of its rights under the Agreement in connection with an Event of Default or such failure.

(3) *Recording.* Each party (i) may electronically or otherwise record telephone conversations of the parties in connection with the Agreement or any potential Transaction, (ii) shall give notice of such potential recording to its relevant personnel and obtain any consent that may be legally required before permitting such personnel to conduct such telephone conversations and (iii) agrees that recordings may be submitted in evidence in any Proceedings relating to the Agreement or any potential Transaction.

(4) *Documents.* So long as either party has or may have any obligation under the Agreement, each party shall, if it is reasonably able and legally in a position to do so and would not thereby materially prejudice its legal or commercial position, promptly make available to the other or to any appropriate government or taxing authority any form, certificate or other document (properly completed and, where appropriate, certified) that is either (a) specified in the Agreement, or (b) reasonably requested in writing in order to allow the other party to make a payment under the Agreement without any deduction or withholding for or on account of any tax or other duty, or with such deduction or withholding at a reduced rate.

10. Miscellaneous

This is a catch-all clause with 11 sub-sections.

(1) Transfer of Rights and Obligations

The transfers stated in this clause are not permitted without the prior written consent of the other party. Such consent is not required where a Corporate Restructuring occurs which does not have asset reduction, tax or other significant adverse effects. No consent is necessary for a party to transfer any Final Settlement Amount due to it from the other party. This provision resembles Section 7 of the ISDA Master Agreement.

(2) *Expenses*

This is an expenses indemnity for a Non-Defaulting Party or an innocent party seeking to enforce or protect its rights following an Event of Default by its counterparty or non-receipt of collateral it expected to receive from them.

(3) *Recording*

This common provision is recommended by the UK Financial Services Authority's *Conduct of Business Sourcebook (2007)*.

(4) *Documents*

The parties conditionally agree to provide to each other or to any government or tax authority such documents as may be stated in the EMA or requested separately to mitigate the effects of withholding tax.

(5) *Remedies.* The rights and remedies provided in the Agreement are cumulative and not exclusive of any rights and remedies provided by law.

(6) *No Waiver.* A failure or delay in exercising (and any partial exercise of) any right or remedy under the Agreement shall not operate as a waiver (or partial waiver) of, and accordingly not preclude or limit any future exercise of that right or remedy.

(7) *Termination.* The Agreement may be terminated by either party upon the giving of not less than twenty days' notice to the other party. Notwithstanding such notice, any Transaction then outstanding shall continue to be subject to the provisions of the Agreement and to that extent the effect of the termination shall occur only when all obligations under the last such Transaction shall have been performed.

(8) *Contractual Currency.* If for any reason a payment is made in a currency other than the Contractual Currency and the amount so paid, converted into the Contractual Currency at the exchange rate prevailing at the time of such payment for the sale of such other currency against the Contractual Currency, as reasonably determined by the payee, falls short of the amount in the Contractual Currency payable under the Agreement, the party owing such amount shall, as a separate and independent obligation, immediately compensate the other party for the shortfall.

(9) *Previous Transactions.* Transactions entered into prior to the effective date of a Master Agreement will be subject to such Master Agreement, individually or by category, to the extent provided in the Special Provisions.

(5) Remedies

This provision is inserted because termination should not be the exclusive remedy of the Non-Defaulting Party. Such party also has the options of leaving the EMA in place or of seeking specific performance of the counterparty's obligations (i.e. where money damages would provide insufficient relief and delivery of securities was required). However, he is unlikely to succeed in an English court as judges are unwilling to "rewrite the terms" of master agreements which promote cash damages as the compensation at close-out rather than delivery of securities.

(6) No waiver

This standard provision is found in many legal agreements. Waivers given under the EMA do not set any precedent for the future.

(7) Termination

The EMA has an unusual termination provision triggered by 20 days' notice by either party. However, this is without prejudice to existing Transactions and total termination of the EMA will only occur when the last payment has been made under the last Transaction.

(8) Contractual Currency

This is a standard provision setting forth obligations to make good currency conversion shortfalls. The ISDA Master Agreement extends this provision to cover return of surpluses made on currency conversions but the EMA does not. Under both Agreements the Contractual Currency is the one stated for payments in a Confirmation.

(9) Previous Transactions

This is a scope of agreement or sweep-in clause which aims to draw in transactions outside the EMA. Such transactions need to be stated in the Special Provisions.

(10) *Agency Transactions.*

(a) *Conditions.* A party may enter into a Transaction,(an "Agency Transaction") as agent (the "Agent") for a third person (a "Principal") only if (i) the party has authority on behalf of that Principal to enter into the Transaction, to perform on behalf of that Principal all of that Principal's obligations and to accept performance of the obligations of the other party and receive all notices and other communications under the Agreement and (ii) when entering into the Transaction and in the relevant Confirmation the party specifies that it is acting as Agent in respect of the Transaction and discloses to the other party the identity of the Principal. If these conditions are not fully satisfied, the party shall be deemed to act as principal.

(b) *Information on Certain Events.* Each party undertakes that, if it enters as Agent into an Agency Transaction, forthwith upon becoming aware (i) of any event or circumstance which constitutes an event as described in Section 6(l)(a)(viii) with respect to the relevant Principal or (ii) of any breach of any of the representations given in Section 5 and paragraph (f) below or of any event or circumstance which has the result that any such representation would be incorrect on the date as of which it was made, it will inform the other party of that fact and will, if so required by the other party, furnish the other party with such additional information as the other party may reasonably request.

(c) *Parties.* Each Agency Transaction shall be a transaction solely between the relevant Principal and the other party. All provisions of the Agreement shall apply separately as between the other party and each Principal for whom the Agent has entered into an Agency Transaction, as if each such Principal were a party to a separate Agreement with the other party, except as provided in paragraph (d) below. A Process Agent appointed by the Agent shall be a Process Agent also for each Principal.

(d) *Notice of Termination.* If an Event of Default or a Change of Circumstances as described in Section 6(2)(a)(ii) or (iii) occurs with respect to the Agent, the other party may give notice pursuant to Section 6(l)(b) or 6(2)(b), respectively, to the Principal with the same effect as if an Event of Default or Change of Circumstances, respectively, had occurred with respect to the Principal.

(10) Agency Transactions

(a) Conditions Agency Transactions are possible under the EMA provided the Agent is fully authorised by the Principal to act on his behalf; its agency capacity is stated in the Confirmation; and it is acting for a disclosed principal. Failure to fulfil these conditions will convert the Agent to a Principal.

(b) Information on Certain Events An Agent must inform the other party of any Insolvency Event affecting the Principal; or of any breach of a Section 5 representation or of the representation in sub-section 10(f) below; and of any event which would invalidate any representation as of the date it was made. The Agent also undertakes to provide any additional information reasonably sought by the other party.

(c) Parties Effectively an Agency Transaction is a transaction between the relevant Principal and the other party as if that Principal had entered into a separate EMA with the other party. A Process Agent appointed by the Agent shall be deemed to be a Process Agent for each Principal.

(d) Notice of Term If an Event of Default or Illegality, Impossibility or Credit Event Upon Restructuring Change of Circumstances event occurs to the Agent, the other party may issue a termination notice to the Principal as if the above events had occurred to the Principal.

(e) *Own Account Transactions.* The foregoing provisions do not affect the operation of the Agreement between the parties hereto in respect of any Transactions into which the Agent may enter on its own account as a principal.

(f) *Representation.* Each party acting as Agent represents to the other in its own name and in the name of the Principal that it will, on each occasion on which it enters or purports to enter into an Agency Transaction, have the authority as described in subsection 10(a)(i) on behalf of the person whom it specifies as the Principal in respect of that Agency Transaction.

(11) *Severability.* In the event that any provision of the Agreement is invalid, illegal or unenforceable under the law of any jurisdiction, the validity, legality and enforceability of the remaining provisions in the Agreement under the law of such jurisdiction, and the validity, legality and enforceability of such and any other provisions under the law of any other jurisdiction shall not in any way be affected thereby. The parties shall, in such event, in good faith negotiate a valid provision the economic effect of which comes as close as possible to that of the invalid, illegal or unenforceable provisions.

(e) Own Account Transactions The Agent may enter into transactions as a principal in its own right under the EMA whereupon these Agency provisions would not apply to it.

(f) Representation Each party when or if acting as Agent under the EMA reaffirms that it has the Principal's authority to act on its behalf whenever it enters into an Agency Transaction.

(11) Severability

This is a standard provision found in many other legal agreements. It lets the EMA remain in effect even if an individual provision therein may become unenforceable. Negotiations between the parties for a substitute provision must be conducted in good faith.

11. Governing Law, Settlement of Disputes, Jurisdiction, Arbitration

(1) *Governing Law.* The Agreement shall be governed by and construed in accordance with the law specified in the Special Provisions or, failing such specification, the law of the country, if identical, in which both parties' principal offices are located when the Master Agreement between them is entered into.

(2) *Settlement of Disputes, Jurisdiction, Arbitration.* Each party irrevocably agrees that in respect of any dispute arising under or related to the Agreement (i) the courts specified in the Special Provisions shall have non-exclusive jurisdiction and each party irrevocably submits to such non-exclusive jurisdiction, or (ii) if so specified in the Special Provisions, any such dispute shall be finally settled by one or more arbitrators appointed and proceeding in accordance with the rules of arbitration specified in the Special Provisions, each party agreeing to comply with such rules. Failing either of such specifications, the courts having jurisdiction in the principal financial centre or, in the absence of a generally recognized financial centre, the capital city of the country whose law governs the Agreement shall have non-exclusive jurisdiction with respect to any suit, action or other proceeding relating to the Agreement (the "Proceedings") and each party irrevocably submits to such non-exclusive jurisdiction.

(3) *Service of Process.* If so specified in the Special Provisions, each party appoints a process agent (the "Process Agent") to receive, for it and on its behalf, service of process in any Proceedings. If for any reason a party's Process Agent is unable to act as such, such party shall promptly notify the other party and within thirty days appoint a substitute process agent which is acceptable to the other party.

(4) *Waiver of Immunity.* The Agreement constitutes a commercial agreement. To the fullest extent permitted by applicable law, each party waives, with respect to itself and its assets, (irrespective of their use or intended use), all immunity on the grounds of sovereignty or otherwise from suit, execution or other legal process and agrees that it will not claim any such immunity in any Proceedings.

11. Governing Law, Settlement of Disputes, Jurisdiction, Arbitration

(1) Governing Law

For domestic agreements, the parties' domestic law will govern assuming they are both in the same jurisdiction. A choice of law is necessary for cross-border transactions and must be stated in the Special Provisions. Alternatively, parties can choose the domestic law of either of them or the law of a third country agreed between them.

(2) Settlement of Disputes, Jurisdiction, Arbitration

Non-exclusive jurisdiction is provided in this clause and each party irrevocably submits to it. The relevant courts must be stated in the Special Provisions. Arbitration proceedings are also possible and disputes may be settled by one or more arbitrators under rules stated in the Special Provisions. Where neither route is stated in the Special Provisions, the fallback is the courts having jurisdiction in the main financial centre or capital city of the country whose law governs the EMA.

(3) Service of Process

Where relevant, Process Agents must be specified in the Special Provisions. Process Agents receive legal documents on behalf of contracting parties who are not incorporated in the jurisdiction whose law governs the EMA. The 30-day time limit to appoint a substitute Process Agent is normal.

(4) Waiver of Immunity

Generally sovereigns and supranationals (who are often established under special charters granting them legal and tax immunities) like to have immunity from being sued and from having their assets confiscated. This right is waived here for the contracting parties. The statement that the EMA is a commercial agreement is an emphasis rarely seen in such documentation.

MASTER AGREEMENT
FOR FINANCIAL TRANSACTIONS

PRODUCT ANNEX
FOR
SECURITIES LOANS
Edition January 2001

This Annex supplements the General Provisions which form part of any Master Agreement for Financial Transactions based on the form published by the Banking Federation of the European Union.

1. Purpose, Applicability

(1) *Purpose.* The purpose of this Annex ("Securities Lending Annex") is to govern Transactions ("Securities Loans") in which one party (the "Lender") lends to the other (the "Borrower") Securities (the "Loaned Securities") for a determined or initially undetermined period of time. Any reference in this Annex to a Transaction shall be construed as a reference to a Securities Loan.

(2) *Applicability.* If this Annex forms part of a Master Agreement between any two parties, such Master Agreement (including this Annex) shall apply to any Securities Loan between such parties which is to be conducted by each party through a Booking Office specified in such Master Agreement in respect of Securities Loans.

Product Annex for Securities Loans

This Annex supplements the EMA's General Provisions. The latest edition of it was published in January 2001.

1. Purpose, Applicability

(1) Purpose

This provision describes a typical securities loan which may be for a fixed term or more likely contracted on an open or on demand basis.

(2) Applicability

This provision brings under the EMA Securities Loans which are subject to this Annex. Booking Offices will be stated in paragraph 5 of the Special Provisions.

2. Deliveries and Payments

(1) *Initial Delivery.* On the date agreed for the delivery of the Loaned Securities (the "Delivery Date"), the Lender shall transfer such Loaned Securities to the Borrower.

(2) *Return.* On the date agreed for the return of the Loaned Securities (the "Return Date"), the Borrower shall transfer to the Lender Securities of the same kind and quantity as the Loaned Securities.

(3) *Interpretation.* Any reference in this Annex to the Loaned Securities or other Securities in the context of the return or retransfer thereof, or to any rights or other assets to be transferred pursuant to Section 3(4), shall be construed so as to mean a reference to Securities, rights or assets of the same kind and quantity as (also referred to below as the "Equivalent" of) such Loaned Securities or other Securities, rights or assets, respectively.

(4) *On Demand Transactions.* The parties may agree that Securities Loans are terminable on demand, in which case the Return Date shall be the date specified in the demand notice sent by either party to the other, provided that the period between the taking effect of such notice and the Return Date so specified shall be not less than the minimum period customarily required for the delivery of Securities of the relevant kind. In the absence of a demand notice, the Return for a Transaction terminable on demand shall be the day which falls 364 days after the Delivery Date.

2. Deliveries and Payments

(1) Initial Delivery

Lender shall deliver Loaned Securities to Borrower on the Delivery Date at the start of the loan. Delivery would be against agreed Margin under the terms of the Margin Maintenance Annex.

(2) Return

On the Return Date Borrower will retransfer the Loaned Securities to Lender and Lender would return the relevant Margin to Borrower under the terms of the Margin Maintenance Annex. The returned securities must be of the same class, type and issuer as the Loaned Securities but need not be the identically numbered securities. In other words, they must be *fungible* securities.

(3) Interpretation

The equivalent nature of the Loaned Securities to be returned or retransferred is emphasised here as to their fungibility.

(4) On Demand Transactions

For an on demand Transaction the Return Date shall be the date stated in the demand notice although the time gap between the notice taking effect and the Return Date itself must be at least the normal minimum settlement time customary in the market concerned. Where no demand notice is issued, the Transaction will automatically terminate 364 days after the Delivery Date. This cut-off was included for tax and regulatory reasons in a number of jurisdictions. Such an automatic cut-off may have systems implications.

(5) *Late Delivery*

(a) *Failure by Lender.* If the Lender fails to transfer the Loaned Securities to the Borrower on the applicable Delivery Date, the Borrower may, at any time while such failure continues:

(i) require the Lender to pay to the Borrower an amount equal to the excess, if any, of the Borrower's Alternative Borrowing Cost over the pro rata portion of the Lending Fee attributable to the period of the delay, each calculated for the period from (and including) the Delivery Date to (but excluding) the earlier of the date on which the Loaned Securities are transferred to the Borrower and the Return Date (which in the case of a Transaction terminable on demand shall be deemed to be the earliest date on which the Loaned Securities would be required to be returned following a demand by the Lender); "Alternative Borrowing Cost" of a party means the cost (including fees and expenses), as determined by such party, which such party has or would have reasonably incurred in borrowing the Equivalent of the Loaned Securities in the market for the relevant period; and

(ii) if the parties have not agreed on measures to promptly remedy the failure, give notice to the Lender that the Return Date shall be advanced so as to occur immediately, whereupon the obligations of the parties to lend or return the Loaned Securities (respectively) shall cease and no deliveries or payments shall be due between them other than, if applicable, pursuant to (i).

(b) *Failure by Borrower.* If the Borrower fails to return the Loaned Securities to the Lender on the applicable Return Date, the Lender may, at any time while such failure continues:

(i) require the Borrower to pay to the Lender an amount equal to the higher of (a) the Lender's Alternative Borrowing Cost and (b) the Lending Fee, each calculated for the period from (and including) the Return Date to (but excluding) the date of actual return of the Loaned Securities or, if earlier, the date specified in the notice, if any, given pursuant to (ii); and

(ii) if the parties have not agreed on measures to promptly remedy the failure, give notice to the Borrower requiring cash settlement in lieu of delivery on a date to be specified in such notice, whereupon the obligation of the Borrower to return the Loaned Securities shall cease and the Borrower shall pay to the Lender an amount equal to the Acquisition Cost for such Securities; "Acquisition Cost" means the cost (including fees and expenses), as determined by the Lender, which the Lender has or would have reasonably incurred in purchasing the Equivalent of the Loaned Securities in the market on the date so specified for cash settlement.

(5) Late Delivery

(a) *Failure by Lender* If the Lender fails to transfer the Loaned Securities to the Borrower on the Delivery Date, the Borrower may:

(i) require the Lender to pay the excess of the Borrower's cost of borrowing the Loaned Securities (including fees and expenses) over the Lending Fee pro rated for the delay. The calculation will be from and including the Delivery Date to but excluding the earlier of the date on which the Loaned Securities are transferred to the Borrower and the Return Date. With on demand Transactions the provisions of Section 2(4) of this Annex would need to be observed; or

(ii) terminate the Transaction immediately with the Borrower giving the Lender notice that the Return Date has been accelerated or brought forward. All their obligations to lend or return Loaned Securities are replaced by the close-out process for the individual transaction.

(b) *Failure by Buyer* If the Borrower fails to transfer the Loaned Securities to the Lender on the Return Date, the Lender may:

(i) require the Borrower to pay the excess of the Lender's cost of borrowing the Loaned Securities over the Lending Fee pro rated for the delay. The calculation will be from and including the Return Date to but excluding the date the Loaned Securities are actually returned or earlier as stated in a notice under Section 2(5)(b)(ii) of this Annex; or

(ii) terminate the Transaction with the Borrower paying cash compensation to the Lender equal to the cost including fees and expenses determined by the Lender for buying in the Loaned Securities in the market on the cash settlement date.

(c) *Partial Delivery.* If the Lender or the Borrower transfers some, but not all, of the Loaned Securities on the date specified in sub-paragraph (a) or (b), respectively, the respective other party may, at its option, either accept such transfer and exercise its rights under those sub-paragraphs with respect to the residual Loaned Securities or decline such acceptance and exercise its rights with respect to all Loaned Securities.

(d) *Remedies.* Beyond the remedies provided in this subsection 5, neither party shall, in the event of any failure by the other party to transfer or return Loaned Securities, be entitled to recover any additional damage as a consequence of such failure, and such failure shall not constitute an Event of Default under Section 6(1)(a)(iii) of the General Provisions. This paragraph (d) is without prejudice to any remedy available in the event of a failure by a party to perform any other obligation (including any obligation to make a payment under this subsection 5).

(6) *Special Events.* If, during the term of a Transaction and in respect of some or all of the Loaned Securities:

(i) a payment of any interest or dividend or any other distribution of money or other property by the issuer of the Loaned Securities (collectively a "Distribution", which term shall include a repayment of principal and a payment in the case of a capital reduction) would, as a result of any change in law or in the application or official interpretation thereof occurring after the date on which such Transaction is entered into, be subject to any deduction or withholding in respect of a tax or other duty or would give rise to a tax credit;

(ii) a notice of early redemption has been validly given;

(iii) a public redemption, exchange, conversion or compensation offer or a public purchase bid is made or announced;

(iv) subscription or other preferential rights which are not freely transferable are granted, or non-fungible property is distributed, to the holders; or

(v) if specified in the Special Provisions, a tax credit or tax entitlement is attached to any interest or dividend paid to the holders (whether or not subparagraph (i) would otherwise apply)

then, subject to any other agreement between the parties, the Return Date for such Securities shall, automatically in the case of (v) and otherwise upon demand by either party, be advanced to the third Business Day before, in the case of (i), (ii) and (v), the expected payment or redemption date or before, in the case of (iii) and (iv), the last day on which such bid or offer may be accepted or the day on which such rights or assets are granted or distributed.

(c) *Partial Delivery* If Lender or Borrower only makes a partial delivery or return of Loaned Securities on their due date, the other party can either choose to accept the partial delivery and exercise its rights in respect of the remaining Loaned Securities or he can reject it and exercise its rights over all the Loaned Securities involved in the Transaction.

(d) *Remedies* Consequential damages for late delivery are excluded as a matter of principle and the EMA basically follows many other master agreements in this respect.

The failure to deliver shall not constitute a Breach of Agreement Event of Default. However, the EMA explicitly provides that the party entitled to the delivery can charge the costs of buying in substitute securities (see Section 2(5)(a)(i) and (b)(i) of this Annex).

This provision does not prevent a party from seeking any other legal remedy in respect of obligations due other than from a failure to deliver.

(6) Special Events

Subject to any other agreement, the Return Date is advanced in a tax credit or the following cases:

(i) a change in law or its interpretation or application results in a withholding tax being levied on an interest or dividend distribution by the issuer of the Loaned Securities; or

(ii) a notice of early redemption is validly issued in respect of the Loaned Securities; or

(iii) a public redemption, exchange, conversion or purchase bid is made or announced or a compensation offer is made; or

(iv) non-freely transferable subscription rights or their like are granted or distributed to Loaned Securities holders; or

(v) if stated in the Special Provisions, a tax credit or entitlement is attached to any interest or dividend paid to holders of the Loaned Securities, whether or not there are withholding tax implications.

The acceleration or early termination is automatic in respect of (v). Otherwise it is on demand by either party whereupon the Return Date will be advanced either to three Business Days before the occurrence of the event or in the case of (iii) or (iv) to the last day on which a bid or offer may be accepted or the day on which the assets or rights are granted.

3. Distributions, Subscription Rights

(1) *Cash Distributions.* If during the term of a Securities Loan any Distribution of money is made by the issuer to the holders of the Loaned Securities, the Borrower shall pay to the Lender, on the date of such Distribution, an amount in the same currency as, and equal to, the amount received by the holders in respect of such Distribution.

(2) *Withholding Taxes Tax Credits.* If a Distribution is subject to withholding tax and/or gives rise to a tax credit, the amount payable by the Borrower under subsection 1 shall be equal to the full amount to which the Lender would be entitled, as previously notified by it, in respect of such Distribution if it were the owner of the Loaned Securities, including the amount of (a) any applicable withholding tax to the extent that the Lender would be entitled to apply for an exemption from, or a refund of, such tax and (b) any tax credit available to the Lender.

(3) *Subscription Rights.* If subscription rights which are freely transferable are granted with respect to the Loaned Securities, the Borrower shall transfer to the Lender, not later than on the third day on which such rights are traded, the Equivalent of the subscription rights attributable to such Loaned Securities. If the rights are not so transferred by such date, the Lender may purchase their Equivalent in the market for the account of the Borrower. Should the Lender be unable so to purchase the rights, it may require the Borrower to pay to it an amount equal to the Market Value of such rights prevailing on the next following trading day for such rights.

(4) *Non-cash Distributions.* Any freely transferable bonus shares, non-cash Distributions and ancillary rights (other than subscription rights) which are issued, made or allotted with respect to the Loaned Securities during the term of a Securities Loan shall be transferred to the Lender on the Return Date.

(5) *Transfer Obligations.* For the avoidance of doubt, the provisions of subsections 1 through 4 shall apply whether or not the Borrower retains the ownership of the Loaned Securities during the term of the Transaction.

3. Distributions, Subscription Rights

(1) Cash Distributions

The Borrower must pay a manufactured dividend to the Lender on income it receives from the issuer of Loaned Securities on the same day he receives it, if possible.

(2) Withholding Taxes, Tax Credits

If payment of a distribution is subject to a withholding tax levied on the issuer, the Borrower must gross up and pay the Lender what it would have been entitled to receive as a distribution had it been the holder of the Loaned Securities. However, the Lender must have previously notified the Borrower of this situation and of any other relevant tax issues such as any tax credit available to the Lender.

(3) Subscription Rights

Subscription rights, like any other freely transferable income distribution, are to be transferred by the Borrower to the Lender. Where this is not done by the third trading day of such rights, the Lender may purchase the equivalent subscription rights in the market for the Borrower's account. If it cannot buy such rights, it can require the Borrower to pay it an amount equal to the Market Value of the subscription rights on the next Business Day.

(4) Non-cash Distributions

Any bonus shares, scrip dividends etc. made during the Securities Loan will be transferred to the Lender on the Return Date, for the sake of convenience.

(5) Transfer Obligations

The above provisions will apply whether or not the Borrower retains ownership of the Loaned Securities throughout the Securities Loan's life. He may have sold, repoed or re-lent the Loaned Securities. Even so the above provisions still apply to him.

4. Lending Fee

The Borrower shall pay to the Lender for each Securities Loan a fee (the "Lending Fee") equal to the rate per annum agreed in respect of such Securities Loan and calculated on the value of the Loaned Securities agreed by the parties for this purpose. The Lending Fee shall be calculated for the period from (and including) the Delivery Date or, if later, the date of actual transfer of the Loaned Securities to the Borrower, to (but excluding) the Return Date or, if later, the date of actual return of the Loaned Securities to the Lender, based on the actual number of days in such period and a 360-day year. Unless otherwise agreed, the Lender shall calculate the Lending Fee at the beginning of each month for the preceding month or, if earlier, on the Return Date, and send the Borrower a statement setting forth such Lending Fee. The Lending Fee shall be payable on the second Business Day following receipt of such statement sent by the Lender.

4. Lending Fee

Borrowers typically pay Lenders a fee for borrowing Loaned Securities. It is based upon the agreed value of the Loaned Securities and calculated on the actual number of days the loan is outstanding divided by a 360-day year. It is calculated from and including the Delivery Date to but excluding the Return Date. Alternatively it can be calculated from and including the day the Loaned Securities were actually delivered to the Borrower to but excluding the day they were actually returned to the Lender.

The Lending Fee is calculated by the Lender at the start of each month for the previous month but, if the parties agree, it can be calculated on the Return Date of a Securities Loan if this is earlier. The Lender will provide the Borrower with a statement of the Lending Fee and it is payable on the second Business Day after the Borrower receives it.

5. Margin Provisions

Any obligations of the parties to transfer cash or Securities as Margin under certain circumstances shall be performed in accordance with the provisions of the applicable Margin Maintenance Annex published by the FBE, or with any other rules to be separately agreed.

5. Margin Provisions

Any obligations of the parties to transfer cash or securities margin shall be done in accordance with the EMA's Margin Maintenance Annex or according to such other rules as the parties may agree.

Suggested Form of Confirmation for Securities Loans

This Confirmation template which is shown in Appendix 3 of this book contains the standard terms for securities loans. It is interesting that Margin Ratio (Haircut) is specified here while it is not in the sample Confirmation in Annex II of the GMRA 2000. Credit Departments set Margin Ratios and it is not normal for them to be specifically documented under the GMRA 2000 or GMSLA documents because they are usually agreed by dealers in the Purchase Price.

MASTER AGREEMENT
FOR FINANCIAL TRANSACTIONS

MARGIN MAINTENANCE ANNEX
Edition 2004

This Annex supplements the General Provisions which form part of any Master Agreement for Financial Transactions based on the form published by the FBE.

1. Net Exposure

(1) *General Principles.* If, at any time when Net Exposure is calculated pursuant to subsection 2, one party (the "Margin Provider") has an Adjusted Net Exposure to the other (the "Margin Recipient") resulting from any Transactions and/or from transfers of Margin pursuant to this Annex, the Margin Recipient may by notice to the Margin Provider require the same to transfer to it cash ("Cash Margin") or Securities ("Margin Securities") acceptable to the Margin Recipient and whose aggregate Market Value, when multiplied by the valuation percentage, if any, agreed between the parties ("Valuation Percentage"), shall be at least equal to the Adjusted Net Exposure. "Adjusted Net Exposure" means the sum of the Net Exposure and any supplementary amount ("Independent Amount") agreed in favour of the Margin Recipient less any Independent Amount agreed in favour of the Margin Provider. Such notice may be given orally or as provided in Section 8(1) of the General Provisions. The Net Exposure will be determined, and accordingly Margin will be required to be transferred, in respect of (a) all such Transactions, (b) specified groups of Transactions, (c) each individual Transaction or (d) otherwise, as agreed by the parties (in the Special Provisions or otherwise), provided that failing such agreement, (b) shall apply in such a manner that all Repurchase Transactions, all Securities Loans and all Derivative Transactions shall each form a separate group of Transactions to which this Annex applies. The "Market Value" of cash shall be the nominal amount thereof, converted, if not denominated in the Base Currency, in accordance with subsection 2. Any reference in this Annex to Transactions shall be construed as a reference to Repurchase Transactions and/or Securities Loans and/or Derivative Transactions.

Margin Maintenance Annex

This Annex adopts a new approach in the market in that it provides common margining terms for repos, securities loans and derivative transactions. It was revised in early 2004 to extend coverage to Derivative Transactions. The Annex supplements the EMA's General Provisions.

1. Net Exposure

(1) General Principles

Following calculation of Net Exposure, the party at risk may call upon the other to provide acceptable cash or securities margin to cover the Net Exposure. Net Exposure is modified by adding any Independent Amount agreed in favour of the Margin Recipient and deducting any Independent Amount in favour of the Margin Provider. The result is called the Adjusted Net Exposure. The parties can choose if the margin shall cover:

(a) **all repo, securities lending or derivative transactions; or**

(b) **specified groups of Transactions; or**

(c) **individual Transactions; or**

(d) **as otherwise agreed by the parties in the Special Provisions.**

However, if the parties do not make a choice, the fallback shall be (b) (i.e. repos, securities loans and derivative transactions forming separate groups).

(2) *Calculation.* The person designated by the parties for this purpose or, failing such designation, each party (each the "Valuation Agent") shall calculate the Net Exposure on each Valuation Date by 11 a.m. Brussels time. The Net Exposure shall be expressed as a positive number if the Valuation Agent would, pursuant to its calculation, be the Margin Recipient, and shall otherwise be expressed as a negative number. All calculations shall be made in the Base Currency; any amount not denominated in the Base Currency shall be converted into the Base Currency at the Applicable Exchange Rate.

(2) Calculation

One or both parties may be the Valuation Agent (note the change from the term Calculation Party in the General Provisions). Net Exposure is to be calculated on each Valuation Day by 11.00 a.m. Brussels time. Intra-day valuations or margin calls are not catered for. All calculations shall be made in the Base Currency. A positive Net Exposure will entail a payment of margin to the Margin Recipient while a negative Net Exposure will involve a payment of margin to the Margin Provider.

(3) *Definitions.* "Net Exposure" means (I) in relation to Repurchase Transactions and Securities Loans the excess (if any), calculated pursuant to subsection 2, of the Liabilities of the Margin Provider over the Liabilities of the Margin Recipient, and (II) in relation to Derivative Transactions the Potential Final Settlement Amount, provided that (a) if the calculation is to be made pursuant to both (I) and (II), the Net Exposure shall be the aggregate of the amounts so calculated, (b) the amount of any prior Adjusted Net Exposure in respect of which a transfer of Margin has already been required, but not completed, shall be subtracted from any Net Exposure subsequently calculated and (c) if both parties act as Valuation Agent and their calculations of Net Exposure differ from each other, (i) the Net Exposure shall be one-half of the difference of the amounts so calculated by both parties (such difference being, for the avoidance of doubt, the sum of the absolute values of such amounts if one is positive and the other negative) and (ii) the Margin Provider shall be the party which has calculated a negative or the lower positive amount;

"Liabilities" means, with respect to a party, the aggregate of

(a) the Market Values of any Securities transferred to that party under a Transaction or pursuant to this Annex 1 and not yet returned to the other party, multiplied (i) in the case of Loaned Securities, by the applicable Margin Ratio and (ii) in the case of Margin Securities, by any applicable Valuation Percentage;

(b) a cash amount equal to the sum of (i) the amount, multiplied by the applicable Margin Ratio, of that party's obligation(s) to pay the Repurchase Price in respect of any Repurchase Transaction if the relevant Valuation Date were the Repurchase Date, and (ii) the Market Value, multiplied by any applicable Valuation Percentage, of any Cash Margin transferred to and not repaid by that party (including unpaid accrued interest on such Cash Margin); and

(c) the cash amount or cash equivalent in respect of any Distribution to be paid or transferred by such party to the other party, but not yet paid or transferred;

"Margin" means either Cash Margin or Margin Securities;

"Margin Ratio" (also called "Haircut") means, with respect to each Repurchase Transaction or Securities Loan, the percentage agreed by the parties by which the Liabilities of the Seller or the Borrower in relation to the Repurchase Price and the Loaned Securities, respectively, are multiplied, as provided under "Liabilities" above, in order to determine the Net Exposure; failing an agreement to that effect, the Margin Ratio shall be equal to (a) with respect to a Repurchase Transaction, the Market Value of the Purchased Securities on the date on which the Transaction was entered into, divided by the Purchase Price, and (b) with respect to a Securities Loan (i) the Market Value, on the date on which the Transaction was entered into, of any Margin to be provided at the commencement of such Securities Loan, multiplied by the applicable Valuation Percentage and divided by the Market Value of the Loaned Securities as of such date, and (ii) if no Margin is provided at the commencement of such Securities Loan, 100 per cent., unless the parties have expressly excluded the provision of Margin for the entire term of the Transaction, in which case the Margin Ratio shall be zero until the Return Date;

"Potential Final Settlement Amount" means the amount which, at the time on each Valuation Date when Net Exposure is calculated in respect of Derivative Transactions pursuant to subsection 2, the Valuation Agent, acting as if it were the Calculation Party (as defined in Section 7(1)(a) of the General Provisions), determines to be equal to the Final Settlement Amount calculated in respect of Derivative Transactions (but excluding Repurchase Transactions and Securities Loans), if the same had to be calculated as of such time and date, such determination to be made in accordance with Section 7(1)(a) of the General Provisions, except that (a) if the determination can be made on the basis of bid and offered quotations, the arithmetic mean of such quotations shall be used for such determination, and (b) the amount of Margin Claims shall be adjusted so as to take into account the applicable Valuation Percentages;

"Valuation Date" means, in respect of calculation of the Net Exposure, each of the dates agreed as such between the parties, and failing such agreement each Business Day.

(3) Definitions

This is a long section.

Net Exposure calculations compare the Liabilities of both parties in respect of repos and securities loans and exclude any margin previously called for but not yet transferred. With Derivative Transactions the Net Exposure is the Potential Final Settlement Amount adjusted in the same manner. Where both parties are Valuation Agent and their Net Exposure figures differ, the difference is split and the Margin Provider will be the party who has calculated a negative amount or lower positive amount.

The definition of Liabilities takes into account the Buyer's or Borrower's obligations to retransfer equivalent securities in line with agreed haircuts and taking into account Distributions received but unpaid to the party owed them. Margin can mean either Cash Margin or Margin Securities.

Margin Ratio basically means the overcollateralisation required to the Loaned Securities transferred to the Borrower.

Valuation Date means each of the dates agreed by the parties for calculating Net Exposure or otherwise each Business Day.

2. Notification of Adjusted Net Exposure and Transfer of Margin

(1) *Notification.* Promptly after determining the Net Exposure, the Valuation Agent shall notify each relevant party of the Adjusted Net Exposure and upon request of a party provide such party with a statement setting forth in reasonable detail the calculation basis of the Adjusted Net Exposure. The notice may be given orally or as provided in Section 8(1) of the General Provisions.

(2) *Transfer.* The Margin Provider shall, upon receipt of the notice referred to in the first sentence of Section 1(1), transfer to the Margin Recipient Margin with an aggregate Market Value at least equal to the Adjusted Net Exposure no later than the date agreed for such transfer, and failing such agreement on the Business Day immediately following receipt of such notice, if such notice is received on a Business Day prior to 11.00 a. m., and otherwise on the second Business Day following such receipt.

(3) *Composition of Margin.* The Margin Provider is entitled to determine the composition of the Margin to be transferred, unless the Margin Recipient has previously paid Cash Margin which has not been repaid or transferred Margin Securities which have not been returned to it, in which case the Margin Provider shall first repay such Cash Margin or return such Margin Securities.

(4) *Cash Margin.* Cash Margin shall be acceptable for the purpose of Section 1 (l) if transferred in the Base Currency or such other currency as the parties may have specified as eligible (in the Special Provisions or otherwise). A payment of Cash Margin shall give rise to a debt owing from the Margin Recipient to the Margin Provider and shall bear interest at such rate, and payable at such times, as agreed by the parties. In the absence of such agreement, that rate shall be equal to the Interbank Rate less 0.10 per cent. per annum, and the interest shall be payable at the end of each calendar month and on each date when the Margin Recipient is required to provide or return Margin.

2. Notification of Adjusted Net Exposure and Transfer of Margin

(1) Notification

The Valuation Agent shall notify the other party of the Adjusted Net Exposure promptly and, if requested, provide a statement, in reasonable detail, showing how the Adjusted Net Exposure was calculated. The notice may be provided orally or by letter, telex, fax or electronic messaging system. It will normally be in writing.

(2) Transfer

When the notice is received, the Margin Provider shall transfer Margin with an aggregate value equal to the Adjusted Net Exposure. The transfer shall occur by the deadline agreed by the parties failing which on the following Business Day if such notice is received by the Margin Provider before 11.00 a.m. on a Business Day and, if not, on the second Business Day following receipt of the notice. This provision does not seem to take into account securities with a longer settlement cycle than two Business Days. However, this will probably not be an issue with two contracting parties in the same domestic market.

(3) Composition of Margin

The Margin Provider is entitled to decide what type of margin it wishes to transfer. However, where the Margin Recipient has previously transferred cash or securities to the Margin Provider the Margin Recipient can insist that these be returned first.

(4) Cash Margin

Cash Margin is payable in the Base Currency or in a currency specified as eligible in the Special Provisions. Payment of Cash Margin represents a debt owed by the Margin Recipient to the Margin Provider. Cash Margin will bear interest at an agreed rate, failing which it shall be Interbank Rate minus 10 basis points per annum. The inclusion of a fallback interest rate is new in collateral agreements. Interest is payable at the end of each calendar month and on each date the Margin Recipient returns Cash Margin.

(5) *Margin Securities.* Margin Securities shall be acceptable for the purpose of Section 1 (l) if Securities of the relevant kind (a) have been specified by the parties as eligible (in the Special Provisions or otherwise) or (b) have an original maturity of not more than five years and are issued by the central government of the country in which the Margin Recipient has its principal office or in which it is organised, incorporated or resident. A transfer of Margin Securities shall give rise to an obligation of the Margin Recipient to the Margin Provider to return such Securities as provided in this Annex.

(6) *Margin Thresholds.* Except in the case of a return of Margin pursuant to subsection 7, a transfer of Margin will take place only (a) to the extent that the Adjusted Net Exposure exceeds the threshold amount, if any, agreed by the parties ("Exposure Threshold") in relation to the Margin Recipient's Net Exposure and (b) if the Market Value of the Margin to be transferred exceeds the minimum amount, if any, agreed for such transfer (the "Minimum Transfer Amount"). In the absence of an agreement on either or both such amounts, such amount, or both, respectively, shall be zero.

(7) *Return of Margin.* Upon satisfaction by a party of all its obligations under Transactions in respect of which Margin is required to be transferred as provided in the fourth sentence of Section 1(1), any Margin previously transferred and not returned shall be returned to the party which transferred it.

(5) Margin Securities

Agreed Margin Securities should be stated in the Special Provisions. Securities with a maturity of less than five years and issued by the Margin Recipient's central government are considered acceptable Margin Securities. A transfer of Margin Securities constitutes an ultimate obligation of the Margin Recipient to retransfer them to the Margin Provider.

(6) Margin Thresholds

Margin transfers may be subject to Exposure Thresholds or Minimum Transfer Amounts. Where not stated, these shall be zero.

(7) Return of Margin

All Margin must be returned when the other party has fully satisfied its obligations under Transactions for which Margin was required (i.e. no Net Exposure is left).

3. Provisions Applicable to Margin Securities

The provisions of Section 3 of the Repurchase Annex (regarding substitution of Purchased Securities) and Sections 2(3), 2(5)(b)(ii) and (d), 2(6) and 3 of the Securities Lending Annex (regarding interpretation, failure to return Loaned Securities, special events, Distributions and subscription rights) shall apply *mutatis mutandis* to Margin Securities transferred pursuant to this Annex, provided that (a) the consent of the Margin Recipient shall not be required for a substitution by the Margin Provider of new Margin Securities acceptable pursuant to Section 2(5) of this Annex for Margin Securities previously transferred and (b) if any of the special events referred to in terminated, but Margin acceptable pursuant to Section 2 (4) or (5) of this Annex shall be substituted for such Securities upon request of either party.

3. Provisions Applicable to Margin Securities

Certain provisions of the Repurchase Annex and the Securities Lending Annex shall apply, *mutatis mutandis*, to Margin Securities. However, if substituted Margin consists of cash or securities previously accepted by the Margin Recipient, their consent is not required again. The occurrence of any of the Special Events in Section 2(6) of the Securities Lending Annex will not lead to termination of the relevant Transaction but acceptable cash or Margin Securities shall be substituted for such securities upon either party's request.

**MASTER AGREEMENT
FOR FINANCIAL TRANSACTIONS**

dated as of_____

between

_____ and _____

("Party A")   ("Party B")

SPECIAL PROVISIONS
Edition 2004

1. Nature of Agreement

This contractual arrangement (the "Special Provisions"), together with the General Provisions (the "General Provisions") and any annex (each an "Annex") referred to below, constitutes a master agreement (the "Master Agreement") under which the parties may enter into financial transactions.

Special Provisions

The Special Provisions are the heart of the EMA and are the only part of the EMA signed by the contracting parties.

This part comprises 5 paragraphs viz:

1. Nature of Agreement

The contractual arrangement of the EMA (i.e. Special Provisions, General Provisions and the Annexes selected in paragraph 2) is defined here.

2. Incorporation of Documents

The following documents, all in the _____ language, published by the FBE are hereby incorporated into and shall accordingly form part of the Master Agreement:

(a) the General Provisions, Edition 2004
(b) the following Annex[es] :

Product Annex[es] for:
Repurchase Transactions, Edition January 2001
Securities Loans, Edition January 2001
Derivative Transactions, Edition 2004
Supplement for Foreign Exchange Transactions, Edition 2004
Supplement for Interest Rate Transactions, Edition 2004
Supplement for Option Transactions, Edition 2004
Margin Maintenance Annex, Edition 2004
Other Supplements (give details)

3. Addresses for notices (Section 8(1) of the General Provisions)

The addresses for notices and other communications between the parties are: ...

2. Incorporation of Documents

In paragraph 2 the documents constituting the EMA are chosen and their language is also stated.

3. Addresses for notices (Section 8(1) of the General Provisions)

This is where the parties' addresses for notices and other communications are inserted.

4. **Governing law, Settlement of Disputes, Jurisdiction, Arbitration (Section 11(1) and (2) of the General Provisions)**

The law governing the Agreement is _____ law.

Settlement of Disputes:

Jurisdiction: The court(s) referred to in Section 11(2) is/are _____.

Arbitration: The rules of arbitration referred to in Section 11(2) are the Rules of Arbitration of [Euro Arbitration - European Center for Financial Dispute Resolution] [the International Chamber of Commerce] §§ [other]§§ [with which each party agrees to comply].

The parties agree to submit those disputes to [a single] [three] arbitrator[s].

Such arbitration shall take place in _____.

The language[s] in which arbitration shall be conducted [is] [are]_____.

5. **Other provisions**

5 · The European Master Agreement

4. Governing law, Settlement of Disputes, Jurisdiction, Arbitration (Section 11(1) and (2) of the General Provisions)

The governing law of the EMA is selected here together along with which courts will have jurisdiction.

Alternatively arbitration details may be inserted instead.

5. Other provisions

This is a miscellaneous provision and typically incorporates the matters referred to in the Appendix (Checklist) which is shown in full in Appendix 3.

The provisions most commonly negotiated are:

- Default Threshold for Cross Default
- whether Automatic Termination is to apply
- Transactions and groups of Transactions covered.

COMPARISON OF THE EMA WITH THE GMSLA 2010

While we have been comparing the EMA with the GMSLA 2010 during this commentary, it is now useful to draw the similarities and differences together.

1. No chosen law

Unlike the GMSLA 2010, the EMA has no chosen law. Its General Provisions allow the parties to choose a governing law in the Special Provisions failing which there is a fallback option. This is the law of the country, if identical, in which both parties' principal offices are located when the EMA is signed.

2. Documentation structure

The GMSLA 2010 has a structure comprising:

(a) a master agreement setting out core provisions applying to Transactions;
(b) a Schedule covering choices for certain stated matters and an opportunity to amend other provisions; and
(c) An Agency Annex and Addendum for Pooled Principal Transactions.

The EMA is similar comprising:

(a) the General Provisions which correspond to the GMSLA 2010 main text;

(b) the Special Provisions to be completed with the bespoke particular requirements of the parties including choice of law and jurisdiction; and

(c) supplemental Annexes to be included as the parties require. Currently the EMA offers product annexes for Repurchase Transactions, Securities Loans and Derivative Transactions (with Supplements for Foreign Exchange Transactions, Interest Rate Transactions and Options) and a Margin Maintenance Annex for them.

3. Scope

The EMA, is wider in scope than the GMSLA 2010. It aims to consolidate into a single set of harmonised documents, agreements covering repos, securities loans and derivative transactions. It also allows for the possibility, by the addition of new product annexes, to expand the scope of the EMA to include other financial transactions in the future. If this aim is achieved, it would enable market players to document potentially all trading transactions under a single master agreement, in other words under a "master master agreement".

Fundamental principles

Certain fundamental principles are common to both agreements viz:

(i) Each agreement constitutes a single contractual relationship explicitly affirming the mutual interdependence of each Transaction entered into under its umbrella.

(ii) The essential legal nature of each non-Derivative Transaction is that of sale and repurchase (repo) or borrowing or lending transaction: in fact, an absolute transfer of title rather than a secured loan.

Common elements in the documentation

Common elements in the documentation include:

(i) basic mechanics and operational details;

(ii) provisions relating to margin maintenance, although note here that the EMA addresses this topic via the separate "Margin Maintenance Annex" which (unlike the GMSLA 2010) sets out common rules regarding margin for repos, securities loans and derivative transactions;

(iii) provisions regulating the treatment of income on repos and securities loans;

(iv) provisions permitting substitution of repoed securities and Loaned Securities;

(v) representations;

(vi) events of default and procedures to apply following a default;

(vii) miscellaneous matters including governing law and jurisdiction including:
- English law and courts for the GMSLA 2010; and
- for the EMA, the requirement on the parties to make a choice in the Special Provisions, essential if the fallback option (see page 425) which would not work in a cross-border context is to be avoided.

Differences

These are as follows.

(1) Events of Default

The GMSLA 2010 does *not* include a cross-default or a default for "restructuring without assumption". The Agreement covers default by reason of regulatory event (i.e. suspension of membership of an exchange or self-regulatory organisation, etc.), and default by reason of failure to perform other obligations. It also provides for a "mini" close-out regime which applies to failure to perform delivery obligations in respect of securities.

The EMA includes a cross-default provision with a materiality threshold designed to avoid technical defaults as well as a default for failure to pay or deliver. The EMA has perhaps a greater latitude on grace periods than the GMSLA 2010 and a separate "Termination due to Change of Circumstances" regime, covering Tax Event, Illegality, Impossibility and Credit Event upon Restructuring.

(2) Consequences of default

The GMSLA 2010 states that the agreement provides a complete statement of the remedies available in respect of a default although it modifies this in its paragraph 27.8. The EMA does not preclude parties from seeking legal redress through other legal means apart from termination but does prohibit seeking redress for consequential losses.

(3) Choice of law

These two forms of agreement do not, of course, exist in a legal vacuum. The laws applicable affect the contractual obligations of the parties under the agreements. This needs stressing with the EMA which leaves the choice of law to the parties' selection as one of the Special Provisions. The parties therefore need to choose a suitable law. With repo and securities lending transactions they should focus on recharacterisation risk under the chosen law. It could be disastrous if the repo or securities loan was recharacterised as a secured loan although this is neutralised in England for repos by the adoption of the European Directive on Collateral Financial Arrangements. As always, legal due diligence is vital.

Despite heavy initial promotion from French and German banks the EMA is still only gradually being used widely in Europe.

The EMA is particularly useful where a counterparty insists on entering into a local law agreement for repos or securities loans.

6

The US Master Securities Loan Agreement (2000)

Christian A. Johnson

Commentary on the Master Securities Loan Agreement (2000 Version) (the "MSLA")

Section by section analysis of the MSLA 2000

Annexes to the MSLA 2000

Schedules A and B of the MSLA 2000

COMMENTARY ON THE MASTER SECURITIES LOAN AGREEMENT (2000 VERSION) (THE "MSLA")

This chapter will annotate the Bond Market Association (now known as the SIFMA) Master Securities Loan Agreement (the "Agreement"). The Agreement is the market standard in the United States for securities lending transactions. As the securities lending market continues to evolve, the Agreement should be flexible enough to accommodate any variety of new securities lending transactions, structures and securities.

For each section of the Agreement, the text is quoted first and explanatory commentary follows immediately opposite. Before presenting the section by section analysis, however, I will start by outlining the evolution and basic structure of the Agreement.

Evolution of the Agreement

As the securities lending market developed in the United States, the documentation of securities lending transactions was done through customised documentation. As time passed, however, the market began to demand more standardised documentation to create legal certainty and streamline the negotiation of master agreements. In May of 1993, the Bond Market Association developed the first version of the Master Securities Loan Agreement:

> The Agreement was first published in May 1993 to provide a basic contractual framework, grounded in market practice, for the rights and obligations of parties to securities loan transactions. The Agreement was designed to address many legal and regulatory concerns present in securities loan transactions, while allowing the parties considerable flexibility, through the use of annexes and schedules, to address specific regulatory or other considerations and to structure the business aspects of their transactions.[1]

Along with the MSLA 1993, the Bond Market Association also published guidance notes to aid users in understanding the purpose behind various provisions.

In 1998, the Bond Market Association published a standard pre-printed form of amendment to the Master Securities Loan Agreement (the "1998 Amendments") and accompanying guidance notes. The Guidance Notes to the 1998 Amendment to the Master Securities Loan Agreement noted that:

---

[1] SIFMA, Master Securities Loan Agreement – Guidance Notes 2000 Version, available at http://www.sifma.org/services/stdforms/pdf/guidance_notes_to_master_securities_loan_agreement.pdf

6. The US Master Securities Loan Agreement (2000)

These amendments, effective on April 1, 1998, not only implement the amendments to the Securities Exchange Act of 1934 (the "Exchange Act") effected by the National Securities Markets Improvement Act of 1996 ("NSMIA"), but also include a number of modifications to Regulation T adopted by the Board in connection with its periodic review of its margin regulations. (p. 1)

In 2000, The Bond Market Association, in conjunction with the Securities Industry Association (now merged together as SIFMA), published the 2000 version of the Master Securities Loan Agreement (hereinafter the "MSLA"). For use within the United States, the MSLA is still considered to be the market standard and has not been replaced or updated. The MSLA was published to update the 1993 version with respect to the following market developments:

(i) legal developments such as relevant changes to the Securities Exchange Act of 1934 and to Regulation T of the Board of Governors of the Federal Reserve System;

(ii) to incorporate revised market practices in the securities lending industry;

(iii) to provide standardised language for optional provisions; and

(iv) to add the Market Value Annex and the Term Loans Annex.[2]

In spite of these changes, the trade groups noted that: "the publication of the revised Agreement should not be construed as a suggestion that counterparties no longer conduct business pursuant to the May 1993 version of the Agreement and the 1998 Amendment thereto."[3]

Structure of the Agreement

The MSLA's basic structure is a printed master form containing provisions for all securities lending transactions between a Lender and a Borrower. It anticipates, although does not require, that the parties will enter into multiple securities lending transactions. The MSLA contains a Schedule A and B and has three different annexes that can be negotiated and included when it is executed between the parties.

Schedule A is used to provide the names and addresses for communications. Schedule B provides a place to provide for defined terms and supplemental provisions, similar to Annex I in the Global Master Repurchase Agreement (2000) or the Schedule to the ISDA Master Agreement.

---

2 Id.
3 Id.

Annex I is also necessary if a party is acting as an agent as it provides key additional representations and warranties, procedures to identify principals and key limitations on the agent's liability. Annex II provides standardised provisions to deal with market value issues for the valuation of Securities. Annex III can be used to provide key provisions to be used for Term Loans.

SECTION BY SECTION ANALYSIS OF THE MSLA 2000

Terms capitalised in this chapter have the same meaning as used in the MSLA. The discussion of the MSLA and annexes also provides common amendments seen in the US securities lending market in the analysis of Schedule B. Chapter 3, written by Paul Harding, on the GMSLA 2000 takes a similar approach.

The annotations in this chapter, for illustration purposes, will assume that there is only one securities lending transaction outstanding between the Borrower and the Lender. The chapter will assume that the Lender will lend 50,000 shares of ABC Company that have a Market Value of $20/per share to the Borrower. The Borrower in turn will pledge Collateral in the form of US Treasury securities that have a Market Value of $1 million. The parties agree to a margin percentage of 105% and a Loan Fee of 5% per annum.

Master Securities Loan Agreement

2000 Version

Dated as of: _____

Between: _____

and _____

1. **Applicability.**

   From time to time the parties hereto may enter into transactions in which one party ("Lender") will lend to the other party ("Borrower") certain Securities (as defined herein) against a transfer of Collateral (as defined herein). Each such transaction shall be referred to herein as a "Loan" and, unless otherwise agreed in writing, shall be governed by this Agreement, including any supplemental terms or conditions contained in an Annex or Schedule hereto and in any other annexes identified herein or therein as applicable hereunder. Capitalized terms not otherwise defined herein shall have the meanings provided in Section 25.

Date block

The MSLA will generally be dated as either the trade date of the first trade between the parties or the date that the MSLA is executed, whichever occurs first. It is usual to date the MSLA as of the date of the first trade between the parties even if it is not signed until several months later. This is based on US practice where the words "as of" mean "with effect from" a specified date.

The legal names of the parties will be entered into this first section of the MSLA. Parties will often add descriptive language such as where they are incorporated or organised.

Section 1 Applicability

This Section sets out the mechanics of a classic securities lending transaction and the obligations of the Borrower and the Lender to each other. The MSLA is written in such a way that either party may be a "Borrower" or a "Lender" depending upon the terms of the transaction. However, a party would normally act in only one of the two capacities for the duration of an executed Agreement. This is because one party typically has a large portfolio of securities available to lend and the other party typically has need to borrow particular securities.

If the parties also enter into a triparty custodial agreement a party can also be designated as a Borrower or a Lender. Paragraph 1 also provides that when parties enter into multiple Loans, all the Loans will be governed by the MSLA.

Neither Section 1 nor any other provision in the MSLA restricts the type or class of securities that can be lent. The MSLA can accommodate the loan of any other type or class of securities. The parties could also, if they chose, amend the Agreement to include other types of assets that could be lent under it.

Although the MSLA could be used for the lending of non-US securities, the Global Master Securities Lending Agreement (2000) or (2010) is much better suited for those types of securities. The MSLA does provide for some key provisions such as tax and contractual currency issues, but is not intended to deal with the myriad of other issues that should be addressed prior to trading such securities.

Using our example, under Section 1, the Lender will lend 50,000 shares of ABC Company having a Market Value of $20 per share against the transfer of Collateral by the Borrower to the Lender. The amount of Collateral to be transferred to the Lender is covered under Section 5 of the MSLA.

2. Loans of Securities.

2.1 Subject to the terms and conditions of this Agreement, Borrower or Lender may, from time to time, seek to initiate a transaction in which Lender will lend Securities to Borrower. Borrower and Lender shall agree on the terms of each Loan (which terms may be amended during the Loan), including the issuer of the Securities, the amount of Securities to be lent, the basis of compensation, the amount of Collateral to be transferred by Borrower, and any additional terms. Such agreement shall be confirmed (a) by a schedule and receipt listing the Loaned Securities provided by Borrower to Lender in accordance with Section 3.2, (b) through any system that compares Loans and in which Borrower and Lender are participants, or (c) in such other manner as may be agreed by Borrower and Lender in writing. Such confirmation (the "Confirmation"), together with the Agreement, shall constitute conclusive evidence of the terms agreed between Borrower and Lender with respect to the Loan to which the Confirmation relates, unless with respect to the Confirmation specific objection is made promptly after receipt thereof. In the event of any inconsistency between the terms of such Confirmation and this Agreement, this Agreement shall prevail unless each party has executed such Confirmation.

2.2 Notwithstanding any other provision in this Agreement regarding when a Loan commences, unless otherwise agreed, a Loan hereunder shall not occur until the Loaned Securities and the Collateral therefor have been transferred in accordance with Section 15.

6. The US Master Securities Loan Agreement (2000)

Section 2 Loans of securities

Section 2 is one of the key operative sections of the MSLA. It describes how to initiate and document a transaction and this section deals with why the parties are entering into the MSLA, i.e. to lend securities. It should be noted that the MSLA does not set out how a transaction must be "initiated". For example it could be initiated orally, through electronic messaging, or through a pre-agreed program of automated trading.

Section 2.1

Section 2.1 sets out the terms that must be agreed upon for a securities lending transaction:

- the issuer of the Securities;
- the amount of Securities to be lent;
- the basis of compensation;
- the amount of Collateral to be transferred by the Borrower;
- any additional terms.

Terms can also be supplemented through the addition of an Annex such as the Term Loan Annex.

Like other types of finance transactions, each of the transactions must be confirmed. The MSLA provides several methods to confirm a transaction in order to be in compliance with Rule 15c3-3 of the Securities Exchange Act. These include (i) by a schedule and receipt; (ii) by any system that compares or matches Loans in which Borrower and Lender are participants; or (iii) any other manner agreed by the Borrower and Lender in writing.

Because of the various ways that a transaction can be confirmed, the MSLA provides for an inconsistency rule that is somewhat different from other forms of Master Agreements. The MSLA provides that it will govern in the event of any inconsistency with a confirmation unless such confirmation has been executed by both parties. This avoids a situation where a party could unilaterally amend the Confirmation without the consent of the other party.

Section 2.2

Section 2.2 provides that a Loan does not begin until both the Securities and the Collateral have been delivered. Under Section 12 (Events of Default), the failure of the Lender to transfer Loaned Securities under Section 2.2 is not a Default. However, if the Borrower were to have transferred Collateral as agreed and the Lender were to fail to return the Collateral as required under Section 4.4 where it had failed to meet its initial obligation to transfer the Loaned Securities, that would be a Default. The rationale for not putting the Lender into default if the Lender fails initially to transfer the Loaned Securities is to avoid terminating all the Loans simply because of a failure at the inception of an individual Loan. Terminating all the Loans would appear to be unnecessary upon such a failure given that the individual Loan concerned never began.

3. **Transfer of Loaned Securities.**

   3.1   Unless otherwise agreed, Lender shall transfer Loaned Securities to Borrower hereunder on or before the Cutoff Time on the date agreed to by Borrower and Lender for the commencement of the Loan.

   3.2   Unless otherwise agreed, Borrower shall provide Lender, for each Loan in which Lender is a Customer, with a schedule and receipt listing the Loaned Securities. Such schedule and receipt may consist of (a) a schedule provided to Borrower by Lender and executed and returned by Borrower when the Loaned Securities are received, (b) in the case of Securities transferred through a Clearing Organization which provides transferors with a notice evidencing such transfer, such notice, or (c) a confirmation or other document provided to Lender by Borrower.

   3.3   Notwithstanding any other provision in this Agreement, the parties hereto agree that they intend the Loans hereunder to be loans of Securities. If, however, any Loan is deemed to be a loan of money by Borrower to Lender, then Borrower shall have, and Lender shall be deemed to have granted, a security interest in the Loaned Securities and the proceeds thereof.

Section 3 Transfer of Loaned Securities

Section 3 provides procedures for the transfer of Loaned Securities. Under Section 3.1, the Loaned Securities are to be transferred on or before the Cutoff Time on an agreed upon date. The Cutoff Time governs the time of transfer for Loaned Securities, Collateral or currency. The definition of Cutoff Time provides that the Cuttoff Time is a time that is agreed to by the parties (i) in Schedule B, (ii) as agreed orally or in writing or (iii) if the terms do not designate a Cutoff Time, it is based on market practice. The parties are free to agree (as described above) to different Cutoff Times for different types or classes of Securities or Collateral. Market Practice is that the Cutoff Time will be in the afternoon, and will vary between 2.00 p.m. Eastern Time and 3.15 p.m. Eastern Time.

Section 3.2

Section 3.2 requires the Borrower to provide the Lender with a schedule and receipt listing the Loaned Securities. This requirement is important in order to comply with Securities Exchange Act Rule 15c3-3(b)(3)(ii). The requirement can be met first by the Lender providing a schedule to the Borrower that is executed and returned by the Borrower. If it is done through a Clearing Organization that provides a transfer or with notice of the transfer, such notice is sufficient. Finally, the Lender can provide the Borrower with a confirmation or other evidence of the transaction.

Section 3.3

Section 3.3 deals with a situation where a transaction may be recharacterised as a loan of money with the Loaned Securities as collateral. If a court were to make such a recharacterisation, the Lender is deemed to have granted a security interest in the Loaned Securities to the Borrower. In the event of such a recharacterisation, such provision is necessary because the MSLA assumes that it is the Borrower that is providing collateral. The Borrower grants the Lender a security interest in the Collateral in Section 4.2.

4. **Collateral.**

   4.1   Unless otherwise agreed, Borrower shall, prior to or concurrently with the transfer of the Loaned Securities to Borrower, but in no case later than the Close of Business on the day of such transfer, transfer to Lender Collateral with a Market Value at least equal to the Margin Percentage of the Market Value of the Loaned Securities.

Section 4 Collateral

Section 4 deals with the transfer of Collateral by the Borrower to the Lender. As opposed to the English law GMLSA documents, the securities lending transaction under the MSLA is actually treated as a secured loan as opposed to a transfer of title. Because of that, it is important that the parties comply with New York law with respect to the Borrower granting a security interest in the Collateral to the Lender (acting as the secured party).

Section 4.1

Section 4.1 sets out the mechanics as to how much Collateral must be transferred to the Lender. The Collateral must be transferred concurrently with the transfer of the Loaned Securities by the Lender, but no later than Close of Business on the day that the Loaned Securities are transferred. The Borrower must transfer Collateral with a Market Value equal to the Margin Percentage of the Market Value of the Loaned Securities. As explained more fully below, Market Value can be defined as form in Annex II, as agreed by the parties, or as defined in Section 25.38 of the MSLA. Margin Percentage, as defined more fully below, is a percentage agreed to by the parties which is typically 105% or more (but not less than 100%).

Using our example, under Section 1, the Lender will lend 50,000 shares of ABC Company having a Market Value of $20 per share against the transfer of Collateral by the Borrower to the Lender for a total amount of $1 million. Assuming a Margin Percentage of 105%, the Borrower will need to transfer Collateral with a Market Value of $1,050,000 ($1,000,000 × 105%).

4.2 The Collateral transferred by Borrower to Lender, as adjusted pursuant to Section 9, shall be security for Borrower's obligations in respect of such Loan and for any other obligations of Borrower to Lender hereunder. Borrower hereby pledges with, assigns to, and grants Lender a continuing first priority security interest in, and a lien upon, the Collateral, which shall attach upon the transfer of the Loaned Securities by Lender to Borrower and which shall cease upon the transfer of the Loaned Securities by Borrower to Lender. In addition to the rights and remedies given to Lender hereunder, Lender shall have all the rights and remedies of a secured party under the UCC. It is understood that Lender may use or invest the Collateral, if such consists of cash, at its own risk, but that (unless Lender is a Broker-Dealer) Lender shall, during the term of any Loan hereunder, segregate Collateral from all securities or other assets in its possession. Lender may Retransfer Collateral only (a) if Lender is a Broker-Dealer or (b) in the event of a Default by Borrower. Segregation of Collateral may be accomplished by appropriate identification on the books and records of Lender if it is a "securities intermediary" within the meaning of the UCC.

Section 4.2

Section 4.2 is another key operative provision because here the Borrower grants to the Lender a security interest in the Collateral securing the Loaned Securities. Please note that the Lender does not give Borrower a security interest in the Loaned Securities (except in situation of a recharacterisation of a transaction involving Cash Collateral as described in Section 3.3).

In addition to any rights and remedies enjoyed by the Lender under the MSLA, Section 4.2 also gives the Lender any rights of a secured party under the New York Uniform Commercial Code.

The MSLA expressly allows a Lender to use or invest Cash Collateral at its own risk. In other words, any losses suffered by the Lender on Cash Collateral is for the account of the Lender. However, unless the Lender is a Broker-Dealer, it is required to segregate the non-Cash Collateral from any securities or assets that it possesses. The Lender may segregate the Collateral on its own books and records if it qualifies as a "securities intermediary" under the New York Uniform Commercial Code. A securities intermediary is defined in Section 8-102(14) of the Uniform Commercial Code as:

> (i) a clearing corporation; or (ii) a person, including a bank or broker, that in the ordinary course of its business maintains securities accounts for others and is acting in that capacity.

Many Lenders, however, will not meet this definition and will need to hold the collateral with a custodian which would probably be a securities intermediary.

A Lender is permitted to Retransfer the Collateral under two situations. First, it is, of course, allowed to Retransfer the Collateral upon an Event of Default by the Borrower, permitting it to liquidate the Collateral where the Borrower fails to return the Loaned Securities. Second, a Broker-Dealer is permitted to Retransfer Collateral pledged to it. Retransfer, as defined in Section 25.43 of the MSLA, provides the Broker-Dealer with usage rights, permitting it to use the Collateral in any way that it wants (i.e. rehypothecate or sell the Collateral) subject to an obligation to return equivalent fungible Collateral (of the same type and class) as required under the MSLA to the Borrower. A Broker-Dealer under the MSLA is defined as any person that is a broker, dealer, municipal securities dealer or government securities broker for purposes of the Securities Exchange Act of 1934. This definition applies to a party, regardless of whether they conduct activities in the US or are required to register with the US Securities and Exchange Commission.

4.3 Except as otherwise provided herein, upon transfer to Lender of the Loaned Securities on the day a Loan is terminated pursuant to Section 6, Lender shall be obligated to transfer the Collateral (as adjusted pursuant to Section 9) to Borrower no later than the Cutoff Time on such day or, if such day is not a day on which a transfer of such Collateral may be effected under Section 15, the next day on which such a transfer may be effected.

4.4 If Borrower transfers Collateral to Lender, as provided in Section 4.1, and Lender does not transfer the Loaned Securities to Borrower, Borrower shall have the absolute right to the return of the Collateral; and if Lender transfers Loaned Securities to Borrower and Borrower does not transfer Collateral to Lender as provided in Section 4.1, Lender shall have the absolute right to the return of the Loaned Securities.

Section 4.3

Section 4.3 deals with the obligations of the Lender with respect to the Collateral upon the termination of a Loan. It requires the Lender to transfer the Collateral back to the Borrower upon the Lender's receipt of the Loaned Securities on the termination date of the loan. The transfer has to be made by the Cutoff Time, which is discussed in detail below.

Section 4.4

Section 4.4 addresses a party's rights where one of the parties fails to make its transfer on the settlement date of the Loan. Therefore, where the Lender does not receive the Collateral after it has transferred the Loaned Securities or the Borrower does not receive the Loaned Securities upon transfer of the Collateral, the performing party has the absolute right to the return of its property. Failure to return either the Loaned Securities or the Collateral would constitute a Default under Section 12.

4.5 Borrower may, upon reasonable notice to Lender (taking into account all relevant factors, including industry practice, the type of Collateral to be substituted, and the applicable method of transfer), substitute Collateral for Collateral securing any Loan or Loans; provided, however, that such substituted Collateral shall (a) consist only of cash, securities or other property that Borrower and Lender agreed would be acceptable Collateral prior to the Loan or Loans and (b) have a Market Value such that the aggregate Market Value of such substituted Collateral, together with all other Collateral for Loans in which the party substituting such Collateral is acting as Borrower, shall equal or exceed the agreed upon Margin Percentage of the Market Value of the Loaned Securities.

Section 4.5

Section 4.5 deals with the substitution rights of the Borrower with respect to Collateral. The Lender, of course, does not have substitution rights given that the whole purpose of a transaction is for the Borrower to borrow specific securities.

The Borrower is allowed to substitute one type of Collateral for another subject to meeting specific requirements. First, the Borrower is required to give reasonable notice. Reasonable notice is particularly important given that the Lender may be using Cash Collateral or, if it is a Broker-Dealer, it is reusing non-Cash Collateral, which it would need to reacquire for the Borrower. No rigid timeframe for the substitution is provided. Instead, the amount of notice required depends upon such things as market practice and the type of Collateral to be substituted.

Second, the Borrower is only permitted to substitute eligible Collateral that was considered to be eligible Collateral prior to the transaction. The MSLA is silent as to a Borrower's right to substitute particular collateral if that collateral was not eligible at the inception of the transaction, even though the parties later agreed that it would be eligible Collateral for future transactions.

The third requirement is that after the substitution, the Lender will have agreed upon the Market Value of Collateral to secure the Loaned Securities. As opposed to making this determination based on what Loan the Collateral in question secured, it is instead done on an aggregate basis across the portfolio. Because the substitution rights are so liberal, there is no reason to trace the collateral that is being substituted out to particular Loaned Securities. As long as the aggregate Market Value of all of the Collateral equals or exceeds the Margin Percentage of the Market Value of the Loaned Securities, after the substitution, the substitution should be permitted.

4.6 Prior to the expiration of any letter of credit supporting Borrower's obligations hereunder, Borrower shall, no later than the Extension Deadline, (a) obtain an extension of the expiration of such letter of credit, (b) replace such letter of credit by providing Lender with a substitute letter of credit in an amount at least equal to the amount of the letter of credit for which it is substituted, or (c) transfer such other Collateral to Lender as may be acceptable to Lender.

Section 4.6

Section 4.6 provides special rules for Collateral in the form of a letter of credit. Letters of credit pose particular problems for a Lender because they can expire, leaving them potentially worthless if they are not renewed. Under Section 4.6, the Borrower is required to take one of three actions prior to the Extension deadline of the letter of credit. The Extension Deadline is defined in Section 25.22 as the "Cutoff Time on the Business Day preceding the day on which the letter of credit expires". Lenders should be alert to the expiration date of a letter of credit and develop a tickler system to alert it ahead of its expiration. This is especially important because the Extension Deadline is only one day prior to the expiration date. The penalty for allowing the Extension Deadline to pass would be an expired letter of credit, which would provide no credit support for the securities loan. A Lender may want to consider amending Section 4.6 to move the date of the Extension Deadline further away from the expiration date of a letter of credit.

The Borrower under Section 4.6 can deal with an expiring letter of credit in three ways. First, it can have the issuing bank extend the expiration date. Second, it can agree to replace the letter of credit with a new one. Third, it can transfer other Collateral to the Lender to replace the expiring letter of credit.

5. **Fees for Loan.**

   5.1   Unless otherwise agreed, (a) Borrower agrees to pay Lender a loan fee (a "Loan Fee"), computed daily on each Loan to the extent such Loan is secured by Collateral other than cash, based on the aggregate Market Value of the Loaned Securities on the day for which such Loan Fee is being computed, and (b) Lender agrees to pay Borrower a fee or rebate (a "Cash Collateral Fee") on Collateral consisting of cash, computed daily based on the amount of cash held by Lender as Collateral, in the case of each of the Loan Fee and the Cash Collateral Fee at such rates as Borrower and Lender may agree. Except as Borrower and Lender may otherwise agree (in the event that cash Collateral is transferred by clearing house funds or otherwise), Loan Fees shall accrue from and including the date on which the Loaned Securities are transferred to Borrower to, but excluding, the date on which such Loaned Securities are returned to Lender, and Cash Collateral Fees shall accrue from and including the date on which the cash Collateral is transferred to Lender to, but excluding, the date on which such cash Collateral is returned to Borrower.

Section 5 Fees for Loan

Section 5 deals with the return the Lender will earn on the Loaned Securities referred to in MSLA generally as a fee. The first type of fee is the fee paid by the Borrower to the Lender where the Borrower has pledged non-cash Collateral, and is referred to as a "Loan Fee". The second type of fee is the fee paid by the Lender to the Borrower if the Borrower has pledged cash Collateral, and is defined as a Cash Collateral Fee in the MSLA.

The most common fee paid historically is the payment of a Loan Fee by the Borrower to the Lender (although the Cash Collateral Fee is becoming more common in the United States). The calculation is substantively similar to an interest charge under a regular loan, although the amount of the fee will vary beyond those factors typically considered for a cash loan such as supply and demand for a particular Loaned Security, collateral flexibility, the size of any manufactured dividends, and the likelihood of the Lender recalling a security early.

The Loan Fee is typically set out in basis points although it could be set out as a percentage instead. The Loan Fee is determined daily on the *aggregate* Market Value of the Loaned Securities. The Loan Fee begins accruing on the date the Loaned Securities are transferred and does not accrue on the date the Loaned Securities are transferred back to the Lender, again similar to the calculation of interest.

Assume that the Loan Fee is 40 basis points, the Market Value of the Loaned Securities is $1,000,000 (and does not vary over the term of the loan), and the securities loan begins on 1st May and ends on 7th May. Because there are seven days between 1st May and 7th May, the Loan Fee will need to be accrued for six days.

The daily amount of the Loan Fee is calculated as follows: $1,000,000 × (0.004/360) = $11.11. The total amount over the term of the loan would equal $11.11 × 6 days = $66.66.

The Cash Collateral Fee is different in that it is paid by the Lender to the Borrower and is based upon the amount of Cash Collateral pledged by the Borrower. The assumption behind the provision is that the Lender will be earning a return on the Cash Collateral and that the Lender will "rebate" part of that fee back to the Borrower. The Lender, however, will be required to pay the Cash Collateral Fee to the Borrower regardless of how much it earns on its investment of the Cash Collateral. The Lender also will be required to return the entire amount of the cash Collateral to the Borrower even if the Lender suffers losses on its reinvestment. During the US financial crisis, AIG, when acting as a Lender, suffered serious losses on its investment of Cash Collateral.

5.2 Unless otherwise agreed, any Loan Fee or Cash Collateral Fee payable hereunder shall be payable:

(a) in the case of any Loan of Securities other than Government Securities, upon the earlier of (i) the fifteenth day of the month following the calendar month in which such fee was incurred and (ii) the termination of all Loans hereunder (or, if a transfer of cash in accordance with Section 15 may not be effected on such fifteenth day or the day of such termination, as the case may be, the next day on which such a transfer may be effected); and

(b) in the case of any Loan of Government Securities, upon the termination of such Loan and at such other times, if any, as may be customary in accordance with market practice.

Notwithstanding the foregoing, all Loan Fees shall be payable by Borrower immediately in the event of a Default hereunder by Borrower and all Cash Collateral Fees shall be payable immediately by Lender in the event of a Default by Lender.

Like the Loan Fee, the Cash Collateral Fee is typically set out in basis points although it could be set out as a percentage instead. The Cash Collateral Fee is determined daily on the amount of cash Collateral outstanding on that date. The Cash Collateral Fee begins accruing on the date the cash Collateral is transferred and does not accrue on the date the cash Collateral is transferred back to the Borrower.

Assume that the Cash Collateral Fee is 20 basis points, the amount of the Cash Collateral is $1,050,000, and the securities loan begins on 1st May and ends on 7th May. Because there are seven days between 1st May and 7th May, the Loan Fee will need to be accrued for six days. The daily amount of the Cash Collateral Fee is calculated as follows: $1,050,000 × (0.002/360) = $5.83. The total amount over the term of the loan would equal $5.83 × 6 days = $34.99.

Section 5.2

The general rule in Section 5.2 is that the Loan Fee or the Cash Collateral Fee is payable on the earlier of (i) the 15th day of the month following such accrual or (ii) the termination of all of the Loans. With respect to fees paid on a loan of Government Securities, the fee is payable upon the termination of a particular loan or as is customary under market practice.

However, wherever a party defaults, Loan Fees or Cash Collateral Fees become immediately payable to the non-defaulting party.

6. **Termination of the Loan.**

  6.1 (a) Unless otherwise agreed, either party may terminate a Loan on a termination date established by notice given to the other party prior to the Close of Business on a Business Day. The termination date established by a termination notice shall be a date no earlier than the standard settlement date that would apply to a purchase or sale of the Loaned Securities (in the case of a notice given by Lender) or the non-cash Collateral securing the Loan (in the case of a notice given by Borrower) entered into at the time of such notice, which date shall, unless Borrower and Lender agree to the contrary, be (i) in the case of Government Securities, the next Business Day following such notice and (ii) in the case of all other Securities, the third Business Day following such notice.

  (b) Notwithstanding paragraph (a) and unless otherwise agreed, Borrower may terminate a Loan on any Business Day by giving notice to Lender and transferring the Loaned Securities to Lender before the Cutoff Time on such Business Day if (i) the Collateral for such Loan consists of cash or Government Securities or (ii) Lender is not permitted, pursuant to Section 4.2, to Retransfer Collateral.

  6.2 Unless otherwise agreed, Borrower shall, on or before the Cutoff Time on the termination date of a Loan, transfer the Loaned Securities to Lender; provided, however, that upon such transfer by Borrower, Lender shall transfer the Collateral (as adjusted pursuant to Section 9) to Borrower in accordance with Section 4.3.

Section 6 Termination of the Loan

The general rule in Section 6 is that *either* party may terminate a securities loan, unless otherwise agreed. In other words, the clause provides the mechanics as to how a Loan is to be terminated if the Loan does not have a fixed term.

Section 6.1 (a)

In Section 6.1(a), to terminate a Loan, a party must give notice of the termination date prior to Close of Business on a Business Day. The termination date, however, cannot be earlier than the standard settlement date with respect to the Loaned Securities or the standard settlement date for the non-cash Collateral. The MSLA assumes that the termination date shall be (i) the third Business Day following notice, (ii) the next Business Day following notice for Government Securities or (iii) as agreed by the parties.

Section 6.1 (b)

Section 6.1(b) provides an exception to 6.1(a) for the Borrower. The Borrower may terminate a Loan on any Business Day by giving notice and transferring the Loaned Securities to the Lender before the Cuttoff Time on such Business Day provided (i) the Collateral is either cash or Government Securities or (ii) the Lender is not permitted to Retransfer the Collateral.

Section 6.2

Under Section 6.2, the Borrower must transfer the Loaned Securities to the Lender. Upon such transfer, the Lender shall transfer the Collateral to the Borrower in accordance with Section 4.3 subject to any necessary adjustment required by Section 9.

7. **Rights in Respect of Loaned Securities and Collateral.**

   7.1   Except as set forth in Sections 8.1 and 8.2 and as otherwise agreed by Borrower and Lender, until Loaned Securities are required to be redelivered to Lender upon termination of a Loan hereunder, Borrower shall have all of the incidents of ownership of the Loaned Securities, including the right to transfer the Loaned Securities to others. Lender hereby waives the right to vote, or to provide any consent or to take any similar action with respect to, the Loaned Securities in the event that the record date or deadline for such vote, consent or other action falls during the term of the Loan.

   7.2   Except as set forth in Sections 8.3 and 8.4 and as otherwise agreed by Borrower and Lender, if Lender may, pursuant to Section 4.2, Retransfer Collateral, Borrower hereby waives the right to vote, or to provide any consent or take any similar action with respect to, any such Collateral in the event that the record date or deadline for such vote, consent or other action falls during the term of a Loan and such Collateral is not required to be returned to Borrower pursuant to Section 4.5 or Section 9.

Section 7 Rights in Respect of Loan

Section 7.1

Section 7.1 treats the Borrower as having "all of the incidents of ownership of the Loaned Securities" even though the Loaned Securities were lent to the Borrower and the Borrower is obligated to return them to the Lender in due course. The Borrower has the right to use the Loaned Securities which would include the right to transfer them to a third party. For example, the Borrower would have the right to sell or lend or repo out the Loaned Securities to a third party or use them as collateral for other of the Lender's obligations. Such rights, however, are limited by Section 8.1 and 8.2 with respect to distributions paid on the Loaned Securities.

Because corporate actions may occur during the period that the Borrower is holding the Loaned Securities, the Lender "waives the right to vote" on the Loaned Securities or "to provide any consent or to or take any similar action with respect to the Loaned Securities". If the Lender wanted to exercise voting rights on the Loaned Securities he would recall them prior to any record date or deadline relating to such corporate actions.

Section 7.2

Section 7.2 deals with a situation in which a Lender has the right to Retransfer Collateral under Section 4.2. In that situation, the Borrower, regardless of whether the Lender has Retransferred the Collateral, waives the right to vote "the Collateral" or "to provide any consent or to take any similar action" with respect to the Collateral. If, however, the Borrower wanted to exercise voting rights on the Collateral he would recall it prior to any record date or deadline relating to such corporate actions.

8. **Distributions.**

   8.1   Lender shall be entitled to receive all Distributions made on or in respect of the Loaned Securities which are not otherwise received by Lender, to the full extent it would be so entitled if the Loaned Securities had not been lent to Borrower.

   8.2   Any cash Distributions made on or in respect of the Loaned Securities, which Lender is entitled to receive pursuant to Section 8.1, shall be paid by the transfer of cash to Lender by Borrower, on the date any such Distribution is paid, in an amount equal to such cash Distribution, so long as Lender is not in Default at the time of such payment. Non-cash Distributions that Lender is entitled to receive pursuant to Section 8.1 shall be added to the Loaned Securities on the date of distribution and shall be considered such for all purposes, except that if the Loan has terminated, Borrower shall forthwith transfer the same to Lender.

Section 8 Distributions

Section 8 deals with Distributions paid on Loaned Securities and non-cash Collateral. Distributions are defined in Section 25.19 to include any distributions made with respect to a Security and includes both cash and non-cash distributions and will be more thoroughly discussed below.

Section 8.1

Section 8.1 provides that the Lender (not the Borrower) is entitled to receive all Distributions made with respect to the Loaned Securities as if the Loaned Securities had not been lent to the Borrower. The language provides that receipt of Distributions is not one of the incidents of ownership that the Borrower enjoys upon borrowing the Loaned Securities. This is also consistent with the language with Section 7.1 and with the Borrower's tax and accounting treatment for the receipt of Distributions.

Section 8.2

Under Section 8.2, to the extent that the Borrower receives any cash Distributions with respect to the Loaned Securities, the Borrower is required to pay those amounts to the Lender on the date that a Distribution is paid. It is important to appreciate, however, that the US Internal Revenue Service may not consider that the cash Distribution has the same characterisation in the hands of the Lender that it had in the hands of the recipient (i.e. the Borrower). This could potentially change any tax benefits enjoyed by the Lender with respect to the Distribution. Please see Chapter 1 for a discussion of US tax law implications.

Section 8.2 clarifies that the Borrower is not obligated to pay over such Distributions to the Lender in the event that the Lender is in Default. Under Section 13.2, the Borrower is entitled to apply any amounts owing to the Lender under Section 8.1 against any amounts owed by the Lender to the Borrower.

If the Borrower receives a non-cash Distribution, the Borrower is then not required to transfer such a non-cash Distribution to the Lender until the Loan is terminated. Such non-cash Distributions would include, for example, a stock dividend. These non-cash Distributions are treated as Loaned Securities. Because of this treatment, the Borrower, for example, would be required to post additional Collateral if the Market Value of the Loaned Securities increased because of the Distribution.

8.3 Borrower shall be entitled to receive all Distributions made on or in respect of non-cash Collateral which are not otherwise received by Borrower, to the full extent it would be so entitled if the Collateral had not been transferred to Lender.

8.4 Any cash Distributions made on or in respect of such Collateral, which Borrower is entitled to receive pursuant to Section 8.3, shall be paid by the transfer of cash to Borrower by Lender, on the date any such Distribution is paid, in an amount equal to such cash Distribution, so long as Borrower is not in Default at the time of such payment. Non-cash Distributions that Borrower is entitled to receive pursuant to Section 8.3 shall be added to the Collateral on the date of distribution and shall be considered such for all purposes, except that if each Loan secured by such Collateral has terminated, Lender shall forthwith transfer the same to Borrower.

Section 8.3

Consistent with the treatment of Distributions in Section 8.1, Section 8.3 provides that the Borrower (not the Lender) is entitled to receive all Distributions made with respect to the non-cash Collateral as if the Collateral had not been transferred to the Lender. The language is consistent with the treatment of the non-cash Collateral as Collateral and with the Lender's tax and accounting treatment for the receipt of Distributions.

Section 8.4

Consistent with the treatment of Distributions to the Lender in Section 8.2, under Section 8.4, to the extent that the Lender receives any cash Distributions with respect to the Collateral, the Lender is required to pay those amounts to the Borrower on the date that a Distribution is paid. Section 8.4 clarifies that the Lender is not obligated to pay over such Distributions to the Borrower in the event that the Borrower is in Default. Under Section 13.2, the Lender is entitled to apply any amounts owing the Borrower under Section 8.3 against any amounts owed by the Lender.

If the Lender receives a non-cash Distribution, the Lender is not required to transfer such non-cash Distribution to the Borrower until the Loan secured by such Collateral is terminated. Such non-cash Distributions would include, for example, a stock dividend. These non-cash Distributions are treated as Collateral for all purposes of the MSLA.

8.5 Unless otherwise agreed by the parties:

(a) If (i) Borrower is required to make a payment (a "Borrower Payment") with respect to cash Distributions on Loaned Securities under Sections 8.1 and 8.2 ("Securities Distributions"), or (ii) Lender is required to make a payment (a "Lender Payment") with respect to cash Distributions on Collateral under Sections 8.3 and 8.4 ("Collateral Distributions"), and (iii) Borrower or Lender, as the case may be ("Payor"), shall be required by law to collect any withholding or other tax, duty, fee, levy or charge required to be deducted or withheld from such Borrower Payment or Lender Payment ("Tax"), then Payor shall (subject to subsections (b) and (c) below), pay such additional amounts as may be necessary in order that the net amount of the Borrower Payment or Lender Payment received by the Lender or Borrower, as the case may be ("Payee"), after payment of such Tax equals the net amount of the Securities Distribution or Collateral Distribution that would have been received if such Securities Distribution or Collateral Distribution had been paid directly to the Payee.

Section 8.5

Section 8.5 describes how the parties deal with a situation in which either the Borrower or the Lender is required to withhold taxes with respect to amounts required to be paid to the other under Section 8.1 or 8.3. For example, assume that the Borrower receives a dividend of $100,000 with respect to the ABC Securities that it has borrowed. Under Section 8.1, the Borrower is obligated to pay $100,000 to the Lender. However, it is possible that the taxing jurisdiction of the Borrower may require the Borrower to withhold taxes on the $100,000 payment. Assuming a 30% withholding rate, the Borrower would then pay only $70,000 to the Lender and $30,000 to the taxing jurisdiction. The premise behind a withholding tax is that the tax is imposed on the recipient of the payment, in this case the Lender. Without Section 8.5, the Lender would therefore only be entitled to a $70,000 payment. However, Section 8.5 shifts the risk of any withholding taxes from the payee to the payor. The withholding jurisdiction would still receive $30,000, but the Borrower would still be required to pay the entire $100,000 to the Lender. This is typically referred to as a gross up provision.

Section 8.5 (a)

Section 8.5(a) provides that if a Lender or Borrower is required to make a payment under Section 8, and if such party is required to withhold taxes on such payment, then the payor is required to make an additional payment (the "gross up payment") to increase the required payment under Section 8 to the payee so that the payee receives the same amount that he would have received if no such withholding had been imposed. It is important to recognise that the payor's taxing authority may view a gross up payment as also subject to withholding, requiring additional gross up payments.

(b) No additional amounts shall be payable to a Payee under subsection (a) above to the extent that Tax would have been imposed on a Securities Distribution or Collateral Distribution paid directly to the Payee.

(c) No additional amounts shall be payable to a Payee under subsection (a) above to the extent that such Payee is entitled to an exemption from, or reduction in the rate of, Tax on a Borrower Payment or Lender Payment subject to the provision of a certificate or other documentation, but has failed timely to provide such certificate or other documentation.

(d) Each party hereto shall be deemed to represent that, as of the commencement of any Loan hereunder, no Tax would be imposed on any cash Distribution paid to it with respect to (i) Loaned Securities subject to a Loan in which it is acting as Lender or (ii) Collateral for any Loan in which it is acting as Borrower, unless such party has given notice to the contrary to the other party hereto (which notice shall specify the rate at which such Tax would be imposed). Each party agrees to notify the other of any change that occurs during the term of a Loan in the rate of any Tax that would be imposed on any such cash Distributions payable to it.

Section 8.5 (b)

Section 8.5(b) relieves a Payor from having to gross up under Section 8.5(a) if the Payee would have been subject to the same withholding had the Payee directly received the original distribution paid to the Payor. This clause is interesting because it presupposes that there would have been no withholding on the original Distribution to the Payee. In the example above, the Borrower would have received the entire $100,000, but would then have withheld the $30,000 and only paid $70,000 to the Lender. If the Lender would have only received $70,000 had it received the distribution directly (because of withholding), the Borrower does not need to make a gross up payment of $30,000 to the Lender.

Participants would be concerned about receiving Distributions that are subject to withholding if they receive them but there would have been no withholding if the amount had been received directly by the original transferees. For example, assume that the Borrower is subject to withholding of $30,000 by the jurisdiction of the issuer of the Loaned Securities on the original Distribution of $100,000 made on the Loaned Securities, but the Lender would not have been subject to withholding on the original Distribution. Under Section 8.1, the Lender would be entitled to the entire $100,000 because the Lender is entitled to receive the same amount of the Distribution that it would have received had it received the original Distribution directly.

Section 8.5 (c)

Under Section 8.5(c), the Payor is also protected from having to make a gross up payment if such withholding could be avoided by the Payee providing the Payor with required certificates or documentation. If the Payee fails to provide such certificates or documentation to the Payor, thus subjecting the Payor to a withholding obligation, the Payor is not required to gross up its payment to the Payee.

Section 8.5(d)

Unless a party gives notice to the contrary, under Section 8.5(d), each party is deemed to make a payor tax representation to the other that no withholding would be required on the payments of a Distribution under Sections 8.1 or 8.3. A misrepresentation under Section 8.5(d) would constitute a Default under Section 12.

8.6 To the extent that, under the provisions of Sections 8.1 through 8.5, (a) a transfer of cash or other property by Borrower would give rise to a Margin Excess or (b) a transfer of cash or other property by Lender would give rise to a Margin Deficit, Borrower or Lender (as the case may be) shall not be obligated to make such transfer of cash or other property in accordance with such Sections, but shall in lieu of such transfer immediately credit the amounts that would have been transferable under such Sections to the account of Lender or Borrower (as the case may be).

Section 8.6

Section 8.6 addresses a situation in which the payment of a Distribution on a Loaned Security or on non-cash Collateral has affected their Market Value creating either a Margin Excess with respect of a transfer to the Borrower or a Margin Deficit with respect to a transfer to the Lender.

For example, with respect to the Margin Excess situation, assume in our scenario that before the payment to the Borrower of a Distribution on the Loaned Securities, such Loaned Securities had a Market Value of $1,000,000. Assume further the Collateral had a Market Value of $1,050,000 (the required Margin Percentage amount). If after a cash Distribution of $100,000 on such Loaned Securities to the Borrower, the Loaned Securities now have a Market Value of only $900,000. The Borrower would then be overcollateralised since it would only be required to provide Collateral equal to $945,000 ($900,000 × 105%). The Borrower would not be required to transfer the Distribution to the Lender, but would instead credit the amount to its account as a reduction of the amount of Collateral.

For example, with respect to the Margin Deficit situation, assume in our situation that before the payment to the Lender of a Distribution on Collateral, such Collateral had a Market Value of $1,050,000 which also equalled its required Margin Percentage. If after a cash Distribution of $100,000 on such Collateral, the Collateral now had a Market Value of only $950,000, the Lender would not be required to transfer the Distribution to the Borrower, but would instead credit the amount to the Borrower as additional Collateral.

9. Mark to Market.

9.1 If Lender is a Customer, Borrower shall daily mark to market any Loan hereunder and in the event that at the Close of Trading on any Business Day the Market Value of the Collateral for any Loan to Borrower shall be less than 100% of the Market Value of all the outstanding Loaned Securities subject to such Loan, Borrower shall transfer additional Collateral no later than the Close of Business on the next Business Day so that the Market Value of such additional Collateral, when added to the Market Value of the other Collateral for such Loan, shall equal 100% of the Market Value of the Loaned Securities.

Section 9 Mark to Market

Section 9.1

Section 9.1 deals with regulatory requirements for a Broker-Dealer. Where a Broker-Dealer borrows securities from a Customer, it is required by Securities Exchange Act Rule 15c3-3 always to pledge Collateral to its Customer/Lender equal to 100% of the daily mark to market value of the Loaned Securities. The provision also requires the Borrower to post the Collateral even though the Lender does not make any margin calls on the Borrower.

9.2　In addition to any rights of Lender under Section 9.1, if at any time the aggregate Market Value of all Collateral for Loans by Lender shall be less than the Margin Percentage of the Market Value of all the outstanding Loaned Securities subject to such Loans (a "Margin Deficit"), Lender may, by notice to Borrower, demand that Borrower transfer to Lender additional Collateral so that the Market Value of such additional Collateral, when added to the Market Value of all other Collateral for such Loans, shall equal or exceed the Margin Percentage of the Market Value of the Loaned Securities.

9.3　Subject to Borrower's obligations under Section 9.1, if at any time the Market Value of all Collateral for Loans to Borrower shall be greater than the Margin Percentage of the Market Value of all the outstanding Loaned Securities subject to such Loans (a "Margin Excess"), Borrower may, by notice to Lender, demand that Lender transfer to Borrower such amount of the Collateral selected by Borrower so that the Market Value of the Collateral for such Loans, after deduction of such amounts, shall thereupon not exceed the Margin Percentage of the Market Value of the Loaned Securities.

Section 9.2 and 9.3

Sections 9.2 and 9.3 are actually the key substantive mark to market margining provisions in Section 9, since Section 9.1 only deals with Broker-Dealer/Customer situations and only provides for a collateralisation of 100%. Another key difference between 9.1 versus 9.2 and 9.3 is that a party must give notice if it believes that it is entitled to a transfer of Collateral. In other words, a party is only obligated to make a collateral transfer under Section 9.2 and 9.3 if it receives notice from the other party.

Section 9.2

Section 9.2 deals with the situation in which the Lender is undercollateralised, referred to in the document as a Margin Deficit. It is important to note that the MSLA implements mark to market margining on an aggregate basis rather than on a Loan by Loan basis. A Margin Deficit occurs when the aggregate Market Value of all the Collateral held by the Lender is less than the Margin Percentage of the Market Value of all the Loaned Securities.

For example, assume that the Borrower has pledged $10 million in cash to the Lender and the Market Value of the Loaned Securities is also $10 million. Assume further that the parties have agreed to a Margin Percentage of 105%. The parties would compare the $10 million in Market Value of the Collateral to the Margin Percentage of the Market Value of the Loaned Securities. The Margin Percentage of the Market Value of the Loaned Securities would equal 105% multiplied by $10 million, which equals $10,500,000. The Borrower would therefore have to pledge $500,000 in additional Collateral to eliminate the Margin Deficit.

Section 9.3

Section 9.3 deals with the situation in which the Lender is overcollateralised, referred to in the MSLA as a Margin Excess. It is important to note that the MSLA implements mark to market margining on an aggregate basis rather than on a Loan by Loan basis. A Margin Excess occurs when the aggregate Market Value of all of the Collateral held by the Lender is greater than the Margin Percentage of the Market Value of all of the Loaned Securities.

For example, assume that the Borrower has pledged $12 million in cash to the Lender and the Market Value of the Loaned Securities is $10 million. Assume further that the parties have agreed to a Margin Percentage of 105%. The parties would compare the $12 million in Market Value of the Collateral to the Margin Percentage of the Market Value of the Loaned Securities. The Margin Percentage of the Market Value of the Loaned Securities would equal 105% multiplied by $10 million, or $10,500,000. The Lender would therefore have to transfer $1,500,000 in Collateral to the Borrower to eliminate the Margin Excess.

9.4   Borrower and Lender may agree, with respect to one or more Loans hereunder, to mark the values to market pursuant to Sections 9.2 and 9.3 by separately valuing the Loaned Securities lent and the Collateral given in respect thereof on a Loan-by-Loan basis.

9.5   Borrower and Lender may agree, with respect to any or all Loans hereunder, that the respective rights of Lender and Borrower under Sections 9.2 and 9.3 may be exercised only where a Margin Excess or Margin Deficit exceeds a specified dollar amount or a specified percentage of the Market Value of the Loaned Securities under such Loans (which amount or percentage shall be agreed to by Borrower and Lender prior to entering into any such Loans).

Section 9.4

Section 9.4 allows the parties to agree to determine the mark to market calculations on a Loan by Loan basis as opposed to an aggregate basis. The parties may want to enter into such an agreement if the Loaned Securities have different Margin Percentages. The Margin Percentages may differ between Loans depending upon the volatility, scarcity or desirability of particular Loaned Securities.

Section 9.5

Section 9.5 introduces a "nuisance" amount concept into the calculations, similar to the concept of a Minimum Transfer Amount in the ISDA Credit Support Annex. Under Section 9.5, the parties can agree that a party may only call for collateral if the Margin Excess or Margin Deficient exceeds a certain amount. Typically such an amount would set out in Schedule B to the MSLA.

Designating such an amount would help minimise the daily margin calls under Sections 9.2 and 9.3 by providing a minimum threshold that needs to be crossed before the right to call for Collateral. For example, if the parties agreed to an amount of $250,000 for the purposes of Section 9.5, a party would not be entitled to make a margin call until the Margin Deficit or Margin Excess exceeded that amount. These provisions are important to minimise the burden placed on operations to make *de minimis* margin transfers.

9.6 If any notice is given by Borrower or Lender under Sections 9.2 or 9.3 at or before the Margin Notice Deadline on any day on which a transfer of Collateral may be effected in accordance with Section 15, the party receiving such notice shall transfer Collateral as provided in such Section no later than the Close of Business on such day. If any such notice is given after the Margin Notice Deadline, the party receiving such notice shall transfer such Collateral no later than the Close of Business on the next Business Day following the day of such notice.

Section 9.6

Under Section 9.6, the party receiving a margin call under Section 9.2 or 9.3 by the "Margin Notice Deadline" must transfer the Collateral by Close of Business on that day. If a party gives notice after the Margin Notice Deadline, then the transferor is given an additional Business Day to make the transfer. Parties negotiating the Margin Notice Deadline obviously should consult carefully with their Collateral Operations departments to ensure that they have not agreed to an impractical time.

Margin Notice Deadline is defined in Section 25.36 to be the time agreed to (i) in a confirmation, (ii) in Schedule B, or (iii) for the purposes of Section 9 by the parties. If the parties have not otherwise agreed, the Margin Notice Deadline shall be based on market practice.

10. Representations.

The parties to this Agreement hereby make the following representations and warranties, which shall continue during the term of any Loan hereunder:

Section 10 Representations

The representations required in Paragraph 10 are typical of those in other master agreements. The representations requested are of sufficient importance such that if they are not true, the requesting party would be unwilling to move forward with the agreement. The representations are important for three reasons. First, if a representation proves to be incorrect or untrue in any material respect, it constitutes an Event of Default under paragraph 12.6 and permits the non-defaulting party to exercise its rights under the Agreement. Second, the representations provide a framework for a party to conduct due diligence with respect to its counterparty. This helps ensure that that there are no undisclosed problems or issues that would prevent it from entering into the MSLA with its counterparty. Finally, requiring a party to make a representation will hopefully limit a party's right to assert later that the agreement is not enforceable as it had acted beyond its powers (ultra vires) and did not have the authority to enter into the MSLA.

The first line of Section 10 states that the parties are making "representations and warranties, which shall continue during the term of any Loan hereunder". Based upon this sentence, the representations and warranties would be true upon execution of the MSLA. In addition, the representations must continue to be true during the term of any Loan. In contrast to some other forms of finance agreements, this would mean that a misrepresentation would occur at any time that a representation becomes untrue. In other finance contracts, a representation is only deemed to be repeated (after execution of the Agreement) or each time a new transaction is done.

The use of the word "warranty" also suggests that the representations must be true at all times when a loan is outstanding. One commentator has noted that:

> **The most assertive take is that offered in the** *Model Stock Purchase Agreement (1995)* and *Model Asset Purchase Agreement (2001)* — **both published by the ABA's Section of Business Law** — **which state that "representations are statements of past or existing facts and warranties are promises that existing or future facts are or will be true." But** *Krys v. Henderson*, **69 S.E.2d 635, 637 (Ga. Ct. App. 1952), is the only case I have found that stands squarely for this distinction.**[4]

---

[4] Kenneth A. Adams (2005) A lesson in drafting contracts, *Business Law Today,* November/December.

10.1 Each party hereto represents and warrants that (a) it has the power to execute and deliver this Agreement, to enter into the Loans contemplated hereby and to perform its obligations hereunder, (b) it has taken all necessary action to authorize such execution, delivery and performance, and (c) this Agreement constitutes a legal, valid and binding obligation enforceable against it in accordance with its terms.

Section 10.1

Section 10.1 deals with the most common (and important) representations requested. Legal opinions provided by a party should also parallel these representations in particular. Sections 10.1(a) and 10.1(b) focus on a party's legal capacity and authority to "execute and deliver" both the MSLA and any Loans. Section 10.1(b) focuses on the party's actions to "authorize such execution, delivery and performance". Both of these representations are particularly important when dealing with less sophisticated parties or when dealing with governmental counterparties or highly regulated entities. Where trades move adversely against such party, their defence in litigation will often centre on whether they had such power and authority to enter into the transactions. Failure to have such capacity and authority could result in the transactions being declared ultra vires or void. Such a defence was raised somewhat successfully by Hammersmith and Fulham (among other London municipalities) in the late 1980s with respect to dealers' efforts to enforce OTC derivatives contracts against the municipalities.

Section 10.1 (c)

Section 10.1(c) is what is referred to as an enforceability or remedies representation. Essentially the party represents that in the event that the MSLA is litigated, a court would find that the Agreement would be enforceable against the party making the representation. This representation could also form the basis for a legal opinion provided by such party to its counterparty.

10.2 Each party hereto represents and warrants that it has not relied on the other for any tax or accounting advice concerning this Agreement and that it has made its own determination as to the tax and accounting treatment of any Loan and any dividends, remuneration or other funds received hereunder.

10.3 Each party hereto represents and warrants that it is acting for its own account unless it expressly specifies otherwise in writing and complies with Section 11.1(b).

10.4 Borrower represents and warrants that it has, or will have at the time of transfer of any Collateral, the right to grant a first priority security interest therein subject to the terms and conditions hereof.

Section 10.2

Section 10.2 is a limited form of "non reliance" representation that has became more and more important after the litigation between Proctor & Gamble and Bankers Trust over certain over-the-counter derivative trades during the 1990s (925 F.Supp. 1040 (S.D. Ohio 1996)). The concern is that a party will represent that it relied to its detriment upon the advice of its counterparty (typically a more sophisticated party such as a dealer) and therefore it should be excused from performance. In other words, its counterparty took advantage of its superior position, perhaps violating a fiduciary duty or even committing fraud. This representation provides some comfort to the more sophisticated party that its counterparty will not be able to raise such a defence. This form of representation can easily be expanded in Schedule B with more detailed and expansive language depending upon the concerns of the parties.

Section 10.3

Section 10.3 provides assurances that each party is acting as principal and not as an undisclosed agent. The representation provides that if it is acting as an agent, that it has complied with Section 11.1(b) and is in compliance with Annex I to the MSLA.

Section 10.4

Section 10.4 centres on one of the key concerns of a Lender. In the event that a Borrower were to go into default, to foreclose upon the Collateral, the Lender would need to have a first priority security interest in the Collateral. Without such a security interest, other creditors of the Borrower may have a competing interest in the Collateral. Therefore the Borrower grants a first priority security interest in the Collateral to the Lender at the time the Collateral is transferred.

10.5 (a) Borrower represents and warrants that it (or the person to whom it relends the Loaned Securities) is borrowing or will borrow Loaned Securities that are Equity Securities for the purpose of making delivery of such Loaned Securities in the case of short sales, failure to receive securities required to be delivered, or as otherwise permitted pursuant to Regulation T as in effect from time to time.

Section 10.5

Historically, parties have been concerned about violating Regulation T that was promulgated by the Board of Governors of the Federal Reserve System. Regulation T regulates credit by brokers and dealers. The 2000 version of the MSLA was revised to reflect amendments to Regulation T that minimised its impact on securities lending. Currently, Section 220.10 of Regulation T deals with securities lending. This appears as follows:

Title 12 of the U.S. Code: Banks and Banking

PART 220—CREDIT BY BROKERS AND DEALERS (REGULATION T)

§ 220.10   Borrowing and lending securities.

(a) Without regard to the other provisions of this part, a creditor may borrow or lend securities for the purpose of making delivery of the securities in the case of short sales, failure to receive securities required to be delivered, or other similar situations. If a creditor reasonably anticipates a short sale or fail transaction, such borrowing may be made up to one standard settlement cycle in advance of trade date.

(b) A creditor may lend foreign securities to a foreign person (or borrow such securities for the purpose of relending them to a foreign person) for any purpose lawful in the country in which they are to be used.

(c) A creditor that is an exempted borrower may lend securities without regard to the other provisions of this part and a creditor may borrow securities from an exempted borrower without regard to the other provisions of this part.

{Reg. T, 63 FR 2826, Jan. 16, 1998}

Section 10.5 (a)

In Section 10.5(a), the Borrower makes several representations about the purpose of its borrowing that conform with the permitted borrowing and lending purposes found in Section 220.10(a) of Regulation T. This representation would ensure that the Loan is in compliance with Regulation T.

(b) Borrower and Lender may agree, as provided in Section 24.2, that Borrower shall not be deemed to have made the representation or warranty in subsection (a) with respect to any Loan. By entering into any such agreement, Lender shall be deemed to have represented and warranted to Borrower (which representation and warranty shall be deemed to be repeated on each day during the term of the Loan) that Lender is either (i) an "exempted borrower" within the meaning of Regulation T or (ii) a member of a national securities exchange or a broker or dealer registered with the U.S. Securities and Exchange Commission that is entering into such Loan to finance its activities as a market maker or an underwriter.

Section 220.10(c) of Regulation T provides that an exempted borrower "may lend securities without regard to the other provisions of this part and a creditor may borrow securities from an exempted borrower without regard to the other provisions of this part" provided that (i) the Lender is either an exempted borrower or (ii) "a member of a national securities exchange or a broker or dealer registered with the U.S. Securities and Exchange Commission that is entering into such Loan to finance its activities as a market maker or an underwriter". Because of this exemption, the parties can agree not to make the representation in Section 10.5(a) without violating Regulation T.

An exempted borrower under Section 220.2 of Regulation T is defined as:

> a member of a national securities exchange or a registered broker or dealer, a substantial portion of whose business consists of transactions with persons other than brokers or dealers, and includes a borrower who:
>
> 1 maintains at least 1000 active accounts on an annual basis for persons other than brokers, dealers, and persons associated with a broker or dealer;
>
> 2 earns at least $10 million in gross revenues on an annual basis from transactions with persons other than brokers, dealers, and persons associated with a broker or dealer; or
>
> 3 earns at least 10 percent of its gross revenues on an annual basis from transactions with persons other than brokers, dealers, and persons associated with a broker or dealer.

10.6 Lender represents and warrants that it has, or will have at the time of transfer of any Loaned Securities, the right to transfer the Loaned Securities subject to the terms and conditions hereof.

Section 10.6

Section 10.6 is the parallel provision for the Borrower with respect to Section 10.4. This section is critical for the Borrower since the whole purpose of a securities Loan, of course, is for the Borrower to have complete control over the Loaned Securities.

11. Covenants.

11.1 Each party agrees either (a) to be liable as principal with respect to its obligations hereunder or (b) to execute and comply fully with the provisions of Annex I (the terms and conditions of which Annex are incorporated herein and made a part hereof).

11.2 Promptly upon (and in any event within seven (7) Business Days after) demand by Lender, Borrower shall furnish Lender with Borrower's most recent publicly-available financial statements and any other financial statements mutually agreed upon by Borrower and Lender. Unless otherwise agreed, if Borrower is subject to the requirements of Rule 17a-5(c) under the Exchange Act, it may satisfy the requirements of this Section by furnishing Lender with its most recent statement required to be furnished to customers pursuant to such Rule.

Section 11 Covenants

In contrast to a traditional bank lending agreement, the covenants in Section 11 of the MSLA are minimal at best. In contrast to a typical loan agreement, securities Loans under the MSLA are fully secured and are terminable on demand or have a relatively short maturity.

Section 11.1

Section 11.1 is used in conjunction with Section 10.3 to ensure that neither party is acting as an undisclosed agent and that the parties are in full compliance with Annex I.

Section 11.2

Section 11.2 requires the Borrower to furnish its "most recent publicly available financial statements" to the Lender. It is important to note that the obligation is not reciprocal upon the Lender to furnish financial statements to the Borrower. This is because the principal concern behind the provision is to give the Lender sufficient information to assess that the Borrower will meet its margining obligations and its obligation to return the Loaned Securities to the Lender upon maturity of the Loan.

12. **Events of Default.**

All Loans hereunder may, at the option of the non-defaulting party (which option shall be deemed to have been exercised immediately upon the occurrence of an Act of Insolvency), be terminated immediately upon the occurrence of any one or more of the following events (individually, a "Default"):

Section 12 Events of Default

Section 12 details the Defaults that would permit a non-defaulting party to exercise its remedies as set forth in Section 13. In general, defaults call into question whether the defaulting party will meet its obligations to its counterparty in the future. In other words, upon the occurrence of any of the events listed in Section 12, the non-defaulting party believes that it would recover more from the Defaulting Party if it were to terminate all the Loans than if it were to wait for them to mature.

Section 12 only permits the non-defaulting party to terminate "all loans" (without, of course, the consent of the Defaulting Party). This would prevent the non-defaulting party from cherry picking transactions that were profitable to it.

It is important to note that the occurrence of a Default does not result in the automatic termination of all of the Loans, except with respect to an Act of Insolvency for the Defaulting Party. This allows the non-defaulting party time to assess whether such an event is sufficiently serious to merit termination. Non-defaulting parties should take care, however, to exercise their rights within a reasonable period of time to avoid a Defaulting Party's argument that the non-defaulting party had waived its right to exercise its remedies (see Section 20 for an additional discussion of waivers).

The Defaults set out in Section 12 also conform with the events of default required under New York Stock Exchange Rule 296 for securities lending involving a member of the Exchange. Rule 296, however, focuses on Acts of Insolvency and does not include the non-Act of Insolvency Defaults found in Section 12 (see www.nyserules.nyse.com, Liquidation of Securities Loans and Borrowing).

Section 12 does not include the following defaults found in Sections 11.6 and 11.7 of the 1993 Master Securities Loan Agreement in order to conform more closely with other similar master agreements:

11.6 if either party shall have been suspended or expelled from membership or participation in any national securities exchange or registered national securities association of which it is a member or other self-regulatory organization to whose rules it is subject or if it is suspended from dealing in securities by any federal or state government agency thereof.

11.7 if either party shall have its license, charter, or other authorization necessary to conduct a material portion of its business withdrawn, suspended or revoked by any applicable federal or state government or agency thereof.

As discussed below, the drafters of the Master Securities Loan Agreement Guidance Notes – 2000 Version suggest that parties might want to consider adding these defaults through Schedule B.

12.1 if any Loaned Securities shall not be transferred to Lender upon termination of the Loan as required by Section 6;

12.2 if any Collateral shall not be transferred to Borrower upon termination of the Loan as required by Sections 4.3 and 6;

12.3 if either party shall fail to transfer Collateral as required by Section 9;

12.4 if either party (a) shall fail to transfer to the other party amounts in respect of Distributions required to be transferred by Section 8, (b) shall have been notified of such failure by the other party prior to the Close of Business on any day, and (c) shall not have cured such failure by the Cutoff Time on the next day after such Close of Business on which a transfer of cash may be effected in accordance with Section 15;

12.5 if an Act of Insolvency occurs with respect to either party;

Sections 12.1, 12.2 and 12.3

Sections 12.1, 12.2 and 12.3 deal with the most fundamental failures of a party to perform under the MSLA. Section 12.1 is perhaps the most important Default for the Lender, allowing it to terminate all the Loans if a Borrower fails to return Loaned Securities. Similarly, Section 12.2 provides important protections for the Borrower where the Lender does not return Collateral. Finally, Section 12.3 ensures that a party may terminate all Loans in the event that its counterparty fails to provide or return Collateral as required by Section 9.

Section 12.4

Section 12.4 provides that it is a Default if a party fails to transfer Distributions to its counterparty pursuant to Section 8. The Section requires, however, that the Defaulting Party be given a one-day cure period after notice for such failure, provided, however, that such notice is received by the Cutoff Time. If notice is not given by the Cutoff Time then presumably the Defaulting Party would have an additional day to cure such failure.

Sections 12.1–12.4

Sections 12.1, 12.2 and 12.4 are loan specific failures, meaning that a failure to perform on only one loan is sufficient to create a default. Section 12.3 is a failure to transfer based on the aggregate value of the Collateral.

Section 12.5

Section 12.5 provides that an Act of Insolvency is an Event of Default. As discussed above, an Act of Insolvency is an automatic Event of Default and results in the immediate termination of all outstanding Loans. What constitutes an Act of Insolvency is discussed in the Section 25.1 analysis.

12.6 if any representation made by either party in respect of this Agreement or any Loan or Loans hereunder shall be incorrect or untrue in any material respect during the term of any Loan hereunder;

12.7 if either party notifies the other of its inability to or its intention not to perform its obligations hereunder or otherwise disaffirms, rejects or repudiates any of its obligations hereunder; or

Section 12.6

Section 12.6 is a Default because of a misrepresentation made in Section 10 or elsewhere in Schedule B or applicable Annexes. Section 12.6 reaffirms that a representation not only needs to be true at the execution of the MSLA but also when any Loan is outstanding.

To be a default, however, the misrepresentation must be "incorrect or untrue in any material respect". The MSLA, however, does not define what is meant by "material". Presumably, a misrepresentation would be material if a party would not have entered into the MSLA or an individual loan had it known that the representation was untrue or incorrect.

Section 12.7

Section 12.7 allows a party to terminate the Loans if its counterparty notifies it that it is unable or unwilling to perform its obligations under the MSLA. It also allows a party to terminate if its counterparty "disaffirms, rejects or repudiates" its obligations to perform. Presumably these actions by the Defaulting Party would occur before that party was actually in default under any of the other provisions. Inevitably, however, a Default eventually would occur under a different sub-section simply through the passage of time combined with a failure to meet its obligations under the MSLA. Assuming that the Defaulting Party does provide an indication to the non-defaulting party that it will not or cannot perform, it allows the non-defaulting party to exercise its remedies earlier than otherwise possible.

12.8 if either party (a) shall fail to perform any material obligation under this Agreement not specifically set forth in clauses 12.1 through 12.7, above, including but not limited to the payment of fees as required by Section 5, and the payment of transfer taxes as required by Section 14, (b) shall have been notified of such failure by the other party prior to the Close of Business on any day, and (c) shall not have cured such failure by the Cutoff Time on the next day after such Close of Business on which a transfer of cash may be effected in accordance with Section 15.

The non-defaulting party shall (except upon the occurrence of an Act of Insolvency) give notice as promptly as practicable to the defaulting party of the exercise of its option to terminate all Loans hereunder pursuant to this Section 12.

Section 12.8

Section 12.8 is a catch all provision that creates a Default upon the failure to perform any "material obligation" other than those described in Sections 12.1 through 12.7. Section 12.8 expressly includes the failure to pay fees under Section 5 and the payment of transfer taxes under Section 14. This provision also has a one-day cure period after notice similar to Section 12.4.

Last clause

The last clause in Section 12 requires the non-defaulting party to give notice of its decision to terminate all of the Loans "as promptly as practicable". Notice is not required upon the occurrence of an Act of Insolvency. A party would therefore be able to exercise its remedies under Section 13 where it was unable to contact the Defaulting Party through no fault of its own.

13. Remedies.

13.1 Upon the occurrence of a Default under Section 12 entitling Lender to terminate all Loans hereunder, Lender shall have the right, in addition to any other remedies provided herein, (a) to purchase a like amount of Loaned Securities ("Replacement Securities") in the principal market for such Loaned Securities in a commercially reasonable manner, (b) to sell any Collateral in the principal market for such Collateral in a commercially reasonable manner and (c) to apply and set off the Collateral and any proceeds thereof (including any amounts drawn under a letter of credit supporting any Loan) against the payment of the purchase price for such Replacement Securities and any amounts due to Lender under Sections 5, 8, 14 and 16. In the event that Lender shall exercise such rights, Borrower's obligation to return a like amount of the Loaned Securities shall terminate. Lender may similarly apply the Collateral and any proceeds thereof to any other obligation of Borrower under this Agreement, including Borrower's obligations with respect to Distributions paid to Borrower (and not forwarded to Lender) in respect of Loaned Securities. In the event that (i) the purchase price of Replacement Securities (plus all other amounts, if any, due to Lender hereunder) exceeds (ii) the amount of the Collateral, Borrower shall be liable to Lender for the amount of such excess together with interest thereon at a rate equal to (A) in the case of purchases of Foreign Securities, LIBOR, (B) in the case of purchases of any other Securities (or other amounts, if any, due to Lender hereunder), the Federal Funds Rate or (C) such other rate as may be specified in Schedule B, in each case as such rate fluctuates from day to day, from the date of such purchase until the date of payment of such excess. As security for Borrower's obligation to pay such excess, Lender shall have, and Borrower hereby grants, a security interest in any property of Borrower then held by or for Lender and a right of setoff with respect to such property and any other amount payable by Lender to Borrower. The purchase price of Replacement Securities purchased under this Section 13.1 shall include, and the proceeds of any sale of Collateral shall be determined after deduction of, broker's fees and commissions and all other reasonable costs, fees and expenses related to such purchase or sale (as the case may be). In the event Lender exercises its rights under this Section 13.1, Lender may elect in its sole discretion, in lieu of purchasing all or a portion of the Replacement Securities or selling all or a portion of the Collateral, to be deemed to have made, respectively, such purchase of Replacement Securities or sale of Collateral for an amount equal to the price therefor on the date of such exercise obtained from a generally recognized source or the last bid quotation from such a source at the most recent Close of Trading. Subject to Section 18, upon the satisfaction of all obligations hereunder, any remaining Collateral shall be returned to Borrower.

Section 13 Remedies

Section 13.1

Section 13.1 deals with the Lender's rights and remedies upon a Default by the Borrower. The first remedy given the Lender puts it into the same position it would have been had the Borrower not defaulted. The Lender may purchase a like amount of Loaned Securities in the market that it lent to the Borrower. In order to fund the replacement of the Loaned Securities, the Lender may sell any Collateral it holds and apply the proceeds against payment of the purchase price. Proceeds would also include any drawdowns on a letter of credit held as Collateral. In addition, the Lender may use these proceeds from the liquidation of the Collateral for any amounts owed by the Borrower to the Lender under Sections 5 (Fees), 8 (Distributions), 14 (Transfer Taxes) and 16 (Contractual Currency).

Section 13.1 requires that the Replacement Securities be purchased in the principal market for such Loaned Securities and that this is done "in commercially reasonable manner". Similarly, Collateral must be sold in the principal market for such Collateral and also sold in a commercially reasonable manner. Failure to complete these steps would result in a claim by the Borrower for the difference between what the Replacement Securities should have cost versus the actual purchase price, and, in the case of Collateral, for the difference between what the Collateral should have been sold for versus the actual proceeds received.

If the Lender does purchase Replacement Securities, the Borrower's obligation to return the Loaned Securities is terminated. This is logical given that the Lender now has the Replacement Securities in place of the Loaned Securities.

Finally, the Lender may apply any remaining proceeds from the liquidation of the Collateral against any other remaining obligations of the Borrower to the Lender under the Agreement.

It is possible, of course, that the purchase price of the Replacement Securities may exceed the proceeds from the liquidation of the Collateral. Section 13.1 provides that the Borrower shall be liable for such excess. For example, assume that the replacement cost of ABC Securities had increased from $1 million to $1.5 million and that the Lender held $1.2 million of Collateral in US Treasury Securities. The Lender would offset the $1.5 million replacement cost of the ABC securities against the $1.2 million in proceeds that it received in liquidating the US Treasuries, leaving an excess owed by the Borrower of $300,000.

Where the Borrower fails to promptly pay such excess, interest will accrue at LIBOR if the Replacement Securities were Foreign Securities. Foreign Securities are securities that are principally settled and cleared outside the United States. If the case of non-Foreign Securities, interest will accrue at the Federal Funds Rate. The parties can also agree in Schedule B to use a different rate rather than LIBOR or the Federal Funds Rate. Based on the example above, interest would accrue on the $300,000 excess at the Federal Funds Rate. Interest would accrue on the $300,000 on the date of purchase and would terminate on the date that the excess is paid. Assume that the Replacement Securities were purchased on 1st March and the $300,000 excess was paid on 7th March. The Borrower would owe six days of interest to the Lender.

As additional protection for the Lender for the payment of the excess by the Borrower, the Borrower is deemed to grant a security interest to the Lender in any other property of the Borrower held by the Lender. This includes property of the Borrower held by the Lender for purposes other than the MSLA. This would permit the Lender also to liquidate any other property of the Borrower to satisfy the excess through a right of set off.

Section 13.1 clarifies that the Lender is entitled to take into account any costs associated with the purchase of Replacement Securities or the sale of Collateral. These costs would cover broker's fees and commission as well as any other reasonable costs, fees or expenses.

Section 13.1 does not require the Lender to purchase Replacement Securities or to liquidate Collateral. The Lender is permitted to deem that he has purchased Replacement Securities and is permitted to deem that he has sold the Collateral. For example, the Lender could still liquidate the Collateral, but not actually purchase the Replacement Securities. It could also purchase the Replacement Securities but retain the Collateral as opposed to liquidating it.

To determine the deemed purchase price of the Replacement Securities and deemed sales price of the Collateral, the Lender is to use (i) "the price therefor on the date of such exercise obtained from a generally recognized source" or (ii) "the last bid quotation from such a source at the most recent Close of Trading". Because the Lender will not be out of pocket for any transaction costs in purchasing Replacement Securities or selling Collateral, the MSLA does not provide that the Lender may adjust these amounts for any deemed transaction costs.

Section 13.1 also clarifies that where the proceeds from the sale of the Collateral exceed the purchase price of the Replacement Securities, the excess Collateral is to be returned to the Borrower. Assuming that the parties have properly margined the loans, it is probable that there would be an excess amount equal to the overcollateralisation.

13.2 Upon the occurrence of a Default under Section 12 entitling Borrower to terminate all Loans hereunder, Borrower shall have the right, in addition to any other remedies provided herein, (a) to purchase a like amount of Collateral ("Replacement Collateral") in the principal market for such Collateral in a commercially reasonable manner, (b) to sell a like amount of the Loaned Securities in the principal market for such Loaned Securities in a commercially reasonable manner and (c) to apply and set off the Loaned Securities and any proceeds thereof against (i) the payment of the purchase price for such Replacement Collateral, (ii) Lender's obligation to return any cash or other Collateral, and (iii) any amounts due to Borrower under Sections 5, 8 and 16. In such event, Borrower may treat the Loaned Securities as its own and Lender's obligation to return a like amount of the Collateral shall terminate; provided, however, that Lender shall immediately return any letters of credit supporting any Loan upon the exercise or deemed exercise by Borrower of its termination rights under Section 12. Borrower may similarly apply the Loaned Securities and any proceeds thereof to any other obligation of Lender under this Agreement, including Lender's obligations with respect to Distributions paid to Lender (and not forwarded to Borrower) in respect of Collateral. In the event that (i) the sales price received from such Loaned Securities is less than (ii) the purchase price of Replacement Collateral (plus the amount of any cash or other Collateral not replaced by Borrower and all other amounts, if any, due to Borrower hereunder), Lender shall be liable to Borrower for the amount of any such deficiency, together with interest on such amounts at a rate equal to (A) in the case of Collateral consisting of Foreign Securities, LIBOR, (B) in the case of Collateral consisting of any other Securities (or other amounts due, if any, to Borrower hereunder), the Federal Funds Rate or (C) such other rate as may be specified in Schedule B, in each case as such rate fluctuates from day to day, from the date of such sale until the date of payment of such deficiency. As security for Lender's obligation to pay such deficiency, Borrower shall have, and Lender hereby grants, a security interest in any property of Lender then held by or for Borrower and a right of setoff with respect to such property and any other amount payable by Borrower to Lender. The purchase price of any Replacement Collateral purchased under this Section 13.2 shall include, and the proceeds of any sale of Loaned Securities shall be determined after deduction of, broker's fees and commissions and all other reasonable costs, fees and expenses related to such purchase or sale (as the case may be). In the event Borrower exercises its rights under this Section 13.2, Borrower may elect in its sole discretion, in lieu of purchasing all or a portion of the Replacement Collateral or selling all or a portion of the Loaned Securities, to be deemed to have made, respectively, such purchase of Replacement Collateral or sale of Loaned Securities for an amount equal to the price therefor on the date of such exercise obtained from a generally recognized source or the last bid quotation from such a source at the most recent Close of Trading. Subject to Section 18, upon the satisfaction of all Lender's obligations hereunder, any remaining Loaned Securities (or remaining cash proceeds thereof) shall be returned to Lender.

Section 13.2

Section 13.2 deals with the Borrower's rights and remedies upon a Default by the Lender. The first remedy given the Borrower puts the Borrower back into the same position it would have been had the Lender not defaulted. Section 13.2 closely parallels the remedy given the Lender upon a Default by the Borrower in Section 13.1.

The Borrower may purchase a like amount of Collateral that it transferred to the Lender. In order to fund the replacement of the Replacement Collateral, the Borrower may sell a like amount of the Loaned Securities and apply the proceeds against payment of the purchase price. In addition, the Borrower may use these proceeds from the liquidation of the Loaned Securities for any amounts owed by the Lender to the Borrower under Sections 5 (Fees), 8 (Distributions), and 16 (Contractual Currency).

Section 13.2 requires that the Replacement Collateral be purchased in the principal market for such Collateral and that it be done "in commercially reasonable manner". Similarly, Loaned Securities must be sold in the principal market for such securities and also sold in a commercially reasonable manner. Failure to do these would result in a claim by the Lender for the difference between what the Replacement Collateral should have cost versus the actual purchase price, and, in the case of the Loaned Securities, for the difference between what the Loaned Securities should have been sold for versus the proceeds actually received.

If the Borrower does purchase Replacement Collateral, the Lender's obligation to return such Collateral is terminated. This is logical given that the Borrower now has the Replacement Collateral in place of the Collateral originally transferred. The Lender is also obligated to return any outstanding Letters of Credit.

Finally, the Borrower may apply any remaining proceeds from the liquidation of the Collateral against any other remaining obligations of the Borrower to the Lender under the MSLA through a right of set off.

It is possible, of course, that the purchase price of the Replacement Collateral may exceed the proceeds from the liquidation of the Loaned Securities. Section 13.2 provides that the Lender shall be liable for such excess. For example, assume that the replacement cost of Collateral consisting of US Treasury Securities was $1.6 million and the market value of the ABC Securities (the Loaned Securities) was $1.25 million. The Borrower would offset the US$1.6 million replacement cost of the US Treasury Securities against the $1.25 million in proceeds that it received in liquidating the ABC Securities, leaving an excess owed by the Lender to the Borrower of $350,000.

In the event that the Lender fails promptly to pay such excess, interest will accrue at LIBOR if the Replacement Collateral was Foreign Securities. Foreign Securities are securities that are principally settled and cleared outside the United States. If the case of non-Foreign Securities, interest will accrue at the Federal Funds Rate. The parties can also agree in Schedule B to use a different rate rather than LIBOR or the Federal Funds Rate. Based on the example above, interest would accrue on the $350,000 excess at the Federal Funds Rate. Interest would accrue on the $350,000 on the date of purchase and would terminate on the date that the excess is paid. Assume that the Replacement Collateral was purchased on 1st March and the $350,000 excess was paid on 7th March. The Lender would owe six days of interest to the Borrower.

As additional protection for the Borrower for the payment of the excess by the Lender, the Lender is deemed to grant a security interest to the Borrower in any other property of the Lender held by the Borrower. This includes property of the Lender held by the Borrower for purposes other than the MSLA. This would permit the Borrower also to liquidate any other property of the Lender to satisfy the excess through a set-off right. Section 13.2 clarifies that the Borrower is entitled to take into account any costs associated with the purchase of Replacement Collateral Securities or the sale of the Loaned Securities. These costs would include broker's fees and commission as well as any other reasonable costs, fees or expenses.

Section 13.2 does not require the Borrower to purchase Replacement Collateral or to liquidate the Loaned Securities. The Borrower is permitted to deem that he has purchased Replacement Collateral and is permitted to deem that he has sold the Loaned Securities. For example, the Borrower could still liquidate the Loaned Securities but not actually purchase the Replacement Collateral. It could also purchase the Replacement Collateral but retain the Loaned Securities as opposed to liquidating them.

To determine the deemed purchase price of the Replacement Collateral and deemed sales price of the Loaned Securities, the Borrower is to use (i) "the price therefore on the date of such exercise obtained from a generally recognized source" or (ii) "the last bid quotation from such a source at the most recent Close of Trading". Because the Borrower will not be out of pocket for any transaction costs in purchasing Replacement Collateral or selling the Loaned Securities, the MSLA does not provide that the Borrower may adjust these deemed amounts for any deemed transaction costs.

Section 13.2 also clarifies that where the proceeds from the sale of the Loaned Securities exceed the purchase price of the Replacement Collateral, the excess Loaned Securities or proceeds from its liquidation are to be returned to the Lender. It is unlikely, however, that there would be excess proceeds because the amount of Collateral transferred should always exceed the Market Value of the Loaned Securities.

13.3 Unless otherwise agreed, the parties acknowledge and agree that (a) the Loaned Securities and any Collateral consisting of Securities are of a type traded in a recognized market, (b) in the absence of a generally recognized source for prices or bid or offer quotations for any security, the non-defaulting party may establish the source therefor in its sole discretion, and (c) all prices and bid and offer quotations shall be increased to include accrued interest to the extent not already included therein (except to the extent contrary to market practice with respect to the relevant Securities).

13.4 In addition to its rights hereunder, the non-defaulting party shall have any rights otherwise available to it under any other agreement or applicable law.

Section 13.3

Section 13.3 is needed to clarify how prices for Loaned Securities and Collateral are to be determined. In clause (a), the parties acknowledge the Loaned Securities and securities Collateral are "of a type traded in a recognized market", facilitating the pricing of these securities by agreeing in advance they are traded in a recognised market. Clause (b) provides for a contingency where there is no generally recognised source for prices, delegating to the non-defaulting party the responsibility of establishing the source for the necessary quotations. Finally, clause (c) clarifies that the prices are to be adjusted for any accrued interest as appropriate.

Section 13.4

Section 13.4. provides that the non-defaulting party enjoys, in addition to the express remedies provided in Section 13, any other rights and remedies available under "any other agreement or applicable law". For example, a non-defaulting party may find a situation in which it may want to claim rights under "restitution" or rescission of the contract or perhaps specific performance.

14. **Transfer Taxes.**

All transfer taxes with respect to the transfer of the Loaned Securities by Lender to Borrower and by Borrower to Lender upon termination of the Loan and with respect to the transfer of Collateral by Borrower to Lender and by Lender to Borrower upon termination of the Loan or pursuant to Section 4.5 or Section 9 shall be paid by Borrower.

Section 14 Transfer taxes

Section 14 reflects market practice with respect to the payment of transfer taxes. Any costs associated with transfer taxes with respect to any transfers between Lender and Borrower are to be paid by the Borrower.

15. **Transfers.**

   15.1   All transfers by either Borrower or Lender of Loaned Securities or Collateral consisting of "financial assets" (within the meaning of the UCC) hereunder shall be by (a) in the case of certificated securities, physical delivery of certificates representing such securities together with duly executed stock and bond transfer powers, as the case may be, with signatures guaranteed by a bank or a member firm of the New York Stock Exchange, Inc., (b) registration of an uncertificated security in the transferee's name by the issuer of such uncertificated security, (c) the crediting by a Clearing Organization of such financial assets to the transferee's "securities account" (within the meaning of the UCC) maintained with such Clearing Organization, or (d) such other means as Borrower and Lender may agree.

Section 15 Transfers

Section 15 defines how securities and collateral are to be transferred. Section 15 was updated in 2000 to account for any relevant changes necessary stemming from the revision of the New York Uniform Commercial Code (the NY UCC).

Section 15.1

Section 15.1 sets out the rules for the transfer of "financial assets" as defined in the NY UCC. Section 8-102(9) of the New York Uniform Commercial Code defines the term financial assets:

> "Financial asset", except as otherwise provided in Section 8--103, means:
>
> (i) a security;
>
> (ii) an obligation of a person or a share, participation, or other interest in a person or in property or an enterprise of a person, which is, or is of a type, dealt in or traded on financial markets, or which is recognized in any area in which it is issued or dealt in as a medium for investment; or
>
> (iii) any property that is held by a securities intermediary for another person in a securities account if the securities intermediary has expressly agreed with the other person that the property is to be treated as a financial asset under this Article. As context requires, the term means either the interest itself or the means by which a person's claim to it is evidenced, including a certificated or uncertificated security, a security certificate, or a security entitlement.

This Section deals with how transfers are to take place for (a) certificated securities, (b) uncertificated securities, or (c) book entry securities transferred through a Clearing Organization. It also permits the parties to agree to any other appropriate processes for effecting transfers of financial assets.

15.2 All transfers of cash hereunder shall be by (a) wire transfer in immediately available, freely transferable funds or (b) such other means as Borrower and Lender may agree.

15.3 All transfers of letters of credit from Borrower to Lender shall be made by physical delivery to Lender of an irrevocable letter of credit issued by a "bank" as defined in Section 3(a)(6)(A)-(C) of the Exchange Act. Transfers of letters of credit from Lender to Borrower shall be made by causing such letters of credit to be returned or by causing the amount of such letters of credit to be reduced to the amount required after such transfer.

15.4 A transfer of Securities, cash or letters of credit may be effected under this Section 15 on any day except (a) a day on which the transferee is closed for business at its address set forth in Schedule A hereto or (b) a day on which a Clearing Organization or wire transfer system is closed, if the facilities of such Clearing Organization or wire transfer system are required to effect such transfer.

15.5 For the avoidance of doubt, the parties agree and acknowledge that the term "securities," as used herein (except in this Section 15), shall include any "security entitlements" with respect to such securities (within the meaning of the UCC). In every transfer of "financial assets" (within the meaning of the UCC) hereunder, the transferor shall take all steps necessary (a) to effect a delivery to the transferee under Section 8-301 of the UCC, or to cause the creation of a security entitlement in favor of the transferee under Section 8-501 of the UCC, (b) to enable the transferee to obtain "control" (within the meaning of Section 8-106 of the UCC), and (c) to provide the transferee with comparable rights under any applicable foreign law or regulation.

Section 15.2

Section 15.2 requires that cash transfers be done through wire transfers or as agreed by the parties.

Section 15.3

Under Section 15.3 transfers of Letters of Credit are relatively straightforward. The Borrower is physically to deliver an "irrevocable" letter of credit to the Lender. When a letter of credit is to be returned to the Borrower, it can be done by returning the letter to the Borrower or by causing the letter of credit to be reduced through an amendment or substitution.

Section 15.4

Section 15.4 provides that transfers can be made on any business day except for those days in which the appropriate entity through which the transfer is to be made is closed.

Section 15.5

Under Section 15.5, the parties agree that the term securities includes any "securities entitlement" as defined in Section 8-102(17) of the New York Uniform Commercial Code. A Securities entitlement is defined as "rights and property interest of an entitlement holder with respect to a financial asset specified in Part 5". The transferor of financial assets also agrees to take all necessary steps under the New York Uniform Commercial Code to protect the transferee's rights in the financial assets transferred.

16. **Contractual Currency.**

    16.1   Borrower and Lender agree that (a) any payment in respect of a Distribution under Section 8 shall be made in the currency in which the underlying Distribution of cash was made, (b) any return of cash shall be made in the currency in which the underlying transfer of cash was made, and (c) any other payment of cash in connection with a Loan under this Agreement shall be in the currency agreed upon by Borrower and Lender in connection with such Loan (the currency established under clause (a), (b) or (c) hereinafter referred to as the "Contractual Currency"). Notwithstanding the foregoing, the payee of any such payment may, at its option, accept tender thereof in any other currency; provided, however, that, to the extent permitted by applicable law, the obligation of the payor to make such payment will be discharged only to the extent of the amount of Contractual Currency that such payee may, consistent with normal banking procedures, purchase with such other currency (after deduction of any premium and costs of exchange) on the banking day next succeeding its receipt of such currency.

Section 16 Contractual Currency

Section 16 is a classic contractual currency clause that is found in many financial contracts.

Section 16.1

Section 16.1 obligates parties to make payments to each other in the Contractual Currency. It sets out the three situations where contractual currencies are relevant in the MSLA. First, a payment made by the recipient of a Distribution should make the pass through payment in the same currency as the "underlying Distribution of Cash was made". This makes sense since the purpose of the Distribution is to pass through the income earned on the Loaned Security or Collateral. For example, if the income on the underlying security was paid in Euros, the Distribution should also be made in Euros. Second, a party should return cash in the same currency in which it received it such as in a return of cash Collateral. Third, a party should make any other payment in the Contractual Currency agreed by both parties.

Although the parties are to make their payments in the Contractual Currency required, the payee may accept payment in a non-Contractual Currency. However, the payor's obligation to make such payment is discharged only to the extent that the payee is able to convert such non-Contractual Currency into the Contractual Currency on the next banking day.

For example, assuming that a payor is obligated to make a transfer of $10 million to the payee. Instead of paying US dollars, the payor instead transfers €7 million. Assuming an exchange rate on the next banking day of $1.4 per Euro, the payor would only be discharged in amount equal to $9.8 million (the difference from the original amount of $10 million Contractual Currency owing and the amount of US dollars purchased of $9.8 million).

It is important to note that a party may make a payment in a non-Contractual Currency because in a dispute, a court may order a judgment to be paid in a non-Contractual Currency (the "Judgment Currency"). Typically the amount of a Judgment Currency awarded, if converted on the date of the judgment into the Contractual Currency, would equal the appropriate amount of Contractual Currency. The problem, however, is that there may be lengthy delays between when the judgment is awarded and when it is actually paid, subjecting the payee to the risk of currency fluctuations between the value of the Judgment Currency and the Contractual Currency.

16.2 If for any reason the amount in the Contractual Currency received under Section 16.1, including amounts received after conversion of any recovery under any judgment or order expressed in a currency other than the Contractual Currency, falls short of the amount in the Contractual Currency due in respect of this Agreement, the party required to make the payment will (unless a Default has occurred and such party is the non-defaulting party) as a separate and independent obligation and to the extent permitted by applicable law, immediately pay such additional amount in the Contractual Currency as may be necessary to compensate for the shortfall.

16.3 If for any reason the amount in the Contractual Currency received under Section 16.1 exceeds the amount in the Contractual Currency due in respect of this Agreement, then the party receiving the payment will (unless a Default has occurred and such party is the non-defaulting party) refund promptly the amount of such excess.

Section 16.2

Section 16.2 deals with the rights of the payee if it receives less than the full amount of the Contractual Currency to which it is entitled. Under Section 16.2, any deficiency constitutes a "separate and independent obligation". The payor is then obligated immediately to pay any such deficiency to the payor.

Section 16.3

Section 16.3 deals with a less likely scenario in which after a payee has converted the payment into the Contractual Currency, it has more of the Contractual Currency than it is entitled to. Under Section 16.3, the payee is obligated to refund any such excess to the payor. This scenario, however, is unlikely, because a payor would most probably convert the payment currency itself into the Contractual Currency prior to payment, transferring only the exact amount of Contractual Currency to the payee.

17. **ERISA.**

Lender shall, if any of the Securities transferred to the Borrower hereunder for any Loan have been or shall be obtained, directly or indirectly, from or using the assets of any Plan, so notify Borrower in writing upon the execution of this Agreement or upon initiation of such Loan under Section 2.1. If Lender so notifies Borrower, then Borrower and Lender shall conduct the Loan in accordance with the terms and conditions of Department of Labor Prohibited Transaction Exemption 81-6 (46 Fed. Reg. 7527, Jan. 23, 1981; as amended, 52 Fed. Reg. 18754, May 19, 1987), or any successor thereto (unless Borrower and Lender have agreed prior to entering into a Loan that such Loan will be conducted in reliance on another exemption, or without relying on any exemption, from the prohibited transaction provisions of Section 406 of the Employee Retirement Income Security Act of 1974, as amended, and Section 4975 of the Internal Revenue Code of 1986, as amended). Without limiting the foregoing and notwithstanding any other provision of this Agreement, if the Loan will be conducted in accordance with Prohibited Transaction Exemption 81-6, then:

17.1 Borrower represents and warrants to Lender that it is either (a) a bank subject to federal or state supervision, (b) a broker-dealer registered under the Exchange Act or (c) exempt from registration under Section 15(a)(1) of the Exchange Act as a dealer in Government Securities.

17.2 Borrower represents and warrants that, during the term of any Loan hereunder, neither Borrower nor any affiliate of Borrower has any discretionary authority or control with respect to the investment of the assets of the Plan involved in the Loan or renders investment advice (within the meaning of 29 C.F.R. Section 2510.3-21(c)) with respect to the assets of the Plan involved in the Loan. Lender agrees that, prior to or at the commencement of any Loan hereunder, it will communicate to Borrower information regarding the Plan sufficient to identify to Borrower any person or persons that have discretionary authority or control with respect to the investment of the assets of the Plan involved in the Loan or that render investment advice (as defined in the preceding sentence) with respect to the assets of the Plan involved in the Loan. In the event Lender fails to communicate and keep current during the term of any Loan such information, Lender rather than Borrower shall be deemed to have made the representation and warranty in the first sentence of this Section 17.2.

Section 17 ERISA

Broker-dealers are concerned that the loan of securities to a Customer that is an employee benefit or similar type of plan may violate restrictions against the use of plan assets under the Employee Retirement Income Security Act of 1974 (ERISA). The United States has stringent rules that protect employee benefit plans, pension plans and similar types of arrangements (a "Plan"), as well as certain entities in which Plans invest, from being taken advantage of by parties that have an interest or certain relationships with the Plan (a "Related Party"). The principle behind this is that a Related Party may have an opportunity to engage in proprietary trading or similar types of behaviour because of the special relationship it has with the Plan, e.g. serving as an investment adviser. Fortunately, there is a specific exemption for securities lending from such concerns set out in Prohibited Transaction Class Exemption 81-6. A copy of the exemption is set out in an exhibit to the US law discussion in Chapter 2 on pages 56–58.

As succinctly summarised in the Master Securities Lending Agreement Guidance Notes (2000 Version):

> **The objectives of Section 17 are (i) to identify transactions raising potential ERISA concerns, (ii) in the case of any Loan involving ERISA Plan assets, to comply with PTE 81-6, unless the parties have determined that they wish to rely on another exemption or proceed without an exemption, and (iii) to provide other requirements appropriate to securities lending transactions involving ERISA plan assets. (p. 17)**

Section 17 first places a duty upon a Lender to notify the Borrower that the Loaned Securities are Plan assets, thus subjecting it to the possible restrictions in ERISA. The parties then agree in such a scenario to comply with the requirements of Exemption 81-6.

Sections 17.1 and 17.2

To ensure such compliance, the Borrower makes a series of representations in Section 17.1 and 17.2 that, if true, would result in the Loan qualifying for Exemption 81-6.

The representations in Section 17.1 are necessary to ensure that the Borrower is a bank or broker-dealer entitled to rely on Exemption 81.6. The representations and agreements required in Section 17.2 are necessary to ensure compliance with clause 1 of Exemption 81-6.

17.3 Borrower shall mark to market daily each Loan hereunder pursuant to Section 9.1 as is required if Lender is a Customer.

17.4 Borrower and Lender agree that:

(a) the term "Collateral" shall mean cash, securities issued or guaranteed by the United States government or its agencies or instrumentalities, or irrevocable bank letters of credit issued by a person other than Borrower or an affiliate thereof;

(b) prior to the making of any Loans hereunder, Borrower shall provide Lender with (i) the most recent available audited statement of Borrower's financial condition and (ii) the most recent available unaudited statement of Borrower's financial condition (if more recent than the most recent audited statement), and each Loan made hereunder shall be deemed a representation by Borrower that there has been no material adverse change in Borrower's financial condition subsequent to the date of the latest financial statements or information furnished in accordance herewith;

(c) the Loan may be terminated by Lender at any time, whereupon Borrower shall deliver the Loaned Securities to Lender within the lesser of (i) the customary delivery period for such Loaned Securities, (ii) five Business Days, and (iii) the time negotiated for such delivery between Borrower and Lender; provided, however, that Borrower and Lender may agree to a longer period only if permitted by Prohibited Transaction Exemption 81-6; and

(d) the Collateral transferred shall be security only for obligations of Borrower to the Plan with respect to Loans, and shall not be security for any obligation of Borrower to any agent or affiliate of the Plan.

Section 17.3

In 17.3, the Borrower covenants to mark to market each of the Loans as required under Section 9.1 of the MSLA. This covenant is important in order to meet the sixth requirement of Exemption 81-6 requiring that the market value of the Collateral transferred by the Borrower to the Lender is not less than 100% of the market value of the Loaned Securities.

Section 17.4

In Section 17.4(a), the definition of Collateral is limited in order to comply with clause 2 of Exemption 81–6.

In Section 17.4(b), the Borrower is required to provide certain information in order to comply with Clause 3 of Exemption 81-6.

In Section 17.4(c), certain termination requirements are imposed to comply with clause 7 of Exemption 81-6.

In Section 17.4(d), the parties agree that the Collateral will only secure the Loan, ensuring that the Collateral only secures the Loan and does not relate to any other transaction outside of the reach of Exemption 81–6.

18. Single Agreement.

Borrower and Lender acknowledge that, and have entered into this Agreement in reliance on the fact that, all Loans hereunder constitute a single business and contractual relationship and have been entered into in consideration of each other. Accordingly, Borrower and Lender hereby agree that payments, deliveries and other transfers made by either of them in respect of any Loan shall be deemed to have been made in consideration of payments, deliveries and other transfers in respect of any other Loan hereunder, and the obligations to make any such payments, deliveries and other transfers may be applied against each other and netted. In addition, Borrower and Lender acknowledge that, and have entered into this Agreement in reliance on the fact that, all Loans hereunder have been entered into in consideration of each other. Accordingly, Borrower and Lender hereby agree that (a) each shall perform all of its obligations in respect of each Loan hereunder, and that a default in the performance of any such obligation by Borrower or by Lender (the "Defaulting Party") in any Loan hereunder shall constitute a default by the Defaulting Party under all such Loans hereunder, and (b) the non-defaulting party shall be entitled to set off claims and apply property held by it in respect of any Loan hereunder against obligations owing to it in respect of any other Loan with the Defaulting Party.

Section 18 Single Agreement

The purpose of Section 18 is to avoid a scenario in bankruptcy or insolvency commonly referred to as "cherry picking". The parties agree that the MSLA and all the underlying Loan transactions should be treated as a single agreement between them and that all loan payments, deliveries and transfers are made in consideration of each other and are nettable with corresponding sums under other loans. A default under one loan between the parties counts as defaults under all of them under their MSLA for the purposes of the single agreement concept. Assuming that an insolvency trustee or judge respects the parties' agreement, the trustee would be unable to accept those Loans favourable to the bankrupt estate and reject those that are unfavourable. As explained in the US law section in Chapter 2, US bankruptcy law and banking insolvency law require a bankruptcy judge or trustee to enforce the "single agreement treatment", enforcing the netting of any amounts owing between the parties with respect to the termination of the various Loans.

19. APPLICABLE LAW.

THIS AGREEMENT SHALL BE GOVERNED AND CONSTRUED IN ACCORDANCE WITH THE LAWS OF THE STATE OF NEW YORK WITHOUT GIVING EFFECT TO THE CONFLICT OF LAW PRINCIPLES THEREOF.

Section 19 APPLICABLE LAW

The MSLA was written with the understanding that New York law would be chosen to govern the Agreement. As explained in the US law section in Chapter 2, both New York state courts and US Federal courts sitting in the State of New York would enforce a choice of New York law. Parties should consult legal counsel where they choose to have the MSLA Agreement governed by any other law than New York law.

20. **Waiver.**

The failure of a party to this Agreement to insist upon strict adherence to any term of this Agreement on any occasion shall not be considered a waiver or deprive that party of the right thereafter to insist upon strict adherence to that term or any other term of this Agreement. All waivers in respect of a Default must be in writing.

Section 20

Section 20 is necessary to overcome a common law presumption that if a party fails to exercise its rights and remedies within a reasonable time period, it risks waiving the right to exercise such rights and remedies in the future. The rationale of the common law rule is that if such a right or remedy was so important, a party would have exercised such right within a reasonable time period. This would avoid a situation in which a non-defaulting party attempts to exercise its rights based on a Default that had occurred much earlier. The concern would be that the non-defaulting party is now attempting to terminate the Loans for a reason other than the Default but is using that earlier Default as a basis for its current actions.

Although it is prudent to include Section 20, most law firms will not opine that such a provision will necessarily be enforced by a court under New York law.

21. **Survival of Remedies.**

All remedies hereunder and all obligations with respect to any Loan shall survive the termination of the relevant Loan, return of Loaned Securities or Collateral and termination of this Agreement.

Section 21 Survival of Remedies

Section 21 ensures that even if all of Loan transactions have been terminated, the Collateral returned or the MSLA terminated, a party will still have a right to pursue any of its remedies under the MSLA. For example, even though all the Loans have been terminated, a party may still have a Contractual Currency claim under Section 16. In spite of this clause, it is prudent for a party not to terminate the MSLA itself even if it has terminated all the underlying Loans or they have matured in the normal course of business.

22. **Notices and Other Communications.**

Any and all notices, statements, demands or other communications hereunder may be given by a party to the other by telephone, mail, facsimile, e-mail, electronic message, telegraph, messenger or otherwise to the individuals and at the facsimile numbers and addresses specified with respect to it in Schedule A hereto, or sent to such party at any other place specified in a notice of change of number or address hereafter received by the other party. Any notice, statement, demand or other communication hereunder will be deemed effective on the day and at the time on which it is received or, if not received, on the day and at the time on which its delivery was in good faith attempted; provided, however, that any notice by a party to the other party by telephone shall be deemed effective only if (a) such notice is followed by written confirmation thereof and (b) at least one of the other means of providing notice that are specifically listed above has previously been attempted in good faith by the notifying party.

Section 22 Notices and Other Communications

Notice provisions are often ignored and underappreciated until a party needs to ensure that it has communicated "officially" with its counterparty. For example, a Default does not occur under Sections 12.4 and 12.8 until the non-defaulting party has given the Defaulting Party notice and a chance to cure the Default. Such notice would not be considered to be effective unless it were given in accordance with Section 22. For an example where notice was not effectively given in the US with respect to an over-the-counter derivative transaction, see *First Nat. Bank of Chicago v. Ackerley Communications, Inc.* (S.D.N.Y. 2001).

Fortunately for the sender (and unfortunately for the recipient), the notice provisions under the MSLA are very generous with respect to how notice can be given in comparison with other master agreements. Methods of giving notice include telephone, mail, facsimile, e-mail, electronic message, telegraph, messenger or otherwise. In addition, notice is considered to have been given (even if not received), if the delivery was done in good faith. Telephone notice is only effective if confirmed in writing and it follows previous use in good faith of the other ways of notification referred to at the start of Section 22.

Because the notice provisions are so liberal, a party may want to consider limiting the method of giving notice, especially for purposes such as terminating the Loans upon the occurrence of a Default. For example, the parties may want to consider requiring notice by mail to have certification and return receipt. It may also want to require that notice only be effective if it is actually documented as received by the recipient.

23. SUBMISSION TO JURISDICTION; WAIVER OF JURY TRIAL.

23.1 EACH PARTY HERETO IRREVOCABLY AND UNCONDITIONALLY (A) SUBMITS TO THE NON-EXCLUSIVE JURISDICTION OF ANY UNITED STATES FEDERAL OR NEW YORK STATE COURT SITTING IN NEW YORK CITY, AND ANY APPELLATE COURT FROM ANY SUCH COURT, SOLELY FOR THE PURPOSE OF ANY SUIT, ACTION OR PROCEEDING BROUGHT TO ENFORCE ITS OBLIGATIONS HEREUNDER OR RELATING IN ANY WAY TO THIS AGREEMENT OR ANY LOAN HEREUNDER AND (B) WAIVES, TO THE FULLEST EXTENT IT MAY EFFECTIVELY DO SO, ANY DEFENSE OF AN INCONVENIENT FORUM TO THE MAINTENANCE OF SUCH ACTION OR PROCEEDING IN ANY SUCH COURT AND ANY RIGHT OF JURISDICTION ON ACCOUNT OF ITS PLACE OF RESIDENCE OR DOMICILE.

23.2 EACH PARTY HERETO HEREBY IRREVOCABLY WAIVES ANY RIGHT THAT IT MAY HAVE TO TRIAL BY JURY IN ANY ACTION, PROCEEDING OR COUNTERCLAIM ARISING OUT OF OR RELATING TO THIS AGREEMENT OR THE TRANSACTIONS CONTEMPLATED HEREBY.

Section 23 SUBMISSION TO JURISDICTION; WAIVER OF JURY TRIAL

Section 23 is important in order to ensure that a New York court would enforce the selection of New York law and take jurisdiction over a dispute. As explained in the discussion of New York law in Chapter 2, a New York court will take jurisdiction over a dispute and will enforce the selection of New York law provided that the parties have chosen New York law and agreed to non-exclusive (or exclusive) jurisdiction in New York.

In addition, because jury trial is a constitutional right in the United States, most parties insist that such a right be waived in the MSLA. Although such jury waivers have been enforced in New York, there have been concerns that such a waiver may not be enforceable in other jurisdictions such as California. Many law firms are also often reluctant to opine that such a waiver is enforceable.

24. Miscellaneous.

24.1 Except as otherwise agreed by the parties, this Agreement supersedes any other agreement between the parties hereto concerning loans of Securities between Borrower and Lender. This Agreement shall not be assigned by either party without the prior written consent of the other party and any attempted assignment without such consent shall be null and void. Subject to the foregoing, this Agreement shall be binding upon and shall inure to the benefit of Borrower and Lender and their respective heirs, representatives, successors and assigns. This Agreement may be terminated by either party upon notice to the other, subject only to fulfillment of any obligations then outstanding. This Agreement shall not be modified, except by an instrument in writing signed by the party against whom enforcement is sought. The parties hereto acknowledge and agree that, in connection with this Agreement and each Loan hereunder, time is of the essence. Each provision and agreement herein shall be treated as separate and independent from any other provision herein and shall be enforceable notwithstanding the unenforceability of any such other provision or agreement.

Section 24.1

Section 24.1 is a disparate group of boilerplate provisions. Although these provisions are always present in finance contracts, they are frequently ignored on the incorrect assumption that they are unimportant. In fact, these boilerplate provisions appear in every finance contract because they typically are included as necessary to deal with unfavourable common law precedents that even if outdated, could still affect litigation results.

The first sentence sets out the rule that the MSLA supersedes any previous agreements with respect to Loans between the parties. This clause eliminates confusion over whether previous agreements or understandings would override the MSLA. It becomes particularly important if the parties encounter ambiguities in the MSLA or its Schedule. To resolve those ambiguities, it would be tempting to appeal to earlier term sheets, negotiations, correspondence, discussions or proposals. For example, the parties may have agreed in earlier negotiations to clauses or terms that were not added to the MSLA. The parties may attempt to interpret the MSLA based on absence of a particular provision. Based upon a strict interpretation of this clause, however, such examples should be irrelevant with respect to interpreting the MSLA.

The second sentence in 24.1 prohibits a party from transferring its interest in the MSLA without the consent of the other party. The remaining party may have serious concerns about a new transferee and should insist on the right to approve such a transfer.

The MSLA may also be terminated at any time by either party, subject only to the outstanding obligations under the MSLA being fulfilled. The 2000 Agreement may only be modified or amended in writing and signed by the party against whom the contract is being enforced. Time is of the essence in the Agreement. Finally, the MSLA provides that each provision can be enforced independently.

24.2 Any agreement between Borrower and Lender pursuant to Section 10.5(b) or Section 25.37 shall be made (a) in writing, (b) orally, if confirmed promptly in writing or through any system that compares Loans and in which Borrower and Lender are participants, or (c) in such other manner as may be agreed by Borrower and Lender in writing.

Section 24.2

24.2 Any agreement between Borrower and Lender pursuant to Section 10.5(b) or Section 25.37 shall be made (a) in writing, (b) orally, if confirmed promptly in writing or through any system that compares Loans and in which Borrower and Lender are participants, or (c) in such other manner as may be agreed by Borrower and Lender in writing.

25. Definitions.

For the purposes hereof:

25.1 "Act of Insolvency" shall mean, with respect to any party, (a) the commencement by such party as debtor of any case or proceeding under any bankruptcy, insolvency, reorganization, liquidation, moratorium, dissolution, delinquency or similar law, or such party's seeking the appointment or election of a receiver, conservator, trustee, custodian or similar official for such party or any substantial part of its property, or the convening of any meeting of creditors for purposes of commencing any such case or proceeding or seeking such an appointment or election, (b) the commencement of any such case or proceeding against such party, or another seeking such an appointment or election, or the filing against a party of an application for a protective decree under the provisions of the Securities Investor Protection Act of 1970, which (i) is consented to or not timely contested by such party, (ii) results in the entry of an order for relief, such an appointment or election, the issuance of such a protective decree or the entry of an order having a similar effect, or (iii) is not dismissed within 15 days, (c) the making by such party of a general assignment for the benefit of creditors, or (d) the admission in writing by such party of such party's inability to pay such party's debts as they become due.

Section 25 Definitions

Section 25.1

The definition of an "Act of Insolvency" is drafted broadly in Section 25.1(a) and should cover any entity organised under US law. If a party is dealing with a counterparty organised under the laws of a jurisdiction outside the United States, it should analyse whether the provision includes any other possible forms of insolvency. The definition also includes a situation in which a case or proceeding is commenced against a party for a protective decree under the Securities Investor Protect Act of 1970.

25.2 "Bankruptcy Code" shall have the meaning assigned in Section 26.1

25.3 "Borrower" shall have the meaning assigned in Section 1.

25.4 "Borrower Payment" shall have the meaning assigned in Section 8.5(a).

25.5 "Broker-Dealer" shall mean any person that is a broker (including a municipal securities broker), dealer, municipal securities dealer, government securities broker or government securities dealer as defined in the Exchange Act, regardless of whether the activities of such person are conducted in the United States or otherwise require such person to register with the U.S. Securities and Exchange Commission or other regulatory body.

Section 25.2

Section 26.1 defines Bankruptcy Code as Title 11 of the United States Code, as amended.

Section 25.3

It should be noted that either party may act as a Borrower or a Lender.

Section 25.4

A Borrower Payment refers to cash Distributions made to the Lender on Loaned Securities as required by Sections 8.1 and 8.2.

Section 25.5

Section 25.5 provides a broad standard definition of a Broker-Dealer. A "broker" under the Securities Exchange Act of 1934 is defined broadly as "any person engaged in the business of effecting transactions in securities for the account of others" (Section 3(a)(4)(A) of the Exchange Act). A dealer under the Exchange Act does not act as an agent like a broker but instead acts as a principal. The Exchange Act defines a dealer as "any person engaged in the business of buying and selling securities for his own account, through a broker or otherwise" (Section 3(a)(5)(A) of the Securities Exchange Act).

25.6 "Business Day" shall mean, with respect to any Loan hereunder, a day on which regular trading occurs in the principal market for the Loaned Securities subject to such Loan, provided, however, that for purposes of determining the Market Value of any Securities hereunder, such term shall mean a day on which regular trading occurs in the principal market for the Securities whose value is being determined. Notwithstanding the foregoing, (a) for purposes of Section 9, "Business Day" shall mean any day on which regular trading occurs in the principal market for any Loaned Securities or for any Collateral consisting of Securities under any outstanding Loan hereunder and "next Business Day" shall mean the next day on which a transfer of Collateral may be effected in accordance with Section 15, and (b) in no event shall a Saturday or Sunday be considered a Business Day.

Section 25.6

Section 25.6 does not provide a general definition of "Business Day". Instead, it is defined in relation to each specific Loan as "a day on which regular trading occurs in the principal market for the Loaned Securities subject to such Loan". In other words, the definition could vary depending on the type and nature of Loaned Securities. In an important proviso, however, a Business Day is limited to a "day on which regular trading occurs in the principal market for the Securities whose value is being determined" for purposes of determining "Market Value" of any Securities. The definition is refined for Collateral in the form of Securities because they are subject to a collateral call and deliverable one Business Day later. The main focus of the definition is on Business Days when there is "regular trading" in order to be able to make required transfers of Securities.

The definition is modified with respect to Section 9 (mark-to-market margining) and Section 15 (transfers). For the purposes of Section 9, it must be a Business Day both for the purposes of Loaned Securities and Collateral consisting of Securities in order to determine an accurate Margin Excess or Margin Deficit. The definition clarifies that for the purposes of Section 9 the term "next Business Day" refers to "the next day on which a transfer of Collateral may be effected in accordance with Section 15".

Finally, the definition clarifies that Saturday or Sunday cannot be a Business Day.

25.7 "Cash Collateral Fee" shall have the meaning assigned in Section 5.1.

25.8 "Clearing Organization" shall mean (a) The Depository Trust Company, or, if agreed to by Borrower and Lender, such other "securities intermediary" (within the meaning of the UCC) at which Borrower (or Borrower's agent) and Lender (or Lender's agent) maintain accounts, or (b) a Federal Reserve Bank, to the extent that it maintains a book-entry system.

25.9 "Close of Business" shall mean the time established by the parties in Schedule B or otherwise orally or in writing or, in the absence of any such agreement, as shall be determined in accordance with market practice.

25.10 "Close of Trading" shall mean, with respect to any Security, the end of the primary trading session established by the principal market for such Security on a Business Day, unless otherwise agreed by the parties.

Section 25.7

The Cash Collateral Fee in Section 5.1 refers to the rebate paid by the Lender to the Borrower with respect to cash Collateral Transferred to the Lender by the Borrower.

Section 25.8

A Clearing Organization is defined as first, The Depository Trust Company. Second, any "securities intermediary" agreed by the parties. A "securities intermediary" is defined in Section 1-108 of the New York Uniform Commercial Code as a "(i) a clearing corporation; or (ii) a person, including a bank or broker, that in the ordinary course of its business maintains securities accounts for others and is acting in that capacity". It can also be a Federal Reserve Bank to the extent that it has a book-entry system for the securities in question.

Section 25.9

Section 25.9 permits the parties to set out the time meant by "Close of Business" in Schedule B, in writing or orally. If the parties do not agree on a time for Close of Business, it will be determined in accordance with market practice.

Section 25.10

The MSLA distinguishes between Close of Trading and Close of Business. Close of Trading is primarily used in the Agreement with respect to determining Market Value. It is defined on a security by security basis and refers to the "end of the primary trading session established by the principal market for such Security". The MSLA provides, however, that the user should still follow market practice if it differs from this definition.

25.11 "Collateral" shall mean, whether now owned or hereafter acquired and to the extent permitted by applicable law, (a) any property which Borrower and Lender agree prior to the Loan shall be acceptable collateral and which is transferred to Lender pursuant to Sections 4 or 9 (including as collateral, for definitional purposes, any letters of credit mutually acceptable to Lender and Borrower), (b) any property substituted therefor pursuant to Section 4.5, (c) all accounts in which such property is deposited and all securities and the like in which any cash collateral is invested or reinvested, and (d) any proceeds of any of the foregoing; *provided, however*, that if Lender is a Customer, "Collateral" shall (subject to Section 17.4(a), if applicable) be limited to cash, U.S. Treasury bills and notes, an irrevocable letter of credit issued by a "bank" (as defined in Section 3(a)(6)(A)-(C) of the Exchange Act), and any other property permitted to serve as collateral securing a loan of securities under Rule 15c3-3 under the Exchange Act or any comparable regulation of the Secretary of the Treasury under Section 15C of the Exchange Act (to the extent that Borrower is subject to such Rule or comparable regulation) pursuant to exemptive, interpretive or no-action relief or otherwise. If any new or different Security shall be exchanged for any Collateral by recapitalization, merger, consolidation or other corporate action, such new or different Security shall, effective upon such exchange, be deemed to become Collateral in substitution for the former Collateral for which such exchange is made. For purposes of return of Collateral by Lender or purchase or sale of Securities pursuant to Section 13, such term shall include Securities of the same issuer, class and quantity as the Collateral initially transferred by Borrower to Lender, as adjusted pursuant to the preceding sentence.

Section 25.11

Section 25.11 sets out the situations in which property held by the Lender shall constitute Collateral under the MSLA. First, it consists of any property that the Borrower and Lender initially agreed would constitute acceptable Collateral and which has been transferred by the Borrower to the Lender under either Section 4 (transferred at the inception of the Loan) or Section 9 (margining).

Second, it consists of any property that is substituted under Section 4.5 by the Borrower for Collateral previously transferred. Third, it also includes the accounts in which the property is deposited. For purposes of cash Collateral, it includes any "securities and the like" in which the Lender has invested or reinvested the cash. Fourth, it includes any proceeds from the liquidation of such Collateral.

Section 25.11 sets out an important restriction, however, as to what constitutes Collateral in situations in which a Lender is a Customer of a Broker-Dealer and the parties are subject to Rule 15c3-3 under the Securities Exchange Act (1934), subject however to any application of Section 17.4 (ERISA provision). In this situation, property will only constitute Collateral if it is Cash, US Treasury Securities or an irrevocable letter of credit issued by a qualifying bank under Rule 15c3-3, and a catch-all provision consisting of any other property permitted under Rule 15c-3.

The definition also deals with a situation in which original securities Collateral has been exchanged for a different Security because of a "recapitalization, merger, consolidation or other action". Such securities shall be deemed to constitute Collateral effective upon the exchange.

Section 25.12 also defines what constitutes Collateral for purposes of returning it to the Borrower or in situations in which the Borrower is purchasing Replacement Collateral under Section 13 of the Agreement. Such Collateral must consist of equivalent Securities, meaning that it must be of the same issuer, class and quantity as the original Collateral, as adjusted for any corporate action as described above.

25.12 "Collateral Distributions" shall have the meaning assigned in Section 8.5(a).

25.13 "Confirmation" shall have the meaning assigned in Section 2.1.

25.14 "Contractual Currency" shall have the meaning assigned in Section 16.1.

Section 25.12

Collateral Distributions are defined in Section 8.5(a). This is where a Lender has received a cash distribution with respect to Collateral and is required to pass that distribution through to the Borrower.

Section 25.13

Section 25.13 defines what is meant by a Confirmation. It is important to note a confirmation only confirms the securities lending transaction entered into between the Borrower and Lender and is used to constitute evidence of this transaction.

Section 25.14

Section 16.1 defines what is meant by Contractual Currency. The concept of a Contractual Currency requires that a party receiving a payment from a counterparty receives the equivalent amount that it was entitled to receive in the Contractual Currency; otherwise the recipient would have a claim for any deficiency after it converts the currency received into the Contractual Currency. Conversely a recipient may need to return any excess amount of Contractual Currency that it receives over the required amount.

25.15 "Customer" shall mean any person that is a customer of Borrower under Rule 15c3-3 under the Exchange Act or any comparable regulation of the Secretary of the Treasury under Section 15C of the Exchange Act (to the extent that Borrower is subject to such Rule or comparable regulation).

Section 25.15

Section 25.15 defines a Customer for purposes of situations in the MSLA involving the application of Rule 15c3-3 of the Exchange Act. A Customer under Rule 15c3-3 is defined as:

> The term *customer* shall mean any person from whom or on whose behalf a broker or dealer has received or acquired or holds funds or securities for the account of that person. The term shall not include a broker or dealer, a municipal securities dealer, or a government securities broker or government securities dealer. The term shall, however, include another broker or dealer to the extent that broker or dealer maintains an omnibus account for the account of customers with the broker or dealer in compliance with Regulation T (12 CFR 220.1 through 220.19). The term shall not include a general partner or director or principal officer of the broker or dealer or any other person to the extent that person has a claim for property or funds which by contract, agreement or understanding, or by operation of law, is part of the capital of the broker or dealer or is subordinated to the claims of creditors of the broker or dealer. In addition, the term shall not include a person to the extent that the person has a claim for security futures products held in a futures account, or any security futures product and any futures product held in a "proprietary account" as defined by the Commodity Futures Trading Commission in § 1.3(y) of this chapter. The term also shall not include a counterparty who has delivered collateral to an OTC derivatives dealer pursuant to a transaction in an eligible OTC derivative instrument, or pursuant to the OTC derivatives dealer's cash management securities activities or ancillary portfolio management securities activities, and who has received a prominent written notice from the OTC derivatives dealer that:
>
> - Rule 15c3-3 – Customer Protection--Reserves and Custody of Securities Page 1 of 13
>
>   http://www.law.uc.edu/CCL/34ActRls/rule15c3-3.html 7/10/2010
>
>   Except as otherwise agreed in writing by the OTC derivatives dealer and the counterparty, the dealer may repledge or otherwise use the collateral in its business;
> - In the event of the OTC derivatives dealer's failure, the counterparty will likely be considered an unsecured creditor of the dealer as to that collateral;
> - The Securities Investor Protection Act of 1970 (15 U.S.C. 78aaa et seq.) does not protect the counterparty; and
> - The collateral will not be subject to the requirements of Rule 8c-1, Rule 15c2-1, Rule 15c3-2, or Rule 15c3-3.

25.16 "Cutoff Time" shall mean a time on a Business Day by which a transfer of cash, securities or other property must be made by Borrower or Lender to the other, as shall be agreed by Borrower and Lender in Schedule B or otherwise orally or in writing or, in the absence of any such agreement, as shall be determined in accordance with market practice.

25.17 "Default" shall have the meaning assigned in Section 12.

25.18 "Defaulting Party" shall have the meaning assigned in Section 18.

25.19 "Distribution" shall mean, with respect to any Security at any time, any distribution made on or in respect of such Security, including, but not limited to: (a) cash and all other property, (b) stock dividends, (c) Securities received as a result of split ups of such Security and distributions in respect thereof, (d) interest payments, (e) all rights to purchase additional Securities, and (f) any cash or other consideration paid or provided by the issuer of such Security in exchange for any vote, consent or the taking of any similar action in respect of such Security (regardless of whether the record date for such vote, consent or other action falls during the term of the Loan). In the event that the holder of a Security is entitled to elect the type of distribution to be received from two or more alternatives, such election shall be made by Lender, in the case of a Distribution in respect of the Loaned Securities, and by Borrower, in the case of a Distribution in respect of Collateral.

6. The US Master Securities Loan Agreement (2000)

Section 25.16

Cutoff Time is defined as the time agreed by the parties in Schedule B, orally or in writing or in accordance with market practice if the parties have not agreed to a time. Cutoff Time provides a deadline for a party to make a transfer as required by the MSLA.

Section 25.17

The laundry list of what constitutes a Default is set forth in Section 12. The occurrence of a Default provides the non-defaulting party with the option of terminating all the securities loans. The termination, however, occurs automatically upon the occurrence of an Act of Insolvency.

Section 25.18

Section 18 is the "Single Agreement" provision in the MSLA. The Defaulting Party is defined therein as a party that defaults in its performance of any of its obligations in respect of any Loan under the Agreement.

Section 25.19

Section 25.19 provides a laundry list of what constitutes a Distribution with respect to a Security. The definition notes that the list is not exclusive, however, and may include similar Distributions as follows:

- cash and all other property,
- stock dividends,
- Securities received as a result of split ups of such Security and distributions in respect thereof,
- interest payments,
- all rights to purchase additional Securities, and
- any cash or other consideration paid or provided by the issuer of such Security in exchange for any vote, consent or the taking of any of such Security (regardless of whether the record date for such vote, consent or other action falls during the term of the Loan).

25.20 "Equity Security" shall mean any security (as defined in the Exchange Act) other than a "nonequity security," as defined in Regulation T.

25.21 "Exchange Act" shall mean the Securities Exchange Act of 1934, as amended.

25.22 "Extension Deadline" shall mean, with respect to a letter of credit, the Cutoff Time on the Business Day preceding the day on which the letter of credit expires.

25.23 "FDIA" shall have the meaning assigned in Section 26.4.

25.24 "FDICIA" shall have the meaning assigned in Section 26.5.

25.25 "Federal Funds Rate" shall mean the rate of interest (expressed as an annual rate), as published in Federal Reserve Statistical Release H.15(519) or any publication substituted therefor, charged for federal funds (dollars in immediately available funds borrowed by banks on an overnight unsecured basis) on that day or, if that day is not a banking day in New York City, on the next preceding banking day.

Section 25.20

The definition of an Equity Security in Section 3(a)(11) of the Securities Exchange Act is set forth succinctly in Rule 3a11-1 as the following:

> The term *equity security* is hereby defined to include any stock or similar security, certificate of interest or participation in any profit sharing agreement, preorganization certificate or subscription, transferable share, voting trust certificate or certificate of deposit for an equity security, limited partnership interest, interest in a joint venture, or certificate of interest in a business trust; any security future on any such security; or any security convertible, with or without consideration into such a security, or carrying any warrant or right to subscribe to or purchase such a security; or any such warrant or right; or any put, call, straddle, or other option or privilege of buying such a security from or selling such a security to another without being bound to do so. (38 FR 11449, May 8, 1973; 67 FR 19671, 19673, Apr. 23, 2002.)

Regulation T defines an non-equity security as the following: "*Non-equity security* means a security that is not an equity security (as defined in section 3(a)(11) of the Act)."

Section 25.21

The Securities Exchange Act of 1934 is codified at 15 USC §§ 78a *et seq.*

Section 25.22

Letters of Credit under applicable law must have an expiration date. The Lender is, therefore, at risk that the Letter of Credit may expire, leaving him unsecured. The Agreement provides in Section 4.6 that a letter of credit must be renewed by the Extension Deadline.

Section 25.23

FDIA is the Federal Deposit Insurance Act, codified in Title 12 of the US Code.

Section 25.24

FDICIA is the Federal Deposit Insurance Corporation Improvement Act, codified in Title 12 of the US Code.

Section 25.25

The definition of Federal Funds Rate in Section 25.25 is a standard definition for this particular overnight rate. The rate is referenced in the remedies section for overdue amounts.

25.26 "Foreign Securities" shall mean, unless otherwise agreed, Securities that are principally cleared and settled outside the United States.

25.27 "Government Securities" shall mean government securities as defined in Section 3(a)(42)(A)-(C) of the Exchange Act.

Section 25.26

The distinguishing feature of a Foreign Security for purposes of the MSLA is whether such security is cleared and settled outside the United States.

Section 25.27

Section 3(a)(42)(A)-(C) of the Exchange Act defines "Government Securities" as:

(a) securities which are direct obligations of, or obligations guaranteed as to principal or interest by, the United States;

(b) securities which are issued or guaranteed by the Tennessee Valley Authority or by corporations in which the United States has a direct or indirect interest and which are designated by the Secretary of the Treasury for exemption as necessary or appropriate in the public interest or for the protection of investors;

(c) securities issued or guaranteed as to principal or interest by any corporation the securities of which are designated, by statute specifically naming such corporation, to constitute exempt securities within the meaning of the laws administered by the Commission;

(d) for purposes of sections 15C and 17A, any put, call, straddle, option, or privilege on a security described in subparagraph (A), (B), or (C) other than a put, call, straddle, option, or privilege--

   (i) that is traded on one or more national securities exchanges; or

   (ii) for which quotations are disseminated through an automated quotation system operated by a registered securities association; or

(e) for purposes of sections 15, 15C, and 17A as applied to a bank, a qualified Canadian government obligation as defined in section 24 of Title 12.

25.28 "Lender" shall have the meaning assigned in Section 1.

25.29 "Lender Payment" shall have the meaning assigned in Section 8.5(a).

25.30 "LIBOR" shall mean for any date, the offered rate for deposits in U.S. dollars for a period of three months which appears on the Reuters Screen LIBO page as of 11:00 a.m., London time, on such date (or, if at least two such rates appear, the arithmetic mean of such rates).

25.31 "Loan" shall have the meaning assigned in Section 1.

25.32 "Loan Fee" shall have the meaning assigned in Section 5.1.

25.33 "Loaned Security" shall mean any Security transferred in a Loan hereunder until such Security (or an identical Security) is transferred back to Lender hereunder, except that, if any new or different Security shall be exchanged for any Loaned Security by recapitalization, merger, consolidation or other corporate action, such new or different Security shall, effective upon such exchange, be deemed to become a Loaned Security in substitution for the former Loaned Security for which such exchange is made. For purposes of return of Loaned Securities by Borrower or purchase or sale of Securities pursuant to Section 13, such term shall include Securities of the same issuer, class and quantity as the Loaned Securities, as adjusted pursuant to the preceding sentence.

Section 25.28

Under the MSLA either party may act as a Lender.

Section 25.29

A Lender Payment refers to cash Distributions to be made on Collateral as required by Sections 8.1 and 8.2.

Section 25.30

LIBOR is a reference interest rate used in the Agreement to calculate interest on certain overdue payments in Section 13.1 and Section 13.2. The definition in Section 25.30 is a standard definition referring the parties to a particular Reuters' trading screen for a rate at a particular time.

Section 25.31

A Loan under the MSLA consists of the transfer of the Loaned Securities to the Borrower, secured by the Collateral pledged by the Borrower, as described in Section 1.

Section 25.32

The Loan Fee is the compensation that the Borrower pays to the Lender for the loan of the Loaned Securities.

Section 25.33

A Loaned Security is a security lent by a Lender to a Borrower under a Loan until such Loaned Security is transferred back to the Lender. Where during the Loan, the Loaned Security has been exchanged for a new Security or Securities because of a recapitalisation, merger, consolidation or other corporate action, the new Security or Securities shall be deemed to be the Loaned Securities.

25.34 "Margin Deficit" shall have the meaning assigned in Section 9.2.

25.35 "Margin Excess" shall have the meaning assigned in Section 9.3.

25.36 "Margin Notice Deadline" shall mean the time agreed to by the parties in the relevant Confirmation, Schedule B hereto or otherwise as the deadline for giving notice requiring same-day satisfaction of mark-to-market obligations as provided in Section 9 hereof (or, in the absence of any such agreement, the deadline for such purposes established in accordance with market practice).

25.37 "Margin Percentage" shall mean, with respect to any Loan as of any date, a percentage agreed by Borrower and Lender, which shall be not less than 100%, unless (a) Borrower and Lender agree otherwise, as provided in Section 24.2, and (b) Lender is not a Customer. Notwithstanding the previous sentence, in the event that the writing or other confirmation evidencing the agreement described in clause (a) does not set out such percentage with respect to any such Loan, the Margin Percentage shall not be a percentage less than the percentage obtained by dividing (i) the Market Value of the Collateral required to be transferred by Borrower to Lender with respect to such Loan at the commencement of the Loan by (ii) the Market Value of the Loaned Securities required to be transferred by Lender to Borrower at the commencement of the Loan.

Section 25.34

Margin Deficit is the amount that the Margin Percentage of the Market Value of the Loaned Securities exceeds the Market Value of the Collateral. Section 9.2 would obligate the Borrower to make a transfer of Collateral to make up the amount of the difference upon Lender's demand.

Section 25.35

Margin Excess is the amount that the Market Value of the Collateral exceeds the Margin Percentage of the Market Value of the Loaned Securities. Section 9.3 would obligate the Lender to make a transfer of Collateral to make up the amount of the excess upon Borrower's demand.

Section 25.36

Under the margining provisions of Section 9, if a party wants to receive a transfer of Collateral on the same day that it makes a collateral call, it needs to provide such notice by the "Margin Notice Deadline". The Margin Notice Deadline means the time agreed to (a) in the relevant Confirmation, (b) in the Schedule or (c) if there is no agreement, the Margin Notice Deadline shall be established in accordance with market practice.

Section 25.37

The Margin Percentage represents the percentage that is multiplied by the Market Value of Loaned Securities in order to determine whether a Margin Deficit or Margin Excess under Section 9 has arisen. The Lender and the Borrower agree to the Margin Percentage which may not be less than 100%. The parties, however, typically agree to a Margin Percentage that is above 100% so that the Lender is over-collateralised with respect to the relevant Loaned Securities. This can be agreed to on a Loan by Loan basis or on an aggregate basis. The definition provides, however, that the parties may agree to a Margin Percentage less than 100% as long as the Borrower is not a Customer (see the commentary on Section 25.15).

Where the parties do not expressly agree to a Margin Percentage, the Margin Percentage shall not be less than the percentage obtained by dividing (i) the Market Value of the Collateral required to be transferred at the inception of the Loan over (ii) the Market Value of the Loaned Securities required to be transferred at that time by the Lender.

25.38 "Market Value" shall have the meaning set forth in Annex II or otherwise agreed to by Borrower and Lender in writing. Notwithstanding the previous sentence, in the event that the meaning of Market Value has not been set forth in Annex II or in any other writing, as described in the previous sentence, Market Value shall be determined in accordance with market practice for the Securities, based on the price for such Securities as of the most recent Close of Trading obtained from a generally recognized source agreed to by the parties or the closing bid quotation at the most recent Close of Trading obtained from such source, plus accrued interest to the extent not included therein (other than any interest credited or transferred to, or applied to the obligations of, the other party pursuant to Section 8, unless market practice with respect to the valuation of such Securities in connection with securities loans is to the contrary). If the relevant quotation did not exist at such Close of Trading, then the Market Value shall be the relevant quotation on the next preceding Close of Trading at which there was such a quotation. The determinations of Market Value provided for in Annex II or in any other writing described in the first sentences of this Section 25.38 or, if applicable, in the preceding sentence shall apply for all purposes under this Agreement, except for purposes of Section 13.

Section 25.38

Under the MSLA it is necessary to know the Market Value of both Collateral and Loaned Securities for purposes of determining the initial transfers at the start of the Loan under Section 4.1; making substitutions under Section 4.5; determining the amount of fees under Section 5.1; and properly margining the Loans under Section 9. Market Value has the meaning set out in Annex II if the parties agree that it is applicable or as otherwise agreed by the parties in writing. The definition of Market Value, however, is not applicable for purposes of termination of a Loan under Section 13.

If the parties have not elected to use Annex II or have not otherwise provided a definition of Market Value, Section 25.38 provides a specific procedure for determining the Market Value of Securities. Market Value is to be determined in accordance with market practice. The Market Value is to be based on the price as of the most recent Close of Trading. It is to be obtained from either "a generally recognized source agreed by the parties" or "the closing bid quotation at the most recent Close of Trading" from such source. Accrued interest, to the extent that it has not already been included in the price, should be added to the Market Value.

If a relevant stock price quotation was not available at the most recent Close of Trading, then the price from the next preceding day should be utilised.

Finally, if Annex II is applicable (or the parties have agreed to the determination of Market Value in another writing), that determination of Market Value shall be applicable for all purposes of the MSLA except for purposes of terminating a Loan.

25.39 "Payee" shall have the meaning assigned in Section 8.5(a).

25.40 "Payor" shall have the meaning assigned in Section 8.5(a).

25.41 "Plan" shall mean: (a) any "employee benefit plan" as defined in Section 3(3) of the Employee Retirement Income Security Act of 1974 which is subject to Part 4 of Subtitle B of Title I of such Act; (b) any "plan" as defined in Section 4975(e)(1) of the Internal Revenue Code of 1986; or (c) any entity the assets of which are deemed to be assets of any such "employee benefit plan" or "plan" by reason of the Department of Labor's plan asset regulation, 29 C.F.R. Section 2510.3-101.

25.42 "Regulation T" shall mean Regulation T of the Board of Governors of the Federal Reserve System, as in effect from time to time.

25.43 "Retransfer" shall mean, with respect to any Collateral, to pledge, repledge, hypothecate, rehypothecate, lend, relend, sell or otherwise transfer such Collateral, or to re-register any such Collateral evidenced by physical certificates in any name other than Borrower's.

25.44 "Securities" shall mean securities or, if agreed by the parties in writing, other assets.

25.45 "Securities Distributions" shall have the meaning assigned in Section 8.5(a).

25.46 "Tax" shall have the meaning assigned in Section 8.5(a).

25.47 "UCC" shall mean the New York Uniform Commercial Code.

Section 25.39

In Section 8.5(a), the Payee is the recipient of a payment required to be made because of a Distribution.

Section 25.40

In Section 8.5(a), the Payor is the transferor of a payment required to be made because of a Distribution.

Section 25.41

The definition of "Plan" in Section 25.41 provides a legal definition of an employee benefit plan or other plans under the Employee Retirement Income Security Act of 1974.

Section 25.42

Regulation T refers to the regulations promulgated by the Board of Governors of the Federal Reserve System found in 12 CFR Part 220 – Credit By Brokers and Dealers. Section 220.10 of Part 220 deals with the borrowing and lending of securities.

Section 25.43

The definition of Retransfer in Section 25.43 is defined as what is commonly known as "use rights" or a right of rehypothecation with respect to Collateral.

Section 25.44

The definition of Securities is drafted very broadly to include not only what is commonly understood to be securities but also to include other assets if agreed to by the parties.

Section 25.45

A Securities Distribution is defined to include cash payments received by the Borrower with respect to Loaned Securities.

Section 25.46

The definition of Tax in Section 8.5(a) is very broad, including any withholding tax or "other tax, duty, fee, levy or charge required to be deducted or withheld from such Borrower Payment or Lender Payment".

Section 25.47

The New York Uniform Commercial Code governs the rights of an obligor and a secured party with respect to Collateral.

26. **Intent.**

26.1 The parties recognize that each Loan hereunder is a "securities contract," as such term is defined in Section 741 of Title 11 of the United States Code (the "Bankruptcy Code"), as amended (except insofar as the type of assets subject to the Loan would render such definition inapplicable).

26.2 It is understood that each and every transfer of funds, securities and other property under this Agreement and each Loan hereunder is a "settlement payment" or a "margin payment," as such terms are used in Sections 362(b)(6) and 546(e) of the Bankruptcy Code.

26.3 It is understood that the rights given to Borrower and Lender hereunder upon a Default by the other constitute the right to cause the liquidation of a securities contract and the right to set off mutual debts and claims in connection with a securities contract, as such terms are used in Sections 555 and 362(b)(6) of the Bankruptcy Code.

26.4 The parties agree and acknowledge that if a party hereto is an "insured depository institution," as such term is defined in the Federal Deposit Insurance Act, as amended ("FDIA"), then each Loan hereunder is a "securities contract" and "qualified financial contract," as such terms are defined in the FDIA and any rules, orders or policy statements thereunder (except insofar as the type of assets subject to the Loan would render such definitions inapplicable).

26.5 It is understood that this Agreement constitutes a "netting contract" as defined in and subject to Title IV of the Federal Deposit Insurance Corporation Improvement Act of 1991 ("FDICIA") and each payment obligation under any Loan hereunder shall constitute a "covered contractual payment entitlement" or "covered contractual payment obligation," respectively, as defined in and subject to FDICIA (except insofar as one or both of the parties is not a "financial institution" as that term is defined in FDICIA).

26.6 Except to the extent required by applicable law or regulation or as otherwise agreed, Borrower and Lender agree that Loans hereunder shall in no event be "exchange contracts" for purposes of the rules of any securities exchange and that Loans hereunder shall not be governed by the buy-in or similar rules of any such exchange, registered national securities association or other self-regulatory organization.

Section 26.1

In order to avoid any legal uncertainty in the event of a bankruptcy of one of the parties, the parties agree in Section 26.1 that upon executing the MSLA each Loan should be characterised as a securities contract under the US Bankruptcy Code in order to take advantage of the close-out netting and other benefits extended to a creditor for a securities contract under the US Bankruptcy Code. Please see the insolvency discussion in the US law section in Chapter 2.

Section 26.2

In order to avoid any legal uncertainty in the event of a bankruptcy of one of the parties, the parties agree in Section 26.2 that upon executing the MSLA that transfers of funds under the Agreement should be characterised as a settlement payment or a margin payment in order to qualify for beneficial treatments under the Bankruptcy Code.

Section 26.3

In order to avoid any legal uncertainty in the event of a bankruptcy of one of the parties, the parties agree in Section 26.3 that upon executing the MSLA, that upon a Default, the non-defaulting party will have the right to liquidate the loans and set off any mutual debts and claims as permitted under the Bankruptcy Code.

Section 26.4

In order to avoid any legal uncertainty in the event of an insolvency of an institution that has deposits insured by the FDIC, the parties agree in Section 26.4 that upon executing the MSLA each Loan should be characterised as a securities contract and a qualified financial contract under the Federal Deposit Insurance Act in order to take advantage of the close-out netting and other benefits extended to a creditor with respect to a securities contract under the Agreement. Please see the insolvency law discussion in the US law section in Chapter 2.

Section 26.5

In order to avoid any legal uncertainty in the event of an insolvency of a financial institution that qualifies for the benefits of FDICIA, the parties agree in Section 26.5 that upon executing the MSLA, the parties will qualify for the preferential treatments under FDICIA given to a netting contract, a covered contractual payment entitlement or a covered contractual payment obligations. Again, please see the insolvency discussion in the U.S. law section in Chapter 2.

Section 26.6

In order to avoid any legal uncertainty over the recharacterization of the Loans, the parties agree in Section 26.6 that the Loans shall not be characterised as exchange contracts in order to avoid being subject to buy-in or similar rules imposed by exchanges and similar organisations.

27. **DISCLOSURE RELATING TO CERTAIN FEDERAL PROTECTIONS.**

   27.1 WITHOUT WAIVING ANY RIGHTS GIVEN TO LENDER HEREUNDER, IT IS UNDERSTOOD AND AGREED THAT THE PROVISIONS OF THE SECURITIES INVESTOR PROTECTION ACT OF 1970 MAY NOT PROTECT LENDER WITH RESPECT TO LOANED SECURITIES HEREUNDER AND THAT, THEREFORE, THE COLLATERAL DELIVERED TO LENDER MAY CONSTITUTE THE ONLY SOURCE OF SATISFACTION OF BORROWER'S OBLIGATIONS IN THE EVENT BORROWER FAILS TO RETURN THE LOANED SECURITIES.

   27.2 LENDER ACKNOWLEDGES THAT, IN CONNECTION WITH LOANS OF GOVERNMENT SECURITIES AND AS OTHERWISE PERMITTED BY APPLICABLE LAW, SOME SECURITIES PROVIDED BY BORROWER AS COLLATERAL UNDER THIS AGREEMENT MAY NOT BE GUARANTEED BY THE UNITED STATES.

By: _____
Title: _____
Date: _____

By: _____
Title: _____
Date: _____

Section 27 DISCLOSURE RELATING TO CERTAIN FEDERAL PROTECTIONS

Section 27.1

The Securities Investor Protection Act of 1970 (SIPA) provides certain protections for accounts of Customers of a Broker-Dealer. Section 27.1 is intended to advise Customers that it may not necessarily provide such protections with respect to Loans made to a Broker-Dealer and that a Customer's only recourse may be to the Collateral transferred with respect to such a Loan.

Section 27.2

Although a superficial reading of the definition of Government Securities may suggest that the payment of interest and principal on such securities is guaranteed by the United States, the parties in Section 27.2 expressly acknowledge that this may not always be the case and that they assume the risk that such payments may not be guaranteed.

Annex I

Party Acting as Agent

This Annex sets forth the terms and conditions governing all transactions in which a party lending or borrowing Securities, as the case may be ("Agent"), in a Loan is acting as agent for one or more third parties (each, a "Principal"). Unless otherwise defined, capitalized terms used but not defined in this Annex shall have the meanings assigned in the Securities Loan Agreement of which it forms a part (such agreement, together with this Annex and any other annexes, schedules or exhibits, referred to as the "Agreement") and, unless otherwise specified, all section references herein are intended to refer to sections of such Securities Loan Agreement.

ANNEXES TO THE MSLA 2000

The drafters of the MSLA developed three annexes to adapt it to three common fact situations. The Annexes standardise the terms of the MSLA for these scenarios, helping to create legal certainty and efficiencies in negotiating the MSLA. Annex I deals with a common situation in which an agent acts for a Principal or several Principals. Annex II deals with defining Market Value for Securities. Finally, Annex III deals with Term Loans. Just like the standard pre-printed MSLA form, each of these Annexes can be amended or modified by making changes through Schedule B.

Annex I Party Acting as Agent

Annex I envisions that an Agent may act for either a Lender or a Borrower under the MSLA. In the GMSLA documents an Agent can only ever act on behalf of a Lender.

In addition, any capitalised terms in Annex I shall have the same meaning, and any section numbers shall refer to the same section numbers, as in the MSLA.

1. **Additional Representations and Warranties.** In addition to the representations and warranties set forth in the Agreement, Agent hereby makes the following representations and warranties, which shall continue during the term of any Loan: Principal has duly authorized Agent to execute and deliver the Agreement on its behalf, has the power to so authorize Agent and to enter into the Loans contemplated by the Agreement and to perform the obligations of Lender or Borrower, as the case may be, under such Loans, and has taken all necessary action to authorize such execution and delivery by Agent and such performance by it.

6. The US Master Securities Loan Agreement (2000)

Section 1

Section 1 of Annex 1 sets forth representations to be made by the Agent. It is important to remember that the making a misrepresentation in Annex I would be treated the same way as a misrepresentation in the MSLA itself for purposes of the occurrence of a Default. This would mean that a non-defaulting party would have the right to terminate all outstanding Loans with a Defaulting Party. In Section 1, the Agent makes several basic representations with respect to its status, authorisation and powers that are standard in the securities industry for transactions using agents:

- the Principal has authorised the Agent to execute and deliver the agreement;
- the Principal has the power to authorise the Agent to enter into Loans on its behalf;
- the Principal has the power to authorise the Agent to perform the obligations of the Principal;
- the Principal has taken all necessary action to authorise the Agent to act as described above.

Typically two Principals will normally enter into the MSLA directly with each other.

However, it has become increasingly common for an Agent to act on behalf of a Lender or several Lenders through a single MSLA 2000. For example, investment managers may act as agent in securities lending transaction on behalf of investment funds that want to lend securities. A custodial bank may act as agent on behalf of its customers that hold lendable securities. A prime broker might act as an agent for hedge funds wanting to borrow certain securities. Annex I provides a market standard approach to modify the MSLA to account for these type of Agent/Principal scenarios. Because the MSLA was not itself written for Agent/Principal scenarios, these changes are necessary in order for an Agent to be able to trade on behalf of its Principals with the other party.

2. **Identification of Principals.** Agent agrees (a) to provide the other party, prior to any Loan under the Agreement, with a written list of Principals for which it intends to act as Agent (which list may be amended in writing from time to time with the consent of the other party), and (b) to provide the other party, before the Close of Business on the next Business Day after agreeing to enter into a Loan, with notice of the specific Principal or Principals for whom it is acting in connection with such Loan. If (i) Agent fails to identify such Principal or Principals prior to the Close of Business on such next Business Day or (ii) the other party shall determine in its sole discretion that any Principal or Principals identified by Agent are not acceptable to it, the other party may reject and rescind any Loan with such Principal or Principals, return to Agent any Collateral or Loaned Securities, as the case may be, previously transferred to the other party and refuse any further performance under such Loan, and Agent shall immediately return to the other party any portion of the Loaned Securities or Collateral, as the case may be, previously transferred to Agent in connection with such Loan; *provided, however*, that (A) the other party shall promptly (and in any event within one Business Day of notice of the specific Principal or Principals) notify Agent of its determination to reject and rescind such Loan and (B) to the extent that any performance was rendered by any party under any Loan rejected by the other party, such party shall remain entitled to any fees or other amounts that would have been payable to it with respect to such performance if such Loan had not been rejected. The other party acknowledges that Agent shall not have any obligation to provide it with confidential information regarding the financial status of its Principals; Agent agrees, however, that it will assist the other party in obtaining from Agent's Principals such information regarding the financial status of such Principals as the other party may reasonably request.

Section 2

Prior to entering into any securities lending transactions, Section 2 requires the Agent to provide to the other party a list of its Principals. This list can be amended from time to time. After entering into a Loan, the Agent must provide to the other party prior to Close of Business on the next Business Day, a list of the Principal or Principals for whom it is acting with respect to an individual Loan. Such an identification of a Principal(s) is important to the other party as part of its due diligence with respect to its counterparty for a particular Loan and for risk exposure purposes. It is also important because failure to disclose that a party is not acting as a Principal is a Default under Section 10.3 of the MSLA (and may also create liability under the common law) unless the Agent enters into and complies with Annex I.

If (i) the Agent fails to provide such Principal identification by Close of Business on the next Business Day or (ii) the other party determines that such a Principal or Principals are not acceptable to it, the other party may (x) reject and rescind such Loan, (y) return to the Agent any previously transferred Loaned Securities or Collateral for such Loan, and (z) refuse any further performance under the Loan. Any rejection of a Loan upon the disclosure of the Principal(s) to the other party must be made to the Agent within one Business Day. Although it is unstated whether such rejection of a Loan, upon identification of the Principal, must be done in good faith (i.e. the other party has good reason for rejecting a particular Principal), such a good faith obligation should be implied. Otherwise, this provision would provide the other party with an option to reject a particular trade for reasons other than the identification of the Principal. Such an obligation should also be implied given that the identities of all possible Principals was known to the other party before entering into any Loans.

Upon the rejection and recission of a Loan, the Agent in turn is obligated to return any Loaned Securities or Collateral. If the Loan is rescinded, the party rejecting the Loan is required to pay any fees or other compensation to the Principal(s) to the extent the Principal(s) had performed under the Loan prior to its rejection.

The Agent is not obligated to provide to the other party any confidential financial information about its Principal(s). The Agent, however, agrees to reasonably assist the other party in obtaining such information.

3. **Limitation of Agent's Liability.** The parties expressly acknowledge that if the representations and warranties of Agent under the Agreement, including this Annex, are true and correct in all material respects during the term of any Loan and Agent otherwise complies with the provisions of this Annex, then (a) Agent's obligations under the Agreement shall not include a guarantee of performance by its Principal or Principals and (b) the other party's remedies shall not include a right of setoff against obligations, if any, of Agent arising in other transactions in which Agent is acting as principal.

4. **Multiple Principals.**

   (a) In the event that Agent proposes to act for more than one Principal hereunder, Agent and the other party shall elect whether (i) to treat Loans under the Agreement as transactions entered into on behalf of separate Principals or (ii) to aggregate such Loans as if they were transactions by a single Principal. Failure to make such an election in writing shall be deemed an election to treat Loans under the Agreement as transactions on behalf of separate Principals.

   (b) In the event that Agent and the other party elect (or are deemed to elect) to treat Loans under the Agreement as transactions on behalf of separate Principals, the parties agree that (i) Agent will provide the other party, together with the notice described in Section 2(b) of this Annex, notice specifying the portion of each Loan allocable to the account of each of the Principals for which it is acting (to the extent that any such Loan is allocable to the account of more than one Principal), (ii) the portion of any individual Loan allocable to each Principal shall be deemed a separate Loan under the Agreement, (iii) the mark to market obligations of Borrower and Lender under the Agreement shall be determined on a Loan-by-Loan basis (unless the parties agree to determine such obligations on a Principal-by-Principal basis), and (iv) Borrower's and Lender's remedies under the Agreement upon the occurrence of a Default shall be determined as if Agent had entered into a separate Agreement with the other party on behalf of each of its Principals.

   (c) In the event that Agent and the other party elect to treat Loans under the Agreement as if they were transactions by a single Principal, the parties agree that (i) Agent's notice under Section 2(b) of this Annex need only identify the names of its Principals but not the portion of each Loan allocable to each Principal's account, (ii) the mark to market obligations of Borrower and Lender under the Agreement shall, subject to any greater requirement imposed by applicable law, be determined on an aggregate basis for all Loans entered into by Agent on behalf of any Principal, and (iii) Borrower's and Lender's remedies upon the occurrence of a Default shall be determined as if all Principals were a single Lender or Borrower, as the case may be.

   (d) Notwithstanding any other provision of the Agreement (including, without limitation, this Annex), the parties agree that any transactions by Agent on behalf of a Plan shall be treated as transactions on behalf of separate Principals in accordance with Section 4(b) of this Annex (and all mark to market obligations of the parties shall be determined on a Loan-by-Loan basis).

Section 3

Limiting the liability of an Agent is important because any possible liability under the MSLA would most certainly be greater than the compensation received by the Agent for its agency duties. Such potential liability could include (i) requiring the Agent to guarantee the performance of its Principal(s) or (ii) permitting the other party a right of set off for its obligations to a Principal against obligations of the Agent, as a principal, to the other party. Section 3 limits an Agent's liability provided that (x) the representations of the Agent are true and correct and (y) the Agent complies with Annex I.

Section 4

Section 4(a) deals with situations involving a MSLA that has multiple principals. Section 4(a) presumes that the other party and the Agent will treat each Loan separately for each individual Principal. The parties, however, may elect to aggregate each of the Loans made to separate Principals as if they were made to a single Principal.

Section 4(b) clarifies the treatment under the MSLA of Loans that are treated as being entered into on a separate Principal by Principal basis. First, if a single Loan is to be allocated between multiple Principals, the Agent is to specify the allocation among the individual Principals. Second, the parties agree that such allocable portion shall be treated as a single Loan. Third, any mark to market margining provisions shall be determined on a Loan by Loan basis, unless the parties agree to do it on a Principal by Principal basis. Fourth, the exercise of any remedies under the MSLA shall be done as if each Principal had entered into a separate MSLA.

Section 4(c) clarifies the treatment under the MSLA of Loans that are deemed to have been entered into with a single Principal. First, although all of the Principals need to be identified with respect to each Loan, the allocation of a Loan to each Principal is not required to be disclosed. Second, any mark to market margining provisions shall be determined on an aggregate basis for all Loans entered into by the Agent on behalf of any Principal. Third, the exercise of any remedies under the MSLA shall be done as if all Principals were a single Principal.

Section 4(d) clarifies that notwithstanding the MSLA and Annex I, any transaction entered into by an Agent on behalf of a Principal that is a Plan as defined in Section 17 of the MSLA, is to be treated as a transaction on behalf of a separate Principal and in accordance with Section 4(b) of the Annex. Mark-to-Market obligations are also to be determined on a Loan by Loan basis.

5. **Interpretation of Terms.** All references to "Lender" or "Borrower," as the case may be, in the Agreement shall, subject to the provisions of this Annex (including, among other provisions, the limitations on Agent's liability in Section 3 of this Annex), be construed to reflect that (i) each Principal shall have, in connection with any Loan or Loans entered into by Agent on its behalf, the rights, responsibilities, privileges and obligations of a "Lender" or "Borrower," as the case may be, directly entering into such Loan or Loans with the other party under the Agreement, and (ii) Agent's Principal or Principals have designated Agent as their sole agent for performance of Lender's obligations to Borrower or Borrower's obligations to Lender, as the case may be, and for receipt of performance by Borrower of its obligations to Lender or Lender of its obligations to Borrower, as the case may be, in connection with any Loan or Loans under the Agreement (including, among other things, as Agent for each Principal in connection with transfers of securities, cash or other property and as agent for giving and receiving all notices under the Agreement). Both Agent and its Principal or Principals shall be deemed "parties" to the Agreement and all references to a "party" or "either party" in the Agreement shall be deemed revised accordingly (and any Default by Agent under the Agreement shall be deemed a Default by Lender or Borrower, as the case may be).

By: _____
Title: _____
Date: _____

By: _____
Title: _____
Date: _____

Section 5

Section 5 clarifies that, subject to Section 3 of Annex I, each Principal is to be treated as a separate Lender or separate Borrower, as the case may be, and be entitled to such Lender's or Borrower's rights, responsibilities, privileges and obligations, as if it had entered into a Loan directly. Section 5 also assumes that the Agent has been designated as the Principal's sole agent with respect to the Agreement. Furthermore, the Agent and any Principal shall be deemed to be parties to the MSLA and any Default by the Agent under the Agreement shall be deemed to be a Default by a Principal acting as Borrower or Lender under it.

Annex II

Market Value

Unless otherwise agreed by Borrower and Lender:

1. If the principal market for the Securities to be valued is a national securities exchange in the United States, their Market Value shall be determined by their last sale price on such exchange at the most recent Close of Trading or, if there was no sale on the Business Day of the most recent Close of Trading, by the last sale price at the Close of Trading on the next preceding Business Day on which there was a sale on such exchange, all as quoted on the Consolidated Tape or, if not quoted on the Consolidated Tape, then as quoted by such exchange.

Annex II Market Value

Under the MSLA it is necessary to know the Market Value of both Collateral and Loaned Securities for purposes of determining the initial transfers at the start of the Loan under Section 4.1; making substitutions under Section 4.5; determining the amount of fees under Section 5.1; and properly margining the Loans under Section 9.

The purpose of Annex II is to provide agreement over how to determine the Market Value of Securities based upon prices or quotations in their principal market. In particular, it provides specific methodologies as to how to determine the Market Value of exchange traded securities, over-the-counter traded securities and foreign securities. The definition of Market Value found in Section 25.38 is only used if the parties have not designated Annex II as applicable or have not provided another definition in writing. The definition provided in Section 25.38 is more general with respect to the sources to be to be used to determine the Market Value of a Security. Annex II, of course, can also be further amended in Schedule B.

Under Annex II, the method of determining Market Value is based upon the principal market for the security to be valued. The methodologies in Annex II provide an objective basis by referring to the last sales price at the most recent Close of Trading in the Security's principal market thus limiting any arguments over valuation.

Section 1

Section 1 applies to a Security whose principal market is a national securities exchange in the United States such as the New York Stock Exchange or the Chicago Stock Exchange. The general rule is that the Market Value of such a Security is based upon "their last sales price on such exchange at the most recent Close of Trading".

If the Security was thinly traded and there was no sale on the Business Day of the most recent Close of Trading, then the parties are to use the last sale price at the Close of Trading on the next preceding Business Day on which there was a sale, all as quoted on Consolidated Tape. Consolidated Tape is "a high-speed, electronic system that constantly reports the latest price and volume data on sales of exchange-listed stocks" (http://www.sec.gov/answers/consolt.htm).

2. If the principal market for the Securities to be valued is the over-the-counter market, and the Securities are quoted on The Nasdaq Stock Market ("Nasdaq"), their Market Value shall be the last sale price on Nasdaq at the most recent Close of Trading or, if the Securities are issues for which last sale prices are not quoted on Nasdaq, the last bid price at such Close of Trading. If the relevant quotation did not exist at such Close of Trading, then the Market Value shall be the relevant quotation on the next preceding Close of Trading at which there was such a quotation.

3. Except as provided in Section 4 of this Annex, if the principal market for the Securities to be valued is the over-the-counter market, and the Securities are not quoted on Nasdaq, their Market Value shall be determined in accordance with market practice for such Securities, based on the price for such Securities as of the most recent Close of Trading obtained from a generally recognized source agreed to by the parties or the closing bid quotation at the most recent Close of Trading obtained from such a source. If the relevant quotation did not exist at such Close of Trading, then the Market Value shall be the relevant quotation on the next preceding Close of Trading at which there was such a quotation.

Section 2

Section 2 applies to a security whose principal market is the over-the-counter market and the Securities are quoted on Nasdaq. Nasdaq is an American stock exchange that has been historically considered to be an "over-the-counter" securities exchange. It now actually more closely resembles the trading done on national exchanges. Section 2 is effectively a provision for using Nasdaq (versus other national exchanges) as a means of determining Market Value as opposed to obtaining a quotation for a Security from a different OTC market maker.

The general rule is that the Market Value of such a Security quoted on Nasdaq is based upon "their last sale price on Nasdaq at the most recent Close of Trading".

If the security was thinly traded and the relevant quotation did not exist at such Close of Trading, then the Market Value shall be the relevant quotation on the next preceding Close of Trading at which there was such a sale quotation.

Section 3

Section 3 is the section that is more relevant to securities whose principal market is the over-the-counter market and such Securities are not quoted on Nasdaq. This is stock trading that is done between market makers for securities that do not trade on organised exchanges.

The general rule is that the Market Value of such a Security is determined "in accordance with market practice for such Securities". The Market Value is to be based upon "the price for such Securities as of the most recent Close of Trading obtained from a generally recognized source agreed to by the parties or the closing bid quotation at the most recent Close of Trading obtained from such a source".

If the security is thinly traded and there is no relevant quotation at the most recent Close of Trading obtained from such a source, then the parties are to use the relevant quotation on the next preceding Business Day on which there was such a quotation.

4. If the Securities to be valued are Foreign Securities, their Market Value shall be determined as of the most recent Close of Trading in accordance with market practice in the principal market for such Securities.

5. The Market Value of a letter of credit shall be the undrawn amount thereof.

6. All determinations of Market Value under Sections 1 through 4 of this Annex shall include, where applicable, accrued interest to the extent not already included therein (other than any interest credited or transferred to, or applied to the obligations of, the other party pursuant to Section 8 of the Agreement), unless market practice with respect to the valuation of such Securities in connection with securities loans is to the contrary.

7. The determinations of Market Value provided for in this Annex shall apply for all purposes under the Agreement, except for purposes of Section 13 of the Agreement.

By: _____
Title: _____
Date: _____

By: _____
Title: _____
Date: _____

Section 4

Section 4 applies to the valuation of Foreign Securities and the valuation method places emphasis on following market practice in the principal market for such Securities.

Section 5

Section 5 states that the general rule for a letter of credit is that its Market Value is equal to its undrawn amount.

Section 6

In Section 6, similar to the definition of Market Value in Section 25.38, the Market Value is to include any accrued interest not already included in the Market Value unless general market practice is otherwise for the valuation of Securities in securities lending.

Section 7

Section 7 clarifies that Annex II is not to be used to determine the Market Value of a Security for purposes of the Section 13 remedies section. This is because Section 13 provides very specific procedures as to how Loaned Securities and Collateral are to be replaced or liquidated upon close-out.

Annex III

Term Loans

This Annex sets forth additional terms and conditions governing Loans designated as "Term Loans" in which Lender lends to Borrower a specific amount of Loaned Securities ("Term Loan Amount") against a pledge of cash Collateral by Borrower for an agreed upon Cash Collateral Fee until a scheduled termination date ("Termination Date"). Unless otherwise defined, capitalized terms used but not defined in this Annex shall have the meanings assigned in the Securities Loan Agreement of which it forms a part (such agreement, together with this Annex and any other annexes, schedules or exhibits, referred to as the "Agreement").

1. The terms of this Annex shall apply to Loans of Equity Securities only if they are designated as Term Loans in a Confirmation therefor provided pursuant to the Agreement and executed by each party, in a schedule to the Agreement or in this Annex. All Loans of Securities other than Equity Securities shall be "Term Loans" subject to this Annex, unless otherwise agreed in a Confirmation or other writing.

2. The Confirmation for a Term Loan shall set forth, in addition to any terms required to be set forth therein under the Agreement, the Term Loan Amount, the Cash Collateral Fee and the Termination Date. Lender and Borrower agree that, except as specifically provided in this Annex, each Term Loan shall be subject to all terms and conditions of the Agreement, including, without limitation, any provisions regarding the parties' respective rights to terminate a Loan.

Annex III Term Loans

Annex III only applies to Loans that are designated as "Term Loans". A Term Loan is a Loan of a specific amount of Loaned Securities for a specific period of time. The Borrower only pledges cash Collateral in a Term Loan and the Borrower earns a Cash Collateral Fee. It should be noted that even though the Term Loan has a scheduled termination date, the Term Loan can still be terminated pursuant to Section 6 of the MSLA.

Section 1

Because Loans of Securities (such as fixed-income securities) other than Equity Securities are typically structured as Term Loans, Annex III deems such Loans to be Term Loans unless the parties agree otherwise. Term Loans are popular for fixed-income securities because it is less likely that they will need to be recalled due to corporate actions, votes or similar actions which are common to Equity Securities.

The parties, however, need to designate a Loan of Equity Securities as a Term Loan if they want Annex III to apply. The designation can be done in a Confirmation, in Schedule B or in a writing executed by each party.

Section 2

Section 2 provides that to be a Term Loan, the parties need to set out the Term Loan Amount, the Cash Collateral Fee and the Termination Date in a Confirmation. The parties should also include in the Confirmation any special terms negotiated between them with respect to a party's right to terminate a Term Loan.

3. In the event that either party exercises its right under the Agreement to terminate a Term Loan on a date (the "Early Termination Date") prior to the Termination Date, Lender and Borrower shall, unless otherwise agreed, use their best efforts to negotiate in good faith a new Term Loan (the "Replacement Loan") of comparable or other Securities, which shall be mutually agreed upon by the parties, with a Market Value equal to the Market Value of the Term Loan Amount under the terminated Term Loan (the "Terminated Loan") as of the Early Termination Date. Such agreement shall, in accordance with Section 2 of this Annex, be confirmed in a new Confirmation at the commencement of the Replacement Loan and be executed by each party. Each Replacement Loan shall be subject to the same terms as the corresponding Terminated Loan, other than with respect to the commencement date and the identity of the Loaned Securities. The Replacement Loan shall commence on the date on which the parties agree which Securities shall be the subject of the Replacement Loan and shall be scheduled to terminate on the scheduled Termination Date of the Terminated Loan.

4. Borrower and Lender agree that, except as provided in Section 5 of this Annex, if the parties enter into a Replacement Loan, the Collateral for the related Terminated Loan need not be returned to Borrower and shall instead serve as Collateral for such Replacement Loan.

Section 3

Even though a Term Loan has a scheduled termination date, the parties still have the right in Section 6 to terminate the Loan (unless they otherwise agree). A need to terminate a Term Loan early might occur because an Equity Security needs to be recalled because of a vote or other corporate action. The need to recall a fixed income security early would be much more unlikely. In spite of this early termination, however, Annex III anticipates that the parties will enter into a Replacement Loan, similar in every way to the Terminated Loan except that comparable instead of identical Securities will constitute the Loaned Securities. Section 3 provides that if a party exercises its right to terminate a Loan earlier than the scheduled termination date, the parties agree to negotiate a new Replacement Loan. This clause is important in order for the parties to preserve the anticipated benefits from reinvesting the cash Collateral and paying the Borrower the Cash Collateral Fee.

Therefore, the Replacement Loan should comprise replacement Loaned Securities that are comparable to the earlier Loaned Securities. It should have a comparable Market Value to the amount of the Terminated Term Loan. Finally, it should have the same terms as the Terminated Loan and should be scheduled to terminate on the same scheduled Termination Date as the Terminated Loan.

Section 4

Section 4 provides that if the parties are going to enter into a Replacement Loan, the cash Collateral for the related Terminated Loan shall serve as the Cash Collateral for the Replacement Loan. Because the parties are obligating themselves to enter into a Replacement Loan upon termination of the Terminated Loan, there should be no need for retransfers of cash Collateral.

5. If the parties are unable to negotiate and enter into a Replacement Loan for some or all of the Term Loan Amount on or before the Early Termination Date, (a) the party requesting termination of the Terminated Loan shall pay to the other party a Breakage Fee computed in accordance with Section 6 of this Annex with respect to that portion of the Term Loan Amount for which a Replacement Loan is not entered into and (b) upon the transfer by Borrower to Lender of the Loaned Securities subject to the Terminated Loan, Lender shall transfer to Borrower Collateral for the Terminated Loan in accordance with and to the extent required under the Agreement, provided that no Default has occurred with respect to Borrower.

6. For purposes of this Annex, the term "Breakage Fee" shall mean a fee agreed by Borrower and Lender in the Confirmation or otherwise orally or in writing. In the absence of any such agreement, the term "Breakage Fee" shall mean, with respect to Loans of Government Securities, a fee equal to the sum of (a) the cost to the non-terminating party (including all fees, expenses and commissions) of entering into replacement transactions and entering into or terminating hedge transactions in connection with or as a result of the termination of the Terminated Loan, and (b) any other loss, damage, cost or expense directly arising or resulting from the termination of the Terminated Loan that is incurred by the non-terminating party (other than consequential losses or costs for lost profits or lost opportunities), as determined by the non-terminating party in a commercially reasonable manner, and (c) any other amounts due and payable by the terminating party to the non-terminating party under the Agreement on the Early Termination Date.

By: _____
Title: _____
Date: _____

By: _____
Title: _____
Date: _____

Section 5

The failure to enter into a Replacement Loan may subject the party requesting an early termination to pay a Breakage Fee. Even though Section 6 permits an early termination of a Term Loan, Annex III is drafted to ensure that the non-terminating party receives the full benefit of the Terminated Loan as if it had not been terminated early. The Breakage Fee effectively makes the non-terminating party whole after taking into account the costs of replacing the Terminated Loan and any other related costs, as set out in Section 6 of Annex III.

Section 5 also clarifies that if a Replacement Loan cannot be negotiated, the Lender needs to transfer the cash Collateral back to the Borrower, provided of course, that the Borrower has returned the Loaned Securities to the Lender. No Default must have occurred to the Borrower or Section 13 remedies might be triggered by the non-defaulting party.

Section 6

Section 6 sets out the definition of a Breakage Fee for purposes of Section 5 of Annex III. It also clarifies that the parties are entitled to amend and modify the definition of Breakage Fee. The definition, however, is only applicable to Loans of Government Securities. In the event that the parties were to do Term Loans using Equity Securities or non-Government Securities, they would need to craft an addition to the definition of a Breakage Fee.

The definition of Breakage Fee is broken into three amounts. The first amount is equal to the cost to a non-terminating party of entering into a replacement transaction. These costs would include all fees, expenses and commissions. It also includes the cost of terminating any hedges entered into in connection with the Terminated Loan.

The second amount includes any "other loss, damage, cost or expense directly arising or resulting from termination of the Terminated Loan". It does not include, however, any "consequential losses or costs for lost profits or lost opportunities". The non-terminating party calculates these in a commercially reasonable manner.

The third amount includes "any other amounts due and payable by the terminating party to the non-terminating party under the Agreement on the Early Termination Date". This is a catch-all provision in relation to other sums.

Schedule A

Names and Addresses for Communications

SCHEDULES A AND B OF THE MSLA 2000

Schedule A Names and Addresses for communication

Schedule A is where the parties' address details for notices and communications are recorded.

Schedule B

Defined Terms and Supplemental Provisions

6. The US Master Securities Loan Agreement (2000)

Schedule of Optional Provisions for Schedule B

As with the ISDA Master Agreement, it is market practice not to make edits, amendments or changes directly to the pre-printed form of the MSLA, other than the addition of the parties' names. Instead, any changes are made as part of Schedule B.

However, in contrast to the ISDA Master Agreement relatively few changes are made in Schedule B. The difference between the ISDA Master Agreement and the MSLA stems primarily from the credit risk taken under the respective documents. Under the ISDA Master Agreement, at least part of the risk exposure between the parties is frequently unsecured and there can be great volatility in contrast to the MSLA where the exposure is completely secured and there is normally little volatility.

In contrast to the ISDA Master Agreement, the drafters of the MSLA did not provide a template for the form of Schedule B. The drafters did provide, however, a series of suggested Schedule B provisions in the 2000 Version Guidance Notes.

Additional Events of Default.

In addition to the events enumerated in Section 12 of the Agreement:

(a) The occurrence of any one or more of the following events shall constitute a Default under the Agreement and entitle the non-defaulting party to exercise the termination rights under Section 12 of the Agreement:
   (i) if either party shall have been suspended or expelled from membership or participation in any national securities exchange, registered national securities association or registered clearing agency of which it is a member or any other self-regulatory organization to whose rules it is subject or if it is suspended from dealing in securities by any federal or state government agency thereof; or
   (ii) if either party shall have its license, charter, or other authorization necessary to conduct a material portion of its business withdrawn, suspended or revoked by any applicable federal or state government or agency thereof.

A form of this event of default was in the previous 1993 version of the MSLA as Sections 11.6 and 11.7, but was removed from the MSLA 2000 in an effort to conform to market practice. Due to the severity of the events set out in clauses (i) and (ii), it would not be unreasonable for a party to insist that it have the right to terminate upon their occurrence. The counter argument would be that as long as the Defaulting Party is still performing under the Loans and is not insolvent, it should not be necessary to terminate the Loans.

(b) The occurrence of any one or more of the following events with respect to an individual Loan (if so agreed in a Confirmation for such Loan that is executed by each party) or with respect to a class of Loans (if so agreed by the parties in writing in this Schedule B or otherwise) shall constitute a Default under the Agreement and entitle the non-defaulting party to exercise the termination rights under Section 12 of the Agreement:

(i) if Loaned Securities shall not, in accordance with Section 3.1 of the Agreement, be transferred to Borrower against the transfer of Collateral on or before the Cutoff Time on the date agreed to by Borrower and Lender for the commencement of such Loan or Loans; or

(ii) if Collateral shall not, in accordance with Section 4.1 of the Agreement, be transferred to Lender against the transfer of Loaned Securities on or before the Cutoff Time on the date agreed to by Borrower and Lender for the commencement of such Loan or Loans.

Unless otherwise agreed, all Loans of Loaned Securities consisting of Securities other than Equity Securities shall be subject to this paragraph (b).

Under Section 12, the failure of the Lender to transfer Loaned Securities or the failure of the Borrower to transfer Collateral at the inception of a Loan is not an event of default. However, it would be if the performing party was to have made a transfer and the non-performing party did not promptly return such Loaned Securities or Collateral after the failed transfer. The intent of the clause is to avoid terminating all the Loans simply because of a failure at the inception of a Loan. Terminating all the Loans would appear to be unnecessary upon such a failure given that the individual Loan concerned never began.

This clause, however, changes that standard and provides that such delivery failures would constitute a Default under the MSLA. The reasoning may be that any failure to perform suggests that future performance may be in jeopardy as well and, therefore, the Loans should all be terminated.

The last clause provides that Equity Securities would not be subject to paragraph (b). Such a clause is typically added in order to maintain consistency with both market practice in the securities lending market and the repo market.

6. The US Master Securities Loan Agreement (2000)

Additional Remedies.

In addition to any other remedies to which a non-defaulting party may be entitled under the Agreement, the defaulting party shall, with respect to an individual Loan (if so agreed in a Confirmation for such Loan that is executed by each party) or with respect to a class of Loans (if so agreed by the parties in writing in this Schedule B or otherwise), be liable to the non-defaulting party for (a) the amount of all reasonable legal or other expenses incurred by the non-defaulting party in connection with or as a result of a Default, (b) damages in an amount equal to the cost (including all fees, expenses and commissions) of entering into replacement transactions and entering into or terminating hedge transactions in connection with or as a result of a Default, and (c) any other loss, damage, cost or expense directly arising or resulting from the occurrence of a Default in respect of a Loan.

Unless otherwise agreed, all Loans of Loaned Securities consisting of Securities other than Equity Securities shall be subject to this Section.

This provision provides additional protection to the non-defaulting party, ensuring that the non-defaulting party is made completely whole by the defaulting party. It captures additional costs and damages that occur as a result of a Default such as (i) enforcement expenses, (ii) costs of entering into replacement transactions or related hedging transactions or (iii) any other costs associated with terminating a Loan.

The last clause provides that Equity Securities would not be subject to this section. Such a clause is typically added in order to maintain consistency with both market practice in the securities lending market and the repo market.

Standard Settlement Date for Foreign Securities.

Notwithstanding Section 6.1(a)(ii) of the Agreement, Borrower and Lender agree that the standard settlement date that would apply to a purchase or sale of Foreign Securities for purposes of the termination provisions of Section 6 of the Agreement shall be the standard settlement date that would apply to a purchase or sale of such Foreign Securities entered into at the time of a termination notice in the principal market for such Foreign Securities.

This particular clause clarifies what the standard settlement date is with respect to the purchase or sale of Foreign Securities for purposes of the termination provisions.

Trading Practices.

Each party shall observe, and the Agreement and each Loan thereunder is subject to, including with regard to (a) the allocation of economic benefits in respect of Loaned Securities and Collateral and (b) buy-in procedures in the case of failures to receive Loaned Securities or Collateral, any uniform practices applicable to securities loans among members of The Bond Market Association and the Securities Industry Association (the "Associations"), as currently in effect, or successor provisions thereto (the "Uniform Practices"), regardless of whether each party is a member of one of the Associations, to the extent that such market practice (including the Uniform Practices) does not conflict with the terms of the Agreement. Notwithstanding the preceding sentence, a party shall not waive its right to exercise its option to terminate all Loans under Section 12 of the Agreement by observing the buy-in procedures described in clause (b) of the preceding sentence.

This clause incorporates into the MSLA uniform market practices that are applicable to the Securities Industry and Financial Markets Association (the successor to The Bond Market Association and the Securities Industry Association), provided that such practices do not conflict with the Agreement. SIFMA has developed a Uniform Practices Manual (available to members of SIFMA at http://www.sifma.org/services/publications/upupdates.shtml) in an effort to develop best practices, create efficiencies and eliminate uncertainties and ambiguities.

No Reliance.

In addition to the representations and warranties set forth in Section 10 of the Agreement, each party hereby makes the following representations and warranties in connection with the Agreement and each Loan thereunder, which shall continue during the term of any such Loan:

(a) unless there is a written agreement with the other party to the contrary, it is not relying on any advice (whether written or oral) of the other party, other than the representations expressly set out in the Agreement;

(b) it has made and will make its own decisions regarding the entering into of any Loan based upon its own judgment and upon advice from such professional advisers as it has deemed it necessary to consult; and

(c) it understands the terms, conditions and risks of each Loan and is willing to assume (financially and otherwise) those risks.

This no reliance clause is similar to the no reliance clauses that are commonly used in other forms of master agreements. The clause was developed in reaction to litigious claims by customers of dealers that they had relied on representations or warranties given by the dealer to them to their detriment.

Restricted or Control Securities.

In addition to the representations and warranties set forth in Section 10 of the Agreement, the following representations and warranties shall apply, unless otherwise agreed by the parties:

(a) On the commencement date for any Loan, Lender represents and warrants that:

(i) Lender is familiar with the provisions of Rule 144 under the Securities Act of 1933 (the "Securities Act");

(ii) Lender is not, and within the preceding three months has not been, an "affiliate" of the issuer of any Loaned Securities as that term is used in Rule 144; and

(iii) Any Loaned Securities transferred to Borrower by Lender are not "restricted securities" within the meaning of Rule 144 or otherwise subject to any legal, regulatory or contractual restrictions on transfer; and

(b) On the date that any Loan is terminated, Borrower represents and warrants that:

(i) Borrower is familiar with the provisions of Rule 144 under the Securities Act;

(ii) Borrower is not, and within the preceding three months has not been, an "affiliate" of the issuer of any Loaned Securities as that term is used in Rule 144; and

(iii) assuming the accuracy and completeness of Lender's representations under subparagraph (a) of this paragraph, any Loaned Securities transferred to Lender by Borrower are not "restricted securities" within the meaning of Rule 144 or otherwise subject to any legal, regulatory or contractual restrictions on transfer.

Rule 144 of the Securities Exchange Act of 1933 provides relief from compliance with certain securities law requirements in an offering of Securities in the United States. However, securities under Rule 144 have certain limitations on their free transferability and would restrict their use in securities lending. A Borrower should ascertain that the Loaned Securities are not subject to these restrictions in order to make sure that it can transfer or liquidate them.

Additional Definitions.

Close of Business

Cutoff Times

Margin Notice Deadline

The Guidance Notes suggest that these definitions need to be defined in Schedule B.

Additional suggested provisions for Schedule B

The following are provisions taken from various forms of Schedule B used in the US securities lending market:

Opening Paragraph

This Schedule B (the "Schedule") forms a part of the Master Securities Loan Agreement dated as of _____ __, 200_ (the "Agreement") between _____ ("Borrower") and **BANK** ("Lender" or Lending Fund"). In the event of any conflict between the terms of this Schedule and any other term of the Agreement, the terms of this Schedule shall prevail. Capitalized terms used but not defined in this Schedule shall have the meanings ascribed to them in the Agreement.

Opening Paragraph – additional example

This Schedule B, dated as of _____ __, 2010, between ("**Party A**") and ("**Party B**") hereby amends and supplements the Master Securities Loan Agreement (2000 Version) dated as of April 26, 2010, including [Annexes IA,] II and III thereto as they may be amended hereby, between Party A and Party B (the "Agreement"). In the event of any conflict between the terms of this Schedule B and the terms of the Agreement, the terms of this Schedule B shall control. All capitalized terms used, but not defined herein, shall have the meanings assigned to them in the Agreement. References herein to Sections are, unless indicated to the contrary, to Sections of the Agreement. In all other respects, the Agreement remains unchanged, and as amended hereby supersedes all prior writings in respect thereof.

Restatement and Amendment of Prior Agreement.

This Master Agreement restates and amends in its entirety the Master Securities Loan Agreement dated as of _____ between the parties hereto (the "Prior Agreement"). Each Confirmation to the Prior Agreement shall be deemed a Confirmation subject to this Agreement, and each Loan subject to such a Confirmation shall be governed hereby.

6. The US Master Securities Loan Agreement (2000)

Existing Loans

All Loans entered into between the parties hereto prior to the date of the Agreement which are outstanding at the date of the Agreement are hereby deemed to have been entered into pursuant to the Agreement and are governed by its terms.

Additional Definitions

For purposes of this Agreement, the parties agree that the terms set forth below shall have the following meanings:

A.	Cutoff Time	3:15 p.m. (New York time)
B.	Close of Business	3:00 p.m. (New York time)
C.	Margin Notice Deadline	10:00 a.m.(New York time)

Revised Definitions

25.1 "Act of Insolvency" shall mean, with respect to any party, (a) the commencement by such party or any parent of such party as debtor of any case or proceeding under any bankruptcy, insolvency, reorganization, liquidation, moratorium, dissolution, delinquency or similar law, or such party's, or any parent of such party's, seeking the appointment or election of a receiver, conservator, trustee, custodian or similar official for such party or any parent of such party, or any substantial part of its property, or the convening of any meeting or creditors for purposes of commencing any such case or proceeding or seeking such an appointment or election, (b) the commencement of any such case or proceeding against such party or any parent of such party, or another seeking such an appointment or election, or the filing against a party or any parent of such party, of an application for a protective decree under the provisions of the Securities Investor Protection Act of 1970, which (i) is consented to or not timely contested by such party or any parent of such party, (ii) results in the entry of an order for relief, such an appointment or election, the issuance of such a protective decree or the entry of an order having a similar effect, or (iii) is not dismissed within 15 days, (c) the making by such party or any parent of such party of a general assignment for the benefit of creditors, or (d) the admission in writing by such party or any parent of such party of such party or any parent of such party's inability to pay such debts as they become due.

25.37 "Margin Percentage" shall mean, with respect to any Loan as of any date, a percentage agreed by Borrower and Lender, which shall be not less than 102% (105% for international equity securities), unless (a) Borrower and Lender agree otherwise, as provided in Section 24.2, and (b) Lender is not a Customer. Notwithstanding the previous sentence, in the event that the writing or other confirmation evidencing the agreement described in clause (a) does not set out such percentage with respect to any such Loan, the Margin Percentage shall not be a percentage less than the percentage obtained by dividing (i) the Market Value of the Collateral required to be transferred by Borrower to Lender with respect to such Loan at the commencement of the Loan by (ii) the Market Value of the Loaned Securities required to be transferred by Lender to Borrower at the commencement of the Loan.

25.38 "Market Value" shall mean,

(a) As to portfolio Securities of a Fund, the "Market Value" of any such Security shall be the value determined by such Fund in accordance with its currently effective prospectus under the Securities Act on each day such Fund shall so compute its net asset value per share; in the event such Fund shall suspend the computation of its net asset value per share in accordance with the provisions of Section 22(e) of the 1940 Act, the "Market Value" of such Security during such suspension shall be determined in good faith by the Board of Directors/Trustees of such Fund in accordance with the 1940 Act.

(b) As to any U.S. Government Security delivered to a Fund as Permitted Collateral, (x) if similar Securities are held by such Fund in a Portfolio, the "Market Value" of the same portfolio Security owned by such Fund as determined in accordance with the foregoing Section (a) of this definition of "Market Value" and (y) if similar Securities are not held by such Fund in a Portfolio, the "Market Value" of such Permitted Collateral, unless otherwise agreed between the Borrower and such Fund, shall be the bid price as quoted in The Wall Street Journal (New York Edition) for the Business Day preceding the date on which such determination is made plus accrued interest to such date, or, if not so quoted on such Business Day, the "Market Value" of such Permitted Collateral shall be the average of the bid and asked prices as quoted by a broker, other than the Borrower, dealing in U.S. Government Securities for the Business Day preceding the date on which such determination is made, plus accrued interest to such date.

(c) Notwithstanding the foregoing, from time to time, the Lender may, when it deems it necessary or advisable to do so, use any industry recognized pricing source rather than using the pricing methodologies set forth in Section 25.38(a) and (b).

The definition in Section 25.6 of the Agreement of the term "Business Day" is hereby replaced with the following:

"Business Day" shall mean, with respect to any Loan hereunder, a day on which regular trading may occur in the principal market for the Loaned Securities subject to such Loan and a day on which the Fedwire for money transfers is open; provided, however, that for purposes of determining the Market Value of any Securities hereunder, such term shall mean a day on which regular trading may occur in the principal market for the Securities whose value is being determined. Notwithstanding the foregoing, (a) for purposes of Section 9, "Business Day" shall mean any day on which regular trading may occur in the principal market for any Loaned Securities or for any Collateral consisting of Securities under any outstanding Loan hereunder and "next Business Day" shall mean the next day on which a transfer of Collateral may be effected in accordance with Section 15 and (b) in no event shall a Saturday or Sunday be considered a Business Day.

With respect to Section 25.36 of the Agreement, "Margin Notice Deadline" shall mean in the case of Loaned Securities that are Government Securities, 10.00 a.m. NYT and in the case of Loaned Securities that are other Securities, 11.30 a.m. NYT.

Confirmation Procedures

Upon agreeing to enter into a Loan hereunder, the Lender shall promptly deliver to the other party a written confirmation of each Loan (a "Confirmation"). The Confirmation shall describe the Loaned Securities (including CUSIP number if any), identify Lender's Agent and Lender and Borrower, and set forth (i) the date borrowed, (ii) the Loan Fee, (iii) the term of the Loan unless the Loan is to be terminable on demand, (iv) the Cash Collateral Fee, (v) the Margin Percentage, and (vi) any additional terms or conditions of the Loan not inconsistent with this Agreement, as amended. The Confirmation, together with this Agreement, as amended, shall constitute conclusive evidence of the terms agreed between Lender and Borrower with respect to the Loan to which the Confirmation relates. In the event of any conflict between the terms of such Confirmation and this Agreement, such Confirmation shall prevail.

Confirmation Procedures Additional Example

The following provision shall be added at the end of Section 2.1.

All Confirmations shall include the following information: (i) a description of the Loaned Securities and Collateral (including CUSIP number or SEDOL number, if any); (ii) the identity of the Lender and Borrower; (iii) the Loan Date, (iv) the Loan Termination Date, unless the Transaction is to be terminable on demand, and (v) any additional terms or conditions of the Agreement, not inconsistent with this Schedule. In addition, upon the transfer of substituted or Additional Collateral by either party, Borrower shall promptly provide notice to the Lender confirming such transfer, including all of the information specified in this paragraph.

Amendments to Section 3

The following provisions are added to Section 3 of the Agreement as follows:

3.4 Any Securities loaned by any Lender to the Borrower, shall, notwithstanding any termination of such loan under this Agreement, continue to be subject to the provision of this Agreement until the Borrower has completely satisfied all of its obligations under this Agreement with respect to the return of such Securities to the Lender.

3.5 The Lender may determine in its sole discretion whether to act as agent for more than one Lending Fund and whether to aggregate such Loans as if they were transactions by a single Lender. In the event that the Lender elects to treat Loans under the Agreement as if they were transactions by a single Lender, then (a) the mark to market obligations of Borrower and Lender under the Agreement shall, subject to any greater requirement imposed by applicable law, be determined on an aggregate basis for all Loans entered into by the Lender on behalf of any Lending Fund, and (b) Borrower's and Lender's remedies upon the occurrence of a Default shall be determined as if all such Lending Funds were a single Lender.

Amendment to Section 6.1

The following provision shall replace Section 6.1 of the Agreement:

Unless otherwise agreed, either party may terminate a Loan on a termination date established by notice given to the other party prior to the Close of Business on a Business Day. The termination date established by a termination notice shall be a date no earlier than the standard settlement date that would apply to a purchase or sale of the Loaned Securities (in the case of a notice given by Lender) or the non-cash Collateral securing the Loan (in the case of a notice given by Borrower) entered into at the time of such notice, which date shall, unless Borrower and Lender agree to the contrary, be in the case of all Securities other than Government Securities, the third Business Day following such notice. All Loaned Securities shall be due for return to Lender on the termination date by 2:30PM

ET. Failure by the Borrower to return the Loaned Securities to the Lender by 2:30PM ET on the termination date will be considered an event of Default. Upon such Default and without further notice to Borrower, Lender will immediately reduce the per diem rate of any Cash Collateral Fee payable to the Borrower to zero or less. In the case of Government Securities, either party may terminate a Loan on any Business Day, by notifying the other party no later than 10:00 a.m. New York City time on the Business Day which is to be the specified termination date.

Borrower and Lender agree that the standard settlement date that would apply to a purchase or sale of Foreign Securities for purposes for the termination provisions of Section 6 of the Agreement shall be the standard settlement date that would apply to a purchase or sale of such Foreign Securities entered into at the time of termination notice in the principal market for such Foreign Securities.

Amendment to Section 7.3

The following provision is added to the Agreement as Section 7.3:

7.3 In the event that a Loaned Security is subject to a corporate action, Borrower agrees to return the Loaned Security to Lender at least 24 hours prior to the expiration date and time of the corporate action election. Borrower must return the Loaned Security to Lender by no later than the close of business on the business day immediately preceding the expiration date. The Lender will not accept the Loaned Security on the expiration date. If the Borrower has not returned the Loaned Security to the Lender by the close of business on the business day immediately preceding the expiration date, then the soonest the Lender will accept the Loaned Security is the close of the processing of the corporate action on the first business day following the processing date. If the Borrower does not comply with the foregoing, Borrower (a) agrees to act on the Lender's instructions regarding the corporate action, (b) shall deliver the resulting entitlements, and (c) will be held liable for any and all damages which may occur as a result of Borrower's failure to have returned the Loaned Security.

Section 9.1 Percentage

Section 9.1 of the Agreement is hereby replaced with the following:

9.1 If Lender is a Customer, Borrower shall daily mark to market any Loan hereunder and in the event that at the Close of Trading on any Business Day the Market Value of the Collateral for any Loan to Borrower shall be less than 102% of the Market Value of all the outstanding Loaned Securities subject to such Loan (105% of the Market Value of all the outstanding international equity Loaned Securities subject to such Loan, unless the collateral posted is in the same currency as the securities on loan), Borrower shall transfer additional Collateral no later than the Close of Business on the next Business Day so that the Market Value of such additional Collateral, when added to the Market Value of the other Collateral for such Loan, shall equal 102% of the Market Value of the Loaned Securities (105% of the Market Value of international equity Loaned Securities).

Qualification to Section 10.1 Enforceability Representation

Section 10.1 is amended to add the following to the end of the last sentence in this section as follows:

", except as may be limited by bankruptcy, insolvency or other laws affecting generally the enforceability of creditors' rights or by equitable principles generally applied."

Additional Borrower Representations

The following provision is added to the Agreement as Section 10.7:

The Borrower represents, warrants, and covenants that:

(a) If a corporation, it is duly organized, validly existing and in good standing under the laws of the state of its incorporation; or, if a partnership, business trust, common law trust, association or other juridical entity, it is duly organized and validly existing under the laws of its jurisdiction of organization.

(b) It is licensed or qualified to transact business in all other jurisdictions wherein it is required to be so licensed or so qualified in order to enter into the agreements contained herein and to perform its covenants and agreements hereunder and has full power and authority to own its properties and to enter into the agreements contained herein and perform its covenants and agreements hereunder.

(c) It is a registered broker-dealer under the Exchange Act and registered as a broker-dealer in all jurisdictions in which it is required to be registered in order to enter into the agreements contained herein and perform its covenants and agreements hereunder.

(d) Neither the execution and delivery of this Agreement nor the consummation of the transactions contemplated herein will violate any applicable provision of any statute, ordinance, regulation, order, judgment or decree of any court or governmental agency, or conflict with or result in any breach of any of the terms of or constitute a default under or result in the termination of or the creation of any lien pursuant to the terms of any contract or agreement to which it is a party or by which it or any of its assets is bound.

(e) The Borrower will not use any Securities borrowed hereunder in connection with any illegal transaction or business and will not use or knowingly permit anyone to use such Securities in such a way as to violate any provision of any federal or state laws, the rules of the SEC, or the constitution, bylaws or rules of any stock exchange or of the Financial Industry Regulatory Authority.

(f) The Borrower acknowledges that each Fund is an investment company registered under the 1940 Act and agrees to conduct the transactions hereunder in conformity with the conditions of the 1940 Act and any rules, interpretations or guidelines thereunder applicable to each Fund.

Additional Borrower Representation

(a) A new Section 10.7 is hereby inserted, as follows:

Each party represents that it is an "exempted borrower" within the meaning of Regulation T ("Reg T"). Reg T defines "exempted borrower" as follows:

Exempted borrower means a member of a national securities exchange or a registered broker or dealer, a substantial portion of whose business consists of transactions with persons other than brokers or dealers, and includes a borrower who –

1 maintains at least 1000 active accounts on an annual basis for persons other than brokers, dealers, and persons associated with a broker or dealer;

2 earns at least $10 million in gross revenues on an annual basis from transactions with persons other than brokers, dealers, and persons associated with a broker or dealer; or

3 earns at least 10 percent of its gross revenue on an annual basis from transactions with persons other than brokers, dealers, and persons associated with a broker or dealer.

Additional Lender Representation

The following provision is added to the Agreement as Section 10.8:

10.8 The Lender represents, warrants, and covenants that:

(a) Each Fund is duly organized and validly existing under the laws of its state of organization, is in good standing under such laws, and has full power and authority to own its properties and to enter into the agreements contained herein and to perform its covenants and agreements hereunder, and has taken all acts necessary to empower its officers and employees to execute this Agreement and to empower its officers and employees and the Lender to perform any duty under this Agreement, including the making and delivery of the representations and covenants contained in this Section 10.8, all subject to the terms and conditions contained in this Agreement.

(b) Each Fund is a registered investment company under the 1940 Act.

(c) Neither the execution and delivery of this Agreement nor the consummation of the transactions contemplated herein will violate any applicable provision of any statute, ordinance, regulation, order, judgment or decree of any court or governmental agency, or conflict with or result in any breach of any of the terms of or constitute a default under or result in the termination of or the creation of any lien pursuant to the terms of any contract or agreement to which it is a party or by which it or any of its assets is bound.

(d) The Lender has complete power and capacity to act for and on behalf of each Lending entity with respect to all matters pertaining to this Agreement.

Section 13 Additional Remedies

The following provisions are added to Section 13 of the Agreement:

Section 13.5 Upon the occurrence of a Default under Section 12.1 of this Agreement, in addition to any other rights available to it under: 1) Section 13 of this Agreement, 2) any other agreement, or 3) applicable law, the Lender may drop the rebate payable to Borrower to zero, regardless of the value of Securities on loan.

6. The US Master Securities Loan Agreement (2000)

Cross Default; Setoff; and Cross Collateral

The following paragraph shall be inserted in Paragraph 18 at the end thereof:

"Each party further agrees that (i) a party's ('X') failure to pay or deliver any amounts as required under any other transaction or agreement with the other party ('Y') (and after giving effect to any defenses or cure periods contained in such transaction or agreement, there occurs a liquidation, an acceleration, or an early termination of all obligations under the master agreement under which multiple transactions may be entered into by the relevant parties (or in the case of any transaction with respect to which no master agreement is in place, such transaction or agreement)) ("Other Obligations") shall constitute an Event of Default hereunder with X as the defaulting party, (ii) upon the occurrence of the event referred to in (i), Y, without prior notice to X, shall have the right to setoff any amounts or obligations owed by X hereunder against any amounts or obligations owed by Y arising under Other Obligations (irrespective of the currency), and (iii) upon the occurrence of the event referred to in (i), as security for the performance by a party of its Other Obligations, it grants to the other party a security interest in all securities and other property (and all proceeds thereof) transferred pursuant to this Agreement, which security interest may be enforced in accordance with the provisions of applicable law or Paragraph 13.2 hereof (applying such Paragraph as if such defaulted Other Obligations were owed hereunder in respect of a Transaction in which X is the Lender)."

Set-Off

Without prejudice to the provisions of Section 13 of the Agreement, each party hereby acknowledges that:

(i) upon the occurrence of an event of Default with respect to a party ("X"), the other party ("Y") will have the right (but not be obliged) without prior notice to X or any other person to set-off or apply any obligation of X owed to Y (whether or not matured or contingent and whether or not arising under the Agreement, and regardless of the currency, place of payment or booking office of the obligation) against any obligation of Y to pay any amount to X pursuant to the Agreement.

(ii) for the purpose of sub-paragraph (i), any obligations so set-off or applied which are not denominated in the U.S. dollars shall be converted into U.S. dollars on the relevant date at a spot rate published by a recognized source on such date.

(iii) for the purposes of sub-paragraph (i), if an obligation of X is unascertained, Y may in good faith estimate that obligation and effect a set-off or application in respect of the amount so estimated, subject to the relevant party accounting to the other when the obligation is ascertained.

(iv) this subparagraph shall not constitute a mortgage, charge, lien or other security interest upon any of the property or assets of either party to the Agreement.

Additional Set-Off Clause Example

A new Section 13.6 is hereby inserted, as follows:

In addition to the remedies available to the nondefaulting party set forth in Paragraph 13 of the Agreement, upon the occurrence of an event of Default with respect to the defaulting party ("Party X"), the non-defaulting party ("Party Y") may, without prior notice to Party X set-off any Obligation (as such term is defined below) owed by Party X to Party Y or any affiliate of Party Y ("Party Y's Set-Off Amount") against any Obligation owed by Party Y or any affiliate of Party Y to Party X ("Party X's Set-Off Amount"). Party Y will give notice to Party X of any set-off effected under this Section.

For purposes of this Section, the term "Obligation" means any sum or obligation, whether arising under this Agreement or otherwise, whether matured or un-matured, whether or not contingent and irrespective of the currency, place of payment or booking office of the sum or obligation.

For this purpose, either Party Y's Set-Off Amount or Party X's Set-Off Amount (or the relevant portion of such amounts) may be converted at Party Y's option into the currency in which the other set-off amount is denominated at the rate of exchange at which Party Y would be able, acting in a reasonable manner and in good faith, to purchase the relevant amount of such currency.

If an Obligation is unascertained, Party Y may in good faith estimate that Obligation and set-off in respect of the estimate, subject to the relevant party accounting to the other when the Obligation is ascertained.

This Section shall be without prejudice and in addition to any right of set-off, combination of accounts, lien or other right to which any party is at any time otherwise entitled (whether by operation of law, contract or otherwise).

Document Deliveries

Each party shall, at the time of execution of the Agreement, deliver to the other party evidence of the authority, incumbency and specimen signature of each party executing this Agreement and the following:

Party Required to Deliver Delivered	Form/Document/ Certificate	Date by Which to be Documents
Party A	A duly executed United States Internal Revenue Service Form W-9 (or successor thereto)	(i) Upon execution of the Agreement; or (ii) upon request
Party B	A duly executed United States Internal Revenue Service W-8IMY, or W-8ECI, or W-8BEN or W-9, as relevant	(i) Upon execution of the Agreement; or (ii) upon request.

Letters of Credit

Notwithstanding Section 25.11 of this Agreement, [Client Name] shall not accept letters of credit as collateral to be transferred to [Client Name], as Lender, by Borrower.

Boilerplate clauses

Process Agent Appointment

Each party hereunder irrevocably appoints as its process agent to receive for it and on its behalf service of process in any proceeding.

Consent to Recording

Each party (i) consents to the recording of the telephone conversations of trading and marketing and/or other personnel of the parties in connection with this Agreement or any potential transaction (ii) agrees to obtain any necessary consent of and give notice of such recording to such personnel of it; and (iii) agrees that recordings may be submitted in evidence in any proceedings relating to this Agreement.

Counterparts

Counterparts. The following provision is added to the Agreement as Section 24.3:

24.3 The Agreement may be executed in any number of counterparts, each of which shall be deemed to be an original, but such counterparts shall, together, constitute only one (1) instrument.

Submission to Jurisdiction.

(a) the word "non" is deleted from Section 23.1(A).

Immunity Waiver

A new section 23.3 is hereby inserted, as follows:

To the extent that either party has or hereafter may acquire any immunity (sovereign or otherwise) from any legal action, suit or proceeding, from jurisdiction of any court or from set off or any legal process (whether service or notice, attachment prior to judgment, attachment in aid of execution of judgment, execution of judgment or otherwise) with respect to itself or any of its property, such party hereby irrevocably waives and agrees not to plead or claim such immunity in respect of any action brought to enforce its obligations under the Agreement or relating in any way to the Agreement or any Loan under the Agreement.

Limitation of Liability

For any Transaction involving a Lender organized as a business trust (or a series thereof) where the trustees, officers, employees or interest holders of such business trust (or series thereof) may be held personally liable for its obligations, Borrower acknowledges and agrees that, to the extent such trustees are regarded as entering into the Agreement, they do so only as trustees and not individually and that the obligations of the Agreement are not binding upon any such trustees, officer, employees or interest holder individually, but are binding only upon the assets and property of said Lender (or series thereof). Borrower hereby agrees that such trustees, officers, employees or interest holders shall not be personally liable under the Agreement and that Borrower shall look solely to the property of the Lending Fund (or series thereof) for the performance of the Agreement or payment of any claim under the Agreement.

Confidentiality

Lender and Borrower are parties to a Nondisclosure Agreement dated _____ in respect to securities lending transactions. That Nondisclosure Agreement is hereby incorporated by reference and governs all confidentiality matters related to the Transactions covered by this Agreement.

Signature Block

IN WITNESS WHEREOF, this Schedule B amends the Agreement and is executed by:

Bank	[Client's Name]
By: _____	By: _____
Name:	Name:
Title:	Title:

Signature Block attestation

IN WITNESS WHEREOF, the parties hereto, through their duly authorized representatives, have executed this Schedule B as of the day and year set forth above.

The credit crunch and possible future developments in the securities lending market

Origins

What happened?

The current position

Possible future developments

The opinions expressed in this chapter are the authors' own.
This is not an extensive treatment of the credit crunch but a summary of significant points.

ORIGINS

A number of commentators have identified the origins of the credit crunch in market deregulation, too light or lax supervision of financial institutions fostering huge competition, cheap money, over-exposure to poorly understood and inaccurately rated structured products and a bonus culture linked to them.

The credit crunch has been the defining event of our times since 9/11. It is not one event but many interconnected ones like a fine web or the pieces of a shattered chandelier, depending upon your point of view. As we have found to our cost the words of E. M. Forster are very true when he said "everything connects".

WHAT HAPPENED?

The credit crunch probably had its direct beginning in February 2007 when HSBC Bank Plc announced heavy losses in its US subsidiary, Household Finance Corporation, particularly in its subprime mortgage book. Indeed commentators generally regard the US subprime mortgage debacle where money was lent at low rates to uncreditworthy borrowers as a major cause of the global credit crunch.

Other factors which contributed to the credit crunch were:

- The collapse of two Bear Stearns hedge funds, heavily leveraged and invested in mortgage backed securities during the summer of 2007.
- The disruption of GBP LIBOR and the high level it reached in the three-month period from August 2007. It was still volatile at times in 2010.
- The drying up of financial market liquidity from August 2007 particularly in the short-term commercial paper market which had a catastrophic effect on structured investment vehicles (SIVs) many of which relied on overnight loans and commercial paper to fund them. Many of these SIVs had to be taken back on to bank balance sheets and their value written down.
- Over 80% of collateralised debt obligation issues going into default since 2007 partly due to inaccurate credit ratings being applied to them.
- The collapse of Northern Rock and its being taken into public ownership in February 2008.
- The collapse of Bear Stearns in the spring of 2008.

- The US government rescues of Freddie Mac and Fannie Mae on 7th September 2008.
- The collapse of Lehman Brothers on 15th September 2008 which put the markets into freefall and was followed by the major rescue of AIG; the collapse of Washington Mutual and the takeover of Wachovia by Wells Fargo.
- The insolvency of the three major Icelandic banks in October 2008 and the subsequent collapse of the Icelandic krona.
- Lloyds Banking Group and the Royal Bank of Scotland PLC going into partial UK government ownership at around the same time.
- A large reduction of the number of active hedge funds in the UK many of which closed their doors because they could not make their target investment returns.

The key event in Europe was really the collapse of Lehman Brothers which still reverberates today. Its administrator said in September 2009 that it could take up to 10 years before litigation relating to the collapse is fully resolved. In the US, it was the extraordinary string of failures in September 2008.

THE CURRENT POSITION

Even though securities lending is a collateralised arrangement it has not escaped regulatory scrutiny. This was partly due to a loosening in collateral requirements and haircuts before the credit crunch. Before September 2008 a wide range of collateral had become acceptable to securities lending market players. In addition haircuts often became "broad brush" and were applied uncritically across the board. So there could be the same 5% haircut for cash and equity indices, which made little sense but it had become a market practice.

When the crisis hit, sudden demands for more collateral and higher haircuts stifled activity and created financial pressure on banks and hedge funds scrambling for securities to meet their obligations.

In the US, one of the causes of the AIG failure came from AIG's losses suffered when it invested cash collateral received in securities lending transactions in high yielding securities.

In March 2010 global regulators working under the aegis of the Bank for International Settlements proposed capital increases for securities lending and daily review by market players of their collateral requirements so as to avoid sudden sharp rises in collateral demand. An additional "supervisory haircut" is also a possibility.

These proposals are now being considered by the Financial Stability Board which makes recommendations on financial matters to the G20.

One of the key developments in OTC derivatives over the past 18 months has been a push by regulators to process as many "standardised" contracts as possible on central clearing counterparty ("CCP") platforms. Latest (December 2010) figures showed that $14 trillion of credit default swap contracts had been cleared through Intercontinental Exchange Inc. (better known as ICE), a leading player in both Europe and the USA.

OTC derivatives are, of course, longer term and often more complex than securities loans which is why regulators have not pushed for them to be cleared on CCPs. However, in June 2009, SecFinex (owned by NYSE Euronext) announced the introduction of centrally cleared services for stock borrowing and lending of European equities in the SecFinex Order Market. The aim was and is to eliminate multi-entity counterparty risk and increase capital efficiency. Spin off benefits were envisaged to be more transparency, full straight-through-processing and more competitive pricing. While there is likely to be far less regulatory impetus for this than for OTC derivatives, it is nonetheless an interesting development.

As we saw in Chapter 1 the hot topic of the credit crunch was short selling and particularly naked short selling. Since 2008 various countries have adopted *ad hoc* measures to protect bearish investors selling vulnerable stocks.

On 2nd March 2010 the Committee of European Securities Regulators proposed an EU-wide standard of public disclosure for any short position greater than 0.5% of the outstanding equity in issue. Two weeks later Germany acted unilaterally by publishing decrees forbidding naked short selling of shares in 10 domestic financial stocks and Eurozone bonds and credit default swaps on those bonds until 31st March 2011. On 25th May Germany extended the ban to naked short selling of *all* domestic stock listed on German stock exchanges. The ban also extended to Eurozone currency derivatives entered into speculatively. On 15th September 2010 the European Commission adopted the 0.2% and 0.5% levels (with further disclosure each time they rise by 0.1%). They are likely to be adopted by 1st July 2012 via Short Selling Directive.

The Dodd–Frank Wall Street Reform and Consumer Protection Act which provides for a comprehensive reform of the US financial industry was signed into law by President Barack Obama on 21st July 2010.

As far as securities lending is concerned the main effects of this Act are likely to be:

- changes to the statutory insolvency regimes for major broker-dealers and other financial institutions;
- risk exposure limitations and additional capital requirements which may result in lower volumes of securities lending in future;

- amendments to the Securities Exchange Act (1934) to prohibit "manipulative" short selling of securities; and
- changes to federal securities laws resulting in additional disclosure for securities lending.

The full implications of this Act will become clear over time. It calls for studies, reports and discretionary rule making by federal regulatory agencies by July 2012.

Finally, back in 2007 when the tripartite acquisition of ABN AMRO Bank NV by Royal Bank of Scotland, Fortis and Banco Santander was in full swing, there was market concern that Fortis shares were being lent so that their borrowers could vote against the acquisition. Short selling was also involved. This type of activity influenced the inclusion of a Borrower Warranty in paragraph 14(e) of the GMSLA 2010 viz:

> it is not entering into a Loan for the primary purpose of obtaining or exercising voting rights in respect of the Loaned Securities.

How this can be practically enforced remains debatable.

POSSIBLE FUTURE DEVELOPMENTS

While securities lending is not without complexity, it is essentially a short-term collateralised product. Nonetheless we consider that the industry is likely to be characterised in future by the following in Europe:

- higher capital costs against trading book risk;
- tighter regulation and higher levels of disclosure within the industry;
- a drive by trade associations to enhance educational training and qualifications in the securities lending space;
- tougher and more differentiated margining requirements across access classes;
- possibly greater use of CCP such as SecFinex.

So, as with OTC derivatives, a greyer and more professional future may also be in store for the global securities lending market.

Appendices

Appendix 1: A facsimile of the Global Master Securities Lending Agreement (2000) reproduced with the kind permission of the International Securities Lending Association

Appendix 2: A facsimile of the Global Master Securities Lending Agreement (2010) reproduced with the kind permission of the International Securities Lending Association

Appendix 3: A facsimile of the European Master Agreement reproduced with the kind permission of the European Banking Federation

Appendix 4: A facsimile of the Master Securities Loan Agreement (2000) reproduced by kind permission of the Securities Industry and Financial Markets Association

APPENDIX 1: A FACSIMILE OF THE GLOBAL MASTER SECURITIES LENDING AGREEMENT (2000) REPRODUCED WITH THE KIND PERMISSION OF THE INTERNATIONAL SECURITIES LENDING ASSOCIATION

VERSION: MAY 2000

GLOBAL MASTER SECURITIES LENDING AGREEMENT

CLIFFORD CHANCE

CONTENTS

1. Applicability 1
2. Interpretation 1
3. Loans Of Securities 5
4. Delivery 5
5. Collateral 7
6. Distributions And Corporate Actions 10
7. Rates Applicable To Loaned Securities And Cash Collateral 11
8. Redelivery Of Equivalent Securities 11
9. Failure To Redeliver 13
10. Set-Off Etc 14
11. Transfer Taxes 17
12. Lender's Warranties 17
13. Borrower's Warranties 18
14. Events Of Default 18
15. Interest On Outstanding Payments 19
16. Transactions Entered Into As Agent 19
17. Termination Of This Agreement 21
18. Single Agreement 21
19. Severance 21
20. Specific Performance 22
21. Notices 22
22. Assignment 22
23. Non-Waiver 22
24. Governing Law And Jurisdiction 23
25. Time 23
26. Recording 23
27. Waiver Of Immunity 23
28. Miscellaneous 23

SCHEDULE 26

AGREEMENT

BETWEEN:

                ("**Party A**") a company incorporated under the laws of
of   acting through a Designated Office; and

                ("**Party B**") a company incorporated under the laws of
of   acting through a Designated Office.

1. **APPLICABILITY**

1.1 From time to time the parties may enter into transactions in which one party ("**Lender**") will transfer to the other ("**Borrower**") securities and financial instruments ("**Securities**") against the transfer of Collateral (as defined in paragraph 2) with a simultaneous agreement by Borrower to transfer to Lender Securities equivalent to such Securities on a fixed date or on demand against the transfer to Borrower by Lender of assets equivalent to such Collateral.

1.2 Each such transaction shall be referred to in this Agreement as a "**Loan**" and shall be governed by the terms of this Agreement, including the supplemental terms and conditions contained in the Schedule and any Addenda or Annexures attached hereto, unless otherwise agreed in writing.

1.3 Either party may perform its obligations under this Agreement either directly or through a Nominee.

2. **INTERPRETATION**

2.1 In this Agreement:-

"**Act of Insolvency**" means in relation to either Party

(i) its making a general assignment for the benefit of, or entering into a reorganisation, arrangement, or composition with creditors; or

(ii) its stating in writing that it is unable to pay its debts as they become due; or

(iii) its seeking, consenting to or acquiescing in the appointment of any trustee, administrator, receiver or liquidator or analogous officer of it or any material part of its property; or

(iv) the presentation or filing of a petition in respect of it (other than by the other Party to this Agreement in respect of any obligation under this Agreement) in any court or before any agency alleging or for the bankruptcy, winding-up or insolvency of such Party (or any analogous proceeding) or seeking any reorganisation, arrangement, composition, re-adjustment, administration, liquidation, dissolution or similar relief under any present or future statute, law or regulation, such petition not having been stayed or dismissed within 30 days of its filing (except in the case of a petition for winding-up or any analogous proceeding in respect of which no such 30 day period shall apply); or

(v) the appointment of a receiver, administrator, liquidator or trustee or analogous officer of such Party over all or any material part of such Party's property; or

(vi) the convening of any meeting of its creditors for the purpose of considering a voluntary arrangement as referred to in Section 3 of the Insolvency Act 1986 (or any analogous proceeding);

"**Alternative Collateral**" means Collateral having a Market Value equal to the Collateral delivered pursuant to paragraph 5 and provided by way of substitution in accordance with the provisions of paragraph 5.3;

"**Base Currency**" means the currency indicated in paragraph 2 of the Schedule;

"**Business Day**" means a day other than a Saturday or a Sunday on which banks and securities markets are open for business generally in each place stated in paragraph 3 of the Schedule and, in relation to the delivery or redelivery of any of the following in relation to any Loan, in the place(s) where the relevant Securities, Equivalent Securities, Collateral or Equivalent Collateral are to be delivered;

"**Cash Collateral**" means Collateral that takes the form of a transfer of currency;

"**Close of Business**" means the time at which the relevant banks, securities exchanges or depositaries close in the business centre in which payment is to be made or Securities or Collateral is to be delivered;

"**Collateral**" means such securities or financial instruments or transfers of currency as are referred to in the table set out under paragraph 1 of the Schedule as being acceptable or any combination thereof as agreed between the Parties in relation to any particular Loan and which are delivered by Borrower to Lender in accordance with this Agreement and shall include Alternative Collateral;

"**Defaulting Party**" shall have the meaning given in paragraph 14;

"**Designated Office**" means the branch or office of a Party which is specified as such in paragraph 4 of the Schedule or such other branch or office as may be agreed to in writing by the Parties;

"**Equivalent** " or "**equivalent to**" in relation to any Securities or Collateral provided under this Agreement means securities, together with cash or other property(in the case of Collateral) as the case may be, of an identical type, nominal value, description and amount to particular Securities or Collateral, as the case may be, so provided. If and to the extent that such Securities or Collateral, as the case may be, consists of securities that are partly paid or have been converted, subdivided, consolidated, made the subject of a takeover, rights of pre-emption, rights to receive securities or a certificate which may at a future date be exchanged for securities, the expression shall include such securities or other assets to which Lender or Borrower as the case may be, is entitled following the occurrence of the relevant event, and, if appropriate, the giving of the relevant notice in accordance with paragraph 6.4 and provided that Lender or Borrower, as the case may be, has paid to the other Party all and any sums due in respect thereof. In the event that such Securities or Collateral, as the case may be, have been redeemed, are partly paid, are the subject of a capitalisation issue or are subject to an event similar to any of the foregoing events described in this paragraph, the expression shall have the following meanings:-

(a) in the case of redemption, a sum of money equivalent to the proceeds of the redemption;

(b) in the case of a call on partly paid securities, securities equivalent to the relevant Loaned Securities or Collateral, as the case may be, provided that Lender shall have paid Borrower, in respect of Loaned Securities, and Borrower shall have paid to Lender, in respect of Collateral, an amount of money equal to the sum due in respect of the call;

(c) in the case of a capitalisation issue, securities equivalent to the relevant Loaned Securities or Collateral, as the case may be, together with the securities allotted by way of bonus thereon;

(d) in the case of any event similar to any of the foregoing events described in this paragraph, securities equivalent to the Loaned Securities or the relevant Collateral, as the case may be, together with or replaced by a sum of money or securities or other property equivalent to that received in respect of such Loaned Securities or Collateral, as the case may be, resulting from such event;

"**Income**" means any interest, dividends or other distributions of any kind whatsoever with respect to any Securities or Collateral;

"**Income Payment Date**", with respect to any Securities or Collateral means the date on which Income is paid in respect of such Securities or Collateral, or, in the case of registered Securities or Collateral, the date by reference to which particular registered holders are identified as being entitled to payment of Income;

"**Letter of Credit**" means an irrevocable, non-negotiable letter of credit in a form, and from a bank, acceptable to Lender;

"**Loaned Securities**" means Securities which are the subject of an outstanding Loan;

"**Margin**" shall have the meaning specified in paragraph 1 of the Schedule with reference to the table set out therein;

"**Market Value**" means:

(a) in relation to the valuation of Securities, Equivalent Securities, Collateral or Equivalent Collateral (other than Cash Collateral or a Letter of Credit):

(i) such price as is equal to the market quotation for the bid price of such Securities, Equivalent Securities, Collateral and/or Equivalent Collateral as derived from a reputable pricing information service reasonably chosen in good faith by Lender; or

(ii) if unavailable the market value thereof as derived from the prices or rates bid by a reputable dealer for the relevant instrument reasonably chosen in good faith by Lender,

in each case at Close of Business on the previous Business Day or, at the option of either Party where in its reasonable opinion there has been an exceptional movement in the price of the asset in question since such time, the latest available price; plus (in each case)

(iii) the aggregate amount of Income which has accrued but not yet been paid in respect of the Securities, Equivalent Securities, Collateral or Equivalent Collateral concerned to the extent not included in such price,

(provided that the price of Securities, Equivalent Securities, Collateral or Equivalent Collateral that are suspended shall (for the purposes of paragraph 5) be nil unless the Parties otherwise agree and (for all other purposes) shall be the price of such Securities, Equivalent Securities, Collateral or Equivalent Collateral, as the case may be, as of Close of Business on the dealing day in the relevant market last preceding the date of suspension or a commercially reasonable price agreed between the Parties;

(b) in relation to a Letter of Credit the face or stated amount of such Letter of Credit; and

(c) in relation to Cash Collateral the amount of the currency concerned;

"**Nominee**" means an agent or a nominee appointed by either Party to accept delivery of, hold or deliver Securities, Equivalent Securities, Collateral and/or Equivalent Collateral or to receive or make payments on its behalf;

"**Non-Defaulting Party**" shall have the meaning given in paragraph 14;

"**Parties**" means Lender and Borrower and "Party" shall be construed accordingly;

"**Posted Collateral**" has the meaning given in paragraph 5.4;

"**Required Collateral Value**" shall have the meaning given in paragraph 5.4;

"**Settlement Date**" means the date upon which Securities are transferred to Borrower in accordance with this Agreement.

2.2 **Headings**

All headings appear for convenience only and shall not affect the interpretation of this Agreement.

2.3 **Market terminology**

Notwithstanding the use of expressions such as "borrow", "lend", "Collateral", "Margin", "redeliver" etc. which are used to reflect terminology used in the market for transactions of the kind provided for in this Agreement, title to Securities "borrowed" or "lent" and "Collateral" provided in accordance with this Agreement shall pass from one Party to another as provided for in this Agreement, the Party obtaining such title being obliged to redeliver Equivalent Securities or Equivalent Collateral as the case may be.

2.4 **Currency conversions**

For the purposes of determining any prices, sums or values (including Market Value, Required Collateral Value, Relevant Value, Bid Value and Offer Value for the purposes of paragraphs 5 and 10 of this Agreement) prices, sums or values stated in currencies other than the Base Currency shall be converted into the Base Currency at the latest available spot rate of exchange quoted by a bank selected by Lender (or if an Event of Default has occurred in relation to Lender, by Borrower) in the London interbank market for the purchase of the Base Currency with the currency concerned on the day on which the calculation is to be made or, if that day is not a Business Day the spot rate of exchange quoted at Close of Business on the immediately preceding Business Day.

2.5 The parties confirm that introduction of and/or substitution (in place of an existing currency) of a new currency as the lawful currency of a country shall not have the effect of altering, or discharging, or excusing performance under, any term of the Agreement or any Loan thereunder, nor give a party the right unilaterally to alter or terminate the Agreement or any Loan thereunder. Securities will for the purposes of this Agreement be regarded as equivalent to other securities notwithstanding that as a result of such introduction and/or substitution those securities have been redenominated into the new currency or the nominal value of the securities has changed in connection with such redenomination.

2.6 **Modifications etc to legislation**

Any reference in this Agreement to an act, regulation or other legislation shall include a reference to any statutory modification or re-enactment thereof for the time being in force.

3. **LOANS OF SECURITIES**

Lender will lend Securities to Borrower, and Borrower will borrow Securities from Lender in accordance with the terms and conditions of this Agreement. The terms of each Loan shall be agreed prior to the commencement of the relevant Loan either orally or in writing (including any agreed form of electronic communication) and confirmed in such form and on such basis as shall be agreed between the Parties. Any confirmation produced by a Party shall not supersede or prevail over the prior oral, written or electronic communication (as the case may be).

4. **DELIVERY**

4.1 **Delivery of Securities on commencement of Loan**

Lender shall procure the delivery of Securities to Borrower or deliver such Securities in accordance with this Agreement and the terms of the relevant Loan. Such Securities shall be deemed to have been delivered by Lender to Borrower on delivery to Borrower or as it shall direct of the relevant instruments of transfer, or in the case of Securities held by an agent or within a clearing or settlement system on the effective instructions to such agent or the operator of such system which result in such Securities being held by the operator of the clearing system for the account of the Borrower or as it shall direct, or by such other means as may be agreed.

4.2 **Requirements to effect delivery**

The Parties shall execute and deliver all necessary documents and give all necessary instructions to procure that all right, title and interest in:

(a) any Securities borrowed pursuant to paragraph 3;

(b) any Equivalent Securities redelivered pursuant to paragraph 8;

(c) any Collateral delivered pursuant to paragraph 5;

(d) any Equivalent Collateral redelivered pursuant to paragraphs 5 or 8;

shall pass from one Party to the other subject to the terms and conditions set out in this Agreement, on delivery or redelivery of the same in accordance with this Agreement with full title guarantee, free from all liens, charges and encumbrances. In the case of Securities, Collateral, Equivalent Securities or Equivalent Collateral title to which is registered in a computer based system which provides for the recording and transfer of title to the same by way of book entries, delivery and transfer of title shall take place in accordance with the rules and procedures of such system as in force from time to time. The Party acquiring such right, title and interest shall have no obligation to return or redeliver any of the assets so acquired but, in so far as any Securities are borrowed or any Collateral is delivered to such Party, such Party shall be obliged, subject to the terms of this Agreement, to redeliver Equivalent Securities or Equivalent Collateral as appropriate.

4.3 **Deliveries to be simultaneous unless otherwise agreed**

Where under the terms of this Agreement a Party is not obliged to make a delivery unless simultaneously a delivery is made to it, subject to and without prejudice to its rights under paragraph 8.6 such Party may from time to time in accordance with market practice and in recognition of the practical difficulties in arranging simultaneous delivery of Securities, Collateral and cash transfers waive its right under this Agreement in respect of simultaneous delivery and/or payment provided that no such waiver (whether by course of conduct or otherwise) in respect of one transaction shall bind it in respect of any other transaction.

4.4 **Deliveries of Income**

In respect of Income being paid in relation to any Loaned Securities or Collateral, Borrower in the case of Income being paid in respect of Loaned Securities and Lender in the case of Income being paid in respect of Collateral shall provide to the other Party, as the case may be, any endorsements or assignments as shall be customary and appropriate to effect the delivery of money or property equivalent to the type and amount of such Income to Lender, irrespective of whether Borrower received the same in respect of any Loaned Securities or to Borrower, irrespective of whether Lender received the same in respect of any Collateral.

5. COLLATERAL

5.1 Delivery of Collateral on commencement of Loan

Subject to the other provisions of this paragraph 5, Borrower undertakes to deliver to or deposit with Lender (or in accordance with Lender's instructions) Collateral simultaneously with delivery of the Securities to which the Loan relates and in any event no later than Close of Business on the Settlement Date. In respect of Collateral comprising securities, such Collateral shall be deemed to have been delivered by Borrower to Lender on delivery to Lender or as it shall direct of the relevant instruments of transfer, or in the case of such securities being held by an agent or within a clearing or settlement system, on the effective instructions to such agent or the operator of such system, which result in such securities being held by the operator of the clearing system for the account of the Lender or as it shall direct, or by such other means as may be agreed.

5.2 Deliveries through payment systems generating automatic payments

Unless otherwise agreed between the Parties, where any Securities, Equivalent Securities, Collateral or Equivalent Collateral (in the form of securities) are transferred through a book entry transfer or settlement system which automatically generates a payment or delivery, or obligation to pay or deliver, against the transfer of such securities, then:-

(i) such automatically generated payment, delivery or obligation shall be treated as a payment or delivery by the transferee to the transferor, and except to the extent that it is applied to discharge an obligation of the transferee to effect payment or delivery, such payment or delivery, or obligation to pay or deliver, shall be deemed to be a transfer of Collateral or redelivery of Equivalent Collateral, as the case may be, made by the transferee until such time as the Collateral or Equivalent Collateral is substituted with other Collateral or Equivalent Collateral if an obligation to deliver other Collateral or redeliver Equivalent Collateral existed immediately prior to the transfer of Securities, Equivalent Securities, Collateral or Equivalent Collateral; and

(ii) the party receiving such substituted Collateral or Equivalent Collateral, or if no obligation to deliver other Collateral or redeliver Equivalent Collateral existed immediately prior to the transfer of Securities, Equivalent Securities, Collateral or Equivalent Collateral, the party receiving the deemed transfer of Collateral or redelivery of Equivalent Collateral, as the case may be, shall cause to be made to the other party for value the same day either, where such transfer is a payment, an irrevocable payment in the amount of such transfer or, where such transfer is a delivery, an irrevocable delivery of securities (or other property, as the case may be) equivalent to such property.

5.3 **Substitutions of Collateral**

Borrower may from time to time call for the repayment of Cash Collateral or the redelivery of Collateral equivalent to any Collateral delivered to Lender prior to the date on which the same would otherwise have been repayable or redeliverable provided that at the time of such repayment or redelivery Borrower shall have delivered or delivers Alternative Collateral acceptable to Lender and Borrower is in compliance with paragraph 5.4 or paragraph 5.5, as applicable.

5.4 **Marking to Market of Collateral during the currency of a Loan on aggregated basis**

Unless paragraph 1.3 of the Schedule indicates that paragraph 5.5 shall apply in lieu of this paragraph 5.4, or unless otherwise agreed between the Parties:-

(i) the aggregate Market Value of the Collateral delivered to or deposited with Lender (excluding any Equivalent Collateral repaid or redelivered under Paragraphs 5.4(ii) or 5.5(ii) (as the case may be)) ("**Posted Collateral**") in respect of all Loans outstanding under this Agreement shall equal the aggregate of the Market Value of the Loaned Securities and the applicable Margin (the "**Required Collateral Value**") in respect of such Loans;

(ii) if at any time on any Business Day the aggregate Market Value of the Posted Collateral in respect of all Loans outstanding under this Agreement exceeds the aggregate of the Required Collateral Values in respect of such Loans, Lender shall (on demand) repay and/or redeliver, as the case may be, to Borrower such Equivalent Collateral as will eliminate the excess;

(iii) if at any time on any Business Day the aggregate Market Value of the Posted Collateral in respect of all Loans outstanding under this Agreement falls below the aggregate of Required Collateral Values in respect of all such Loans, Borrower shall (on demand) provide such further Collateral to Lender as will eliminate the deficiency.

5.5 **Marking to Market of Collateral during the currency of a Loan on a Loan by Loan basis**

If paragraph 1.3 of the Schedule indicates this paragraph 5.5 shall apply in lieu of paragraph 5.4, the Posted Collateral in respect of any Loan shall bear from day to day and at any time the same proportion to the Market Value of the Loaned Securities as the Posted Collateral bore at the commencement of such Loan. Accordingly:

(i) the Market Value of the Posted Collateral to be delivered or deposited while the Loan continues shall be equal to the Required Collateral Value;

(ii) if at any time on any Business Day the Market Value of the Posted Collateral in respect of any Loan exceeds the Required Collateral Value in respect of such Loan,

Lender shall (on demand) repay and/or redeliver, as the case may be, to Borrower such Equivalent Collateral as will eliminate the excess; and

(iii) if at any time on any Business Day the Market Value of the Posted Collateral falls below the Required Collateral Value, Borrower shall (on demand) provide such further Collateral to Lender as will eliminate the deficiency.

5.6 **Requirements to redeliver excess Collateral**

Where paragraph 5.4 applies, unless paragraph 1.4 of the Schedule indicates that this paragraph 5.6 does not apply, if a Party (the "**first Party**") would, but for this paragraph 5.6, be required under paragraph 5.4 to provide further Collateral or redeliver Equivalent Collateral in circumstances where the other Party (the "**second Party**") would, but for this paragraph 5.6, also be required to or provide Collateral or redeliver Equivalent Collateral under paragraph 5.4, then the Market Value of the Collateral or Equivalent Collateral deliverable by the first Party ("**X**") shall be set-off against the Market Value of the Collateral or Equivalent Collateral deliverable by the second Party ("**Y**") and the only obligation of the Parties under paragraph 5.4 shall be, where X exceeds Y, an obligation of the first Party, or where Y exceeds X, an obligation of the second Party to repay and/or (as the case may be) redeliver Equivalent Collateral or to deliver further Collateral having a Market Value equal to the difference between X and Y.

5.7 Where Equivalent Collateral is repaid or redelivered (as the case may be) or further Collateral is provided by a Party under paragraph 5.6, the Parties shall agree to which Loan or Loans such repayment, redelivery or further provision is to be attributed and failing agreement it shall be attributed, as determined by the Party making such repayment, redelivery or further provision to the earliest outstanding Loan and, in the case of a repayment or redelivery up to the point at which the Market Value of Collateral in respect of such Loan equals the Required Collateral Value in respect of such Loan, and then to the next earliest outstanding Loan up to the similar point and so on.

5.8 **Timing of repayments of excess Collateral or deliveries of further Collateral**

Where any Equivalent Collateral falls to be repaid or redelivered (as the case may be) or further Collateral is to be provided under this paragraph 5, unless otherwise agreed between the Parties, it shall be delivered on the same Business Day as the relevant demand. Equivalent Collateral comprising securities shall be deemed to have been delivered by Lender to Borrower on delivery to Borrower or as it shall direct of the relevant instruments of transfer, or in the case of such securities being held by an agent or within a clearing or settlement system on the effective instructions to such agent or the operator of such system which result in such securities being held by the operator of the clearing system for the account of the Borrower or as it shall direct or by such other means as may be agreed.

5.9 **Substitutions and extensions of Letters of Credit**

Where Collateral is a Letter of Credit, Lender may by notice to Borrower require that Borrower, on the Business Day following the date of delivery of such notice, substitute

Collateral consisting of cash or other Collateral acceptable to Lender for the Letter of Credit. Prior to the expiration of any Letter of Credit supporting Borrower's obligations hereunder, Borrower shall, no later than 10.30a.m. UK time on the second Business Day prior to the date such Letter of Credit expires, obtain an extension of the expiration of such Letter of Credit or replace such Letter of Credit by providing Lender with a substitute Letter of Credit in an amount at least equal to the amount of the Letter of Credit for which it is substituted.

6. **DISTRIBUTIONS AND CORPORATE ACTIONS**

6.1 **Manufactured Payments**

Where Income is paid in relation to any Loaned Securities or Collateral (other than Cash Collateral) on or by reference to an Income Payment Date Borrower, in the case of Loaned Securities, and Lender, in the case of Collateral, shall, on the date of the payment of such Income, or on such other date as the Parties may from time to time agree, (the "**Relevant Payment Date**") pay and deliver a sum of money or property equivalent to the type and amount of such Income that, in the case of Loaned Securities, Lender would have been entitled to receive had such Securities not been loaned to Borrower and had been retained by Lender on the Income Payment Date, and, in the case of Collateral, Borrower would have been entitled to receive had such Collateral not been provided to Lender and had been retained by Borrower on the Income Payment Date unless a different sum is agreed between the Parties.

6.2 **Income in the form of Securities**

Where Income, in the form of securities, is paid in relation to any Loaned Securities or Collateral, such securities shall be added to such Loaned Securities or Collateral (and shall constitute Loaned Securities or Collateral, as the case may be, and be part of the relevant Loan) and will not be delivered to Lender, in the case of Loaned Securities, or to Borrower, in the case of Collateral, until the end of the relevant Loan, provided that the Lender or Borrower (as the case may be) fulfils their obligations under paragraph 5.4 or 5.5 (as applicable) with respect to the additional Loaned Securities or Collateral, as the case may be.

6.3 **Exercise of voting rights**

Where any voting rights fall to be exercised in relation to any Loaned Securities or Collateral, neither Borrower, in the case of Equivalent Securities, nor Lender, in the case of Equivalent Collateral, shall have any obligation to arrange for voting rights of that kind to be exercised in accordance with the instructions of the other Party in relation to the Securities borrowed by it or transferred to it by way of Collateral, as the case may be, unless otherwise agreed between the Parties.

6.4 **Corporate actions**

Where, in respect of any Loaned Securities or any Collateral, any rights relating to conversion, sub-division, consolidation, pre-emption, rights arising under a takeover offer, rights to receive securities or a certificate which may at a future date be exchanged for securities or other rights, including those requiring election by the holder for the time being of such Securities or Collateral, become exercisable prior to the redelivery of Equivalent Securities or Equivalent Collateral, then Lender or Borrower, as the case may be, may, within a reasonable time before the latest time for the exercise of the right or option give written notice to the other Party that on redelivery of Equivalent Securities or Equivalent Collateral, as the case may be, it wishes to receive Equivalent Securities or Equivalent Collateral in such form as will arise if the right is exercised or, in the case of a right which may be exercised in more than one manner, is exercised as is specified in such written notice.

7. **RATES APPLICABLE TO LOANED SECURITIES AND CASH COLLATERAL**

7.1 **Rates in respect of Loaned Securities**

In respect of each Loan, Borrower shall pay to Lender, in the manner prescribed in sub-paragraph 7.3, sums calculated by applying such rate as shall be agreed between the Parties from time to time to the daily Market Value of the Loaned Securities.

7.2 **Rates in respect of Cash Collateral**

Where Cash Collateral is deposited with Lender in respect of any Loan, Lender shall pay to Borrower, in the manner prescribed in paragraph 7.3, sums calculated by applying such rates as shall be agreed between the Parties from time to time to the amount of such Cash Collateral. Any such payment due to Borrower may be set-off against any payment due to Lender pursuant to paragraph 7.1.

7.3 **Payment of rates**

In respect of each Loan, the payments referred to in paragraph 7.1 and 7.2 shall accrue daily in respect of the period commencing on and inclusive of the Settlement Date and terminating on and exclusive of the Business Day upon which Equivalent Securities are redelivered or Cash Collateral is repaid. Unless otherwise agreed, the sums so accruing in respect of each calendar month shall be paid in arrear by the relevant Party not later than the Business Day which is one week after the last Business Day of the calendar month to which such payments relate or such other date as the Parties shall from time to time agree.

8. **REDELIVERY OF EQUIVALENT SECURITIES**

8.1 **Delivery of Equivalent Securities on termination of a Loan**

Borrower shall procure the redelivery of Equivalent Securities to Lender or redeliver Equivalent Securities in accordance with this Agreement and the terms of the relevant Loan on termination of the Loan. Such Equivalent Securities shall be deemed to have been delivered by Borrower to Lender on delivery to Lender or as it shall direct of the relevant instruments of transfer, or in the case of Equivalent Securities held by an agent or within a clearing or settlement system on the effective instructions to such agent or the operator of such system which result in such Equivalent Securities being held by the operator of the clearing system for the account of the Lender or as it shall direct, or by such other means as may be agreed. For the avoidance of doubt any reference in this Agreement or in any other agreement or communication between the Parties (howsoever expressed) to an obligation to redeliver or account for or act in relation to Loaned Securities shall accordingly be construed as a reference to an obligation to redeliver or account for or act in relation to Equivalent Securities.

8.2 **Lender's right to terminate a Loan**

Subject to paragraph 10 and the terms of the relevant Loan, Lender shall be entitled to terminate a Loan and to call for the redelivery of all or any Equivalent Securities at any time by giving notice on any Business Day of not less than the standard settlement time for such Equivalent Securities on the exchange or in the clearing organisation through which the Loaned Securities were originally delivered. Borrower shall redeliver such Equivalent Securities not later than the expiry of such notice in accordance with Lender's instructions.

8.3 **Borrower's right to terminate a Loan**

Subject to the terms of the relevant Loan, Borrower shall be entitled at any time to terminate a Loan and to redeliver all and any Equivalent Securities due and outstanding to Lender in accordance with Lender's instructions and Lender shall accept such redelivery.

8.4 **Redelivery of Equivalent Collateral on termination of a Loan**

On the date and time that Equivalent Securities are required to be redelivered by Borrower on the termination of a Loan, Lender shall simultaneously (subject to paragraph 5.4 if applicable) repay to Borrower any Cash Collateral or, as the case may be, redeliver Collateral equivalent to the Collateral provided by Borrower pursuant to paragraph 5 in respect of such Loan. For the avoidance of doubt any reference in this Agreement or in any other agreement or communication between the Parties (however expressed) to an obligation to redeliver or account for or act in relation to Collateral shall accordingly be construed as a reference to an obligation to redeliver or account for or act in relation to Equivalent Collateral.

8.5 **Redelivery of Letters of Credit**

Where a Letter of Credit is provided by way of Collateral, the obligation to redeliver Equivalent Collateral is satisfied by Lender redelivering for cancellation the Letter of Credit so provided, or where the Letter of Credit is provided in respect of more than one Loan, by Lender consenting to a reduction in the value of the Letter of Credit.

8.6 **Redelivery obligations to be reciprocal**

Neither Party shall be obliged to make delivery (or make a payment as the case may be) to the other unless it is satisfied that the other Party will make such delivery (or make an appropriate payment as the case may be) to it. If it is not so satisfied (whether because an Event of Default has occurred in respect of the other Party or otherwise) it shall notify the other party and unless that other Party has made arrangements which are sufficient to assure full delivery (or the appropriate payment as the case may be) to the notifying Party, the notifying Party shall (provided it is itself in a position, and willing, to perform its own obligations) be entitled to withhold delivery (or payment, as the case may be) to the other Party.

9. FAILURE TO REDELIVER

9.1 Borrower's failure to redeliver Equivalent Securities

(i) If Borrower does not redeliver Equivalent Securities in accordance with paragraph 8.1 or 8.2, Lender may elect to continue the Loan (which Loan, for the avoidance of doubt, shall continue to be taken into account for the purposes of paragraph 5.4 or 5.5 as applicable) provided that if Lender does not elect to continue the Loan, Lender may either by written notice to Borrower terminate the Loan forthwith and the Parties' delivery and payment obligations in respect thereof (in which case sub-paragraph (ii) below shall apply) or serve a notice of an Event of Default in accordance with paragraph 14.

(ii) Upon service of a notice to terminate the relevant Loan pursuant to paragraph 9.1(i):-

   (a) there shall be set-off against the Market Value of the Equivalent Securities concerned such amount of Posted Collateral chosen by Lender (calculated at its Market Value) as is equal thereto;

   (b) the Parties delivery and payment obligations in relation to such assets which are set-off shall terminate;

   (c) in the event that the Market Value of the Posted Collateral set-off is less than the Market Value of the Equivalent Securities concerned Borrower shall account to Lender for the shortfall; and

   (d) Borrower shall account to Lender for the total costs and expenses incurred by Lender as a result thereof as set out in paragraphs 9.3 and 9.4 from the time the notice is effective.

9.2 Lender's failure to Redeliver Equivalent Collateral

(i) If Lender does not redeliver Equivalent Collateral in accordance with paragraph 8.4 or 8.5, Borrower may either by written notice to Lender terminate the Loan forthwith and the Parties' delivery and payment obligations in respect thereof (in which case sub-paragraph (ii) below shall apply) or serve a notice of an Event of Default in accordance with paragraph 14.

(ii) Upon service of a notice to terminate the relevant Loan pursuant to paragraph 9.2(i):-

   (a) there shall be set-off against the Market Value of the Equivalent Collateral concerned the Market Value of the Loaned Securities;

   (b) the Parties delivery and payment obligations in relation to such assets which are set-off shall terminate;

(c) in the event that the Market Value of the Loaned Securities held by Borrower is less than the Market Value of the Equivalent Collateral concerned Lender shall account to Borrower for the shortfall; and

(d) Lender shall account to Borrower for the total costs and expenses incurred by Borrower as a result thereof as set out in paragraphs 9.3 and 9.4 from the time the notice is effective.

9.3 **Failure by either Party to redeliver**

This provision applies in the event that a Party (the "**Transferor**") fails to meet a redelivery obligation within the standard settlement time for the asset concerned on the exchange or in the clearing organisation through which the asset equivalent to the asset concerned was originally delivered or within such other period as may be agreed between the Parties. In such situation, in addition to the Parties' rights under the general law and this Agreement where the other Party (the "**Transferee**") incurs interest, overdraft or similar costs and expenses the Transferor agrees to pay on demand and hold harmless the Transferee with respect to all such costs and expenses which arise directly from such failure excluding (i) such costs and expenses which arise from the negligence or wilful default of the Transferee and (ii) any indirect or consequential losses. It is agreed by the Parties that any costs reasonably and properly incurred by a Party arising in respect of the failure of a Party to meet its obligations under a transaction to sell or deliver securities resulting from the failure of the Transferor to fulfil its redelivery obligations is to be treated as a direct cost or expense for the purposes of this paragraph.

9.4 **Exercise of buy-in on failure to redeliver**

In the event that as a result of the failure of the Transferor to fulfil its redelivery obligations a "buy-in" is exercised against the Transferee, then the Transferor shall account to the Transferee for the total costs and expenses reasonably incurred by the Transferee as a result of such "buy-in".

10. **SET-OFF ETC**

10.1 **Definitions for paragraph 10**

In this paragraph 10:

"**Bid Price**" in relation to Equivalent Securities or Equivalent Collateral means the best available bid price on the most appropriate market in a standard size;

"**Bid Value**" subject to paragraph 10.5 means:-

(a) in relation to Collateral equivalent to Collateral in the form of a Letter of Credit zero and in relation to Cash Collateral the amount of the currency concerned; and

(b) in relation to Equivalent Securities or Collateral equivalent to all other types of Collateral the amount which would be received on a sale of such Equivalent Securities or Equivalent Collateral at the Bid Price at Close of Business on the relevant Business Day less all costs, fees and expenses that would be incurred in connection therewith, calculated on the assumption that the aggregate thereof is the least that could reasonably be expected to be paid in order to carry out such sale or realisation and adding thereto the amount of any interest, dividends, distributions or other amounts, in the case of Equivalent Securities, paid to Borrower and in respect of which equivalent amounts have not been paid to Lender and in the case of Equivalent Collateral, paid to Lender and in respect of which equivalent amounts have not been paid to Borrower, in accordance with paragraph 6.1 prior to such time in respect of such Equivalent Securities, Equivalent Collateral or the original Securities or Collateral held, gross of all and any tax deducted or paid in respect thereof;

"**Offer Price**" in relation to Equivalent Securities or Equivalent Collateral means the best available offer price on the most appropriate market in a standard size;

"**Offer Value**" subject to paragraph 10.5 means:-

(a) in relation to Collateral equivalent to Collateral in the form of a Letter of Credit zero and in relation to Cash Collateral the amount of the currency concerned; and

(b) in relation to Equivalent Securities or Collateral equivalent to all other types of Collateral the amount it would cost to buy such Equivalent Securities or Equivalent Collateral at the Offer Price at Close of Business on the relevant Business Day together with all costs, fees and expenses that would be incurred in connection therewith, calculated on the assumption that the aggregate thereof is the least that could reasonably be expected to be paid in order to carry out the transaction and adding thereto the amount of any interest, dividends, distributions or other amounts, in the case of Equivalent Securities, paid to Borrower and in respect of which equivalent amounts have not been paid to Lender and in the case of Equivalent Collateral, paid to Lender and in respect of which equivalent amounts have not been paid to Borrower, in accordance with paragraph 6.1 prior to such time in respect of such Equivalent Securities, Equivalent Collateral or the original Securities or Collateral held, gross of all and any tax deducted or paid in respect thereof;

10.2 **Termination of delivery obligations upon Event of Default**

Subject to paragraph 9, if an Event of Default occurs in relation to either Party, the Parties' delivery and payment obligations (and any other obligations they have under this Agreement) shall be accelerated so as to require performance thereof at the time such Event of Default occurs (the date of which shall be the "**Termination Date**" for the purposes of this clause) so that performance of such delivery and payment obligations shall be effected only in accordance with the following provisions:

(i) the Relevant Value of the securities which would have been required to be delivered but for such termination (or payment to be made, as the case may be) by each Party shall be established in accordance with paragraph 10.3; and

(ii) on the basis of the Relevant Values so established, an account shall be taken (as at the Termination Date) of what is due from each Party to the other and (on the basis that each Party's claim against the other in respect of delivery of Equivalent Securities or Equivalent Collateral or any cash payment equals the Relevant Value thereof) the sums due from one Party shall be set-off against the sums due from the other and only the balance of the account shall be payable (by the Party having the claim valued at the lower amount pursuant to the foregoing) and such balance shall be payable on the Termination Date.

If the Bid Value is greater than the Offer Value, and the Non-Defaulting Party had delivered to the Defaulting Party a Letter of Credit, the Defaulting Party shall draw on the Letter of Credit to the extent of the balance due and shall subsequently redeliver for cancellation the Letter of Credit so provided.

If the Offer Value is greater than the Bid Value, and the Defaulting Party had delivered to the Non-Defaulting Party a Letter of Credit, the Non-Defaulting Party shall draw on the Letter of Credit to the extent of the balance due and shall subsequently redeliver for cancellation the Letter of Credit so provided.

In all other circumstances, where a Letter of Credit has been provided to a Party, such Party shall redeliver for cancellation the Letter of Credit so provided.

10.3 **Determination of delivery values upon Event of Default**

For the purposes of paragraph 10.2 the **"Relevant Value"**:-

(i) of any securities to be delivered by the Defaulting Party shall, subject to paragraph 10.5 below, equal the Offer Value of such securities; and

(ii) of any securities to be delivered to the Defaulting Party shall, subject to paragraph 10.5 below, equal the Bid Value of such securities.

10.4 For the purposes of paragraph 10.3, but subject to paragraph 10.5, the Bid Value and Offer Value of any securities shall be calculated for securities of the relevant description (as determined by the Non-Defaulting Party) as of the first Business Day following the Termination Date, or if the relevant Event of Default occurs outside the normal business hours of such market, on the second Business Day following the Termination Date (the **"Default Valuation Time"**);

10.5 Where the Non-Defaulting Party has following the occurrence of an Event of Default but prior to the close of business on the fifth Business Day following the Termination Date purchased securities forming part of the same issue and being of an identical type and description to those to be delivered by the Defaulting Party or sold securities forming part of the same issue and being of an identical type and description to those to be delivered by him to the Defaulting Party, the cost of such purchase or the proceeds of such sale, as the case may be, (taking into account all reasonable costs, fees and expenses that would be incurred in connection therewith) shall (together with any amounts owing pursuant to paragraph 6.1) be treated as the Offer Value or Bid Value, as the case may be, of the amount of securities to be delivered which is equivalent to the amount of the securities so bought or sold, as the case may be, for the purposes of this paragraph 10, so that where the amount of securities to be delivered is more than the amount so bought or sold as the case may be, the Offer Value or Bid Value as the case may be, of the balance shall be valued in accordance with paragraph 10.4.

10.6 Any reference in this paragraph 10 to securities shall include any asset other than cash provided by way of Collateral.

10.7 **Other costs, expenses and interest payable in consequence of an Event of Default**

The Defaulting Party shall be liable to the Non-Defaulting Party for the amount of all reasonable legal and other professional expenses incurred by the Non-Defaulting Party in connection with or as a consequence of an Event of Default, together with interest thereon at the one-month London Inter Bank Offered Rate as quoted on a reputable financial information service ("**LIBOR**") as of 11.00 am, London Time, on the date on which it is to be determined or, in the case of an expense attributable to a particular transaction and where the parties have previously agreed a rate of interest for the transaction, that rate of interest if it is greater than LIBOR. The rate of LIBOR applicable to each month or part thereof that any sum payable pursuant to this paragraph 10.7 remains outstanding is the rate of LIBOR determined on the first Business Day of any such period of one month or any part thereof. Interest will accrue daily on a compound basis and will be calculated according to the actual number of days elapsed.

11. **TRANSFER TAXES**

Borrower hereby undertakes promptly to pay and account for any transfer or similar duties or taxes chargeable in connection with any transaction effected pursuant to or contemplated by this Agreement, and shall indemnify and keep indemnified Lender against any liability arising as a result of Borrower's failure to do so.

12. **LENDER'S WARRANTIES**

Each Party hereby warrants and undertakes to the other on a continuing basis to the intent that such warranties shall survive the completion of any transaction contemplated herein that, where acting as a Lender:

(a) it is duly authorised and empowered to perform its duties and obligations under this Agreement;

(b) it is not restricted under the terms of its constitution or in any other manner from lending Securities in accordance with this Agreement or from otherwise performing its obligations hereunder;

(c) it is absolutely entitled to pass full legal and beneficial ownership of all Securities provided by it hereunder to Borrower free from all liens, charges and encumbrances; and

(d) it is acting as principal in respect of this Agreement or, subject to paragraph 16, as agent and the conditions referred to in paragraph 16.2 will be fulfilled in respect of any Loan which it makes as agent.

13. **BORROWER'S WARRANTIES**

Each Party hereby warrants and undertakes to the other on a continuing basis to the intent that such warranties shall survive the completion of any transaction contemplated herein that, where acting as a Borrower:

(a) it has all necessary licenses and approvals, and is duly authorised and empowered, to perform its duties and obligations under this Agreement and will do nothing prejudicial to the continuation of such authorisation, licences or approvals;

(b) it is not restricted under the terms of its constitution or in any other manner from borrowing Securities in accordance with this Agreement or from otherwise performing its obligations hereunder;

(c) it is absolutely entitled to pass full legal and beneficial ownership of all Collateral provided by it hereunder to Lender free from all liens, charges and encumbrances; and

(d) it is acting as principal in respect of this Agreement.

14. **EVENTS OF DEFAULT**

14.1 Each of the following events occurring in relation to either Party (the "**Defaulting Party**", the other Party being the "**Non-Defaulting Party**") shall be an Event of Default for the purpose of paragraph 10 but only (subject to sub-paragraph (v) below) where the Non-Defaulting Party serves written notice on the Defaulting Party:-

(i) Borrower or Lender failing to pay or repay Cash Collateral or deliver Collateral or redeliver Equivalent Collateral or Lender failing to deliver Securities upon the due date;

(ii) Lender or Borrower failing to comply with its obligations under paragraph 5;

(iii) Lender or Borrower failing to comply with its obligations under paragraph 6.1;

(iv) Borrower failing to comply with its obligations to deliver Equivalent Securities in accordance with paragraph 8;

(v) an Act of Insolvency occurring with respect to Lender or Borrower, an Act of Insolvency which is the presentation of a petition for winding up or any analogous proceeding or the appointment of a liquidator or analogous officer of the Defaulting Party not requiring the Non-Defaulting Party to serve written notice on the Defaulting Party;

(vi) any representation or warranty made by Lender or Borrower being incorrect or untrue in any material respect when made or repeated or deemed to have been made or repeated;

(vii) Lender or Borrower admitting to the other that it is unable to, or it intends not to, perform any of its obligations under this Agreement and/or in respect of any Loan;

(viii) Lender (if applicable) or Borrower being declared in default or being suspended or expelled from membership of or participation in, any securities exchange or association or suspended or prohibited from dealing in securities by any regulatory authority;

(ix) any of the assets of Lender or Borrower or the assets of investors held by or to the order of Lender or Borrower being transferred or ordered to be transferred to a trustee (or a person exercising similar functions) by a regulatory authority pursuant to any securities regulating legislation, or

(x) Lender or Borrower failing to perform any other of its obligations under this Agreement and not remedying such failure within 30 days after the Non-Defaulting Party serves written notice requiring it to remedy such failure.

14.2 Each Party shall notify the other (in writing) if an Event of Default or an event which, with the passage of time and/or upon the serving of a written notice as referred to above, would be an Event of Default, occurs in relation to it.

14.3 The provisions of this Agreement constitute a complete statement of the remedies available to each Party in respect of any Event of Default.

14.4 Subject to paragraph 9.3 and 10.7, neither Party may claim any sum by way of consequential loss or damage in the event of failure by the other party to perform any of its obligations under this Agreement.

15. **INTEREST ON OUTSTANDING PAYMENTS**

In the event of either Party failing to remit sums in accordance with this Agreement such Party hereby undertakes to pay to the other Party upon demand interest (before as well as after judgment) on the net balance due and outstanding, for the period commencing on and inclusive of the original due date for payment to (but excluding) the date of actual payment, in the same currency as the principal sum and at the rate referred to in paragraph 10.7. Interest will accrue daily on a compound basis and will be calculated according to the actual number of days elapsed.

16. **TRANSACTIONS ENTERED INTO AS AGENT**

16.1 **Power for Lender to enter into Loans as agent**

Subject to the following provisions of this paragraph, Lender may (if so indicated in paragraph 6 of the Schedule) enter into Loans as agent (in such capacity, the "**Agent**") for a third person (a "**Principal**"), whether as custodian or investment manager or otherwise (a Loan so entered into being referred to in this paragraph as an "**Agency Transaction**").

16.2 **Conditions for agency loan**

A Lender may enter into an Agency Transaction if, but only if:-

(i) it specifies that Loan as an Agency Transaction at the time when it enters into it;

(ii) it enters into that Loan on behalf of a single Principal whose identity is disclosed to Borrower (whether by name or by reference to a code or identifier which the Parties have agreed will be used to refer to a specified Principal) at the time when it enters into the Loan or as otherwise agreed between the Parties; and

(iii) it has at the time when the Loan is entered into actual authority to enter into the Loan and to perform on behalf of that Principal all of that Principal's obligations under the agreement referred to in paragraph 16.4(ii).

16.3 **Notification by Lender of certain events affecting the principal**

Lender undertakes that, if it enters as agent into an Agency Transaction, forthwith upon becoming aware:-

(i) of any event which constitutes an Act of Insolvency with respect to the relevant Principal; or

(ii) of any breach of any of the warranties given in paragraph 16.5 or of any event or circumstance which has the result that any such warranty would be untrue if repeated by reference to the then current facts;

it will inform Borrower of that fact and will, if so required by Borrower, furnish it with such additional information as it may reasonably request.

16.4 **Status of agency transaction**

(i) Each Agency Transaction shall be a transaction between the relevant Principal and Borrower and no person other than the relevant Principal and Borrower shall be a party to or have any rights or obligations under an Agency Transaction. Without limiting the foregoing, Lender shall not be liable as principal for the performance of an Agency Transaction, but this is without prejudice to any liability of Lender under any other provision of this clause; and

(ii) all the provisions of the Agreement shall apply separately as between Borrower and each Principal for whom the Agent has entered into an Agency transaction or Agency Transactions as if each such Principal were a party to a separate agreement with Borrower in all respects identical with this Agreement other than this paragraph and as if the Principal were Lender in respect of that agreement;

PROVIDED THAT

if there occurs in relation to the Agent an Event of Default or an event which would constitute an Event of Default if Borrower served written notice under any sub-clause of paragraph 14, Borrower shall be entitled by giving written notice to the Principal (which notice shall be validly given if given to Lender in accordance with paragraph 21) to declare that by reason of that event an Event of Default is to be treated as occurring in relation to the Principal. If Borrower gives such a notice then an Event of Default shall be treated as occurring in relation to the Principal at the time when the notice is deemed to be given; and if the Principal is neither incorporated in nor has established a place of business in Great Britain, the Principal shall for the purposes of the agreement referred to in paragraph 16.4(ii) be deemed to have appointed as its agent to receive on its behalf service of process in the courts of England the Agent, or if the Agent is neither incorporated nor has established a place of business in Great Britain, the person appointed by the Agent for the purposes of this Agreement, or such other person as the Principal may from time to time specify in a written notice given to the other Party.

The foregoing provisions of this paragraph do not affect the operation of the Agreement as between Borrower and Lender in respect of any transactions into which Lender may enter on its own account as principal.

16.5 **Warranty of authority by Lender acting as agent**

Lender warrants to Borrower that it will, on every occasion on which it enters or purports to enter into a transaction as an Agency Transaction, have been duly authorised to enter into that Loan and perform the obligations arising under such transaction on behalf of the person whom it specifies as the Principal in respect of that transaction and to perform on behalf of that person all the obligations of that person under the agreement referred to in paragraph 16.4(ii).

17. **TERMINATION OF THIS AGREEMENT**

Each Party shall have the right to terminate this Agreement by giving not less than 15 Business Days' notice in writing to the other Party (which notice shall specify the date of termination) subject to an obligation to ensure that all Loans which have been entered into but not discharged at the time such notice is given are duly discharged in accordance with this Agreement.

18. **SINGLE AGREEMENT**

Each Party acknowledges that, and has entered into this Agreement and will enter into each Loan in consideration of and in reliance upon the fact that, all Loans constitute a single business and contractual relationship and are made in consideration of each other. Accordingly, each Party agrees:

(i) to perform all of its obligations in respect of each Loan, and that a default in the performance of any such obligations shall constitute a default by it in respect of all Loans; and

(ii) that payments, deliveries and other transfers made by either of them in respect of any Loan shall be deemed to have been made in consideration of payments, deliveries and other transfers in respect of any other Loan.

19. **SEVERANCE**

If any provision of this Agreement is declared by any judicial or other competent authority to be void or otherwise unenforceable, that provision shall be severed from the Agreement and the remaining provisions of this Agreement shall remain in full force and effect. The Agreement shall, however, thereafter be amended by the Parties in such reasonable manner so as to achieve as far as possible, without illegality, the intention of the Parties with respect to that severed provision.

20. **SPECIFIC PERFORMANCE**

    Each Party agrees that in relation to legal proceedings it will not seek specific performance of the other Party's obligation to deliver or redeliver Securities, Equivalent Securities, Collateral or Equivalent Collateral but without prejudice to any other rights it may have.

21. **NOTICES**

    21.1 Any notice or other communication in respect of this Agreement may be given in any manner set forth below to the address or number or in accordance with the electronic messaging system details set out in paragraph 4 of the Schedule and will be deemed effective as indicated:

    (i) if in writing and delivered in person or by courier, on the date it is delivered;

    (ii) if sent by telex, on the date the recipient's answerback is received;

    (iii) if sent by facsimile transmission, on the date that transmission is received by a responsible employee of the recipient in legible form (it being agreed that the burden of proving receipt will be on the sender and will not be met by a transmission report generated by the sender's facsimile machine);

    (iv) if sent by certified or registered mail (airmail, if overseas) or the equivalent (return receipt requested), on the date that mail is delivered or its delivery is attempted; or

    (v) if sent by electronic messaging system, on the date that electronic message is received,

    unless the date of that delivery (or attempted delivery) or the receipt, as applicable, is not a Business Day or that communication is delivered (or attempted) or received, as applicable, after the Close of Business on a Business Day, in which case that communication shall be deemed given and effective on the first following day that is a Business Day.

    21.2 Either party may by notice to the other change the address, telex or facsimile number or electronic messaging system details at which notices or other communications are to be given to it.

22. **ASSIGNMENT**

    Neither Party may charge assign or transfer all or any of its rights or obligations hereunder without the prior consent of the other Party.

23. **NON-WAIVER**

    No failure or delay by either Party (whether by course of conduct or otherwise) to exercise any right, power or privilege hereunder shall operate as a waiver thereof nor shall any single or partial exercise of any right, power or privilege preclude any other or further exercise thereof or the exercise of any other right, power or privilege as herein provided.

24. GOVERNING LAW AND JURISDICTION

24.1 This Agreement is governed by, and shall be construed in accordance with, English law.

24.2 The courts of England have exclusive jurisdiction to hear and decide any suit, action or proceedings, and to settle any disputes, which may arise out of or in connection with this Agreement (respectively, "**Proceedings**" and "**Disputes**") and, for these purposes, each party irrevocably submits to the jurisdiction of the courts of England.

24.3 Each party irrevocably waives any objection which it might at any time have to the courts of England being nominated as the forum to hear and decide any Proceedings and to settle any Disputes and agrees not to claim that the courts of England are not a convenient or appropriate forum.

24.4 Each of Party A and Party B hereby respectively appoints the person identified in paragraph 5 of the Schedule pertaining to the relevant Party as its agent to receive on its behalf service of process in the courts of England. If such an agent ceases to be an agent of Party A or party B, as the case may be, the relevant Party shall promptly appoint, and notify the other Party of the identity of its new agent in England.

25. TIME

Time shall be of the essence of the Agreement.

26. RECORDING

The Parties agree that each may record all telephone conversations between them.

27. WAIVER OF IMMUNITY

Each Party hereby waives all immunity (whether on the basis of sovereignty or otherwise) from jurisdiction, attachment (both before and after judgement) and execution to which it might otherwise be entitled in any action or proceeding in the courts of England or of any other country or jurisdiction relating in any way to this Agreement and agrees that it will not raise, claim or cause to be pleaded any such immunity at or in respect of any such action or proceeding.

28. MISCELLANEOUS

28.1 This Agreement constitutes the entire agreement and understanding of the Parties with respect to its subject matter and supersedes all oral communication and prior writings with respect thereto.

28.2 The Party (the "**Relevant Party**") who has prepared the text of this Agreement for execution (as indicated in paragraph 7 of the Schedule) warrants and undertakes to the other Party that such text conforms exactly to the text of the standard form Global Master Securities Lending Agreement posted by the International Securities Lenders Association on its website on 7 May 2000 except as notified by the Relevant Party to the other Party in writing prior to the execution of this Agreement.

28.3 No amendment in respect of this Agreement will be effective unless in writing (including a writing evidenced by a facsimile transmission) and executed by each of the Parties or confirmed by an exchange of telexes or electronic messages on an electronic messaging system.

28.4 The obligations of the Parties under this Agreement will survive the termination of any Loan.

28.5 The warranties contained in paragraphs 12, 13, 16 and 28.2 will survive termination of this Agreement for so long as any obligations of either of the Parties pursuant to this Agreement remain outstanding.

28.6 Except as provided in this Agreement, the rights, powers, remedies and privileges provided in this Agreement are cumulative and not exclusive of any rights, powers, remedies and privileges provided by law.

28.7 This Agreement (and each amendment in respect of it) may be executed and delivered in counterparts (including by facsimile transmission), each of which will be deemed an original.

28.8 A person who is not a party to this Agreement has no right under the Contracts (Rights of Third Parties) Act 1999 to enforce any terms of this Agreement, but this does not affect any right or remedy of a third party which exists or is available apart from that Act.

EXECUTED by the **PARTIES**

SIGNED BY)
)
DULY AUTHORISED FOR AND)
ON BEHALF OF)

SIGNED BY)
)
DULY AUTHORISED FOR AND)
ON BEHALF OF)

SCHEDULE

1. **Collateral**

   1.1 The securities, financial instruments and deposits of currency set out in the table below with a cross marked next to them are acceptable forms of Collateral under this Agreement.

   1.2 Unless otherwise agreed between the Parties, the Market Value of the Collateral delivered pursuant to paragraph 5 by Borrower to Lender under the terms and conditions of this Agreement shall on each Business Day represent not less than the Market Value of the Loaned Securities together with the percentage contained in the row of the table below corresponding to the particular form of Collateral, referred to in this Agreement as the "**Margin**".

Security/Financial Instrument/Deposit of Currency	Mark "X" if acceptable form of Collateral	Margin (%)

   1.3 Basis of Margin Maintenance:

   Paragraph 5.4 (aggregation) shall not apply* ☐

   The assumption is that paragraph 5.4 (aggregation) applies unless the box is ticked.

   1.4 Paragraph 5.6 (netting of obligations to deliver Collateral and redeliver Equivalent Collateral) shall not apply* ☐

   If paragraph 5.4 applies, the assumption is that paragraph 5.6 (netting) applies unless the box is ticked.

2. **Base Currency**

   The Base Currency applicable to this Agreement is

3. **Places of Business**

   (See definition of Business Day.)

4. **Designated Office and Address for Notices**

   (A) **Designated office of Party A:**

   Address for notices or communications to Party A:

Address:

Attention:

Facsimile No:

Telephone No:

Electronic Messaging System Details:

(B) **Designated office of Party B:**

Address for notices or communications to Party B:

Address:

Attention:

Facsimile No:

Telephone No:

Electronic Messaging System Details:

5. (A) **Agent of Party A for Service of Process**

Name:

Address:

(B) **Agent of Party B for Service of Process**

Name:

Address:

6. **Agency**

- Paragraph 16 may apply to Party A* ☐

- Paragraph 16 may apply to Party B* ☐

7. **Party Preparing this Agreement**

Party A* ☐

Party B* ☐

APPENDIX 2: A FACSIMILE OF THE GLOBAL MASTER SECURITIES LENDING AGREEMENT (2010) REPRODUCED WITH THE KIND PERMISSION OF THE INTERNATIONAL SECURITIES LENDING ASSOCIATION

VERSION: JANUARY 2010

ISLA
INTERNATIONAL
SECURITIES
LENDING
ASSOCIATION

GLOBAL MASTER SECURITIES LENDING AGREEMENT

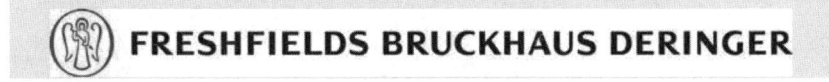

FRESHFIELDS BRUCKHAUS DERINGER

CONTENTS

CLAUSE		PAGE
1.	APPLICABILITY	3
2.	INTERPRETATION	3
3.	LOANS OF SECURITIES	9
4.	DELIVERY	9
5.	COLLATERAL	10
6.	DISTRIBUTIONS AND CORPORATE ACTIONS	13
7.	RATES APPLICABLE TO LOANED SECURITIES AND CASH COLLATERAL	15
8.	DELIVERY OF EQUIVALENT SECURITIES	16
9.	FAILURE TO DELIVER	17
10.	EVENTS OF DEFAULT	18
11.	CONSEQUENCES OF AN EVENT OF DEFAULT	19
12.	TAXES	23
13.	LENDER'S WARRANTIES	25
14.	BORROWER'S WARRANTIES	25
15.	INTEREST ON OUTSTANDING PAYMENTS	25
16.	TERMINATION OF THIS AGREEMENT	26
17.	SINGLE AGREEMENT	26
18.	SEVERANCE	26
19.	SPECIFIC PERFORMANCE	26
20.	NOTICES	26
21.	ASSIGNMENT	27
22.	NON-WAIVER	27
23.	GOVERNING LAW AND JURISDICTION	27
24.	TIME	28
25.	RECORDING	28
26.	WAIVER OF IMMUNITY	28
27.	MISCELLANEOUS	28
SCHEDULE		31
AGENCY ANNEX		34
ADDENDUM FOR POOLED PRINCIPAL AGENCY LOANS		37

AGREEMENT

BETWEEN:

(***Party A***) a company incorporated under the laws of acting through one or more Designated Offices; and

(***Party B***) a company incorporated under the laws of acting through one or more Designated Offices.

1. APPLICABILITY

1.1 From time to time the Parties acting through one or more Designated Offices may enter into transactions in which one party (***Lender***) will transfer to the other (***Borrower***) securities and financial instruments (***Securities***) against the transfer of Collateral (as defined in paragraph 2) with a simultaneous agreement by Borrower to transfer to Lender Securities equivalent to such Securities on a fixed date or on demand against the transfer to Borrower by Lender of assets equivalent to such Collateral.

1.2 Each such transaction shall be referred to in this Agreement as a ***Loan*** and shall be governed by the terms of this Agreement, including the supplemental terms and conditions contained in the Schedule and any Addenda or Annexes attached hereto, unless otherwise agreed in writing. In the event of any inconsistency between the provisions of an Addendum or Annex and this Agreement, the provisions of such Addendum or Annex shall prevail unless the Parties otherwise agree.

1.3 Either Party may perform its obligations under this Agreement either directly or through a Nominee.

2. INTERPRETATION

2.1 In this Agreement:

Act of Insolvency means in relation to either Party:

(a) its making a general assignment for the benefit of, or entering into a reorganisation, arrangement, or composition with creditors; or

(b) its stating in writing that it is unable to pay its debts as they become due; or

(c) its seeking, consenting to or acquiescing in the appointment of any trustee, administrator, receiver or liquidator or analogous officer of it or any material part of its property; or

(d) the presentation or filing of a petition in respect of it (other than by the other Party to this Agreement in respect of any obligation under this Agreement) in any court or before any agency alleging or for the bankruptcy, winding-up or insolvency of such Party (or any analogous proceeding) or seeking any reorganisation, arrangement, composition, re-adjustment, administration, liquidation, dissolution or similar relief under any present or future statute, law or regulation, such petition not having been stayed or dismissed within 30 days of its filing (except in the case of a petition for winding-up or any analogous proceeding in respect of which no such 30 day period shall apply); or

(e) the appointment of a receiver, administrator, liquidator or trustee or analogous officer of such Party over all or any material part of such Party's property; or

(f) the convening of any meeting of its creditors for the purpose of considering a voluntary arrangement as referred to in Section 3 of the Insolvency Act 1986 (or any analogous proceeding);

Agency Annex means the Annex to this Agreement published by the International Securities Lending Association and providing for Lender to act as agent for a third party in respect of one or more Loans;

Alternative Collateral means Collateral having a Market Value equal to the Collateral delivered pursuant to paragraph 5 and provided by way of substitution in accordance with the provisions of paragraph 5.3;

Applicable Law means the laws, rules and regulations (including double taxation conventions) of any relevant jurisdiction, including published practice of any government or other taxing authority in connection with such laws, rules and regulations;

Automatic Early Termination has the meaning given in paragraph 10.1(d);

Base Currency means the currency indicated in paragraph 2 of the Schedule;

Business Day means:

(a) in relation to Delivery in respect of any Loan, a day other than a Saturday or a Sunday on which banks and securities markets are open for business generally in the place(s) where the relevant Securities, Equivalent Securities, Collateral or Equivalent Collateral are to be delivered;

(b) in relation to any payments under this Agreement, a day other than a Saturday or a Sunday on which banks are open for business generally in the principal financial centre of the country of which the currency in which the payment is denominated is the official currency and, if different, in the place where any account designated by the Parties for the making or receipt of the payment is situated (or, in the case of a payment in euro, a day on which TARGET operates);

(c) in relation to a notice or other communication served under this Agreement, any day other than a Saturday or a Sunday on which banks are open for business generally in the place designated for delivery in accordance with paragraph 3 of the Schedule; and

(d) in any other case, a day other than a Saturday or a Sunday on which banks are open for business generally in each place stated in paragraph 6 of the Schedule;

Buy-In means any arrangement under which, in the event of a seller or transferor failing to deliver securities to the buyer or transferee, the buyer or transferee of such securities is entitled under the terms of such arrangement to buy or otherwise acquire securities equivalent to such securities and to recover the cost of so doing from the seller or transferor;

Cash Collateral means Collateral taking the form of a transfer of currency;

Close of Business means the time at which the relevant banks, securities settlement systems or depositaries close in the business centre in which payment is to be made or Securities or Collateral is to be delivered;

Collateral means such securities or financial instruments or transfers of currency as are referred to in the table set out under paragraph 1 of the Schedule as being acceptable or any combination thereof as agreed between the Parties in relation to any particular Loan and which are delivered by Borrower to Lender in accordance with this Agreement and shall include Alternative Collateral;

Defaulting Party has the meaning given in paragraph 10;

Delivery in relation to any Securities or Collateral or Equivalent Securities or Equivalent Collateral comprising Securities means:

(a)   in the case of Securities held by a Nominee or within a clearing or settlement system, the crediting of such Securities to an account of the Borrower or Lender, as the case may be, or as it shall direct, or,

(b)   in the case of Securities otherwise held, the delivery to Borrower or Lender, as the case may be, or as the transferee shall direct of the relevant instruments of transfer, or

(c)   by such other means as may be agreed,

and ***deliver*** shall be construed accordingly;

Designated Office means the branch or office of a Party which is specified as such in paragraph 6 of the Schedule or such other branch or office as may be agreed to in writing by the Parties;

Equivalent or ***equivalent to*** in relation to any Loaned Securities or Collateral (whether Cash Collateral or Non-Cash Collateral) provided under this Agreement means Securities or other property, of an identical type, nominal value, description and amount to particular Loaned Securities or Collateral (as the case may be) so provided. If and to the extent that such Loaned Securities or Collateral (as the case may be) consists of Securities that are partly paid or have been converted, subdivided, consolidated, made the subject of a takeover, rights of pre-emption, rights to receive securities or a certificate which may at a future date be exchanged for Securities, the expression shall include such Securities or other assets to which Lender or Borrower (as the case may be) is entitled following the occurrence of the relevant event, and, if appropriate, the giving of the relevant notice in accordance with paragraph 6.7 and provided that Lender or Borrower (as the case may be) has paid to the other Party all and any sums due in respect thereof. In the event that such Loaned Securities or Collateral (as the case may be) have been redeemed, are partly paid, are the subject of a capitalisation issue or are subject to an event similar to any of the foregoing events described in this paragraph, the expression shall have the following meanings:

(a) in the case of redemption, a sum of money equivalent to the proceeds of the redemption;

(b) in the case of a call on partly-paid Securities, Securities equivalent to the relevant Loaned Securities or Collateral, as the case may be, provided that Lender shall have paid Borrower, in respect of Loaned Securities, and Borrower shall have paid to Lender, in respect of Collateral, an amount of money equal to the sum due in respect of the call;

(c) in the case of a capitalisation issue, Securities equivalent to the relevant Loaned Securities or Collateral, as the case may be, together with the securities allotted by way of bonus thereon;

(d) in the case of any event similar to any of the foregoing events described in this paragraph, Securities equivalent to the Loaned Securities or the relevant Collateral, as the case may be, together with or replaced by a sum of money or Securities or other property equivalent to that received in respect of such Loaned Securities or Collateral, as the case may be, resulting from such event;

Income means any interest, dividends or other distributions of any kind whatsoever with respect to any Securities or Collateral;

Income Record Date, with respect to any Securities or Collateral, means the date by reference to which holders of such Securities or Collateral are identified as being entitled to payment of Income;

Letter of Credit means an irrevocable, non-negotiable letter of credit in a form, and from a bank, acceptable to Lender;

Loaned Securities means Securities which are the subject of an outstanding Loan;

Margin has the meaning specified in paragraph 1 of the Schedule with reference to the table set out therein;

Market Value means:

(a) in relation to the valuation of Securities, Equivalent Securities, Collateral or Equivalent Collateral (other than Cash Collateral or a Letter of Credit):

(i) such price as is equal to the market quotation for the mid price of such Securities, Equivalent Securities, Collateral and/or Equivalent Collateral as derived from a reputable pricing information service reasonably chosen in good faith by Lender; or

(ii) if unavailable the market value thereof as derived from the mid price or rate bid by a reputable dealer for the relevant instrument reasonably chosen in good faith by Lender,

in each case at Close of Business on the previous Business Day, or as specified in the Schedule, unless agreed otherwise or, at the option of either Party where in its reasonable opinion there has been an exceptional movement in the price of the asset in question since such time, the latest available price, plus (in each case):

(iii) the aggregate amount of Income which has accrued but not yet been paid in respect of the Securities, Equivalent Securities, Collateral or Equivalent Collateral concerned to the extent not included in such price,

provided that the price of Securities, Equivalent Securities, Collateral or Equivalent Collateral that are suspended or that cannot legally be transferred or that are transferred or required to be transferred to a government, trustee or third party (whether by reason of nationalisation, expropriation or otherwise) shall for all purposes be a commercially reasonable price agreed between the Parties, or absent agreement, be a price provided by a third party dealer agreed between the Parties, or if the Parties do not agree a third party dealer then a price based on quotations provided by the Reference Dealers. If more than three quotations are provided, the Market Value will be the arithmetic mean of the prices, without regard to the quotations having the highest and lowest prices. If three quotations are provided, the Market Value will be the quotation remaining after disregarding the highest and lowest quotations. For this purpose, if more than one quotation has the same highest or lowest price, then one of such quotations shall be disregarded. If fewer than three quotations are provided, the Market Value of the relevant Securities, Equivalent Securities, Collateral or Equivalent Collateral shall be determined by the Party making the determination of Market Value acting reasonably;

(b) in relation to a Letter of Credit the face or stated amount of such Letter of Credit; and

(c) in relation to Cash Collateral the amount of the currency concerned;

Nominee means a nominee or agent appointed by either Party to accept delivery of, hold or deliver Securities, Equivalent Securities, Collateral and/or Equivalent Collateral or to receive or make payments on its behalf;

Non-Cash Collateral means Collateral other than Cash Collateral;

Non-Defaulting Party has the meaning given in paragraph 10;

Notification Time means the time specified in paragraph 1.5 of the Schedule;

Parties means Lender and Borrower and *Party* shall be construed accordingly;

Posted Collateral has the meaning given in paragraph 5.4;

Reference Dealers means, in relation to any Securities, Equivalent Securities, Collateral or Equivalent Collateral, four leading dealers in the relevant securities selected by the Party making the determination of Market Value in good faith;

Required Collateral Value has the meaning given in paragraph 5.4;

Sales Tax means value added tax and any other Tax of a similar nature (including, without limitation, any sales tax of any relevant jurisdiction);

Settlement Date means the date upon which Securities are due to be transferred to Borrower in accordance with this Agreement;

Stamp Tax means any stamp, transfer, registration, documentation or similar Tax; and

Tax means any present or future tax, levy, impost, duty, charge, assessment or fee of any nature (including interest, penalties and additions thereto) imposed by any government or other taxing authority in respect of any transaction effected pursuant to or contemplated by, or any payment under or in respect of, this Agreement.

2.2 **Headings**

All headings appear for convenience only and shall not affect the interpretation of this Agreement.

2.3 **Market terminology**

Notwithstanding the use of expressions such as "borrow", "lend", "Collateral", "Margin" etc. which are used to reflect terminology used in the market for transactions of the kind provided for in this Agreement, title to Securities "borrowed" or "lent" and "Collateral" provided in accordance with this Agreement shall pass from one Party to another as provided for in this Agreement, the Party obtaining such title being obliged to deliver Equivalent Securities or Equivalent Collateral as the case may be.

2.4 **Currency conversions**

Subject to paragraph 11, for the purposes of determining any prices, sums or values (including Market Value and Required Collateral Value) prices, sums or values stated in currencies other than the Base Currency shall be converted into the Base Currency at the latest available spot rate of exchange quoted by a bank selected by Lender (or if an Event of Default has occurred in relation to Lender, by Borrower) in the London inter-bank market for the purchase of the Base Currency with the currency concerned on the day on which the calculation is to be made or, if that day is not a Business Day, the spot rate of exchange quoted at Close of Business on the immediately preceding Business Day on which such a quotation was available.

2.5 The Parties confirm that introduction of and/or substitution (in place of an existing currency) of a new currency as the lawful currency of a country shall not have the effect of altering, or discharging, or excusing performance under, any term of the Agreement or any Loan thereunder, nor give a Party the right unilaterally to alter or terminate the Agreement or any Loan thereunder. Securities will for the purposes of this Agreement be regarded as equivalent to other securities notwithstanding that as a result of such introduction and/or substitution those securities have been redenominated into the new currency or the nominal value of the securities has changed in connection with such redenomination.

2.6 **Modifications etc. to legislation**

Any reference in this Agreement to an act, regulation or other legislation shall include a reference to any statutory modification or re-enactment thereof for the time being in force.

Appendices

3. **LOANS OF SECURITIES**

   Lender will lend Securities to Borrower, and Borrower will borrow Securities from Lender in accordance with the terms and conditions of this Agreement. The terms of each Loan shall be agreed prior to the commencement of the relevant Loan either orally or in writing (including any agreed form of electronic communication) and confirmed in such form and on such basis as shall be agreed between the Parties. Unless otherwise agreed, any confirmation produced by a Party shall not supersede or prevail over the prior oral, written or electronic communication (as the case may be).

4. **DELIVERY**

   4.1 **Delivery of Securities on commencement of Loan**

   Lender shall procure the Delivery of Securities to Borrower or deliver such Securities in accordance with this Agreement and the terms of the relevant Loan.

   4.2 **Requirements to effect Delivery**

   The Parties shall execute and deliver all necessary documents and give all necessary instructions to procure that all right, title and interest in:

   (a) any Securities borrowed pursuant to paragraph 3;

   (b) any Equivalent Securities delivered pursuant to paragraph 8;

   (c) any Collateral delivered pursuant to paragraph 5;

   (d) any Equivalent Collateral delivered pursuant to paragraphs 5 or 8;

   shall pass from one Party to the other subject to the terms and conditions set out in this Agreement, on delivery of the same in accordance with this Agreement with full title guarantee, free from all liens, charges and encumbrances. In the case of Securities, Collateral, Equivalent Securities or Equivalent Collateral title to which is registered in a computer-based system which provides for the recording and transfer of title to the same by way of book entries, delivery and transfer of title shall take place in accordance with the rules and procedures of such system as in force from time to time. The Party acquiring such right, title and interest shall have no obligation to return or deliver any of the assets so acquired but, in so far as any Securities are borrowed by or any Collateral is delivered to such Party, such Party shall be obliged, subject to the terms of this Agreement, to deliver Equivalent Securities or Equivalent Collateral as appropriate.

   4.3 **Deliveries to be simultaneous unless otherwise agreed**

   Where under the terms of this Agreement a Party is not obliged to make a Delivery unless simultaneously a Delivery is made to it, subject to and without prejudice to its rights under paragraph 8.6, such Party may from time to time in accordance with market practice and in recognition of the practical difficulties in arranging simultaneous delivery of Securities, Collateral and cash transfers, waive its right under this Agreement in respect of simultaneous delivery and/or payment provided that no such waiver (whether by course of conduct or otherwise) in respect of one transaction shall bind it in respect of any other transaction.

4.4 Deliveries of Income

In respect of Income being paid in relation to any Loaned Securities or Collateral, Borrower (in the case of Income being paid in respect of Loaned Securities) and Lender (in the case of Income being paid in respect of Collateral) shall provide to the other Party, as the case may be, any endorsements or assignments as shall be customary and appropriate to effect, in accordance with paragraph 6, the payment or delivery of money or property in respect of such Income to Lender, irrespective of whether Borrower received such endorsements or assignments in respect of any Loaned Securities, or to Borrower, irrespective of whether Lender received such endorsements or assignments in respect of any Collateral.

5. COLLATERAL

5.1 Delivery of Collateral on commencement of Loan

Subject to the other provisions of this paragraph 5, Borrower undertakes to deliver to or deposit with Lender (or in accordance with Lender's instructions) Collateral simultaneously with Delivery of the Securities to which the Loan relates and in any event no later than Close of Business on the Settlement Date.

5.2 Deliveries through securities settlement systems generating automatic payments

Unless otherwise agreed between the Parties, where any Securities, Equivalent Securities, Collateral or Equivalent Collateral (in the form of securities) are transferred through a book entry transfer or settlement system which automatically generates a payment or delivery, or obligation to pay or deliver, against the transfer of such securities, then:

(a) such automatically generated payment, delivery or obligation shall be treated as a payment or delivery by the transferee to the transferor, and except to the extent that it is applied to discharge an obligation of the transferee to effect payment or delivery, such payment or delivery, or obligation to pay or deliver, shall be deemed to be a transfer of Collateral or delivery of Equivalent Collateral, as the case may be, made by the transferee until such time as the Collateral or Equivalent Collateral is substituted with other Collateral or Equivalent Collateral if an obligation to deliver other Collateral or deliver Equivalent Collateral existed immediately prior to the transfer of Securities, Equivalent Securities, Collateral or Equivalent Collateral; and

(b) the Party receiving such substituted Collateral or Equivalent Collateral, or if no obligation to deliver other Collateral or redeliver Equivalent Collateral existed immediately prior to the transfer of Securities, Equivalent Securities, Collateral or Equivalent Collateral, the Party receiving the deemed transfer of Collateral or Delivery of Equivalent Collateral, as the case may be, shall cause to be made to the other Party for value the same day either, where such transfer is a payment, an irrevocable payment in the amount of such transfer or, where such transfer is a Delivery, an irrevocable Delivery of securities (or other property, as the case may be) equivalent to such property.

Appendices

5.3 **Substitutions of Collateral**

Borrower may from time to time call for the repayment of Cash Collateral or the Delivery of Collateral equivalent to any Collateral delivered to Lender prior to the date on which the same would otherwise have been repayable or deliverable provided that at or prior to the time of such repayment or Delivery Borrower shall have delivered Alternative Collateral acceptable to Lender and Borrower is in compliance with paragraph 5.4 or paragraph 5.5, as applicable.

5.4 **Marking to Market of Collateral during the currency of a Loan on aggregated basis**

Unless paragraph 1.3 of the Schedule indicates that paragraph 5.5 shall apply in lieu of this paragraph 5.4, or unless otherwise agreed between the Parties:

(a) the aggregate Market Value of the Collateral delivered to or deposited with Lender (excluding any Equivalent Collateral repaid or delivered under paragraphs 5.4(b) or 5.5(b) (as the case may be)) (*Posted Collateral*) in respect of all Loans outstanding under this Agreement shall equal the aggregate of the Market Value of Securities equivalent to the Loaned Securities and the applicable Margin (the *Required Collateral Value*) in respect of such Loans;

(b) if at any time on any Business Day the aggregate Market Value of the Posted Collateral in respect of all Loans outstanding under this Agreement together with: (i) all amounts due and payable by the Lender under this Agreement but which are unpaid; and (ii) if agreed between the parties and if the Income Record Date has occurred in respect of any Non-Cash Collateral, the amount or Market Value of Income payable in respect of such Non-Cash Collateral exceeds the aggregate of the Required Collateral Values in respect of such Loans together with: (i) all amounts due and payable by the Borrower under this Agreement but which are unpaid; and (ii) if agreed between the parties and if the Income Record Date has occurred in respect of any securities equivalent to Loaned Securities, the amount or Market Value of Income payable in respect of such Equivalent Securities, Lender shall (on demand) repay and/or deliver, as the case may be, to Borrower such Equivalent Collateral as will eliminate the excess;

(c) if at any time on any Business Day the aggregate Market Value of the Posted Collateral in respect of all Loans outstanding under this Agreement together with: (i) all amounts due and payable by the Lender under this Agreement but which are unpaid; and (ii) if agreed between the parties and if the Income Record Date has occurred in respect of any Non-Cash Collateral, the amount or Market Value of Income payable in respect of such Non-Cash Collateral falls below the aggregate of Required Collateral Values in respect of all such Loans together with: (i) all amounts due and payable by the Borrower under this Agreement but which are unpaid; and (ii) if agreed between the parties and if the Income Record Date has occurred in respect of Securities equivalent to any Loaned Securities, the amount or Market Value of Income payable in respect of such Equivalent Securities, Borrower shall (on demand) provide such further Collateral to Lender as will eliminate the deficiency;

(d) where a Party acts as both Lender and Borrower under this Agreement, the provisions of paragraphs 5.4(b) and 5.4(c) shall apply separately (and without duplication) in respect of Loans entered into by that Party as Lender and Loans entered into by that Party as Borrower.

5.5 **Marking to Market of Collateral during the currency of a Loan on a Loan by Loan basis**

If paragraph 1.3 of the Schedule indicates this paragraph 5.5 shall apply in lieu of paragraph 5.4, the Posted Collateral in respect of any Loan shall bear from day to day and at any time the same proportion to the Market Value of Securities equivalent to the Loaned Securities as the Posted Collateral bore at the commencement of such Loan. Accordingly:

(a) the Market Value of the Posted Collateral to be delivered or deposited while the Loan continues shall be equal to the Required Collateral Value;

(b) if at any time on any Business Day the Market Value of the Posted Collateral in respect of any Loan together with: (i) all amounts due and payable by the Lender in respect of that Loan but which are unpaid; and (ii) if agreed between the parties and if the Income Record Date has occurred in respect of any Non-Cash Collateral, the amount or Market Value of Income payable in respect of such Non-Cash Collateral exceeds the Required Collateral Value in respect of such Loan together with: (i) all amounts due and payable by the Borrower in respect of that Loan; and (ii) if agreed between the parties and if the Income Record Date has occurred in respect of Securities equivalent to any Loaned Securities, the amount or Market Value of Income payable in respect of such Equivalent Securities, Lender shall (on demand) repay and/or deliver, as the case may be, to Borrower such Equivalent Collateral as will eliminate the excess; and

(c) if at any time on any Business Day the Market Value of the Posted Collateral together with: (i) all amounts due any payable by the Lender in respect of that Loan; and (ii) if agreed between the parties and if the Income Record Date has occurred in respect of any Non-Cash Collateral, the amount or Market Value of Income payable in respect of such Non-Cash Collateral falls below the Required Collateral Value together with: (i) all amounts due and payable by the Borrower in respect of that Loan; and (ii) if agreed between the parties and if the Income Record Date has occurred in respect of Securities equivalent to any Loaned Securities, the amount or Market Value of Income payable in respect of such Equivalent Securities, Borrower shall (on demand) provide such further Collateral to Lender as will eliminate the deficiency.

5.6 **Requirements to deliver excess Collateral**

Where paragraph 5.4 applies, unless paragraph 1.4 of the Schedule indicates that this paragraph 5.6 does not apply, if a Party (the *first Party*) would, but for this paragraph 5.6, be required under paragraph 5.4 to provide further Collateral or deliver Equivalent Collateral in circumstances where the other Party (the *second Party*) would, but for this paragraph 5.6, also be required to or provide Collateral or deliver Equivalent Collateral under paragraph 5.4, then the Market Value of the Collateral or Equivalent Collateral deliverable by the first Party (*X*) shall be set off against the Market Value of the Collateral or Equivalent Collateral deliverable by the second

Party (*Y*) and the only obligation of the Parties under paragraph 5.4 shall be, where X exceeds Y, an obligation of the first Party, or where Y exceeds X, an obligation of the second Party to repay and/or (as the case may be) deliver Equivalent Collateral or to deliver further Collateral having a Market Value equal to the difference between X and Y.

5.7 Where Equivalent Collateral is repaid or delivered (as the case may be) or further Collateral is provided by a Party under paragraph 5.6, the Parties shall agree to which Loan or Loans such repayment, delivery or further provision is to be attributed and failing agreement it shall be attributed, as determined by the Party making such repayment, delivery or further provision to the earliest outstanding Loan and, in the case of a repayment or delivery up to the point at which the Market Value of Collateral in respect of such Loan equals the Required Collateral Value in respect of such Loan, and then to the next earliest outstanding Loan up to the similar point and so on.

5.8 **Timing of repayments of excess Collateral or deliveries of further Collateral**

Where any Equivalent Collateral falls to be repaid or delivered (as the case may be) or further Collateral is to be provided under this paragraph 5, unless otherwise provided or agreed between the Parties, if the relevant demand is received by the Notification Time specified in paragraph 1.5 of the Schedule, then the delivery shall be made not later than the Close of Business on the same Business Day; if a demand is received after the Notification Time, then the relevant delivery shall be made not later than the Close of Business on the next Business Day after the date such demand is received.

5.9 **Substitutions and extensions of Letters of Credit**

Where Collateral is a Letter of Credit, Lender may by notice to Borrower require that Borrower, on the third Business Day following the date of delivery of such notice (or by such other time as the Parties may agree), substitute Collateral consisting of cash or other Collateral acceptable to Lender for the Letter of Credit. Prior to the expiration of any Letter of Credit supporting Borrower's obligations hereunder, Borrower shall, no later than 10.30 a.m. UK time on the second Business Day prior to the date such Letter of Credit expires (or by such other time as the Parties may agree), obtain an extension of the expiration of such Letter of Credit or replace such Letter of Credit by providing Lender with a substitute Letter of Credit in an amount at least equal to the amount of the Letter of Credit for which it is substituted.

6. **DISTRIBUTIONS AND CORPORATE ACTIONS**

6.1 In this paragraph 6, references to an amount of Income *received* by any Party in respect of any Loaned Securities or Non-Cash Collateral shall be to an amount received from the issuer after any applicable withholding or deduction for or on account of Tax.

6.2 **Manufactured payments in respect of Loaned Securities**

Where the term of a Loan extends over an Income Record Date in respect of any Loaned Securities, Borrower shall, on the date such Income is paid by the issuer, or on such other date as the Parties may from time to time agree, pay or deliver to Lender such sum of money or property as is agreed between the Parties or, failing such agreement, a sum of money or property equivalent to (and in the same currency as) the type and amount of such Income that would be received by Lender in respect of such Loaned Securities assuming such Securities were not loaned to Borrower and were retained by Lender on the Income Record Date.

6.3   **Manufactured payments in respect of Non-Cash Collateral**

Where Non-Cash Collateral is delivered by Borrower to Lender and an Income Record Date in respect of such Non-Cash Collateral occurs before Equivalent Collateral is delivered by Lender to Borrower, Lender shall on the date such Income is paid, or on such other date as the Parties may from time to time agree, pay or deliver to Borrower a sum of money or property as is agreed between the Parties or, failing such agreement, a sum of money or property equivalent to (and in the same currency as) the type and amount of such Income that would be received by Lender in respect of such Non-Cash Collateral assuming Lender:

(a)   retained the Non-Cash Collateral on the Income Record Date; and

(b)   is not entitled to any credit, benefit or other relief in respect of Tax under any Applicable Law.

6.4   **Indemnity for failure to redeliver Equivalent Non-Cash Collateral**

Unless paragraph 1.6 of the Schedule indicates that this paragraph does not apply, where:

(a)   prior to any Income Record Date in relation to Non-Cash Collateral, Borrower has in accordance with paragraph 5.3 called for the Delivery of Equivalent Non-Cash Collateral;

(b)   Borrower has given notice of such call to Lender so as to be effective, at the latest, five hours before the Close of Business on the last Business Day on which Lender would customarily be required to initiate settlement of the Non-Cash Collateral to enable settlement to take place on the Business Day immediately preceding the relevant Income Record Date;

(c)   Borrower has provided reasonable details to Lender of the Non-Cash Collateral, the relevant Income Record Date and the proposed Alternative Collateral;

(d)   Lender, acting reasonably, has determined that such Alternative Collateral is acceptable to it and Borrower shall have delivered or delivers such Alternative Collateral to Lender; and

(e)   Lender has failed to make reasonable efforts to transfer Equivalent Non-Cash Collateral to Borrower prior to such Income Record Date,

Lender shall indemnify Borrower in respect of any cost, loss or damage (excluding any indirect or consequential loss or damage or any amount otherwise compensated by Lender, including pursuant to paragraphs 6.3 and/or 9.3) suffered by Borrower that it would not have suffered had the relevant Equivalent Non-Cash Collateral been transferred to Borrower prior to such Income Record Date.

6.5   **Income in the form of Securities**

Where Income, in the form of securities, is paid in relation to any Loaned Securities or Collateral, such securities shall be added to such Loaned Securities or Collateral (and shall constitute Loaned Securities or Collateral, as the case may be, and be part of the relevant Loan) and will not be delivered to Lender, in the case of Loaned Securities, or to Borrower, in the case of Collateral, until the end of the relevant Loan, provided that the Lender or Borrower (as the case may be) fulfils its obligations under paragraph 5.4 or 5.5 (as applicable) with respect to the additional Loaned Securities or Collateral, as the case may be.

6.6   **Exercise of voting rights**

Where any voting rights fall to be exercised in relation to any Loaned Securities or Collateral, neither Borrower, in the case of Equivalent Securities, nor Lender, in the case of Equivalent Collateral, shall have any obligation to arrange for voting rights of that kind to be exercised in accordance with the instructions of the other Party in relation to the Securities borrowed by it or transferred to it by way of Collateral, as the case may be, unless otherwise agreed between the Parties.

6.7   **Corporate actions**

Where, in respect of any Loaned Securities or any Collateral, any rights relating to conversion, sub-division, consolidation, pre-emption, rights arising under a takeover offer, rights to receive securities or a certificate which may at a future date be exchanged for securities or other rights, including those requiring election by the holder for the time being of such Securities or Collateral, become exercisable prior to the delivery of Equivalent Securities or Equivalent Collateral, then Lender or Borrower, as the case may be, may, within a reasonable time before the latest time for the exercise of the right or option give written notice to the other Party that on delivery of Equivalent Securities or Equivalent Collateral, as the case may be, it wishes to receive Equivalent Securities or Equivalent Collateral in such form as will arise if the right is exercised or, in the case of a right which may be exercised in more than one manner, is exercised as is specified in such written notice.

7.   **RATES APPLICABLE TO LOANED SECURITIES AND CASH COLLATERAL**

7.1   **Rates in respect of Loaned Securities**

In respect of each Loan, Borrower shall pay to Lender, in the manner prescribed in sub-paragraph 7.3, sums calculated by applying such rate as shall be agreed between the Parties from time to time to the daily Market Value of the Loaned Securities.

7.2   **Rates in respect of Cash Collateral**

Where Cash Collateral is deposited with Lender in respect of any Loan, Lender shall pay to Borrower, in the manner prescribed in paragraph 7.3, sums calculated by applying such rates as shall be agreed between the Parties from time to time to the amount of such Cash Collateral. Any such payment due to Borrower may be set-off against any payment due to Lender pursuant to paragraph 7.1.

7.3   **Payment of rates**

In respect of each Loan, the payments referred to in paragraph 7.1 and 7.2 shall accrue daily in respect of the period commencing on and inclusive of the Settlement Date and terminating on and exclusive of the Business Day upon which Equivalent Securities are delivered or Cash Collateral is repaid. Unless otherwise agreed, the sums so accruing in respect of each calendar month shall be paid in arrears by the relevant Party not later than the Business Day which is the tenth Business Day after the last Business Day of the calendar month to which such payments relate or such other date as the Parties shall from time to time agree.

8. DELIVERY OF EQUIVALENT SECURITIES

8.1 Lender's right to terminate a Loan

Subject to paragraph 11 and the terms of the relevant Loan, Lender shall be entitled to terminate a Loan and to call for the delivery of all or any Equivalent Securities at any time by giving notice on any Business Day of not less than the standard settlement time for such Equivalent Securities on the exchange or in the clearing organisation through which the Loaned Securities were originally delivered. Borrower shall deliver such Equivalent Securities not later than the expiry of such notice in accordance with Lender's instructions.

8.2 Borrower's right to terminate a Loan

Subject to the terms of the relevant Loan, Borrower shall be entitled at any time to terminate a Loan and to deliver all and any Equivalent Securities due and outstanding to Lender in accordance with Lender's instructions and Lender shall accept such delivery.

8.3 Delivery of Equivalent Securities on termination of a Loan

Borrower shall procure the Delivery of Equivalent Securities to Lender or deliver Equivalent Securities in accordance with this Agreement and the terms of the relevant Loan on termination of the Loan. For the avoidance of doubt any reference in this Agreement or in any other agreement or communication between the Parties (howsoever expressed) to an obligation to deliver or account for or act in relation to Loaned Securities shall accordingly be construed as a reference to an obligation to deliver or account for or act in relation to Equivalent Securities.

8.4 Delivery of Equivalent Collateral on termination of a Loan

On the date and time that Equivalent Securities are required to be delivered by Borrower on the termination of a Loan, Lender shall simultaneously (subject to paragraph 5.4 if applicable) repay to Borrower any Cash Collateral or, as the case may be, deliver Collateral equivalent to the Collateral provided by Borrower pursuant to paragraph 5 in respect of such Loan. For the avoidance of doubt any reference in this Agreement or in any other agreement or communication between the Parties (however expressed) to an obligation to deliver or account for or act in relation to Collateral shall accordingly be construed as a reference to an obligation to deliver or account for or act in relation to Equivalent Collateral.

8.5 Delivery of Letters of Credit

Where a Letter of Credit is provided by way of Collateral, the obligation to deliver Equivalent Collateral is satisfied by Lender delivering for cancellation the Letter of Credit so provided, or where the Letter of Credit is provided in respect of more than one Loan, by Lender consenting to a reduction in the value of the Letter of Credit.

8.6   **Delivery obligations to be reciprocal**

Neither Party shall be obliged to make delivery (or make a payment as the case may be) to the other unless it is satisfied that the other Party will make such delivery (or make an appropriate payment as the case may be) to it. If it is not so satisfied (whether because an Event of Default has occurred in respect of the other Party or otherwise) it shall notify the other Party and unless that other Party has made arrangements which are sufficient to assure full delivery (or the appropriate payment as the case may be) to the notifying Party, the notifying Party shall (provided it is itself in a position, and willing, to perform its own obligations) be entitled to withhold delivery (or payment, as the case may be) to the other Party until such arrangements to assure full delivery (or the appropriate payment as the case may be) are made.

9. **FAILURE TO DELIVER**

9.1   **Borrower's failure to deliver Equivalent Securities**

If Borrower fails to deliver Equivalent Securities in accordance with paragraph 8.3 Lender may:

(a)   elect to continue the Loan (which, for the avoidance of doubt, shall continue to be taken into account for the purposes of paragraph 5.4 or 5.5 as applicable); or

(b)   at any time while such failure continues, by written notice to Borrower declare that that Loan (but only that Loan) shall be terminated immediately in accordance with paragraph 11.2 as if (i) an Event of Default had occurred in relation to the Borrower, (ii) references to the Termination Date were to the date on which notice was given under this sub-paragraph, and (iii) the Loan were the only Loan outstanding. For the avoidance of doubt, any such failure shall not constitute an Event of Default (including under paragraph 10.1(i)) unless the Parties otherwise agree.

9.2   **Lender's failure to deliver Equivalent Collateral**

If Lender fails to deliver Equivalent Collateral comprising Non-Cash Collateral in accordance with paragraph 8.4 or 8.5, Borrower may:

(a)   elect to continue the Loan (which, for the avoidance of doubt, shall continue to be taken into account for the purposes of paragraph 5.4 or 5.5 as applicable); or

(b)   at any time while such failure continues, by written notice to Lender declare that that Loan (but only that Loan) shall be terminated immediately in accordance with paragraph 11.2 as if (i) an Event of Default had occurred in relation to the Lender, (ii) references to the Termination Date were to the date on which notice was given under this sub-paragraph, and (iii) the Loan were the only Loan outstanding. For the avoidance of doubt, any such failure shall not constitute an Event of Default (including under paragraph 10.1(i)) unless the Parties otherwise agree.

9.3 Failure by either Party to deliver

Where a Party (the *Transferor*) fails to deliver Equivalent Securities or Equivalent Collateral by the time required under this Agreement or within such other period as may be agreed between the Transferor and the other Party (the *Transferee*) and the Transferee:

(a)   incurs interest, overdraft or similar costs and expenses; or

(b)   incurs costs and expenses as a direct result of a Buy-in exercised against it by a third party,

then the Transferor agrees to pay within one Business Day of a demand from the Transferee and hold harmless the Transferee with respect to all reasonable costs and expenses listed in sub-paragraphs (a) and (b) above properly incurred which arise directly from such failure other than (i) such costs and expenses which arise from the negligence or wilful default of the Transferee and (ii) any indirect or consequential losses.

10. EVENTS OF DEFAULT

10.1   Each of the following events occurring and continuing in relation to either Party (the *Defaulting Party*, the other Party being the *Non-Defaulting Party*) shall be an Event of Default but only (subject to sub-paragraph 10.1(d)) where the Non-Defaulting Party serves written notice on the Defaulting Party:

(a)   Borrower or Lender failing to pay or repay Cash Collateral or to deliver Collateral on commencement of the Loan under paragraph 5.1 or to deliver further Collateral under paragraph 5.4 or 5.5;

(b)   Lender or Borrower failing to comply with its obligations under paragraph 6.2 or 6.3 upon the due date and not remedying such failure within three Business Days after the Non-Defaulting Party serves written notice requiring it to remedy such failure;

(c)   Lender or Borrower failing to pay any sum due under paragraph 9.1(b), 9.2(b) or 9.3 upon the due date;

(d)   an Act of Insolvency occurring with respect to Lender or Borrower, provided that, where the Parties have specified in paragraph 5 of the Schedule that Automatic Early Termination shall apply, an Act of Insolvency which is the presentation of a petition for winding up or any analogous proceeding or the appointment of a liquidator or analogous officer of the Defaulting Party shall not require the Non-Defaulting Party to serve written notice on the Defaulting Party (*Automatic Early Termination*);

(e)   any warranty made by Lender or Borrower in paragraph 13 or paragraphs 14(a) to 14(d) being incorrect or untrue in any material respect when made or repeated or deemed to have been made or repeated;

Appendices

(f) Lender or Borrower admitting to the other that it is unable to, or it intends not to, perform any of its obligations under this Agreement and/or in respect of any Loan where such failure to perform would with the service of notice or lapse of time constitute an Event of Default;

(g) all or any material part of the assets of Lender or Borrower being transferred or ordered to be transferred to a trustee (or a person exercising similar functions) by a regulatory authority pursuant to any legislation;

(h) Lender (if applicable) or Borrower being declared in default or being suspended or expelled from membership of or participation in, any securities exchange or suspended or prohibited from dealing in securities by any regulatory authority, in each case on the grounds that it has failed to meet any requirements relating to financial resources or credit rating; or

(i) Lender or Borrower failing to perform any other of its obligations under this Agreement and not remedying such failure within 30 days after the Non-Defaulting Party serves written notice requiring it to remedy such failure.

10.2 Each Party shall notify the other (in writing) if an Event of Default or an event which, with the passage of time and/or upon the serving of a written notice as referred to above, would be an Event of Default, occurs in relation to it.

10.3 The provisions of this Agreement constitute a complete statement of the remedies available to each Party in respect of any Event of Default.

10.4 Subject to paragraphs 9 and 11, neither Party may claim any sum by way of consequential loss or damage in the event of failure by the other Party to perform any of its obligations under this Agreement.

11. CONSEQUENCES OF AN EVENT OF DEFAULT

11.1 If an Event of Default occurs in relation to either Party then paragraphs 11.2 to 11.7 below shall apply.

11.2 The Parties' delivery and payment obligations (and any other obligations they have under this Agreement) shall be accelerated so as to require performance thereof at the time such Event of Default occurs (the date of which shall be the *Termination Date*) so that performance of such delivery and payment obligations shall be effected only in accordance with the following provisions.

(a) The Default Market Value of the Equivalent Securities and Equivalent Non-Cash Collateral to be delivered and the amount of any Cash Collateral (including sums accrued) to be repaid and any other cash (including interest accrued) to be paid by each Party shall be established by the Non-Defaulting Party in accordance with paragraph 11.4 and deemed as at the Termination Date.

(b) On the basis of the sums so established, an account shall be taken (as at the Termination Date) of what is due from each Party to the other under this Agreement (on the basis that each Party's claim against the other in respect of delivery of Equivalent Securities or Equivalent Non-Cash Collateral equal to the Default Market Value thereof) and the sums due from one Party shall be set off against the sums due from the other and only the balance of the account shall be payable (by the Party having the claim valued at the lower amount pursuant to the foregoing) and such balance shall be payable on the next following Business Day after such account has been taken and such sums have been set off in accordance with this paragraph. For the purposes of this calculation, any sum not denominated in the Base Currency shall be converted into the Base Currency at the Spot Rate prevailing at such dates and times determined by the Non-Defaulting Party acting reasonably.

(c) If the balance under sub-paragraph (b) above is payable by the Non-Defaulting Party and the Non-Defaulting Party had delivered to the Defaulting Party a Letter of Credit, the Defaulting Party shall draw on the Letter of Credit to the extent of the balance due and shall subsequently deliver for cancellation the Letter of Credit so provided.

(d) If the balance under sub-paragraph (b) above is payable by the Defaulting Party and the Defaulting Party had delivered to the Non-Defaulting Party a Letter of Credit, the Non-Defaulting Party shall draw on the Letter of Credit to the extent of the balance due and shall subsequently deliver for cancellation the Letter of Credit so provided.

(e) In all other circumstances, where a Letter of Credit has been provided to a Party, such Party shall deliver for cancellation the Letter of Credit so provided.

11.3 For the purposes of this Agreement, the *Default Market Value* of any Equivalent Collateral in the form of a Letter of Credit shall be zero and of any Equivalent Securities or any other Equivalent Non-Cash Collateral shall be determined in accordance with paragraphs 11.4 to 11.6 below, and for this purpose:

(a) the *Appropriate Market* means, in relation to securities of any description, the market which is the most appropriate market for securities of that description, as determined by the Non-Defaulting Party;

(b) the *Default Valuation Time* means, in relation to an Event of Default, the close of business in the Appropriate Market on the fifth dealing day after the day on which that Event of Default occurs or, where that Event of Default is the occurrence of an Act of Insolvency in respect of which under paragraph 10.1(d) no notice is required from the Non-Defaulting Party in order for such event to constitute an Event of Default, the close of business on the fifth dealing day after the day on which the Non-Defaulting Party first became aware of the occurrence of such Event of Default;

(c) *Deliverable Securities* means Equivalent Securities or Equivalent Non-Cash Collateral to be delivered by the Defaulting Party;

(d) *Net Value* means at any time, in relation to any Deliverable Securities or Receivable Securities, the amount which, in the reasonable opinion of the Non-Defaulting Party, represents their fair market value, having regard to such pricing sources and methods (which may include, without limitation, available prices for securities with similar maturities, terms and credit characteristics as the relevant Equivalent Securities or Equivalent Collateral) plus, in the case of Deliverable Securities, all Transaction Costs incurred or reasonably anticipated in connection with the purchase or sale of such securities;

(e) **Receivable Securities** means Equivalent Securities or Equivalent Non-Cash Collateral to be delivered to the Defaulting Party; and

(f) **Transaction Costs** in relation to any transaction contemplated in paragraph 11.4 or 11.5 means the reasonable costs, commissions (including internal commissions), fees and expenses (including any mark-up or mark-down or premium paid for guaranteed delivery) incurred or reasonably anticipated in connection with the purchase of Deliverable Securities or sale of Receivable Securities, calculated on the assumption that the aggregate thereof is the least that could reasonably be expected to be paid in order to carry out the transaction.

11.4 If between the Termination Date and the Default Valuation Time:

(a) the Non-Defaulting Party has sold, in the case of Receivable Securities, or purchased, in the case of Deliverable Securities, securities which form part of the same issue and are of an identical type and description as those Equivalent Securities or that Equivalent Collateral, (and regardless as to whether or not such sales or purchases have settled) the Non-Defaulting Party may elect to treat as the Default Market Value:

(i) in the case of Receivable Securities, the net proceeds of such sale after deducting all Transaction Costs; provided that, where the securities sold are not identical in amount to the Equivalent Securities or Equivalent Collateral, the Non-Defaulting Party may, acting in good faith, either (A) elect to treat such net proceeds of sale divided by the amount of securities sold and multiplied by the amount of the Equivalent Securities or Equivalent Collateral as the Default Market Value or (B) elect to treat such net proceeds of sale of the Equivalent Securities or Equivalent Collateral actually sold as the Default Market Value of that proportion of the Equivalent Securities or Equivalent Collateral, and, in the case of (B), the Default Market Value of the balance of the Equivalent Securities or Equivalent Collateral shall be determined separately in accordance with the provisions of this paragraph 11.4; or

(ii) in the case of Deliverable Securities, the aggregate cost of such purchase, including all Transaction Costs; provided that, where the securities purchased are not identical in amount to the Equivalent Securities or Equivalent Collateral, the Non-Defaulting Party may, acting in good faith, either (A) elect to treat such aggregate cost divided by the amount of securities purchased and multiplied by the amount of the Equivalent Securities or Equivalent Collateral as the Default Market Value or (B) elect to treat the aggregate cost of purchasing the Equivalent Securities or Equivalent Collateral actually purchased as the Default Market Value of that proportion of the Equivalent Securities or Equivalent Collateral, and, in the case of (B), the Default Market Value of the balance of the Equivalent Securities or Equivalent Collateral shall be determined separately in accordance with the provisions of this paragraph 11.4;

(b) the Non-Defaulting Party has received, in the case of Deliverable Securities, offer quotations or, in the case of Receivable Securities, bid quotations in respect of securities of the relevant description from two or more market makers or regular dealers in the Appropriate Market in a commercially reasonable size (as determined by the Non-Defaulting Party) the Non-Defaulting Party may elect to treat as the Default Market Value of the relevant Equivalent Securities or Equivalent Collateral:

(i) the price quoted (or where more than one price is so quoted, the arithmetic mean of the prices so quoted) by each of them for, in the case of Deliverable Securities, the sale by the relevant market marker or dealer of such securities or, in the case of Receivable Securities, the purchase by the relevant market maker or dealer of such securities, provided that such price or prices quoted may be adjusted in a commercially reasonable manner by the Non-Defaulting Party to reflect accrued but unpaid coupons not reflected in the price or prices quoted in respect of such Securities;

(ii) after deducting, in the case of Receivable Securities or adding in the case of Deliverable Securities the Transaction Costs which would be incurred or reasonably anticipated in connection with such transaction.

11.5 If, acting in good faith, either (A) the Non-Defaulting Party has endeavoured but been unable to sell or purchase securities in accordance with paragraph 11.4(a) above or to obtain quotations in accordance with paragraph 11.4(b) above (or both) or (B) the Non-Defaulting Party has determined that it would not be commercially reasonable to sell or purchase securities at the prices bid or offered or to obtain such quotations, or that it would not be commercially reasonable to use any quotations which it has obtained under paragraph 11.4(b) above the Non-Defaulting Party may determine the Net Value of the relevant Equivalent Securities or Equivalent Collateral (which shall be specified) and the Non-Defaulting Party may elect to treat such Net Value as the Default Market Value of the relevant Equivalent Securities or Equivalent Collateral.

11.6 To the extent that the Non-Defaulting Party has not determined the Default Market Value in accordance with paragraph 11.4, the Default Market Value of the relevant Equivalent Securities or Equivalent Collateral shall be an amount equal to their Net Value at the Default Valuation Time; provided that, if at the Default Valuation Time the Non-Defaulting Party reasonably determines that, owing to circumstances affecting the market in the Equivalent Securities or Equivalent Collateral in question, it is not reasonably practicable for the Non-Defaulting Party to determine a Net Value of such Equivalent Securities or Equivalent Collateral which is commercially reasonable (by reason of lack of tradable prices or otherwise), the Default Market Value of such Equivalent Securities or Equivalent Collateral shall be an amount equal to their Net Value as determined by the Non-Defaulting Party as soon as reasonably practicable after the Default Valuation Time.

Appendices

Other costs, expenses and interest payable in consequence of an Event of Default

11.7 The Defaulting Party shall be liable to the Non-Defaulting Party for the amount of all reasonable legal and other professional expenses incurred by the Non-Defaulting Party in connection with or as a consequence of an Event of Default, together with interest thereon at such rate as is agreed by the Parties and specified in paragraph 10 of the Schedule or, failing such agreement, the overnight London Inter Bank Offered Rate as quoted on a reputable financial information service (*LIBOR*) as at 11.00 a.m., London time, on the date on which it is to be determined or, in the case of an expense attributable to a particular transaction and, where the Parties have previously agreed a rate of interest for the transaction, that rate of interest if it is greater than LIBOR. Interest will accrue daily on a compound basis.

Set-off

11.8 Any amount payable to one Party (the *Payee*) by the other Party (the *Payer*) under paragraph 11.2(b) may, at the option of the Non-Defaulting Party, be reduced by its set-off against any amount payable (whether at such time or in the future or upon the occurrence of a contingency) by the Payee to the Payer (irrespective of the currency, place of payment or booking office of the obligation) under any other agreement between the Payee and the Payer or instrument or undertaking issued or executed by one Party to, or in favour of, the other Party. If an obligation is unascertained, the Non-Defaulting Party may in good faith estimate that obligation and set off in respect of the estimate, subject to accounting to the other Party when the obligation is ascertained. Nothing in this paragraph shall be effective to create a charge or other security interest. This paragraph shall be without prejudice and in addition to any right of set-off, combination of accounts, lien or other right to which any Party is at any time otherwise entitled (whether by operation of law, contract or otherwise).

12. TAXES

Withholding, gross-up and provision of information

12.1 All payments under this Agreement shall be made without any deduction or withholding for or on account of any Tax unless such deduction or withholding is required by any Applicable Law.

12.2 Except as otherwise agreed, if the paying Party is so required to deduct or withhold, then that Party (*Payer*) shall:

   (a) promptly notify the other Party (*Recipient*) of such requirement;

   (b) pay or otherwise account for the full amount required to be deducted or withheld to the relevant authority;

   (c) upon written demand of Recipient, forward to Recipient documentation reasonably acceptable to Recipient, evidencing such payment to such authorities; and

   (d) other than in respect of any payment made by Lender to Borrower under paragraph 6.3, pay to Recipient, in addition to the payment to which Recipient is otherwise entitled under this Agreement, such additional amount as is necessary to ensure that the amount actually received by Recipient (after taking account of such withholding or deduction) will equal the amount Recipient would have received had no such deduction or withholding been required; provided Payer will not be required to pay any additional amount to Recipient under this sub-paragraph (d) to the extent it would not be required to be paid but for the failure by Recipient to comply with or perform any obligation under paragraph 12.3.

12.3 Each Party agrees that it will upon written demand of the other Party deliver to such other Party (or to any government or other taxing authority as such other Party directs), any form or document and provide such other cooperation or assistance as may (in either case) reasonably be required in order to allow such other Party to make a payment under this Agreement without any deduction or withholding for or on account of any Tax or with such deduction or withholding at a reduced rate (so long as the completion, execution or submission of such form or document, or the provision of such cooperation or assistance, would not materially prejudice the legal or commercial position of the Party in receipt of such demand). Any such form or document shall be accurate and completed in a manner reasonably satisfactory to such other Party and shall be executed and delivered with any reasonably required certification by such date as is agreed between the Parties or, failing such agreement, as soon as reasonably practicable.

Stamp Tax

12.4 Unless otherwise agreed, Borrower hereby undertakes promptly to pay and account for any Stamp Tax chargeable in connection with any transaction effected pursuant to or contemplated by this Agreement (other than any Stamp Tax that would not be chargeable but for Lender's failure to comply with its obligations under this Agreement).

12.5 Borrower shall indemnify and keep indemnified Lender against any liability arising as a result of Borrower's failure to comply with its obligations under paragraph 12.4.

Sales Tax

12.6 All sums payable by one Party to another under this Agreement are exclusive of any Sales Tax chargeable on any supply to which such sums relate and an amount equal to such Sales Tax shall in each case be paid by the Party making such payment on receipt of an appropriate Sales Tax invoice.

Retrospective changes in law

12.7 Unless otherwise agreed, amounts payable by one Party to another under this Agreement shall be determined by reference to Applicable Law as at the date of the relevant payment and no adjustment shall be made to amounts paid under this Agreement as a result of:

(a) any retrospective change in Applicable Law which is announced or enacted after the date of the relevant payment; or

(b) any decision of a court of competent jurisdiction which is made after the date of the relevant payment (other than where such decision results from an action taken with respect to this Agreement or amounts paid or payable under this Agreement).

Appendices

13. **LENDER'S WARRANTIES**

    Each Party hereby warrants and undertakes to the other on a continuing basis to the intent that such warranties shall survive the completion of any transaction contemplated herein that, where acting as a Lender:

    (a) it is duly authorised and empowered to perform its duties and obligations under this Agreement;

    (b) it is not restricted under the terms of its constitution or in any other manner from lending Securities in accordance with this Agreement or from otherwise performing its obligations hereunder;

    (c) it is absolutely entitled to pass full legal and beneficial ownership of all Securities provided by it hereunder to Borrower free from all liens, charges and encumbrances; and

    (d) it is acting as principal in respect of this Agreement, other than in respect of an Agency Loan.

14. **BORROWER'S WARRANTIES**

    Each Party hereby warrants and undertakes to the other on a continuing basis to the intent that such warranties shall survive the completion of any transaction contemplated herein that, where acting as a Borrower:

    (a) it has all necessary licences and approvals, and is duly authorised and empowered, to perform its duties and obligations under this Agreement and will do nothing prejudicial to the continuation of such authorisation, licences or approvals;

    (b) it is not restricted under the terms of its constitution or in any other manner from borrowing Securities in accordance with this Agreement or from otherwise performing its obligations hereunder;

    (c) it is absolutely entitled to pass full legal and beneficial ownership of all Collateral provided by it hereunder to Lender free from all liens, charges and encumbrances;

    (d) it is acting as principal in respect of this Agreement; and

    (e) it is not entering into a Loan for the primary purpose of obtaining or exercising voting rights in respect of the Loaned Securities.

15. **INTEREST ON OUTSTANDING PAYMENTS**

    In the event of either Party failing to remit sums in accordance with this Agreement such Party hereby undertakes to pay to the other Party upon demand interest (before as well as after judgment) on the net balance due and outstanding, for the period commencing on and inclusive of the original due date for payment to (but excluding) the date of actual payment, in the same currency as the principal sum and at the rate referred to in paragraph 11.7. Interest will accrue daily on a compound basis and will be calculated according to the actual number of days elapsed. No interest shall be payable under this paragraph in respect of any day on which one Party endeavours to make a payment to the other Party but the other Party is unable to receive it.

16. **TERMINATION OF THIS AGREEMENT**

Each Party shall have the right to terminate this Agreement by giving not less than 15 Business Days' notice in writing to the other Party (which notice shall specify the date of termination) subject to an obligation to ensure that all Loans which have been entered into but not discharged at the time such notice is given are duly discharged in accordance with this Agreement.

17. **SINGLE AGREEMENT**

Each Party acknowledges that, and has entered into this Agreement and will enter into each Loan in consideration of and in reliance upon the fact that, all Loans constitute a single business and contractual relationship and are made in consideration of each other. Accordingly, each Party agrees:

(a) to perform all of its obligations in respect of each Loan, and that a default in the performance of any such obligations shall constitute a default by it in respect of all Loans, subject always to the other provisions of the Agreement; and

(b) that payments, deliveries and other transfers made by either of them in respect of any Loan shall be deemed to have been made in consideration of payments, deliveries and other transfers in respect of any other Loan.

18. **SEVERANCE**

If any provision of this Agreement is declared by any judicial or other competent authority to be void or otherwise unenforceable, that provision shall be severed from the Agreement and the remaining provisions of this Agreement shall remain in full force and effect. The Agreement shall, however, thereafter be amended by the Parties in such reasonable manner so as to achieve as far as possible, without illegality, the intention of the Parties with respect to that severed provision.

19. **SPECIFIC PERFORMANCE**

Each Party agrees that in relation to legal proceedings it will not seek specific performance of the other Party's obligation to deliver Securities, Equivalent Securities, Collateral or Equivalent Collateral but without prejudice to any other rights it may have.

20. **NOTICES**

20.1 Any notice or other communication in respect of this Agreement may be given in any manner set forth below to the address or number or in accordance with the electronic messaging system details set out in paragraph 5 of the Schedule and will be deemed effective as indicated:

(a) if in writing and delivered in person or by courier, on the date it is delivered;

(b) if sent by facsimile transmission, on the date that transmission is received by a responsible employee of the recipient in legible form (it being agreed that the burden of proving receipt will be on the sender and will not be met by a transmission report generated by the sender's facsimile machine);

(c) if sent by certified or registered mail (airmail, if overseas) or the equivalent (return receipt requested), on the date that mail is delivered or its delivery is attempted; or

(d) if sent by electronic messaging system, on the date that electronic message is received,

unless the date of that delivery (or attempted delivery) or the receipt, as applicable, is not a Business Day or that communication is delivered (or attempted) or received, as applicable, after the Close of Business on a Business Day, in which case that communication shall be deemed given and effective on the first following day that is a Business Day.

20.2 Either Party may by notice to the other change the address or facsimile number or electronic messaging system details at which notices or other communications are to be given to it.

21. ASSIGNMENT

21.1 Subject to paragraph 21.2, neither Party may charge, assign or otherwise deal with all or any of its rights or obligations hereunder without the prior consent of the other Party.

21.2 Paragraph 21.1 shall not preclude a party from charging, assigning or otherwise dealing with all or any part of its interest in any sum payable to it under paragraph 11.2(b) or 11.7.

22. NON-WAIVER

No failure or delay by either Party (whether by course of conduct or otherwise) to exercise any right, power or privilege hereunder shall operate as a waiver thereof nor shall any single or partial exercise of any right, power or privilege preclude any other or further exercise thereof or the exercise of any other right, power or privilege as herein provided.

23. GOVERNING LAW AND JURISDICTION

23.1 This Agreement and any non-contractual obligations arising out of or in connection with this Agreement shall be governed by, and shall be construed in accordance with, English law.

23.2 The courts of England have exclusive jurisdiction to hear and decide any suit, action or proceedings, and to settle any disputes or any non-contractual obligation which may arise out of or in connection with this Agreement (respectively, **Proceedings** and **Disputes**) and, for these purposes, each Party irrevocably submits to the jurisdiction of the courts of England.

23.3 Each Party irrevocably waives any objection which it might at any time have to the courts of England being nominated as the forum to hear and decide any Proceedings and to settle any Disputes and agrees not to claim that the courts of England are not a convenient or appropriate forum.

23.4 Each Party hereby respectively appoints the person identified in paragraph 7 of the Schedule pertaining to the relevant Party as its agent to receive on its behalf service of process in the courts of England. If such an agent ceases to be an agent of a Party, the relevant Party shall promptly appoint, and notify the other Party of the identity of its new agent in England.

24. TIME

Time shall be of the essence of the Agreement.

25. RECORDING

The Parties agree that each may record all telephone conversations between them.

26. WAIVER OF IMMUNITY

Each Party hereby waives all immunity (whether on the basis of sovereignty or otherwise) from jurisdiction, attachment (both before and after judgement) and execution to which it might otherwise be entitled in any action or proceeding in the courts of England or of any other country or jurisdiction relating in any way to this Agreement and agrees that it will not raise, claim or cause to be pleaded any such immunity at or in respect of any such action or proceeding.

27. MISCELLANEOUS

27.1 This Agreement constitutes the entire agreement and understanding of the Parties with respect to its subject matter and supersedes all oral communication and prior writings with respect thereto.

27.2 The Party (the **Relevant Party**) who has prepared the text of this Agreement for execution (as indicated in paragraph 9 of the Schedule) warrants and undertakes to the other Party that such text conforms exactly to the text of the standard form Global Master Securities Lending Agreement (2009 version) posted by the International Securities Lending Association on its website except as notified by the Relevant Party to the other Party in writing prior to the execution of this Agreement.

27.3 Unless otherwise provided for in this Agreement, no amendment in respect of this Agreement will be effective unless in writing (including a writing evidenced by a facsimile transmission) and executed by each of the Parties or confirmed by an exchange of telexes or electronic messages on an electronic messaging system.

27.4 The Parties agree that where paragraph 11 of the Schedule indicates that this paragraph 27.4 applies, this Agreement shall apply to all loans which are outstanding as at the date of this Agreement and which are subject to the securities lending agreement or agreements specified in paragraph 11 of the Schedule, and such Loans shall be treated as if they had been entered into under this Agreement, and the terms of such loans are amended accordingly with effect from the date of this Agreement.

27.5 The Parties agree that where paragraph 12 of the Schedule indicates that this paragraph 27.5 applies, each may use the services of a third party vendor to automate the processing of Loans under this Agreement and that any data relating to such Loans received from the other Party may be disclosed to such third party vendors.

27.6 The obligations of the Parties under this Agreement will survive the termination of any Loan.

27.7 The warranties contained in paragraphs 13, 14 and 27.2 and in the Agency Annex will survive termination of this Agreement for so long as any obligations of either of the Parties pursuant to this Agreement remain outstanding.

27.8 Except as provided in this Agreement, the rights, powers, remedies and privileges provided in this Agreement are cumulative and not exclusive of any rights, powers, remedies and privileges provided by law.

27.9 This Agreement (and each amendment in respect of it) may be executed and delivered in counterparts (including by facsimile transmission), each of which will be deemed an original.

27.10 A person who is not a party to this Agreement has no right under the Contracts (Rights of Third Parties) Act 1999 to enforce any terms of this Agreement, but this does not affect any right or remedy of a third party which exists or is available apart from that Act.

EXECUTED by the **PARTIES**

SIGNED by)
)
duly authorised for and)
on behalf of)

SIGNED by)
)
duly authorised for and)
on behalf of)

SCHEDULE

1. **COLLATERAL**

    1.1   The securities, financial instruments and deposits of currency set out in the table below with a cross marked next to them are acceptable forms of Collateral under this Agreement.

    1.2   Unless otherwise agreed between the Parties, the Market Value of the Collateral delivered pursuant to paragraph 5 by Borrower to Lender under the terms and conditions of this Agreement shall on each Business Day represent not less than the Market Value of the Loaned Securities together with the percentage contained in the row of the table below corresponding to the particular form of Collateral, referred to in this Agreement as the *Margin*.

Security/Financial Instrument/ Deposit of Currency	Mark "X" if acceptable form of Collateral	Margin (%)

    1.3   Basis of Margin Maintenance:

    Paragraph 5.4 (aggregation) shall not apply* ☐

    Paragraph 5.4 (aggregation) applies unless the box is ticked.

    1.4   Paragraph 5.6 (netting of obligations to deliver Collateral and redeliver Equivalent Collateral) shall not apply* ☐

    Paragraph 5.6 (netting) applies unless the box is ticked

    1.5   For the purposes of Paragraph 5.8, Notification Time means by ☐ , London time.

    1.6   Paragraph 6.4 (indemnity for failure to redeliver Equivalent Non-Cash Collateral) shall not apply* ☐

    Paragraph 6.4 (indemnity for failure to redeliver Equivalent Non-Cash Collateral) applies unless the box is ticked.

---

* Delete as appropriate.
* Delete as appropriate.
* Delete as appropriate.

2. **BASE CURRENCY**

The Base Currency applicable to this Agreement is   provided that if that currency ceases to be freely convertible the Base Currency shall be [US Dollars] [Euro] [specify other currency]*

3. **PLACES OF BUSINESS**

(See definition of Business Day.)

4. **MARKET VALUE**

(See definition of Market Value.)

5. **EVENTS OF DEFAULT**

Automatic Early Termination shall apply in respect of Party A ☐

Automatic Early Termination shall apply in respect of Party B ☐

6. **DESIGNATED OFFICE AND ADDRESS FOR NOTICES**

(a) **Designated office of Party A:**

Address for notices or communications to Party A:

Address:

Attention:

Facsimile No:

Telephone No:

Electronic Messaging System Details:

(b) **Designated office of Party B:**

Address for notices or communications to Party B:

Address:

Attention:

Facsimile No:

Telephone No:

Electronic Messaging System Details:

7. (a) **Agent of Party A for Service of Process**

Name:

Address:

(b) **Agent of Party B for Service of Process**

Name:

Address:

8. **AGENCY**

– Party A [may][will always]* act as agent ☐

– Party B [may][will always]* act as agent ☐

– The Addendum for Pooled Principal Transactions may apply to Party A ☐

– The Addendum for Pooled Principal Transactions may apply to Party B ☐

9. **PARTY PREPARING THIS AGREEMENT**

Party A ☐

Party B ☐

10. **DEFAULT INTEREST**

Rate of default interest:

11. **EXISTING LOANS**

Paragraph 27.4 applies* ☐

[Overseas Securities Lenders Agreement dated]*

[Global Master Securities Lending Agreements dated]*

12. **AUTOMATION**

Paragraph 27.5 applies* ☐

---

* Delete as appropriate.

AGENCY ANNEX

1. TRANSACTIONS ENTERED INTO AS AGENT

1.1 Power for Lender to enter into Loans as agent

Subject to the following provisions of this paragraph, Lender may enter into Loans as agent (in such capacity, the *Agent*) for a third person (a *Principal*), whether as custodian or investment manager or otherwise (a Loan so entered into being referred to in this paragraph as an *Agency Loan*).

If the Lender has indicated in paragraph 8 of the Schedule that it may act as Agent, it must identify each Loan in respect of which it acts as Agent as an Agency Loan at the time it is entered into. If the Lender has indicated in paragraph 8 of the Schedule that it will always act as Agent, it need not identify each Loan as an Agency Loan.

1.2 [Pooled Principal transactions

The Lender may enter into an Agency Loan on behalf of more than [one] Principal and accordingly the addendum hereto for pooled principal transactions shall apply.]*

1.3 Conditions for Agency Loan

A Lender may enter into an Agency Loan if, but only if:

(a) it provides to Borrower, prior to effecting any Agency Loan, such information in its possession necessary to complete all required fields in the format generally used in the industry, or as otherwise agreed by Agent and Borrower (*Agreed Format*), and will use its best efforts to provide to Borrower any optional information that may be requested by the Borrower for the purpose of identifying such Principal (all such information being the *Principal Information*). Agent represents and warrants that the Principal Information is true and accurate to the best of its knowledge and has been provided to it by Principal;

(b) it enters into that Loan on behalf of a single Principal whose identity is disclosed to Borrower (whether by name or by reference to a code or identifier which the Parties have agreed will be used to refer to a specified Principal) either at the time when it enters into the Loan or before the Close of Business on the next Business Day after the date on which Loaned Securities are transferred to the Borrower in the Agreed Format or as otherwise agreed between the Parties; and

(c) it has at the time when the Loan is entered into actual authority to enter into the Loan and to perform on behalf of that Principal all of that Principal's obligations under the agreement referred to in paragraph 1.5(b) below.

Agent agrees that it will not effect any Loan with Borrower on behalf of any Principal unless Borrower has notified Agent of Borrower's approval of such Principal, and has not notified Agent that it has withdrawn such approval (such Principal, an *Approved Principal*), with both such notifications in the Agreed Format.

---

* Delete as appropriate.

Borrower acknowledges that Agent shall not have any obligation to provide it with confidential information regarding the financial status of its Principals; Agent agrees, however, that it will assist Borrower in obtaining from Agent's Principals such information regarding the financial status of such Principals as Borrower may reasonably request.

1.4 **Notification by Agent of certain events affecting any Principal**

Agent undertakes that, if it enters as agent into an Agency Loan, forthwith upon becoming aware:

(a) of any event which constitutes an Act of Insolvency with respect to the relevant Principal; or

(b) of any breach of any of the warranties given in paragraph 1.6 below or of any event or circumstance which results in any such warranty being untrue if repeated by reference to the then current facts,

it will inform Borrower of that fact and will, if so required by Borrower, furnish it with such additional information as it may reasonably request to the extent that such information is readily obtainable by Agent.

1.5 **Status of Agency Loan**

(a) Each Agency Loan shall be a transaction between the relevant Principal and Borrower and no person other than the relevant Principal and Borrower shall be a party to or have any rights or obligations under an Agency Loan. Without limiting the foregoing, Agent shall not be liable as principal for the performance of an Agency Loan, but this is without prejudice to any liability of Agent under any other provision of this Annex; and

(b) all the provisions of the Agreement shall apply separately as between Borrower and each Principal for whom the Agent has entered into an Agency Loan or Agency Loans as if each such Principal were a party to a separate agreement with Borrower in all respects identical with this Agreement other than this Annex and as if the Principal were Lender in respect of that agreement; provided that

(i) if there occurs in relation to the Agent an Event of Default or an event which would constitute an Event of Default if Borrower served written notice under any sub-clause of paragraph 10 of the Agreement, Borrower shall be entitled by giving written notice to the Principal (which notice shall be validly given if given in accordance with paragraph 20 of the Agreement) to declare that by reason of that event an Event of Default is to be treated as occurring in relation to the Principal. If Borrower gives such a notice then an Event of Default shall be treated as occurring in relation to the Principal at the time when the notice is deemed to be given; and

(ii) if the Principal is neither incorporated in nor has established a place of business in Great Britain, the Principal shall for the purposes of the agreement referred to in paragraph 1.5(b) above be deemed to have appointed as its agent to receive on its behalf service of process in the courts of England the Agent, or if the Agent is neither incorporated nor has established a place of business in Great Britain, the person appointed by the Agent for the purposes of this Agreement, or such other person as the Principal may from time to time specify in a written notice given to the other Party.

If Lender has indicated in paragraph 6 of the Schedule that it may enter into Loans as agent, the foregoing provisions of this paragraph do not affect the operation of the Agreement as between Borrower and Lender in respect of any Loans into which Lender may enter on its own account as principal.

1.6 **Warranty of authority by Lender acting as Agent**

Agent warrants to Borrower that it will, on every occasion on which it enters or purports to enter into a Loan as an Agency Loan, have been duly authorised to enter into that Loan and perform the obligations arising under such Loan on behalf of the Principal in respect of that Loan and to perform on behalf of the Principal all the obligations of that person under the agreement referred to in paragraph 1.5(b) above.

ADDENDUM FOR POOLED PRINCIPAL AGENCY LOANS

1. SCOPE

This addendum applies where the Agent wishes to enter into an Agency Loan on behalf of more than one Principal. The Agency Annex shall apply to such a Loan subject to the modifications and additional terms and conditions contained in paragraph 2 to 7 below.

2. INTERPRETATION

2.1 In this addendum:

(a) *Collateral Transfer* has the meaning given in paragraph 5.1 below;

(b) if at any time on any Business Day the aggregate Market Value of Posted Collateral in respect of all Agency Loans outstanding with a Principal under the Agreement exceeds the aggregate of the Required Collateral Value in respect of such Agency Loans, Borrower has a *Net Loan Exposure* to that Principal equal to that excess; if at any time on any Business Day the aggregate Market Value of Posted Collateral in respect of all Agency Loans outstanding under the Agreement with a Principal falls below the aggregate of the Required Collateral Value in respect of such Agency Loans, that Principal has a *Net Loan Exposure* to Borrower for such Agency Loans equal to that deficiency;

(c) *Pooled Principal* has the meaning given in paragraph 6(a) below; and

(d) *Pooled Loan* has the meaning given in paragraph 6(a) below.

3. MODIFICATIONS TO THE AGENCY ANNEX

3.1 Paragraph 1.3(b) of the Agency Annex is deleted and replaced by the following:

"it enters into that Loan on behalf of one or more Principals and at or before the time when it enters into the Loan it discloses to Borrower the identity and the jurisdiction of incorporation, organisation or establishment of each such Principal (and such disclosure may be made either directly or by reference to a code or identifier which the Parties have agreed will be used to refer to a specified Principal);".

3.2 Paragraph 1.3(c) of the Agency Annex is deleted and replaced by the following:

"it has at the time when the Loan is entered into actual authority to enter into the Loan on behalf of each Principal and to perform on behalf of each Principal all of that Principal's obligations under the Agreement".

4. ALLOCATION OF AGENCY LOANS

4.1 The Agent undertakes that if, at the time of entering into an Agency Loan, the Agent has not allocated the Loan to a Principal, it will allocate the Loan before the Settlement Date for that Agency Loan either to a single Principal or to several Principals, each of whom shall be responsible for only that part of the Agency Loan which has been allocated to it. Promptly following such allocation, the Agent shall notify Borrower of the Principal or Principals (whether by name or reference to a code or identifier which the Parties have agreed will be used to refer to a specified Principal) to which that Loan or part of that Loan has been allocated.

4.2   Upon allocation of a Loan in accordance with paragraph 4.1 above or otherwise, with effect from the date on which the Loan was entered into:

(a)   where the allocation is to a single Principal, the Loan shall be deemed to have been entered into between Borrower and that Principal; and

(b)   where the allocation is to two or more Principals, a separate Loan shall be deemed to have been entered into between Borrower and each such Principal with respect to the appropriate proportion of the Loan.

4.3   If the Agent shall fail to perform its obligations under paragraph 4.2 above then for the purposes of assessing any damage suffered by Borrower (but for no other purpose) it shall be assumed that, if the Loan concerned (to the extent not allocated) had been allocated in accordance with that paragraph, all the terms of the Loan would have been duly performed.

5.   ALLOCATION OF COLLATERAL

5.1   Unless the Agent expressly allocates (a) a deposit or delivery of Posted Collateral or (b) a repayment of Cash Collateral or a redelivery of Equivalent Collateral (each a *Collateral Transfer*) before such time, the Agent shall, at the time of making or receiving that Collateral Transfer, be deemed to have allocated any Collateral Transfer in accordance with paragraph 6.3 below.

5.2 (a) If the Agent has made a Collateral Transfer on behalf of more than one Pooled Principal, that Collateral Transfer shall be allocated in proportion to Borrower's Net Loan Exposure in respect of each Pooled Principal at the Agent's close of business on the Business Day before the Collateral Transfer is made; and

(b)   if the Agent has received a Collateral Transfer on behalf of more than one Pooled Principal, that Collateral Transfer shall be allocated in proportion to each Pooled Principal's Net Loan Exposure in respect of Borrower at the Agent's close of business on the Business Day before the Collateral Transfer is made.

(c)   Sub-paragraphs (a) and (b) shall not apply in respect of any Collateral Transfer which is effected or deemed to have been effected under paragraph 6.3 below.

6.   POOLED PRINCIPALS: REBALANCING OF MARGIN

6.1   Where the Agent acts on behalf of more than one Principal, the Parties may agree that, as regards all (but not some only) outstanding Agency Loans with those Principals, or with such of those Principals as they may agree (*Pooled Principals*, such Agency Loans being *Pooled Loans*), any Collateral Transfers are to be made on an aggregate net basis.

6.2   Paragraphs 6.3 to 6.5 below shall have effect for the purpose of ensuring that Posted Collateral is, so far as is practicable, transferred and held uniformly, as between the respective Pooled Principals, in respect of all Pooled Loans for the time being outstanding under the Agreement.

6.3   At or as soon as practicable after the Agent's close of business on each Business Day on which Pooled Loans are outstanding (or at such other times as the Parties may from time to time agree) there shall be effected such Collateral Transfers as shall ensure that immediately thereafter:

(a) in respect of all Pooled Principals which have a Net Loan Exposure to Borrower, the amount of Collateral then deliverable or Cash Collateral then payable by Borrower to each such Pooled Principal is equal to such proportion of the aggregate amount of Collateral then deliverable or Cash Collateral then payable, to all such Pooled Principals as corresponds to the proportion which the Net Loan Exposure of the relevant Pooled Principal bears to the aggregate of the Net Loan Exposures of all Pooled Principals to Borrower; and

(b) in respect of all Pooled Principals to which Borrower has a Net Loan Exposure, the aggregate amount of Equivalent Collateral then deliverable or repayable by each such Pooled Principal to Borrower is equal to such proportion of the aggregate amount of Equivalent Collateral then deliverable or repayable by all such Pooled Principals as corresponds to the proportion which the Net Loan Exposure of Borrower to the relevant Pooled Principal bears to the aggregate of the Net Loan Exposures of Borrower to all Pooled Principals.

6.4 Collateral Transfers effected under paragraph 6.3 shall be effected (and if not so effected shall be deemed to have been so effected) by appropriations made by the Agent and shall be reflected by entries in accounting and other records maintained by the Agent. Accordingly, it shall not be necessary for payments of cash or deliveries of Securities to be made through any settlement system for the purpose of such Collateral Transfers. Without limiting the generality of the foregoing, the Agent is hereby authorised and instructed by Borrower to do all such things on behalf of Borrower as may be necessary or expedient to effect and record the receipt on behalf of Borrower of cash and Securities from, and the delivery on behalf of Borrower of cash and Securities to, Pooled Principals in the course or for the purposes of any Collateral Transfer effected under that paragraph.

6.5 Promptly following the Collateral Transfers effected under paragraph 6.3 above, and as at the Agent's close of business on any Business Day, the Agent shall prepare a statement showing in respect of each Pooled Principal the amount of cash Collateral which has been paid, and the amount of non-cash Collateral of each description which have been transferred, by or to that Pooled Principal immediately after those Collateral Transfers. If Borrower so requests, the Agent shall deliver to Borrower a copy of the statement so prepared in a format and to a timetable generally used in the market.

7. WARRANTIES

7.1 The Agent warrants to Borrower that:

(a) all notifications provided to Borrower under paragraph 4.1 above and all statements provided to the other party under paragraph 6.5 above shall be complete and accurate in all material respects;

(b) at the time of allocating an Agency Loan in accordance with paragraph 4.1 above, each Principal or Principals to whom the Agent has allocated that Agency Loan or any part of that Agency Loan is duly authorised to enter into the Agency Loans contemplated by this Agreement and to perform its obligations thereunder; and

(c) at the time of allocating an Agency Loan in accordance with paragraph 4.1 above, no Event of Default or event which would constitute an Event of Default with the service of a Default Notice or other written notice under paragraph 14 of the Agreement has occurred in relation to any Principal or Principals to whom the Agent has allocated that Agency Loan or any part of that Agency Loan.

APPENDIX 3: A FACSIMILE OF THE EUROPEAN MASTER AGREEMENT REPRODUCED WITH THE KIND PERMISSION OF THE EUROPEAN BANKING FEDERATION

FBE

FEDERATION BANCAIRE DE L'UNION EUROPEENNE
BANKING FEDERATION OF THE EUROPEAN UNION
BANKENVEREINIGUNG DER EUROPÄISCHEN UNION

in co-operation with

EUROPEAN SAVINGS BANKS GROUP
GROUPEMENT EUROPEEN DES CAISSES D'EPARGNE
EUROPÄISCHE SPARKASSENVEREINIGUNG

EUROPEAN ASSOCIATION OF COOPERATIVE BANKS
GROUPEMENT EUROPEEN DES BANQUES COOPERATIVES
EUROPÄISCHE VEREINIGUNG DER GENOSSENSCHAFTSBANKEN

MASTER AGREEMENT FOR FINANCIAL TRANSACTIONS

GENERAL PROVISIONS
Edition 2004

1. Purpose, Structure, Interpretation

(1) Purpose, Applicability. The provisions set out in this document (the "General Provisions") are intended to govern financial transactions (each a "Transaction") under any Master Agreement for Financial Transactions (each a "Master Agreement") based on the form published by the Banking Federation of the European Union ("FBE"). The provisions of a Master Agreement shall apply to the extent that they are incorporated by the parties into the terms of a Transaction or type of Transactions between them.

(2) Structure. A Master Agreement consists of (i) an agreement between the parties thereto providing a basis for Transactions between them (the "Special Provisions"), (ii) these General Provisions, (iii) any annexes thereto (each an "Annex"), being Annexes concerning particular types of Transactions ("Product Annexes") or concerning other matters and (iv) any supplements to the Product Annexes (each a "Supplement"). If no Special Provisions have been agreed, these General Provisions (together with, if applicable, any Annexes and any Supplements thereto) shall constitute a Master Agreement governing all Transactions into the terms of which they have been incorporated. Each Master Agreement and the terms agreed in respect of all Transactions there under shall collectively be referred to herein as the "Agreement".

(3) Interpretation. In the event of any conflict between different parts of the Agreement, (i) any Annex shall prevail over the General Provisions, (ii) the Special Provisions shall prevail over the General Provisions and any Annex and (iii) the terms agreed in respect of an individual Transaction shall, in respect of that Transaction only, prevail over all other terms of the Agreement. Unless otherwise specified, all references herein or in any Annex to Sections are to Sections of these General Provisions or such Annex, respectively. Certain expressions used in the Agreement are defined at the places indicated in the Index of Defined Terms published by the FBE in connection with these General Provisions.

(4) Single Agreement. The Agreement constitutes a single contractual relationship. Accordingly, (i) each obligation of a party under any Transaction is incurred and performed in consideration of the obligations incurred and to be performed by the other party under all Transactions, and (ii) unless otherwise agreed, a failure by a party to perform an obligation under any Transaction shall constitute a failure to perform under the Agreement as a whole.

The parties enter into the Master Agreement between them and each Transaction there under in reliance on these principles, which they consider fundamental to their risk assessment.

(5) Modifications. Any modification of these General Provisions or any modified or new Annex which the FBE may promulgate in the future may become effective between the parties to a Master Agreement by each party notifying its acceptance in the manner designated by the FBE.

2. Transactions

(1) Form. A Transaction may be entered into orally or by any other means of communication.

(2) Confirmation. Upon the parties having agreed on a Transaction each party shall promptly send to the other a confirmation (a "Confirmation") of such Transaction in the

manner specified in Section 8(1). The absence of either or both Confirmations shall not affect the validity of the Transaction.

3. Payments, Deliveries and Related Definitions

(1) Date, Place, Manner. Each party shall make the payments and deliveries to be made by it at the time, date and place and to the account agreed in respect of the Transaction concerned and in the manner customary for payments or deliveries of the relevant kind. Each payment shall be made in the currency agreed in respect thereof (the "Contractual Currency"), free of all costs and in funds which are freely available on the due date. Each party may change its account for receiving a payment or delivery by giving notice to the other at least ten Business Days prior to the scheduled date for the relevant payment or delivery, unless the other party reasonably objects to such change and gives timely notice thereof.

(2) Transfer of Title. Retransfer of Securities.

(a) Transfer of Title. Unless otherwise agreed, any delivery or transfer of securities or other financial instruments ("Securities") or any other assets (including, in respect of Derivative Transactions, any other underlying assets of such Transactions) by a party to the other pursuant to the Agreement shall constitute a transfer to such other party of the unrestricted title to such Securities and/or assets or, if customary in the place where delivery is to be effected, of a legal position (such as a co-ownership interest in a collective holding of Securities, the position as beneficiary of a trust or another form of beneficial ownership) which is the functional equivalent of such title (including, in each case, an unrestricted right to dispose of such Securities and/or assets) and not the creation of a security interest; the use of the terms "margin" or "substitution" shall not be construed as indicating an agreement to the contrary. The transferor of any Securities and/or assets shall, accordingly, (i) not retain in respect of those Securities and/or assets any ownership interest, security interest or right to dispose and (ii) execute all documents reasonably required to effect such full transfer. As far as transfer of Securities is concerned, if registered Securities are to be transferred, the transferee may dispose of the Securities received before the transfer is entered into the relevant register; if the entry depends upon a circumstance beyond the transferor's reasonable control, the transferor does not warrant that such entry will be effected.

(b) Retransfer of Securities. An obligation to return or retransfer any Securities is an obligation to transfer Securities of the same kind as such Securities. Securities are "of the same kind" as other Securities if they are of the same issuer and the same type and nominal value and represent identical rights as such other Securities; if all such other Securities have been redeemed, redenominated, exchanged, converted, subdivided, consolidated or been the subject of a capital increase, capital reduction, call on partly paid securities or event similar to any of the foregoing, Securities "of the same kind" means the amount of Securities, money and other property (together "Substitute Assets") received in respect of such other Securities as a result of such event (provided that if any sum had to be paid in order to receive such Substitute Assets, an obligation to transfer them shall be conditional upon payment by the transferee of such sum to the transferor).

(3) Conditions Precedent. Each payment or delivery obligation of a party is subject to the conditions precedent that (i) no Event of Default or event which by the lapse of time or the giving of notice (or both) may become an Event of Default with respect to the other party has occurred and is continuing and (ii) no notice of termination has been given in respect of the relevant Transaction because of a Change of Circumstances.

(4) Payment Netting. If on any date both parties would otherwise be required to make payments in the same currency in respect of the same Transaction, the mutual payment obligations shall automatically be set off against each other and the party owing the higher amount shall pay to the other the difference between the amounts owed. The parties may agree that this principle shall apply in respect of two or more Transactions or one or more types of Transactions or that it shall apply also in respect of mutual obligations to deliver assets which are fungible with each other. If and so long as a single currency can be expressed in different currency units (such as the euro unit and national currency units under the principles governing the transition to European Economic and Monetary Union), the principle set forth in the first sentence of this subsection shall apply only if both payments are to be made in the same unit.

(5) Late Payment. If in respect of a Transaction a party fails to make a payment to the other when due (and, for the avoidance of doubt, without being entitled to withhold such payment), interest, payable on demand, shall accrue (before and after judgment) at the Default Rate on the amount outstanding, calculated for the period from (and including) the due date to (but excluding) the day on which such payment is received. "Default Rate" means the higher of (a) the Interbank Rate and (b) the cost to the other party, as certified by it, of funding the relevant amount, in each case plus any interest surcharge which may be agreed in the Special Provisions. "Interbank Rate" means the interbank offered interest rate charged by prime banks to each other for overnight deposits at the place of payment and in the currency of the amount outstanding for each day on which interest is to be charged (being, if an amount in euros is outstanding, the Euro Overnight Index Average ("EONIA") Rate calculated by the European Central Bank).

(6) Business Day Convention. If any payment or delivery date, any determination or valuation date, any commencement or termination date or any exercise date agreed between the parties which is deemed to be a Business Day is not a Business Day, payments, deliveries, determinations or valuations shall be made or, as the case may be, the commencement date, the termination date or the exercise date shall be deemed to occur, as elected in respect of the relevant Transaction, on (a) the immediately preceding Business Day ("Preceding"), (b) the immediately following Business Day ("Following"), or (c) the immediately following Business Day, unless such day falls in the next calendar month, in which case the relevant payment, delivery, determination or valuation shall be made

or, as the case may be, the relevant commencement date, termination date or exercise date shall be deemed to occur on the immediately preceding Business Day ("Modified Following" or "Modified"), provided that failing such election, (b) shall apply.

(7) *Business Day Definition*. "Business Day" means (a) in relation to any payment in euros a day on which all relevant parts of TARGET are operational to effect such a payment, (b) in relation to any payment in any other currency a day (other than a Saturday or a Sunday) on which commercial banks are open for business (including payments in the currency concerned as well as dealings in foreign exchange and foreign currency deposits) in the place(s) agreed in relation to the relevant Transaction or, if not so agreed, in the place where the relevant account is located and, if different, in the principal financial centre, if any, of the currency of such payment, (c) in relation to any delivery of Securities, (i) where a Transaction is to be settled through a securities settlement system, a day on which such securities settlement system is open for business in the place where delivery of the Securities is to be effected, and (ii) where a Transaction is to be settled in a way other than (i), a day (other than a Saturday or a Sunday) on which commercial banks are open for business in the place where delivery of the Securities is to be effected, (d) in relation to any delivery of any assets other than Securities, a day (other than a Saturday or a Sunday) on which commercial banks are open for business in the place where delivery of the relevant assets is to be effected or any other day agreed between the parties in the Confirmation of the relevant Transactions or otherwise, (e) in relation to any valuation, a day on which an up-to-date valuation based on the agreed price sources can reasonably be carried out, and (f) in relation to any notice or other communication, a day (other than a Saturday or Sunday) on which commercial banks are open for business in the city specified in the address provided by the recipient pursuant to Section 8(1).

(8) *Market Value*. "Market Value" means in respect of any Securities as of any time on any date, (a) the price for such Securities then quoted through and obtainable from a generally recognised source agreed to by the parties and (b) failing such agreement or such quotation (i) if the Securities are listed on a stock exchange and not then suspended, their price last quoted on such exchange; (ii) if the Securities are not so listed, but have, on the main market on which they are traded, the price published or made public by a central bank or an entity of undisputed authority on such day, such price last published or made public; and (iii) in any other case, the average of the bid and offer prices for such Securities, as of such time on such date, as established by two leading market participants other than the parties, in each of the cases listed in (a) and (b) together with (if not included in such price) any interest accrued on such Securities as of that date.

4. Taxes

(1) *Withholding Tax*. If a party is or will be obliged to deduct or withhold an amount for or on account of any tax or other duty from a payment which it is to make, it shall pay to the other party such additional amounts as are necessary to ensure that such other party receives the full amount to which it would have been entitled at the time of such payment if no deduction or withholding had been required. This shall not apply if the tax or duty concerned is imposed or levied (a) by or on behalf or for the account of the jurisdiction (or a tax authority of or resident in the jurisdiction) in which the Booking Office of the payee (or its place of residence, if the payee is an individual) is located, (b) pursuant to (directly or indirectly) an obligation imposed by a treaty to which such jurisdiction is a party, or by a regulation or directive enacted under such treaty, or (c) because the payee has failed to perform its obligation under Section l0(4)(b).

(2) *Documentary Tax*. Subject to Section 10(2), each party shall pay any stamp, documentary or similar tax or duty payable with respect to the Agreement (a "Documentary Tax") and imposed upon it in the jurisdiction in which its Booking Office or place of residence is located and shall indemnify the other party for any Documentary Tax payable in such jurisdiction and imposed upon the other party, unless the Booking Office of such other party (or its place of residence, if the other party is an individual) is also located in such jurisdiction.

5. Representations

(1) *Representations*. Each party represents to the other, as of the date on which it enters into a Master Agreement and as of each date on which a Transaction is entered into, that:

(a) *Status*. It is validly existing under the laws of its organisation or incorporation;

(b) *Corporate Action*. It is duly authorised to execute and deliver, and perform its obligations under, the Agreement;

(c) *No Violation or Conflict*. The execution, delivery and performance of the Agreement do not violate or conflict with any provision of law, judgment or government or court order applicable to it, or any provision of its constitutional documents;

(d) *Consents*. All governmental and other consents which are required to be obtained by it with respect to the Agreement have been obtained and are in full force and effect;

(e) *Obligations Binding*. Its obligations under the Agreement are legal, valid and binding;

(f) *Absence of Certain Events*. No Event of Default or event which by the lapse of time or the giving of notice (or both) may become an Event of Default and, to its knowledge, no Change of Circumstances with respect to it has occurred and is continuing;

(g) *Absence of Litigation*. There is not pending or, to its knowledge, threatened against it any action, suit or proceeding before any court, tribunal, arbitrator or governmental or other authority that is likely to affect the legality, validity, binding effect or enforceability against it of the Agreement or its ability to perform its obligations under the Agreement;

(h) *No Reliance*. It has the necessary knowledge and experience to assess the benefits and risks incurred in each Transaction and has not relied for such purpose on the other party;

(i) *Margin*. It has full title to the Securities transferred, as margin or collateral, to the other party under the Agreement and that such Securities shall be free and clear of any lien, security interest or any other right which may affect the right of the other party to dispose freely of such Securities.

(2) *Applicability to Guarantor*. If a third person specified in the Special Provisions or in a Confirmation as Guarantor (a "Guarantor") has, in an instrument specified in the Special Provisions or otherwise agreed between the parties, given a guarantee or other credit support in respect of any obligations of either party under the Agreement (a "Guarantee"), then the representations of such party in respect of itself and the Agreement pursuant to subsection 1(a) through (i) shall *mutatis mutandis* apply also to the Guarantor and the Guarantee.

6. Termination

(1) *Termination due to an Event of Default*.

(a) *Event of Default*. The occurrence of any of the following events in respect of a party shall constitute an event of default ("Event of Default"):

(i) *Failure to Pay or Deliver*. The party fails to make, when due, any payment or delivery under the Agreement and such failure continues for three Business Days after the day on which notice of such failure is given to the party;

(ii) *Failure to Provide or Return Margin or Collateral*. The party fails to provide or return, when due, margin or collateral required to be provided or returned by it under the Agreement;

(iii) *Other Breach of Agreement*. The party fails to perform, when due, any other obligation under the Agreement and such failure continues for thirty days after the day on which notice of such failure is given to the party;

(iv) *Misrepresentation*. Any representation by the party in the Agreement proves to have been incorrect on the date as of which it was made and the other party determines in good faith that, as a result thereof (or of the matters of fact or law which were not correctly stated), the balance of its risks and benefits under the Agreement is materially adversely affected;

(v) *Default under Specified Transactions*. If the parties have, in the Special Provisions, specified any Transactions ("Specified Transactions") to which this Section 6(l)(a)(v) will apply, the party fails to make a payment or a delivery under any such Specified Transaction and such failure (A) results in the liquidation or early termination of, or an acceleration of obligations under, such Specified Transaction or (B) continues beyond any applicable grace period (or, if there is no such period, for at least three Business Days) after the last payment or delivery date of such Specified Transaction, provided, in either case, that such failure is not caused by circumstances which, if occurring under the Agreement, would constitute a Change of Circumstances as described in subsection 2(a)(ii);

(vi) *Cross Default*. Any payment obligation of the party in respect of borrowed money (whether incurred by it as primary or secondary obligor and whether arising from one or more contracts or instruments) in an aggregate amount of not less than the applicable Default Threshold (A) has become, or may be declared, due and payable prior to the stated maturity thereof as a result of any default or similar event (however described) which has occurred in respect of the party or (B) has not been performed for more than seven days after its due date and, in either case, the other party has reasonable grounds to conclude that the financial obligations of the party under the Agreement may not be performed. "Default Threshold" means the amount specified as such in the Special Provisions in respect of a party or, in the absence of such specification, 1 per cent. of such party's equity (meaning the sum of its capital, disclosed reserves and retained earnings, determined in accordance with generally accepted accounting principles applicable to that party, as reported in its most recent published audited financial statements);

(vii) *Restructuring Without Assumption*. The party is subject to a Corporate Restructuring and the Successor Entity fails to assume all obligations of such party under the Agreement. "Corporate Restructuring" means, with respect to such party, any consolidation or amalgamation with, or merger into, or demerger, or transfer of all or substantially all assets to, another person, or an agreement providing for any of the foregoing, and "Successor Entity" means the person which results from, survives or is the transferee in, such Corporate Restructuring;

(viii) *Insolvency Events*. (1) The party is dissolved or has a resolution passed for its dissolution (other than, in either case, pursuant to a Corporate Restructuring resulting in a solvent Successor Entity); (2) the party commences an Insolvency Proceeding against itself or takes any corporate action to authorize such Insolvency Proceeding; (3) a governmental or judicial authority or self-regulatory organisation having jurisdiction over the party in a Specified Jurisdiction (a "Competent Authority") commences an Insolvency Proceeding with respect to the party; (4) a Competent Authority takes any action under any bankruptcy, insolvency or similar law or any banking, insurance or similar law governing the operation of the party which is likely to prevent the party from performing when due its payment or delivery obligations under the Agreement; (5) a person other than a Competent Authority commences an Insolvency Proceeding against the party in a Specified Jurisdiction and such action (A) results in a Judgment of Insolvency, or (B) is not dismissed or stayed within thirty days following the action or event commencing the Insolvency Proceeding, unless the commencement of such Proceedings by such person or under the given circumstances is obviously inadmissible or frivolous; (6) the party is bankrupt or insolvent as defined under any bankruptcy or insolvency law applicable to it in a

Specified Jurisdiction; (7) the party makes a general assignment for the benefit of, or enters into a composition or amicable settlement with, its creditors generally; (8) the party is generally unable to pay its debts as they fall due; or (9) the party causes or is subject to any event which, under the laws of the Specified Jurisdiction, has an effect which is analogous to any of the events specified in Nos. (1) to (8). "Insolvency Proceeding" means a mandatory or voluntary proceeding seeking a judgment, order or arrangement of insolvency, bankruptcy, composition, amicable settlement, rehabilitation, reorganisation, administration, dissolution or liquidation with respect to a party or its assets or seeking the appointment of a receiver, liquidator, administrator or similar official for such party or for all or any substantial part its assets under any bankruptcy, insolvency or similar law or any banking, insurance or similar law governing the operation of the party; the expression does not include a solvent corporate reorganisation. An Insolvency Proceeding is "commenced" if a petition to conduct such proceeding is presented to or filed with, or (where no such petition is required) a decision to conduct such proceeding is taken by, a competent court, authority, corporate body or person. "Judgment of Insolvency" means any judgment, order or arrangement instituting an Insolvency Proceeding. "Specified Jurisdiction" in relation to a party means the jurisdiction of that party's organisation, incorporation, principal office or residence and any additional jurisdiction that may be specified with respect to that party in the Special Provisions;

(ix) *Repudiation of Obligations.* The party declares that it will not perform any material obligation under the Agreement or under any Specified Transaction (otherwise than as part of a bona fide dispute as to the existence, nature or extent of such obligation);

(x) *Guarantee Ineffective.* A Guarantee given with respect to the party is not in full force and effect, except if it has ceased to be in effect (i) in accordance with its terms, (ii) upon satisfaction of all of the party's obligations secured by such Guarantee or (iii) with the consent of the other party.

(b) *Termination.* If an Event of Default occurs with respect to a party (the "Defaulting Party") and is continuing, the other party (the "Non-Defaulting Party") may, by giving not more than twenty days' notice specifying the relevant Event of Default, terminate all outstanding Transactions, but not part thereof only, with effect as from a date (the "Early Termination Date") to be designated by it in such notice. Notwithstanding the foregoing, unless otherwise specified in the Special Provisions, all Transactions shall terminate, and the Early Termination Date shall occur, automatically in the case of an Event of Default mentioned in paragraph (a)(viii)(l), (2), (3), (5)(A) or, to the extent analogous thereto, (9) as of the time immediately preceding the relevant event or action.

(2) *Termination due to Change of Circumstances.*

(a) *Change of Circumstances.* The occurrence of any of the following events or circumstances in respect of a party shall constitute a change of circumstances ("Change of Circumstances"):

(i) *Tax Event.* As a result of the entry into force of any new law or regulation or of any change in law or any other provision of mandatory effect or change in the application or official interpretation thereof occurring after the date on which a Transaction is entered into, or as a result of a Corporate Restructuring of either party not falling under subsection 1(a)(vii), the party would, on or before the next due date relating to such Transaction, (A) be required to pay additional amounts pursuant to Section 4(1) with regard to a payment which it is obliged to make, other than a payment of interest pursuant to Section 3(5), or (B) receive a payment, other than a payment of interest pursuant to Section 3(5), from which an amount is required to be deducted for or on account of a tax or duty and no additional amount is required to be paid in respect of such tax or duty under Section 4(1), other than by reason of Section 4(l)(c);

(ii) *Illegality, Impossibility.* As a result of the entry into force of any new law or regulation or of any change in law or any other provision of mandatory effect or change in the application or official interpretation thereof or, if so specified in the Special Provisions, as a result of an Impossibility Event, in each case occurring after the date on which a Transaction is entered into,

it becomes, or is likely to become, unlawful or impossible for the party (A) to make, or receive, a payment or delivery in respect of such Transaction when due or to punctually comply with any other material obligation under the Agreement relating to such Transaction or (B) to perform any obligation to provide margin or collateral as and when required to be provided by it under the Agreement; "Impossibility Event" means any catastrophe, armed conflict, act of terrorism, riot or any other circumstance beyond the party's reasonable control affecting the operations of the party;

(iii) *Credit Event upon Restructuring.* If the party is subject to a Corporate Restructuring, the creditworthiness of the Successor Entity is materially weaker than that of the party immediately before the Corporate Restructuring.

(b) *Termination.* If a Change of Circumstances occurs with respect to a party (the "Affected Party"), the Affected Party in the case of paragraph (a)(i) or (ii), and the other party (the "Non-Affected Party") in the case of paragraph (a)(ii) or (iii) may, subject to the limitations set forth below, by giving not more than twenty days' notice, terminate the Transaction(s) affected by such change, with effect as from a date (the "Early Termination Date") to be designated by it in such notice, it being understood that, in the case of paragraph (a)(iii), all Transactions will be deemed so affected. If, without prejudice to any agreement between the parties on the provision of margin or collateral, either party determines that as a result of such termination its credit exposure to the other party is significantly increased, it may, not later than one week after the effective date of the notice of termination, by giving notice to the other party require such other party to provide, within one week after receipt of such last-mentioned notice, margin or collateral reasonably acceptable to it in such amount as to be at least equal to the increase in credit exposure under the Agreement, as determined by it. In the cases of paragraph (a)(i) and (ii), the right to terminate shall be subject to the following limitations: (i) the Early Termination Date may not be earlier than thirty days before the date on which the Change of Circumstances becomes effective, and (ii) the Affected Party may, unless it would otherwise be required to pay additional amounts as contemplated by paragraph (a)(i)(A), give notice of termination only after a period of thirty days has expired following a notice by it informing the other party of such event and if the situation (if capable of remedy) has not been remedied within such period (by way of an agreed transfer of the affected Transactions to another Booking Office or otherwise).

(3) *Applicability to Guarantor*. If a Guarantee has been given with respect to a party and any of the events described in subsections l(a)(iii) through (ix) and 2(a) occurs with respect to the relevant Guarantor or such Guarantee, the occurrence of such event shall have the same effect as if it had occurred with respect to such party or the Agreement, respectively.

(4) *Effect of Termination*. In the event of a termination pursuant to this Section 6, neither party shall be obliged to make any further payment or delivery under the terminated Transaction(s) which would have become due on or after the Early Termination Date or to provide or return margin or collateral which would otherwise be required to be provided or returned under the Agreement and related to the terminated Transaction(s). These obligations shall be replaced by an obligation of either party to pay the Final Settlement Amount in accordance with Section 7.

(5) *Event of Default and Change of Circumstances*. If an event or circumstance which would otherwise constitute or give rise to an Event of Default also constitutes a Change of Circumstances as referred to in subsection 2(a)(ii), it will be treated as a Change of Circumstances and will not constitute an Event of Default, except that any event as described in subsection 1(a)(viii) will always be treated as an Event of Default and not as a Change of Circumstances.

7.   Final Settlement Amount

(1) *Calculation*.

(a) *Procedure and Bases of Calculation*. Upon termination pursuant to Section 6, the Non-Defaulting Party or, as the case may be, the Non-Affected Party or, if there are two Affected Parties, each party (each the "Calculation Party") shall as soon as reasonably possible calculate the Final Settlement Amount.

"Final Settlement Amount" means, subject to subsection 2(b)(i), the amount determined by the Calculation Party to be equal to, as of the Early Termination Date, (A) the sum of all Transaction Values which are positive for it, the Amounts Due owed to it and its Margin Claims less (B) the sum of the absolute amounts of all Transaction Values which are negative for it, the Amounts Due owed by it and the Margin Claims of the other party;

"Amounts Due" owed by a party means the sum of (i) any amounts that were required to be paid by such party under any Transaction, but not paid, (ii) the Default Value, as of the agreed delivery date, of each asset that was required to be delivered by such party under any Transaction, but not delivered (in either case regardless of whether or not the party was entitled to withhold such payment or delivery, by virtue of Section 3(3) or for any other reason) and (iii) interest on the amounts specified in (i) and (ii) from (and including) the due date of the relevant payment or delivery to (but excluding) the Early Termination Date at the Interbank Rate or, if Section 3(5) is applicable, the Default Rate; Margin Claims shall be disregarded for the determination of Amounts Due;

"Default Value" means, in respect of any assets (including Securities or, in respect of Derivative Transactions, any other underlying assets of such Transactions) on any given date, an amount equal to (A) if the assets are or were to be delivered by the Calculation Party, the net proceeds (after deducting fees and expenses) which the Calculation Party has or could have reasonably received when selling assets of the same kind and quantity in the market on such date, (B) if the assets are or were to be delivered to the Calculation Party, the cost (including fees and expenses) which the Calculation Party has or would have reasonably incurred in purchasing assets of the same kind and quantity in the market on such date, and (C) if a market price for such assets cannot be determined, an amount which the Calculation Party determines in good faith to be its total losses and costs (or gains, in which case expressed as a negative number) in connection with such assets;

"Margin Claims" means, as of the Early Termination Date, the aggregate of the amount of cash paid and the Default Value of Securities transferred, as margin or collateral, by a party and not repaid or retransferred to it, plus any interest accrued on such cash at the rate agreed in respect thereof;

"Transaction Value" means, with respect to any Transaction or group of Transactions, an amount equal to, at the option of the Calculation Party, (i) the loss incurred (expressed as a positive number) or gain realized (expressed as a negative number) by the Calculation Party as a result of the termination of such Transaction(s), or (ii) the arithmetic mean of the quotations for replacement or hedge transactions on the Quotation Date obtained by the Calculation Party from not less than two leading market participants. In the case of (ii), each such quotation shall be expressed as the amount which the market participant would pay or receive on the Quotation Date if such market participant were to assume, as from the Quotation Date, the rights and obligations of the other party (or their economic equivalent) under the relevant Transaction(s); the resulting amount shall be expressed as a positive number if it would be payable to the market participant, and shall otherwise be expressed as a negative number. If, in such case, no or only one quotation can reasonably be obtained, the Transaction Value shall be determined pursuant to (i).

"Quotation Date" means the Early Termination Date, except that in the event of an automatic termination as provided in Section 6(1)(b), the Quotation Date shall be the date designated as such by the Non-Defaulting Party, which shall be not later than the fifth Business Day after the day on which the Non-Defaulting Party became aware of the event which caused such automatic termination.

(b) *Conversion.* Any Amounts Due, Default Value, Margin Claims and Transaction Value not denominated in the Base Currency shall be converted into the Base Currency at the Applicable Exchange Rate. "Base Currency" means the euro, unless otherwise agreed. "Applicable Exchange Rate" means the arithmetic mean of the respective rates at which the person calculating or converting an amount pursuant to the Agreement is reasonably able to (i) purchase the relevant other currency with, and (ii) sell such currency for, the Base Currency on the date as of which such amount is calculated or converted.

(2) *Payment Obligations.*

(a) *One Calculation Party.* If one party only acts as Calculation Party, the Final Settlement Amount, as calculated by it, shall be paid (i) to that party by the other party if it is a positive number and (ii) by that party to the other party if it is a negative number; in the latter case the amount payable shall be the absolute value of the Final Settlement Amount.

(b) *Two Calculation Parties.* If both parties act as Calculation Party and their calculations of the Final Settlement Amount differ from each other, the Final Settlement Amount shall (i) be equal to one-half of the difference between the amounts so calculated by both parties (such difference being, for the avoidance of doubt, the sum of the absolute values of such amounts if one is positive and the other negative) and (ii) be paid by the party which has calculated a negative or the lower positive amount.

(3) *Notification and Due Date.*

(a) *Notification.* The Calculation Party shall notify as soon as reasonably possible the other party of the Final Settlement Amount calculated by it and provide to such other party a statement setting forth in reasonable detail the basis upon which the Final Settlement Amount was determined.

(b) *Due Date.* The Final Settlement Amount shall be payable immediately upon receipt of the notification mentioned in paragraph (a) if termination occurs as a result of an Event of Default, and otherwise within two Business Days following such receipt, but in either case not before the Early Termination Date. It shall bear interest as from the Early Termination Date to the date on which the payment is due at the Interbank Rate and thereafter at the Default Rate.

(4) *Set-Off.* The Non-Defaulting Party may set off its obligation (if any) to pay the Final Settlement Amount against any actual or contingent claims ("Counterclaims") which it has against the Defaulting Party on any legal grounds whatsoever (including by virtue of any financing or other contract). For the purpose of calculating the value of the Counterclaims, the Non-Defaulting Party shall, (i) to the extent that they are not payable in the Base Currency, convert them into the Base Currency at the Applicable Exchange Rate, (ii) to the extent that they are contingent or unascertained, take into account for such calculation their potential amount, if ascertainable, or otherwise a reasonable estimate thereof, (iii) to the extent that they are claims other than for the payment of money, determine their value in money and convert them into a money claim expressed in the Base Currency and (iv) to the extent that they are not yet due and payable, determine their present value (also having regard to interest claims). The provisions of this subsection 4 relating to Counterclaims against a Defaulting Party shall apply *mutatis mutandis* to Counterclaims against an Affected Party if termination occurred pursuant to Section 6(2)(a)(ii) or (iii).

8. Notices

(1) *Manner of Giving Notices.* Unless otherwise specified in the Agreement, any notice or other communication under the Agreement shall be made by letter, telex, telefax or any electronic messaging system agreed to by the parties in the Special Provisions to the address (if any) previously specified by the addressee.

(2) *Effectiveness.* Every notice or other communication made in accordance with subsection 1 shall be effective (a) if made by letter or telefax, upon receipt by the addressee, (b) if made by telex, upon receipt by the sender of the addressee's answerback at the end of transmission, and (c) if made by an electronic messaging system, upon receipt of that electronic message, provided that if, in any such case, such notice or other communication is not received on a Business Day or is received after the close of business on a Business Day, it shall take effect on the first following day that is a Business Day.

(3) *Change of Address.* Either party may by notice to the other change the address, telex or telefax number or electronic messaging system details at which notices or other communications are to be given to it.

9. Booking Offices

(1) *Extent of Obligations.* If a party enters into a Transaction through a Booking Office other than its principal office, its obligations in respect of that Transaction shall constitute obligations of such party as a whole, to the same extent as if they had been entered through such party's principal office. Such party shall not be obliged, however, to perform such obligations through any of its other offices if performance through that Booking Office is unlawful or impossible by virtue of any of the events described in Section 6(2)(a)(ii).

(2) *Change of Booking Office.* Neither party may change a Booking Office without the prior written consent of the other party.

(3) *Definition.* "Booking Office" of a party means the office agreed by the parties through which such party is acting for the relevant Transaction, provided that if no such office is agreed in respect of a party, such party's principal office (or, in the absence of a principal office, such party's registered office or place of residence) shall be deemed to be the Booking Office.

10. Miscellaneous

(1) Transfer of Rights and Obligations. No rights or obligations under the Agreement may be transferred, charged or otherwise disposed of to or in favour of any third person without the prior consent of the other party given in the manner specified in Section 8(1), except that no such consent shall be required in the case of a transfer of all or substantially all assets of a party in connection with a Corporate Restructuring which does not involve a change of the tax status relevant to the Agreement and does not otherwise adversely affect the interests of the other party to any significant extent.

The limitation provided in the preceding sentence shall not apply to a party's right to receive the Final Settlement Amount or to be indemnified pursuant to subsection 2.

(2) Expenses. A Defaulting Party and a party failing to make a payment or delivery when due shall on demand indemnify the other party for all reasonable expenses, including legal fees, incurred by the other party for the enforcement or protection of its rights under the Agreement in connection with an Event of Default or such failure.

(3) Recording. Each party (i) may electronically or otherwise record telephone conversations of the parties in connection with the Agreement or any potential Transaction, (ii) shall give notice of such potential recording to its relevant personnel and obtain any consent that may be legally required before permitting such personnel to conduct such telephone conversations and (iii) agrees that recordings may be submitted in evidence in any Proceedings relating to the Agreement or any potential Transaction.

(4) Documents. So long as either party has or may have any obligation under the Agreement, each party shall, if it is reasonably able and legally in a position to do so and would not thereby materially prejudice its legal or commercial position, promptly make available to the other or to any appropriate government or taxing authority any form, certificate or other document (properly completed and, where appropriate, certified) that is either (a) specified in the Agreement, or (b) reasonably requested in writing in order to allow the other party to make a payment under the Agreement without any deduction or withholding for or on account of any tax or other duty, or with such deduction or withholding at a reduced rate.

(5) Remedies. The rights and remedies provided in the Agreement are cumulative and not exclusive of any rights and remedies provided by law.

(6) No Waiver. A failure or delay in exercising (and any partial exercise of) any right or remedy under the Agreement shall not operate as a waiver (or partial waiver) of, and accordingly not preclude or limit any future exercise of, that right or remedy.

(7) Termination. The Agreement may be terminated by either party upon the giving of not less than twenty days' notice to the other party. Notwithstanding such notice, any Transaction then outstanding shall continue to be subject to the provisions of the Agreement and to that extent the effect of the termination shall occur only when all obligations under the last such Transaction shall have been performed.

(8) Contractual Currency. If for any reason a payment is made in a currency other than the Contractual Currency and the amount so paid, converted into the Contractual Currency at the exchange rate prevailing at the time of such payment for the sale of such other currency against the Contractual Currency, as reasonably determined by the payee, falls short of the amount in the Contractual Currency payable under the Agreement, the party owing such amount shall, as a separate and independent obligation, immediately compensate the other party for the shortfall.

(9) Previous Transactions. Transactions entered into prior to the effective date of a Master Agreement will be subject to such Master Agreement, individually or by category, to the extent provided in the Special Provisions.

(10) Agency Transactions.

(a) Conditions. A party may enter into a Transaction (an "Agency Transaction") as agent (the "Agent") for a third person (a "Principal") only if (i) the party has authority on behalf of that Principal to enter into the Transaction, to perform on behalf of that Principal all of that Principal's obligations and to accept performance of the obligations of the other party and receive all notices and other communications under the Agreement and (ii) when entering into the Transaction and in the relevant Confirmation the party specifies that it is acting as Agent in respect of the Transaction and discloses to the other party the identity of the Principal. If these conditions are not fully satisfied, the party shall be deemed to act as principal.

(b) Information on Certain Events. Each party undertakes that, if it enters as Agent into an Agency Transaction, forthwith upon becoming aware (i) of any event or circumstance which constitutes an event as described in Section 6(1)(a)(viii) with respect to the relevant Principal or (ii) of any breach of any of the representations given in Section 5 and paragraph (f) below or of any event or circumstance which has the result that any such representation would be incorrect on the date as of which it was made, it will inform the other party of that fact and will, if so required by the other party, furnish the other party with such additional information as the other party may reasonably request.

(c) Parties. Each Agency Transaction shall be a transaction solely between the relevant Principal and the other party. All provisions of the Agreement shall apply separately as between the other party and each Principal for whom the Agent has entered into an Agency Transaction, as if each such Principal were a party to a separate Agreement with the other party, except as provided in paragraph (d) below. A Process Agent appointed by the Agent shall be a Process Agent also for each Principal.

(d) Notice of Termination. If an Event of Default or a Change of Circumstances as described in Section 6(2)(a)(ii) or (iii) occurs with respect to the Agent, the other party may give notice pursuant to Section 6(1)(b) or 6(2)(b), respectively, to the Principal with the same effect as if an

Event of Default or Change of Circumstances, respectively, had occurred with respect to the Principal.

(e)   Own Account Transactions. The foregoing provisions do not affect the operation of the Agreement between the parties hereto in respect of any Transactions into which the Agent may enter on its own account as a principal.

(f)   Representation. Each party acting as Agent represents to the other in its own name and in the name of the Principal that it will, on each occasion on which it enters or purports to enter into an Agency Transaction, have the authority as described in subsection 10(a)(i) on behalf of the person whom it specifies as the Principal in respect of that Agency Transaction.

(11)   Severability. In the event that any provision of the Agreement is invalid, illegal or unenforceable under the law of any jurisdiction, the validity, legality and enforceability of the remaining provisions in the Agreement under the law of such jurisdiction, and the validity, legality and enforceability of such and any other provisions under the law of any other jurisdiction shall not in any way be affected thereby. The parties shall, in such event, in good faith negotiate a valid provision the economic effect of which comes as close as possible to that of the invalid, illegal or unenforceable provisions.

11.   Governing Law, Settlement of Disputes, Jurisdiction, Arbitration

(1)   Governing Law. The Agreement shall be governed by and construed in accordance with the law specified in the Special Provisions or, failing such specification, the law of the country, if identical, in which both parties' principal offices are located when the Master Agreement between them is entered into.

(2)   Settlement of Disputes, Jurisdiction, Arbitration. Each party irrevocably agrees that in respect of any dispute arising under or related to the Agreement (i) the courts specified in the Special Provisions shall have non-exclusive jurisdiction and each party irrevocably submits to such non-exclusive jurisdiction, or (ii) if so specified in the Special Provisions, any such dispute shall be finally settled by one or more arbitrators appointed and proceeding in accordance with the rules of arbitration specified in the Special Provisions, each party agreeing to comply with such rules.

Failing either of such specifications, the courts having jurisdiction in the principal financial centre or, in the absence of a generally recognized financial centre, the capital city of the country whose law governs the Agreement shall have non-exclusive jurisdiction with respect to any suit, action or other proceeding relating to the Agreement (the "Proceedings") and each party irrevocably submits to such non-exclusive jurisdiction.

(3)   Service of Process. If so specified in the Special Provisions, each party appoints a process agent (the "Process Agent") to receive, for it and on its behalf, service of process in any Proceedings. If for any reason a party's Process Agent is unable to act as such, such party shall promptly notify the other party and within thirty days appoint a substitute process agent which is acceptable to the other party.

(4)   Waiver of Immunity. The Agreement constitutes a commercial agreement. To the fullest extent permitted by applicable law, each party waives, with respect to itself and its assets (irrespective of their use or intended use), all immunity on the grounds of sovereignty or otherwise from suit, execution or other legal process and agrees that it will not claim any such immunity in any Proceedings.

FEDERATION BANCAIRE DE L'UNION EUROPEENNE
BANKING FEDERATION OF THE EUROPEAN UNION
BANKENVEREINIGUNG DER EUROPÄISCHEN UNION

in co-operation with

EUROPEAN SAVINGS BANKS GROUP
GROUPEMENT EUROPEEN DES CAISSES D'EPARGNE
EUROPÄISCHE SPARKASSENVEREINIGUNG

EUROPEAN ASSOCIATION OF COOPERATIVE BANKS
GROUPEMENT EUROPEEN DES BANQUES COOPERATIVES
EUROPÄISCHE VEREINIGUNG DER GENOSSENSCHAFTSBANKEN

MASTER AGREEMENT FOR FINANCIAL TRANSACTIONS

PRODUCT ANNEX FOR REPURCHASE TRANSACTIONS

Edition January 2001

This Annex supplements the General Provisions which form part of any Master Agreement for Financial Transactions based on the form published by the Banking Federation of the European Union.

1. Purpose, Applicability

(1) Purpose. The purpose of this Annex ("Repurchase Annex") is to govern Transactions ("Repurchase Transactions") in which one party (the "Seller") sells to the other (the "Buyer") Securities against payment of an agreed price (the "Purchase Price") and in which the Buyer sells to the Seller Securities of the same kind and quantity as such Securities against payment of another agreed price for delivery and payment at a specified later date or on demand. Any reference in this Annex to a Transaction shall be construed as a reference to a Repurchase Transaction.

(2) Applicability. If this Annex forms part of a Master Agreement between any two parties, such Master Agreement (including this Annex) shall apply to any Repurchase Transaction between such parties which is to be conducted by each party through a Booking Office specified in such Master Agreement in respect of Repurchase Transactions.

2. Deliveries and Payments

(1) Purchase. On the settlement date agreed for the purchase of Securities by the Buyer under a Transaction (the "Purchase Date"), the Seller shall transfer to the Buyer the Securities sold in that Transaction (the "Purchased Securities") against simultaneous payment of the Purchase Price.

(2) Repurchase. On the settlement date agreed for the repurchase of the Purchased Securities (the "Repurchase Date"), the Buyer shall transfer to the Seller Securities of the same kind and quantity as the Purchased Securities against simultaneous payment of the Repurchase Price.

(3) Definitions, Interpretation. "Repurchase Price" means the sum of the Purchase Price and the Price Differential. "Price Differential" means for any Transaction the aggregate amount obtained by applying the pricing rate agreed for such Transaction and expressed as a percentage per annum (the "Pricing Rate") to the Purchase Price for the actual number of days during the period from (and including) the Purchase Date to (but excluding) the Repurchase Date, on a 360-day or 365-day basis in accordance with market practice or on any other basis agreed between the parties. A payment shall be "simultaneous" if it occurs as part of a delivery-versus-payment system or, should the use of such system in the given circumstances not be customary, if it occurs on the same day as the transfer of the relevant Securities. Any reference in this Annex to the Purchased Securities or other Securities in the context of the return or retransfer thereof, or to any rights or other assets to be transferred pursuant to Section 4(4), shall be construed so as to mean a reference to Securities, rights or assets of the same kind and quantity as (also referred to below as the "Equivalent" of) such Purchased Securities or other Securities, rights or assets, respectively.

Copyright © 2001 FBE

Product Annex for Repurchase Transactions - 2001

(4) *On Demand Transactions*. The parties may agree that Transactions are terminable on demand, in which case the Repurchase Date shall be the date specified in the demand notice sent by either party to the other, provided that the period between the taking effect of such notice and the Repurchase Date so specified shall be not less than the minimum period customarily required for the payment of money and the delivery of Securities of the relevant kind. In the absence of a demand notice, the Repurchase Date for a Transaction terminable on demand shall be the day which falls 364 days after the Purchase Date.

(5) *Late Payment*. If the Purchase Price or the Repurchase Price is not paid when due, the interest payable pursuant to Section 3(5) of the General Provisions shall be calculated at the higher of the Default Rate and the Pricing Rate, without prejudice to the application of Section 6(l)(a)(i) of the General Provisions.

(6) *Late Delivery*

(a) *Failure by Seller* If the Seller fails to transfer the Purchased Securities to the Buyer on the applicable Purchase Date, the Buyer may, at any time while such failure continues:

(i) if it has paid the Purchase Price to the Seller, require the Seller immediately to repay the sum so paid;

(ii) require the Seller to pay to the Buyer an amount equal to the excess, if any, of the Buyer's Borrowing Cost over the pro rata portion of the Price Differential attributable to the period of the delay, each calculated for the period from (and including) the Purchase Date to (but excluding) the earlier of the date on which the Purchased Securities are transferred to the Buyer and the Repurchase Date (which in the case of a Transaction terminable on demand shall be deemed to be the earliest date on which the Purchased Securities would be required to be returned following a demand by the Seller); "Borrowing Cost" of a party means the cost (including fees and expenses), as determined by such party, which such party has or would have reasonably incurred in borrowing the Equivalent of the Purchased Securities in the market for the relevant period; and

(iii) if the parties have not agreed on measures to promptly remedy the failure, give notice that the Repurchase Date shall be advanced so as to occur immediately, whereupon the mutual obligations originally agreed by the parties under the relevant Transaction shall be netted, so that no payments or deliveries are due except that the Seller shall pay to the Buyer (in addition to complying with its obligations pursuant to (i) and (ii), if applicable) an amount equal to the Price Differential for the period from (and including) the Purchase Date to (but excluding) the Repurchase Date so advanced.

(b) *Failure by Buyer*. If the Buyer fails to return the Purchased Securities to the Seller on the applicable Repurchase Date, the Seller may, at any time while such failure continues:

(i) if it has paid the Repurchase Price to the Buyer, require the Buyer immediately to repay the sum so paid;

(ii) require the Buyer to pay to the Seller an amount equal to the excess, if any, of the Seller's Borrowing Cost over the amount receivable if the Repurchase Price were placed on deposit at the Interbank Rate, each calculated for the period from (and including) the Repurchase Date to (but excluding) the date of actual return of the Purchased Securities or, if earlier, the date specified in the notice, if any, given pursuant to (iii); and

(iii) if the parties have not agreed on measures to promptly remedy the failure, give notice requiring cash settlement in lieu of delivery on a date to be specified in such notice, whereupon the obligations of the parties originally agreed in respect of the Repurchase Date shall cease, and the Buyer shall (A) pay to the Seller (in addition to complying with its obligations pursuant to (i) and (ii), if applicable) an amount equal to the excess, if any, of the Alternative Purchase Cost for such Securities over the Repurchase Price or, as the case may be, (B) be entitled to receive from the Seller the excess, if any, of the Repurchase Price over such Alternative Purchase Cost; "Alternative Purchase Cost" means the cost (including fees and expenses), as determined by the Seller, which the Seller has or would have reasonably incurred in purchasing the Equivalent of the Purchased Securities in the market on the date so specified for cash settlement.

(c) *Remedies* Beyond the remedies provided in this subsection 6, neither party shall, in the event of any failure by the other party to transfer or return Purchased Securities, be entitled to recover any additional damage as a consequence of such failure, and such failure shall not constitute an Event of Default under Section 6(l)(a)(iii) of the General Provisions. This paragraph (c) is without prejudice to any remedy available in the event of any failure by a party to perform any other obligation (including any obligation to make a payment under this subsection 6) when due.

(7) *Special Events* If, during the term of a Transaction and in respect of some or all of the Purchased Securities:

(i) a payment of any interest or dividend or any other distribution of money or other property by the issuer of the Purchased Securities (collectively a "Distribution", which term shall include a repayment of principal and a payment in the case of a capital reduction) would, as a result of any change in law or in the application or official interpretation thereof occurring after the date on which such Transaction is entered into, be subject to any deduction or withholding in respect of a tax or other duty or would give rise to a tax credit;

(ii) a notice of early redemption has been validly given;

(iii) a public redemption, exchange, conversion or compensation offer or a public purchase bid is made or announced;

(iv) subscription or other rights or assets which are not freely transferable are granted or distributed to the holders; or

(v) if specified in the Special Provisions, a tax credit or tax entitlement is attached to any interest or dividend paid to the holders (whether or not subparagraph (i) would otherwise apply) then, subject to any other agreement between the parties, the Repurchase Date for such Securities shall, automatically in the case of (v) and otherwise upon demand by either party, be advanced to the third Business Day before, in the case of (i), (ii) and (v), the expected payment or redemption date or before, in the case of (iii) and (iv), the last day on which such bid or offer may be accepted or the day on which such rights or assets are granted or distributed.

3. Substitution

(1) General Principle. The Seller may, at its cost and with the consent of the Buyer, substitute for any Purchased Securities other Securities ("New Securities") which at the time at which the parties agree to such substitution have a Market Value at least equal to the Market Value of the Purchased Securities for which they are substituted.

(2) No Novation. The substitution shall have no novation effect on the relevant Transaction, and the Transaction shall continue in effect, except that the New Securities will be deemed to be Purchased Securities instead of the Securities that are replaced.

(3) Simultaneous Retransfer. The substitution will be carried out by simultaneous transfer of the New Securities in exchange for the Purchased Securities to be replaced.

4. Distributions, Subscription Rights

(1) Cash Distributions. If during the term of a Transaction any Distribution of money is made by the issuer to the holders of the Purchased Securities, the Buyer shall pay to the Seller, on the date of such Distribution, an amount in the same currency as, and equal to, the amount received by the holders in respect of such Distribution.

(2) Withholding Taxes Tax Credits If a Distribution is subject to withholding tax and/or gives rise to a tax credit, the amount payable by the Buyer under subsection 1 shall be equal to the full amount to which the Seller would be entitled, as previously notified by it, in respect of such Distribution if it were the owner of the Purchased Securities, including the amount of (a) any applicable withholding tax to the extent that the Seller would be entitled to apply for an exemption from, or a refund of, such tax and (b) any tax credit available to the Seller.

(3) Subscription Rights if subscription rights which are freely transferable are granted with respect to the Purchased Securities, the Buyer shall transfer to the Seller, not later than on the third day on which such rights are traded, the Equivalent of the subscription rights attributable to such Purchased Securities. If the rights are not so transferred by such date, the Seller may purchase their Equivalent in the market for the account of the Buyer. Should the Seller be unable so to purchase the rights, it may require the Buyer to pay to it an amount equal to the Market Value of such rights prevailing on the next following trading day for such rights.

(4) Non-cash Distributions Any freely transferable bonus shares, non-cash Distributions and ancillary rights (other than subscription rights) which are issued, made or allotted with respect to the Purchased Securities during the term of a Transaction shall be transferred to the Seller on the Repurchase Date.

(5) Transfer Obligations For the avoidance of doubt, the provisions of subsections 1 through 4 shall apply whether or not the Buyer retains the ownership of the Purchased Securities during the term of the Transaction.

5. Specific Terms for Buy/Sell Back Transactions

(1) Applicability, Definitions Transactions shall be subject to this Section 5 if they are identified as Buy/Sell Back Transactions. "Buy/Sell Back Transactions" are Repurchase Transactions for which the Purchase Price and the Repurchase Price are each composed of (a) a price quoted exclusive of Accrued Interest (being the "Clean Price", payable on the Purchase Date, and the "Forward Price", also called "Sell Back Price", payable on the Repurchase Date) and (b) Accrued Interest, calculated as of the Purchase Date when payable together with the Clean Price and calculated as of the Repurchase Date when payable together with the Forward Price. "Accrued Interest" means the accrued portion, as of the relevant date of calculation, of the interest (if any) payable by the issuer of the Purchased Securities in respect of such Securities.

(2) Interpretation In the event of any conflict, this Section 5 shall, with respect to Buy/Sell Back Transactions, prevail over any other terms of this Annex. For Buy/Sell Back Transactions, (a) any reference in the Agreement to the Purchase Price shall be construed as referring to the Clean Price plus Accrued Interest paid or payable on the Purchase Date and (b) any reference in the Agreement to the Repurchase Price shall, notwithstanding the definition of that term in Section 2 (3), be construed as referring to the agreed Forward Price plus Accrued Interest paid or payable on the Repurchase Date or, as the case may be, to the adjusted Forward Price calculated pursuant to subsection 5 (to which no Accrued Interest shall be added).

(3) Confirmation the Confirmation of a Buy/Sell Back Transaction shall specify), the Forward Price and the Pricing Rate.

(4) Distributions Section 4(1) shall apply to Buy/Sell Back Transactions only if specifically so agreed.

(5) Adjusted Forward Price In relation to a date other than the originally agreed Repurchase Date, for example in relation to a Repurchase Date advanced in accordance with Section ^{2}(6)(a)(iii) or Section 2(7), the Forward Price shall be equal to:

(a) the Repurchase Price as defined in Section 2(3), less (except if the parties have agreed that Section 4 (1) shall apply)

(b) the sum of (i) the amount of any Distribution in respect of the Purchased Securities made by the issuer on a date falling between the Purchase Date and the Repurchase

Date, and (ii) the aggregate amount obtained by daily application of the Pricing Rate for the relevant Transaction to such amount from (and including) the date of the Distribution to (but excluding) such advanced or postponed Repurchase Date.

6. Margin Maintenance, Repricing

(1) Margin Provisions any obligations of the parties to transfer cash or Securities as Margin under certain circumstances shall be performed in accordance with the provisions of the applicable Margin Maintenance Annex published by the FBE, or with any other rules to be separately agreed.

(2) Repricing If the parties agree on the repricing of one or more Transactions (the "Original Transactions") instead of a transfer of Margin, then

(a) the Repurchase Date of each Original Transaction shall be deemed advanced to the date as of which the repricing is to occur (the "Repricing Date"),

(b) a new Transaction (the "New Transaction") shall be deemed entered into under which (i) Purchased Securities shall be the Equivalent of those purchased under the Original Transaction, (ii) the Purchase Date shall be the Repricing Date, (iii) the Purchase Price shall be equal to the Market Value of such Securities on the Repricing Date divided by the Margin Ratio, if any, applicable to the Original Transaction, as agreed pursuant to the applicable Margin Maintenance Annex, and (iv) the Repurchase Date, the Pricing Rate, the Margin Ratio and, subject to the above, the other terms shall be identical to the ones of the Original Transaction, and

(c) the obligations to pay the Purchase Price and to transfer the Purchased Securities under the New Transaction shall be discharged by setting them off against the obligations to pay the Repurchase Price and to retransfer the Equivalent of the Purchased Securities under the Original Transaction, so that only a net cash amount shall be payable by one party to the other on the Repricing Date or, if that is not practicable, on the next Business Day.

- 5 -

Suggested form of Confirmation

To:
From:
Date:

We refer to our telephone conversation and hereby confirm our agreement to enter into a Repurchase Transaction [in the form of a Buy/Sell Back Transaction] [which shall be subject to the FBE Master Agreement for Financial Transactions between us].
The terms of the Transaction are as follows:

Reference Number:
Transaction Date

Seller:
Buyer:

Purchase Date:
Repurchase Date: [(date)][on demand]

Purchased Securities (designation, type):
Securities Code:
Amount/Number of Purchased Securities:

Purchase Price:
[Clean Price:]
[Accrued Interest payable on Purchase Date:]
Pricing Rate: % p.a.
[Forward Price (Sell Back Price):]
[Accrued Interest payable on
Repurchase Date:]
[Distribution amount payable to Seller:] [Gross without deduction][plus % tax credit][net after deduction of... % withholding tax]

[Eligible Margin:] [Cash Margin: (specify currency)]
 [Margin Securities: (specify type)]
 [other: (specify details)]
[Margin Ratio (Haircut)[6]

Buyer's account:
Seller's account:
Delivery system:

[Agency:] The Transaction is an Agency Transaction. [Name of Agent] is acting as agent for [name or identifier of Principal]]
[Additional provisions:]

Please confirm that the foregoing correctly sets forth the terms of our agreement by countersigning this Confirmation and returning it to [ ] or by sending us a confirmation substantially similar to this Confirmation, which confirmation sets forth the material terms of the Transaction to which this Confirmation relates and indicates agreement to those terms.

Yours sincerely,

1,2,3,4 Relevant only for Buy/Sell Back Transactions. The terms "Forward Price" and Sell Back Price" (note 3) have the same meaning; either or both may be used.
5 Relevant if eligible Margin is not specified in the Special Provisions.
6 The terms "Margin Ratio" and "Haircut" have the same meaning; either or both may be used.

Copyright © 2001 FBE   Product Annex for Repurchase Transactions - 2001

FEDERATION BANCAIRE DE L'UNION EUROPEENNE
BANKING FEDERATION OF THE EUROPEAN UNION
BANKENVEREINIGUNG DER EUROPÄISCHEN UNION

in co-operation with

EUROPEAN SAVINGS BANKS GROUP
GROUPEMENT EUROPEEN DES CAISSES D'EPARGNE
EUROPÄISCHE SPARKASSENVEREINIGUNG

EUROPEAN ASSOCIATION OF COOPERATIVE BANKS
GROUPEMENT EUROPEEN DES BANQUES COOPERATIVES
EUROPÄISCHE VEREINIGUNG DER GENOSSENSCHAFTSBANKEN

MASTER AGREEMENT FOR FINANCIAL TRANSACTIONS

PRODUCT ANNEX FOR SECURITIES LOANS

Edition January 2001

This Annex supplements the General Provisions which form part of any Master Agreement for Financial Transactions based on the form published by the Banking Federation of the European Union.

1. Purpose, Applicability

(1) Purpose. The purpose of this Annex ("Securities Lending Annex") is to govern Transactions ("Securities Loans") in which one party (the "Lender") lends to the other (the "Borrower") Securities (the "Loaned Securities") for a determined or initially undetermined period of time. Any reference in this Annex to a Transaction shall be construed as a reference to a Securities Loan.

(2) Applicability. If this Annex forms part of a Master Agreement between any two parties, such Master Agreement (including this Annex) shall apply to any Securities Loan between such parties which is to be conducted by each party through a Booking Office specified in such Master Agreement in respect of Securities Loans.

2. Deliveries and Returns

(1) Initial Delivery. On the date agreed for the delivery of the Loaned Securities (the "Delivery Date"), the Lender shall transfer such Loaned Securities to the Borrower.

(2) Return. On the date agreed for the return of the Loaned Securities (the "Return Date"), the Borrower shall transfer to the Lender Securities of the same kind and quantity as the Loaned Securities.

(3) Interpretation. Any reference in this Annex to the Loaned Securities or other Securities in the context of the return or retransfer thereof, or to any rights or other assets to be transferred pursuant to Section 3(4), shall be construed so as to mean a reference to Securities, rights or assets of the same kind and quantity as (also referred to below as the "Equivalent" of) such Loaned Securities or other Securities, rights or assets, respectively.

(4) On Demand Transactions. The parties may agree that Securities Loans are terminable on demand, in which case the Return Date shall be the date specified in the demand notice sent by either party to the other, provided that the period between the taking effect of such notice and the Return Date so specified shall be not less than the minimum period customarily required for the delivery of Securities of the relevant kind. In the absence of a demand notice, the Return Date for a Transaction terminable on demand shall be the day which falls 364 days after the Delivery Date.

(5) Late Delivery

(a) *Failure by Lender.* If the Lender fails to transfer the Loaned Securities to the Borrower on the applicable Delivery Date, the Borrower may, at any time while such failure continues:

(i) require the Lender to pay to the Borrower an amount equal to the excess, if any, of the Borrower's Alternative Borrowing Cost over the pro rata portion of the Lending Fee attributable to the period of the delay, each calculated for the period from (and including) the Delivery Date to (but excluding) the earlier of the date on which the Loaned Securities are transferred to the Borrower and the Return Date (which in the case of a Transaction terminable on demand shall be deemed to be the earliest date on which the

Loaned Securities would be required to be returned following a demand by the Lender); "Alternative Borrowing Cost" of a party means the cost (including fees and expenses), as determined by such party, which such party has or would have reasonably incurred in borrowing the Equivalent of the Loaned Securities in the market for the relevant period; and

(ii) if the parties have not agreed on measures to promptly remedy the failure, give notice to the Lender that the Return Date shall be advanced so as to occur immediately, whereupon the obligations of the parties to lend or return the Loaned Securities (respectively) shall cease and no deliveries or payments shall be due between them other than, if applicable, pursuant to (i).

(b) *Failure by Borrower*. If the Borrower fails to return the Loaned Securities on the applicable Return Date, the Lender may, at any time while such failure continues:

(i) require the Borrower to pay to the Lender an amount equal to the higher of (a) the Lender's Alternative Borrowing Cost and (b) the Lending Fee, each calculated for the period from (and including) the Return Date to (but excluding) the date of actual return of the Loaned Securities or, if earlier, the date specified in the notice, if any, given pursuant to (ii); and

(ii) if the parties have not agreed on measures to promptly remedy the failure, give notice to the Borrower requiring cash settlement in lieu of delivery on a date to be specified in such notice, whereupon the obligation of the Borrower to return the Loaned Securities shall cease and the Borrower shall pay to the Lender an amount equal to the Acquisition Cost for such Securities; "Acquisition Cost" means the cost (including fees and expenses), as determined by the Lender, which the Lender has or would have reasonably incurred in purchasing the Equivalent of the Loaned Securities in the market on the date so specified for cash settlement.

(c) *Partial Delivery*. If the Lender or the Borrower transfers some, but not all, of the Loaned Securities on the date specified in sub-paragraph (a) or (b), respectively, the respective other party may, at its option, either accept such transfer and exercise its rights under those sub-paragraphs with respect to the residual Loaned Securities or decline such acceptance and exercise its rights with respect to all Loaned Securities.

(d) *Remedies*. Beyond the remedies provided in this subsection 5, neither party shall in the event of any failure by the other party to transfer or return Loaned Securities, be entitled to recover any additional damage as a consequence of such failure, and such failure shall
not constitute an Event of Default under Section 6(l)(a)(iii) of the General Provisions. This paragraph (d) is without prejudice to any remedy available in the event of a failure by a party to perform any other obligation (including any obligation to make a payment under this subsection 5).

(6) *Special Events*. If, during the term of a Transaction and in respect of some or all of the Loaned Securities:

(i) a payment of any interest or dividend or any other distribution of money or other property by the issuer of the Loaned Securities (collectively a "Distribution", which term shall include a repayment of principal and a payment in the case of a capital reduction) would, as a result of any change in law or in the application or official interpretation thereof occurring after the date on which such Transaction is entered into, be subject to any deduction or withholding in respect of a tax or other duty or would give rise to a tax credit;

(ii) a notice of early redemption has been validly given;

(iii) a public redemption, exchange, conversion or compensation offer or a public purchase bid is made or announced;

(iv) subscription or other preferential rights which are not freely transferable are granted, or non-fungible property is distributed, to the holders; or

(v) if specified in the Special Provisions, a tax credit or tax entitlement is attached to any interest or dividend paid to the holders (whether or not subparagraph (i) would otherwise apply)

then, subject to any other agreement between the parties, the Return Date for such Securities shall, automatically in the case of (v) and otherwise upon demand by either party, be advanced to the third Business Day before, in the case of (i), (ii) and (v), the expected payment or redemption date or before, in the case of (iii) and (iv), the last day on which such bid or offer may be accepted or the day on which such rights or assets are granted or distributed.

3. **Distributions, Subscription Rights**

(1) Cash Distributions. If during the term of a Securities Loan any Distribution of money is made by the issuer to the holders of the Loaned Securities, the Borrower shall pay to the Lender, on the date of such Distribution, an amount in the same currency as, and equal to, the amount received by the holders in respect of such Distribution.

(2) Withholding Taxes Tax Credits If a Distribution is subject to withholding tax and/or gives rise to a tax credit, the amount payable by the Borrower under subsection 1 shall be equal to the full amount to which the Lender would be entitled, as previously notified by it, in respect of such Distribution if it were the owner of the Loaned Securities, including the amount of (a) any applicable withholding tax to the extent that the Lender would be entitled to apply for an exemption from, or a refund of, such tax and (b) any tax credit available to the Lender.

(3) Subscription Rights. If subscription rights which are freely transferable are granted with respect to the Loaned Securities, the Borrower shall transfer to the Lender not later than on the third day on which such rights are traded, the Equivalent of the subscription rights attributable to such Loaned Securities. If the rights are not so transferred by such date, the Lender may purchase their Equivalent in the market for the account of the Borrower. Should the Lender be unable so to purchase the rights, it may require the Borrower to pay to it an amount equal to the Market Value of such rights prevailing on the next following trading day for such rights.

Copyright © 2001 FBE

Product Annex for Securities Loans - 2001

(4) Non-cash Distributions Any freely transferable bonus shares, non-cash Distributions and ancillary rights (other than subscription rights) which are issued, made or allotted with respect to the Loaned Securities during the term of a Securities Loan shall be transferred to the Lender on the Return Date.

(5) Transfer Obligations For the avoidance of doubt, the provisions of subsections 1 through 4 shall apply whether or not the Borrower retains the ownership of the Loaned Securities during the term of the Transaction.

4.   Lending Fee

The Borrower shall pay to the Lender for each Securities Loan a fee (the "Lending Fee") equal to the rate per annum agreed in respect of such Securities Loan and calculated on the value of the Loaned Securities agreed by the parties for this purpose. The Lending Fee shall be calculated for the period from (and including) the Delivery Date or, if later, the date of actual transfer of the Loaned Securities to the Borrower, to (but excluding) the Return Date or, if later, the date of actual return of the Loaned Securities to the Lender, based on the actual number of days in such period and a 360-day year. Unless otherwise agreed, the Lender shall calculate the Lending Fee at the beginning of each month for the preceding month or, if earlier, on the Return Date, and send the Borrower a statement setting forth such Lending Fee. The Lending Fee shall be payable on the second Business Day following the receipt of such statement sent by the Lender.

5.   Margin Provisions

Any obligations of the parties to transfer cash or Securities as Margin under certain circumstances shall be performed in accordance with the provisions of the applicable Margin Maintenance Annex published by the FBE, or with any other rules to be separately agreed.

Suggested form of Confirmation

To:

From:

Date:

We refer to our telephone conversation and hereby confirm our agreement to enter into a Securities Loan Transaction [which shall be subject to the FBE Master Agreement for Financial Transactions between us]. The terms of the Transaction are as follows:

Reference Number:
Transaction Date:

Lender:
Borrower:

Delivery Date:
Return Date: [.....(date)] [on demand]

Loaned Securities (designation, type):
Securities Code:
Amount/Number of Loaned Securities:

Lending Fee Rate: ... % p.a.
Value of the Loaned Securities for purposes
of Lending Fee calculation:
[Distribution amount payable to Lender:]   [Gross without deduction] [plus ... % tax credit] [net
                                                      after deduction of... % withholding tax]

[Margin:][1]   [Cash Margin: ... (specify currency and amount)]
                                                      [Margin Securities: ... (specify type and amount);
                                                      applicable Valuation Percentage: %]
                                                      [other: ... (specify details)]

[Margin Ratio (Haircut)[2]:

Borrower's account:

Lender's account:

Delivery system:
[Agency: The Transaction is an Agency Transaction. [Name of Agent] is
                                                      acting as agent for [name or identifier of Principal]].

[Additional provisions:]

Please confirm that the foregoing correctly sets forth the terms of our agreement by countersigning this Confirmation and returning it to [   ] or by sending us a confirmation substantially similar to this Confirmation, which confirmation sets forth the material terms of the Securities Loan to which this Confirmation relates and indicates agreement to those terms.

Yours sincerely

Copyright © 2001 FBE   Product Annex for Securities Loans - 2001

[1] Relevant if Margin is to be provided in respect of the relevant individual Transaction
[2] The terms "Margin Ratio" and "Haircut" have the same meaning; either or both may be used

FBE

FEDERATION BANCAIRE DE L'UNION EUROPEENNE
BANKING FEDERATION OF THE EUROPEAN UNION
BANKENVEREINIGUNG DER EUROPÄISCHEN UNION

in co-operation with

EUROPEAN SAVINGS BANKS GROUP
GROUPEMENT EUROPEEN DES CAISSES D'EPARGNE
EUROPÄISCHE SPARKASSENVEREINIGUNG

EUROPEAN ASSOCIATION OF COOPERATIVE BANKS
GROUPEMENT EUROPEEN DES BANQUES COOPERATIVES
EUROPÄISCHE VEREINIGUNG DER GENOSSENSCHAFTSBANKEN

MASTER AGREEMENT
FOR FINANCIAL TRANSACTIONS

MARGIN MAINTENANCE ANNEX
Edition 2004

This Annex supplements the General Provisions which form part of any Master Agreement for Financial Transactions based on the form published by the FBE.

1. Net Exposure

(1) General Principles. If, at any time when Net Exposure is calculated pursuant to subsection 2, one party (the "Margin Provider") has an Adjusted Net Exposure to the other (the "Margin Recipient") resulting from any Transactions and/or from transfers of Margin pursuant to this Annex, the Margin Recipient may by notice to the Margin Provider require the same to transfer to it cash ("Cash Margin") or Securities ("Margin Securities") acceptable to the Margin Recipient and whose aggregate Market Value, when multiplied by the valuation percentage, if any, agreed between the parties ("Valuation Percentage"), shall be at least equal to the Adjusted Net Exposure. "Adjusted Net Exposure" means the sum of the Net Exposure and any supplementary amount ("Independent Amount") agreed in favour of the Margin Recipient less any Independent Amount agreed in favour of the Margin Provider. Such notice may be given orally or as provided in Section 8(1) of the General Provisions. The Net Exposure will be determined, and accordingly Margin will be required to be transferred, in respect of (a) all such Transactions, (b) specified groups of Transactions, (c) each individual Transaction or (d) otherwise, as agreed by the parties (in the Special Provisions or otherwise), provided that failing such agreement, (b) shall apply in such a manner that all Repurchase Transactions, all Securities Loans and all Derivative Transactions shall each form a separate group of Transactions to which this Annex applies. The "Market Value" of cash shall be the nominal amount thereof, converted, if not denominated in the Base Currency, in accordance with subsection 2. Any reference in this Annex to Transactions shall be construed as a reference to Repurchase Transactions and/or Securities Loans and/or Derivative Transactions.

(2) Calculation. The person designated by the parties for this purpose or, failing such designation, each party (each the "Valuation Agent") shall calculate the Net Exposure on each Valuation Date by 11 a.m. Brussels time. The Net Exposure shall be expressed as a positive number if the Valuation Agent would, pursuant to its calculation, be the Margin Recipient, and shall otherwise be expressed as a negative number. All calculations shall be made in the Base Currency; any amount not denominated in the Base Currency shall be converted into the Base Currency at the Applicable Exchange Rate.

(3) Definitions. "Net Exposure" means (I) in relation to Repurchase Transactions and Securities Loans the excess (if any), calculated pursuant to subsection 2, of the Liabilities of the Margin Provider over the Liabilities of the Margin Recipient, and (II) in relation to Derivative Transactions the Potential Final Settlement Amount, provided that (a) if the calculation is to be made pursuant to both (I) and (II), the Net Exposure shall be the aggregate of the amounts so calculated, (b) the amount of any prior Adjusted Net Exposure in respect of which a transfer of Margin has already been required, but not completed, shall be subtracted from any Net Exposure subsequently calculated and (c) if both parties act as Valuation Agent and their calculations of Net Exposure differ from each other, (i) the Net Exposure shall be one-half of the difference of the amounts so calculated by both parties (such difference being, for the avoidance of doubt, the sum of the absolute values of such amounts if one is positive and the other negative) and (ii) the Margin Provider shall be the party which has calculated a negative or the lower positive amount;"Liabilities" means, with respect to a party, the aggregate of

(a) the Market Values of any Securities transferred to that party under a Transaction or pursuant to this Annex and not yet returned to the other party, multiplied (i) in the case of Loaned Securities, by the applicable Margin Ratio and (ii) in the case of Margin Securities, by any applicable Valuation Percentage;

Copyright © 2004 FBE

Margin Maintenance Annex - 2004

(b) a cash amount equal to the sum of (i) the amount, multiplied by the applicable Margin Ratio, of that party's obligation(s) to pay the Repurchase Price in respect of any Repurchase Transaction if the relevant Valuation Date were the Repurchase Date, and (ii) the Market Value, multiplied by any applicable Valuation Percentage, of any Cash Margin transferred to and not repaid by that party (including unpaid accrued interest on such Cash Margin); and

(c) the cash amount or cash equivalent in respect of any Distribution to be paid or transferred by such party to the other party, but not yet paid or transferred;
"Margin" means either Cash Margin or Margin Securities;

"Margin Ratio" (also called "Haircut") means, with respect to each Repurchase Transaction or Securities Loan, the percentage agreed by the parties by which the Liabilities of the Seller or the Borrower in relation to the Repurchase Price and the Loaned Securities, respectively, are multiplied, as provided under "Liabilities" above, in order to determine the Net Exposure; failing an agreement to that effect, the Margin Ratio shall be equal to (a) with respect to a Repurchase Transaction, the Market Value of the Purchased Securities on the date on which the Transaction was entered into, divided by the Purchase Price, and (b) with respect to a Securities Loan (i) the Market Value, on the date on which the Transaction was entered into, of any Margin to be provided at the commencement of such Securities Loan, multiplied by the applicable Valuation Percentage and divided by the Market Value of the Loaned Securities as of such date, and (ii) if no Margin is provided at the commencement of such Securities Loan, 100 per cent., unless the parties have expressly excluded the provision of Margin for the entire term of the Transaction, in which case the Margin Ratio shall be zero until the Return Date;

"Potential Final Settlement Amount" means the amount which, at the time on each Valuation Date when Net Exposure is calculated in respect of Derivative Transactions pursuant to subsection 2, the Valuation Agent, acting as if it were the Calculation Party (as defined in Section 7(1)(a) of the General Provisions), determines to be equal to the Final Settlement Amount calculated in respect of Derivative Transactions (but excluding Repurchase Transactions and Securities Loans), if the same had to be calculated as of such time and date, such determination to be made in accordance with Section 7(1)(a) of the General Provisions, except that (a) if the determination can be made on the basis of bid and offered quotations, the arithmetic mean of such quotations shall be used for such determination, and (b) the amount of Margin Claims shall be adjusted so as to take into account the applicable Valuation Percentages;
"Valuation Date" means, in respect of calculation of the Net Exposure, each of the dates agreed as such between the parties, and failing such agreement each Business Day.

2. Notification of Adjusted Net Exposure and Transfer of Margin

(1) *Notification.* Promptly after determining the Net Exposure, the Valuation Agent shall notify each relevant party of the Adjusted Net Exposure and upon request of a party provide such party with a statement setting forth in reasonable detail the calculation basis of the Adjusted Net Exposure. The notice may be given orally or as provided in Section 8(1) of the General Provisions.

(2) *Transfer.* The Margin Provider shall, upon receipt of the notice referred to in the first sentence of Section 1(1), transfer to the Margin Recipient Margin with an aggregate Market Value at least equal to the Adjusted Net Exposure no later than the date agreed for such transfer, and failing such agreement on the Business Day immediately following receipt of such notice, if such notice is received on a Business Day prior to 11.00 a. m., and otherwise on the second Business Day following such receipt.

(3) *Composition of Margin.* The Margin Provider is entitled to determine the composition of the Margin to be transferred, unless the Margin Recipient has previously paid Cash Margin which has not been repaid or transferred Margin Securities which have not been returned to it, in which case the Margin Provider shall first repay such Cash Margin or return such Margin Securities.

(4) *Cash Margin.* Cash Margin shall be acceptable for the purpose of Section 1 (1) if transferred in the Base Currency or such other currency as the parties may have specified as eligible (in the Special Provisions or otherwise). A payment of Cash Margin shall give rise to a debt owing from the Margin Recipient to the Margin Provider and shall bear interest at such rate, and payable at such times, as agreed by the parties. In the absence of such agreement, that rate shall be equal to the Interbank Rate less 0.10 per cent. per annum, and the interest shall be payable at the end of each calendar month and on each date when the Margin Recipient is required to provide or return Margin.

(5) *Margin Securities.* Margin Securities shall be acceptable for the purpose of Section 1(1) if Securities of the relevant kind (a) have been specified by the parties as eligible (in the Special Provisions or otherwise) or (b) have an original maturity of not more than five years and are issued by the central government of the country in which the Margin Recipient has its principal office or in which it is organised, incorporated or resident. A transfer of Margin Securities shall give rise to an obligation of the Margin Recipient to the Margin Provider to return such Securities as provided in this Annex.

(6) *Margin Thresholds.* Except in the case of a return of Margin pursuant to subsection 7, a transfer of Margin will take place only (a) to the extent that the Adjusted Net Exposure exceeds the threshold amount, if any, agreed by the parties ("Exposure Threshold") in relation to the Margin Recipient's Net Exposure and (b) if the Market Value of the Margin to be transferred exceeds the minimum amount, if any, agreed for such transfer (the "Minimum Transfer Amount"). In the absence of an agreement on either or both such amounts, such amount, or both, respectively, shall be zero.

(7) *Return of Margin.* Upon satisfaction by a party of all its obligations under Transactions in respect of which Margin is required to be transferred as provided in

the fourth sentence of Section 1(1), any Margin previously transferred and not returned shall be returned to the party which transferred it.

3.   Provisions Applicable to Margin Securities

The provisions of Section 3 of the Repurchase Annex (regarding substitution of Purchased Securities) and Sections 2(3), 2(5)(b)(ii) and (d), 2(6) and 3 of the Securities Lending Annex (regarding interpretation, failure to return Loaned Securities, special events, Distributions and subscription rights) shall apply *mutatis mutandis* to Margin Securities transferred pursuant to this Annex, provided that (a) the consent of the Margin Recipient shall not be required for a substitution by the Margin Provider of new Margin Securities acceptable pursuant to Section 2(5) of this Annex for Margin Securities previously transferred and (b) if any of the special events referred to in Section 2(6) of the Securities Lending Annex occurs in relation to Margin Securities, the relevant Transaction shall not be modified or terminated, but Margin acceptable pursuant to Section 2(4) or (5) of this Annex shall be substituted for such Securities upon request of either party.

FBE

FEDERATION BANCAIRE DE L'UNION EUROPEENNE
BANKING FEDERATION OF THE EUROPEAN UNION
BANKENVEREINIGUNG DER EUROPÄISCHEN UNION

in co-operation with

EUROPEAN SAVINGS BANKS GROUP
GROUPEMENT EUROPEEN DES CAISSES D'EPARGNE
EUROPÄISCHE SPARKASSENVEREINIGUNG

EUROPEAN ASSOCIATION OF COOPERATIVE BANKS
GROUPEMENT EUROPEEN DES BANQUES COOPERATIVES
EUROPÄISCHE VEREINIGUNG DER GENOSSENSCHAFTSBANKEN

MASTER AGREEMENT
FOR FINANCIAL TRANSACTIONS

PRODUCT ANNEX FOR DERIVATIVE TRANSACTIONS
Edition 2004

This Annex, together with any Supplement thereto, supplements the General Provisions which form part of any Master Agreement for Financial Transactions based on the form published by the FBE.

1. Purpose, Applicability

(1) Purpose. The purpose of this Annex ("Derivatives Annex") is to govern Transactions ("Derivative Transactions") which are (a) over-the-counter market transactions, including, but not limited to, forward, swap, option, cap, floor, and collar transactions, any combination of these and any other similar transactions, the object of which is (i) the exchange of amounts of money denominated in different currencies, (ii) the delivery or transfer of currencies, securities, financial instruments, commodities, precious metals, energy (including but not limited to gas and electricity) or any other assets, (iii) the payment of money, if either the obligation to make such payment, or the amount thereof, is contingent upon market-related, credit-related or other events or circumstances, (including, but not limited to, the level of interest or exchange rates, credit spreads, prices, market or economic indices, statistics, weather conditions, economic conditions or any other measurement), (iv) any combination of the foregoing, or (b) any transaction referred to in Section 1(2)(a) of this Annex.

(2) Applicability. If this Annex forms part of a Master Agreement between any two parties, such Master Agreement (including this Annex) shall apply to any Derivative Transaction between such parties which is to be conducted by each party through a Booking Office specified in such Master Agreement in respect of Derivative Transactions and which either (a) has been entered into subject to the terms of such Master Agreement (whether or not the transaction is of a type referred to in Section 1(1)(a) of this Annex), or (b) is a Foreign Exchange Transaction if the parties have specified in Section 2 of the Special Provisions that the Foreign Exchange Supplement shall be incorporated into this Annex, or (c) is of a type specified in the Special Provisions as being a type to which this Annex shall apply.

2. Other Market Standard Documentation

If the parties have, in the Special Provisions, a Confirmation or otherwise, incorporated into the terms of a Transaction any Market Standard Documentation, in whole or in part, such documentation (or parts thereof) so incorporated shall apply to such Transaction. For the avoidance of doubt, the terms of such Market Standard Documentation shall, unless the parties have agreed otherwise, be construed in accordance with the law agreed by the parties in Section 4 of the Special Provisions to govern the Master Agreement. "Market Standard Documentation" means a documentation (including, but not limited to, any documentation published by a member association of the FBE or by an industry association) which sets out for different types of Transactions the terms and technical characteristics relating to such Transactions and which may include one or more definitions, lists of definitions, addenda (including, but not limited to, samples of Confirmation) or provisions for use in connection with other market standard master agreements.

3. Margin Provisions

Any obligations of the parties to transfer cash or Securities as Margin under certain circumstances shall be performed in accordance with the provisions of the applicable Margin Maintenance Annex or with any other rules to be separately agreed.

4. Definitions common to Supplements to this Annex

"Calculation Agent" means the party or any other third person specified as such in respect of the relevant Transaction; the Calculation Agent shall make all calculations, adjustments, determinations, estimates, anticipations or selections in good faith and in a reasonable manner;

"Cash Settlement Currency" means the euro, unless otherwise agreed;

"Effective Date" means the date agreed as such between the parties in respect of the relevant Transaction or, failing such agreement, the Trade Date; the Effective Date is the first day of the term of the Transaction and shall not be subject to adjustments in accordance with Section 3(6) of the General Provisions, unless otherwise specified by the parties;

"Exchange" means the regulated or organised exchange(s) or the quotation system(s) for any underlying asset or any underlying measurement of a Transaction, agreed as such between the parties. This definition shall be subject to any modification which may be agreed in any Confirmation or agreed between the parties in a separate document (including any applicable Supplement) or otherwise;

"Exchange Business Day" means a day on which the Exchange(s) is/are open for trading. If any payment or delivery date, any determination or valuation date, any commencement or termination date or any exercise date agreed between the parties which is deemed to be an Exchange Business Day is not an Exchange Business Day, the provisions of Section 3(6) of the General Provisions shall be applicable provided that for purposes of application of those provisions, references to a "Business Day" shall be deemed to be references to an "Exchange Business Day";

"Market Disruption Convention" means any provisions incorporated in any Confirmation or agreed between the parties in a separate document (including any applicable Supplement) or otherwise, providing for the consequences of a Market Disruption Event occurring and continuing at the Valuation Time on any Valuation Date;

"Market Disruption Event" means in respect of any underlying asset or measurement of a Transaction and to the extent such underlying asset or measurement is subject to quotations, the situation where the Calculation Agent ascertains during the one-half hour period that ends at the relevant Valuation Time any suspension of quotations or any material limitation of trading (in particular by reason of movements in prices exceeding the limits allowed by any relevant exchange(s), or any relevant central bank or any market undertaking or otherwise) on the relevant exchange(s), of the underlying asset or measurement or, as the case may be, of any future or option contract relating to the underlying asset or measurement. This definition shall be subject to any modification which may be agreed in any Confirmation or agreed between the parties in a separate document (including any applicable Supplement) or otherwise;

"Settlement Date" means, subject to any modifications made in an applicable Supplement and to adjustments in accordance with Section 3(6) of the General Provisions, each date agreed between the parties upon which payments, deliveries or transfers shall be made in respect of the relevant Transaction;

a payment shall be "simultaneous" if it occurs as part of a delivery-versus-payment system or, should such system not exist or the use of such system in the given circumstances not be customary, if it occurs on the same day as the delivery or transfer of currencies, securities, financial instruments, commodities, precious metals, energy or any other assets;

"Termination Date" means the date agreed as such between the parties in respect of the relevant Transaction or, failing such agreement, the last Settlement Date of the Transaction; the Termination Date is the last day of the term of the Transaction and shall not be subject to adjustments in accordance with Section 3(6) of the General Provisions, unless otherwise specified by the parties;

"Trade Date" means the date on which the parties enter into the relevant Transaction;

"Valuation Date" means, subject to adjustments in accordance with the applicable Market Disruption Convention or Section 3(6) of the General Provisions, (i) the date agreed as such between the parties on which the relevant prices, interest rates, exchange rates, credit spreads, market or economic indices, statistics, weather conditions, economic conditions or any other measurement are to be determined in respect of the relevant Transaction or, failing such agreement, (ii) the date so specified in the applicable Supplement;

"Valuation Time" means the time agreed as such between the parties in respect of the relevant Transaction or, failing such agreement, the close of business on the Valuation Date.

FEDERATION BANCAIRE DE L'UNION EUROPEENNE
BANKING FEDERATION OF THE EUROPEAN UNION
BANKENVEREINIGUNG DER EUROPÄISCHEN UNION

in co-operation with

EUROPEAN SAVINGS BANKS GROUP
GROUPEMENT EUROPEEN DES CAISSES D'EPARGNE
EUROPÄISCHE SPARKASSENVEREINIGUNG

EUROPEAN ASSOCIATION OF COOPERATIVE BANKS
GROUPEMENT EUROPEEN DES BANQUES COOPERATIVES
EUROPÄISCHE VEREINIGUNG DER GENOSSENSCHAFTSBANKEN

MASTER AGREEMENT FOR FINANCIAL TRANSACTIONS

SUPPLEMENT TO THE DERIVATIVES ANNEX

FOREIGN EXCHANGE TRANSACTIONS
Edition 2004

This Supplement complements the General Provisions and the Derivatives Annex which form part of a Master Agreement for Financial Transactions based on the form published by the FBE.

1. Purpose, Interpretation

(1) Purpose. The purpose of this Supplement ("Foreign Exchange Supplement") is to govern Foreign Exchange Transactions, which means a Foreign Exchange Spot, Foreign Exchange Forward, Non-Deliverable Foreign Exchange Forward, Foreign Exchange Option, Non-Deliverable Foreign Exchange Option or any other Transaction so agreed by the parties in respect of the individual Transaction or in the Special Provisions.

(2) Interpretation. This Supplement forms an integral part of the Derivatives Annex. The term "Annex" as used in Section 1(3) of the General Provisions should be construed as to include this Supplement. In the event of any conflict between different parts of the Derivatives Annex and this Supplement, this Supplement shall prevail.

2. Foreign Exchange Transactions

"Foreign Exchange Spot" means a Transaction in which one party (the "Seller") sells to the other (the "Buyer") a specified amount of a specified currency (the "Reference Currency") against payment of an agreed amount of a specified different currency (the "Settlement Currency"), and both obligations are settled on a spot basis.

"Foreign Exchange Forward" means a Transaction in which the Seller sells to the Buyer a specified amount of the Reference Currency against payment of an agreed amount of the Settlement Currency, and both obligations are settled on a specified later date.

"Non-Deliverable Foreign Exchange Forward" means a Transaction in which the Seller sells to the Buyer a specified amount of the Reference Currency, which is a non-convertible, non-transferable or thinly traded currency, against payment of an agreed amount of the Settlement Currency, and both obligations are settled by the payment by the Seller or, as the case may be, the Buyer of the Settlement Currency Amount based on the difference between the agreed price for the Settlement Currency and the price for the Settlement Currency on a specified later date.

"Foreign Exchange Option" means an Option Transaction in which the Seller grants to the Buyer against payment of the Premium the right to purchase, in the case of a Call, or sell, in the case of a Put, a specified amount of the Reference Currency (the "Call Currency" in the case of a Call and the "Put Currency" in the case of a Put) against payment of an agreed amount of the Settlement Currency (the "Put Currency" in the case of a Call and the "Call Currency" in the case of a Put). The Option Transaction may be settled by (i), in the case of a Foreign Exchange Option to which "Physical Settlement" applies (the "Physically Settled Foreign Exchange Option"), delivering or transferring a specified amount of the Reference Currency against payment of an agreed amount of the Settlement Currency or (ii), in the case of a Foreign Exchange Option to which "Cash Settlement" applies (the "Cash Settled Foreign Exchange Option"), paying the Cash Settlement Amount based on the difference between the agreed price for the Settlement Currency and the price for the Settlement Currency on the Valuation Date.

"Non-Deliverable Foreign Exchange Option" means an Option Transaction in which the Seller grants to the Buyer against payment of the Premium the right to purchase, in the case of a Call, or sell, in the case of a

Copyright © 2004 FBE

Foreign Exchange Transactions - 2004

Put, a specified amount of the Reference Currency, which is a non-convertible, non-transferable or thinly traded currency, (the "Call Currency" in the case of a Call and the "Put Currency" in the case of a Put) against payment of an agreed amount of the Settlement Currency (the "Put Currency" in the case of a Call and the "Call Currency" in the case of a Put), and both obligations are settled by paying the Cash Settlement Amount based on the difference between the agreed price for the Settlement Currency and the price for the Settlement Currency on the Valuation Date.

3. Deliveries and Payments

(1) *Foreign Exchange Spot and Foreign Exchange Forward*. On the agreed Settlement Date for the Foreign Exchange Spot or the Foreign Exchange Forward the Seller shall deliver or transfer to the Buyer the specified amount of the Reference Currency and the Buyer shall deliver or transfer to the Seller the agreed amount of the Settlement Currency.

(2) *Non-Deliverable Foreign Exchange Forward*. On the agreed Settlement Date for the Non-Deliverable Foreign Exchange Forward, the Seller shall pay to the Buyer the absolute value of the Settlement Currency Amount, if such amount is a negative number, and the Buyer shall pay to the Seller the Settlement Currency Amount, if such amount is a positive number.

"Settlement Currency Amount" means an amount expressed in the Settlement Currency calculated on the basis of the following formula:

$$\left[\text{Agreed Amount of the Settlement Currency} \times \left(1 - \frac{\text{Forward Rate}}{\text{Settlement Currency Rate}} \right) \right]$$

(3) *Physically Settled Foreign Exchange Option*. On the agreed Premium Payment Date for the Physically Settled Foreign Exchange Option the Buyer shall pay to the Seller the Premium. If the Physically Settled Foreign Exchange Option is exercised or deemed to be exercised, on the agreed Settlement Date of the Option Transaction, the Seller shall deliver or transfer to the Buyer the specified amount of the Reference Currency against simultaneous payment of the agreed amount of the Settlement Currency.

(4) *Non-Deliverable Foreign Exchange Option and Cash Settled Foreign Exchange Option*. On the agreed Premium Payment Date for the Non-Deliverable Foreign Exchange Option or the Cash Settled Foreign Exchange Option the Buyer shall pay to the Seller the Premium. If the Option Transaction is exercised or deemed to be exercised, on the agreed Settlement Date for the Non-Deliverable Foreign Exchange Option or the Cash Settled Foreign Exchange Option, the Seller shall pay to the Buyer the Cash Settlement Amount, if such amount is a positive number.

"Cash Settlement Amount" means an amount expressed in the Settlement Currency and calculated as follows, (i) in the case of an Option Transaction where the Reference Currency is the Put Currency and the Settlement Currency is the Call Currency:

$$\left[\text{Agreed Amount of the Call Currency} \times \left(\frac{\text{Settlement CurrencyRate} - \text{Strike Price}}{\text{Settlement CurrencyRate}} \right) \right]$$

and (ii) in the case of an Option Transaction where the Reference Currency is the Call Currency and the Settlement Currency is the Put Currency:

$$\left[\text{Agreed Amount of the Put Currency} \times \left(1 - \frac{\text{Strike Price} - \text{Settlement Currency Rate}}{\text{Settlement Currency Rate}} \right) \right]$$

(5) *Definitions.* "Forward Rate" means the forward foreign exchange rate agreed as such between the parties, such rate shall be expressed as an amount of the Reference Currency per one unit of the Settlement Currency.

"Settlement Currency Rate" means the foreign exchange rate expressed as an amount of the Reference Currency per one unit of the Settlement Currency as determined by the Calculation Agent on the Valuation Date for the Valuation Time based on the currency exchange rate for the Reference Currency and the Settlement Currency (the "Currency Pair") (i) quoted through and obtainable from the Price Source specified in the agreed Currency Rate Option or, failing such agreement, (ii) determined by the Calculation Agent. "Currency Rate Option" means the foreign exchange rate agreed by the parties by reference to the publication, screen or web page of an information vendor or any other price source (the "Price Source").

"Strike Price" means the foreign exchange rate agreed between the parties at which the Currency Pair shall be exchanged if an Option Transaction is exercised or deemed to be exercised; such rate shall be expressed as an amount of the Reference Currency per one unit of the Settlement Currency.

4. Provisions applicable to Option Transactions

Unless otherwise defined in this Supplement, any term relating to Option Transactions is to be construed in accordance with the applicable Options Supplement published by the FBE.

FEDERATION BANCAIRE DE L'UNION EUROPEENNE
BANKING FEDERATION OF THE EUROPEAN UNION
BANKENVEREINIGUNG DER EUROPÄISCHEN UNION

in co-operation with

EUROPEAN SAVINGS BANKS GROUP
GROUPEMENT EUROPEEN DES CAISSES D'EPARGNE
EUROPÄISCHE SPARKASSENVEREINIGUNG

EUROPEAN ASSOCIATION OF COOPERATIVE BANKS
GROUPEMENT EUROPEEN DES BANQUES COOPERATIVES
EUROPÄISCHE VEREINIGUNG DER GENOSSENSCHAFTSBANKEN

MASTER AGREEMENT FOR FINANCIAL TRANSACTIONS

SUPPLEMENT TO THE DERIVATIVES ANNEX

OPTION TRANSACTIONS
Edition 2004

This Supplement complements the General Provisions, the Derivatives Annex and each Supplement to such Annex which form part of a Master Agreement for Financial Transactions based on the form published by the FBE.

1. Purpose, Interpretation

(1) Purpose. The purpose of this Supplement ("Options Supplement") is to govern Transactions ("Option Transactions") in which one party (the "Seller") grants to the other party (the "Buyer"), against payment of an agreed premium (the "Premium") or any other consideration, the right (the "Option") to

(a) purchase, in the case of a Call, or sell, in the case of a Put, a specified amount, quantity or number of currencies, securities, financial instruments, commodities, precious metals, energy or any other assets (an "Underlying Asset") against payment of an agreed price, whereby both obligations are to be settled (i) by delivering or transferring the specified amount, quantity or number of the Underlying Asset against payment of the agreed price, in the case of an Option Transaction to which "Physical Settlement" applies, or (ii) in the case of an Option Transaction to which "Cash Settlement" applies, by paying a Cash Settlement Amount based on the difference of the agreed price (the "Strike Price") for the Underlying Asset and the price (the "Settlement Price") for such Underlying Asset on the Valuation Date,

(b) request the payment of a Cash Settlement Amount based on the difference of an agreed level (the "Strike Level") of interest or exchange rates, credit spreads, prices, market or economic indices, statistics, weather conditions, economic conditions or any other measurement (an "Underlying Measurement") and the level (the "Settlement Level") of such Underlying Measurement on the Valuation Date,

(c) cause an underlying Transaction (the "Underlying Transaction") to become effective, whereby the Underlying Transaction is to be settled (i) by making all payments and deliveries or transfers to be made by the parties in accordance with the terms of the Underlying Transaction, in the case of an Option Transaction to which "Physical Settlement" applies or (ii), in the case of an Option Transaction to which "Cash Settlement" applies, by paying a Cash Settlement Amount based on the value of the Underlying Transaction on the Valuation Date, if such value, from the Buyer's perspective, is a positive number, or

(d) terminate a specified Transaction to the effect that all obligations under the terminated Transaction or under the Agreement related to the terminated Transaction, which otherwise would have become due on or after the Exercise Date shall be replaced by an obligation to pay a Cash Settlement Amount based on the value of the terminated Transaction and owed by the Seller if such amount is a positive number and by the Buyer if such amount is a negative number.

(2) Interpretation. This Supplement forms an integral part of the Derivatives Annex. The term "Annex" as used in Section 1(3) of the General Provisions should be construed as to include this Supplement. In the event of any conflict between different parts of the Derivatives Annex and this Supplement, this Supplement shall prevail.

2. Option Transactions

(1) Styles. "American Option" means an Option Transaction in which the Option is exercisable on each Exercise Business Day during a period from (and including) the Commencement Date to (and including) the Expiration Date.

"Bermuda Option" means an Option Transaction in which the Option is exercisable on each Exercise

- 2 -

Business Day so agreed to between the parties (each a "Scheduled Exercise Date") and on the Expiration Date, subject to adjustments in accordance with Section 3(6) of the General Provisions. "European Option" means an Option Transaction in which the Option is exercisable on the Expiration Date.

"Asian Option" means an American Option, Bermuda Option or European Option in which the Settlement Price or the Settlement Level is calculated on the Valuation Date as the average of prices or levels determined for the Underlying Asset or Underlying Measurement on each Averaging Date.

(2) *Types.* "Call" means an Option Transaction that, upon exercise (i), in case of Section 1(1)(a)(i) of this Supplement, obliges the Seller to deliver or transfer the specified amount, quantity or number of the Underlying Asset against payment of the agreed price, or (ii), in case of Section 1(1)(a)(ii) or 1(1)(b) of this Supplement, entitles the Buyer to request payment of the Cash Settlement Amount if the Settlement Price exceeds the Strike Price or the Settlement Level exceeds the Strike Level.

"Put" means an Option Transaction that, upon exercise (i), in case of Section 1(1)(a)(i) of this Supplement, obliges the Buyer to deliver or transfer the specified amount, quantity or number of the Underlying Asset against payment of the agreed price, or (ii), in case of Section 1(1)(a)(ii) or 1(1)(b) of this Supplement, entitles the Buyer to request payment of the Cash Settlement Amount if the Strike Price exceeds the Settlement Price or the Strike Level exceeds the Settlement Level.

(3) *Definitions of Dates.* "Expiration Date" means the Exercise Business Day agreed between the parties beyond which an Option can not be exercised any more, subject to adjustments in accordance with Section 3(6) of the General Provisions.

"Commencement Date" means the Exercise Business Day agreed as such between the parties (subject to adjustments in accordance with Section 3(6) of the General Provisions) or, failing such agreement, the Trade Date.

"Averaging Date" means each date agreed as such between the parties (subject to adjustments in accordance with Section 3(6) of the General Provisions) or, failing any agreement, each Exercise Business Day from (and including) the Commencement Date to (and including) the Expiration Date.

"Exercise Date" means each Exercise Business Day on which an Option is exercised or deemed to be exercised.

"Exercise Business Day" means each day during the Exercise Period on which an Option may be exercised, that is either (a) a Business Day (as defined in Section 3(7) of the General Provisions) in (i) the place(s) agreed between the parties or, failing such agreement, (ii) the place(s) determined pursuant to the terms of any applicable Supplement or, failing such terms (iii) the city specified in the address of the Seller's Office or (b) an Exchange Business Day.

"Valuation Date" means the Exercise Business Day agreed as such between the parties (subject to adjustments in accordance with Section 3(6) of the General Provisions) or failing such agreement, the Exercise Date.

3. **Premium**

The Buyer shall pay to the Seller the Premium on the date or dates (each a "Premium Payment Date") agreed between the parties (subject to adjustments in accordance

with Section 3(6) of the General Provisions) or, failing such agreement, the date that is two Business Days immediately following the Trade Date.

4. **Exercise**

(1) *Exercise by Notice.* The Buyer is entitled to exercise an Option by giving notice (the "Exercise Notice"), which may be given orally, including by telephone, to the Seller's Office during the Exercise Period. An Exercise Notice is irrevocable. If an Exercise Notice is given orally, the Buyer shall promptly send to the Seller a confirmation of such notice in the manner specified in Section 8(1) of the General Provisions. The absence of such confirmation shall not affect the validity of the exercise of the Option.

"Seller's Office" means the office and contact details specified as such in the terms of an Option Transaction or, if none is specified, the office through which the Seller enters into the relevant Option Transaction.

(2) *Exercise Period.* "Exercise Period" means the period from (and including) the Earliest Exercise Time to (and including) the Latest Exercise Time on a day that is, (i) in the case of an European Option, the Expiration Date, (ii) in the case of an American Option, each Exercise Business Day from (and including) the Commencement Date to (and including) the Expiration Date and (iii) in the case of a Bermuda Option the Expiration Date and each Scheduled Exercise Date.

"Earliest Exercise Time" means the time agreed as such pursuant to the terms of an Option Transaction or, failing such agreement, 11:00 a.m. local time in the city specified in the address of the Seller's Office.

"Latest Exercise Time" means the time agreed as such pursuant to the terms of an Option Transaction or, failing such agreement, close of business in the city specified in the address of the Seller's Office.

(3) *Exercise Time.* An Exercise Notice which is received by the Seller at any time other than on an Exercise Business Day during the Exercise Period shall be invalid, unless such notice is received (i) prior to the Earliest Exercise Time on an Exercise Business Day, in which case it shall be deemed to be received at the Earliest Exercise Time, (ii) in respect of an European Option only, on any Exercise Business Day prior to the Expiration Date, in which case such notice shall be deemed to be received at the Earliest Exercise Time on the Expiration Date or (iii) in respect of an American Option only, after the Latest Exercise Time on an Exercise Business Day other than the Expiration Date, in which case it shall be deemed received at the Earliest Exercise Time on the following Exercise Business Day.

(4) *Automatic Exercise.* If the parties agree to apply "Automatic Exercise" to an Option Transaction, then the unexercised amount or number of the Underlying Asset or the unexercised number of Options under such Option Transaction ("Unexercised Quantity") shall be deemed to be automatically exercised at the Latest Exercise Time on the Expiration Date if at such time the Buyer would be entitled to request payment of the Cash Settlement Amount, unless the Buyer notifies the Seller prior to such time at the Seller's Office, orally, including by telephone, or in

writing, that it does not wish Automatic Exercise to apply.

(5) *Conditional Exercise.* The parties may specify in relation to an Option Transaction that the Option may only be exercised if a specified event has occurred ("Knock-in Event") or not occurred ("Knock-out Event") or if the price of the Underlying Asset or the level of the Underlying Measurement agreed as such between the parties ("Barrier") has been reached or crossed or not.

(6) *Partial Exercise.* If the parties agree to apply "Partial Exercise" to an Option Transaction, then the Buyer shall be entitled to exercise less than the entire amount or number of Options, provided that the Exercise Notice specifies the amount or number (the "Exercise Quantity") of Options exercised. Any Exercise Quantity must be (i) equal to or greater than the minimum quantity agreed between the parties (the "Minimum Exercise Quantity") and (ii) equal to or an integral multiple of the number agreed between the parties (the "Integral Multiple") in respect of the relevant Option Transaction. Any exercise (i) which does not specify an Exercise Quantity will be deemed to be an exercise of the Unexercised Quantity, (ii) of less than the Minimum Exercise Quantity is invalid, (iii) which refers to an Exercise Quantity which is not equal to or an integral multiple of the Integral Multiple will be deemed to be an exercise of a number of Options equal to the nearest smaller integral multiple of the Integral Multiple.

(7) *Multiple Exercise.* If the parties agree to apply "Multiple Exercise" to an American Option or Bermuda Option, then the Buyer shall be entitled to exercise parts of or the entire Unexercised Quantity once or several times during the Exercise Period, provided that any Exercise Notice specifies the Exercise Quantity. Except for the exercise of the entire Unexercised Quantity on the Expiration Date, any Exercise Quantity must be (i) equal to or greater than the Minimum Exercise Quantity, (ii) equal to or less than the maximum quantity agreed between the parties (the "Maximum Exercise Quantity") and (iii) equal to or an integral multiple of the Integral Multiple, each as agreed in respect of the relevant Option Transaction. Any exercise (i) which does not specify an Exercise Quantity will be deemed to be an exercise of the Unexercised Quantity, (ii) of more than the Maximum Exercise Quantity will be deemed to be an exercise of the Maximum Exercise Quantity, (iii) of less than the Minimum Exercise Quantity is invalid and (iv) which refers to an Exercise Quantity which is not equal to or an integral multiple of the Integral Multiple will be deemed to be an exercise of a number of Options equal to the nearest smaller integral multiple of the Integral Multiple. As a consequence of any such exercise of Options in a quantity of less than the Unexercised Quantity the Unexercised Quantity shall be reduced accordingly.

5. Cash Settlement

(1) *Cash Settlement Amount.* "Cash Settlement Amount" means the amount agreed between the parties or, failing such agreement, an amount in the Cash Settlement Currency determined by the Calculation Agent on the Valuation Date in accordance with the applicable Cash Settlement Method.
"Cash Settlement Method" means (a) the methodology or formula agreed between the parties in respect of the individual Option Transaction or defined in any applicable Supplement or, failing such agreement or Supplement, (b), in case of Section 1(1)(a)(ii) or 1(1)(b) of this Supplement, the following method: the Cash Settlement Amount shall be calculated by the Calculation Agent on the Valuation Date based on the Settlement Price or Settlement Level determined on such date or, in case of Asian Options, on each Averaging Date; the Cash Settlement Amount shall be equal to the product of (i) the difference between the Settlement Price and the Strike Price or, as the case may be, the Settlement Level and the Strike Level and (ii), in case of Section 1(1)(b) of this Supplement, the agreed amount per unit of the Underlying Measurement, (iii) the Exercise Quantity and (iv) the agreed factor, if any, (c), in case of Section 1(1)(c) or 1(1)(d) of this Supplement, the method specified in Section 7(1)(a) of the General Provisions and applied as if the Buyer were the Calculation Party.

(2) *Payment of the Cash Settlement Amount.* The Cash Settlement Amount shall be paid on the Settlement Date agreed as such between the parties or, failing such agreement, two Business Days following the Valuation Date.

6. Taxes and Duties.

If "Physical Settlement" applies to an Option Transaction, the Buyer shall bear all taxes and duties necessarily falling due in connection with the delivery or transfer of the Underlying Asset.

FEDERATION BANCAIRE DE L'UNION EUROPEENNE
BANKING FEDERATION OF THE EUROPEAN UNION
BANKENVEREINIGUNG DER EUROPÄISCHEN UNION

in co-operation with

EUROPEAN SAVINGS BANKS GROUP
GROUPEMENT EUROPEEN DES CAISSES D'EPARGNE
EUROPÄISCHE SPARKASSENVEREINIGUNG

EUROPEAN ASSOCIATION OF COOPERATIVE BANKS
GROUPEMENT EUROPEEN DES BANQUES COOPERATIVES
EUROPÄISCHE VEREINIGUNG DER GENOSSENSCHAFTSBANKEN

MASTER AGREEMENT FOR FINANCIAL TRANSACTIONS

SUPPLEMENT TO THE DERIVATIVES ANNEX

INTEREST RATE TRANSACTIONS
Edition 2004

This Supplement complements the General Provisions and the Derivatives Annex which form part of a Master Agreement for Financial Transactions based on the form published by the FBE.

1. Purpose, Interpretation

(1) Purpose. The purpose of this Supplement ("Interest Rate Supplement") is to govern Interest Rate Transactions, which means an Interest Rate Swap, Cross Currency Rate Swap, Forward Rate Agreement, Interest Rate Cap, Interest Rate Floor, Interest Rate Swaption or any other Transaction so agreed by the parties in respect of an individual Transaction or in the Special Provisions.

(2) Interpretation. This Supplement forms an integral part of the Derivatives Annex. The term "Annex" as used in Section 1(3) of the General Provisions should be construed as to include this Supplement. In the event of any conflict between different parts of the Derivatives Annex and this Supplement, this Supplement shall prevail.

2. Interest Rate Transactions

"Interest Rate Swap" means a Transaction in which (a) one party pays, once or periodically, amounts of money (the "Floating Amounts") in a specified currency calculated on a specified notional amount (the "Notional Amount") in such currency and a specified Floating Rate, and (b) the other party pays, once or periodically, either (i) amounts of money (the "Fixed Amounts") in the same currency calculated on the same Notional Amount and a specified Fixed Rate or (ii) Floating Amounts in the same currency calculated on the same Notional Amount and a different Floating Rate.

"Cross Currency Rate Swap" means a Transaction in which (a) one party pays, once or periodically, Floating Amounts or Fixed Amounts in a specified currency calculated on a specified notional amount (the "Currency Amount") in such currency, and (b) the other party pays, once or periodically, Floating Amounts or Fixed Amounts in a different currency calculated on a Currency Amount in such different currency.

"Forward Rate Agreement" or "FRA" means a Transaction in which one party (the "Seller") or the other party (the "Buyer") pays, once or periodically, Floating Amounts in a specified currency calculated on a Notional Amount in such currency and the difference between the Floating Rate and the Fixed Rate.

"Interest Rate Cap" means a Transaction in which the Seller pays to the Buyer against payment of an agreed premium, once or periodically, Floating Amounts in a specified currency calculated on a Notional Amount in such currency and the difference between the Floating Rate and the Fixed Rate, if such amount is a positive number.

"Interest Rate Floor" means a Transaction in which the Seller pays to the Buyer against payment of an agreed premium, once or periodically, Floating Amounts in a specified currency calculated on a Notional Amount in such currency and the difference between the Floating Rate and the Fixed Rate, if such amount is a negative number.

"Interest Rate Swaption" means an Option Transaction in which the Seller grants to the Buyer against payment of a Premium the right to cause the underlying Interest Rate Transaction (the "Underlying Transaction") to become effective, whereby the Underlying Transaction is to be settled (i) by making all payments and deliveries or transfers to be made by the parties in accordance with the terms of the Underlying Transaction, in the case of an Interest Rate Swaption to which "Physical Settlement" applies (the "Physically Settled Interest Rate Swaption") or (ii), in the case of an Interest Rate Swaption to which "Cash Settlement" applies (the "Cash Settled Interest

Rate Swaption"), by paying the Cash Settlement Amount based on the value of the Underlying Transaction on the Valuation Date, if such value, from the Buyer's perspective, is a positive number.

3. Deliveries and Payments

(1) *Interest Rate Swap and Cross Currency Rate Swap.* On each agreed Settlement Date for the payment of a Floating Amount, the party (the "Floating Amount Payer") that owes such amount shall pay the Floating Amount and on each Settlement Date for the payment of a Fixed Amount, the party (the "Fixed Amount Payer") that owes such amount shall pay the Fixed Amount.

(2) *Forward Rate Agreement.* On each agreed Settlement Date for the payment of a Floating Amount, the Seller shall pay to the Buyer the Floating Amount if such amount is a positive number and the Buyer shall pay to the Seller the Floating Amount if such amount is a negative number.

(3) *Interest Rate Cap and Interest Rate Floor.* On each agreed Settlement Date for the payment of a premium, the Buyer shall pay to the Seller the agreed premium. On each agreed Settlement Date for the payment of a Floating Amount, the Seller under an Interest Rate Cap shall pay to the Buyer the Floating Amount if such amount is a positive number and the Seller under an Interest Rate Floor shall pay to the Buyer the Floating Amount if such amount is a negative number.

(4) *Physically Settled Interest Rate Swaption.* On each agreed Premium Payment Date for a Physically Settled Interest Rate Swaption, the Buyer shall pay to the Seller the Premium. If a Physically Settled Interest Rate Swaption is exercised or deemed to be exercised, on each agreed Settlement Date for the payment of a Floating Amount under the Underlying Transaction, the Floating Amount Payer shall pay the Floating Amount and on each Settlement Date agreed for the payment of a Fixed Amount under the Underlying Transaction, the Fixed Amount Payer shall pay the Fixed Amount.

(5) *Cash Settled Interest Rate Swaption.* On each agreed Premium Payment Date for a Cash Settled Interest Rate Swaption, the Buyer shall pay to the Seller the Premium. If a Cash Settled Interest Rate Swaption is exercised or deemed to be exercised, on the Settlement Date for the Cash Settled Interest Rate Swaption, the Seller shall pay to the Buyer the Cash Settlement Amount, if such amount is a positive number. The Cash Settlement Amount is (a) the amount agreed as such between the parties or, failing such agreement, (b) an amount in the Cash Settlement Currency equal to the value of the Underlying Transaction as determined by the Calculation Agent on the Valuation Date in accordance with (i) the Cash Settlement Method agreed between the parties in respect of the relevant Option Transaction or, failing such agreement, (ii) Section 7(1)(a) of the General Provisions and applied as if the Buyer were the Calculation Party.

4. Calculation of Fixed Amounts and Floating Amounts

(1) *Fixed Amounts.* The Fixed Amount payable on a Settlement Date of a Fixed Amount is the amount (a) agreed to by the parties in respect of that Settlement Date or the Calculation Period relating to that Settlement Date or, failing such agreement, (b) equal to the product of (i) the Calculation Amount (ii) the Fixed Rate, and (iii) the Day Count Fraction elected by the parties in respect of the Fixed Amounts.

(2) *Floating Amounts.* The Floating Amount payable on a Settlement Date of a Floating Amount is the amount (a), if neither "Compounding" nor "Flat Compounding" is elected in respect of the relevant Transaction, equal to the product of (i) the Calculation Amount, (ii) the Floating Rate (plus or minus a spread), and (iii) the Day Count Fraction elected by the parties in respect of Floating Amounts; or (b), if "Compounding" is elected in respect of the relevant Transaction, equal to the sum of the Compounding Period Amounts calculated for each Compounding Period in the Calculation Period relating to that Settlement Date; or (c), if "Flat Compounding" is elected in respect of the relevant Transaction, equal to the sum of (i) the Basic Compounding Period Amounts and (ii) the Additional Compounding Period Amounts, each calculated for each Compounding Period in the Calculation Period relating to that Settlement Date. For the purposes of the calculation of the Floating Amount and where "Compounding" or "Flat Compounding" is elected in respect of the relevant Transaction:

"Compounding Period" means, in relation to a Calculation Period, each period beginning with, and including, the Effective Date or a Compounding Date and ending with, but excluding, the next following Compounding Date or Termination Date.

"Compounding Date" means each day during the term of the relevant Transaction agreed as such by the parties, subject to adjustments in accordance with Section 3(6) of the General Provisions applicable to Period End Dates in respect of the Transaction.

"Compounding Period Amount" means, for each Compounding Period, an amount equal to the product of (i) the Adjusted Calculation Amount, (ii) the Floating Rate (plus or minus a spread), and (iii) the Day Count Fraction elected by the parties in respect of Floating Amounts.

"Adjusted Calculation Amount" means (i) in relation to the first Compounding Period in the Calculation Period, the Calculation Amount for this Calculation Period and (ii) in relation to each succeeding Compounding Period in this Calculation Period, an amount equal to the sum of the Calculation Amount for this Calculation Period and the Compounding Period Amounts for each of the preceding Compounding Periods in this Calculation Period.

"Basic Compounding Period Amount" means, for each Compounding Period, an amount calculated in accordance with the method indicated in subsection 2(a) above.

"Additional Compounding Period Amount" means, for each Compounding Period, an amount equal to the product of (i) the Flat Compounding Amount, (ii) the Floating Rate, and (iii) the Day Count Fraction elected by the parties in respect of Floating Amounts.

"Flat Compounding Amount" means (i) in relation to the first Compounding Period in the Calculation Period, zero and (ii) in relation to each succeeding Compounding Period in this Calculation Period, an amount equal to the sum of the Basic Compounding Period Amounts and the

Additional Compounding Period Amounts for each of the preceding Compounding Periods in this Calculation Period.

(3) *Calculation Amount*. "Calculation Amount" means the Notional Amount or, as the case may be, the Currency Amount expressed in a specified currency agreed to by the parties in respect of the relevant Settlement Date or the Calculation Period relating to that Settlement Date.

(4) *Fixed Rate*. "Fixed Rate" means the interest rate expressed as a decimal figure equal to a per annum rate agreed by the parties in respect of the relevant Settlement Date or the Calculation Period relating to that Settlement Date.

(5) *Floating Rate*. "Floating Rate" means (a) in respect of a Forward Rate Agreement, Interest Rate Cap and Interest Rate Floor, the difference between (i) the interest rate determined in the manner described in (b) below and (ii) the Fixed Rate, in each case expressed as a decimal figure equal to a per annum rate, and (b) in respect of all other Interest Rate Transactions (i) the interest rate expressed as a decimal figure equal to a per annum rate agreed by the parties in respect of the relevant Settlement Date or the Calculation Period or Compounding Period relating to that Settlement Date, or, failing such agreement, (ii) if the parties agreed to a specified Floating Rate Option and either (x) only one Reset Date has been agreed by the parties in respect of the relevant Settlement Date or the Calculation Period or Compounding Period relating to that Settlement Date, the Settlement Interest Rate on that Reset Date, or (y) more than one Reset Date has been agreed by the parties in respect of the relevant Settlement Date or the Calculation Period or Compounding Period relating to that Settlement Date, the arithmetic mean of the Settlement Interest Rates for each of those Reset Dates, or (z) more than one Reset Date and "Weighted Average" has been agreed by the parties in respect of the relevant Settlement Date or the Calculation Period or Compounding Period relating to that Settlement Date, the weighted arithmetic mean of the Settlement Interest Rates for each of those Reset Dates calculated by (x) multiplying each Settlement Interest Rate by the number of days such Settlement Interest Rate is in effect, (y) determining the sum of those products, and (z) dividing such sum by the number of days in the relevant Calculation Period or Compounding Period.

"Settlement Interest Rate" means the interest rate expressed as a decimal figure equal to a per annum rate as determined on or in respect of the relevant Reset Date on the basis of the interest rate (i) quoted through and obtained from the Price Source specified in the agreed Floating Rate Option or, failing such agreement, (ii) determined by the Calculation Agent.

"Floating Rate Option" means the interest rate agreed by the parties by reference to the publication, screen or web page of an information vendor or any other price source (the "Price Source").

"Reset Date" means, subject to adjustments in accordance with Section 3(6) of the General Provisions, each day (i) agreed as such by the parties in respect of the relevant Transaction or (ii) determined by applying the agreed Floating Rate Option, subject to the provisions of paragraph 8 below.

(6) *Rounding*. Any interest rate used for calculating a Floating Amount or Fixed Amount shall, if not already an integral number, be rounded up or down to the nearest fifth decimal place. If the sixth decimal place is equal to five, the fifth decimal place shall be rounded up.

(7) *Day Count Fraction*. "Day Count Fraction" means, as elected by the parties in respect of calculating the Fixed Amounts or Floating Amounts or Compounding Period Amounts:

(a) "1/1" means the fraction whose numerator is 1 and whose denominator is 1.

(b) "Actual/360" means the fraction whose numerator is the actual number of days elapsed during the Calculation Period or Compounding Period and whose denominator is 360.

(c) "30E/360" means the fraction whose numerator is the number of days elapsed during the Calculation Period or Compounding Period, calculated on the basis of a year comprising 12 months of 30 days and whose denominator is 360. If the last day of the Calculation Period or Compounding Period is the last day of the month of February, the number of days elapsed during such month shall be taken as the actual number of days.

(d) "30/360" means the fraction whose numerator is the number of days elapsed during the Calculation Period or Compounding Period, calculated on the basis of a year comprising 12 months of 30 days and whose denominator is 360. If the last day of the Calculation Period or Compounding Period is the 31st day of a month and the first day of the Calculation Period or Compounding Period is a day other than the 30th or 31st day of a month, the last month of the period shall be deemed to be a month of 31 days. If the last day of the Calculation Period or Compounding Period is the last day of the month of February, the number of days elapsed during such month shall be taken as the actual number of days.

(e) "360/360 (German Master)" means the fraction whose numerator is the number of days elapsed during the Calculation Period or Compounding Period, calculated on the basis of 360-day year with 12 months of 30 days and whose denominator is 360.

(f) "Actual/365" means the fraction whose numerator is the actual number of days elapsed during the Calculation Period or Compounding Period and whose denominator is 365 or 366 in the case of a leap year. If part of the Calculation Period or Compounding Period should fall in a leap year, Actual/365 shall mean the sum of (i) the fraction whose numerator is the actual number of days elapsed during the non-leap year and whose denominator is 365 and (ii) the fraction whose numerator is the number of actual days elapsed during the leap year and whose denominator is 366.

(g) "Actual/Fixed 365" means the fraction whose numerator is the actual number of days elapsed during the Calculation Period or Compounding Period and whose denominator is 365.

(h) "365/365 (German Master)" means the fraction whose numerator is the number of days elapsed during the Calculation Period or Compounding Period and whose denominator is 365 or 366 in the case of a leap year.

(i) "Actual/Actual AFB/FBF Master Agreement)" means the fraction whose numerator is the actual number of days elapsed during the Calculation Period or Compounding Period and whose denominator is 365 (or 366 if 29 February falls within the Calculation Period or Compounding Period). If the Calculation Period or Compounding Period is a term of more than one year, the basis shall be calculated as follows: (a) the number of complete years shall be counted back from the last day of the Calculation Period or Compounding Period and (b) this number shall be increased by the fraction for the relevant period calculated as shown above.

(8) *Determination of the Settlement Interest Rate.* Where a Floating Rate is to be determined by reference to a specified Floating Rate Option, the Calculation Agent shall notify the other party or, as the case may be, each party the Settlement Interest Rate and the Floating Rate calculated therefrom on the Reset Date or promptly thereafter. If on a Reset Date a Price Source Disruption Event occurs and the Calculation Agent determines that such event is material, (a) if only one Reset Date has been agreed by the parties in respect of the relevant Settlement Date or the Calculation Period or Compounding Period relating to that Settlement Date, the Reset Date shall be postponed to the first succeeding Business Day on which there is no Price Source Disruption Event, unless there is a Price Source Disruption Event relating to the relevant Floating Rate Option on each of the five Business Days immediately following the Reset Date, in which case such fifth Business Day shall be deemed to be the Reset Date and the Calculation Agent shall determine the Settlement Interest Rate on that fifth Business Day; or (b) if more than one Reset Date has been agreed by the parties in respect of the relevant Settlement Date or the Calculation Period or Compounding Period relating to that Settlement Date, that Reset Date should be omitted and deemed to be not a relevant Reset Date, provided that if through operation of this provision there would not be a Reset Date, then (a) above will apply.

(9) *Price Source Disruption and Price Source Conversion.* "Price Source Disruption Event" means any failure of the relevant Price Source to announce, display or publish the interest rate for the relevant Floating Rate Option or any other information necessary for determining the interest rate or a temporary or permanent discontinuance or unavailability of the Price Source. If the relevant Price Source has ceased to announce, display or publish the interest rate for the relevant Floating Rate Option and (i) if an alternative price source (the "Successor Price Source") has been agreed by the parties for the relevant Transaction or, failing such agreement, (ii) if a Successor Price Source is officially designated in the information vendor's publication, screen or web page or by the sponsor of the Floating Rate Option, the Calculation Agent will determine the Settlement Interest Rate by reference to that Successor Price Source. If no such Successor Price Source has been agreed or designated, the Calculation Agent will determine the Settlement Interest Rate by reference to a new Floating Rate Option agreed by the parties.

(10) *Correction of Published Interest Rates.* Where a Floating Rate is to be determined by reference to a specified Floating Rate Option, in the event that an interest rate announced, displayed or published by the relevant information vendor and used by the Calculation Agent for determining the Settlement Interest Rate is subsequently corrected and announced, displayed or published within thirty Business Days after the relevant Reset Date, the Calculation Agent shall notify the other party or, as the case may be, each party of the Settlement Interest Rate, the Floating Rate calculated there from and the Floating Amount payable as a result of that correction.

(11) *Calculation Period, Period End Date.* "Calculation Period" means each period beginning with, and including, the Effective Date or a Period End Date and ending with, but excluding, the next following Period End Date or Termination Date. "Period End Date" means (a) each day during the term of the Transaction agreed as such by the parties, or (b) if "Eurodollar Convention" has been agreed by the parties, each day during the term of the Transaction that numerically corresponds with the preceding applicable Period End Date or Effective Date in the calendar month that is the specified number of months after the month in which such preceding applicable Period End Date or Effective Date occurred, provided that if there is no numerically corresponding day in the calendar month in which such Period End Date should occur, Period End Date will be the last Business Day of that calendar month and all subsequent Period End Dates will be the last Business Day of the calendar month that is the specified number of months after the month in which the preceding applicable Period End Date occurred and, failing such agreements, (c) each Settlement Date, in each case subject to adjustments in accordance with Section 3(6) of the General Provisions which shall apply accordingly, provided that no such adjustment applies if "No Adjustment" has been agreed by the parties.

(12) *Settlement Date.* "Settlement Date" means in respect of the payment of a Floating Amount or Fixed Amount either (a) each day during the term of the Transaction agreed by the parties upon which the payment of a Floating Amount or a Fixed Amount shall be made, or (b) if "Delayed Payment" is agreed between the parties, each date that is the specified number of days after the applicable Period End Date or Termination Date, or (c) if "Early Payment" is agreed between the parties, each date that is the specified number of days prior to the applicable Period End Date or Termination Date or, failing such agreements, (d) each Period End Date, in each case subject to adjustments in accordance with Section 3(6) of the General Provisions.

5.   Provisions applicable to Option Transactions

Unless otherwise defined in this Supplement, any term relating to Option Transactions is to be construed in accordance with the applicable Options Supplement published by the FBE.

FEDERATION BANCAIRE DE L'UNION EUROPEENNE
BANKING FEDERATION OF THE EUROPEAN UNION
BANKENVEREINIGUNG DER EUROPÄISCHEN UNION

in co-operation with

EUROPEAN SAVINGS BANKS GROUP
GROUPEMENT EUROPEEN DES CAISSES D'EPARGNE
EUROPÄISCHE SPARKASSENVEREINIGUNG

EUROPEAN ASSOCIATION OF COOPERATIVE BANKS
GROUPEMENT EUROPEEN DES BANQUES COOPERATIVES
EUROPÄISCHE VEREINIGUNG DER GENOSSENSCHAFTSBANKEN

MASTER AGREEMENT
FOR FINANCIAL TRANSACTIONS

dated as of _____

between

_____ and _____
("Party A")   ("Party B")

SPECIAL PROVISIONS
Edition 2004

1. Nature of Agreement

This contractual arrangement (the "Special Provisions"), together with the General Provisions (the "General Provisions") and any annex (each an "Annex") referred to below, constitutes a master agreement (the "Master Agreement") under which the parties may enter into financial transactions.

2. Incorporation of Documents

The following documents, all in the _____ language, published by the FBE are hereby incorporated into and shall accordingly form part of the Master Agreement:

(a) the General Provisions, Edition 2004
(b) the following Annex[es][1]

Product Annex[es] for :
Repurchase Transactions, Edition January 2001
Securities Loans, Edition January 2001
Derivative Transactions, Edition 2004
Supplement for Foreign Exchange Transactions, Edition 2004
Supplement for Interest Rate Transactions, Edition 2004
Supplement for Option Transactions, Edition 2004
Margin Maintenance Annex, Edition 2004
Other Supplements (give details)

---

[1] Delete and/or complete the references in this paragraph (b) as appropriate

Copyright © 2004 FBE

3. **Addresses for notices (Section 8(1) of the General Provisions)**

The addresses for notices and other communications between the parties are: ...

4. **Governing law, Settlement of Disputes, Jurisdiction, Arbitration (Section 11(1) and (2) of the General Provisions)**

The law governing the Agreement is _____ law.

Settlement of Disputes:

Jurisdiction[2]:   The court(s) referred to in Section 11(2) is/are _____.

Arbitration[3]:   The rules of arbitration referred to in Section 11(2) are the Rules of Arbitration of[4] [Euro Arbitration – European Center for Financial Dispute Resolution] [the International Chamber of Commerce] [§§] [other][§§] [with which each party agrees to comply].

The parties agree to submit those disputes to [a single] [three] arbitrator[s].

Such arbitration shall take place in _____.

The language[s] in which arbitration shall be conducted [is] [are] _____.

5. **Other provisions**

_____[5]

_____   _____
(Name of Party A)   (Name of Party B)

By: By:

_____   _____
Name(s):   Name(s):
Title(s):   Title(s):

---

[2] Delete if not applicable
[3] Delete if not applicable
[4] If arbitration is selected, specify which rules apply
[5] Insert amendments (which may be provisions from the attached Appendix) or state "None"

Copyright © 2004 FBE   Special provisions - 2004

Appendix (Checklist)
Elections and Amendments[6]

I. General Provisions

(1)   Section 3(4) (Payment Netting)

The principle set forth in Section 3(4), first sentence, of the General Provisions is hereby extended so as to apply also to:

- mutual payments in the same currency in respect of [the following types of Transactions: ...][all types of Transactions] and

- mutual deliveries of assets that are fungible with each other and are due in respect of [the same Transaction] [the following types of Transactions: ...] [all types of Transactions].

(2)   Section 3(5) (Late Payment)

The interest surcharge referred to in Section 3(5) shall be ... per cent per annum.

(3)   Section 3(8) (Market Value)

The price source for determining the Market Value of Securities shall be...

(4)   Section 5(2) (Guarantor/Guarantee)

Guarantor means

   in relation to Party A: ... (whose jurisdiction of organisation/incorporation is ...)
   in relation to Party B: ... (whose jurisdiction of organisation/incorporation is ...).

Guarantee means

   in relation to Party A: ...
   in relation to Party B: ...

(5)   Section 6(1)(a)(v) (Default under Specified Transactions)

Section 6(1)(a)(v) will apply to [Party A][Party B][both parties] and "Specified Transactions" are ..... (e.g.: derivative and other trading transactions (to be specified) entered into with the other party to the Agreement and/or with any third party).

(6)   Section 6(1)(a)(vi) (Cross Default)

Section 6(1)(a)(vi) shall not apply/apply only to Party [A] [B] and not to the other party/apply with the following modifications:

The Default Threshold is:

   in relation to Party A: ...
   in relation to Party B: ...

(7)   Section 6(1)(a)(viii) (Insolvency Events)

The following shall, in addition to each party's country of organisation, incorporation, principal office or residence, be a Specified Jurisdiction:

   in relation to Party A: ...
   in relation to Party B: ...

Sub-paragraph (viii) (5) (B) shall not apply/shall apply with a period of ... days instead of thirty days/shall apply only to Party [A] [B].

---

[6]   These provisions refer to clauses of the Master Agreement contemplating possible choices or modifications to be made in the Special Provisions. When any such provision is not inserted, the relevant fall back provision specified in the Master Agreement will apply. Parties may insert these provisions (or any other clause amending the terms of the Master Agreement) in paragraph no 5 (Other provisions) of the Special Provisions

(8)   Section 6(1)(b) (Automatic Termination)

Section 6(1)(b), second sentence, shall not apply/shall apply only in relation to Party [A][B].

(9)   Section 6(2)(a) (Change of Circumstances)

Section 6(2)(a)(ii) shall extend to an Impossibility Event.

(10) Section 7(1)(b) (Conversion)

"Base Currency" means...

(11) Section 8(1) (Manner of Giving Notices)

The electronic messaging system(s) for purposes of Section 8(1) is/are: ...

(12) Section 9(1) (Booking Offices)

Booking Offices may be

    in relation to Party A: - for Repurchase Transactions: ...
                                        - for Securities Loans: ...
                                        - for Derivative Transactions.....

    in relation to Party B: - for Repurchase Transactions: ...
                                        - for Securities Loans: ...
                                        - for Derivative Transactions.....

(13) Section 10(4) (Documents)

The following documents shall be delivered by Party A and Party B, respectively, by the dates specified below:

	Type of document	To be delivered by (date)
Party A:	......	......
Party B:	......	......

(14) Section 10(9) (Previous Transactions)

[Specify relevant transactions (if any) and further details (e.g. effect/cessation of effect of contractual terms governing previous transactions)]

(15) Section 11(3) (Service of Process)

The Process Agent (Section 11(3)) is

    in relation to Party A: ...
    in relation to Party B: ...

II. Margin Maintenance Annex

(1)   Transactions and groups of Transactions covered

Net Exposure shall be calculated, and Margin transferred, in respect of the following Booking Offices and types of Transactions:

(i)   [all Booking Offices in the aggregate]
      [each Booking Office of Party A/B][7]
      [each pair of Booking Offices of Party A and Party B][8]
      [other arrangement]

---

[7] If one Party acts through more than one office
[8] If both parties act through more than one office

(ii) [the aggregate of all Repurchase Transactions, Securities Loans and Derivative Transactions],
[the aggregate of all Repurchase Transactions, of all Securities Loans and of all Derivative Transactions in each case separately],
[the aggregate of all Transactions relating to fixed income Securities, of all Transactions relating to equity Securities and of Derivative Transactions, in each case separately],
[each Transaction separately],
[other arrangement].

(2) Eligible Margin

Cash Margin: eligible currencies (other than the Base Currency):

Currency	Valuation Percentage	Transferring party	
[ ]	[ ]%	[Party A]	[Party B]

Interest payable on Cash Margin:

Margin Securities:

	Eligible Securities	Valuation Percentage	Transferring party	
(i)	Negotiable debt obligations issued by the Government of [ ] having an original maturity at issuance of not more than [one year]	[ ]%	[Party A]	[Party B]
(ii)	Negotiable debt obligations issued by the Government of [ ] having an original maturity at issuance of more than [one year] but not more than 10 years	[ ]%	[Party A]	[Party B]
(iii)	Other:		[Party A]	[Party B]

(3) "Valuation Agent" means: ...

(4) Valuation Procedure

(a) "Valuation Date" means each [Business Day/Monday...]

(b) "Independent Amount" means
- with respect to Party A: ...
- with respect to Party B: ...

(c) "Exposure Threshold" means:
- in relation to the Net Exposure of Party B to Party A: ...
- in relation to the Net Exposure of Party A to Party B: ...

(d) "Minimum Transfer Amount" means: ...

(5) Margin Transfer Deadline

The date by which transfers of Margin have to be effected pursuant to Section 2(2) of the Margin Maintenance Annex shall be...

III. Other Annexes

Repurchase Annex

Section 2(7)(v) shall apply.

Securities Lending Annex

Section 2(6)(v) shall apply.

Derivatives Annex

<u>Section 1(2)(b)</u>

The provisions of Section 1(2)(b) of the Derivatives Annex shall not apply to foreign exchange transactions settling within two Business Days following the date/one Business Day following the date/on the same Business Day[9] on which the transaction is concluded.

<u>Section 1(2)(c)</u>

The provisions of Section 1(2)(c) of the Derivatives Annex shall apply to the following types of Derivative Transactions:

<u>types of Derivative Transactions</u>
[   ].

<u>Section 2</u>

The Market Standard Documentation(s) set out below shall be incorporated into the terms of the following types of Derivative Transactions:

<u>Market Standard Documentation(s)</u>   <u>types of Derivative Transactions</u>
[   ]   [   ].

The terms in the Market Standard Documentation(s) which have been incorporated into the terms of a Derivative Transaction shall be construed in accordance with the following law(s) as set out below:

<u>Market Standard Documentation(s)</u>   <u>law</u>
[   ]   [   ].

---

[9] Delete where not applicable

FBE

FEDERATION BANCAIRE DE L'UNION EUROPEENNE
BANKING FEDERATION OF THE EUROPEAN UNION
BANKENVEREINIGUNG DER EUROPÄISCHEN UNION

in co-operation with

EUROPEAN SAVINGS BANKS GROUP
GROUPEMENT EUROPEEN DES CAISSES D'EPARGNE
EUROPÄISCHE SPARKASSENVEREINIGUNG

EUROPEAN ASSOCIATION OF COOPERATIVE BANKS
GROUPEMENT EUROPEEN DES BANQUES COOPERATIVES
EUROPÄISCHE VEREINIGUNG DER GENOSSENSCHAFTSBANKEN

MASTER AGREEMENT FOR FINANCIAL TRANSACTIONS

INDEX OF DEFINED TERMS
Edition 2004

This index sets forth the documents and sections in which the terms listed below are defined.

As used in this index,
SP means Special Provisions,
GP means General Provisions,
REPO means Product Annex for Repurchase Transactions,
SL means Product Annex for Securities Loans,
D means Product Annex for Derivative Transactions,
MMA means Margin Maintenance Annex,
SIR means Supplement to the Derivatives Annex - Interest Rate Transactions,
SFX means Supplement to the Derivatives Annex - Foreign Exchange Transactions,
SO means supplement to the Derivatives Annex - Option Transactions.

Numbers not in parentheses are references to sections of the relevant document; numbers and letters in parentheses are references to subsections and paragraphs.

Copyright © 2004 FBE

Index of Defined Terms - 2004

A.
Accrued Interest REPO 5(1)
Acquisition Cost SL 2(5)(b)(ii)
Additional Compounding Period Amount SIR 4(2)
Adjusted Calculation Amount SIR 4(2)
Adjusted Net Exposure MMA 1(1)
Affected Party GP 6(2)(b)
Agency Transaction GP 10(10)(a)
Agent GP 10(10)(a)
Agreement GP 1(2)
Alternative Borrowing Cost SL 2(5)(a)(i)
Alternative Purchase Cost REPO 2(6)(b)(iii)
American Option SO 2(1)
Amounts Due GP 7(1)(a)
Annex SP1; GP1(2)
Applicable Exchange Rate GP 7(l)(b)
Asian Option SO 2(1)
Automatic Exercise SO 4(4)
Averaging Date SO 2(3)

B.
Barrier SO 4(5)
Base Currency GP 7(l)(b)
Basic Compounding Period Amount SIR 4(2)
Bermuda Option SO 2(1)
Booking Office GP 9(3)
Borrower SL 1(1)
Borrowing Cost REPO 2(6)(a)(ii)
Business Day GP 3(7)
Buyer REPO 1(1); SO 1(1); SFX 2; SIR 2
Buy/Sell Back Transactions REPO 5(1)

C.
Calculation Agent D 4
Calculation Amount SIR 4(3)
Calculation Party GP 7(1)(a)
Calculation Period SIR 4(11)
Call SO 2(2)
Call Currency SFX 2
Cash Margin MMA 1(1)
Cash Settled Foreign Exchange Option SFX 2
Cash Settled Interest Rate Swaption SIR 2
Cash Settlement SO 1(1)(a)(ii); SO 1(1)(c)(ii); SFX 2; SIR 2
Cash Settlement Amount SO 5(1); SFX 3(4)
Cash Settlement Currency D 4
Cash Settlement Method SO 5(1)
Change of Circumstances GP 6(2)(a)
Clean Price REPO 5(1)
Commence GP 6(1)(a)(viii)
Commencement Date SO 2(3)
Competent Authority GP 6(1)(a)(viii)(3)
Compounding SIR 4(2)
Compounding Date SIR 4(2)
Compounding Period SIR 4(2)
Compounding Period Amount SIR 4(2)
Confirmation GP 2(2)
Contractual Currency GP 3(1)
Corporate Restructuring GP 6(1)(a)(vii)
Counterclaims GP 7(4)
Cross Currency Rate Swap SIR 2
Currency Amount SIR 2
Currency Pair SFX 3(5)
Currency Rate Option SFX 3(5)

- 3 -

D.
Day Count Fraction (1/1; Actual/360; 30E/360; 30/360; 360/360 (German Master); Actual/365; Actual/Fixed 365; 365/365 (German Master); Actual/Actual (AFB / FBF Master Agreement)) SIR 4(7)
Default Rate GP 3(5)
Default Threshold GP 6(1)(a)(vi)
Default Value GP 7(l)(a)
Defaulting Party GP 6(1)(b)
Delayed Payment SIR 4(12)
Delivery Date SL 2(1)
Derivative Transactions D 1(1)
Derivatives Annex D 1(1)
Distribution REPO 2(7)(i); SL 2(6)(i)
Documentary Tax GP 4(2)

E.
Earliest Exercise Time SO 4(2)
Early Payment SIR 4(12)
Early Termination Date GP 6(l)(b); GP 6(2)(b)
Effective Date D 4
EONIA GP 3(5)
Equivalent REPO 2(3); SL 2(3)
Eurodollar Convention SIR 4(11)
European Option SO 2(1)
Event of Default GP 6(l)(a)
Exchange D 4
Exchange Business Day D 4
Exercise Business Day SO 2(3)
Exercise Date SO 5(2)
Exercise Notice SO 4(1)
Exercise Period SO 4(2)
Exercise Quantity SO 4(6)
Expiration Date SO 2 (3)
Exposure Threshold MMA 2(6)

F.
FBE GP 1(1)
Flat Compounding Amount SIR 4(2)
Final Settlement Amount GP 7(l)(a)
Fixed Amount Payer SIR 3(1)
Fixed Amounts SIR 2
Fixed Rate SIR 4(4)
Flat Compounding SIR 4(2)
Floating Amount Payer SIR 3(1)
Floating Amounts SIR 2
Floating Rate SIR 4(5)
Floating Rate Option SIR 4(5)
Following GP 3(6)(b)
Foreign Exchange Forward SFX 2
Foreign Exchange Option SFX 2
Foreign Exchange Spot SFX 2
Foreign Exchange Supplement SFX 1(1)
Foreign Exchange Transactions SFX 1(1)
Forward Price REPO 5(1)
Forward Rate SFX 3(5)
Forward Rate Agreement (FRA) SIR 2

G.
General Provisions SP 1; GP 1(1)
Guarantee GP 5(2)
Guarantor GP 5(2)

H.
Haircut MMA 1(3)

- 4 -

I.
Impossibility Event GP 6(2)(a)(ii)
Independent Amount MMA 1(1)
Insolvency Proceeding GP 6(1)(a)(viii)
Integral Multiple SO 4(6)
Interbank Rate GP 3(5)
Interest Rate Cap SIR 2
Interest Rate Floor SIR 2
Interest Rate Supplement SIR 1(1)
Interest Rate Transactions SIR 1(1)
Interest Rate Swap SIR 2
Interest Rate Swaption SIR 2

J.
Judgment of Insolvency GP 6(1)(a)(viii)

K.
Kind ("of the same kind") GP 3(2)(b)
Knock-in Event SO 4(5)
Knock-out Event SO 4(5)

L.
Latest Exercise Time SO 4(2)
Lender SL 1(1)
Lending Fee SL 4
Liabilities MMA 1(3)
Loaned Securities SL 1(1)

M.
Margin MMA 1(3)
Margin Claim GP 7(l)(a)
Margin Ratio MMA 1(3)
Margin Provider MMA 1(1)
Margin Recipient MMA 1(1)
Margin Securities MMA 1(1)
Market Disruption Convention D 4
Market Disruption Event D 4
Market Standard Documentation D 2
Market Value GP 3(8); MMA 1(1)
Master Agreement SP 1; GP 1(1)
Maximum Exercise Quantity SO 4(7)
Minimum Exercise Quantity SO 4(6)
Minimum Transfer Amount MMA 2(6)
Modified, Modified Following GP 3(6)(c)
Multiple Exercise SO 4(7)

N.
Net Exposure MMA 1(3)
New Securities REPO 3(1)
New Transaction REPO 6(2)(b)
No Adjustment SIR 4(11)
Non-Affected Party GP 6(2)(b)
Non-Defaulting Party GP 6(l)(b)
Non-Deliverable Foreign Exchange Forward SFX 2
Non-Deliverable Foreign Exchange Option SFX 2
Notional Amount SIR 2

0.
Option SO 1(1)
Option Transactions SO 1(1)
Options Supplement SO 1(1)
Original Transactions REPO 6(2)

P.

Partial Exercise SO 4(6)
Period End Date SIR 4(11)
Physical Settlement SO 1(1)(a)(i); SO 1(1)(c)(i); SFX 2; SIR 2
Physically Settled Foreign Exchange Option SFX 2
Physically Settled Interest Rate Swaption SIR 2
Potential Final Settlement Amount MMA 1(3)
Preceding GP 3(6)(a)
Premium SO 1(1)
Premium Payment Date SO 3
Price Differential REPO 2(3)
Price Source SFX 3(5); SIR 4(5)
Price Source Disruption Event SIR 4(9)
Pricing Rate REPO 2(3)
Principal GP 10(10)(a)
Proceedings GP 11(2)
Process Agent GP 11(3)
Product Annexes GP 1(2)
Purchase Date REPO 2(1)
Purchase Price REPO 1(1)
Purchased Securities REPO 2(1)
Put SO 2(2)
Put Currency SFX 2

Q.

Quotation Date GP 7(1)(a)

R.

Reference Currency SFX 2
Repricing Date REPO 6(2)(a)
Repurchase Annex REPO 1(1)
Repurchase Date REPO 2(2)
Repurchase Price REPO 2(3)
Repurchase Transactions REPO 1(1)
Reset Date SIR 4(5)
Return Date SL 2(2)

S.

Scheduled Exercise Date SO 2(1)
Securities GP 3(2)(a)
Securities Lending Annex SL 1(1)
Securities Loans SL 1(1)
Sell Back Price REPO 5(1)
Seller REPO 1(1); SO 1(1); SFX 2; SIR 2
Seller's Office SO 4(1)
Settlement Currency SFX 2
Settlement Currency Amount SFX 3(2)
Settlement Currency Rate SFX 3(5)
Settlement Date D 4; SIR 4(12)
Settlement Interest Rate SIR 4(5)
Settlement Level SO 1(1)(b)
Settlement Price SO 1(1)(a)(ii)
simultaneous REPO 2(3); D 4
Special Provisions GP 1(2); SP I
Specified Jurisdiction GP 6(l)(a)(viii)
Specified Transactions GP 6(l)(a)(v)
Strike Level SO 1(1)(b)
Strike Price SO 1(1)(a); SFX 3(5)
Substitute Assets GP 3(2)(b)
Successor Entity GP 6(l)(a)(vii)
Successor Price Source SIR 4(9)

T.
Termination Date D 4
Trade Date D 4
Transaction GP 1(1)
Transaction Value GP 7(1)(a)

U.
Underlying Asset SO 1(1)(a)
Underlying Measurement SO 1(1)(b)
Underlying Transaction SO 1(1)(c); SIR 2
Unexercised Quantity SO 4(4)

V.
Valuation Agent MMA 1(2);
Valuation Date MMA 1(3); D 4; SO 5(2)
Valuation Percentage MMA 1(1)
Valuation Time D 4

W.
Weighted Average SIR 4(5)

APPENDIX 4: A FACSIMILE OF THE MASTER SECURITIES LOAN AGREEMENT (2000) REPRODUCED BY KIND PERMISSION OF THE SECURITIES INDUSTRY AND FINANCIAL MARKETS ASSOCIATION

Master Securities Loan Agreement

2000 Version

Dated as of: _____

Between: _____

and _____

1. **Applicability.**

    From time to time the parties hereto may enter into transactions in which one party ("Lender") will lend to the other party ("Borrower") certain Securities (as defined herein) against a transfer of Collateral (as defined herein). Each such transaction shall be referred to herein as a "Loan" and, unless otherwise agreed in writing, shall be governed by this Agreement, including any supplemental terms or conditions contained in an Annex or Schedule hereto and in any other annexes identified herein or therein as applicable hereunder. Capitalized terms not otherwise defined herein shall have the meanings provided in Section 25.

2. **Loans of Securities.**

    2.1 Subject to the terms and conditions of this Agreement, Borrower or Lender may, from time to time, seek to initiate a transaction in which Lender will lend Securities to Borrower. Borrower and Lender shall agree on the terms of each Loan (which terms may be amended during the Loan), including the issuer of the Securities, the amount of Securities to be lent, the basis of compensation, the amount of Collateral to be transferred by Borrower, and any additional terms. Such agreement shall be confirmed (a) by a schedule and receipt listing the Loaned Securities provided by Borrower to Lender in accordance with Section 3.2, (b) through any system that compares Loans and in which Borrower and Lender are participants, or (c) in such other manner as may be agreed by Borrower and Lender in writing. Such confirmation (the "Confirmation"), together with the Agreement, shall constitute conclusive evidence of the terms agreed between Borrower and Lender with respect to the Loan to which the Confirmation relates, unless with respect to the Confirmation specific objection is made promptly after receipt thereof. In the event of any inconsistency between the terms of such Confirmation and this Agreement, this Agreement shall prevail unless each party has executed such Confirmation.

    2.2 Notwithstanding any other provision in this Agreement regarding when a Loan commences, unless otherwise agreed, a Loan hereunder shall not occur until the Loaned Securities and the Collateral therefor have been transferred in accordance with Section 15.

3. **Transfer of Loaned Securities.**

   3.1 Unless otherwise agreed, Lender shall transfer Loaned Securities to Borrower hereunder on or before the Cutoff Time on the date agreed to by Borrower and Lender for the commencement of the Loan.

   3.2 Unless otherwise agreed, Borrower shall provide Lender, for each Loan in which Lender is a Customer, with a schedule and receipt listing the Loaned Securities. Such schedule and receipt may consist of (a) a schedule provided to Borrower by Lender and executed and returned by Borrower when the Loaned Securities are received, (b) in the case of Securities transferred through a Clearing Organization which provides transferors with a notice evidencing such transfer, such notice, or (c) a confirmation or other document provided to Lender by Borrower.

   3.3 Notwithstanding any other provision in this Agreement, the parties hereto agree that they intend the Loans hereunder to be loans of Securities. If, however, any Loan is deemed to be a loan of money by Borrower to Lender, then Borrower shall have, and Lender shall be deemed to have granted, a security interest in the Loaned Securities and the proceeds thereof.

4. **Collateral.**

   4.1 Unless otherwise agreed, Borrower shall, prior to or concurrently with the transfer of the Loaned Securities to Borrower, but in no case later than the Close of Business on the day of such transfer, transfer to Lender Collateral with a Market Value at least equal to the Margin Percentage of the Market Value of the Loaned Securities.

   4.2 The Collateral transferred by Borrower to Lender, as adjusted pursuant to Section 9, shall be security for Borrower's obligations in respect of such Loan and for any other obligations of Borrower to Lender hereunder. Borrower hereby pledges with, assigns to, and grants Lender a continuing first priority security interest in, and a lien upon, the Collateral, which shall attach upon the transfer of the Loaned Securities by Lender to Borrower and which shall cease upon the transfer of the Loaned Securities by Borrower to Lender. In addition to the rights and remedies given to Lender hereunder, Lender shall have all the rights and remedies of a secured party under the UCC. It is understood that Lender may use or invest the Collateral, if such consists of cash, at its own risk, but that (unless Lender is a Broker-Dealer) Lender shall, during the term of any Loan hereunder, segregate Collateral from all securities or other assets in its possession. Lender may Retransfer Collateral only (a) if Lender is a Broker-Dealer or (b) in the event of a Default by Borrower. Segregation of Collateral may be accomplished by appropriate identification on the books and records of Lender if it is a "securities intermediary" within the meaning of the UCC.

   4.3 Except as otherwise provided herein, upon transfer to Lender of the Loaned Securities on the day a Loan is terminated pursuant to Section 6, Lender shall be obligated to transfer the Collateral (as adjusted pursuant to Section 9) to Borrower no later than the Cutoff Time on such day or, if such day is not a day on which a transfer of such Collateral may be effected under Section 15, the next day on which such a transfer may be effected.

   4.4 If Borrower transfers Collateral to Lender, as provided in Section 4.1, and Lender does not transfer the Loaned Securities to Borrower, Borrower shall have the absolute right to the return of the Collateral; and if Lender transfers Loaned Securities to Borrower and

2 ■ 2000 Master Securities Loan Agreement

Appendices

Borrower does not transfer Collateral to Lender as provided in Section 4.1, Lender shall have the absolute right to the return of the Loaned Securities.

4.5 Borrower may, upon reasonable notice to Lender (taking into account all relevant factors, including industry practice, the type of Collateral to be substituted, and the applicable method of transfer), substitute Collateral for Collateral securing any Loan or Loans; provided, however, that such substituted Collateral shall (a) consist only of cash, securities or other property that Borrower and Lender agreed would be acceptable Collateral prior to the Loan or Loans and (b) have a Market Value such that the aggregate Market Value of such substituted Collateral, together with all other Collateral for Loans in which the party substituting such Collateral is acting as Borrower, shall equal or exceed the agreed upon Margin Percentage of the Market Value of the Loaned Securities.

4.6 Prior to the expiration of any letter of credit supporting Borrower's obligations hereunder, Borrower shall, no later than the Extension Deadline, (a) obtain an extension of the expiration of such letter of credit, (b) replace such letter of credit by providing Lender with a substitute letter of credit in an amount at least equal to the amount of the letter of credit for which it is substituted, or (c) transfer such other Collateral to Lender as may be acceptable to Lender.

5. Fees for Loan.

5.1 Unless otherwise agreed, (a) Borrower agrees to pay Lender a loan fee (a "Loan Fee"), computed daily on each Loan to the extent such Loan is secured by Collateral other than cash, based on the aggregate Market Value of the Loaned Securities on the day for which such Loan Fee is being computed, and (b) Lender agrees to pay Borrower a fee or rebate (a "Cash Collateral Fee") on Collateral consisting of cash, computed daily based on the amount of cash held by Lender as Collateral, in the case of each of the Loan Fee and the Cash Collateral Fee at such rates as Borrower and Lender may agree. Except as Borrower and Lender may otherwise agree (in the event that cash Collateral is transferred by clearing house funds or otherwise), Loan Fees shall accrue from and including the date on which the Loaned Securities are transferred to Borrower to, but excluding, the date on which such Loaned Securities are returned to Lender, and Cash Collateral Fees shall accrue from and including the date on which the cash Collateral is transferred to Lender to, but excluding, the date on which such cash Collateral is returned to Borrower.

5.2 Unless otherwise agreed, any Loan Fee or Cash Collateral Fee payable hereunder shall be payable:

(a) in the case of any Loan of Securities other than Government Securities, upon the earlier of (i) the fifteenth day of the month following the calendar month in which such fee was incurred and (ii) the termination of all Loans hereunder (or, if a transfer of cash in accordance with Section 15 may not be effected on such fifteenth day or the day of such termination, as the case may be, the next day on which such a transfer may be effected); and

(b) in the case of any Loan of Government Securities, upon the termination of such Loan and at such other times, if any, as may be customary in accordance with market practice.

2000 Master Securities Loan Agreement ■ 3

Notwithstanding the foregoing, all Loan Fees shall be payable by Borrower immediately in the event of a Default hereunder by Borrower and all Cash Collateral Fees shall be payable immediately by Lender in the event of a Default by Lender.

6. **Termination of the Loan.**

    6.1   (a)   Unless otherwise agreed, either party may terminate a Loan on a termination date established by notice given to the other party prior to the Close of Business on a Business Day. The termination date established by a termination notice shall be a date no earlier than the standard settlement date that would apply to a purchase or sale of the Loaned Securities (in the case of a notice given by Lender) or the non-cash Collateral securing the Loan (in the case of a notice given by Borrower) entered into at the time of such notice, which date shall, unless Borrower and Lender agree to the contrary, be (i) in the case of Government Securities, the next Business Day following such notice and (ii) in the case of all other Securities, the third Business Day following such notice.

    (b)   Notwithstanding paragraph (a) and unless otherwise agreed, Borrower may terminate a Loan on any Business Day by giving notice to Lender and transferring the Loaned Securities to Lender before the Cutoff Time on such Business Day if (i) the Collateral for such Loan consists of cash or Government Securities or (ii) Lender is not permitted, pursuant to Section 4.2, to Retransfer Collateral.

    6.2   Unless otherwise agreed, Borrower shall, on or before the Cutoff Time on the termination date of a Loan, transfer the Loaned Securities to Lender; provided, however, that upon such transfer by Borrower, Lender shall transfer the Collateral (as adjusted pursuant to Section 9) to Borrower in accordance with Section 4.3.

7. **Rights in Respect of Loaned Securities and Collateral.**

    7.1   Except as set forth in Sections 8.1 and 8.2 and as otherwise agreed by Borrower and Lender, until Loaned Securities are required to be redelivered to Lender upon termination of a Loan hereunder, Borrower shall have all of the incidents of ownership of the Loaned Securities, including the right to transfer the Loaned Securities to others. Lender hereby waives the right to vote, or to provide any consent or to take any similar action with respect to, the Loaned Securities in the event that the record date or deadline for such vote, consent or other action falls during the term of the Loan.

    7.2   Except as set forth in Sections 8.3 and 8.4 and as otherwise agreed by Borrower and Lender, if Lender may, pursuant to Section 4.2, Retransfer Collateral, Borrower hereby waives the right to vote, or to provide any consent or take any similar action with respect to, any such Collateral in the event that the record date or deadline for such vote, consent or other action falls during the term of a Loan and such Collateral is not required to be returned to Borrower pursuant to Section 4.5 or Section 9.

8. **Distributions.**

    8.1   Lender shall be entitled to receive all Distributions made on or in respect of the Loaned Securities which are not otherwise received by Lender, to the full extent it would be so entitled if the Loaned Securities had not been lent to Borrower.

8.2 Any cash Distributions made on or in respect of the Loaned Securities, which Lender is entitled to receive pursuant to Section 8.1, shall be paid by the transfer of cash to Lender by Borrower, on the date any such Distribution is paid, in an amount equal to such cash Distribution, so long as Lender is not in Default at the time of such payment. Non-cash Distributions that Lender is entitled to receive pursuant to Section 8.1 shall be added to the Loaned Securities on the date of distribution and shall be considered such for all purposes, except that if the Loan has terminated, Borrower shall forthwith transfer the same to Lender.

8.3 Borrower shall be entitled to receive all Distributions made on or in respect of non-cash Collateral which are not otherwise received by Borrower, to the full extent it would be so entitled if the Collateral had not been transferred to Lender.

8.4 Any cash Distributions made on or in respect of such Collateral, which Borrower is entitled to receive pursuant to Section 8.3, shall be paid by the transfer of cash to Borrower by Lender, on the date any such Distribution is paid, in an amount equal to such cash Distribution, so long as Borrower is not in Default at the time of such payment. Non-cash Distributions that Borrower is entitled to receive pursuant to Section 8.3 shall be added to the Collateral on the date of distribution and shall be considered such for all purposes, except that if each Loan secured by such Collateral has terminated, Lender shall forthwith transfer the same to Borrower.

8.5 Unless otherwise agreed by the parties:

(a) If (i) Borrower is required to make a payment (a "Borrower Payment") with respect to cash Distributions on Loaned Securities under Sections 8.1 and 8.2 ("Securities Distributions"), or (ii) Lender is required to make a payment (a "Lender Payment") with respect to cash Distributions on Collateral under Sections 8.3 and 8.4 ("Collateral Distributions"), and (iii) Borrower or Lender, as the case may be ("Payor"), shall be required by law to collect any withholding or other tax, duty, fee, levy or charge required to be deducted or withheld from such Borrower Payment or Lender Payment ("Tax"), then Payor shall (subject to subsections (b) and (c) below), pay such additional amounts as may be necessary in order that the net amount of the Borrower Payment or Lender Payment received by the Lender or Borrower, as the case may be ("Payee"), after payment of such Tax equals the net amount of the Securities Distribution or Collateral Distribution that would have been received if such Securities Distribution or Collateral Distribution had been paid directly to the Payee.

(b) No additional amounts shall be payable to a Payee under subsection (a) above to the extent that Tax would have been imposed on a Securities Distribution or Collateral Distribution paid directly to the Payee.

(c) No additional amounts shall be payable to a Payee under subsection (a) above to the extent that such Payee is entitled to an exemption from, or reduction in the rate of, Tax on a Borrower Payment or Lender Payment subject to the provision of a certificate or other documentation, but has failed timely to provide such certificate or other documentation.

(d) Each party hereto shall be deemed to represent that, as of the commencement of any Loan hereunder, no Tax would be imposed on any cash Distribution paid to it with respect to (i) Loaned Securities subject to a Loan in which it is acting as

Lender or (ii) Collateral for any Loan in which it is acting as Borrower, unless such party has given notice to the contrary to the other party hereto (which notice shall specify the rate at which such Tax would be imposed). Each party agrees to notify the other of any change that occurs during the term of a Loan in the rate of any Tax that would be imposed on any such cash Distributions payable to it.

8.6   To the extent that, under the provisions of Sections 8.1 through 8.5, (a) a transfer of cash or other property by Borrower would give rise to a Margin Excess or (b) a transfer of cash or other property by Lender would give rise to a Margin Deficit, Borrower or Lender (as the case may be) shall not be obligated to make such transfer of cash or other property in accordance with such Sections, but shall in lieu of such transfer immediately credit the amounts that would have been transferable under such Sections to the account of Lender or Borrower (as the case may be).

9. Mark to Market.

9.1   If Lender is a Customer, Borrower shall daily mark to market any Loan hereunder and in the event that at the Close of Trading on any Business Day the Market Value of the Collateral for any Loan to Borrower shall be less than 100% of the Market Value of all the outstanding Loaned Securities subject to such Loan, Borrower shall transfer additional Collateral no later than the Close of Business on the next Business Day so that the Market Value of such additional Collateral, when added to the Market Value of the other Collateral for such Loan, shall equal 100% of the Market Value of the Loaned Securities.

9.2   In addition to any rights of Lender under Section 9.1, if at any time the aggregate Market Value of all Collateral for Loans by Lender shall be less than the Margin Percentage of the Market Value of all the outstanding Loaned Securities subject to such Loans (a "Margin Deficit"), Lender may, by notice to Borrower, demand that Borrower transfer to Lender additional Collateral so that the Market Value of such additional Collateral, when added to the Market Value of all other Collateral for such Loans, shall equal or exceed the Margin Percentage of the Market Value of the Loaned Securities.

9.3   Subject to Borrower's obligations under Section 9.1, if at any time the Market Value of all Collateral for Loans to Borrower shall be greater than the Margin Percentage of the Market Value of all the outstanding Loaned Securities subject to such Loans (a "Margin Excess"), Borrower may, by notice to Lender, demand that Lender transfer to Borrower such amount of the Collateral selected by Borrower so that the Market Value of the Collateral for such Loans, after deduction of such amounts, shall thereupon not exceed the Margin Percentage of the Market Value of the Loaned Securities.

9.4   Borrower and Lender may agree, with respect to one or more Loans hereunder, to mark the values to market pursuant to Sections 9.2 and 9.3 by separately valuing the Loaned Securities lent and the Collateral given in respect thereof on a Loan-by-Loan basis.

9.5   Borrower and Lender may agree, with respect to any or all Loans hereunder, that the respective rights of Lender and Borrower under Sections 9.2 and 9.3 may be exercised only where a Margin Excess or Margin Deficit exceeds a specified dollar amount or a specified percentage of the Market Value of the Loaned Securities under such Loans (which amount or percentage shall be agreed to by Borrower and Lender prior to entering into any such Loans).

9.6　If any notice is given by Borrower or Lender under Sections 9.2 or 9.3 at or before the Margin Notice Deadline on any day on which a transfer of Collateral may be effected in accordance with Section 15, the party receiving such notice shall transfer Collateral as provided in such Section no later than the Close of Business on such day. If any such notice is given after the Margin Notice Deadline, the party receiving such notice shall transfer such Collateral no later than the Close of Business on the next Business Day following the day of such notice.

10. Representations.

The parties to this Agreement hereby make the following representations and warranties, which shall continue during the term of any Loan hereunder:

10.1　Each party hereto represents and warrants that (a) it has the power to execute and deliver this Agreement, to enter into the Loans contemplated hereby and to perform its obligations hereunder, (b) it has taken all necessary action to authorize such execution, delivery and performance, and (c) this Agreement constitutes a legal, valid and binding obligation enforceable against it in accordance with its terms.

10.2　Each party hereto represents and warrants that it has not relied on the other for any tax or accounting advice concerning this Agreement and that it has made its own determination as to the tax and accounting treatment of any Loan and any dividends, remuneration or other funds received hereunder.

10.3　Each party hereto represents and warrants that it is acting for its own account unless it expressly specifies otherwise in writing and complies with Section 11.1(b).

10.4　Borrower represents and warrants that it has, or will have at the time of transfer of any Collateral, the right to grant a first priority security interest therein subject to the terms and conditions hereof.

10.5　(a)　Borrower represents and warrants that it (or the person to whom it relends the Loaned Securities) is borrowing or will borrow Loaned Securities that are Equity Securities for the purpose of making delivery of such Loaned Securities in the case of short sales, failure to receive securities required to be delivered, or as otherwise permitted pursuant to Regulation T as in effect from time to time.

(b)　Borrower and Lender may agree, as provided in Section 24.2, that Borrower shall not be deemed to have made the representation or warranty in subsection (a) with respect to any Loan. By entering into any such agreement, Lender shall be deemed to have represented and warranted to Borrower (which representation and warranty shall be deemed to be repeated on each day during the term of the Loan) that Lender is either (i) an "exempted borrower" within the meaning of Regulation T or (ii) a member of a national securities exchange or a broker or dealer registered with the U.S. Securities and Exchange Commission that is entering into such Loan to finance its activities as a market maker or an underwriter.

10.6　Lender represents and warrants that it has, or will have at the time of transfer of any Loaned Securities, the right to transfer the Loaned Securities subject to the terms and conditions hereof.

11. Covenants.

11.1 Each party agrees either (a) to be liable as principal with respect to its obligations hereunder or (b) to execute and comply fully with the provisions of Annex I (the terms and conditions of which Annex are incorporated herein and made a part hereof).

11.2 Promptly upon (and in any event within seven (7) Business Days after) demand by Lender, Borrower shall furnish Lender with Borrower's most recent publicly-available financial statements and any other financial statements mutually agreed upon by Borrower and Lender. Unless otherwise agreed, if Borrower is subject to the requirements of Rule 17a-5(c) under the Exchange Act, it may satisfy the requirements of this Section by furnishing Lender with its most recent statement required to be furnished to customers pursuant to such Rule.

12. Events of Default.

All Loans hereunder may, at the option of the non-defaulting party (which option shall be deemed to have been exercised immediately upon the occurrence of an Act of Insolvency), be terminated immediately upon the occurrence of any one or more of the following events (individually, a "Default"):

12.1 if any Loaned Securities shall not be transferred to Lender upon termination of the Loan as required by Section 6;

12.2 if any Collateral shall not be transferred to Borrower upon termination of the Loan as required by Sections 4.3 and 6;

12.3 if either party shall fail to transfer Collateral as required by Section 9;

12.4 if either party (a) shall fail to transfer to the other party amounts in respect of Distributions required to be transferred by Section 8, (b) shall have been notified of such failure by the other party prior to the Close of Business on any day, and (c) shall not have cured such failure by the Cutoff Time on the next day after such Close of Business on which a transfer of cash may be effected in accordance with Section 15;

12.5 if an Act of Insolvency occurs with respect to either party;

12.6 if any representation made by either party in respect of this Agreement or any Loan or Loans hereunder shall be incorrect or untrue in any material respect during the term of any Loan hereunder;

12.7 if either party notifies the other of its inability to or its intention not to perform its obligations hereunder or otherwise disaffirms, rejects or repudiates any of its obligations hereunder; or

12.8 if either party (a) shall fail to perform any material obligation under this Agreement not specifically set forth in clauses 12.1 through 12.7, above, including but not limited to the payment of fees as required by Section 5, and the payment of transfer taxes as required by Section 14, (b) shall have been notified of such failure by the other party prior to the Close of Business on any day, and (c) shall not have cured such failure by the Cutoff Time on the next day after such Close of Business on which a transfer of cash may be effected in accordance with Section 15.

The non-defaulting party shall (except upon the occurrence of an Act of Insolvency) give notice as promptly as practicable to the defaulting party of the exercise of its option to terminate all Loans hereunder pursuant to this Section 12.

13. **Remedies.**

    13.1 Upon the occurrence of a Default under Section 12 entitling Lender to terminate all Loans hereunder, Lender shall have the right, in addition to any other remedies provided herein, (a) to purchase a like amount of Loaned Securities ("Replacement Securities") in the principal market for such Loaned Securities in a commercially reasonable manner, (b) to sell any Collateral in the principal market for such Collateral in a commercially reasonable manner and (c) to apply and set off the Collateral and any proceeds thereof (including any amounts drawn under a letter of credit supporting any Loan) against the payment of the purchase price for such Replacement Securities and any amounts due to Lender under Sections 5, 8, 14 and 16. In the event that Lender shall exercise such rights, Borrower's obligation to return a like amount of the Loaned Securities shall terminate. Lender may similarly apply the Collateral and any proceeds thereof to any other obligation of Borrower under this Agreement, including Borrower's obligations with respect to Distributions paid to Borrower (and not forwarded to Lender) in respect of Loaned Securities. In the event that (i) the purchase price of Replacement Securities (plus all other amounts, if any, due to Lender hereunder) exceeds (ii) the amount of the Collateral, Borrower shall be liable to Lender for the amount of such excess together with interest thereon at a rate equal to (A) in the case of purchases of Foreign Securities, LIBOR, (B) in the case of purchases of any other Securities (or other amounts, if any, due to Lender hereunder), the Federal Funds Rate or (C) such other rate as may be specified in Schedule B, in each case as such rate fluctuates from day to day, from the date of such purchase until the date of payment of such excess. As security for Borrower's obligation to pay such excess, Lender shall have, and Borrower hereby grants, a security interest in any property of Borrower then held by or for Lender and a right of setoff with respect to such property and any other amount payable by Lender to Borrower. The purchase price of Replacement Securities purchased under this Section 13.1 shall include, and the proceeds of any sale of Collateral shall be determined after deduction of, broker's fees and commissions and all other reasonable costs, fees and expenses related to such purchase or sale (as the case may be). In the event Lender exercises its rights under this Section 13.1, Lender may elect in its sole discretion, in lieu of purchasing all or a portion of the Replacement Securities or selling all or a portion of the Collateral, to be deemed to have made, respectively, such purchase of Replacement Securities or sale of Collateral for an amount equal to the price therefor on the date of such exercise obtained from a generally recognized source or the last bid quotation from such a source at the most recent Close of Trading. Subject to Section 18, upon the satisfaction of all obligations hereunder, any remaining Collateral shall be returned to Borrower.

    13.2 Upon the occurrence of a Default under Section 12 entitling Borrower to terminate all Loans hereunder, Borrower shall have the right, in addition to any other remedies provided herein, (a) to purchase a like amount of Collateral ("Replacement Collateral") in the principal market for such Collateral in a commercially reasonable manner, (b) to sell a like amount of the Loaned Securities in the principal market for such Loaned Securities in a commercially reasonable manner and (c) to apply and set off the Loaned Securities and any proceeds thereof against (i) the payment of the purchase price for such Replacement Collateral, (ii) Lender's obligation to return any cash or other Collateral, and (iii) any amounts due to Borrower under Sections 5, 8 and 16. In such event, Borrower may treat the Loaned Securities as its own and Lender's obligation to return a like amount of the Collateral shall terminate; provided, however, that Lender shall immediately return any letters of credit supporting any Loan upon the exercise or deemed exercise by Borrower of its termination rights under Section 12. Borrower may similarly apply the Loaned Securities and any proceeds thereof to any other obligation of Lender under this Agreement, including Lender's obligations with respect to Distributions paid to Lender (and not forwarded to Borrower) in respect of Collateral. In the event that (i) the sales price received from such Loaned Securities is less than (ii) the purchase price of Replacement Collateral (plus the amount of any cash or other Collateral not replaced by Borrower and all other amounts, if any, due to Borrower hereunder), Lender shall be liable to Borrower for the amount of any such deficiency, together with interest on such amounts at a rate equal to (A) in the case of Collateral consisting of Foreign Securities, LIBOR, (B) in the case of Collateral consisting of any other Securities (or other amounts due, if any, to Borrower hereunder), the Federal Funds Rate or (C) such other rate as may be specified in Schedule B, in each case as such rate fluctuates from day to day, from the date of such sale until the date of payment of such deficiency. As security for Lender's obligation to pay such deficiency, Borrower shall have, and Lender hereby grants, a security interest in any property of Lender then held by or for Borrower and a right of setoff with respect to such property and any other amount payable by Borrower to Lender. The purchase price of any Replacement Collateral purchased under this Section 13.2 shall include, and the proceeds of any sale of Loaned Securities shall be determined after deduction of, broker's fees and commissions and all other reasonable costs, fees and expenses related to such purchase or sale (as the case may be). In the event Borrower exercises its rights under this Section 13.2, Borrower may elect in its sole discretion, in lieu of purchasing all or a portion of the Replacement Collateral or selling all or a portion of the Loaned Securities, to be deemed to have made, respectively, such purchase of Replacement Collateral or sale of Loaned Securities for an amount equal to the price therefor on the date of such exercise obtained from a generally recognized source or the last bid quotation from such a source at the most recent Close of Trading. Subject to Section 18, upon the satisfaction of all Lender's obligations hereunder, any remaining Loaned Securities (or remaining cash proceeds thereof) shall be returned to Lender.

13.3 Unless otherwise agreed, the parties acknowledge and agree that (a) the Loaned Securities and any Collateral consisting of Securities are of a type traded in a recognized market, (b) in the absence of a generally recognized source for prices or bid or offer quotations for any security, the non-defaulting party may establish the source therefor in its sole discretion, and (c) all prices and bid and offer quotations shall be increased to include accrued interest to the extent not already included therein (except to the extent contrary to market practice with respect to the relevant Securities).

13.4 In addition to its rights hereunder, the non-defaulting party shall have any rights otherwise available to it under any other agreement or applicable law.

14. Transfer Taxes.

All transfer taxes with respect to the transfer of the Loaned Securities by Lender to Borrower and by Borrower to Lender upon termination of the Loan and with respect to the transfer of Collateral by Borrower to Lender and by Lender to Borrower upon termination of the Loan or pursuant to Section 4.5 or Section 9 shall be paid by Borrower.

15. **Transfers.**

   15.1 All transfers by either Borrower or Lender of Loaned Securities or Collateral consisting of "financial assets" (within the meaning of the UCC) hereunder shall be by (a) in the case of certificated securities, physical delivery of certificates representing such securities together with duly executed stock and bond transfer powers, as the case may be, with signatures guaranteed by a bank or a member firm of the New York Stock Exchange, Inc., (b) registration of an uncertificated security in the transferee's name by the issuer of such uncertificated security, (c) the crediting by a Clearing Organization of such financial assets to the transferee's "securities account" (within the meaning of the UCC) maintained with such Clearing Organization, or (d) such other means as Borrower and Lender may agree.

   15.2 All transfers of cash hereunder shall be by (a) wire transfer in immediately available, freely transferable funds or (b) such other means as Borrower and Lender may agree.

   15.3 All transfers of letters of credit from Borrower to Lender shall be made by physical delivery to Lender of an irrevocable letter of credit issued by a "bank" as defined in Section 3(a)(6)(A)-(C) of the Exchange Act. Transfers of letters of credit from Lender to Borrower shall be made by causing such letters of credit to be returned or by causing the amount of such letters of credit to be reduced to the amount required after such transfer.

   15.4 A transfer of Securities, cash or letters of credit may be effected under this Section 15 on any day except (a) a day on which the transferee is closed for business at its address set forth in Schedule A hereto or (b) a day on which a Clearing Organization or wire transfer system is closed, if the facilities of such Clearing Organization or wire transfer system are required to effect such transfer.

   15.5 For the avoidance of doubt, the parties agree and acknowledge that the term "securities," as used herein (except in this Section 15), shall include any "security entitlements" with respect to such securities (within the meaning of the UCC). In every transfer of "financial assets" (within the meaning of the UCC) hereunder, the transferor shall take all steps necessary (a) to effect a delivery to the transferee under Section 8-301 of the UCC, or to cause the creation of a security entitlement in favor of the transferee under Section 8-501 of the UCC, (b) to enable the transferee to obtain "control" (within the meaning of Section 8-106 of the UCC), and (c) to provide the transferee with comparable rights under any applicable foreign law or regulation.

16. **Contractual Currency.**

   16.1 Borrower and Lender agree that (a) any payment in respect of a Distribution under Section 8 shall be made in the currency in which the underlying Distribution of cash was made, (b) any return of cash shall be made in the currency in which the underlying transfer of cash was made, and (c) any other payment of cash in connection with a Loan under this Agreement shall be in the currency agreed upon by Borrower and Lender in connection with such Loan (the currency established under clause (a), (b) or (c) hereinafter referred to as the "Contractual Currency"). Notwithstanding the foregoing, the payee of any such payment may, at its option, accept tender thereof in any other currency; provided, however, that, to the extent permitted by applicable law, the obligation of the payor to make such payment will be discharged only to the extent of the amount of Contractual Currency that such payee may, consistent with normal banking procedures, purchase with such other currency (after deduction of any premium and costs of exchange) on the banking day next succeeding its receipt of such currency.

16.2 If for any reason the amount in the Contractual Currency received under Section 16.1, including amounts received after conversion of any recovery under any judgment or order expressed in a currency other than the Contractual Currency, falls short of the amount in the Contractual Currency due in respect of this Agreement, the party required to make the payment will (unless a Default has occurred and such party is the non-defaulting party) as a separate and independent obligation and to the extent permitted by applicable law, immediately pay such additional amount in the Contractual Currency as may be necessary to compensate for the shortfall.

16.3 If for any reason the amount in the Contractual Currency received under Section 16.1 exceeds the amount in the Contractual Currency due in respect of this Agreement, then the party receiving the payment will (unless a Default has occurred and such party is the non-defaulting party) refund promptly the amount of such excess.

17. ERISA.

Lender shall, if any of the Securities transferred to the Borrower hereunder for any Loan have been or shall be obtained, directly or indirectly, from or using the assets of any Plan, so notify Borrower in writing upon the execution of this Agreement or upon initiation of such Loan under Section 2.1. If Lender so notifies Borrower, then Borrower and Lender shall conduct the Loan in accordance with the terms and conditions of Department of Labor Prohibited Transaction Exemption 81-6 (46 Fed. Reg. 7527, Jan. 23, 1981; as amended, 52 Fed. Reg. 18754, May 19, 1987), or any successor thereto (unless Borrower and Lender have agreed prior to entering into a Loan that such Loan will be conducted in reliance on another exemption, or without relying on any exemption, from the prohibited transaction provisions of Section 406 of the Employee Retirement Income Security Act of 1974, as amended, and Section 4975 of the Internal Revenue Code of 1986, as amended). Without limiting the foregoing and notwithstanding any other provision of this Agreement, if the Loan will be conducted in accordance with Prohibited Transaction Exemption 81-6, then:

17.1 Borrower represents and warrants to Lender that it is either (a) a bank subject to federal or state supervision, (b) a broker-dealer registered under the Exchange Act or (c) exempt from registration under Section 15(a)(1) of the Exchange Act as a dealer in Government Securities.

17.2 Borrower represents and warrants that, during the term of any Loan hereunder, neither Borrower nor any affiliate of Borrower has any discretionary authority or control with respect to the investment of the assets of the Plan involved in the Loan or renders investment advice (within the meaning of 29 C.F.R. Section 2510.3-21(c)) with respect to the assets of the Plan involved in the Loan. Lender agrees that, prior to or at the commencement of any Loan hereunder, it will communicate to Borrower information regarding the Plan sufficient to identify to Borrower any person or persons that have discretionary authority or control with respect to the investment of the assets of the Plan involved in the Loan or that render investment advice (as defined in the preceding sentence) with respect to the assets of the Plan involved in the Loan. In the event Lender fails to communicate and keep current during the term of any Loan such information, Lender rather than Borrower shall be deemed to have made the representation and warranty in the first sentence of this Section 17.2.

17.3   Borrower shall mark to market daily each Loan hereunder pursuant to Section 9.1 as is required if Lender is a Customer.

17.4   Borrower and Lender agree that:

   (a)   the term "Collateral" shall mean cash, securities issued or guaranteed by the United States government or its agencies or instrumentalities, or irrevocable bank letters of credit issued by a person other than Borrower or an affiliate thereof;

   (b)   prior to the making of any Loans hereunder, Borrower shall provide Lender with (i) the most recent available audited statement of Borrower's financial condition and (ii) the most recent available unaudited statement of Borrower's financial condition (if more recent than the most recent audited statement), and each Loan made hereunder shall be deemed a representation by Borrower that there has been no material adverse change in Borrower's financial condition subsequent to the date of the latest financial statements or information furnished in accordance herewith;

   (c)   the Loan may be terminated by Lender at any time, whereupon Borrower shall deliver the Loaned Securities to Lender within the lesser of (i) the customary delivery period for such Loaned Securities, (ii) five Business Days, and (iii) the time negotiated for such delivery between Borrower and Lender; provided, however, that Borrower and Lender may agree to a longer period only if permitted by Prohibited Transaction Exemption 81-6; and

   (d)   the Collateral transferred shall be security only for obligations of Borrower to the Plan with respect to Loans, and shall not be security for any obligation of Borrower to any agent or affiliate of the Plan.

18.   Single Agreement.

Borrower and Lender acknowledge that, and have entered into this Agreement in reliance on the fact that, all Loans hereunder constitute a single business and contractual relationship and have been entered into in consideration of each other. Accordingly, Borrower and Lender hereby agree that payments, deliveries and other transfers made by either of them in respect of any Loan shall be deemed to have been made in consideration of payments, deliveries and other transfers in respect of any other Loan hereunder, and the obligations to make any such payments, deliveries and other transfers may be applied against each other and netted. In addition, Borrower and Lender acknowledge that, and have entered into this Agreement in reliance on the fact that, all Loans hereunder have been entered into in consideration of each other. Accordingly, Borrower and Lender hereby agree that (a) each shall perform all of its obligations in respect of each Loan hereunder, and that a default in the performance of any such obligation by Borrower or by Lender (the "Defaulting Party") in any Loan hereunder shall constitute a default by the Defaulting Party under all such Loans hereunder, and (b) the non-defaulting party shall be entitled to set off claims and apply property held by it in respect of any Loan hereunder against obligations owing to it in respect of any other Loan with the Defaulting Party.

19.   APPLICABLE LAW.

THIS AGREEMENT SHALL BE GOVERNED AND CONSTRUED IN ACCORDANCE WITH THE LAWS OF THE STATE OF NEW YORK WITHOUT GIVING EFFECT TO THE CONFLICT OF LAW PRINCIPLES THEREOF.

20. Waiver.

The failure of a party to this Agreement to insist upon strict adherence to any term of this Agreement on any occasion shall not be considered a waiver or deprive that party of the right thereafter to insist upon strict adherence to that term or any other term of this Agreement. All waivers in respect of a Default must be in writing.

21. Survival of Remedies.

All remedies hereunder and all obligations with respect to any Loan shall survive the termination of the relevant Loan, return of Loaned Securities or Collateral and termination of this Agreement.

22. Notices and Other Communications.

Any and all notices, statements, demands or other communications hereunder may be given by a party to the other by telephone, mail, facsimile, e-mail, electronic message, telegraph, messenger or otherwise to the individuals and at the facsimile numbers and addresses specified with respect to it in Schedule A hereto, or sent to such party at any other place specified in a notice of change of number or address hereafter received by the other party. Any notice, statement, demand or other communication hereunder will be deemed effective on the day and at the time on which it is received or, if not received, on the day and at the time on which its delivery was in good faith attempted; provided, however, that any notice by a party to the other party by telephone shall be deemed effective only if (a) such notice is followed by written confirmation thereof and (b) at least one of the other means of providing notice that are specifically listed above has previously been attempted in good faith by the notifying party.

23. SUBMISSION TO JURISDICTION; WAIVER OF JURY TRIAL.

23.1 EACH PARTY HERETO IRREVOCABLY AND UNCONDITIONALLY (A) SUBMITS TO THE NON-EXCLUSIVE JURISDICTION OF ANY UNITED STATES FEDERAL OR NEW YORK STATE COURT SITTING IN NEW YORK CITY, AND ANY APPELLATE COURT FROM ANY SUCH COURT, SOLELY FOR THE PURPOSE OF ANY SUIT, ACTION OR PROCEEDING BROUGHT TO ENFORCE ITS OBLIGATIONS HEREUNDER OR RELATING IN ANY WAY TO THIS AGREEMENT OR ANY LOAN HEREUNDER AND (B) WAIVES, TO THE FULLEST EXTENT IT MAY EFFECTIVELY DO SO, ANY DEFENSE OF AN INCONVENIENT FORUM TO THE MAINTENANCE OF SUCH ACTION OR PROCEEDING IN ANY SUCH COURT AND ANY RIGHT OF JURISDICTION ON ACCOUNT OF ITS PLACE OF RESIDENCE OR DOMICILE.

23.2 EACH PARTY HERETO HEREBY IRREVOCABLY WAIVES ANY RIGHT THAT IT MAY HAVE TO TRIAL BY JURY IN ANY ACTION, PROCEEDING OR COUNTERCLAIM ARISING OUT OF OR RELATING TO THIS AGREEMENT OR THE TRANSACTIONS CONTEMPLATED HEREBY.

24. Miscellaneous.

24.1 Except as otherwise agreed by the parties, this Agreement supersedes any other agreement between the parties hereto concerning loans of Securities between Borrower and Lender. This Agreement shall not be assigned by either party without the prior written consent of the other party and any attempted assignment without such consent shall be null and void. Subject to the foregoing, this Agreement shall be binding upon and shall inure to the benefit of Borrower and Lender and their respective heirs, representatives, successors and assigns. This Agreement may be terminated by either party upon notice to the other, subject only to fulfillment of any obligations then outstanding. This Agreement shall not be modified, except by an instrument in writing signed by the party against whom enforcement is sought. The parties hereto acknowledge and agree that, in connection with this Agreement and each Loan hereunder, time is of the essence. Each provision and agreement herein shall be treated as separate and independent from any other provision herein and shall be enforceable notwithstanding the unenforceability of any such other provision or agreement.

24.2 Any agreement between Borrower and Lender pursuant to Section 10.5(b) or Section 25.37 shall be made (a) in writing, (b) orally, if confirmed promptly in writing or through any system that compares Loans and in which Borrower and Lender are participants, or (c) in such other manner as may be agreed by Borrower and Lender in writing.

25. Definitions.

For the purposes hereof:

25.1 "Act of Insolvency" shall mean, with respect to any party, (a) the commencement by such party as debtor of any case or proceeding under any bankruptcy, insolvency, reorganization, liquidation, moratorium, dissolution, delinquency or similar law, or such party's seeking the appointment or election of a receiver, conservator, trustee, custodian or similar official for such party or any substantial part of its property, or the convening of any meeting of creditors for purposes of commencing any such case or proceeding or seeking such an appointment or election, (b) the commencement of any such case or proceeding against such party, or another seeking such an appointment or election, or the filing against a party of an application for a protective decree under the provisions of the Securities Investor Protection Act of 1970, which (i) is consented to or not timely contested by such party, (ii) results in the entry of an order for relief, such an appointment or election, the issuance of such a protective decree or the entry of an order having a similar effect, or (iii) is not dismissed within 15 days, (c) the making by such party of a general assignment for the benefit of creditors, or (d) the admission in writing by such party of such party's inability to pay such party's debts as they become due.

25.2 "Bankruptcy Code" shall have the meaning assigned in Section 26.1

25.3 "Borrower" shall have the meaning assigned in Section 1.

25.4 "Borrower Payment" shall have the meaning assigned in Section 8.5(a).

25.5 "Broker-Dealer" shall mean any person that is a broker (including a municipal securities broker), dealer, municipal securities dealer, government securities broker or government securities dealer as defined in the Exchange Act, regardless of whether the activities of such person are conducted in the United States or otherwise require such person to register with the U.S. Securities and Exchange Commission or other regulatory body.

25.6 "Business Day" shall mean, with respect to any Loan hereunder, a day on which regular trading occurs in the principal market for the Loaned Securities subject to such Loan, provided, however, that for purposes of determining the Market Value of any Securities hereunder, such term shall mean a day on which regular trading occurs in the principal market for the Securities whose value is being determined. Notwithstanding the foregoing, (a) for purposes of Section 9, "Business Day" shall mean any day on which regular trading occurs in the principal market for any Loaned Securities or for any Collateral consisting of Securities under any outstanding Loan hereunder and "next Business Day" shall mean the next day on which a transfer of Collateral may be effected in accordance with Section 15, and (b) in no event shall a Saturday or Sunday be considered a Business Day.

25.7 "Cash Collateral Fee" shall have the meaning assigned in Section 5.1.

25.8 "Clearing Organization" shall mean (a) The Depository Trust Company, or, if agreed to by Borrower and Lender, such other "securities intermediary" (within the meaning of the UCC) at which Borrower (or Borrower's agent) and Lender (or Lender's agent) maintain accounts, or (b) a Federal Reserve Bank, to the extent that it maintains a book-entry system.

25.9 "Close of Business" shall mean the time established by the parties in Schedule B or otherwise orally or in writing or, in the absence of any such agreement, as shall be determined in accordance with market practice.

25.10 "Close of Trading" shall mean, with respect to any Security, the end of the primary trading session established by the principal market for such Security on a Business Day, unless otherwise agreed by the parties.

25.11 "Collateral" shall mean, whether now owned or hereafter acquired and to the extent permitted by applicable law, (a) any property which Borrower and Lender agree prior to the Loan shall be acceptable collateral and which is transferred to Lender pursuant to Sections 4 or 9 (including as collateral, for definitional purposes, any letters of credit mutually acceptable to Lender and Borrower), (b) any property substituted therefor pursuant to Section 4.5, (c) all accounts in which such property is deposited and all securities and the like in which any cash collateral is invested or reinvested, and (d) any proceeds of any of the foregoing; *provided, however,* that if Lender is a Customer, "Collateral" shall (subject to Section 17.4(a), if applicable) be limited to cash, U.S. Treasury bills and notes, an irrevocable letter of credit issued by a "bank" (as defined in Section 3(a)(6)(A)-(C) of the Exchange Act), and any other property permitted to serve as collateral securing a loan of securities under Rule 15c3-3 under the Exchange Act or any comparable regulation of the Secretary of the Treasury under Section 15C of the Exchange Act (to the extent that Borrower is subject to such Rule or comparable regulation) pursuant to exemptive, interpretive or no-action relief or otherwise. If any new or different Security shall be exchanged for any Collateral by recapitalization, merger, consolidation or other corporate action, such new or different Security shall, effective upon such exchange, be deemed to become Collateral in substitution for the former Collateral for which such exchange is made. For purposes of return of Collateral by Lender or purchase or sale of Securities pursuant to Section 13, such term shall include Securities of the same issuer, class and quantity as the Collateral initially transferred by Borrower to Lender, as adjusted pursuant to the preceding sentence.

25.12 "Collateral Distributions" shall have the meaning assigned in Section 8.5(a).

25.13 "Confirmation" shall have the meaning assigned in Section 2.1.

25.14 "Contractual Currency" shall have the meaning assigned in Section 16.1.

Appendices

25.15 "Customer" shall mean any person that is a customer of Borrower under Rule 15c3-3 under the Exchange Act or any comparable regulation of the Secretary of the Treasury under Section 15C of the Exchange Act (to the extent that Borrower is subject to such Rule or comparable regulation).

25.16 "Cutoff Time" shall mean a time on a Business Day by which a transfer of cash, securities or other property must be made by Borrower or Lender to the other, as shall be agreed by Borrower and Lender in Schedule B or otherwise orally or in writing or, in the absence of any such agreement, as shall be determined in accordance with market practice.

25.17 "Default" shall have the meaning assigned in Section 12.

25.18 "Defaulting Party" shall have the meaning assigned in Section 18.

25.19 "Distribution" shall mean, with respect to any Security at any time, any distribution made on or in respect of such Security, including, but not limited to: (a) cash and all other property, (b) stock dividends, (c) Securities received as a result of split ups of such Security and distributions in respect thereof, (d) interest payments, (e) all rights to purchase additional Securities, and (f) any cash or other consideration paid or provided by the issuer of such Security in exchange for any vote, consent or the taking of any similar action in respect of such Security (regardless of whether the record date for such vote, consent or other action falls during the term of the Loan). In the event that the holder of a Security is entitled to elect the type of distribution to be received from two or more alternatives, such election shall be made by Lender, in the case of a Distribution in respect of the Loaned Securities, and by Borrower, in the case of a Distribution in respect of Collateral.

25.20 "Equity Security" shall mean any security (as defined in the Exchange Act) other than a "nonequity security," as defined in Regulation T.

25.21 "Exchange Act" shall mean the Securities Exchange Act of 1934, as amended.

25.22 "Extension Deadline" shall mean, with respect to a letter of credit, the Cutoff Time on the Business Day preceding the day on which the letter of credit expires.

25.23 "FDIA" shall have the meaning assigned in Section 26.4.

25.24 "FDICIA" shall have the meaning assigned in Section 26.5.

25.25 "Federal Funds Rate" shall mean the rate of interest (expressed as an annual rate), as published in Federal Reserve Statistical Release H.15(519) or any publication substituted therefor, charged for federal funds (dollars in immediately available funds borrowed by banks on an overnight unsecured basis) on that day or, if that day is not a banking day in New York City, on the next preceding banking day.

25.26 "Foreign Securities" shall mean, unless otherwise agreed, Securities that are principally cleared and settled outside the United States.

25.27 "Government Securities" shall mean government securities as defined in Section 3(a)(42)(A)-(C) of the Exchange Act.

25.28 "Lender" shall have the meaning assigned in Section 1.

25.29 "Lender Payment" shall have the meaning assigned in Section 8.5(a).

25.30 "LIBOR" shall mean for any date, the offered rate for deposits in U.S. dollars for a period of three months which appears on the Reuters Screen LIBO page as of 11:00 a.m., London time, on such date (or, if at least two such rates appear, the arithmetic mean of such rates).

25.31 "Loan" shall have the meaning assigned in Section 1.

25.32 "Loan Fee" shall have the meaning assigned in Section 5.1.

25.33 "Loaned Security" shall mean any Security transferred in a Loan hereunder until such Security (or an identical Security) is transferred back to Lender hereunder, except that, if any new or different Security shall be exchanged for any Loaned Security by recapitalization, merger, consolidation or other corporate action, such new or different Security shall, effective upon such exchange, be deemed to become a Loaned Security in substitution for the former Loaned Security for which such exchange is made. For purposes of return of Loaned Securities by Borrower or purchase or sale of Securities pursuant to Section 13, such term shall include Securities of the same issuer, class and quantity as the Loaned Securities, as adjusted pursuant to the preceding sentence.

25.34 "Margin Deficit" shall have the meaning assigned in Section 9.2.

25.35 "Margin Excess" shall have the meaning assigned in Section 9.3.

25.36 "Margin Notice Deadline" shall mean the time agreed to by the parties in the relevant Confirmation, Schedule B hereto or otherwise as the deadline for giving notice requiring same-day satisfaction of mark-to-market obligations as provided in Section 9 hereof (or, in the absence of any such agreement, the deadline for such purposes established in accordance with market practice).

25.37 "Margin Percentage" shall mean, with respect to any Loan as of any date, a percentage agreed by Borrower and Lender, which shall be not less than 100%, unless (a) Borrower and Lender agree otherwise, as provided in Section 24.2, and (b) Lender is not a Customer. Notwithstanding the previous sentence, in the event that the writing or other confirmation evidencing the agreement described in clause (a) does not set out such percentage with respect to any such Loan, the Margin Percentage shall not be a percentage less than the percentage obtained by dividing (i) the Market Value of the Collateral required to be transferred by Borrower to Lender with respect to such Loan at the commencement of the Loan by (ii) the Market Value of the Loaned Securities required to be transferred by Lender to Borrower at the commencement of the Loan.

25.38 "Market Value" shall have the meaning set forth in Annex II or otherwise agreed to by Borrower and Lender in writing. Notwithstanding the previous sentence, in the event that the meaning of Market Value has not been set forth in Annex II or in any other writing, as described in the previous sentence, Market Value shall be determined in accordance with market practice for the Securities, based on the price for such Securities as of the most recent Close of Trading obtained from a generally recognized source agreed to by the parties or the closing bid quotation at the most recent Close of Trading obtained from such source, plus accrued interest to the extent not included therein (other than any interest credited or transferred to, or applied to the obligations of, the other party pursuant to Section 8, unless market practice with respect to the valuation of such Securities in connection with securities loans is to the contrary). If the relevant quotation did not exist at such Close of Trading, then the Market Value shall be the relevant quotation on the next preceding Close of Trading at which there was such a quotation. The determinations of Market Value provided for in Annex II or in any other writing described in the first sentences of this Section 25.38 or, if applicable, in the preceding sentence shall apply for all purposes under this Agreement, except for purposes of Section 13.

25.39 "Payee" shall have the meaning assigned in Section 8.5(a).

25.40 "Payor" shall have the meaning assigned in Section 8.5(a).

25.41 "Plan" shall mean: (a) any "employee benefit plan" as defined in Section 3(3) of the Employee Retirement Income Security Act of 1974 which is subject to Part 4 of Subtitle B of Title I of such Act; (b) any "plan" as defined in Section 4975(e)(1) of the Internal Revenue Code of 1986; or (c) any entity the assets of which are deemed to be assets of any such "employee benefit plan" or "plan" by reason of the Department of Labor's plan asset regulation, 29 C.F.R. Section 2510.3-101.

25.42 "Regulation T" shall mean Regulation T of the Board of Governors of the Federal Reserve System, as in effect from time to time.

25.43 "Retransfer" shall mean, with respect to any Collateral, to pledge, repledge, hypothecate, rehypothecate, lend, relend, sell or otherwise transfer such Collateral, or to re-register any such Collateral evidenced by physical certificates in any name other than Borrower's.

25.44 "Securities" shall mean securities or, if agreed by the parties in writing, other assets.

25.45 "Securities Distributions" shall have the meaning assigned in Section 8.5(a).

25.46 "Tax" shall have the meaning assigned in Section 8.5(a).

25.47 "UCC" shall mean the New York Uniform Commercial Code.

26. Intent.

26.1 The parties recognize that each Loan hereunder is a "securities contract," as such term is defined in Section 741 of Title 11 of the United States Code (the "Bankruptcy Code"), as amended (except insofar as the type of assets subject to the Loan would render such definition inapplicable).

26.2 It is understood that each and every transfer of funds, securities and other property under this Agreement and each Loan hereunder is a "settlement payment" or a "margin payment," as such terms are used in Sections 362(b)(6) and 546(e) of the Bankruptcy Code.

26.3 It is understood that the rights given to Borrower and Lender hereunder upon a Default by the other constitute the right to cause the liquidation of a securities contract and the right to set off mutual debts and claims in connection with a securities contract, as such terms are used in Sections 555 and 362(b)(6) of the Bankruptcy Code.

26.4 The parties agree and acknowledge that if a party hereto is an "insured depository institution," as such term is defined in the Federal Deposit Insurance Act, as amended ("FDIA"), then each Loan hereunder is a "securities contract" and "qualified financial contract," as such terms are defined in the FDIA and any rules, orders or policy statements thereunder (except insofar as the type of assets subject to the Loan would render such definitions inapplicable).

26.5 It is understood that this Agreement constitutes a "netting contract" as defined in and subject to Title IV of the Federal Deposit Insurance Corporation Improvement Act of 1991 ("FDICIA") and each payment obligation under any Loan hereunder shall constitute a "covered contractual payment entitlement" or "covered contractual payment obligation," respectively, as defined in and subject to FDICIA (except insofar as one or both of the parties is not a "financial institution" as that term is defined in FDICIA).

26.6 Except to the extent required by applicable law or regulation or as otherwise agreed, Borrower and Lender agree that Loans hereunder shall in no event be "exchange contracts" for purposes of the rules of any securities exchange and that Loans hereunder shall not be governed by the buy-in or similar rules of any such exchange, registered national securities association or other self-regulatory organization.

27. **DISCLOSURE RELATING TO CERTAIN FEDERAL PROTECTIONS.**

27.1 **WITHOUT WAIVING ANY RIGHTS GIVEN TO LENDER HEREUNDER, IT IS UNDERSTOOD AND AGREED THAT THE PROVISIONS OF THE SECURITIES INVESTOR PROTECTION ACT OF 1970 MAY NOT PROTECT LENDER WITH RESPECT TO LOANED SECURITIES HEREUNDER AND THAT, THEREFORE, THE COLLATERAL DELIVERED TO LENDER MAY CONSTITUTE THE ONLY SOURCE OF SATISFACTION OF BORROWER'S OBLIGATIONS IN THE EVENT BORROWER FAILS TO RETURN THE LOANED SECURITIES.**

27.2 **LENDER ACKNOWLEDGES THAT, IN CONNECTION WITH LOANS OF GOVERNMENT SECURITIES AND AS OTHERWISE PERMITTED BY APPLICABLE LAW, SOME SECURITIES PROVIDED BY BORROWER AS COLLATERAL UNDER THIS AGREEMENT MAY NOT BE GUARANTEED BY THE UNITED STATES.**

By: _____
Title: _____
Date: _____

By: _____
Title: _____
Date: _____

Appendices

Annex I

Party Acting as Agent

This Annex sets forth the terms and conditions governing all transactions in which a party lending or borrowing Securities, as the case may be ("Agent"), in a Loan is acting as agent for one or more third parties (each, a "Principal"). Unless otherwise defined, capitalized terms used but not defined in this Annex shall have the meanings assigned in the Securities Loan Agreement of which it forms a part (such agreement, together with this Annex and any other annexes, schedules or exhibits, referred to as the "Agreement") and, unless otherwise specified, all section references herein are intended to refer to sections of such Securities Loan Agreement.

1. **Additional Representations and Warranties.** In addition to the representations and warranties set forth in the Agreement, Agent hereby makes the following representations and warranties, which shall continue during the term of any Loan: Principal has duly authorized Agent to execute and deliver the Agreement on its behalf, has the power to so authorize Agent and to enter into the Loans contemplated by the Agreement and to perform the obligations of Lender or Borrower, as the case may be, under such Loans, and has taken all necessary action to authorize such execution and delivery by Agent and such performance by it.

2. **Identification of Principals.** Agent agrees (a) to provide the other party, prior to any Loan under the Agreement, with a written list of Principals for which it intends to act as Agent (which list may be amended in writing from time to time with the consent of the other party), and (b) to provide the other party, before the Close of Business on the next Business Day after agreeing to enter into a Loan, with notice of the specific Principal or Principals for whom it is acting in connection with such Loan. If (i) Agent fails to identify such Principal or Principals prior to the Close of Business on such next Business Day or (ii) the other party shall determine in its sole discretion that any Principal or Principals identified by Agent are not acceptable to it, the other party may reject and rescind any Loan with such Principal or Principals, return to Agent any Collateral or Loaned Securities, as the case may be, previously transferred to the other party and refuse any further performance under such Loan, and Agent shall immediately return to the other party any portion of the Loaned Securities or Collateral, as the case may be, previously transferred to Agent in connection with such Loan; *provided, however*, that (A) the other party shall promptly (and in any event within one Business Day of notice of the specific Principal or Principals) notify Agent of its determination to reject and rescind such Loan and (B) to the extent that any performance was rendered by any party under any Loan rejected by the other party, such party shall remain entitled to any fees or other amounts that would have been payable to it with respect to such performance if such Loan had not been rejected. The other party acknowledges that Agent shall not have any obligation to provide it with confidential information regarding the financial status of its Principals; Agent agrees, however, that it will assist the other party in obtaining from Agent's Principals such information regarding the financial status of such Principals as the other party may reasonably request.

3. **Limitation of Agent's Liability.** The parties expressly acknowledge that if the representations and warranties of Agent under the Agreement, including this Annex, are true and correct in all material respects during the term of any Loan and Agent otherwise complies with the provisions of this Annex, then (a) Agent's obligations under the Agreement shall not include a guarantee of performance by its Principal or Principals and (b) the other party's remedies shall not include a right of setoff against obligations, if any, of Agent arising in other transactions in which Agent is acting as principal.

4. **Multiple Principals.**

    (a) In the event that Agent proposes to act for more than one Principal hereunder, Agent and the other party shall elect whether (i) to treat Loans under the Agreement as transactions entered into on behalf of separate Principals or (ii) to aggregate such Loans as if they were transactions by a single Principal. Failure to make such an election in writing shall be deemed an election to treat Loans under the Agreement as transactions on behalf of separate Principals.

    (b) In the event that Agent and the other party elect (or are deemed to elect) to treat Loans under the Agreement as transactions on behalf of separate Principals, the parties agree that (i) Agent will provide the other party, together with the notice described in Section 2(b) of this Annex, notice specifying the portion of each Loan allocable to the account of each of the Principals for which it is acting (to the extent that any such Loan is allocable to the account of more than one Principal), (ii) the portion of any individual Loan allocable to each Principal shall be deemed a separate Loan under the Agreement, (iii) the mark to market obligations of Borrower and Lender under the Agreement shall be determined on a Loan-by-Loan basis (unless the parties agree to determine such obligations on a Principal-by-Principal basis), and (iv) Borrower's and Lender's remedies under the Agreement upon the occurrence of a Default shall be determined as if Agent had entered into a separate Agreement with the other party on behalf of each of its Principals.

    (c) In the event that Agent and the other party elect to treat Loans under the Agreement as if they were transactions by a single Principal, the parties agree that (i) Agent's notice under Section 2(b) of this Annex need only identify the names of its Principals but not the portion of each Loan allocable to each Principal's account, (ii) the mark to market obligations of Borrower and Lender under the Agreement shall, subject to any greater requirement imposed by applicable law, be determined on an aggregate basis for all Loans entered into by Agent on behalf of any Principal, and (iii) Borrower's and Lender's remedies upon the occurrence of a Default shall be determined as if all Principals were a single Lender or Borrower, as the case may be.

    (d) Notwithstanding any other provision of the Agreement (including, without limitation, this Annex), the parties agree that any transactions by Agent on behalf of a Plan shall be treated as transactions on behalf of separate Principals in accordance with Section 4(b) of this Annex (and all mark to market obligations of the parties shall be determined on a Loan-by-Loan basis).

5. **Interpretation of Terms.** All references to "Lender" or "Borrower," as the case may be, in the Agreement shall, subject to the provisions of this Annex (including, among other provisions, the limitations on Agent's liability in Section 3 of this Annex), be construed to reflect that (i) each Principal shall have, in connection with any Loan or Loans entered into by Agent on its behalf, the rights, responsibilities, privileges and obligations of a "Lender" or "Borrower," as the case may be, directly entering into such Loan or Loans with the other party under the Agreement, and (ii) Agent's Principal or Principals have designated Agent as their sole agent for performance of Lender's obligations to Borrower or Borrower's obligations to Lender, as the case may be, and for receipt of performance by Borrower of its obligations to Lender or Lender of its obligations to Borrower, as the case may be, in connection with any Loan or Loans under the Agreement (including, among other things, as Agent for each Principal in connection with transfers of securities, cash or other property and as agent for giving and receiving all notices under the Agreement). Both Agent and its Principal or Principals shall be deemed "parties" to the Agreement and all references to a "party" or "either party" in the Agreement shall be deemed revised accordingly (and any

Default by Agent under the Agreement shall be deemed a Default by Lender or Borrower, as the case may be).

By: _____
Title: _____
Date: _____

By: _____
Title: _____
Date: _____

Annex II

Market Value

Unless otherwise agreed by Borrower and Lender:

1. If the principal market for the Securities to be valued is a national securities exchange in the United States, their Market Value shall be determined by their last sale price on such exchange at the most recent Close of Trading or, if there was no sale on the Business Day of the most recent Close of Trading, by the last sale price at the Close of Trading on the next preceding Business Day on which there was a sale on such exchange, all as quoted on the Consolidated Tape or, if not quoted on the Consolidated Tape, then as quoted by such exchange.

2. If the principal market for the Securities to be valued is the over-the-counter market, and the Securities are quoted on The Nasdaq Stock Market ("Nasdaq"), their Market Value shall be the last sale price on Nasdaq at the most recent Close of Trading or, if the Securities are issues for which last sale prices are not quoted on Nasdaq, the last bid price at such Close of Trading. If the relevant quotation did not exist at such Close of Trading, then the Market Value shall be the relevant quotation on the next preceding Close of Trading at which there was such a quotation.

3. Except as provided in Section 4 of this Annex, if the principal market for the Securities to be valued is the over-the-counter market, and the Securities are not quoted on Nasdaq, their Market Value shall be determined in accordance with market practice for such Securities, based on the price for such Securities as of the most recent Close of Trading obtained from a generally recognized source agreed to by the parties or the closing bid quotation at the most recent Close of Trading obtained from such a source. If the relevant quotation did not exist at such Close of Trading, then the Market Value shall be the relevant quotation on the next preceding Close of Trading at which there was such a quotation.

4. If the Securities to be valued are Foreign Securities, their Market Value shall be determined as of the most recent Close of Trading in accordance with market practice in the principal market for such Securities.

5. The Market Value of a letter of credit shall be the undrawn amount thereof.

6. All determinations of Market Value under Sections 1 through 4 of this Annex shall include, where applicable, accrued interest to the extent not already included therein (other than any interest credited or transferred to, or applied to the obligations of, the other party pursuant to Section 8 of the Agreement), unless market practice with respect to the valuation of such Securities in connection with securities loans is to the contrary.

7. The determinations of Market Value provided for in this Annex shall apply for all purposes under the Agreement, except for purposes of Section 13 of the Agreement.

By: _____
Title: _____
Date: _____

By: _____
Title: _____
Date: _____

Annex III

Term Loans

This Annex sets forth additional terms and conditions governing Loans designated as "Term Loans" in which Lender lends to Borrower a specific amount of Loaned Securities ("Term Loan Amount") against a pledge of cash Collateral by Borrower for an agreed upon Cash Collateral Fee until a scheduled termination date ("Termination Date"). Unless otherwise defined, capitalized terms used but not defined in this Annex shall have the meanings assigned in the Securities Loan Agreement of which it forms a part (such agreement, together with this Annex and any other annexes, schedules or exhibits, referred to as the "Agreement").

1. The terms of this Annex shall apply to Loans of Equity Securities only if they are designated as Term Loans in a Confirmation therefor provided pursuant to the Agreement and executed by each party, in a schedule to the Agreement or in this Annex. All Loans of Securities other than Equity Securities shall be "Term Loans" subject to this Annex, unless otherwise agreed in a Confirmation or other writing.

2. The Confirmation for a Term Loan shall set forth, in addition to any terms required to be set forth therein under the Agreement, the Term Loan Amount, the Cash Collateral Fee and the Termination Date. Lender and Borrower agree that, except as specifically provided in this Annex, each Term Loan shall be subject to all terms and conditions of the Agreement, including, without limitation, any provisions regarding the parties' respective rights to terminate a Loan.

3. In the event that either party exercises its right under the Agreement to terminate a Term Loan on a date (the "Early Termination Date") prior to the Termination Date, Lender and Borrower shall, unless otherwise agreed, use their best efforts to negotiate in good faith a new Term Loan (the "Replacement Loan") of comparable or other Securities, which shall be mutually agreed upon by the parties, with a Market Value equal to the Market Value of the Term Loan Amount under the terminated Term Loan (the "Terminated Loan") as of the Early Termination Date. Such agreement shall, in accordance with Section 2 of this Annex, be confirmed in a new Confirmation at the commencement of the Replacement Loan and be executed by each party. Each Replacement Loan shall be subject to the same terms as the corresponding Terminated Loan, other than with respect to the commencement date and the identity of the Loaned Securities. The Replacement Loan shall commence on the date on which the parties agree which Securities shall be the subject of the Replacement Loan and shall be scheduled to terminate on the scheduled Termination Date of the Terminated Loan.

4. Borrower and Lender agree that, except as provided in Section 5 of this Annex, if the parties enter into a Replacement Loan, the Collateral for the related Terminated Loan need not be returned to Borrower and shall instead serve as Collateral for such Replacement Loan.

5. If the parties are unable to negotiate and enter into a Replacement Loan for some or all of the Term Loan Amount on or before the Early Termination Date, (a) the party requesting termination of the Terminated Loan shall pay to the other party a Breakage Fee computed in accordance with Section 6 of this Annex with respect to that portion of the Term Loan Amount for which a Replacement Loan is not entered into and (b) upon the transfer by Borrower to Lender of the Loaned Securities subject to the Terminated Loan, Lender shall transfer to Borrower Collateral for the Terminated Loan in accordance with and to the extent required under the Agreement, provided that no Default has occurred with respect to Borrower.

6. For purposes of this Annex, the term "Breakage Fee" shall mean a fee agreed by Borrower and Lender in the Confirmation or otherwise orally or in writing. In the absence of any such agreement, the term "Breakage Fee" shall mean, with respect to Loans of Government Securities, a fee equal to the sum of (a) the cost to the non-terminating party (including all fees, expenses and commissions) of entering into replacement transactions and entering into or terminating hedge transactions in connection with or as a result of the termination of the Terminated Loan, and (b) any other loss, damage, cost or expense directly arising or resulting from the termination of the Terminated Loan that is incurred by the non-terminating party (other than consequential losses or costs for lost profits or lost opportunities), as determined by the non-terminating party in a commercially reasonable manner, and (c) any other amounts due and payable by the terminating party to the non-terminating party under the Agreement on the Early Termination Date.

By: _____
Title: _____
Date: _____

By: _____
Title: _____
Date: _____

Schedule A

Names and Addresses for Communications

Schedule B

Defined Terms and Supplemental Provisions

Bibliography

Paul C. Harding

Bank of England Repo and Stock Lending Committee, Securities Borrowing and Lending Code of Guidance (July 2009 edition).

Mark C. Faulkner, *An Introduction to Securities Lending* (ISLA, 2004).

Goodwin Procter Alert dated 30 July 2010 on the Dodd–Frank Wall Street Reform and Consumer Protection Act (2010).

International Capital Market Association: European market survey number 19 (June 2010).

International Securities Lending Association, Guidance Notes to the Global Master Securities Lending Agreement (2000).

International Securities Lending Association, Guidance Notes to the Global Master Securities Lending Agreement (2010).

Kathleen Tyson-Quah (ed.), *Cross-Border Securities: Repo, Lending and Collateralisation* (Sweet & Maxwell, 1997).

Securities Lending: Your questions answered (ISLA, 2009).

Securities Lending Transactions: Market Development and Implications (IOSCO and CPSS, 1999).

Elizabeth Uwaifo, Customising Securities Lending Documentation: Chapter 9 of Kathleen Tyson-Quah (ed.), *Cross-Border Securities: Repo, Lending and Collateralisation* (Sweet & Maxwell, 1997).

Christian A. Johnson

Securities Industry and Financial Markets Association:
- *Guidance Notes—Annex VIII: Transactions in Equity Securities.*
- *Guidance Notes to the Amendment to the Master Securities Loan Agreement 2000 Version.*
- *Guidance Notes to the Amendment to the Master Securities Loan Agreement 1998 Version.*

Secondary sources

Duffie, Darrell Garleanu, Nicolae and Lasse Heje Pedersen, *Securities Lending, Shorting and Pricing* (Stanford University, 2002).

Mark C. Faulkner, *An Introduction to Securities Lending* (ISLA, Third Edition 2006).

International Organization of Securities Commissions and Bank for International Settlements, *Securities Lending Transactions: Market Development and Implications* (July 1999).

Kahn, Sabrina and Jeffrey Trencher, *Risk and Return in Securities Lending: An Introduction* (State Street Corporation, May 2002).

Kahn, Sabrina and Jeffrey Trencher, *Securities Lending and the Asset/Liability Concept*, (State Street Corporation, March 2002).

John J. Piccitto, Risk in Securities Lending, "Risk in the harsh light of day", *ISF Magazine* (1st Quarter, 2002).

Securities Industry Association and the Risk Management Association, STP Securities Lending Subcommittee, White Paper (March 2003).

Securities Lending: Your Questions Answered (ISLA, 2009).

Index

ABN AMRO 619
accrued income 207, 357
Act of Insolvency *see* insolvency
Additional Termination Events 369
administration freezes 35
agent intermediaries 10–11, 36–42
Agent Lender Disclosure (ALD) 41–2
agent transactions (EMA) 388–91
agent transactions (GMSLA 2000) 136–9, 159–61, 177–85
   collateral 181–3
   confidential information 178, 183
   initiation and confirmation 179
   Pooled Principals 181–3
   records and statements 183
   representations and warranties 180–1
   scope and interpretation 179
   termination/substitution rights 184–5
agent transactions (GMSLA 2010) 308–35
   amendments 323
   automation 311
   collateral 326–7
   conditions for agency loan 314–15
   default interest 311
   interpretation 321
   loan allocation 324–5
   margin rebalancing 328–33
   notices 316–17
   Pooled Principals 320–33
   scope and interpretation 321
   status of agency loan 318–19
   warranties 318–19, 334–5
agent transactions (MSLA) 570–9
   identification of principals 574–5
   interpretation of terms 578–9
   limitation of liability 576–7
   multiple principals 576–7
AIG 617
amendments
   GMSLA (2000) 149, 162–85
   GMSLA (2010) 289, 323
applicability
   EMA 344, 394–5
   GMSLA (2000) 65

   GMSLA (2010) 193
   MSLA 434–5
arbitrage trading 7, 15–17
arbitration 392–3
assignment
   GMSLA (2000) 142–3, 169–70
   GMSLA (2010) 282–3
automatic early termination 197, 305
avoiding power 50

Bankers Trust 481
bankruptcy *see* insolvency
base currency *see* currency conversions
Bear Stearns 616
best execution requirements 38–40
bid price 115
bid value 115, 121
Big Bang 7
Bond Market Association 430–1
bonus securities 237
Booking Offices 382–3
breakage fees 590–1
broker dealers 11, 12
business days 69, 199, 354–7, 543, 602–3
buy in 199

capital gains tax *see* taxation
cash collateral 69, 75, 103, 199, 223, 239, 443
   fees 451, 453, 545
cash driven transactions 2
cash margin 414–15
cash transfers 513
central clearing counterparty (CCP) 618
central securities depositories 10
change of circumstances 368–9, 371, 373
Clayton's Case 229
clearing houses 10, 545, 618
close of business 69, 201
close out netting *see* set off
collateral allocation letters 40–1
collateral (EMA) *see* margining (EMA)
collateral (GMSLA 2000) 86–97, 154–7, 163–4, 170
   agent transactions 181–3

Index

collateral (GMSLA 2000) (*continued*)
   cash collateral 69, 75, 103
   cross collaterisation 175
   delivery on commencement of loan 87–9, 95
   excess collateral 95, 164
   interest rates 103
   Market Value 75
   marking to market 91–3
   posted collateral 77
   redelivery on termination of loan 107
   schedule 154–7
   substituting 67, 71, 89, 163
collateral (GMSLA 2010) 201, 209, 221–9, 294–6
   cash collateral 199, 223, 239
   excess collateral 229
   interest rates 239
   margining 227
   Market Value 225–7
   marking to market 224–7
   notification time 209
   schedule 294–9
collateral (MSLA) 440–9, 546–7
   losses on cash collateral 443
   retransfers 443, 455
   return of 445
   rights in respect of 456–7
   substitution rights 447
conditions precedent 352–3
confidentiality 178, 183, 613
confirmations 18
   agent transactions 179
   EMA 348–9, 407
   GMSLA (2000) 81, 164
   GMSLA (2010) 214–15
   MSLA 436–7, 549, 587, 603–4
contractual currency *see* currency conversions
control securities 599
convertible bond arbitrage 15
corporate actions 20–1
   EMA 342
   GMSLA (2000) 71, 98–101, 164–6
   GMSLA (2010) 203, 221–7
   MSLA 457, 605
costs and expenses 39, 125, 259, 266–7, 384–5
counterparty risk 5, 7, 24–5
covenants 488–9
covering short positions 14
credit crunch 616–19
credit departments 17
Credit Event Upon Merger 369
Credit Event Upon Restructuring 369, 371
credit risk 11
CREST system 19
cross collaterisation 175, 609
Cross Product Master Agreement 51

cross border transfers 24
cross default 175, 365, 609
currency conversions
   EMA 376–7, 386–7
   GMSLA (2000) 69, 79, 157
   GMSLA (2010) 197, 213, 300–1
   MSLA 514–17, 549
custodian banks 10–11, 36–7
customer, definition 549, 551
Cutoff Times 439, 493, 553

daylight risk 19, 26
dealing process 8–10, 16–21
default *see* Events of Default
delivery (EMA) 350–7, 396–401
   initial delivery 397
   late delivery 398–401
   On Demand Transactions 397
   partial delivery 401
   remedies 401
   returned securities 397
   special events 401
delivery (GMSLA 2000) 83–5
delivery (GMSLA 2010) 201, 216–19, 240–3
delivery of income 85, 219
Depository Trust and Clearing Corporation 41–2, 545
deregulation 616
Designated Office
   GMSLA (2000) 63, 71, 159
   GMSLA (2010) 191, 201, 303, 306–7
disclosures to Federal protections 568–9
dividends/distributions 9, 16, 20–1, 28
   delivery 85, 219
   EMA 402–3
   in the form of securities 99
   GMSLA (2000) 73, 99, 164–5
   GMSLA (2010) 205, 231–3
   MSLA 458–67, 553
      and margin 467
   non cash collateral 232–3
   payment dates 73, 205
   reinvestment arbitrage 16
   reinvestment of interest 39
   right to the coupon 33–4
   taxation 22, 23–4
documentary tax 358–9
Dodd–Frank Act 3–4, 618–19
Drysdale Securities 7

EMA 338–428
   agency transactions 388–91
   applicability 344–5, 394–5
   background 338
   benefits 339
   Booking Offices 382–3
   compared to GMSLA (2010) 425–8
   contractual currency 386–7

definitions 345
delivery 350–7, 396–401
distributions 402–3
documents 384–5
Events of Default 363–7, 373, 427
expenses 384–5
fees 404–5
final settlement amount 374–9
General Provisions 340–1, 345
goals 338
governing law 338, 392–3, 424–5, 425, 427–8
incorporation of documents 422–3
interpretation 344–5
jurisdiction 338, 392–3, 424–5, 425, 427–8
margin maintenance 342, 406–19
modifications 346–7
no waiver clause 386–7
notices 380–1, 422–3
payments 350–7, 376–7, 396–401
Product Annex 341–2, 345, 394–407
remedies 386–7
representations 360–1, 390–1
scope 426
severability 390–1
single agreement concept 346–7
Special Provisions 341, 345, 420–5
structure 340–2, 344–5, 425–6
subscription rights 342, 402–3
taxes 358–9
termination 362–73, 386–7
    agency transactions 388–9
transactions 348–9
transfer of rights 384–5
voting rights 342
waiver of immunity 392–3
employee plan assets 55–8
enforceability representation 606
equity of redemption 33
equity security 555
Equivalent
    GMSLA (2000) 71, 105
    GMSLA (2010) 203, 241
ERISA 518–21
European securities lending market 8
Events of Default (EMA) 363–7, 373, 427
    Default Value 374–5
Events of Default (GMSLA 2000) 36, 115, 119–23, 130–3, 168–9
    costs, expenses and interest 125
    defaulting party 71
    delivery values 121–3
    letters of credit 119
    Relevant Values 119
    termination of obligations 119
Events of Default (GMSLA 2010) 36, 245, 247, 250–67, 304–5

consequences 254–67
costs, expenses and interest 259, 266–7
defaulting party 201
grace periods 251
Market Values 258–65
Events of Default (MSLA) 477, 490–7, 553
    Additional Events of Default 595–6
    interest rates 501, 505, 555, 559
    price determination 507
    remedies 498–507, 597, 608–11
    replacement collateral 503, 505
    replacement securities 499, 501
exempted borrowers 607
expenses 39, 125, 259, 266–7, 384–5
Extension Deadlines 449

failure to deliver 20
    buy in exercise 113
    by borrower 109, 245
    by either party 113, 249
    by lender 111, 247
    EMA 363
    GMSLA (2000) 109–13, 167
    GMSLA (2010) 234–5, 244–9
    MSLA 437
Fannie Mae 617
Federal Deposit Insurance Act (FDIA) 46, 51–2
Federal Deposit Insurance Corporation Improvement Act (FDICIA) 53–4
Federal Funds Rate 555
Federal Home Loan Banks 46
fees 8, 9, 18, 39
    cash collateral 451, 453, 545
    EMA 404–5
    GMSLA (2000) 102–3
    GMSLA (2010) 239
    MSLA 450–3, 559
        breakage fees 590–1
    taxation 23
final settlement amount (EMA) 374–9
fixed term loans 17
force majeure 172–3
foreign securities 557
    standard settlement date 597
Freddie Mac 617
free of payment settlement 19
FSA (Financial Services Authority) 6, 31
fungible securities 8, 353

General Provisions (EMA) 340–1, 345
gilt edged securities 2, 43
global margining 95, 170–1, 229, 297
GMSLA (2000)
    agent transactions 136–9, 159–61, 177–85
    amendments 149, 162–85
    applicability 65
    assignment 142–3, 169–70
    borrower's warranties 128–9

Index

GMSLA (2000) (*continued*)
  collateral 86–97, 154–7, 163–4, 170
  corporate actions 71, 98–101, 164–6
  delivery 83–5
  Designated Office 63, 71, 159
  Event of Default 36, 115, 119–23, 130–3, 168–9
  excess amounts 176–7
  failure to redeliver 109–13, 167
  force majeure 172–3
  governing law and jurisdiction 144–5
  governing practices 173–4
  interest on outstanding payments 134–5
  interpretation 67–79, 162–3
  labour dispute events 172–3
  lender's warranties 128–9, 168
  loans of securities 81
  miscellaneous 148–51
  non waiver clause 144–5
  notices 142–3
  rates applicable 102–3
  recording telephone conversations 144–5, 170
  redelivery of equivalent securities 105–7, 166
  scope of agreement 171
  set off 114–25, 174–5
  severance 140–1
  signing block 152–3
  single agreement concept 140–1
  specific performance 142–3
  termination of agreement 105, 140–1
  third party rights 151
  Threshold 172
  time 144–5
  transfer taxes 126–7, 167–8
  waiver of immunity 144, 147
  warranties 128–9, 150–1, 168
GMSLA (2010)
  agent transactions 308–35
  amendments 289
  applicability 193
  assignment 282–3
  collateral 221–9, 294–6
  compared to GMSLA (2000) 188–9
  corporate actions 203, 221–7
  delivery 201, 216–19, 240–3
  Designated Office 191, 201, 303, 306–7
  Events of Default 36, 250–67, 304–5
  governing law 282–3
  interest on outstanding payments 276, 277
  interpretation 194–213
  jurisdiction 282–3
  loans of securities 214–15
  non waiver 282–3
  notices 280–1, 307
  rates applicable 238–9
  recording 282, 285

  severance 280–1
  signing block 293
  single agreement 278, 279
  specific performance 280, 281
  taxes 268–71
  termination 243, 276, 277
  third party rights 291
  time 282, 285
  waiver of immunity 286–7
  warranties 273, 275, 289, 291
Goldman Sachs 13
governing law *see* jurisdiction
government securities 557
guarantee ineffective 367

haircuts 617
headings 79, 213
hedge funds 617
history of securities lending 2, 6–8
Household Finance Corporation 616
HSBC 616

Icelandic Banks 617
icing securities 17
Illegality 369
immunity waiver 612
Impossibility 369
income *see* dividends/distributions
indemnities 37
index arbitrage 16
insolvency
  administration freezes 35
  EMA 365
  GMSLA (2000) 67, 162–3
  GMSLA (2010) 195
  MSLA 493, 539, 567, 601–2
  US banking insolvency law 51
  US Bankruptcy Code 46–52, 541, 567
insolvency risk 32–3, 35
intent 566–7
Intercontinental Exchange (ICE) 618
interest rates 8–9, 103, 239, 311
  GMSLA (2000) 134–5
  GMSLA (2010) 276, 277
  MSLA 501, 505, 555, 559
  reinvestment of interest 39
intermediaries 10–14
  best execution requirements 38–40
  borrowers' preferences 13
  broker dealers 11, 12
  central securities depositories 10
  clearing houses 10, 545, 618
  collateral allocation letters 40–1
  custodian banks 10–11, 36–7
  indemnities 37
  legal issues 36–42
  main lenders 13
  pooling arrangements 40

Index

prime brokers 10, 11, 13
principal intermediaries 11
services provided 10, 11–12, 36–7
specialist intermediaries 12–13
see also agent transactions
interpretation
   EMA 344–5
   GMSLA (2000) 67–79, 162–3
   GMSLA (2010) 194–213
ISLA (International Securities Lenders Association) 5, 6

Judgment Currency 515
jurisdiction 44–5
   EMA 338, 392–3, 424–5, 425, 427–8
   GMSLA (2000) 144–5
   GMSLA (2010) 282–3
   MSLA 532–3

labour dispute events 172–3
legal capacity 31, 54
legal issues (UK) 31–43
   administration freezes 35
   agency arrangements 36–42
   breach of negative pledge 35
   close out netting 35–6
   enforcement formalities 34
   legal capacity 31
   proceeds on enforcement 34
   right to the coupon 33–4
   right to deal with the securities 33, 34
   substance over form 33
   title transfer 32–5
   see also jurisdiction; regulation
legal issues (US) 44–58, 524–5
   avoiding power 50
   banking insolvency law 51
   Bankruptcy Code 46–52
   definition of securities contracts 47
   employee plan assets 55–8
   enforcement 44–6
   legal capacity 54
   master netting contracts 50–1
   preference payments 50
   repo transactions 45
   right to terminate and liquidate 49–50
   Securities Investor Protection Corporation (SIPC) 46, 50
   severability 55
   termination 51–2
   see also jurisdiction; regulation
legal opinions 43, 185–6, 188, 479
legal risk 26–7
Lehman Brothers 4–6, 617
letters of credit
   delivery/redelivery 107, 243
   expiry 449
   GMSLA (2000) 73, 75, 97, 119, 163

GMSLA (2010) 205, 207
   market value 115, 117, 205
   MSLA 449, 513, 555, 611
LIBOR 559
limitation of liability 612–13
liquidity risk 12, 14–15
Lloyds Banking Group 617
loaned securities
   GMSLA (2000) 73
   GMSLA (2010) 205

main lenders 13
manipulative short selling 3
manufactured dividends *see* dividends/distributions
margining (EMA) 342, 406–19
   cash margin 414–15
   composition of margin 414–15
   definitions 412–13
   Margin Claims 374–5
   margin securities 416–17, 418–19
   net exposure calculation 408–11
   notification of net exposure 414–15
   return of margin 416–17
      failure to return 363
   Thresholds 416–17
   transfer of margin 414–15
margining (GMSLA 2000) 73, 91–5, 154–7, 170–2
margining (GMSLA 2010) 205, 227, 229, 297, 328–33
margining (MSLA) 440–1, 560–1
   and distributions 467
   marking to market 468–75
   notice deadlines 475
   nuisance amount concept 476
market making 14–15
market risk 25
market terminology 79, 213
Market Value
   EMA 356–7
   GMSLA (2000) 75, 91, 115–17, 258–65
   GMSLA (2010) 207, 225–7, 303
   letters of credit 115, 117, 205
   MSLA 562–3, 580–5, 602–3
marking to market
   GMSLA (2000) 91–3
   GMSLA (2010) 224–7
   MSLA 468–75, 605–6
master netting contracts 50–1
Master Repurchase Agreement 51
matching owners and borrowers 12
maturity of a transaction 8
Maxwell, Robert 7
Merrill Lynch 54
Mirror Group 7
misrepresentation 363
modification to legislation 79, 213

Index

MSLA
  Act of Insolvency 493, 539, 567, 601–2
  agent transactions 570–9
  applicability 434–5
  applicable law 524–5
  collateral 440–9, 546–7
  contractual currency 514–17, 549
  covenants 488–9
  definitions 538–65, 601–3
  disclosures to Federal protections 568–9
  distributions 458–67, 553
  document deliveries 611
  ERISA 518–21
  Events of Default 477, 490–7, 553
    Additional Events of Default 595–6
    remedies 498–507, 597, 608–11
  evolution 430–1
  existing loans 601
  fees 450–3, 559
    breakage fees 590–1
  intent 566–7
  jurisdiction 532–3
  loans of securities 436–7, 559
  Market Value 562–3, 580–5, 602–3
  marking to market 468–75, 605–6
  notices 530–1
  opening paragraph 600
  previous agreements 535, 600
  Regulation T 483, 485, 565
  replacement loans 589, 591
  representations and warranties 476–87, 598–600, 606–8
  rights 456–7, 605
  set off 609–11
  signature block 613
  single agreement concept 522–3, 553
  structure 431–2
  survival of remedies 528–9
  term loans 586–91
  termination 454–5, 535, 589, 604–5
  trading practices 598
  transfer taxes 508–9
  transfers 438–9, 510–13, 535, 604
  waivers 526–7, 612
    of jury trial 532–3

negative pledge 35
netting *see* set off
New York law *see* legal issues (US)
no reliance clause 598–9
no waiver clause 144–5, 282–3, 386–7
nominees
  GMSLA (2000) 77
  GMSLA (2010) 207
non defaulting party
  GMSLA (2000) 77
  GMSLA (2010) 209
non reliance representations 481

Northern Rock 616
notices
  EMA 380–1, 422–3
  GMSLA (2000) 142–3
  GMSLA (2010) 280–1, 307, 316–17
  MSLA 475, 530–1
nuisance amount concept 476

offer price 117
offer value 117, 121
open loans 17
operational risk 25–6
Orange County 54

partialling transactions 20
parties
  GMSLA (2000) 77
  GMSLA (2010) 209
pay to hold 18
payment 27
  dates 73, 205
  EMA 350–7, 376–7, 396–401
  fees and interest 103
  late payment 354–5
performance date 121
pledges 32–3, 34
  negative pledge 35
pooling arrangements 40, 181–3, 320–33
preference payments 50
pricing *see* fees
prime brokers 10, 11, 13
principal intermediaries 11
Process Agents 159, 171, 611
Proctor & Gamble 481
Product Annex 341–2, 345, 394–407

Quotation Date 374–5

RBS 617
reasons for borrowing 14–17
recall risk 12
recharacterisation risk 33–5, 45
reciprocal obligations 107, 243
recording telephone conversations 144–5, 170, 282, 285, 611–12
records and statements 183
reference dealers 209
regulation 2–4, 6–7
  see also legal issues
Regulation T 483, 485, 565
relative value arbitrage 15
replacement loans 589, 591
repo trading 2, 6, 9, 27–8, 45
representations and warranties
  agent transactions 180–1
  EMA 360–1, 390–1
  GMSLA (2000) 128–9, 150–1, 168
  GMSLA (2010) 251, 273–5, 289–91, 318–19, 334–5

Index

MSLA 476–87, 598–600, 606–8
repudiation of obligations 367
restricted securities 599
revaluation process 19
rights issues *see* corporate actions
risk 24–7
    counterparty risk 5, 7, 24–5
    credit risk 11
    daylight risk 19, 26
    insolvency risk 32–3, 35
    legal risk 26–7
    liquidity risk 12, 14–15
    market risk 25
    operational risk 25–6
    recall risk 12
    recharacterisation risk 33–5, 45

sales tax 209, 271
scope of agreements 171, 179, 321, 426
SecFinex 618
securities driven transactions 2
Securities Investor Protection Corporation (SIPC) 46, 50
Securities Lending and Repo Committee 6
Securities Lending Set Off Protocol 188
set off
    EMA 352–3, 378–9
    enforceability 35–6
    GMSLA (2000) 114–25, 174–5
    GMSLA (2010) 266–7
    MSLA 609–11
settlement 6, 7, 18–19
    CREST system 19
    dates 77, 209
    operational risk 25–6
severability 55
    EMA 390–1
    GMSLA (2000) 140–1
    GMSLA (2010) 280–1
shaping transactions 20
short selling
    controversy 2
    covering short positions 14
    and the credit crunch 618
    regulations and Directive 2–4
simultaneous delivery 85
single agreement concept
    EMA 346–7
    GMSLA (2000) 140–1
    GMSLA (2010) 278, 279
    MSLA 522–3, 553
Special Provisions 341, 345, 420–5
specialist intermediaries 12–13
specific performance 142–3, 280, 281
stamp tax 22, 211, 271
strategies for borrowing 14–17
structured investment vehicles (SIVs) 616
subscription rights 342, 402–3
substance over form 33
substitute collateral 67, 71, 89, 163, 447

survival of remedies 528–9
suspended securities 75, 207

takeover offers *see* corporate actions
tax arbitrage 16
Tax Event (EMA) 369, 371
taxation 21–4, 211
    dividends 22, 24
    documentary tax 358–9
    EMA 358–9, 369, 402–3
    GMSLA (2000) 126–7, 167–8, 176, 185
    GMSLA (2010) 268–71, 336
    MSLA 508–9
    sales tax 209, 271
    stamp tax 22, 211, 271
    in the UK 21–2, 185, 336
    in the US 23–4
term 17, 28
term loans 586–91
termination 19–20, 51–2
    agency transactions 184–5, 388–9
    automatic early termination 197, 305
    borrower's rights 105, 241
    EMA 362–73, 386–7, 388–9
    GMSLA (2000) 105, 121, 140–1, 184–5
    GMSLA (2010) 241, 243, 276, 277
    lender's rights 105, 241
    MSLA 454–5, 535, 589, 604–5
third party rights 151, 291
Thresholds 172, 416–17
time 144–5
time zones 19, 26
title transfer 32–5, 83–5
trading practices 598
transaction process 8–10, 17–21
Transaction Value 374–5
transfer taxes 21–2, 23, 126–7, 167–8, 508–9
transfer of title 350–1
triparty custodial agreements 435

UBS 13
ultra vires 31, 54
US banking insolvency law 51
US Bankruptcy Code 46–52, 541, 567

voting rights 4, 20–1
    EMA 342
    GMSLA (2000) 101, 165–6
    GMSLA (2010) 237
    MSLA 457

waivers
    EMA 392–3
    GMSLA (2000) 144, 147
    GMSLA (2010) 286–7
    MSLA 526–7, 612
    of jury trial 532–3
warranties *see* representations and warranties
withholding tax 22, 24, 176, 269, 358–9, 369, 402–3

THE MASTERING SERIES

MASTERING FINANCIAL MODELLING in Microsoft® Excel — ALASTAIR L. DAY
9780273708063

MASTERING CREDIT DERIVATIVES — ANDREW KASAPIS
9780273714859

MASTERING FINANCIAL CALCULATIONS — BOB STEINER
9780273704447

MASTERING RISK MODELLING — ALASTAIR L. DAY
9780273719298

MASTERING FINANCIAL MANAGEMENT — CLIVE MARSH
9780273724544

MASTERING FINANCIAL MATHEMATICS in Microsoft® Excel — ALASTAIR L. DAY
9780273730330

MASTERING THE ISDA® MASTER AGREEMENTS (1992 and 2002) — PAUL C. HARDING
9780273725206

MASTERING OPERATIONAL RISK — TONY BLUNDEN & JOHN THIRLWELL
9780273727323

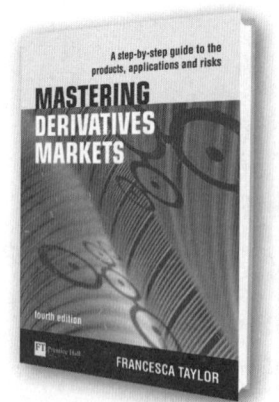

MASTERING DERIVATIVES MARKETS — FRANCESCA TAYLOR
9780273735670

MASTERING INVESTMENT BANKING SECURITIES — NATASHA KOZUL
9780273744795

PRACTICAL
COMPREHENSIVE
ESSENTIAL

Available now from
http://www.pearsoned.co.uk

FT Prentice Hall
FINANCIAL TIMES